CLASSIC
CONTRIBUTIONS IN
THE ADDICTIONS

CLASSIC CONTRIBUTIONS IN THE ADDICTIONS

Edited, with Commentary, by

HOWARD SHAFFER, PH.D.

and

**MILTON EARL BURGLASS,
M.D., M.P.H., M. DIV.**

*The Department of Psychiatry,
Harvard Medical School
at The Cambridge Hospital*

BRUNNER/MAZEL, *Publishers* • New York

Library of Congress Cataloging in Publications Data
Main entry under title:

Classic contributions in the addictions.

    Bibliography: p.
    1. Drug abuse—Addresses, essays, lectures. 2. Drug abuse—Treatment—Addresses, essays, lectures. 3. Narcotic habit—Addresses, essays, lectures. I. Shaffer, Howard, 1948–
II. Burglass, Milton Earl, 1941- . [DNLM: 1. Drug dependence—Collected works. WM
270 C614] HV5801.C55   616.86'3   80-39589
ISBN 0-87630-260-6

Published by
BRUNNER/MAZEL, INC.
19 Union Square
New York, New York 10003

MANUFACTURED IN THE UNITED STATES OF AMERICA

To
Linda and David,
H.S.

Janice, Chloë, and Blue,
M.E.B.

and

To
Marshall Jones and Sidney Diamond,
who first taught us that asking
the right questions
is more important than
giving answers.

FOREWORD

In recent years there have been increasing efforts to define and establish as an organized, specific discipline the study of the use of intoxicants and the dysfunctional consequences of that use. Most notable of these efforts has been the establishment in the public sector of the National Institute on Drug Abuse (NIDA) and the National Institute on Alcoholism and Alcohol Abuse (NIAAA), and in the private sector of The Drug Abuse Council, Inc. (DAC), funded by The Ford Foundation, Carnegie Corporation, Commonwealth Fund, Kaiser Foundation, and Equitable Life Assurance Company from 1972 to 1978. While NIDA and NIAAA have awarded career teacher and career research grants specifically in the field of intoxicant use, the DAC explicitly established a fellowship program, one of whose goals was to arrive at a coherent definition of this field as a discipline.

These efforts represent a substantial beginning to a formidable task. Not the least of the problems faced is the ubiquity of intoxicant use. It is almost as if one were attempting to establish a discipline for the study of eating. Practically every known culture has made regular use of one intoxicant or another. While every member of every group may not partake, as he or she must of food, the majority has done so in ways almost as diverse and with almost as many subsequent difficulties as with food. In fact, the arguments around the "proper" use of intoxicants are somewhat similar to those around the "proper" use of food, that is, what, how much, how to, and when. Substances accepted by one group are not accepted by another; even the same substance is used differently by different groups at different times. Only the most clearly destructive results of use are universally accepted as misuse.

Except for the most extreme cases, the difficulty in differentiating between use and misuse is a basic problem. Are we seeking a discipline to study the results of misuse and ways to isolate and define clear-cut syndromes and their antecedents, and treatment, or are we attempting to study the entire phenomenon of intoxicant use? Recently, this large question has been further broadened through efforts to think about intoxicant use as habitual behavior, particularly when it is regular and potentially troublesome, and compare it to other habitual behaviors. Despite the enormity of the task, these efforts have begun to bear fruit. While there is not yet a Department of Intoxicant Studies at any university, there are recognized leaders in this field, some knowledgeable in the entire field and some in highly specific areas, as is true in other disciplines.

The development of a discipline of intoxicant use has been hampered by two particular difficulties that I would like to mention, both of which, I believe, will be resolved in part by the publication of this volume. The first is the extent to which the field has been used as a political football, not only in this country but elsewhere. Using concerns about intoxicant use for political advantage is not a new game, although in this country former President Nixon probably raised it to its apogee or nadir, depending on one's point of view. The fears around cocaine use by blacks at the turn of the century, the passage of the Harrison Narcotic Act in 1914, the spate of bills in the fifties calling for draconian penalties against drug users, and even the Whisky Rebellion of 1794 are examples of earlier political use of the intoxicant problem. I am not sure that it was true then, but I am sure that now the political seductiveness of the intoxicant issue acts to impede the field's development as a coherent discipline.

The second difficulty I would like to mention is the lack of an integrated and available intellectual and scientific literature. It has been hard for interested laymen and professionals in the field to know where to turn for an overview that represents the solid work in the field. It is easy to romanticize with Beaudelaire, deQuincey, and Coleridge or to be impressed with the thoroughness and grasp of Terry and Pellens or the prescience of Lindesmith, but such individual efforts do not provide the roots for a consolidated field. Good work has been done; some books have been published, but more often articles have been scattered through the journals of a dozen or more specialized fields.

The present volume is one remedy for that situation. I believe that the publication of a work that brings together many valuable contributions to the study of intoxicant use helps with the political problem, as it is my conviction that the lack of intellectual respectability has been contributory to easy political usage.

Norman E. Zinberg, M.D.

PREFACE

During the past few years, we have been actively involved with addiction treatment, theory, and research. We also have been teaching courses in the "addictions" at the undergraduate, graduate, and applied or inservice training levels. Our experiences have demonstrated the need for an organized volume that contains the major contributions to the addiction treatment theory literature. We have experienced repeatedly the frustrations of searching for articles, compiling syllabi listing hard-to-find articles, and sending reluctant students to libraries' reference desks. The sparsity of quality scientific literature in the field of addictions has contributed to our frustration. The present volume is offered as a partial solution to this problem.

Classic Contributions in the Addictions is offered to provide perspective and insight into the origins of contemporary substance abuse treatment and theory. Often, the field of addictions has been considered to be zealous, political, and even irrational. In some cases this is certainly true; however, much of addiction treatment and research has its roots in well developed theory and empirical analysis. In fact, some major recurrent themes in contemporary addiction treatment resonate with the thoughts of those who have provided the context for current drug treatment. The contributions made by these individuals are landmark. This book is an attempt to identify and organize this body of work into a single text. Some of these papers have changed the flow of history. Indeed, the papers selected for this text were included based on the following measure: the ideas expressed or implied in these works have significantly changed—or in some cases we believe will change—the fields of addiction theory, research, and practice. As a consequence, the contributions contained herein provide a major creative perspective on the history of knowledge about addiction. Like the field, these articles originate from a variety of disciplines and do not specifically endorse any one position or point of view regarding the etiology or treatment of substance abuse.

Most practitioners who study the addictions tend to study the problem from their ideological frame of reference. For example, psychiatrists tend to read psychiatric journals; psychologists tend to read psychological journals; social workers tend to read social work journals, etc. It is no surprise, then, that psychological theory begets further psychological theory, and no major bridges are crossed. Since substance abuse does not have an operative paradigm, treatment and theory lack the comprehensivity that can be obtained only by crossing the broad lines that separate the various intellectual disciplines. We believe that *Classic Contributions* is a first step in that direction.

Classic Contributions in the Addictions is intended for all those who seek knowledge and information about (a) substance use and abuse; (b) the causes and treatments of addiction; and (c) the history and roots of contemporary addiction literature. We believe that it can be a major adjunct to texts in pharmacology, psychology, sociology, and addiction, as well as a major source for inservice training programs designed to teach and communicate information about the etiology, ideology, and treatment of substance abuse.

The sections of the book that follow are thematic and not chronological. These sections are somewhat arbitrary, but do reflect the grouping of selections that discuss similar substantive issues. Some overlap is present, and some gaps exist. Thankfully, a working knowledge of the field does not require comprehensive, inclusive coverage of its constituent parts.

Caveats and Disclaimers: What This Book Is Not

Because of spatial, organizational and traditional precedent, the present volume does not include selections from the areas of alcoholism, overeating, or smoking. Also, some areas within the field of substance abuse were self-limiting (e.g., *some* factions of the self-help movement) since these activities were *not* expressed in written work that was disseminated through the field's formal channels (i.e., journal articles or books). Further, we have elected to limit the variety of perspectives that are represented in this volume; specifically, selections from the criminal justice point of view, prevention, acupuncture and opiate antagonist literature have been restricted. In the main, all of these areas are considered integral parts of the field of substance abuse or addictive behavior. These areas have not been excluded from the present volume because we believe they are of lesser importance; they have been eliminated as a result of organizational strategies that include considerations such as space, price, and the interests of potential readers. We anticipate that future projects will organize this literature in a manner similar to the present text.

The present anthology emphasizes opiate use. This focus is not the result of our chauvanism with respect to other drugs of abuse, but rather the practical consequence of historical precedents favoring conceptual and empirical interest in opiate use and abuse. This bias is the consequence of (a) the long-standing social interest in opiate use and (b) the only recent proliferation and abuse pattern of the non-alcohol, hypnotic-sedative drugs (Valium, Placidyl, Nembutal, etc.). Similarly, we refer to "addiction" throughout this text; this reference to addiction is in keeping with tradition and not an unequivocal acceptance or reification of this construct. Our position will be explicated in more detail in the introduction and epilogue chapters that follow.

ACKNOWLEDGMENTS

We would like to take this opportunity to acknowledge those individuals who helped make this volume possible. Thanks are extended to Dr. John A. Renner, Jr., for providing the forum, encouragement, and feedback that helped nourish the original idea for this collection. Thanks are also extended to Dr. Edward Khantzian, Janice Kauffman, Dr. Thomas J. Paolino, Jr., Charles Neuhaus and the staff of The Cambridge Hospital Drug Problems Resource Center for their support and helpful comments on earlier drafts of our work.

We would also like to take this opportunity to commend and thank the staff members of the Harvard University Library System for their cooperation and assistance in locating the materials that were necessary to complete this project.

Special thanks are extended to our colleague and friend Dr. Norman Zinberg for his advice, counsel, support, and critical feedback regarding the selection of articles and substance of original material for this volume. However, we accept responsibility for the final selections and original positions expressed in this text.

Very special thanks and heartfelt appreciation are extended to Carolyn Dyer for her diligent efforts in the coordination of gaining permission to reprint previously published material. Moreover, we would like to thank her for being patient when we were impatient, and organized when we were disorganized. Without her help, this entire project would have been impossible.

We do not want to forget our students, patients and clients for they are the main reason that we originally embarked on this project. These individuals have challenged and provoked our thinking; they have been pupils and teachers concurrently. It is with sincere gratitude that we share the hope that a better understanding of addictive behavior will lead to interventions that will improve the quality of life for those who are struggling against their impulses.

Lastly, we would like to thank each of the contributors and the corresponding publishers for their permission to reprint these materials.

Howard Shaffer
Milton Earl Burglass
Harvard Medical School at
The Cambridge Hospital

CONTENTS

Someone saw Nasrudin searching for something on the ground.

"What have you lost, Mulla?" he asked.

"My key," said the Mulla.

So they both went down on their knees and looked for it.

After a time the other man asked: "Where exactly did you drop it?"

"In my own house."

"Then why are you looking here?"

"There is more light here than inside my own house."

—from *The Exploits of the Incomparable
Mulla Nasrudin,* by Idries Shah.

INTRODUCTION:

THE NATURAL HISTORY OF IDEAS IN THE TREATMENT OF THE ADDICTIONS

Milton Earl Burglass and Howard Shaffer

Certain individuals use certain substances in certain ways thought at certain times to be unacceptable by certain other individuals for reasons both certain and uncertain.

Both the phenomenon described above and the field of endeavor and inquiry of which it is the object are today known as the addictions. The *phenomenon* has a long cultural history; the *field* which has grown up around it is of recent origin. Throughout history society has demonstrated an interest in regulating the substances ingested by its members. The development of this interest can be traced in the succession of religious and secular rules, laws, sanctions, and policies that have served to define certain substances as being acceptable or unacceptable either as "food" or "drugs" and certain forms and patterns of ingestion as proper use or abuse. Contemporary society, scientifically informed and religiously pluralistic, continues this tradition of regulating ingestible substances, though now less explicitly in the name of religion as in earlier times and more so in the cause of public health and safety. The ill-specified nature of these latter-day causes and the zeal and fervor with which regulatory activities are pursued have led some observers to characterize our present food and drug laws, their medical and scientific "justifications" notwithstanding, as religious in intent, purpose and effect, as being in fact the dietary and liturgical laws of the modern secular religion of science.

In this century, as the church yielded to the state primary responsibility for the promulgation of values and the regulation of individual conduct, the phenomenon of the addictions came to be seen as the social problem of addiction and as such the object of formal inquiry and intervention. Social concern to prevent or stop individuals from using certain substances in certain ways has prompted many and varied theories of both the cause and treatment of addiction. The earliest of these emphasized personal responsibility; the moral turpitude of the individual was cited as the cause; and addiction, like poverty and ignorance, was understood as the consequence of spiritual weakness. As society became increasingly urban, a widening segment of the population became exposed to so-called "dangerous drugs" in the cities and some individuals fell under their influence. Less personally condemning theories were soon supplied by the fledgling fields of psychology and psychiatry. Moral turpitude gradually yielded to psychological defect as the preferred explanation for an individual's addiction (Abraham, 1908; Rado, 1926). And addicts came to be seen as *patients* to be cured by treatment rather than as *sinners* to be saved by piety.

The Great Depression of the 1930s and the Second World War in the 1940s stimulated society's appreciation of the role of external conditions and forces in shaping individual behavior; consequently, social and environmental theories emerged to explain the social problem of addiction in the 1940s and 1950s (e.g., Lindesmith, 1947). The 1960s brought wide prosperity, profound cultural changes, and unprecedented drug use at all levels of society. The attending dissolution of the social value consensus, the perceived inadequacy of the then-current social and psychological models to explain or solve the problem at the individual or social level, and the growing fascination with technology perhaps explain the appeal of the behavioral theories that appeared in the 1960s. In the 1970s, although recreational drug use became somewhat more acceptable culturally as it became more prevalent, explanations and solutions were still thought necessary for the statistically small but numerically large number of individuals whose drug use was perceived to have disabling, disruptive social and individual consequences. Theories appeared which, further minimizing personal responsibility, cited causes at the involuntary physiological (Dole & Nyswander, 1965, 1966; Goldstein & Goldstein, 1968) and cultural (Brecher, 1972; Szasz, 1974) levels.

The analysis of broad cultural/historical factors can provide considerable insight into *why* knowledge about the phenomenon of the addictions has taken the various forms it has. But to understand *how* this knowledge grows and develops we must examine the addictions field and consider the structures and processes whereby its knowledge base is generated, disseminated, and utilized by researchers and practitioners.

The following discussion, then, is a functional description of the knowledge transfer system in the field as it is today. Our purpose is not to criticize; rather, we hope that a candid description of the current situation will provide those working in the field with a better understanding of the factors that influence research, theory and practice.

THE CRISIS OF CATEGORIES

Ideas about the phenomenon of the addictions are to be found (a) in statements of problems wanting solution through research and/or direct intervention; (b) in the forms in which these problems are stated; and (c) in the assumptions, presuppositions, and forms of said research and intervention.

Every problem addressed by the addictions field and hence every idea about the phenomenon of addiction derives from the particular perspective and frame of reference of the individual(s) who formulate it. Thus, pharmacologists understand the addictions as a set of pharmacological problems involving such pharmacological categories as drugs, tolerance, or binding sites. Psychologists and psychiatrists are wont to read into the phenomenon problems of learning, compulsion, or ego function. Physiologists posit problems of withdrawal, metabolism, or target organ effects. Sociologists see processes of social regulation, peer pressure, and/or environmental forces. Politicians, lawyers, and law enforcement agents define problems involving controlled substances, criminals, and/or deterrence. At present, no single theory dominates thinking in the field or informs social intervention. Older theories or remnants thereof are still applied in diagnosis and treatment. Nonetheless, current theory and practice, despite the extreme diversity and often strident discord in the field, reflect a growing consensus on the importance of using scientific methods in both research and practice, and on modeling the older, established scientific disciplines.

As an intellectual activity, scholarship in the addictions is a relatively new endeavor. It reflects as well as molds current conceptions and explanations of the phenomenon. Progress in the field takes place when the explanatory categories employed are capable of illuminating a more thorough understanding of the phenomenon under study and are thereby relatively validated by the research that follows. Conversely, new ideas generated from the application of such facilitating categories tend to in question these very categories and their presuppositions. This leads ultimately to a basic questioning of the adequacy of existing categories for the present stage of research. The outcome is a crisis of categories. In the more mature natural sciences this crisis is averted or readily resolved through reference to the set of rules of method and practice adopted in consensus by the particular community of scientists. According to Kuhn (1962), this set of rules or "paradigm" (a) acts as a screen through which only those aspects of experience that are consistent with the paradigm are filtered, and (b) delimits the relevant questions one might pose about experience.

After reviewing the current state of theory, research, and practice, recent theorists (Gambino & Shaffer, 1979; Shaffer, 1977; Shaffer & Gambino, 1979) have concluded that the addictions field lacks a paradigm, and that:

> (1) There is a lack of interface between theory-research and practice (i.e., a prescribed procedure for the translation of the former into the latter); (2) a disregard for the difference between extant theories of addiction which purport to explain the causes of addiction and the need for theories which provide effective strategies for the treatment of the problem associated with addiction (i.e., socially recognizable dysfunctional behavior); and (3) the failure of practitioners to rely upon their own clinical experiences to develop an explicit and viable theory of practice for the treatment of addiction. That is, practitioners have not made explicit the implicit rules that govern their actions with clients, evaluated the effectiveness of those rules, or utilized the valuable knowledge and experience gained through practice to effect the development of an appropriate practice theory (Shaffer & Gambino, 1979, p. 299).

Precisely because it lacks a paradigm, the field is in a state of crisis with regard to the basic categories by which it gathers data and assembles its ideas into theory. Thus, the various discipline-specific ideas and theories can neither disprove nor invalidate one another. These perspectives simply coexist; each has its loyal adherents; each pursues its particular version of truth about the addictions in its own way. Absent the ordering function of a paradigm, one elementary scheme for ordering ideas in the addictions would be to group these according to the source discipline, perspective, or special interest of the individuals who introduce them to the field. While such a scheme might meet a heuristic need for organization and clarification and facilitate the comparing and contrasting of ideas within each group, it would not address the present crisis of categories in the field. To attain clarity with regard to this crisis is, we think, of vital importance for the field. The present chapter is intended to play a catalytic role in that process. We shall begin by examining the current state of knowledge about the phenomenon of the addictions.

Subsequently, we shall consider the knowledge transfer system of the field—specifically, certain aspects of its generation, dissemination, and utilization functions.

The Addictions as an Immature Field of Inquiry

Ravetz (1971) has described as *immature* those fields of human inquiry whose theory, methods, and practices have yet to attain the rigor and consistency of the physical sciences. His analysis of the consequences of the condition of immaturity for the social sciences has direct application to our present description of the natural history of ideas in the addictions. Because this field lacks an integrative, operative paradigm, it lacks its own facts—facts not in the sense of independent units of knowledge about the state of its object of inquiry, the phenomenon of the addictions, but facts considered as a particular sort of assertion about the object of inquiry which may (perhaps imperfectly) correspond to its actual state. "Not all facts are, or become genuine scientific knowledge; they must survive lengthy and rigorous processes of testing and transformation. These take place in the course of the evolution of the different components of a solved problem" (Ravetz, 1971, p. 192).

Ravetz argues that for an assertion to attain fact status it must possess three properties: significance, stability, and invariance (1971, p. 188). An assertion has *significance* if it is noticed by someone and judged to be of at least potential interest and value for the field. Such recognition presupposes the assertion's fundamental intelligibility for at least some workers in the field. In the addictions, most of the proffered assertions would be considered insignificant—even incomprehensible—by at least some workers. Consider, for example, Wikler's (1973) masterful theoretical statement on the etiology of addiction in which he integrates complex and subtle ideas derived from pharmacology, learning theory, and physiology. Wikler, a physician-researcher, first published this paper in a medical journal. Yet, to comprehend his argument one requires a level of knowledge of pharmacology, learning-theory, and physiology quite beyond that held by even the typical physician-reader. While this paper and others of its type are often referenced in technical works about the addictions, for most workers in the field such assertions are unintelligible and therefore lack significance.

The *stability* of an assertion refers to its capacity for reproduction, i.e., to generate other ideas, to further specify existing problems, or to define new problems or subproblems. Consider the long life and many progeny of Rado's (1933) application of psychoanalytic theory to the phenomenon of the addictions. His assertions about the compulsive aspects of an individual's drug use have provided an enduring motif for subsequent theorists and practitioners in psychoanalysis, as well as in psychiatry, psychology, sociology, and social work. Clearly these notions of compulsion and dependence have been stable and useful ideas for a wide variety of thinkers in the addictions.

The property of *invariance* is defined by Ravetz (1971) as follows:

> We have seen how science advances through the investigation of problems; how each problem is concerned with the drawing of conclusions about certain classes of intellectually constructed things and events; and how these classes, existing only through the determination of their properties, change even in the course of the investigation of a single problem. When a solved problem has been presented to the community, and new work is done on its basis, then the objects of investigation will necessarily change, sometimes only slightly, but sometimes drastically. In a retrospect on the original problem, even after a brief period of development, its argument will be seen as concerning objects which no longer exist. There is then the question of whether it can be translated or recast so as to relate to the newer objects descended from the original ones, and still be an adequate foundation for a conclusion. If not, then the original conclusion is rejected as dealing with non-objects, or as ascribing false properties to real objects. But if such a translation or recasting is possible, then the original solved problem is seen to have contained some element which is invariant with respect to the changes in the objects of investigation (pp. 188-189).

Gendreau and Gendreau (1970) traced the history of the "addictive personality" through its various manifestations and expressions in personality theory and as a motif in theory derived from other paradigms. That drug use (to the point of dependence) might reflect a predisposition or stable trait of the individual drug user was long and widely held to be a useful and valuable idea in drug treatment. Though clearly significant and stable, the idea has come to be rejected for referring to a nonobject (Gendreau & Gendreau, 1970, 1971); it thus fails to attain fact status for lack of the property of invariance.

The addictions is a strongly theoretical field in which the objects of investigation and intervention are continuously and rapidly changing. Few assertions become facts. Libraries are being filled with research reports, theoretical statements, and philosophical manifestos; all of these are products of hard work and considerable expense, and some of inspiration as well. Nevertheless, one can find few, if any, facts. Though one or another group of related ideas may enjoy a momentary ascendency on the basis of merit or facilitation by a constellation of economic, political, and cultural forces (both internal and external to the field), none can validly claim to be determining and defining for the entire field. Theorists in the field have avoided the construction of the type of comprehensive theory characteristic of the early years of psychology and psychiatry. Instead, the emphasis has been on developing mini-theories limited to elucidating one or a limited number of factors or dimensions of the phenomenon. With few exceptions (cf. Burglass, Bremer & Evans, 1975a, 1975b; Wikler, 1973), multifactorial models of addiction have not been constructed, despite the recognized utility of model building for the development of psychological theory (Chapanis, 1961; Lachman, 1960; Simon & Newell, 1963). Distinct groups of related ideas have been creatively combined, even integrated (rarely), across disciplinary lines. Thus there are psycho-pharmacological, socio-political, behavioral-neurological, and other hyphenated ideas and theories about the phenomenon of the addictions. Although the hyphen itself signifies an unacknowledged paradigm, no explicit paradigm yet exists which provides for the hyphenization of all of the discipline-specific paradigms presently generating ideas about the addictions.

FACTORS INFLUENCING THE GENERATION OF IDEAS

Ideas in the field arise from research and from the experience of practitioners providing treatment services to individuals with so-called drug problems. Research in the treatment of the addictions addresses three formal types of problems: scientific, technical, and practical. An example of a *scientific* problem would be the nature of the opiate receptor in the brain; development of a long acting, orally effective narcotic antagonist would constitute a *technical* problem; and treatment of the polydrug client in an outpatient setting a *practical* problem.

Scientific and technical problems are typically investigated by researchers trained in the disciplines that formulate the terms of these problems. Practical problems are usually investigated by treatment practitioners using a variety of unarticulated paradigms and representing heterogenous viewpoints and interests. Knowledge about practical problems has derived more from clinical experience than from direct research. The nature of practical problems in the addictions, particularly their economic and political aspects, has dictated a merging of research and intervention that has not in every instance facilitated the work of either. Research efforts on all three types of problems, as well as treatment practice, have been significantly influenced by the way such activities are funded.

Funding in the addictions in the main is centralized and governmental. While the centralization of sources *could* facilitate long-range planning and the development of comprehensive solutions, governmental funding, operating through the mechanisms of contracts and grant awards, is typically short-term. Thus, there is little continuity of ideas, the people who generate them, or the programs in which the thoughts are expressed or realized. Ideas, therefore, tend to be less than fully developed or verified. According to Pelz (1967), maximal scientific achievement is likely to be realized in those research environments that manage to maintain a "creative tension" between sources of challenge and security. The addictions field certainly contains many challenges for its workers but provides little security beyond whatever comfort and stability may be derived from the pursuit of specialized research in a narrow area. It is perhaps not surprising that few ideas attain fact status under the existing system.

Because funding sources are governmental, their priorities and decisions can be influenced as much by political factors as by the merits of the proposed projects. The recent trend toward decentralization of federal funding, with the mandated involvement of state, county, and municipal governments and regulatory agencies, has only compounded the problem and made more complex the already difficult and demanding grant application and contract award procedures.

Competition for funds is keen among the field's diverse interest groups, each with an agenda for research and intervention informed by its own particular conceptions of the problem and the field. The sheer complexity of the funding process acts to reward only the most diligent applicants, who not surprisingly are usually those whose proposals are better formulated and more conventionally or elegantly articulated—in other words, the degreed professionals. The less traditional, countercultural, or alternative methods and perspectives often espoused by nondegreed professionals are often at a stylistic disadvantage and, despite their merits, may fail to win funding.

In today's technocratic view of science as a basic factor of production, many practically valuable scientific results are treated as a sort of commodity to be produced under contract. The vast majority of the public funds given to the addictions flows directly or indirectly from the National Institute on Drug Abuse (NIDA). Chartered in 1973 as the principal conduit for federal funds for the addictions, the agency is mandated to provide

> leadership, policies, and goals for the federal effort in the prevention, control and treatment of narcotic addiction and drug abuse, and the rehabilitation of affected individuals. In carrying

out these responsibilities the Institute: (1) conducts and supports research on the biological, psychological, sociological and epidemiological aspects of narcotic addiction and drug abuse; (2) supports the training of professional and paraprofessional personnel in prevention, treatment and control of drug abuse; (3) conducts and supports research on the development and improvement of drug abuse services delivery, administration, and financing, and supports services, programs, and projects . . . ; (4) collaborates with and provides technical assistance to state authorities and Regional Offices and supports state and community efforts in planning, establishing, maintaining, coordinating and evaluating more effective narcotic addiction and drug abuse programs; (5) collaborates with, provides assistance to, and encourages other federal agencies, national, foreign, state and local organizations, hospitals and volunteer groups to facilitate and extend programs for the prevention of narcotic addiction, and for the care, treatment, and rehabilitation of addicted persons; (6) provides information on narcotic addiction and drug abuse to the public and to the scientific community (*Federal Register*, 1974, pp. 1656-1658).

In addition to funding treatment services, NIDA supports directed and nondirected research. Directed research is typically initiated by the agency with contracts for its execution awarded to individual or institutional researchers. Nondirected research is funded by means of grant awards to individual investigators for projects of their own conception. Grant applications are evaluated in a peer review process and awards are made on the proposal's merits and relevance to current federal funding priorities. While such grant awards, strictly speaking, are not contracts for specialized products, prospective researchers soon learn the wisdom of tailoring their interests and proposals to fit the prevailing funding priorities of the agency. In order to sustain a research effort and maintain a staff in the face of annually shifting priorities, the contractor-researcher is obliged to become somewhat of an entrepreneur who juggles a portfolio of grants and contracts—existing, extendable, renewable, or prospective—from various offices in one or more agencies. The capital of this precarious research business is the agency contacts and whatever credibility the researcher manages to accrue with those who make the funding decisions. Such conditions are not always conducive to the production of high quality research, and much of the work can be self-serving so long as it satisfies the administrative and political needs of the agency contacts. Talented individuals often feel pressured to maintain a stream of output or "product" (agency jargon) without particular regard for its utility or validity for the field.

Researchers, as chief investigators, usually are obliged to administer their own projects, a task for which most are ill-suited by experience, training, or inclination. They are saddled with demanding administrative responsibilities which leave little time for reflective thinking, conceptual construction, or other creative work; yet, they are expected to produce a steady flow of reports and publications as proof of continued competence and activity. It is no wonder that much of the federally funded research "product" contributes little to the advancement of knowledge in the field (see Wachtel, 1980, for an interesting discussion of this issue in psychology). For when a research contractor sets the goals of the "shop" to be the renewal or gaining of grants and contracts, the survival of the shop and researcher often can be assured only at the expense of the development of valuable ideas.

Because funding sources prefer to support research conducted in a treatment context, patients tend to become subjects in research studies and research subjects tend to be patients in treatment programs. When this happens clinical principles may be compromised by research needs, and research designs may be hampered or thwarted by treatment considerations. Either way the consequences are less than desirable. Patients may suffer unnecessarily, and ideas may be tested in a less than rigorous fashion.

DISSEMINATION AND UTILIZATION PROCESSES

Dissemination refers to the process whereby knowledge—generated through basic and applied research or derived from treatment experience—finds its way through formal and informal channels to the individuals or groups who will utilize it in further research or treatment. *Utilization* refers to what happens when knowledge arrives at its destination, i.e., how it is received, transformed, and consumed by the user. Dissemination and utilization (D&U), while two distinct processes, are so interrelated that discussion of these is facilitated by their simultaneous consideration, as if both were aspects of a single process.

Considering the magnitude of resources invested by the public and private sectors of society in the development of knowledge in all fields, it is astonishing how little is known about the ways such knowledge is used or applied to the actual practices of the field(s) for which it is generated. As a research field, D&U can be said to be in its infancy. One of the more prolific of the few full-time D&U researchers, Ronald Havelock, and his colleagues have studied the D&U functions of a wide range of governmental and private agencies, institutions, and programs (Harary & Havelock, 1972; Havelock, 1973; Havelock & Guskin, 1969; Havelock & Lingwood, 1973; Havelock & Markowitz, 1971) and have evolved a theoretical model of the knowledge transfer process. This model specifies six sets of functions that are necessary for knowledge producers (researchers) and consumers (users) to work together in one need domain as an integrated problem-solving system:

(1) *User Self-Servicing*—activities that facilitate the user's awareness of (a) the need for solutions to specified problems and (b) the availability of resources.

(2) *Need Processing*—activities required for the communication of user needs to resource persons and systems.

(3) *Solution Building*—activities serving the research and development enterprise.

(4) *Solution Processing*—activities of dissemination and diffusion whereby solutional ideas are transformed, translated, and transmitted to user systems.

(5) *Microsystem Building*—activities that enable researchers and users to interact on a small scale.

(6) *Macrosystem Building*—activities that facilitate system governance, e.g., system mapping and system monitoring. (See Havelock and Lingwood, 1973, for a detailed exposition of this theoretical model and its application to four very different federal agencies.)

No comprehensive study of the D&U process in the addictions or even in NIDA has yet been done. While such an enormous task is beyond the scope of the present chapter, we shall refer to elements of Havelock's model in the following discussion of selected aspects of structure and process that influence the dissemination and utilization of knowledge in the addictions.

Formal Channels of Dissemination

The *formal* channels provide for a rapid dissemination of research results, theoretical formulations, and evaluative studies. In a maximal knowledge transfer system the formal channels would also carry communications *from* users *to* resource systems. The *informal* channels transmit the methods and style of a field to a restricted audience in an interpersonal context. What gets into the formal channels, i.e., in journals and other publications, conferences, and formal training, is in large part determined by judgments made on the basis of principles transmitted in the informal channels. The latter are the subtle, but sophisticated aspects of the craft knowledge constituting the methods of the field. "Yet the criteria on whose basis editors and referees assess papers appear nowhere in the public channel itself" (Ravetz, 1971, p. 177). In the addictions the formal channels serve aspects of the knowledge transfer functions of need processing, solution building, and solution processing.

Publications. The field has some two dozen periodicals devoted exclusively to the problems of the addictions. The quality of these varies considerably, ranging from excellent refereed journals to inferior controlled circulation publications edited by one or another interest group and containing informational or general interest articles often more polemic than scholarly in tone. Beyond the routine required circulation audits, the distribution and utilization of these periodicals have not been analyzed. Articles and reports about the addictions regularly appear in the journals and publications of those disciplines actively engaged in the field. In a study of psychiatric research output, Brodie and Sabshin (1973) reported that between 1965 and 1973 drug abuse moved from 19th to 1st among 21 categories of papers published in the field's two leading journals or presented at its two most prestigious research conferences. Our own cursory review of the cumulative indices of journals in psychology, medicine, and pharmacology for the past five years suggests a similar trend in these disciplines. Of course, the fact that more and more articles about the addictions are being published in specialty journals and those of other disciplines does not necessarily mean that the ideas in those articles are actually reaching and being utilized by workers in the field. Probably more psychiatrists and psychologists are reading about the addictions today than ten years ago, but only a small percentage of these professionals work in the field. To our knowledge, no analysis of the reading or study habits of addiction workers in general has been done.

Government funding for research or treatment projects with few exceptions requires that results be reported to someone somewhere in written form. The ultimate fate of such reports is in large part unknown. A few are published by the funding agencies as monographs or included with related papers in an edited volume. Such publications are rarely marketed through bookstores; these are sometimes distributed gratis to presumably interested individuals and institutions or are simply kept in stock and made available upon request. The NIDA publication of reports prepared by and for the agency, because these are printed by the Government Printing Office and distributed through the Superintendent of Documents, are often slow to appear and may be many months or even years behind the current state of knowledge in the field. NIDA also provides information for practitioners through reports and mono-graphs prepared by the Center for the Study of Narcotics Addiction and Drug Abuse and the Center for Drug Abuse Information. The National Clearinghouse for Drug Abuse Information abstracts the current liter-ature and publishes these in a Research Issues series. The agency also operates data collection and filing services that draw from ongoing re-search projects, clearinghouses, library collections, and other data bases. Agency sponsored regional and national task forces and review com-mittees also collect and synthesize data generated in funded projects. State-of-the-art monographs and condensations of recent findings are distributed to policymakers, professional practitioners, and in more or less well translated versions, to the general public. To our knowledge, no systematic mechanism exists for the periodic review and updating of data bases; hence, field requests for information from these sources may yield materials of varying consistency, age, and value.

Conferences. A number of symposia, meetings, and conferences devoted to topics in the addictions are held each year. Most of these gatherings are convened under the auspices of one of the various professional or academic organizations whose members are active in the addictions field. Such conferences promote microsystem building and offer an excellent opportunity for relatively like-minded researchers and practitioners to share ideas, but rarely do these serve as forums for a multiperspective discussion of addiction. The principal multidisciplinary national confer-ence devoted to all aspects of the addictions has been funded by the federal government since 1968. This annual gathering is mandated to be a forum where workers of different theoretical and philosophical persuasions can come together to share ideas and collaborate in the development of policy and programs. The conference organizers solicit presentations of research reports and theory papers via a widely pub-licized call for abstracts. Submitted abstracts are then reviewed by topic-specific task forces comprised ideally of interested individuals from re-search, treatment, or training programs across the nation. The papers thus selected are delivered at the conference as individual presentations or, more commonly, as one of a panel of related papers. The conference generally invites high ranking government and agency officials in the addictions to make policy presentations at plenary sessions.

Attendance at these conferences has increased significantly in recent years. The 1978 National Drug Abuse Conference, organized around the theme of a multicultural view of drug abuse, attracted over 3,000 participants to Seattle for the five-day event. Over the past four years, conference organizers and sponsoring agencies have made an effort to broaden the base of attendance and participation to include representatives from racial, ethnic, and sexual minority groups; special interest factions; and the self-help movement. The provision of scholarships has encouraged agencies to send more nondegreed professionals. As might be expected, the nature and quality of presentations given at these conferences vary considerably. The same panel may have a data-based, statistically analyzed research report back-to-back with a subjective, conceptual, or philosophical statement. There have been as yet no formal studies of the knowledge transfer processes or practical consequences of these conferences.

What participants actually learn (if anything) at such conferences can be but an object of speculation. Based on our own experience as participants and observers at these events and on that of staff members in programs with which we have been associated, we can state that these conferences *do provide* for information exchange and thus at least potentially facilitate the development of ideas in the field. Recent conferences have provided a forum for the orderly and not-so-orderly expression of a broad spectrum of political ideas and perspectives. The presence of agency officials and politicians has afforded participants a potential means for having their views translated into policy and programming.

Neither the conferences nor any other structure or activity in the field appears to serve the functions of enhancing awareness of, mapping, monitoring, or otherwise governing the knowledge transfer macrosystem in the addictions.

Informal Channels of Dissemination

Training. Urgent calls from the public and private sectors for immediate solutions to putative drug problems have augmented the field's innate tendency to expand. The growing need for workers has generated great demand for training at all levels, but particularly for the front-line treatment workers who provide services directly to program clients. In the most common form of program organization, direct client services are provided by workers with less than complete formal training or graduate education. The workers with full professional training in counseling, social work, psychology, or psychiatry are typically employed as supervisors of front-line workers or in administrative roles. *These less than fully trained front-line workers are the true treatment practitioners in the addictions.* Because they are supervised and directed by more senior, and/or better trained staff members, these practitioners work much as technicians. One characteristic of the work of a technician is that successful use of a technique does not require a command of the theory of that technique. Training in its use, then, can be given in the form of precepts rather than principles. Lacking facts, the addiction field has a diverse and at times bewildering body of knowledge from which to draw for training purposes. Consequently, much of the knowledge that comes to be standardized for training purposes is contained in aphorisms and techniques.

Since there is no single standard text in the addictions, trainees are taught the precepts, techniques, philosophy, and aphorisms of that "school" of treatment to which their teachers ascribe. Much of the skill thought requisite for the would-be treatment practitioner is resistant to orderly formulation (see Mills, 1959, and Elton, 1967, for discussions of this problem in sociology and history, respectively). Oakeshott (1967) states of such craft training: "In every ability there is an ingredient which cannot be resolved into information, and in some skills this may be the greater part of the knowledge required for their practice" (p. 112). Thus, training in the addictions field contains a clear element of indoctrination, and trainees are all too often obliged to believe in order to understand.

Accountability and quality assurance requirements imposed by the third parties who fund treatment services have pressured the field to present its craft knowledge as a formalized body of doctrine imitating a mature science. Without such form, the required evaluation and cert-ification tasks would be virtually impossible, and stable hierarchies and institutions could not be maintained. The learning of standardized ver-sions of this already dilute body of knowledge leaves the front-line prac-titioner somewhat ill-equipped to understand—let alone intervene in—the complex phenomenon of addiction.

There are many fine practitioners in the addictions; few, however, became expert through formal academic channels since academic and clinical training programs traditionally have not provided trainees with opportunities to gain significant experience with drug dependent clients. Consequently, skills in the addictions have tended to be acquired in-ductively—leaving practitioners unable to articulate (a) the principles of their craft (Shaffer & Gambino, 1979) or (b) explicit models to guide the training of practitioners-to-be. In some programs, particularly those organized around the self-help concept, formal training has been con-sidered less valuable than the "life experience" and commitment of the practitioner. In such programs, clients and counselors are matched on the basis of their common membership in a social, racial, or ethnic col-lective; for example, ex-addict with ex-addict, woman with woman, black with black, etc. However, as Van Utt and Burglass (1978) note, the collectivist matching of a client with an *inexperienced or incompletely trained counselor*, despite its current political and economic expedience, *can* result in (a) the creation of an artificial therapeutic focus on stereotyped collectivist concerns, (b) an obscuring of the ultimate therapeutic goal by fostering dependence on the collectivist identification, and (c) an increased probability of a loss of objectivity in transference and countertransference issues.

In recent years NIDA has modified its funding "guidelines" to reflect the agency's growing emphasis on training for all levels of program personnel. A network of NIDA-developed regional training centers offers courses in addiction theory and practice, program management, and research topics. The agency also provides educational assistance to programs in the form of on-site training curricula, fellowships for degreed professionals, and technical consultations.

The development of academic training programs has not been limited by the conceptual and applied chaos in the field. Grants and contracts have been preferentially awarded to individuals with formal agency or institutional (especially academic) affiliations. In fact, on occasion, otherwise questionable training activities have derived legitimacy and prestige from such academic affiliations. A number of undergraduate, graduate, and nondegreed professional programs have emerged; these are taught by a curious mixture of educational enterpreneurs (e.g., philosophers, social reformers, pharmacists, and clinicians). Graduates of such programs often become "manpower units"—commodities to be utilized as drug treatment practitioners, "in-house experts," or addiction consultants—instead of well-grounded clinicians sensitive to the complex and often counterintuitive human problems associated with compulsive drug use. Further, these fledgling practitioners must often work in relative clinical isolation; that is, there may be little support or help available to them to deal with what is considered, in more elite circles, to be an undesirable treatment population. Nonetheless, most clients, whose choice of service providers is limited to one or another of the certified treatment programs authorized to deal with their particular drug problem, must take what they get or get nothing.

Supervision. More so than does formal training, individual supervision shapes the clinical thinking of the front-line treatment practitioner. This remnant of the apprenticeship system in the learned professions is a prominent feature in the training of physicians, psychologists, psychiatrists, social workers, and counselors. It provides an intense interpersonal context for the transmission of both information and the more subtle craft elements of method and practice of the professions. (See Hess, 1980, and Lambert, 1980, for detailed consideration of the supervision process from the perspectives of training and research, respectively.)

As a learning experience, supervision is not, however, without its limitations. De la Torre and Appelbaum (1974) have noted the tendency for supervisees in psychiatry to think in clichés and aphorisms that reflect the views of their supervisors. If, as is common in psychiatry and psychology but uncommon in addiction treatment programs, trainees are exposed to several supervisors of different clinical schools, the use of clichés will be but a stage in the trainee's acquisition of knowledge. However, if trainees have but one or two supervisors or have several of like persuasion, clichéd thinking is apt to be an enduring characteristic of their clinical reasoning. The typical drug treatment program is obliged to provide supervision for its front-line practitioners, but supervision competes, often unsuccessfully, for the already scarce time of the program's senior staff of fully trained professionals, and with the current pattern of close (often marginal) funding, allocations for outside supervision services are necessarily limited. Consequently, for many programs, supervision is necessarily provided by less than fully trained practitioners. These "supervisors" may have no formal training in supervision and but little more clinical experience than those they supervise. It is a fact of life for many drug treatment programs that supervision exists more on paper than in practice.

In the delivery of services there is often a significant discrepancy between the level of theoretical understanding and technical skill of a program's clinical professionals and that of its front-line practitioners. Beyond the obvious implications for the quality of treatment services, another significant consequence of this knowledge and performance gap is that the clinical directors of a program may have little idea about what *actually* goes on in the encounters between the program's practitioners and their clients. Evaluation of treatment outcome and process is thereby seriously compromised.

Invisible Colleges. Crane (1969, 1970, 1972) has examined the role of social organization and personal influence in the diffusion of knowledge within scientific fields. The term "invisible colleges" has been applied to subgroups of workers in a field who through personal communications exchange and transmit information in the field. This informal communications network linking groups of collaborators across institutional and geographical lines also serves to recruit and socialize new members, to define and prioritize research problems, and to stimulate interest and commitment to the field among its members. While a rigorous sociological analysis of knowledge in the addictions has yet to be done, we think that there is good evidence for the existence of invisible colleges in this field. Informal examination of the composition of editorial and advisory boards and conference, program, and grant review committees suggests that their members are drawn from a relatively small pool of workers.

Again, although no formal study has been made of the field's publication citation patterns, our review of the literature for this volume indicates that there are distinct subgroups of researchers who cite each other's work over and over, and who study closely related problems. The invisible college influences knowledge transfer *directly*, because it is itself an informal channel for the transmission of ideas among its members and *indirectly*, because the influence exerted by its members in other informal and formal channels affects the dissemination and utilization of knowledge for the entire field.

Knowledge Utilization in Clinical Practice

Given the condition of knowledge about the phenomenon of addiction, the work of treatment practitioners necessarily embodies some aspects of an eclectic model. In its *content* this model is more a multitheoretical than an interdisciplinary or integrated one. Presented in supervision and training with a bewildering array of diverse and often contradictory theoretical points and perspectives, practitioners learn to select the more appealing or useful features of these for clinical application. How these theory fragments are combined and reconciled is determined in part by the clinical context and in part by the *structure* of the eclectic model, i.e., its relatively atheoretical aspects which reflect the worker's rules of practice. Degreed professionals in the field tend to work in accordance with the rules of practice characteristic of their disciplines; nonetheless, they, too, may be unable to specify these implicit rules beyond being merely "sound clinical principles" or "standard clinical practice." Front-line practitioners, because they have not acquired the professional's methodical approach to practice and do not share a well-defined professional identity, are even more apt to work intuitively. Whereas the content of their therapy, i.e., its theoretical basis and techniques, *appears* eclectic, practitioners may have no structure for organizing their clinical thinking; thus, their work with clients may lack formal consistency.

Dimond, Havens, and Jones (1978) have formulated a conceptual framework for the practice of eclectic psychotherapy. This "clinical process" involves (a) the use of theory, (b) assessment, (c) goal-setting, (d) intervention, and (e) evaluation. The use of such a structure to guide clinical work can provide a practitioner with a consistent role definition, while allowing for the specific means of treatment to be drawn from the entire body of relevant knowledge (Havens & Dimond, 1976). Using this model, we shall now consider to what extent the work of the front-line practitioner is truly eclectic.

Theory. Certainly, all practitioners make use of theory, even if implicitly, in their work with clients. Ideally, they would use their knowledge base *prescriptively,* i.e., drawing upon only those aspects of theory thought to be useful for a particular client. Unfortunately, because they are trained as technicians, front-line practitioners tend to view clients rather stereotypically, seeing each as an instance of a general clinical "type," e.g., as a "character disorder," or a "hustler" or a "wounded bird." Trained with precepts and aphorisms, they may recognize clinical entities only when these present in florid form. Conversely, because they have often been given only an overview or introduction to a clinical topic, they may find that particular characteristic, syndrome, or diagnostic entity in every client they encounter. Some front-line workers will have personal difficulty with their perceived lack of status, power, and knowledge and may define and defend a negative theoretical position that is little more than a rejection or refutation of whatever theories they are offered in training or supervision.

Many programs are funded to deliver only specified forms of treatment, e.g., methadone maintenance, barbiturate detoxification, or concept therapy. In such programs, front-line workers are in effect *told* what theoretical base to use in their clinical work. Even in multimodality programs, the overall style and form of treatment tend to be defined by senior professional clinicians. In a drug treatment program operated under the auspices of a medical school or hospital department of psychiatry, a front-line practitioner might find it difficult and uncomfortable to operate from a widely divergent clinical perspective.

Assessment. In an eclectic process, assessment provides the means of diagnosis which in turn yields a prescriptive treatment. In programs where the client population is closely specified, e.g., female sedative users or black adolescent heroin users, clinical assessment may not be thought of great importance or necessity. All clients may be thought to have the same problem. Even in programs organized around a broader conception of psychological problems, the fact that clients present or are referred for drug-related problems may suggest that comprehensive assessment of individuals and their needs merits but little attention. Front-line workers in such programs will not develop the assessment skills necessary for the proper practice of prescriptive eclectic therapy.

Goal-setting. Traditionally, the explicit or implicit goal set for clients in drug treatment programs has been abstinence. Few theorists or clinicians (cf. Zinberg, Harding, & Winkeller, 1977) acknowledge controlled drug use as an acceptable goal for clients. If, then, all clients are expected to become abstinent, the practitioner need spend no time working with an individual in the process of goal-setting. In a truly eclectic model, goal-setting work with a client is a necessary means of individualizing treatment prescriptions. In the typical drug program, practitioners will learn very little about this process, and when confronted with an atypical case, for example, a drug-dependent person with a valid chronic pain syndrome, they may impose unrealistic expectations on the client.

Intervention. The intervention skill of front-line practitioners is limited by the type of technical training they receive. They may speak only one clinical language, i.e., they may have access to but one set of conceptions, one vocabulary, or one interpersonal therapeutic style. Thus, a client may get what the practitioner has to offer, rather than the practitioner's supplying what the client needs. For example, a self-consciously religious client may have difficulty finding a practitioner who knows how to say what he/she knows about drugs and human behavior in a religiously oriented language. In all too many cases the practitioner's limited ability to translate from one conceptual idiom to another means that the effect of the intervention on the client is rather like that of shining a bright red light into an ear!

Evaluation. It is little wonder that practitioners rarely internalize a structure for evaluating their work with clients at the levels of either the utterance, interchange, session, or course of treatment. *If* all clients are viewed stereotypically, *if* a comprehensive assessment is not made, *if* the goal of treatment is always the same, and *if* the practitioner has only one therapeutic style to offer the client, *then* the in-process evaluation of treatment efforts will *add* little or nothing, precisely because it can *change* little or nothing. Evaluation of outcomes is commonly left for research professionals, and only rarely does this knowledge reach the practitioner. When it does, it is likely to be buried in an inscrutable research report. Because many of the policies and procedures in drug treatment are dictated by governmental and other funding sources, treatment outcome research findings are of less value for practitioners than these might be in a more flexible, responsive setting. (See Goldstein et al., 1975, for an interesting example of this problem in methadone maintenance treatment.)

In summary, the work of the front-line treatment practitioner cannot properly be considered as eclectic. Though it may reflect a multitheoretical view of drug problems, the individualized, prescriptive aspects requisite to an eclectic approach are thwarted by constraints imposed by the structure of the treatment delivery system and by the practitioner's lack of an organizing framework for clinical practice.

CONCLUSIONS

In this chapter we have attempted to provide an overview of the structures and processes which shape the generation, dissemination, and utilization of ideas in the addictions, considered both as a scientific discipline and as a field of practice. Within this framework, a number of themes can be identified.

(1) A crisis of categories exists within the body of knowledge associated with the phenomenon of the addictions. Specifically, this crisis is characterized by (a) the absence of an accepted paradigm; (b) the consequent paucity of facts; (c) the lack of integration between theory, research, and practice; and (d) the failure to successfully coordinate the solution of scientific, technical, and practical problems.

(2) Very little is known about the processes of dissemination and utilization of knowledge in the field. Increasing our understanding of these activities through empirical and theoretical research of the D&U system in the addictions would likely increase the efficiency of this system and consequently maximize the utility of knowledge generated by the field. Maximal utilization of knowledge would in turn facilitate the identification and development of facts, a necessary precondition for the maturation of the field.

(3) The growth of knowledge in the addictions does not appear to be adequately described by either (a) the traditional understanding of science, in which new ideas progress in logical sequence from antecedent formulations through the processes of hypothesis formulation and testing; (b) Price's view (1970) that new ideas in a field need not develop sequentially but may arise from any previous work; (c) Kuhn's paradigmatic model (1962) in which cumulative growth ("normal science") is punctuated with periods of discontinuity and disagreement which result in the formulation of a new set of rules (paradigm) for inquiry; (d) Kroeber's view (1957) that the rapid expansion of knowledge in a field leads to the exhaustion of the ideas that initially stimulated its growth; or (e) Toulmin's theory (1963, 1967), wherein continual change in the objects and methods of inquiry results in a "selective perpetuation of preferred intellectual variants" that enables an old idea to survive or to be reintroduced after new facts are established. (For a brilliant illustration of this last point as applied to the development of the concept of the "borderline personality," see Mack, 1975.)

Perhaps a future model which combines or integrates aspects of each of these theories will explain the development of ideas in the addictions. Alternatively, any and all formulations about *scientific* knowledge may be inappropriate and inapplicable to knowledge in the addictions.

(4) Knowledge and practice in the addictions have been and are *profoundly* affected by broad cultural factors external to the field and by the unparalleled and unprecedented influence of government in defining and funding research and in regulating practice.

(5) The clinical work of the front-line treatment practitioner, despite its great diversity of form and content, does not reflect a *truly* eclectic, prescriptive model of therapy. Although no theoretical consensus exists among practitioners in the field, what clients *actually* receive in the various treatment programs is for the most part different versions of more of the same.

We believe that the articles that follow are examples of outstandingly creative efforts to initiate, organize, and communicate important ideas about the phenomenon of the addictions. Taken together, these works provide an historical perspective on thinking about the phenomenon during the modern era, clarify our understanding of past and present treatment practices in the field, and by identifying the accomplishments and deficiencies of the past, facilitate the achievements of the future.

Lastly, we affirm our personal commitment to the development of knowledge in the field, for it is *precisely* in immature fields such as the addictions where the greatest challenges in research and practice are to be found.

REFERENCES

ABRAHAM, K. The psychological relation between sexuality and alcoholism. In *Selected papers of Karl Abraham.* New York: Basic Books, 1960. (Originally published, 1908.)

BRECHER, E. M. *Licit and illicit drugs.* Boston: Little, Brown, 1972.

BRODIE, K., & SABSHIN, M. Overview of trends in psychiatric research. *American Journal of Psychiatry,* 1973, *130,* 1301-1318.

BURGLASS, M. E., BREMER, D. H., & EVANS, R. J. *Opiate dependency cycle.* Cambridge, Mass.: Correctional Solutions Foundation Press, 1975a.

BURGLASS, M. E., BREMER, D. H., & EVANS, R. J. *Sedative-hypnotic dependency cycle.* Cambridge, Mass.: Correctional Solutions Foundation Press, 1975b.

CHAPANIS, A. Men, machines, and models. *American Psychologist,* 1961, *16,* 113-131.

CRANE, D. Social structure in a group of scientists: A test of the "invisible college" hypothesis. *American Sociological Review,* 1969, *34,* 335-352.

CRANE, D. The nature of scientific communication and influence: A theoretical model. *International Social Science Journal,* 1970, *22,* 28-41.

CRANE, D. *Invisible colleges: Diffusion of knowledge in scientific communities.* Chicago: University of Chicago Press, 1972.

DE LA TORRE, J., & APPELBAUM, A. Use and misuse of clichés in clinical supervision. *Archives of General Psychiatry,* 1974, *31,* 302-306.

DIMOND, R. E., & HAVENS, R. A. Restructuring psychotherapy: Toward a prescriptive eclecticism. *Professional Psychology,* 1975, *6,* 193-200.

DIMOND, R. E., HAVENS, R. A., & JONES, A. C. A conceptual framework for the practice of prescriptive eclecticism in psychotherapy. *American Psychologist,* 1978, *33,* 239-248.

DOLE, V. P., & NYSWANDER, M. A medical treatment for diacetylmorphine (heroin) addiction. *Journal of the American Medical Association,* 1965, *193,* 80-84.

DOLE, V. P., & NYSWANDER, M. E. Rehabilitation of heroin addicts after blockade with methadone. *New York State Journal of Medicine,* 1966, 2011-2017.

ELTON, G. R. *The practice of history.* London: Collins (The Fontana Library), 1967.

Federal Register, 1974, *39*(8), 1656-1658.

GAMBINO, B., & SHAFFER, H. The concept of paradigm and the treatment of addiction. *Professional Psychology*, 1979, *10*, 207-223.
GENDREAU, P., & GENDREAU, L. P. The "addiction-prone" personality: A study of Canadian heroin addicts. *Canadian Journal of Behavioural Science*, 1970, *2*, 18-25.
GENDREAU, P., & GENDREAU, L. P. Research design and narcotic addiction proneness. *Canadian Psychiatric Association Journal*, 1971, *16*, 265-267.
GOLDSTEIN, A., & GOLDSTEIN, D. B. Enzyme expansion theory of drug tolerance and physical dependence. In A. Wikler (Ed.), *The addictive states*. Baltimore: Williams and Wilkins, 1968.
GOLDSTEIN, A., HANSTEEN, R. W., & HORNS, W. H. Control of methadone dosage by patients. *Journal of the American Medical Association*, 1975, *234*, 734-737.
HARARY, R., & HAVELOCK, R. Anatomy of a communication arc. *Human Relations*, 1972, *25*, 413-426.
HAVELOCK, R. G. *What do we know from research about the process of research utilization*. Ann Arbor: Center for Research on Utilization of Scientific Knowledge, Institute for Social Research, University of Michigan, 1973.
HAVELOCK, R. G. & GUSKIN, A. *Planning for innovation through dissemination and utilization of knowledge*. Ann Arbor: Center for Research on Utilization of Scientific Knowledge, Institute for Social Research, University of Michigan, 1973.
HAVELOCK, R. G., & LINGWOOD, D. A. *Research utilization programs: A comparison of D & U functions among federal agencies*. Ann Arbor: Center for Research on Utilization of Scientific Knowledge, Institute for Social Research, University of Michigan, 1973.
HAVELOCK, R. G., & MARKOWITZ, E. A. *A national problem-solving system: Highway safety researchers and decision makers*. Ann Arbor: Center for Research on Utilization of Scientific Knowledge, Institute for Social Research, University of Michigan, 1971.
HAVENS, R. A., & DIMOND, R. E. The clinical cube. *Professional Psychology*, 1976, *7*, 403-405.
HESS, A. K. Training models and the nature of psychotherapy supervision. In A. K. Hess (Ed.), *Psychotherapy supervision: Theory, research and practice*. New York: Wiley, 1980.
KROEBER, A. L. *Style and civilizations*. Ithaca, N.Y.: Cornell University Press, 1957.
KUHN, T. S. *The structure of scientific revolutions*. Chicago: University of Chicago Press, 1962.
LACHMAN, R. The model in theory construction. *Psychological Review*, 1960, *67*, 113-129.
LAMBERT, M. J. Research and the supervisory process. In A. K. Hess (Ed.), *Psychotherapy supervision: Theory, research and practice*. New York: Wiley, 1980.
LAZARE, A. Psychiatric examination in the walk-in clinic. *Archives of General Psychiatry*, 1976, *33*, 96-102.
LINDESMITH, A. R. *Opiate addiction*. Bloomington, Indiana: Princia Press, 1947.
MACK, J. E. Borderline states: An historical perspective. In J. E. Mack (Ed.), *Borderline states in psychiatry*. New York: Grune & Stratton, 1975.
MILLS, C. W. *The sociological imagination*. London: Oxford University Press, 1959.
OAKESHOTT, M. Learning and teaching. In R. S. Peters (Ed.), *The concept of education*. London: Routledge and Kegan Paul, 1967.
PELZ, D. C. Creative tensions in the research and development climate. *Science*, 1967, *157*, 160-165.
PRICE, D. J. DES. Citation measures of hard science, soft science, technology and nonscience. In C. Nelson & D. Pollock (Eds.), *Communication among scientists and engineers*. Lexington, Mass.: D. C. Heath, 1970.
RADO, S. The psychic effects of intoxicants: An attempt to evolve a psychoanalytic theory of morbid cravings. *International Journal of Psychoanalysis*, 1926, *7*, 396-413.
RADO, S. The psychoanalysis of pharmacothymia (drug addiction). *Psychoanalytic Quarterly*, 1933, *2*, 1-23.
RAVETZ, J. R. *Scientific knowledge and its social problems*. New York: Oxford University Press, 1971.
SHAFFER, H. Theories of addiction: In search of a paradigm. In H. Shaffer (Ed.), *Myths and realities: A book about drug users*. Boston: Zucker, 1977.
SHAFFER, H., & GAMBINO, B. Addiction paradigms II: Theory, research and practice.

Journal of Psychedelic Drugs, 1979, *11,* 299-304.

SIMON, H. A., & NEWELL, A. The uses and limitations of models. In M. Marx (Ed.), *Theories in contemporary psychology.* New York: Macmillan, 1963.

SZASZ, T. *Ceremonial Chemistry.* New York: Anchor Press/Doubleday, 1974.

TOULMIN, S. *Foresight and understanding.* New York: Harper and Row (Torchbook Series), 1963.

TOULMIN, S. Conceptual revolutions in science. In R. S. Cohen & M. W. Warofsky (Eds.), *Boston studies in the philosophy of science, 3,* 331-347. Dordrecht, Holland: D. Reidel, 1967.

VAN UTT, G., & BURGLASS, M. E. The collectivist issue in client-therapist matching. In D. Smith (Ed.), *A multicultural view of drug abuse.* Cambridge, Mass.: Schenkman, 1978.

WACHTEL, P. L. Investigation and its discontents. Some constraints on progress in psychological research. *American Psychologist,* 1980, *35,* 399-408.

WIKLER, A. Dynamics of drug dependence. Implications of a conditioning theory for research and treatment. *Archives of General Psychiatry,* 1973, *28,* 611-616.

ZINBERG, N. E., HARDING, W. M., & WINKELLER, M. A study of social regulatory mechanisms in controlled illicit drug users. *Journal of Drug Issues,* 1977, 7(2), 117-133.

CLASSIC CONTRIBUTIONS IN THE ADDICTIONS

Section I

PERSPECTIVES ON HISTORY AND RELATED SOCIAL POLICY

Each of the articles included in this section has double significance: each made a classic contribution to the substantive knowledge of the addictions field and each classically embodies a different one of the major approaches to social policy formation. Brecher's work (1972) was done in the tradition of liberal reform; it affirms the validity of the phenomenon of the addictions and the legitimacy of the addictions field, but condemns and thereby seeks to reform the drug policies of both society and the field. Szasz (1974) acknowledges the existence of the phenomenon of the addictions, but denies any validity whatsoever to the addictions field. He provides a total reconceptualization of the phenomenon and thus advocates a radical reformulation of social policy. Weil (1972) affirms the validity of both the phenomenon and the field. Taking the traditional approach to policy formation, his advocacy of the positive value of certain drug experiences is itself a new social policy.

It has been said that "passion makes history while reason hides from it." The history of the addictions proclaims in corollary form that passion makes social policy while reason reforms it. The passions that find expression in society's policies regarding drug use always claim to have their "reasons," and similarly, the "reasons" offered for policy reform typically deny their roots in passion. In 1967, when Brecher and the editors of *Consumer Reports* undertook to prepare a comprehensive report on illicit drug use in America, they were responding to what they perceived to be the "intolerable" and destructive nature of the current drug scene. They were concerned in particular to clarify the distinction between the supposed direct pharmacological effects of illicit drugs and

3

the vastly more destructive indirect effects of ill-conceived, largely irrational drug laws, policies, and social attitudes.

Licit and Illicit Drugs (Brecher, 1972) presented an integrated historical review of the pharmacological, legal and social effects of drug use and drug policy, and concluded by offering a set of specific policy recommendations designed to minimize the adversity of these effects at each level. Brecher stated that these recommendations, while admittedly containing no final solutions to the many problems of illicit drug use at any level, would hopefully "point the way to both short-term and long-term improvements in the present critical situation" (p. x). The book was a "first" in the sense that it offered an unbiased account of the development of a problem that at the time was widely thought to be a unique consequence of various ill-specified cultural, social, and economic conditions and forces, all utterly without precedent in American social history. Moreover, in style and tone, the book was directed to the growing mass market of lay readers whose increasing drug use made them eager for a dose of the straight truth about drug effects and use. It cited the inconsistencies and incompatibilities of previous drug policies and clearly illustrated the ways in which society's fear of drugs and efforts to suppress their use, sale, manufacture, or importation had in the past resulted in the unintended consequences of (a) increasing interest in and use of drugs, (b) creating new drug problems, and (c) compounding of the effects of existing drug problems by the imposition of punitive legal and economic sanctions against users. By commissioning the book, Consumers Union hoped to provide (a) a warning to policymakers about the folly of reimplementing expedient and easy solutions that had failed repeatedly in the past, (b) a background on the problem to enable citizens to better evaluate subsequent proposals for change, and (c) a body of reliable and trustworthy scientific information about drugs for use by community leaders, educators, parents, and the many young people disillusioned by the lies and distortions of previous indoctrination disguised as drug "education."

That the book is finally a manifesto for *reform* of existing social policy is revealed in its policy prescriptions which, although cogent and far-reaching, nonetheless reflect a tacit assumption of the legitimacy of society's regulating the individual's use of certain substances in certain ways, its unquestioned acceptance of "the published scientific literature" as *the* appropriate source of knowledge and basis for its conclusions about drugs and drug use, and its unequivocal affirmation of heroin as an "addicting" drug, a conclusion implying acceptance of the deterministic view of human behavior characteristic of all reform thinking and programming.

That *Licit and Illicit Drugs* takes its place in the mainstream tradition of the liberal reform approach to social policy in no way diminishes its importance for the general public or the significance of its contribution to knowledge about the phenomenon of the addictions. Despite the book's wide appeal and continuing acceptance by the general public as "the whole truth and nothing but the truth," about drugs, it is difficult to locate its point of impact on treatment policy and practice. Clearly, government has neither heeded Brecher's warnings nor implemented his recommendations, and in that sense his caveats are as fresh and relevant in 1981 as they were in 1972. Nonetheless, *Licit and Illicit Drugs* stands as a classic in the field of social policy analysis and sets a standard by which future contributions will be measured for years to come.

For the past 20 years Thomas Szasz has been elaborating a body of provocative and controversial theory and criticism dealing with such topics as the myth of mental illness (1961), involuntary psychiatric commitment (1963, 1977a), forensic psychiatry (1965a), the practice of autonomous psychotherapy (1965b), the mental health movement (1970a, 1970b), drug addiction (1974), schizophrenia (1976), and the theology of medicine (1977b). His views, variously characterized as "antipsychiatric," "radical," and "libertarian," have been heatedly debated in popular, academic, and professional settings and criticized from philosophical (Glaser, 1965), legal (Moore, 1975), and nosological (Roth, 1976; Pies, 1979) perspectives. A brilliant theorist, Szasz is a well-grounded and disciplined thinker; nonetheless, he defies easy classification. His stand on addiction is, indeed, *radical* in that his argument pierces what he maintains to be the superficial and self-serving formulations of psychiatry and social policy, plumbs the depths of ethics, and comes to rest squarely at the roots of the problem in legal and political philosophy. Szasz is an academic psychiatrist and practicing psychoanalyst; yet, he resolutely repudiates any and all psychiatric, physiological, or other medical formulations of addiction or characterizations of drug addicts.

As suggested by the title of his 1974 study of addiction, *Ceremonial Chemistry. The Ritual Persecution of Drugs, Addicts and Pushers,* he views the problem as "religious" in nature. However, his arguments and use of traditional categories from religion and (in particular) theology are not as well-grounded and informed as others of his made from different disciplinary bases, e.g., history or philosophy. He maintains that "the so-called drug-abuse problem is an integral part of our present social ethic, which accepts 'protections' and repressions justified by appeals to health similar to those that medieval societies accepted when they were justified by appeals to faith" (1977b, p. 38). The problem exists because individuals have allowed the medical and psychiatric professions to assume responsibility for the health and protection of their bodies and minds. Whereas this unwise and largely unwitting delegation of authority and abdication of personal responsibility may have eased the burdens of self-determination and autonomy, it has also facilitated the development of what Szasz sees as a "pharmocratic" version of the therapeutic state in which personal liberty has been eroded by the new religion constituted by medicine and psychiatry. Here, doctors maintain their priestly prerogatives through their near-absolute power to define individuals and their behavior as they see fit and their exclusive control of the sacred substances that mediate the new "salvation" of mental health, viz., drugs. Analogizing from an historical analysis of early religions, the Inquisition, and witchcraft, Szasz uses his usual razor-sharp language to forge a succession of brilliant syllogisms into an elegant and elaborate proof for his position.

Because he is outspoken, often stridently so, it is easy for one to take issue with Szasz, but it is another matter entirely to thoroughly refute him. Because his work is so complex with multiple lines and levels of argument being advanced simultaneously or in parallel, he is often misread and even more often misunderstood. Since he is a master word-smith and a brilliant logician with a scholar's knowledge of history, philosophy, and political theory, one can find in the literature many replies, retorts, and comments on carefully selected aspects of Szasz's views, but only a rare well-argued refutation (see Moore, 1975, for an elegantly constructed critique of the myth of mental illness).

Szasz's views of the addiction *field* are simple and straightforward: he categorically denounces it as an illegitimate endeavor. His impact on the field, therefore, is not easily measured. Although his arguments have been given considerable thought by theorists and practitioners, and although his point of view enjoys an enduring stylishness in many circles, any "true believers" would, like Szasz himself, necessarily refrain or desist from participating in any form of drug treatment activity. The large scale acceptance of Szasz's views on addiction would result in the deregulation of medical and psychiatric practice and therefore of all drugs, and with this the eventual disappearance of the addictions field. For a few, his words are like a beacon in the dark night. He issues a summons for the radical reformulation of current psychiatric theory and practice, existing legal and social theories of persons, and the interpersonal and institutional structures of society. For all, Szasz's penetrating and provocative analyses should help catalyze an examination of those aspects of personal conduct and professional practice which, *precisely* because they seem so "obviously" true, therefore require periodic reconsideration.

When Weil's *The Natural Mind* appeared in 1972, it was quickly adopted as the manifesto of the pro-drug counterculture. His brilliant characterization of the subtle marijuana-induced "high state" and its particular mode of "stoned" thinking greatly facilitated marijuana's acceptance as a safe and useful drug and as a valuable means of expanding consciousness. Along with that of Tart (1971, 1972a, 1972b, 1975) and Zinberg (1974, 1977), Weil's work on drug-induced states was instrumental in effecting the subtle but enormously significant shift in the view of these from *altered* states to *alternate* states of consciousness. Thus freed from the limiting definition of "normal" consciousness implicit in the old altered-state concept, alternate states of consciousness became a legitimate subject of scientific inquiry.

Weil's advocacy, explicit or implicit, of the value and utility of certain drug experiences places him across a social policy slashmark from the religious and political leaders and others who have opposed the use of all or selected drugs. Such a value-advocacy position, regardless of valence, i.e., whether pro- or anti-drug use, is the hallmark of the *traditional* approach to social policy. In this model social policy evolves through a succession of policy confrontations of the category versus anti-category type wherein aspects of individual life-styles are emphasized and relatively prescribed or proscribed. The model specifies a more or less narrow range of acceptable forms, and tends to result in a low tolerance of diversity.

In summary, the works of Brecher, Szasz, and Weil each made notable contributions to the substantive knowledge in the addiction *field*. Of equal importance, however, in our consideration of the historical development of the *phenomenon* of the addictions are the different approaches to social policy formation embodied in the work of each.

REFERENCES

BRECHER, E. M. *Licit and Illicit Drugs.* Boston: Little, Brown, 1972.
GLASER, F. G. The dichotomy game: A further consideration of the writings of Dr. Thomas Szasz. *American Journal of Psychiatry,* 1965, *121*, 1069-1074.
MOORE, M. S. Some myths about "mental illness." *Archives of General Psychiatry,* 1975, *32*, 1483-1497.
PIES, R. On myths and counter-myths. *Archives of General Psychiatry,* 1979, *36*, 139-144.
ROTH, M. Schizophrenia and the theories of Thomas Szasz. *British Journal of Psychiatry,* 1976, *129*, 317-326.
SZASZ, T. S. *The Myth of Mental Illness. Foundations of a Theory of Personal Conduct.* New York: Hoeber/Harper, 1961.
SZASZ, T. S. *Law, Liberty, and Psychiatry. An Inquiry into the Social Uses of Mental Health Practices.* New York: Macmillan, 1963.
SZASZ, T. S. *Psychiatric Justice.* New York: Macmillan, 1965a.
SZASZ, T. S. *The Ethics of Psychoanalysis. The Theory and Method of Autonomous Psychotherapy.* New York: Basic Books, 1965b.

SZASZ, T. S. *The Manufacture of Madness. A Comparative Study of the Inquisition and the Mental Health Movement.* New York: Harper & Row, 1970a.

SZASZ, T. S. *Ideology and Insanity. Essays on the Psychiatric Dehumanization of Man.* New York: Anchor/Doubleday, 1970b.

SZASZ, T. S. *Ceremonial Chemistry. The Ritual Persecution of Drugs, Addicts and Pushers.* New York: Anchor Press/Doubleday, 1974.

SZASZ, T. S. *Schizophrenia: The Sacred Symbol of Psychiatry.* New York: Basic Books, 1976.

SZASZ, T. S. *Psychiatric Slavery. When Confinement and Coercion Masquerade as Cure.* New York: Free Press, 1977a.

SZASZ, T. S. *The Theology of Medicine. The Political-Philosophical Foundations of Medical Ethics.* Baton Rouge: Louisiana State University Press, 1977b.

TART, C. *On Being Stoned: A Psychological Study of Marijuana Intoxication.* Palo Alto, California: Science and Behavior Books, 1971.

TART, C. *Altered States of Consciousness: A Book of Readings.* (2nd ed.) New York: Doubleday, 1972a.

TART, C. States of consciousness and state-specific sciences. *Science,* 1972b, *176,* 1203-1210.

TART, C. *States of Consciousness.* New York: Dutton, 1975.

WEIL, A. T. *The Natural Mind: A New Way of Looking at Drugs and the Higher Consciousness.* Boston: Houghton Mifflin, 1972.

WEIL, A. T. When the sun dies. *Harper's,* November, 1973, pp. 46-58.

ZINBERG, N. E. *"High" States: A Beginning Study.* Washington, D.C.: Drug Abuse Council, 1974.

ZINBERG, N. E., HARDING, W. M., & WINKELLER, M. A study of social regulatory mechanisms in controlled illicit drug users. *Journal of Drug Issues,* 1977, *7,* 117-133.

1

SELECTIONS FROM *LICIT AND ILLICIT DRUGS*

Edward M. Brecher and the Editors of *Consumer Reports*

NINETEENTH-CENTURY AMERICA—A "DOPE FIEND'S PARADISE"

The United States of America during the nineteenth century could quite properly be described as a "dope fiend's paradise."

Opium was on legal sale conveniently and at low prices throughout the century; morphine came into common use during and after the Civil War; and heroin was marketed toward the end of the century. These opiates and countless pharmaceutical preparations containing them "were as freely accessible as aspirin is today."[1] They flowed mostly through five broad channels of distribution, all of them quite legal:

(1) Physicians dispensed opiates directly to patients, or wrote prescriptions for them.

(2) Drugstores sold opiates over the counter to customers without a prescription.

(3) Grocery and general stores as well as pharmacies stocked and sold opiates. An 1883-1885 survey of the state of Iowa, which then had a population of less than 2,000,000, found 3,000 stores in the state where opiates were on sale—and this did not include the physicians who dispensed opiates directly.[2]

(4) For users unable or unwilling to patronize a nearby store, opiates could be ordered by mail.

(5) Finally, there were countless patent medicines on the market containing opium or morphine. They were sold under such names as Ayer's Cherry Pectoral, Mrs. Winslow's Soothing Syrup, Darby's Carminative, Godfrey's Cordial, McMunn's Elixir of Opium, Dover's Powder,[3] and so on. Some were teething syrups for young children, some were "soothing syrups," some were recommended for diarrhea and dysentery or for "women's trouble." They were widely advertised in newspapers and magazines and on billboards as "pain killers," "cough mixtures," "women's friends," "consumption cures," and so on.[4] One wholesale drug house, it is said, distributed more than 600 proprietary medicines and other products containing opiates.[5]

Most of the opium consumed in the United States during the nineteenth century was legally imported. Morphine was legally manufactured here from the imported opium.[6] But opium poppies were also legally grown within the United States. One early reference—perhaps the earliest—was in a letter from a Philadelphia physician, Dr. Thomas Bond, who wrote to Pennsylvania farmer on August 24, 1781: "The opium you sent is pure and of good quality. I hope you will take care of the seed."[7] During the War of 1812, opium was scarce, but "some parties produced it in New Hampshire and sold the product at from $10 to $12 per pound."[8]

In 1871 a Massachusetts official reported:

> There are so many channels through which the drug may be brought into the State, that I suppose it would be almost impossible to determine how much foreign opium is used here; but it may easily be shown that the home production increases every year. Opium has been recently made from white poppies, cultivated for the purpose, in Vermont, New Hampshire, and Connecticut, the annual production being estimated by hundreds of pounds, and this has generally been absorbed in the communities where it is made. It has also been brought here from Florida and Louisiana, while comparatively large quantities are regularly sent east from California and Arizona, where its cultivation is becoming an important branch of industry, ten acres of poppies being said to yield, in Arizona, twelve hundred pounds of opium.[9]

Opium was also produced in the Confederate states (Virginia, Tennessee, South Carolina, Georgia)[10] during the Civil War—and perhaps thereafter. Though some states outlawed it earlier, Congress did not ban the cultivation of opium poppies nationally until 1942.[11]

The nineteenth-century distribution system reached into towns, villages, and hamlets as well as the large cities. A New England physician-druggist wrote about 1870:

> In this town I began business twenty years since. The population then at 10,000 has increased only inconsiderably, but my sales have advanced from 50 pounds of opium the first year to 300 pounds now; and of laudanum [opium in alcohol] four times upon what was formerly required. About 50 regular purchasers come to my shop, and as many more, perhaps, are divided among the other three apothecaries in the place. Some country dealers also have their quota of dependents.[12]

A correspondent for the Portland (Maine) *Press* had this to say about opium users in 1868: "In the little village of Auburn . . . at least fifty such (as counted up by a resident apothecary) regularly purchase their supplies hereabouts; and the country grocers too, not a few of them, find occasion for keeping themselves supplied with a stock."[13]

A survey of 10,000 prescriptions filled by thirty-five Boston drugstores in 1888 revealed that 1,481 of them contained opiates. Among prescriptions refilled three or more times, 78 percent contained opiates.[14]

One Massachusetts druggist, asked to review his opiate sales, added a picturesque detail. He had only one steady customer, he reported—and that a noted temperance lecturer."[15]

Nor was the Middle West different from New England. The *Annual Report* of the Michigan State Board of Health for 1878 reported three opium eaters in the village of Huron (population 437), four opium eaters and one morphine eater in the village of Otisville(population 1,365), 18 opium eaters and 20 morphine eaters in the town of Hillsdale (population 4,189), and so on around the state.[16] Some children were included in the statistics.

Though called "opium eaters" in the medical literature, most nineteenth-century opium users (including Thomas De Quincey, author of *Confessions of an English Opium-Eater*) were in fact opium drinkers; they drank laudanum or other opiate liquids. Similarly "morphine eaters" included many who took morphine by injection or in other ways. In a number of the quotations which follow, "opium eaters" refers generally to morphine as well as opium users. Opium *smokers*, however, were considered to be in a separate category.

The nineteenth-century use of opiates was more or less the same in Britain. A classic report on the English industrial system, *The Factory System Illustrated* (1842), by W. Dodd, noted that factory workers of the time used opiates—notably laudanum—to quiet crying babies.[17]

In the official *Report of the Medical Officer of the Privy Council* for 1864 it was observed: "To push the sale of opiate . . . is the great aim of some enterprising wholesale merchants. By druggists it is considered the leading article."[18] The report also noted the giving of opiates to infants;[19] Karl Marx, citing this report in *Capital* (1867), spoke of the English working-class custom of "dosing children with opiates."[20]

In 1873 an English physician reported:

> . . . Amongst the three millions and three-quarters [people in London] there are to be found some persons here and there who take [opium] as a luxury, though by far the greater number of those who take it in anything like quantity do so for some old neuralgia or rheumatic malady, and began under medical advice. Neither is it to be found over the agricultural or manufacturing districts, save in the most scattered and casual way. The genuine opium-eating districts are the ague and fen districts of Norfolk and Lincolnshire. There it is not casual, accidental, or rare, but popular, habitual, and common. Anyone who visits such a town as Louth or Wisbeach, and strolls about the streets on a Saturday evening, watching the country people as they do their marketing, may soon satisfy himself that the crowds in the chemists' shops come for opium; and they have a peculiar way of getting it. They go in, lay down their money, and receive the opium pills in exchange without saying a word. For instance, I was at Wisbeach one evening in August 1871; went into a chemist's shop; laid a penny on the counter. The chemist said—"The best?" I nodded. He gave me a pill-box and took up the penny; and so the purchase was completed without my having uttered a syllable. You offer money, and get opium as a matter of course. This may show how familiar the custom is. . . .
>
> In these districts it is taken by people of all classes, but especially by the poor and miserable, and by those who in other districts would seek comfort from gin or beer.[21]

Godfrey's Cordial—a mixture of opium, molasses for sweetening, and sassafras for flavoring—was especially popular in England. Dr. C. Fraser Brockington reports that in mid-nineteenth-century Coventry, ten gallons of Godfrey's Cordial—enough for 12,000 doses—was sold weekly, and was administered to 3,000 infants under two years of age.

> Even greater quantities of opium mixtures were said to be sold in Nottingham. . . . Every surgeon in Marshland testified to the fact that "there was not a labourer's house in which the bottle of opium was not to be seen, and not a child, but who got it in some form." . . . Wholesale druggists reported the sale of immense quantities of opium; a retail druggist dispensed up to 200 pounds a year—in pills and penny sticks or as Godfrey's Cor-

dial. . . . To some extent this was a practice which had been taken on during the years when malaria was indigneous in the Fens and when, a century before, the poppy had been cultivated for the London market.[22]

The nonmedicinal use of opiates, while legal in both the United States and England, was not considered respectable. Indeed, as an anonymous but perceptive and well-informed American writer noted in the *Catholic World* for September 1881, it was as disreputable as drinking alcoholic beverages—and much harder to detect:

> The gentleman who would not be seen in a bar-room, however respectable, or who would not purchase liquor and use it at home, lest the odor might be detected upon his person, procures his supply of morphia and has it in his pocket ready for instantaneous use. It is odorless and occupies but little space. . . . He zealously guards his secret from his nearest friend—for popular wisdom has branded as a disgrace that which he regards as a misfortune. . . .[23]

Opiate use was also frowned upon in some circles as *immoral*—a vice akin to dancing, smoking, theater-going, gambling, or sexual promiscuity. But while deemed immoral, it is important to note that opiate use in the nineteenth century was not subject to the moral sanctions current today. Employees were not fired for addiction. Wives did not divorce their addicted husbands, or husbands their addicted wives. Children were not taken from their homes and lodged in foster homes or institutions because one or both parents were addicted. Addicts continued to participate fully in the life of the community. Addicted children and young people continued to go to school, Sunday School, and college. Thus, the nineteenth century avoided one of the most disastrous effects of current narcotics laws and attitudes—the rise of a deviant addict subculture, cut off from respectable society and without a "road back" to respectability.

Our nineteenth-century forbears correctly perceived the major objection to the opiates. *They are addicting.* Though the word "addiction" was seldom used during the nineteenth century, the phenomenon was well understood. The true nature of the narcotic evil becomes visible, the *Catholic World* article pointed out, when someone who has been using an opiate for some time

> attempts to give up its use. Suddenly his eyes are opened to his folly and he realizes the startling fact that he is in the coils of a a serpent as merciless as the boa-constrictor and as relentless as

fate. With a firm determination to free himself he discontinues its use. Now his sufferings begin and steadily increase until they become unbearable. The tortures of Dives are his; but unlike that miser, he has only to stretch forth his hand to find oceans with which to satisfy his thirst. That human nature is not often equal to so extraordinary a self-denial affords little cause for astonishment. .˙. . Again and again he essays release from a bondage so humiliating, but meets with failure only, and at last submits to his fate—a confirmed opium-eater.[24]

The terms "addicting" and "addiction" will be further discussed later.

Our nineteenth-century forbears also perceived opiate use as a "will-weakening" vice—for surely, they insisted, a man or woman of strong will could stop if he tried hard enough. The fact was generally known that addicts deprived of their opiates (when hospitalized for some illness unrelated to their addiction, for example) would lie or even steal to get their drug, and addicts "cured" of their addiction repeatedly relapsed. Hence there was much talk of the *moral degeneration* caused by the opiates.

Nevertheless, there was very little popular support for a law banning these substances. "Powerful organizations for the suppression . . . of alcoholic stimulants exist throughout the land,"[25] the 1881 article in the *Catholic World* noted, but there were no similar anti-opiate organizations.

The reason for this lack of demand for opiate prohibition was quite simple: the drugs were not viewed as a menace to society and, as we shall demonstrate in subsequent chapters, they were not in fact a menace.

REFERENCES

1. HUBERT S. HOWE, "A Physician's Blueprint for the Management and Prevention of Narcotic Addiction," *New York State Journal of Medicine*, 55 (February 1, 1955): 341-348.
2. CHARLES E. TERRY and MILDRED PELLENS, *The Opium Problem* (New York: Committee on Drug Addictions, Bureau of Social Hygiene, Inc., 1928), p. 18. Hereinafter cited as *Terry and Pellens*.
3. Ibid., pp. 61, 96.
4. Ibid., pp.75, 123.
5. CHARLES B. TOWNS, "The Peril of the Drug Habit," *Century Magazine*, 84 (1912): 580-587.
6. *Terry and Pellens*, p. 670.
7. *Proceedings, American Pharmaceutical Association*, 13 (1865): 51.
8. PERRY M. LICHTENSTEIN, "Thirteen Years' Observation on Drug Addiction at the Tombs Prison," *Narcotic Education*, ed. H. S. Middlemiss, *Proceedings of the First World Conference on Narcotic Education, July 5-9, 1926, Philadelphia*, (Washington, D.C., 1926), p. 123.
9. S. DANA HAYS, quoted in *Annual Report of the State Board of Health, Massachusetts* (1871), cited in *Terry and Pellens*, p. 7.

10. D. M. R. CULBRITH, *Materia Medica and Pharmacology*, 3rd ed. (1903), cited in *Terry and Pellens*, p. 7.
11. Opium Poppy Control Act of 1912, Public Law No. 400, 78th Cong.
12. Quoted by Alonzo Calkins, *Opium and the Opium Appetite* (Philadelphia, 1871), cited in *Terry and Pellens*, p. 6.
13. Quoted by Calkins, *Opium and the Opium Appetite*.
14. VIRGIL G. EATON, "How the Opium Habit is Acquired," *Popular Science Monthly*, 33 (1888): 606, cited in Alfred R. Lindesmith, *Opiate Addiction* (Evanston, Ill.: Principal Press, 1947), p. 105.
15. Quoted by F. E. OLIVER, *Annual Report of the State Board of Health, Massachusetts* (1871), cited in *Terry and Pellens*, p. 9.
16. *Annual Report, Michigan State Board of Health* (1878), Table 1, cited in *Terry and Pellens*, p. 12.
17. W. DODD, *The Factory System Illustrated* (1812), p. 149, cited in E. P. THOMPSON, *The Making of the English Working Class*, 1966 ed. (New York: Vintage Books, 1963), p. 328.
18. "Report By Dr. Henry Julian Hunter on the Excessive Mortality of Infants in Some Rural Districts of England," in *Public Health, Reports of the Medical Officer of the Privy Council*, 6th Report (1864), p. 459, cited in Karl Marx, *Capital*, ed. Friedrich Engels, trans. Samuel Moore and Edward Aveling (Moscow: Progress Publishers, 1965), 1, 399.
19. Ibid., p. 460.
20. Karl Marx, *Capital*, 1, 399.
21. *Medical Times and Gazette*, 2 (London: July 19, 1879): 73.
22. C. FRASER BROCKINGTON, *Public Health in the Nineteenth Century* (London: E. & S. Livingstone, Ltd., 1965), pp. 225, 226.
23. Anon., "The Opium Habit," in *Catholic World*, 33 (September, 1881): 828.
24. Ibid., p. 829.
25. Ibid., p. 834.

LEARNING FROM MISTAKES: SIX CAVEATS

This nation's drug laws and policies have not been working well; on that simple statement almost all Americans seem agreed. During the fifty-seven years since passage of the Harrison Narcotic Act, heroin has become a national menace; its use has even spread to the middle calss and the suburbs. After a third of a century of escalating penalties against marijuana and of antimarijuana propaganda, marijuana has reached an unprecedented peak of popularity. After a decade of agitation and legislation, LSD—a drug few people had even heard of before 1962—is now known universally and used by hundreds of thousands, even high-school students. The barbiturates, which a generation ago were thought of as sedatives, useful for calming and for sleep, have become "thrill drugs." So have the amphetamines, once used mainly to enable people to work longer hours at hard jobs.

These changes, clearly, are not the result of changes in the chemical composition of the drugs. They are the result of mistaken laws and policies, of mistaken attitudes toward drugs, and of futile, however well-intentioned, efforts to "stamp out the drug menace." This Consumers Union Report, accordingly, has been only partly concerned with the "drug problem." Large portions of our work have focused instead on what Dr. Helen Nowlis has aptly called "the *drug problem* problem"—the damage that results from the ways in which society has approached the drug problem.

To summarize here the entire contents of this Report would be an impossible undertaking. We therefore present instead a series of brief reminders of some of the central themes developed earlier, plus drug-by-drug recommendations growing out of those themes.

Our recommendations are not intended as a blueprint for solving overnight either "the drug problem" or "the *drug problem* problem." Rather, each proposal is put forward as an approach worthy of consideration and trial. As the drug scene changes, new recommendations will no doubt be called for. Consumers Union expects to report such changes and to make additional recommendations in the pages of *Consumer Reports*.

Mistakes in drug laws, policies, and attitudes are discussed and documented throughout this Report. Among the steps which might correct them, we suggest the following.

(1) Stop emphasizing measures designed to keep drugs away from people.

Prohibition—trying to keep drugs away from people—began with the enforcement of the 1914 Harrison Narcotic Act, and it has remained the dominant theme of both antidrug legislation and antidrug propaganda ever since.

Prohibition does not work. As the United States learned from 1920 to 1933, it didn't work with alcohol. As the country has been learning since 1914, it doesn't work with heroin. It isn't working today with marijuana, LSD, or any of the other illicit drugs. Nor is prohibition likely to prove more effective in the future.

What prohibition does accomplish is to raise prices and thus to attract more entrepreneurs to the black market. If the drug is addicting and the price escalation is carried to outrageous extremes (as in the case of heroin), addicts resort to crime to finance their purchases—at a tragic cost, not only in dollars but in community disruption.

What prohibition also achieves is to convert the market from relatively bland, bulky substances to more hazardous concentrates which are more readily smugglable and marketable—from opium smoking to heroin mainlining, from coca leaves to cocaine, from marijuana to hashish.

Again, prohibition opens the door to adulterated and contaminated drugs—methyl alcohol, "ginger jake," pseudo-LSD, adulterated heroin.

Worst of all, excessive reliance on prohibition, on laws and law enforcement, lulls the country decade after decade into a false confidence that nothing more need be done—except to pass yet another law, or to hire a few hundred more narcotics agents, or to license the agents to break down doors without knocking first, and so on.

This is not, obviously, a justification for repealing *all* drug laws tomorrow. A nation that has not learned to keep away from some drugs and to use others wisely cannot be taught those essential lessons merely by repealing drug laws. What is needed in the legal arena are two fresh insights:

• Physicians have a maxim: *Nihil nocere.* It means that a physician must guard against doing more harm than good. A *Nihil nocere* guideline is needed for drug laws and law enforcement. A law-enforcement policy that converts marijuana smokers into LSD or heroin users, to cite an obvious example, should be abandoned. The same is true of a law that turns marijuana smokers into convicts and ex-convicts, with all that the prison experience and the prison record implies. Nor can much be said in favor of a law-enforcement policy that results in raising the price of a nickel's worth of heroin to five dollars—with the further result that addicts must steal vast amounts in order to buy their heroin. A complete revision of laws and enforcement policies in the spirit of the *nihil nocere* principle is called for. Laws and law enforcement cannot solve the drug problem; they should not be allowed to exacerbate it.

• A realistic understanding of what laws can and cannot do is needed. Laws cannot work miracles. They cannot, for example, keep heroin away from heroin addicts, nor marijuana away from marijuana smokers. The most laws can do in these cases is to punish and to alienate. Accordingly, laws and enforcement policies should be revised to concentrate on *achievable* goals. For example, in countries where heroin addicts do not have to patronize and support a black market, law-enforcement efforts can be directed solely toward curbing the flow of heroin to *nonaddicts*. Surely this is the essential goal.

In sum, valuable resources and energies should no longer be wasted chasing prohibition will-o'-the-wisps. Those goals that cannot be achieved by law enforcement should be assigned to other instrumentalities such as education and social reform.

(2) Stop publicizing the horrors of the "drug menace." Scare publicity has been the second cornerstone of national policy, along with law enforcement, since 1914. The effort to frighten people away from illicit drugs has publicized and thus popularized the drugs attacked. The impact on

young eyes and ears of the constant drumming of drug news stories and antidrug messages is clearly discernible—just look around.* As shown throughout this Report, sensationalist publicity is not only ineffective but counterproductive. Both the peril and the warning function as lures. At the same time, the antidrug campaigns have inflamed the hostile emotions of many non-drug users, making it harder to win support for calm, rational, nonpunitive, *effective* drug policies.

(3) *Stop increasing the damage done by drugs.* Current drug laws and policies make drugs more rather than less damaging in many ways. The

---

*Ken Sobol wrote in the New York *Village Voice,* October 21, 1971: "In the past week we were entertained [on television] by seven dope discussion/documentaries, a dope agony ballet, two dope poetry readings, innumerable anti-dope commercials, and three dramatic series shows centering around junkies. Not to mention Rona Barrett revealing Hollywood's latest hophead horror, a variety show host wittily confusing grass and grass, Jim Jensen crackling gravely as he narrated the [New York Police Department's] 'biggest raid of the week' bit, LeRoi Jones accusing the Pope of dealing, and countless other pieces of programs. Reds, greens, ups, downs, agony, ecstasy, sniff, smoke, mainline, degradation, or reha-bilitation—you name it, we had it, as usual.

"All of these items began with the assumption that since dope is an evil, its horrors must be portrayed as graphically as possible in order to educate the viewer. But the moraliz-ing—that drugs are bad, or that *Dope Is Exciting!*—like everything else on tv, dope 'edu-cation' is show biz. And like all show biz, it is glamorous from first, content second. One National Football League anti-drug spot begins with exciting field action, while up tempo, big band jazz blares over. Then, as the music recedes, the camera picks out one player smashing an opposing ballcarrier and we hear his voice over: 'This is Mike Reid . . . That's the way I like to crack down, I'd like to rack up the drug traffic, too.' Up jazz, building to crash climax. It's all groovy sounds and fast action, only slightly interrupted by some rich jock's [anti-drug comments]. Wham, bam, dope, man! Dope is so exciting that even the anti-dope swings.

"That impression is enhanced by the fact that only beautiful, vibrant people turn to drugs on entertainment tv. Last Friday, for one example, among many, the 'D.A.,' a new NBC law and order hour, had a show about a junkie witness. She was, of course, young, beautiful, intelligent, and paying for her mistakes. Decadence sells better than ever these days. It makes people romantically exciting, cool, tragic and *plugged in*—beautiful people, that is.

"Even documentary dope can be a gas. In Frederick Wiseman's 'Hospital,' shown last week on NET, a long sequence (which I am pulling out of context) shows a badtripping teenaged boy in the emergency room. He screams, moans, shakes, crawls in his own puke, begs the doctors not to let him die. All genuine, all riveting. Yet at the same time completely unreal, because the tv screen automatically distances us and makes it a performance—a show about a kid connecting with life in the rawest, most primal way. And again, I think that what may remain in the mind from it is the generalized excitement of that elemental connection, rather than its individual real-life horror. Because tv is not real life, and while it is surprisingly easy to ignore someone else's horror on film, it is no trick at all to get excited by it.

"So there you are. A small piece of last week's junk action. Next week there will be more of the same, and more the week after, and so on, until we have theoretically been 'educated' or frightened off dope—or on to it. Because if McLuhan is at all right, then some people are going about this all wrong. Maybe there is no right way to treat dope on television as it is presently constituted, but I wish to hell someone in a foundation or school somewhere would at least sit down and worry about it."

alleged justification for this is, of course, to *deter* people from using drugs. Thus, the sale or possession of hypodermic needles without prescription is a criminal offense—a policy which leads to the use of nonsterile needles, to the sharing of needles, and to epidemics of hepatitis and other crippling, sometimes fatal, needle-borne diseases. Contaminated and adulterated illicit drugs circulate as freely as pure illicit drugs, with no greater penalty for selling them and no effective system for warning users against them. Only trifling efforts are made to find and eliminate the cause of the hundreds of deaths each year among heroin mainliners—deaths falsely attributed to "overdose." The establishment of methadone maintenance programs for heroin addicts is resisted and delayed in part because some people *want* heroin addiction to lead to disaster—as a deterrent to others. Loss of employment, expulsion from school, and exclusion from respectable society similarly serve to increase the damage done by drugs—and over all of the other penalties hovers society's ultimate sanction, imprisonment, the most damaging of all consequences of illicit drug use.

These and other drug laws and policies have succeeded in making drug use more damaging in the United States than in other countries, and vastly more damaging today than in the United States of a century ago. But as deterrents against drug use, these policies clearly have failed.

Accordingly, future efforts should be directed toward *minimizing* the damage done by drugs. A substantial part of that damage stems not from the chemistry of the drugs but from the ignorant and imprudent ways in which they are used, the settings in which they are used, the laws punishing their use, society's attitudes toward users, and so on. Once a policy of minimizing damage is adopted and conscientiously pursued, a substantial part of the "drug meance" will be eliminated—even though many people may continue to use drugs.

The choice is clear: to continue trying, ineffectively, to stamp out illicit drug use by making it as damaging as possible, or to seek to minimize the damage done by drugs, licit and illicit alike.*

---

*The first faint harbingers of a trend toward lessening drug damage are beginning to appear. Some people who thought a few years ago that imprisonment or death was good enough for "drug fiends" whose skin color was different or who lived in another part of town have begun to change their minds as they realize that the users of illicit drugs include their own children. Actions by both Congress and a number of state legislatures to reduce marijuana possession penalties in 1970 and 1971 were straws in this breeze of change. The concern expressed in 1971 for veterans returning from Vietnam addicted to heroin was another straw. The problem of minimizing the damage done by *licit* drugs, such as nicotine and alcohol, also attracted Congressional attention in 1970 and 1971; cigarette advertisng was banned from television and new alcoholism treatment and research programs were authorized. Several states repealed their laws making public drunkenness a crime punishable by imprisonment.

(4) Stop misclassifying drugs. Misclassification lies close to the heart of the drug problem, for what teachers tell students about a drug, and how judges sentence drug-law violators, both depend on how the drug is classified. Most official and unofficial classifications of drugs are illogical and capricious; they therefore make a mockery of drug-law enforcement and bring drug education into disrepute.

A major error of the current drug classification system is that it treats alcohol and nicotine—two of the most harmful drugs—essentially as non-drugs.* Equating marijuana with heroin is a second shocking example—for it helps to encourage the switch from marijuana to heroin.

The entire jerry-built structure of official drug classification rests on a series of Congressional enactments beginning in 1914 and reaching a climax in the Comprehensive Drug Abuse Prevention and Control Act of 1970. The misclassifications built into this Act were not the results of scientific study but represented compromises between Senate and House committees, between Republican and Democratic legislators, between Congress and the Nixon administration. Worse yet, the Act authorizes the *Attorney General* of the United States to alter the classifications from time to time. Yet judges are bound by this political rather than scientific system of classification in assessing penalties; and educational programs generally take their cue from the official classification.

Propaganda programs contribute to the classification chaos in another way; they accent the distinction between licit and illicit drugs, while failing to draw distinctions between more hazardous and less hazardous illicit drugs. The result is to facilitate the use of the more hazardous illicit drugs.

A sound classification program should concern itself with *modes* of drug use as well as drugs themselves; it should recognize, for example, the vast difference between sniffing, smoking, or swallowing a drug and mainlining it. Society, laws, and law-enforcement policies already differentiate the occasional drinker of a glass of wine or beer, the social drinker, the problem drinker, the spree drinker, the chronic drunk, and the alcoholic. Similar distinctions should be made with respect to various modes of use of marijuana, LSD, the barbiturates, and the amphetamines. It is one thing to get stoned on marijuana on Saturday night; it is quite another to stay stoned all day every day. A sensible drug clas-

---

*Some young people, baffled by the illogic, have concluded that corrupt legislators must have adopted the classifications to protect the tobacco and alcohol industries. Such distrust is perhaps understandable, though ignorance rather than venality seems the more likely explanation. The fact remains, however, that a significant part of American agriculture and industry is engaged, with government support, in the production and marketing of nicotine and alcohol products.

sification program would not only recognize but stress the difference.

Once a reasonable approach is adopted to the classification of drugs and modes of drug use, educators can begin to plan a *believable* program of drug education, based on truth—on what is known and not known. Such a program will be confirmed by what young people see around them, and by what they experience if and when they try drugs themselves. It will therefore no longer bring down ridicule and disrepute upon the whole concept of drug education. Until drugs are sensibly reclassified, no amount of public-relations expertise will restore credibility to governmental, medical, and educational drug pronouncements.

(5) Stop viewing the drug problem as primarily a national problem, to be solved on a national scale. In fact, as workers in the drug scene confirm, the "drug problem" is a collection of local problems. The predominant drugs differ from place to place and from time to time. Effective solutions to problems also vary; a plan that works now for New York City may not be applicable to upstate New York and vice versa. With respect to education and propaganda, the need for local wisdom and local control is particularly pressing. Warning children against drugs readily available to them is a risky business at best, requiring careful, truthful, unsensational approaches. Warning children against drugs used elsewhere, of which they may never have heard, can be like warning them against putting beans in their ears. The role of anti-glue-sniffing warnings in popularizing glue-sniffing is the most striking of many examples.

The errors in drug policy under review here are also generalizations that may or may not be relevant in a particular community. An essential preliminary step in any local drug education program should be to identify the errors in policy currently being committed *locally*—and, if possible, to correct them locally.

(6) Stop pursuing the goal of stamping out illicit drug use. If, in 1937, efforts had been undertaken to *reduce* marijuana smoking over a period of years rather than to try to eradicate it immediately, such a program might well have succeeded. Instead, one of the greatest drug explosions in history—the marijuana eruption of the 1960s—was triggered.

Attempts to stamp out illicit drug use tend to increase both drug use and drug damage. Here LSD is the prime example.

Finally, as we have shown, efforts to stamp out one drug shift users to another—from marijuana to LSD and heroin, from heroin to alcohol.

These, then, are the major mistakes in drug policy as we see them. This Consumers Union Report contains no panaceas for resolving them. But getting to work at correcting these six errors, promptly and ungrudgingly, would surely be a major step in the right direction.

POLICY ISSUES AND RECOMMENDATIONS

Narcotics. The one overwhelming objection to opium, morphine, heroin, and the other narcotics is the fact that they are addicting. The other disastrous effects of narcotics addiction on mind, body, and society are primarily the results of laws and policies.

Many American morphine and heroin addicts prior to 1914 led long, healthy, respectable, productive lives despite addiction—and so do a few addicts today. The sorry plight of most heroin addicts in the United States today results primarily from the high price of heroin, the contamination and adulteration of the heroin available on the black market, the mainlining of the drug instead of safer modes of use, the laws against heroin and the ways in which they are enforced, the imprisonment of addicts, society's attitudes toward addicts, and other nonpharmacological factors. It was the enforcement of the Harrison Act of 1914 that converted opiate addiction from what it had long been—a misfortune and a disgrace—into a disaster.

The time has come to recognize what should have been obvious since 1914—that heroin is a drug most users go right on using despite the threat of imprisonment, despite actual imprisonment for years, despite repeated "cures" and long-term residence in rehabilitation centers, and despite the risks of disease and even death. Heroin is a drug for which addicts will prostitute themselves. It is also a drug to which most addicts return despite a sincere desire to "stay clean," a firm resolve to stay clean, an overwhelming effort to stay clean—and even a success (sometimes enforced by confinement) in staying clean for weeks, months, or years. This is what is meant by the statement that heroin is an addicting drug.

The first and most important step in solving the heroin problem, accordingly, is to recognize at long last what addiction to heroin means. Society must stop expecting that any significant proportion of addicts will become ex-addicts by an act of will, or by spending five years in prison, or a year or two in a prison-like California, New York State, or federal "drug treatment center," or even in a "therapeutic community" like Synanon, Daytop, Phoenix House, Odyssey House, or any of the others.

Almost all heroin addicts, it is true, do stop taking heroin from time to time. But almost all subsequently relapse. Among those who do not relapse, roughly half become skid-row alcoholics. By publicizing the few conspicuous exceptions—the handful of successful ex-heroin addicts—and by assuming that others need only follow in their footsteps, harm is done in at least three tragic ways.

(1) Another generation of young people is persuaded that heroin addiction is temporary. They are falsely assured that the worst that can happen to them if they get hooked on heroin is that they may have to spend a year or two in a drug treatment center, or, better yet, in a therapeutic community like Synanon or Daytop—after which they will emerge, heads high, as certified ex-addicts.

(2) Hundreds of millions of dollars are wasted on vast "treatment programs" that almost totally fail to curb subsequent heroin use by addicts, while more pressing measures are skimped on.

(3) Law-enforcement resources are wasted on futile efforts to keep heroin away from heroin addicts instead of concentrating on the essential task: keeping heroin away from nonaddicts.

The ideal solution to the heroin problem, of course, would be a *cure* for opiate addiction—some means of erasing altogether both the physiological and the psychological traces of past drug use. But no such cure exists, nor is there one on the horizon—and there exist no clues to where such a miracle cure might be found. Accordingly, while scientists who want to search for a cure should certainly be encouraged to do so, it is folly to base national policy on the hope that they may succeed.

There is one major exception to the rule that most heroin addicts go right on using heroin or returning to heroin. A heroin addict can comfortably do without his drug if supplied with a related drug. Methadone is one such drug. Unlike heroin, it can be effectively taken orally rather than by injection; it need be taken only once a day instead of several times; it is legal; it is cheap; and it has other advantages. Like heroin, it has very little effect on either mind or body if taken regularly. An estimated 25,000 ex-heroin addicts were taking legal methadone instead of black-market heroin in 1971, and the number was rapidly growing.

Methadone maintenance is not a panacea. But it frees addicts from the heroin incubus, which is ruining their lives, and it is therefore capable of turning a majority of heroin addicts into law-abiding citizens (like pre-1914 addicts). One of the reasons it succeeds, of course, is that it is itself an addicting drug—that is, a drug that must be taken daily.

The conversion of heroin addicts into methadone maintenance patients is proceeding too slowly. Some communities have no methadone maintenance program; most programs have long waiting lists. Putting an addict on a waiting list for methadone has been likened to putting a drowning man on a waiting list for artificial respiration.

Ideally, addicts should be given a choice of treatment modalities, a choice between methadone maintenance and other programs offering a similar likelihood of rehabilitation. But first those effective alternatives must be found. Consumers Union enthusiastically endorses laboratory and clinical research into effective alternatives to methadone maintenance, including both drug-free approaches and rehabilitation programs using drugs other than methadone. But large sums should not again be spent on alternatives which—since the early "opiate cures" of the nineteenth century—have already repeatedly demonstrated their worthlessness. A program should be considered experimental until it has proved its effectiveness; there should be no further mass failures, such as the California and New York State programs, into which vast sums have been sunk with barely a trace of benefits.

To date, no program other than methadone maintenance has demonstrated its ability to rehabilitate more than a minute proportion of addicts. Failure rates in nonmethadone programs range from 90 to 100 precent, even when entrance is limited to select groups of highly motivated addicts. The failures return to the American black-market system of heroin distribution, paying exorbitant prices for dangerously adulterated and contaminated heroin. Surely methadone maintenance is better than that.

It is shocking, of course, to think of tens of thousands of newly addicted young people and of addicted Vietnam veterans taking a narcotic such as methadone daily, for months, years, perhaps for the rest of their lives. No one can look forward to such a prospect with satisfaction. But no better solution is in sight. And the alternative for those who are not rehabilitated by existing methods is a return to black-market heroin.

The heroin black market must be abolished in the only way it can be abolished: by eliminating the demand for black-market heroin.

On the central issue of narcotics addiction, accordingly, Consumers Union recommends (1) that United States drug policies and practices be promptly revised to insure that no narcotics addict need get his drug from the black market; (2) that methadone maintenance be promptly made available under medical auspices to every narcotics addict who applies for it; (3) that other forms of narcotics maintenance, including opium, morphine, and heroin maintenance, be made available along with methadone maintenance under medical auspices on a carefully planned, experimental basis.

The third of these recommendations—that opium, morphine, and heroin as well as methadone be made available to addicts under well-planned experimental conditions—is based in part on the unassailable fact that an addict is personally far better off on legal, low-cost, medicinally pure opium, morphine, or heroin than he is on exorbitantly priced, dangerously adulterated, and contaminated black-market heroin.

Similarly, society is better off when addicts receive their drugs legally and at low cost or free of charge.

Finally, reliable scientific data on the relative advantages and disadvantages of various maintenance drugs under actual conditions of use in the United States can be secured only by comparative-use studies. The experimental programs should be designed to determine, if possible on a blind or double-blind basis, (a) whether any other drug has any advantages over methadone for general use in narcotics maintenance programs, and (b) whether any particular subcategories of patients may do better on opium, morphine, heroin, or some other maintenance drug rather than on methadone. The tests should be designed to determine whether it is the heroin molecule itself or the mystique surrounding it that makes the difference.

The comparative trials should also be designed to determine whether, as in Britain, there is a proper role for *injectable* methadone in maintenance programs, or for other routes of administration (such as smoking) for the various opiates. Oral morphine and oral heroin should be among the drugs submitted to double-blind trials in competition with oral methadone.

Consumers Union's recommendation for experimental opium, morphine, and heroin maintenance programs is not based on any confidence that they will prove superior to maintenance on methadone or on newer, longer-acting versions of methadone (such as acetyl-alpha-methadol). All of the data so far indicate that methadone is very nearly the ideal maintenance drug—fully effective by mouth, effective for a full twenty-four hours, effective in stable doses, with minimal side effects, and with its safety, effectiveness, and acceptability to addicts already proved under actual field conditions in some 25,000 patients. But the ready availability of an excellent maintenance drug is *not* a sound reason for abandoning the search for an even better maintenance drug. And even if, in the end, the trials of opium, morphine, and heroin maintenance merely buttress the conclusion that methadone is the maintenance drug of choice, the research will have served a useful purpose, for oral methadone has so far only proved its worth in competition with black-market heroin. The next challenge oral methadone should be required to meet is a carefully controlled comparison with legal opium, morphine, and heroin, with injectable methadone, and perhaps with other drugs.*

Further, Consumers Union calls for three immediate steps to be taken

---

*Including dipipanone, pethidine [meperidine, Demerol], dextromoramide, levorphanol—all of which are narcotics and all of which are being tried as maintenance drugs in Britain.

in connection with the tragic deaths of many hundreds of heroin users each year from so-called "overdose."

First, the dangerously wrong "heroin overdose" myth must be promptly exploded once and for all. Addicts and the public alike must be warned that sudden death can follow the intravenous injection of mixtures containing very little heroin—or possibly none at all.

Second, heroin addicts throughout the country should be warned by all means available, including the fullest possible use of the mass media, that deaths falsely attributed to heroin overdose *may* be due to injecting heroin while drunk on alcohol or barbiturates. Although the evidence linking the many hundreds of so-called "heroin overdose" deaths to alcohol and the barbiturates is not conclusive, the evidence *is* conclusive that an addict who injects heroin while drunk on alcohol or barbiturates is running a far greater risk than one who shoots up while sober. *This* should be the public health message.

Third, a full-scale research program must be promptly launched, under capable scientific leadership, to determine what is in fact causing these hundreds of deaths annually, and what measures can be taken to lower the addict death rate. These deaths must be viewed not merely as arguments against injecting heroin, but as the tragic events they are. Society must seek ways to avert them, just as ways are sought to prevent the untimely deaths of nonaddicts.

Cocaine and the amphetamines. These twin drugs must be considered together. In general, the less said about them, the better. Antiamphetamine laws and campaigns have been among the major factors popularizing the amphetamines and recent law-enforcement efforts to suppress the amphetamines have opened wide the door to cocaine.

Among drug users and potential drug users, two facts about the amphetamines are worth stressing. First, they are much less likely to prove damaging if taken in modest doses; hence the dosage should be kept down. Second, they should be taken orally if at all; the *injection* of amphetamines or cocaine in large doses constitutes one of the most damaging forms of drug use known to man. The failure to draw these distinctions between small and large doses, between oral and intravenous use, discredits drug propaganda programs and encourages the "speed-freak" phenomenon.

The latest data from the youth drug scene suggest that the speed-freak phenomenon—that is, the injection of amphetamines in large doses—has passed its peak. Many speed freaks are turning to heroin instead, and the recruitment of new speed freaks is falling off. If a fresh antiamphetamine campaign is not launched, there is every reason to hope that the next wave of youthful drug users will engage in less damaging forms of drug use. But a revival of the antiamphetamine campaign could well sabotage this hopeful outlook.

The barbiturates and alcohol. These are pharmacologically a single problem. Both make you drunk in the same way; both can be addicting in the same way; both can produce hangovers, and delirium tremens can occur after withdrawal from excessive and persistent use. The barbiturates have the effect, in most respects, of solid alcohol—and alcohol is from the pharmacological point of view a kind of liquid barbiturate. The persistent, excessive use of alcohol and barbiturates ranks with the speed-freak phenomenon in damage wrought, and affects vastly more people.

The great majority of users of alcoholic beverages are able to do so occasionally, in moderation, and with minimal adverse effects. But roughly 10 percent of the users become alcoholics (alcohol addicts) or "problem drinkers," with disastrous results to themselves and to society. As with the use of other addicting drugs, no one using alcohol can foretell if or when he will be among the addicted.

Alcohol Prohibition failed woefully from 1920 to 1933. Barbiturate repression is no more successful today. For these as for most other drugs, the ideal solution is to raise a generation of young people whose *needs* for such drugs are minimal. At moments when life is rich and challenging, who wants a mood-altering drug?

As an interim measure, Consumers Union recommends that the advertising and promotion of alcoholic beverages be prohibited. An appropriate hazard notice should be required on all alcoholic beverage labels; like the warning on cigarette packages, it might not deter use of alcohol, but such a notice would at least indicate society's recognition of the potentially harmful nature of alcoholic beverages.

Other interim measures that might palliate this country's alcohol problem—a far larger problem, no matter how measured, than all other drug problems added together—are beyond the scope of this Report.

In particular, the problem of driving automobiles and using machinery while drunk on alcohol is a major menace. A solution to the drunken-driving problem is urgently needed, along with a solution to the problem of driving while under the influence of other drugs. Prohibition of drugs, like prohibition of alcohol, is *not* the answer.

Nicotine. This, too, is an addicting drug. "The confirmed smoker acts under a compulsion which is quite comparable to that of the heroin user."[1] Just as some heroin addicts can and do stop, so some cigarette smokers can and do stop. But the disastrous effect of basing public policy on these exceptional cases is evident from that fact that cigarette consumption, after seven years of anticigarette drives urging voluntary abstinence, is close to its all-time high.

The other evil effect of failure to recognize that nicotine is an addicting drug is that it encourages young people to start smoking. A majority of teen-age smokers have been persuaded, at least in part by anticigarette campaigns, that they will be able to smoke for a few years and then "kick the habit" when they are ready to quit. It is hard to imagine a nastier trap than this one that society has set for its own children.

The anticigarette campaigns have succeeded in persuading both adults and teen-agers that cigarette smoking causes lung cancer and is damaging to health in numerous other ways. But this conviction is not deterring tens of millions of adults and teen-agers from smoking cigarettes. Despite the highly impressive anticigarette ads on television and other well-planned campaigns, the proportion of smokers among seventeen- and eighteen-year-olds is almost as high as among adults.

It is uncertain whether a ban on cigarette advertising by itself would significantly reduce the numbers of new recruits to cigarette smoking. But, while it may not by itself be sufficient, such a ban is a necessary precondition if other anticigarette measures are to be effective. This is the practical ground that leads Consumers Union to recommend that all cigarette advertising and promotion—including point-of-sale displays and cigarette vending machines—be banned altogether.

There is also an ethical ground for our recommendation; it is immoral to permit the advertising of an addicting product that causes lung cancer and other diseases.

In the absence of effective ways to curb cigarette smoking, a safer substitute for nicotine is needed. So far, scientists have hardly even begun to look for one. When they do start to look, the odds are excellent that they will find a safer nicotine substitute, as well as safer ways of using nicotine itself.

Prescription drugs. Adults are securing mind-affecting drugs on prescription in vast quantities—stimulants, sedatives, hypnotics, tranquilizers, and others. Whether they are getting too many, or not enough, or the wrong ones, deserves objective research.

Many members of the generation under thirty are using, among others, the same drugs their elders get on prescription—but without bothering to get a prescription first. If young adults continue this practice as they mature, many prescription drugs may gradually become "nondrugs" like caffeine, nicotine, and alcohol. This, indeed, may already be happening.

LSD. Until 1962, this drug was a promising adjunct to psychotherapy, tried out on thousands of patients with few adverse effects. Then came the anti-LSD campaign and the anti-LSD laws, which helped convert LSD from a psychotherapeutic novelty to an illicit drug popular even among high-school students. The anti-LSD publicity, the scare campaigns, and the laws also helped convert what had been until 1962 a relatively unknown and innocuous drug into a quite damaging one. As in the case of heroin, legal and social rather than pharmacological factors account for most of the LSD tragedies of the 1960s.

Now that the furor has died down, LSD appears to be becoming less damaging again. The latest data indicate that it is not (as was supposed) a way of life, but a stage through which some drug users pass. Most users either discontinue LSD altogether after a few months or years or else reduce their consumption to a few "trips" a year.

The scattered data available so far indicate that LSD use has not benefited users as much as they suppose—nor has it damaged them as much as has been alleged.

It is still too early to map out a sensible program for making the LSD experience legally available to those who want it for self-betterment and self-exploration ("mind expansion"). That time, however, may come. Meanwhile, experimental use of LSD in therapy for alcoholism, for the palliation of terminal cancer, and perhaps for other indications, should be revived and objectively evaluated.

As matters stand, with only "street LSD" of unknown strength and purity available, and in the absence of skilled supervision, no prudent person will take LSD—just as no prudent person will get dead drunk on alcohol. And it is the height of imprudence to take LSD more than a few times a year—just as it is the height of imprudence to get drunk frequently. For schizophrenics, for borderline schizoid personalities, and perhaps for some others, LSD may prove particularly damaging.

Laws, policies, and attitudes should accordingly be shaped to minimize the damage done by LSD and LSD-like drugs to those imprudent enough to take them. Repressive and punitive laws that add the damage done by imprisonment and criminalization to whatever damage may be done by LSD are irrational and counterproductive.

Marijuana. It is now much too late to debate the issue: marijuana *versus* no marijuana. Marijuana is here to stay. No conceivable law-enforcement program can curb its availability. Accordingly, we offer these seven recommendations.

(1) Consumers Union recommends the immediate repeal of all federal laws governing the growing, processing, transportation, sale, possession, and use of marijuana.

(2) Consumers Union recommends that each of the fifty states similarly

repeal its existing marijuana laws and pass new laws legalizing the cultivation, processing, and orderly marketing of marijuana—subject to appropriate regulations.

The term "legalization of marijuana" means many things to many people. As used here, it means that marijuana should be classed as a licit rather than an illicit drug.

We do *not* recommend legalization because we believe that marijuana is "safe" or "harmless." No drug is safe or harmless to all people at all dosage levels or under all conditions of use. Our recommendation arises out of the conviction that an orderly system of legal distribution and licit use will have notable advantages for both users and nonusers over the present marijuana black market. In particular it will separate the channels of marijuana distribution from heroin channels and from the channels of distribution of other illicit drugs. Even more important, it will end the criminalization and alienation of young people and the damage done to them by arrest, conviction, and imprisonment for marijuana offenses.

Three major questions are not answered by the above recommendation:

• What *kind* of distribution system should be substituted for the present black-market system?
• What specific regulations should govern the new system?
• What should be the respective roles of the state and federal governments?

Most discussions of legalizing marijuana anticipate that distribution will be turned over to the tobacco companies, or the alcoholic beverage companies, or to similar large commercial enterprises. We urge instead that individual states experiment with a wide range of distribution patterns.

Marijuana grows readily in fields, along highways, in backyards, in window boxes, and even in suitably illuminated closets and cellars. An informal distribution system has grown up that is, in considerable part, a sharing among friends, and that is patterend after native arts-and-crafts enterprise rather than large-scale commercial enterprise. If legalizing marijuana should mean turning over production and distribution exclusively to the tobacco companies or to other corporate giants, it is questionable whether all marijuana smokers would readily patronize such a system. Some would no doubt continue to harvest and distribute their own, illegally, just as mountaineers and others continue to make and sell their own whiskey. Bootlegging does not encourage respect for law.

Unfortunately, no body of experience exists in any Western country which might serve as a guide or model for an acceptable system of marijuana distribution. In the absence of experience, neither the states nor the federal government can foretell how a system will work. We therefore believe that the fifty states—at least in the beginning—should be left free to devise their own systems and that a wide range of alternative systems should be tried out. Among the possibilities are distribution through a statewide marijuana monopoly (private or public), through small-scale enterprises resembling arts-and-crafts centers, through alcohol channels, and through tobacco channels.

The fifty states should similarly consider alternative answers to other pressing questions. At what age should young people be allowed to buy marijuana legally? Should only one grade and strength be permitted, or should varying strengths be legally marketable? Should marijuana smoking be permitted in public or only in private? If in public, should it be permitted in cocktail lounges, taverns, bars, and roadhouses or only in places where alcoholic beverages are *not* sold? How can the problem of operating an automobile or other machinery while under the influence of marijuana best be handled? Only a wide range of experience can provide the answers needed for wise long-term decisions on these and related issues.

This does not mean, however, that the federal government should play no role. Experience in other fields has shown federal regulation to have great advantages; and this is almost certain to prove true with marijuana regulation as experience with various regulatory approaches accumulates.

(3) Consumers Union therefore recommends that a national marijuana commisiion be established to help provide the states with needed research information, to monitor the various plans evolved by the states, and to build, eventually, the best features of those plans into federal marijuana legislation.

Adequately staffed and funded, the commission should coordinate federal and state research programs, including ongoing controlled studies into long-term effects of marijuana use.

If some aspect of one state's plan proves disastrous, the commission should recommend a federal law prohibiting the practice nationally. If some other aspect of a state's law proves to be an outstanding success, the successful feature can in due course be accepted as national policy and embodied in federal laws or regualtions. Four possibilities in particular should concern the national marijuana commission from the beginning:

- A law making it a federal offense to transport marijuana into a state in violation of that state's own laws. (A similar provision concerning the transportation of intoxicating liquors is contained in Section 2 of the Twenty-first Amendment to the United States Constitution, which repealed the Eighteenth [Alcohol Prohibition] Amendment.)
- A law setting national standards of marijuana strength and purity.
- A law banning the advertising or promotion of marijuana anywhere in the United States.
- A law requiring a detailed warning notice on all marijuana package labels. Such a warning, like the warning on cigarette packages, is unlikely to deter use; but it will serve to remind users that the legalization of marijuana does not constitute official approval of marijuana or assurance of the drug's harmlessness.

Such a hybrid of state experimentation plus federal intervention is hardly a tidy arrangement, but our system of government has never been noted for its tidiness. In fact, as a welcome result of this untidiness, it is possible for a state to experiment with a new policy without the entire country being subjected to that experimentation.* Our marijuana proposals are designed to take the greatest possible advantage of this freedom to experiment—while also making it possible to terminate experiments that go sour and to adopt nationally those that succeed.

During the period of transition, the marijuana debate will no doubt wax even hotter than it has in the past. Even more attention will be focused on marijuana—even more people will be attracted to the drug. Perhaps it will prove unfortunate, but it is equally possible that one effect of the greater concern with marijuana will be a lessening of use of other drugs, licit as well as illicit. This may prove a major gain.

(4) Consumers Union recommends that state and federal taxes on marijuana be kept moderate, and that tax proceeds be devoted primarily to drug research, drug education, and other measures specifically designed to minimize the damage done by alcohol, nicotine, marijuana, heroin, and other drugs.

Both Congress and state legislatures over the years have tended to tax alcoholic beverages and cigarettes for all that the traffic will bear—in

---

* United States Supreme Court Justice Louis D. Brandeis wrote (1931): "It is one of the happy incidents of the federal system that a single courageous State may, if its citizens choose, serve as a laboratory; and try novel social and economic experiments without risk to the rest of the country."[2]

part on the theory that high prices may deter use. As we have shown, however, high drug prices do *not* deter use. High taxes similarly would be unlikely to deter marijuana use. Rather, their effect very probably would be to encourage the bootlegging and smuggling of marijuana to avoid the tax, as whiskey is bootlegged and cigarettes are smuggled today.

It is hardly likely, of course, that Congress will repeal federal marijuana laws tomorrow, or that state legislatures will legalize marijuana without lengthy debate. Some delay may be tolerable—provided that interim measures are taken to end the cruelty and irrationality of current laws. We accordingly propose these interim measures, which we urge Congress and the states to adopt *without* delay:

(5) Consumers Union recommends an immediate end to imprisonment as a punishment for marijuana possession and for furnishing marijuana to friends.*

This recommendation rests on the *nihil nocere* principle set forth above. The imprisonment of youthful marijuana users has not curbed marijuana smoking. It does more harm than good. When a physician finds that his prescription is doing more harm than good, he withdraws the prescription.

The usual argument for continuing to imprison marijuana offenders—that the results of further scientific research should be awaited—is sophistical and brings both the law and scientific research into disrepute. What it tells young marijuana smokers, in effect, is something like this: "We will continue to imprison you for marijuana offenses because scientists are searching feverishly for some justification for imprisoning marijuana smokers, and they will no doubt find one some day." Even if marijuana ultimately proves as damaging as alcohol, which seems very unlikely, imprisonment is hardly the treatment of choice for users.

(6) Consumers Union recommends, pending legalization of marijuana, that marijuana possession and sharing be immediately made civil violations rather than criminal acts. Including marijuana offenses under the criminal law has two major adverse effects on marijuana smokers, even if there is no imprisonment. First, a criminal record bars an indi-

---

* From the 1970 *Interim Report* of Canada's Le Dain Commission: "There is obviously a big difference between selling the drug for monetary consideration and giving it to a friend. Selling it at cost to an acquaintance is different from selling it to a variety of people to make a profit. Selling it on a small scale to make a marginal profit—perhaps to support one's own usage—is not the same as organizing and controlling a large entrepreneurial organization. As can be seen, trafficking activities range along a spectrum from a kind of act not far removed in seriousness from simple possession to the extensive activities of the stereotyped exploiter and profiteer whose image led to the kinds of penalties associated with trafficking."[3]

vidual from government employment and from a wide variety of other jobs and activities. Second, engaging in criminal behavior has a subtle but significant effect on the self-image of individuals. Because they are criminals under the law, they begin to think of themselves as criminals. Lacking respect for the marijuana laws, they may lose respect for other laws as well. Taking marijuana possession and sharing offenses out of the criminal law altogether will contribute to respect for law.

(7) Consumers Union recommends that those now serving prison terms for possession of or sharing marijuana be set free, and that such marijuana offenses be expunged from all legal records. It is hard to think of a more dramatic way to demonstrate this country's earnest desire to bridge the generation gap and to right grievous miscarriages of justice. Respect for law will surely increase.

REFERENCES

1. VINCENT P. DOLE, personal communication.
2. U. S. Supreme Court Justice Louis D. Brandeis, dissenting opinion, *New State Ice Company* v. *Ernest A. Liebmann*, 1931 (285 U.S. 311).
3. *Le Dain Commission Interim Report*, p. 182.

2

THE DISCOVERY OF DRUG ADDICTION

Thomas Szasz

Ever since pharmacology and psychiatry became accepted as modern medical disciplines—that is, since about the last quarter of the nineteenth century—chemists and physicians, psychologists and psychiatrists, politicians and pharmaceutical manufacturers, all have searched, in vain of course, for non-addictive drugs to relieve pain, to induce sleep, and to stimulate wakefulness. This search is based on the dual premises that addiction is a condition caused by drugs, and that some drugs are more, and others less, "addictive." This view epitomizes the confusion between the pharmacological effects of drugs and their practical uses.

When a drug deadens pain, induces sleep, or stimulates wakefulness, and when people know that there are drugs that do these things, then some persons may—depending on their personal and social circumstances and desires—develop an interest in using such drugs. Why many people habitually use such drugs, and countless other substances, need not for the moment concern us here, other than to note that the reason cannot be said to be because the drugs are "addictive." It is the other way around: we call certain drugs "addictive" because people like to use them—just as we call ether and gasoline "flammable" because they are easily ignited. It is therefore just as absurd to search for non-addictive drugs that produce euphoria as it would be to search for non-flammable liquids that are easy to ignite.

Reprinted with permission of Doubleday & Company, Inc. from *Ceremonial Chemistry*, by T. Szasz, New York: Anchor Press/Doubleday, 1974, 3-18. Copyright © 1974 by Thomas Szasz.

Our contemporary confusion regarding drug abuse and drug addiction is an integral part of our confusion regarding religion. Any idea or act that gives men and women a sense of what their life is about or for—that, in other words, gives their existence meaning and purpose—is, properly speaking, religious. Science, medicine, and especially health and therapy are thus admirably suited to function as quasi-religious ideas, values, and pursuits. It is necessary, therefore, to distinguish between science as science, and science as religion (sometimes called "scientism").

Since the use and avoidance of certain substances has to do with prescriptions and prohibitions, with what is legal or licit and illegal or illicit, the so-called "problem" of drug abuse or drug addiction has two aspects: religious (legal) and scientific (medical). Actually, however, since the factual or scientific aspects of this subject are negligible, the problem is, for all practical purposes, almost entirely religious or moral.[1] A simple example will amplify the nature of the distinction, and the confusion, to which I am referring.

As some persons seek or avoid alcohol and tobacco, heroin and marijuana, so others seek or avoid kosher wine and holy water. The differences between kosher wine and non-kosher wine, holy water and ordinary water, are ceremonial, not chemical. Although it would be idiotic to look for the property of kosherness in wine, or for the property of holiness in water, this does not mean that there is no such thing as kosher wine or holy water. Kosher wine is wine that is ritually clean according to Jewish law. Holy water is water blessed by a Catholic priest. This creates a certain demand for such wine and water by people who want this sort of thing; at the same time, and for precisely the same reason, such wine and water are rejected by those who do not believe in their use.

Similarly, the important differences between heroin and alcohol, or marijuana and tobacco—as far as "drug abuse" is concerned—are not chemical but ceremonial. In other words, heroin and marijuana are approached and avoided not because they are more "addictive" or more "dangerous" than alcohol and tobacco, but because they are more "holy" or "unholy"—as the case may be.

The single most important issue in coming to grips with the problem of drug use and drug avoidance is, in my opinion, the medical perspective on moral conduct. As I have shown elsewhere,[2] the psychiatric claim that personal conduct is not volitional but reflexive—in short, that human beings are not subjects but objects, not persons but organisms—was first staked out in relation to acts that were socially disturbing and could conventionally be called "mad" or "insane."

The pioneering eighteenth-century "alienists" managed the first factories for manufacturing madmen, and developed the earliest advertising campaigns for selling "insanity" by renaming badness as madness, and then offering to dispose of it. The famous nineteenth-century "neuropsychiatrists" made decisive advances in both the production and promotion of madness, establishing the "reality" of the modern concept of "mental illness": first, they progressively metaphorized disagreeable conduct and forbidden desire as disease—thus creating more and more mental diseases; second, they literalized this medical metaphor, insisting that disapproved behavior was not merely *like* a disease, but that it *was* a disease—thus confusing others, and perhaps themselves as well, regarding the differences between bodily and behavioral "abnormalities."

By the time the twentieth century was ushered in—thanks in large part to the work of Freud and the modern "psychologists"—madness was bursting through the walls of the insane asylums and was being discovered in clinics and doctors' offices, in literature and art, and in the "psychopathology of everyday life." Since the First World War, the enemies of this psychiatrization of man—in particular, religion and common sense—have lost their nerve; now they no longer even try to resist the opportunistic theories and oppressive technologies of modern "behavioral science."

Thus, by the time the contemporary American drug-abuseologists, legislators, and psychiatrists came on the scene, the contact lenses that refracted deviance as disease were so deeply embedded into the corneas of the American people that they could be pried loose only with the greatest effort; and only by leaving both the laity and the professionals so painfully wounded and temporarily blinded that they could hardly be expected to tolerate such interference with their vision, much less to impose such painful self-enlightenment on themselves.

The result was that when, in the post-Prohibition, post-Second World War, better-living-through-chemistry era, the so-called drug problem "hit" America, the phenomena it presented could be apprehended only as refracted through these irremovable contact lenses. Those who used drugs could not help themselves. Since they were the victims of their irresistible impulses, they needed others to protect them from these impulses. This made it logical and reasonable for politicians and psychiatrists to advocate "drug controls." And since none of this has "worked"—as how could it have?—the blame for it all could at least be affixed to those who sold illicit drugs: they were called "pushers" and were persecuted in the horrifying manner in which men wallowing in the conviction of their own virtuousness have always persecuted those about whose wickedness they could entertain no doubts.

Presumably some persons have always "abused" certain drugs—alcohol for millennia, opiates for centuries. However, only in the twentieth century have certain patterns of drug use been labeled as "addictions." Traditionally, the term "addiction" has meant simply a strong inclination toward certain kinds of conduct, with little or no pejorative meaning attached to it. Thus, the *Oxford English Dictionary* offers such pre-twentieth-century examples of the use of this term as being addicted "to civil affairs," "to useful reading"—and also "to bad habits." Being addicted to drugs is not among the definitions listed.

Until quite recently, then, the term "addiction" was understood to refer to a habit, good or bad as the case might be, actually more often the former. This usage saved people from the confusion into which the contemporary meaning of this term has inevitably led.

Although the term "addiction" is still often used to describe habits, usually of an undesirable sort, its meaning has become so expanded and transformed that it is now used to refer to almost any kind of illegal, immoral, or undesirable association with certain kinds of drugs. For example, a person who has smoked but a single marijuana cigarette, or even one who has not used any habit-forming or illegal drug at all, may be considered to be a drug abuser or drug addict: this is the case when a person, found to be in possession of illicit drugs, is accused by the legal and medical authorities who "examine" him of using (rather than with selling or merely carrying) these substances, and is convicted in a court of law on a charge of "drug abuse" or "drug addiction."

In short—during the past half-century, and especially during recent decades—the noun "addict" has lost its denotative meaning and reference to persons engaged in certain *habits*, and has become transformed into a stigmatizing label possessing only pejorative meaning referring to certain *persons*. The term "addict" has thus been added to our lexicon of stigmatizing labels—such as "Jew," which could mean either a person professing a certain religion or a "Christ killer" who himself should be killed; or "Negro," which could mean either a black-skinned person or a savage who ought to be kept in actual or social slavery. More specifically still, the word "addict" has been added to our psychiatric vocabulary of stigmatizing diagnoses, taking its place alongside such terms as "insane," "psychotic," "schizophrenic," and so forth.

This conceptual, cultural, and semantic transformation in the use and meaning of the term "addiction" is also reflected in its remarkably recent appearance on what psychiatrists regard as the authoritative or official lists of mental diseases or psychiatric diagnoses. The first edition of Kraepelin's classic textbook, published in 1883, lists neither drug intoxication nor drug addiction in its inventory of mental disease.[3] The second edition, published in 1887, mentions "chronic intoxications," and itemizes "alcoholism" and "morphinism," but still does not mention addiction. Four years later, in the fourth edition, "cocainism" is added to the intoxications, but addiction is still not mentioned. ("Homosexuality," however, is now added to the list.) The sixth edition, published in 1899, includes both "acute" and "chronic intoxications," noting specifically the three drugs listed previously; the same diagnoses are listed in the eighth edition, published between 1909 and 1915, with addiction still conspicuously absent.

In Bleuler's famous *Textbook of Psychiatry*, first published in 1916, "toxic psychoses" are listed among the diagnoses, but addiction is not. In the United States, the Retreat for the Insane in Hartford, Connecticut, had, in 1888, a system of classification that included "masturbation insanity" and "alcoholic insanity," but did not include intoxications or addiction. In the United States, the diagnosis of "drug addiction" became officially recognized only in 1934, when it was included for the first time among the "mental illnesses" listed in the American Psychiatric Association's *Standard Classified Nomenclature of Diseases*.[4]

The most authoritative text on the history of psychiatry, and the one most widely used today in American medical schools and psychiatric residency programs, is *A History of Psychiatry* by Gregory Zilboorg. In the index to this book, first published in 1941, there are no entries for "addiction" or "drug addiction."[5]

Ceremonial performances—such as partaking of the Holy Communion, celebrating Yom Kippur, or saluting the flag—articulate certain communal values. By participating in the ceremonial, the individual affirms his membership in the group; by refusing to participate in it, he affirms his rejection of, or withdrawal from, the group.

To understand ceremonial chemistry, we must therefore distinguish between the chemical or medical effects of drugs and the ceremonial or moral aspects of drug use. On the face of it, this is an easy enough distinction to make. If it is elusive nevertheless, it is so because—as we shall have opportunity to observe—it is a distinction we now often make at the peril of losing our valued membership in family, profession, or other group upon which our self-esteem, if not our very livelihood, depends.

The subject matter of textbooks of pharmacology is the chemical effects of various drugs on the body, especially on the human body; and, more narrowly, the use of drugs for the treatment of diseases. There is, of course, an ethical premise implicit even in this—seemingly purely medical—perspective, but this premise is so self-evident that we usually consider it unnecessary to articulate it: namely, that we regard certain drugs as "therapeutic" and seek to develop such drugs with the understanding that they are helpful to the person (patient) who uses them—and not, say, to the pathogenic microorganisms that infect or infest him, or to the cancerous cells to which he is host. A textbook of pharmacology written for pneumococci or spirochetes would not be the same as one written for human beings. The basic and yet tacit moral assumption to which I point here is that pharmacology is an applied scientific discipline—applied, that is, to the welfare of the sick patient, as that welfare is generally understood, and implemented, by the patient himself.

Nevertheless, all recent textbooks of pharmacology contain material within their pages totally inconsistent and incompatible with this aim and premise, and sharply in conflict with the ostensible intellectual task of the student or practitioner of pharmacology. I refer to the fact that all such textbooks contain a chapter on drug addiction and drug abuse.

In the fourth edition of Goodman and Gilman's *The Pharmacological Basis of Therapeutics,* Jerome H. Jaffe, a psychiatrist, defines "drug abuse" as ". . . the use, usually by self-administration, of any drug in a manner that deviates from approved medical or social patterns within a given culture."[6]

Implicitly, then, drug abuse is accepted by Jaffe, and by Goodman and Gilman—as indeed it is by nearly everyone, nearly everywhere today—as a disease whose diagnosis and treatment are the legitimate concern of the physician. But let us note carefully just what drug abuse is. Jaffe himself defines it as any deviation "from approved medical or social patterns" of drug use. We are thus immediately plunged into the innermost depths of the mythology of mental illness: for just as socially disapproved pharmacological behavior constitutes "drug abuse," and is officially recognized as an illness by a medical profession that is a licensed agency of the state, so socially disapproved sexual behavior constitutes "perversion" and is also officially recognized as an illness; and so, more generally, socially disapproved personal behavior of any kind constitutes "mental illness" which is also officially recognized as an illness—"like any other." What is particularly interesting and important about all these "illnesses"—that is, about drug abuse, sex abuse, and mental illness generally—is that few if any of the "patients" suffering from them recognize that they are sick; and that, perhaps because of this reason, these "patients" may be and frequently are "treated" against their will.[7]

As I see it, and indeed as Jaffe's own definition of it acknowledges, drug abuse is a matter of conventionality; hence, it is a subject that belongs to anthropology and sociology, religion and law, ethics and criminology—but surely not to pharmacology.

Moreover, inasmuch as drug abuse deals with disapproved or prohibited patterns of drug use, it resembles not the therapeutic use of drugs given to treat sick patients, but the toxic use of drugs given to healthy people to poison them. Some types of "drug abuse" could thus be viewed as acts of self-poisoning standing in the same sort of logical relationship to acts of criminal poisoning as suicide stands to homicide. But if this is so, why not also include, in textbooks of pharmacology, chapters on how to deal with those who "abuse" drugs not by poisoning themselves but by poisoning others? This, of course, seems like an absurd idea. Why? Because people who *poison other people* are criminals. What we do with them is not a problem for science or pharmacology to solve, but a decision for legislators and the courts to make. But is it any less absurd to include, in the compass of medicine or pharmacology, the problem of what to do with those persons who *poison themselves*, or who do not even harm themselves but merely violate certain social norms or legal rules?

It is clear, of course, that behind this normative or legal dimension of the drug problem there lies a biological one to which pharmacology may indeed rightfully address itself. Regardless of how a chemical substance gets into a person's body—whether through the intervention of a physician, as in ordinary medical treatment; or through self-administration, as is typically the case in drug abuse and drug addiction; or through the intervention of some malefactor, as in cases of criminal poisoning—that substance will have certain effects which we can understand better, and mitigate more successfully, if we rely on pharmacological knowledge and methods. All this is obvious. What is perhaps not so obvious is that by focusing on the chemistry of drugs we may obscure—indeed we may want to obscure—the simple fact that in some instances we deal with persons who consider themselves ill and wish to be medicated under medical control, while in others we deal with persons who do not consider themselves ill but wish to medicate themselves under their own control. The toxicological effects of drugs thus belong properly to a discussion of their other biological effects, as do the pharmacological and other measures useful for counteracting their toxicity; whereas the social and legal interventions imposed on persons called "drug abusers" or "drug addicts" have no legitimate place at all in textbooks of pharmacology.

Pharmacology, let us not forget, is the science of drug use—that is, of the healing (therapeutic) and harming (toxic) effects of drugs. If, nevertheless, textbooks of pharmacology legitimately contain a chapter on drug abuse and drug addiction, then, by the same token, textbooks of gynecology and urology should contain a chapter on prostitution; textbooks of physiology, a chapter on perversion; textbooks of genetics, a chapter on the racial inferiority of Jews and Negroes; textbooks of mathematics, a chapter on gambling syndicates; and, of course, textbooks of astronomy, a chapter on sun worship.

The mythology of psychiatry has corrupted not only our common sense and the law but also our language and pharmacology. To be sure, as are all such corruptions and confusions, this one is not something imposed on us by conspiring or scheming psychiatrists; instead, it is simply another manifestation of the deepseated human need for magic and religion, for ceremonial and ritual, and of the covert (unconscious) expression of this need in what we self-deceivingly think is the "science" of pharmacology.

Not until we distinguish more clearly than we now do between the chemical and ceremonial uses and effects of drugs shall we be able to begin a sensible description and a reasonable discussion of so-called problems of drug abuse and drug addiction.

It is now widely recognized and accepted that our language both reflects and shapes our experience. This sophistication has, however, had no appreciable effect on our contemporary attitudes and policies toward social problems in which the verbal shaping of the "problem" itself constitutes much or even all of the ensuing problem. We seemed to have learned little or nothing from the fact that we had no problem with drugs until we quite literally talked ourselves into having one: we declared first this and then that drug "bad" and "dangerous"; gave them nasty names like "dope" and "narcotic"; and passed laws prohibiting their use. The result: our present "problems of drug abuse and drug addiction."

The plain historical facts are that before 1914 there was no "drug problem" in the United States; nor did we have a name for it. Today there is an immense drug problem in the United States, and we have lots of names for it. Which came first: "the problem of drug abuse" or its name? It is the same as asking which came first: the chicken or the egg? All we can be sure of now is that the more chickens, the more eggs, and vice versa; and similarly, the more problems, the more names for them, and vice versa. My point is simply that our drug abuse experts, legislators, psychiatrists, and other professional guardians of our medical morals have been operating chicken hatcheries: they continue—partly by means of certain characteristic, tactical abuses of our language—to manufacture and maintain the "drug problem" they ostensibly try to solve. The following excerpts from the popular and professional press—and my comments on them—illustrate and support this contention.

From an editorial in *Science*, entitled "Death from Heroin":

Drug abuse, which was once predominantly a disease of Harlem, is now a plague that is spreading to the suburbs. Drug use has been glamorized, while descriptions of the dreadful consequences have been muted. . . . Two relatively new methods seem promising. One is the use of methadone. A second approach is a psychiatric one, which emphasizes attitudinal changes and utilizes ex-addicts to give emotional support to those who wish to stop. . . . This nation should provide the funds to move vigorously against a spreading plague.[8]

Deaths caused by the prohibition of heroin, and especially by the contaminants added to it on the illicit market, are here falsely attributed to heroin itself; the use of heroin is called a "disease," and its spread from blacks to whites is called a "plague"; the use of methadone is considered to be a perfectly legitimate type of medical treatment for the heroin habit, while no mention is made of the fact that the use of heroin originated as a treatment for the morphine habit. Furthermore, psychiatric interventions with persons stigmatized as "drug abusers" and "drug addicts" are here misrepresented as "help" which the "patients" want in order to stop taking illegal drugs, whereas it is actually something imposed on them by law by those who want them to stop this habit; and the policies of psychiatrically harassing persons who take illegal drugs, and of using tax monies to supply them with legal drugs (such as methadone), are accepted unquestioningly and uncritically as medically indicated and morally justified.

From a report in the *Syracuse Herald-Journal* entitled "New Drug Offers Hope: May Immunize Heroin Addicts":

The drug is EN-1639A from laboratories in Garden City, N.Y. Industry sources confirmed the firm is close to clinical testing, the last step before marketing of a new drug. . . . EN-1639A has already been tested on some human subjects at the federal drug rehabilitation and addiction center at Lexington, Ky. Officials there believe the new drug could wipe out addiction the way vaccines have eliminated smallpox.[9]

This is an illustration of some of the consequences of mistaking metaphor for the thing metaphorized. Addiction is no longer *like* a plague; it *is* a plague. A drug compulsorily administered to addicts is no longer *like* a vaccine; it *is* a vaccine.

From a report in *The New York Times* entitled "Amphetamines Used by a Physician to Lift Moods of Famous Patients":

For many years Dr. Max Jacobson, a 72-year old general practitioner in New York, has been injecting amphetamine—the powerful stimulant the drug culture calls "speed"—into the veins of
dozens of the country's most celebrated artists, writers, politicians, and jet-setters. . . . Dr. Jacobson is the best known of a
small number of New York doctors who specialize in prescribing
and administering amphetamines not to treat disease but to boost
the mood of healthy patients. Far from the typical picture of
rag-tag youths dosing themselves with illegally obtained drugs,
the story of Dr. Jacobson and his patients is one of wealthy and
famous adults depending on a licensed physician for their completely legal injections. . . . The most famous of the doctor's
patients were President and Mrs. Kennedy. . . . In 1961, for
example, he went with the President to Vienna for the summit
meeting with Khrushchev and, Dr. Jacobson said in an interview,
gave the President injections there. . . . Once, when Dr. Jacobson
was in the audience for the Boston try-out of Mr. [Alan Jay]
Lerner's "On a Clear Day," he turned to Mrs. Burton Lane, the
wife of the musical's composer, and made a boast that many
persons said he often makes. As Mrs. Lane recalled it, Dr. Jacobson pointed to his tie clip, a PT-109 insignia, and said, "Do
you know where I got this? I worked with the Kennedys. I trav-
elled with the Kennedys. I treated the Kennedys. Jack Kennedy.
Jacqueline Kennedy. They never could have made it without
me. They gave me this in gratitude." . . . Jacqueline Kennedy
Onassis confirmed through a spokesman that she had been
treated by Dr. Jacobson but declined to elaborate.[10]

The medicalization of the English language has here progressed so
far that we have not only "sick patients" but also "healthy patients"; and
that we have "treatments" not only for making sick persons better but
also for making healthy persons more energetic. To be sure, these distinctions apply only to the powerful and the wealthy: when they take
psychoactive drugs, they are still respected political leaders who, in their
spare time, wage war on drug abuse; when the powerless and the poor
take the same drugs, they are "dope fiends" bent on destroying the
nation. The ancient Latin adage *Quod licet Jovi, non licet bovi* ("What is
permitted to Jove is not permitted to the cow") is, perhaps, more relevant
to our understanding of the uses of licit and illicit drugs than all the
chemical facts and fantasies about drug abuse assembled in textbooks
of pharmacology and psychiatry.

In an address at the annual legislative dinner of the Empire State
Chamber of Commerce, Governor Nelson Rockefeller declares: "We,

the citizens, are imprisoned by pushers. I want to put the pushers in prison so we can come out, ladies and gentlemen."[11]

Glester Hinds, the head of Harlem's People's Civic and Welfare Association, commenting on Governor Rockefeller's proposal for mandatory life sentences without parole for heroin pushers, states: "I don't think the Governor went far enough. It should be included in his bill as capital punishment because these murderers need to be gotten rid of completely."[12]

Dr. George W. McMurray, pastor of the Mother African Methodist Episcopal Zion Church, commends Rockefeller for his "forthright stand against addiction," which he calls a "subtle form of genocidal execution."[13]

William F. Buckley, in a column on Governor Rockefeller's proposals for dealing with heroin pushers, writes: "One shrinks from the medieval concern to design modes of death particularly appropriate to the crime of the offender. . . . But it is not, I should think, inappropriate to suggest that a condign means of ridding the world of convicted heroin pushers is to prescribe an overdose. It happens that it is a humane way of dying, if one defines humane as relatively painless. And, of course, there is a rabbinical satisfaction in the idea that the pusher should leave this world in such circumstances as he has caused others to leave it. . . ."[14]

Here we are told, by a variety of authorities, that citizens are imprisoned by pushers, when, in fact, the citizens' safety is imperiled by legislators and politicians who, by prohibiting the sale and use of heroin, create the crimes associated with the illegal market in it; that pushers are "murderers" who should be executed, when, in fact, pushers commit no harm, much less murder, and when there is no death penalty in New York State even for first-degree murder; that "addiction is a form of genocidal execution," when, in fact, it is an expression of self-determination; and that heroin pushers are murderers who should be killed by giving them an overdose of heroin, again advocating the death sentence for metaphorical murderers even though there is no such sentence for literal murderers.

From an address by Rep. James M. Hanley (D.-N.Y.) before the Baldwinsville, N.Y., Chamber of Commerce:

> Rep. Hanley called the 60,000 known drug addicts in the U.S. only "the visible portion of the iceberg," and expressed concern over unknown present and potential addicts, asking "how many vermin are infesting our high schools and colleges," pushing this junk on our unwary youth?[15]

Rep. Hanley here uses the same metaphor for condemning persons who use or sell illegal drugs that the Nazis used to justify murdering Jews by poisoned gas—namely, that the persecuted persons are not human beings but "vermin."

From a Letter to the Editor of *The New York Times* by Steven Jonas, M.D., Assistant Professor of Community Medicine at the State University of New York, Stony Brook, Long Island:

> Governor Rockefeller's new proposal for dealing with the drug problem by attacking sellers [by imposing mandatory life sentences on those who sell "dangerous drugs"] are strongly supported by epidemiological theory. Heroin addiction in particular is much like a communicable disease, even though noninfectious. There are a host, man, an agent, heroin, and identifiable environmental factors, just like there are in infectious communicable diseases. Furthermore, there is a vector, or carrier, or the agent, the pusher (and dealer), who may or may not be infected himself. Thus heroin addiction is similar in many ways to diseases such as malaria with its identifiable vector, the mosquito.[16]

A physician who is a professor in a medical school here asserts that heroin addiction is like malaria, that heroin is like a parasite, and that the person who sells heroin is like a mosquito. The verminization of the human being, begun by the Health Ministry of National Socialist Germany, is thus continued—without any public recognition that it is—through the American war on "drug abuse."

Clearly, the differences between the past and the present—the traditional moral and the modern medical—uses of the term "addict" could hardly be greater. In the first case, we have a *description*—a *name*—not entirely value-free, to be sure, but identifying mainly a particular habit on the part of the person to whom it is applied. In the second case, we have an *ascription*—an *epithet*—not entirely fact-free, to be sure (unless it is used mistakenly or mendaciously), but identifying mainly a particular *judgment* on the part of the person making it. In its descriptive sense, the term "addiction" tells us something about what the "addict" does *to himself;* in its ascriptive sense, it tells us something about what those making the judgment plan to do *to him.*

I have made this same sort of distinction—between fact and value, description and ascription, self-definition and definition by others—in several of my previous works. In particular, I have tried to show that there are not only two different psychiatries, voluntary and involuntary—but that they are antagonistic to one another; and I have tried to demonstrate that to confuse and combine these two can lead only to mystification for the psychiatrists and misfortune for the so-called patients.[17] Nowhere could these distinctions be more obvious than in the area of so-called drug abuse and drug addiction: for the facts here, quite simply are that some people want to take some drugs which some others do not want them to take. The drug users—called "drug abusers" or "drug addicts" by the authorities—regard their drugs as their allies, and those who try to deprive them of the drugs as their adversaries; whereas the politicians, psychiatrists, and ex-addicts—who call themselves "experts on drug abuse and drug addiction"—regard the prohibited drugs as their enemies, the persons who use them as their "patients," and their own coercive interventions as "treatments."

It seems to me that a great deal of current thinking and writing about addiction is vitiated—is made meaningless, misleading, and mischievous—by a persistent failure or refusal to make the distinctions outlined above. Assertions are made, rejoinders are offered, and the whole subject is hotly debated, without bothering to scrutinize what is meant by the terms "addict" and "addiction." One reason for all this is that it is much easier to examine the chemical effects of a drug a person uses than the social effects of a ceremony he performs.

It requires intelligence to understand the chemistry of a drug one takes, but it requires courage to understand the ceremony one performs; and while it requires intelligence to understand the chemistry of a drug others take, it requires both courage and tolerance to understand the ceremony they perform. Intelligence, courage, and tolerance are all in short supply, decreasing in that order. So long as that remains the human condition, the so-called human sciences will continue to lag far behind the natural sciences.

To understand holy water, we must of course examine priests and parishioners, not water; and to understand abused and addictive drugs, we must examine doctors and addicts, politicians and populations, not drugs. Clearly, some situations are more favorable for such an enterprise than others. One could not very well study holy water in medieval Italy or Spain, especially if one was, and hoped to remain, a good Catholic. In the same way, one cannot very well study opium and heroin, or marijuana and methadone, in the U.S.A. or U.S.S.R., especially if one is, and hopes to remain, a loyal physician whose duty is to help combat the "plague" of drug abuse and drug addiction.

Social ceremonies serve to unite individuals in groups. They often perform this function well, albeit at a high cost to certain individuals in the system, or to certain values cherished by the group. Because the scrutiny of ceremonials tends to weaken their cohesive powers, it is perceived as a threat to the group. Herein lies the basic limitation to the feasibility and influence of the analysis of ritual, whether magical or medical.

REFERENCES

1. See THOMAS SZASZ, The ethics of addiction, *Harper's Magazine*, April 1972, pp. 74-79, and Bad habits are not diseases, *Lancet*, 2:83–84 (July 8), 1972.
2. See, especially, THOMAS SZASZ, *The Myth of Mental Illness*, New York: Hoeber-Harper, 1961, and *Ideology and Insanity*. Garden City, New York: Doubleday Anchor, 1970.
3. See KARL MENNINGER, *The Vital Balance*, New York: Viking, 1963, pp. 419–489.
4. Ibid., p. 474.
5. GREGORY ZILBOORG, *A History of Medical Psychology*, New York: Norton, 1941, pp. 591–606.
6. JEROME H. JAFFE, "Drug Addiction and Drug Abuse," in Louis Goodman and Alfred Gilman (Eds.), *The Pharmacological Basis of Therapeutics*, Fourth Edition, New York: Macmillan, 1970, p. 276.
7. In this connection, see THOMAS SZASZ, *Law, Liberty, and Psychiatry*, New York: Macmillan, 1963, and *Psychiatric Justice*, New York: Macmillan, 1965.
8. PHILIP H. ABELSON, Death from heroin (editorial), *Science*, 168:1289 (June 12), 1970.
9. JARED STOUT, New drug offers hope: May immunize heroin addicts, *Syracuse Herald-Journal*, Dec. 23, 1971, p. 1.
10. BOYCE RENSENBERGER, Amphetamines used by a physician to life moods of famous patients, *The New York Times*, Dec. 4, 1972, pp. 1 and 34.
11. JOHN A. HAMILTON, Hooked on histrionics, *The New York Times*, Feb. 12, 1973, p. 27.
12. Black leaders demand stiff drug penalties, *Human Events*, Feb. 17, 1973, p. 3.
13. Ibid.
14. WILLIAM F. BUCKLEY, JR., Rockefeller's proposal, *Syracuse Post-Standard*, Feb. 15, 1973, p. 5.
15. THOMAS ADAMS, Hanley urges stiffer pentalties for drug abusers, *Syracuse Herald-Journal*, March 23, 1968, p. 2.
16. STEVEN JONAS, Dealing with drugs (letter to the editor), *The New York Times*, Jan. 12, 1973, p. 30.
17. See THOMAS SZASZ, *Ideology and Insanity*, Garden City, N.Y.: Doubleday Anchor, 1970, especially pp. 218–245; and *The Age of Madness*, Garden City, N.Y.: Doubleday Anchor, 1973.

3

THE TOPOGRAPHY OF STRAIGHTLAND

Andrew Weil

Previously I wrote that I "do not now have any special case to make for or against the use of drugs." It may have occurred to some readers, however, that I seem to have a case to make for something. And so I do. While I am not for or against the use of drugs, I make no secret of my belief that it is good to learn to spend time consciously in states of consciousness other than the ordinary waking state. In fact, this bias underlies much of what I have written up to now. Earlier I made no effort to justify this point of view except to note occasional examples of the positive implications of consciousness alteration (such as the possibility of voluntary control of the autonomic nervous system). Now I wish to give a formal explanation. The essence of what I have to say is simply this: altered states of consciousness, consciously entered, seem to me to be doors to ways of using the mind that are better than those most of us follow most of the time. I will use the term *stoned* to designate these better ways and the term *straight* to designate the ordinary ways.

I am well aware that these terms have many meanings far removed from the specific ones intended here. *Straight* can mean "honest," "not curved," "not homosexual," or even (in the subcultural slang of the previous generation) "in possession of illegal drugs." To many people *stoned* simply denotes "very intoxicated," usually on alcohol. But in the contemporary counterculture, these words are familiar designations for types of thinking, so that one hears such usages as "stoned humor," referring to funniness based on a particular kind of perception with no connotation of intoxication. Because *straight* and *stoned* are the terms now used by persons who actually experience the difference, I prefer them to any invented words. Other terms have been suggested to me ("unenlightened" vs. "enlightened"; "linear" vs. "nonlinear"; "rational" vs. "nonrational"), but they seem to me cumbersome and less natural. I will continue to talk about straight thinking and stoned thinking and request the reader to regard these as technical terms to be defined in this chapter and the next.

The relative merits of straight versus stoned thinking is by far the most important of all the garbled issues of the drug controversy, and it is also the most anxiety-provoking. The anxiety arises entirely from ego-centered consciousness because it concerns the deeply felt issue of self-esteem. When people who use drugs claim to have reached higher levels of consciousness or greater awareness, they automatically produce negative thoughts of lower levels of consciousness and lesser awareness in people who do not use drugs. Thus, these groups become polarized and begin to fight with each other symbolically, ritually, or even physically. When people are fighting they often fail to notice important things, such as the evidence that higher levels of consciousness exist and are available to all of us.

If we can detach ourselves from the controversy over drugs, we will come to see that it is a battle over unreal issues in which the real issues—the ones that matter to us as individuals—are completely skewed. Pro- and anti-drug forces are polarized in appearance, but in reality both are partly right and both are partly wrong. The more we start to talk about consciousness rather than about drugs, the more, I think, we will be able to see how much in agreement we are.

I will here be talking about two very different ways of using the mind, but I will never be talking about two different groups of people. It seems to me that stoned thinking, like daydreaming, is a natural component of consciousness that all of us have available to us all the time. Therefore, I am uninterested in questions like, Are you more stoned that I am? or, Is he more stoned than you? The only question worth thinking about is, In the moment-to-moment situations of everyday life do I use my mind in a stoned way or in a straight way?

I will attempt to depict straight thinking, first by listing its characteristics, then by giving examples of conceptions that it has produced in our world. I will describe stoned thinking in a similar way. At the outset I must emphasize that stoned thinking predominates naturally in states of consciousness other than the ordinary, ego-centered waking state; consequently, it correlates with drug use only to the extent that drugs are used intelligently as tools to enter altered states of consciousness. I know a great many persons who use a great many drugs and yet think in straight ways most of the time. (In fact, excessive use of drugs is, itself, a pattern of behavior arising from straight conceptions.) On the other hand, I know a number of people who are very stoned in their thinking and yet have never used drugs; they make use of other methods of getting into altered states of consciousness. I know no people who are stoned and who do not spend significant portions of their mental life in nonordinary states of consciousness.

Straight thinking is ordinary thinking. It is what all of us do most of the time with our minds when we are normally alert and functioning in the world. It is what our conventional educational systems reward us for doing well. It is the kind of thinking that predominates in most of the institutions of our society at the present time. We are so used to it that many of us do not suspect the existence of another way of interpreting our perceptions of the world around us.

I understand straight thinking for two reasons. First, like everyone I know, I engage in it frequently. Second, over the past few years, as I have more consciously explored other states of consciousness, I have become acutely aware of the straightness of much of the thinking in areas I am most familiar with: particularly science, medicine, and government. Wherever it appears, this kind of thinking has five easily identifiable characteristics, which I prefer to describe as "tendencies," since they vary in strength of expression but are always present in some degree.

1. *A tendency to know things through the intellect rather than through some other faculty of the mind*

A person using his mind in a straight way tends to forget that his intellect is only one component of his mind; therefore, he thinks he knows something when he understands it intellectually. The counterculture in contemporary America violently opposes this attitude and insists that direct experience is the only valid source of knowledge. In its more extreme forms, this insistence looks like simple anti-intellectualism and clearly frightens intellectuals. But in its most positive aspects, the countercultural emphasis on direct experience seems to me a breath of fresh air that is beginning to dispel some of the stagnation of intellectual life in our society. Indeed, those in academic communities who are open to new ways of thinking recognize its potential value to their own fields of inquiry. For example, Dr. Thomas R. Blackburn, a professor of chemistry, wrote in an article in *Science* in June 1971:

. . . the salient feature of the counterculture is its epistemology of direct sensuous experience, subjectivity, and respect for intuition—especially intuitive knowledge based on a "naive" openness to nature and to other people. Both on its own merits and as a reaction to the abuses of technology, the movement has attracted increasing numbers of intelligent and creative students and professional people. I believe that science as a creative endeavor cannot survive the loss of these people; nor, without them, can science contribute to the solution of the staggering social and ecological problems that we face.

. . . much of the criticism directed at the current scientific model of nature is quite valid. If society is to begin to enjoy the promise of the "scientific revolution," or even to survive in a tolerable form, science must change.[1]

Having identified with the role of intellectual for much of my life, I have found it difficult to accept the fact that my intellect is a hindrance to the kind of development of my mind I now wish to undertake. But I now understand that the intellect is merely the thought producer of the mind and that thoughts are not realities. In order to perceive reality directly, one must sooner or later learn how to abandon the intellect and disengage oneself from the thoughts it produces incessantly. All instructional materials on meditation stress this theme. For example, in his manual, *Concentration and Meditation, Christmas Humphreys* warns the beginner:

A more difficult problem, because entirely new, will be the claims of the intellect, which, with the antagonism displayed by every vehicle when it is sought for the first time to bring it under control, will fight for self-existence with an amazing variety of subtle wiles and unsound arguments. With an arrogance peculiar to itself it will strive to persuade the meditator that in this sphere alone lies truth, and it is all too noticeable that the West as a whole is a victim of this arrogance. Yet the intellect in itself is but a moulder of forms, and sooner or later consciousness must rise above the limitations which form implies . . . To such an extent are most of us dominated by the intellect, or "thought-machine," that in the early stages of meditation we fail to appreciate how it is deceiving us. Many a student imagines, for example, that he is meditating upon his chosen subject, only to find on strict analysis that the real object of his meditation is "I am meditating upon so and so!"[2]

Perhaps the most effective stratagem of the intellect is to convince its owner that it is equivalent to the mind; if one accepts this notion, abandoning the intellect becomes equivalent to losing one's mind. For this reason, intellectuals tend to look upon persons who have gone beyond the intellect as unfortunates who have suffered a mental catastrophe, even though those persons may have greater awareness than any intellectual can have.

Being able to abandon the intellect at will in order to experience certain things directly does not mean losing the intellect permanently. It is always there, always producing its endless chains of associated thoughts, and always available for use. And thoughts can be useful. After all, it was my intellect that led me to mescaline by way of Huxley's *Doors of Perception* (although the motivation to read up on the subject originated in a nonrational intuition that mescaline was somehow important to me). But once the intellect leads us to the brink of an experience, it has served its function, and we must let go of it; otherwise, we never have the experience and never come to know what we are talking about.

As a hallmark of straight thinking, attachment to the intellect is especially visible in American academic communities. In my first year at Harvard College I was a student in the Linguistics Department, under the chairmanship of the late Joshua Whatmough. In one of the lectures I attended in his course, "Language," he ridiculed the idea that there could be such a thing as an "ineffable" experience. If an experience could not be expressed in words, he told the class, it could not exist. He was very sure of himself and obviously unwilling to be contradicted. But a few weeks before, when I had tried mescaline for the second time, I had had an experience that certainly felt ineffable to me. There seemed to be no point in trying to convey anything of its nature to Professor Whatmough; instead I transferred out of the Linguistics Department into psychology, where people turned out to be even less interested in conscious experience. It should not be surprising that large numbers of young people, who are beginning to discover the advantages of direct experience, are becoming much less tolerant of the conventional academic exercises of American colleges. As one's thinking becomes less straight by virtue of conscious time spent out of ordinary waking consciousness (regardless of the means used to get out), one is no longer content with intellectual, verbal description of reality; direct experience becomes more and more worth seeking. This is my own finding based on my own experience (if you will, on my personal research), and I cannot expect any reader to accept it as true until he can confirm it from his own experience. All I can do is present an intellectual argument explaining why it is true, which might lead the reader to design the appropriate experiments to test the proposition. To claim that my argument proved the proposition would be to fall into the same error of thinking that so many university professors make.

In any case, here is the argument: the essence of intellection is the generation of hypotheses about reality by a process of inductive reasoning—that is, by generalizing from observation. Only by direct experience can we confirm or reject these hypotheses with confidence. This kind of testing by actual trial is the strict meaning of the word *proof*, as one can detect in such uses as "proving grounds." In fact, the exception that proves the rule is not, as in the popular mind, the one that is always there and thus establishes proof automatically but rather the one that *tries* the worthiness of the hypothesis. If the conclusion about reality reached intellectually fails the test of confrontation with reality, then it must be rejected. Until the test is carried out, the hypothesis must be regarded as no more than a hypothesis. Some hypotheses are wrong—that is, divergent from reality. If a wrong hypothesis is used as the premise of subsequent intellectual activity or behavior, that activity and behavior will also be wrong, and the wrongness will increase the further one goes from the erroneous hypothesis. This significant risk of building wrong hypotheses into one's conceptual framework is the trouble with straight thinking. It arises directly from this first characteristic of straight thinking: identification of the mind with the intellect and acceptance of intellectual descriptions of reality as true without submitting them to the proof of trial by actual experiment. This false identification is itself an aspect of a more general false identification: the confusion of the mind with ordinary, ego-centered waking consciousness. In fact, all of the other characteristics of straight thinking follow from this ultimate confusion because they are really characteristics of the ego and its thought-producing component, the intellect.*

2. *A tendency to be attached to the senses and through them to external reality*
   Our senses bring us a great deal of information every moment about

---

* These considerations explain to me a number of interesting reactions I have seen people have to drugs. To the extent that an individual takes a drug to get himself out of ego-centered consciousness (that is, to the extent that he is set to interpret the pharmacologic effects of the drug as an opportunity to experience some other sort of consciousness), to that extent will his ego rightly perceive the effects of the drug as threatening. Persons who are strongly attached to their egos, especially when trying drugs for the first time or learning to use them, may defend themselves from this perceived threat with a resurgence of intellectual activity. For example, when I first began smoking marihuana regularly with friends (in 1965-66), our highs, though enjoyable, were extremely verbal, often taken up with long runs of punning. It was only after several years that I was able to learn to use marihuana as an occasion for entering a meditative state in which I could ignore the verbal productions of my intellect. Similarly, I have seen individuals become compulsive punners on first exposure to hallucinogens, attain insight that this behavior represents resistance to letting go, and on subsequent occasions learn to be quiet under the influence of the drug. These observations are consistent with the supposition that attachment to intellect is a way of holding on to ego-centered consciousness and thus remaining straight.

the reality outside our heads. These sensory data are the primary source of information for ego consciousness and the intellect. In fact, the ego seems unable to disengage itself from the moment-to-moment inflow of sensations arising from external reality. Consequently, it is only in states of consciousness other than the ordinary waking state that we can have the experience of being detached from these sensations. As I suggested earlier, detachment from external reality is a common characteristic of many altered states of consciousness. Most of us understand this correlation so well that we say a man is "somewhere else" when he is daydreaming (that is, when he is in a light trance and is tuned out of external reality), and we assure ourselves that a subject is in a trance by waving a hand in front of his open eyes and getting no response. Where is a person's consciousness when it is "somewhere else"? If our conscious life is totally attached to our sensory perceptions of external reality, it is very likely that we will come to equate reality with external reality, just as we tend to equate mind with intellect, and consciousness with ordinary waking consciousness. The very existence of altered states of consciousness is a powerful piece of evidence that "proves" the rule equating reality with external reality and finds it wanting.

The experience of people who learn to retain conscious memories of trances, dreams, highs, and meditations is that another kind of reality exists, perhaps with many variations, that we can call internal or nonordinary reality. It is precisely that aspect of reality we are unconscious of when in the ordinary waking state, and the unconscious mind is precisely that part of the mind that pays attention to it.

In the contact I have had with academic psychiatry in several "good" institutions in Boston and San Francisco, I have been struck by the fact that many psychiatrists, even though they talk constantly of the unconscious mind and are always speculating on the unconscious thoughts of their patients, appear to know this part of the mind only as an intellectual construct and not as a direct experience. Furthermore, many of them appear to be quite frightened of patients who actually live in their unconscious minds, particularly if patients have made this contact by using drugs. This anxiety among psychiatrists is a significant problem in the profession as it is now constituted and is clearly the source of the irrationality that pervades much psychiatric thinking about drugs and altered states of consciousness—the kind of irrationality we examined previously in considering arguments made by psychiatrists against the use of drugs.

It is also clear that this kind of fear is not restricted to any profession. Any mind functioning in a straight way feels threatened by the implications of states of consciousness that point to the existence of another kind of reality. The ego rightly senses the threat implied to its dominion by the fact of an unconscious mind that can perceive an internal reality. Yet nonordinary reality can be experienced even though it cannot be understood intellectually. And this concept of a reality that is beyond human knowledge but nevertheless can be experienced directly seems to me to be the precise sense of the word *mystery* as it is used to describe rites like the Eleusinian mysteries of ancient Greece.

We have an excellent example of the incomprehensibility of nonordinary reality from the point of view of ego consciousness in the popular book *The Teachings of Don Juan* by Carlos Castaneda. In 1965 Castaneda apprenticed himself to a Yaqui Indian witch doctor *(brujo)* from central Mexico who initiated him into mysteries associated with several magic plants. Among the plants was the devil's weed *(Datura inoxia)*, a relative of plants like belladonna, henbane, and deadly nightshade, all of which contain similar alkaloids and all of which were used in medieval witchcraft ceremonies to trigger unusual states of consciousness. A common experience of participants in these ceremonies was that of flying through the air. Under don Juan's direction, and like the witches of old, Castaneda anointed his body with an extract of devil's-weed mixed with fat. He described his subsequent experience as follows:

> Don Juan kept staring at me. I took a step toward him. My legs were rubbery and long, extremely long. I took another step. My knee joints felt springy, like a vault pole; they shook and vibrated and contracted elastically. I moved forward. The motion of my body was slow and shaky; it was more like a tremor forward and up. I looked down and saw don Juan sitting below me, way below me. The momentum carried me forward one more step, which was even more elastic and longer than the preceding one. And from there I soared. I remember coming down once; then I pushed up with both feet, sprang backward, and glided on my back. I saw the dark sky above me and the clouds going by me. I jerked my body so I could look down. I saw the dark mass of the mountains. My speed was extraordinary. My arms were fixed, folded against my sides. My head was the directional unit. If I kept it bent backward I made vertical circles. I changed directions by turning my head to the side. I enjoyed such freedom and swiftness as I had never known before.

The experience ended with Castaneda coming down to earth, becoming sick, and losing awareness. The next day he had the following conversation with his mentor:

> . . . I had to ask him, "Did I really fly, don Juan?"
> "That is what you told me." Didn't you?"

"I know, don Juan. I mean, did my body fly? Did I take off like a bird?"

"You always ask me questions I cannot answer. You flew. That is what the second portion of the devil's weed is for. As you take more of it, you will learn to fly perfectly. It is not a simple matter. A man *flies* with the help of the second portion of the devil's weed. That is all I can tell you. What you want to know makes no sense. Birds fly like birds and a man who has taken the devil's weed flies as such."

"As birds do?"

"No, he flies as a man who has taken the weed."

"Then I didn't really fly, don Juan. I flew in my mind alone. Where was my body?"

"In the bushes," he replied cuttingly, but immediately broke into laughter again. "The trouble with you is that you understand things in only one way. You don't think a man flies; and yet a brujo can move a thousand miles in one second to see what is going on. He can deliver a blow to his enemies long distances away. So, does he or doesn't he fly?"

"You see, don Juan, you and I are differently oriented. Suppose, for the sake of argument, one of my fellow students had been here with me when I took the devil's weed. Would he have been able to see me flying?"

"There you go again with your questions about what would happen if . . . It is useless to talk that way. If your friend, or anybody else, takes the second portion of the weed all he can do is fly. Now, if he had simply watched you, he might have seen you flying, or he might not. That depends on the man."

"But what I mean, don Juan, is that if you and I look at a bird and see it fly, we agree that it is flying. But if two of my friends had seen me flying as I did last night, would they have agreed that I was flying?"

"Well, they might have. You agree that birds fly because you have seen them flying. Flying is a common thing with birds. But you will not agree on many other things birds do, because you have never seen birds doing them. If your friends knew about men flying with the devil's weed, then they would agree."

"Let's put it another way, don Juan. What I meant to say is that if I had tied myself to a rock with a heavy chain I would have flown just the same, because my body had nothing to do with my flying."

Don Juan looked at me incredulously. "If you tie yourself to a rock," he said, "I'm afraid you will have to fly holding the rock with its heavy chain."[3]

Castaneda never seems to get the point that his experience of non-ordinary reality is no less real for being unverifiable in the realm of ordinary experience. Internal reality, in all of its varied forms, is a different order of reality that is self-validating. And the most elementary requirement for getting in touch with it is simple withdrawal of attention from sensory attachment to external reality.

It should not be surprising to learn, therefore, that such withdrawal is emphasized in all instructional materials on meditation. In fact, Patanjali in his ancient codification of yoga listed sense withdrawal (Pratyahara) as one of the basic eight "limbs" of the system. A modern commentator on his aphorisms writes:

> Pratyahara is a detaching of the mind from the sense-organs. The word means "gathering towards." It checks the outgoing powers of the mind and turns them inwards. It is a gathering in and integration of the previously scattered mental energies. In Pratyahara one frees oneself from the thraldom of the sense-organs.[4]

The experience of sense withdrawal is one we have all had if we have ever fallen into a reverie in a room with a ticking clock. The clock continues to tick, the ear continues to hear it, but the mind ceases to pay attention. Masters of meditation assure us that with practice we can learn to detach our minds at will from all of our senses. The worth of this accomplishment is stated tersely in the *Bhagavad-Gita,* in which Krishna (the Hindu analog of Jesus) says: "The tortoise can draw in his legs:/ The seer can draw in his senses. I call him illumined."[5]

As a final comment on the matter of sensory attachment as a defining characteristic of straight thinking, I would note that drug experiences, particularly with marihuana and hallucinogens, may be more or less determined by sensations arising from external reality and that there is no question in my mind that sensory or "esthetic" experiences with drugs are less profound than other kinds. Just as a surge of intellectual activity may serve as a defensive maneuver of the ego to strengthen its control of experience when that control is threatened, so may absorption in sensory phenomena serve the same function. Psychiatrists who have used drugs like LSD in psychotherapy stress the importance of guiding patients beyond the realm of esthetic experience into the deeper and more interesting realms of the psyche.

3. *A tendency to pay attention to outward forms rather than to inner contents and thus to lapse into materialism*

Attachment to senses, as we have seen, leads to acceptance of the hypothesis that external reality constitutes all of reality. Concomitant with the acceptance of this false premise is the belief that something has been experienced or known when its outward appearance has registered on the mind through the senses. It is this ultimate confusion of appearance with reality that necessarily leads to materialistic formulations of man and the cosmos. By *materialism* I do not mean a passion for acquiring color television sets, although the acquisitive lust of modern Americans may well be a symptom of what I have in mind. Rather, I mean the tendency to see material reality as more important or more basic than nonmaterial reality—a tendency I have pointed out in previous chapters in connection with the notions of pharmacologists about the relationship between events in the physical body and brain and conscious experiences.

The essence of materialism is the attribution of causality to external, physical reality. In this way, psychosis becomes a matter of disordered biochemistry or brain function; a high is due to the presence of a drug in the body; infectious disease is caused by germs, and so on. The problem with formulations of this kind is simply that they do not work. They fail to give us the power to describe, predict, and control the phenomena of external reality, as we saw again and again in our earlier analyses of conventional theories of drugs. Incorrect attribution of causality—so easy to spot in pharmacological descriptions of drug effects once one knows to look for it—is nothing more than a specific instance of the more general error of thinking I have described as the equation of reality with external, material reality.

Since this false equation is, itself, a consequence of the equation of consciousness with ego, it should be clear how the initial divergence from reality of a general premise grows with subsequent reasoning based upon that premise. Materialistic conceptions are so divergent from reality that they leave us unable to modify the world around us except for the worse. (I will give specific examples in a few moments.) Still, they are not the end of the chain of false reasoning I have called straight thinking; the compounding of errors goes on to its logical conclusion.

4. *A tendency to perceive differences rather than similarities between phenomena*

A root function of the intellect is discrimination and classification—a function based upon the perception of differences in the appearances of things. This kind of intellectual activity has been very prominent in Western science, particularly in its analysis of the natural history of the world around us. Of course, there are times when it is useful to distinguish a mushroom from a toadstool or a white oak from a black oak. But the intellect, by itself, cannot stop doing this sort of thing, with the result that persons attached to intellect cannot stop perceiving differences. By contrast, persons who forsake ego consciousness, even for a moment, often have an overwhelming sense of the essential similarity of all things; indeed, this direct perception of unity is the very heart of mystic experience. It is not that the apparent differences disappear; rather, the mind experiences a sort of figure-ground reversal in which what had previously been sensed unconsciously as background becomes the central fact of perception. All people who have this experience directly (not those who understand it intellectually) testify that it is accompanied by powerful feelings of joy.

The ultimate distinction made by the intellect is that between *self* and *not-self;* the sense of *I* as distinct from everything else in the universe is the very root of ego consciousness. Furthermore, in the ego's own terms, all that is not-self is potentially threatening because it has the capacity to undermine the whole conceptual scheme built up so carefully by the intellect. Consequently, people who have not yet learned to let go of ego consciousness must necessarily experience the profound sense of isolation that some philosophers consider the normal human condition. Along with this existential loneliness comes the inevitable conviction that one is surrounded by a hostile universe. Everything out there that is not-self seems bent on destroying the fragile, isolated bubble of self. The joy that invariably accompanies mystic experience (or any other kind of ego loss) is simply the natural emotion that wells up when this sense of fearful isolation ends.

These thoughts are not merely theological abstractions. Let me illustrate them with an example from my own experience. Like many of my friends, I projected my sense of the hostility of nature onto certain insects, and while my fear of them did not approach phobic proportions, it was sufficient to keep me from relaxing completely in a wild setting. Although I did not understand it at the time, these feelings arose entirely from my conceiving of these insects (particularly bees and wasps) as fundamentally different from myself and, "therefore," able to harm me. Two years ago, during an LSD trip, I found myself extremely high and unattached to my ego in a field with many bees. For the first time in my life I experienced these creatures as essentially similar to myself and was able to see in them extraordinary beauty I had never before noticed. Since that time, I have learned to extend that feeling to most other insects, many of which I now regard as friends and sources of pleasure. Especially interesting is my find that the insects themselves appear to behave differently toward me. I now live in a country house around which hundreds of wasps and bees build their nests, and although I have frequent contact with them, even removing their nests when necessary from locations with heavy human traffic, I have never been stung and appear to cause them no discomfort or alarm. Needless to say, this change (which had its origin in an altered state of consciousness triggered by a drug) has been a source of great joy.

It is probably not necessary for me to point out that the tendency of the ego to focus on the differences rather than the similarities between itself and things out there causes far worse troubles than those with insects. The unsatisfactoriness of many human relationships and all acts of inhumanity are traceable directly to the same root problem. In fact, the mental step required before a human being commits violence against another human being appears to be definition of the other person as "other" or "different." This process seems all too natural when our minds are functioning in a straight way.

5. *A tendency to negative thinking, pessimism, and despair*

Undiluted straight thinking leads inevitably to despair. When one is living alone in a hostile universe, unable to change anything except for the worse, one can only lapse into increasingly negative and impotent states. The misunderstanding of cause and effect that materialism represents automatically condemns the straight thinker to imprisonment in a darkening reality, and it is all too clear that this is precisely the experience of many contemporary Americans. Whether we have long hair or short hair, many of us can see nothing but imminent disaster in whatever direction we look—whether at the economy, at politics, at conditions in cities, at our own bodies, and, especially, at our own minds. And it is terribly hard for the straight mind to comprehend that negative thinking is self-confirming. The more one is set to interpret preceptions negatively, the more evidence one finds that disaster is imminent; the more evidence one finds, the stronger one's conviction grows that this way of looking at things is right. Specifically because the ego cannot see the reality of nonordinary reality, straight thinkers cannot find the true causes of the negative manifestations of their own ways of perceiving. For the truth is that external phenomena are caused not by things out there (even though it looks that way to the ego) but rather by things in here—that is, in the unconscious mind, from which we are cut off whenever we think straight. All of the nightmares that contemporary ego consciousness can dream up—the nuclear holocausts, ecological dooms, race wars, physical illnesses, and psychiatric catastrophes—will continue to come closer and closer to actual manifestation as long as the mental patterns that create them continue.

And this is, at last, the end of the chain of false logic that is straight thinking. Identification of consciousness with ego consciousness leads to confusion of mind with intellect, to acceptance of appearance as reality, to materialistic formulations of the interaction of mind and matter, to isolation and fear, to increasingly negative conceptions of reality, and, ultimately and very logically, to disaster. I do not know the etymology of the word *straight* in this context, but it seems to me a singularly appropriate adjective. Straight thinking is straight in the way an interstate highway is straight: unlike a winding country road it does not follow the natural contours of reality. And in its ever-widening divergence from reality it leads straight to impotence, despair, and death.

At this point I must hasten to add a note of reassurance. I have been talking about straight *thinking*, not straight thinkers. I am not condemning all of us to hell. All of us are straight thinkers some of the time, but all of us are stoned thinkers, too. What I have just described are characteristics and consequences of pure straight thinking, unmodified by interaction with our unconscious life. The fact is that all of us spend time in nonordinary states of consciousness whether we use drugs or not; the trouble is, simply, that most of us have been discouraged from maintaining continuous awareness of these states. Thus we tend to compartmentalize and isolate those very factors that can temper ego consciousness and get us out of the straight bind. Many of us get locked into ordinary consciousness, but no one lacks the key to freedom.

It is one thing to characterize straight thinking, another to see it at work in everyday life. Here follow actual examples of conceptions produced by straight logic that all of us might subscribe to.

1. The Use of Insecticides to Control Insects

In describing my experiences with insects, I emphasized that the process was purely internal: I changed my fears of insects and the nature of their interaction with me by doing certain things inside my head—in particular, by experiencing the insects I was afraid of through a state of consciousness other than my usual ego-centered one. An alternative was available to me, of course, one that I had made frequent use of in the past. I could have picked up an aerosol can of insecticide and killed the insects that came near me. I now find the alternative unacceptable, and I made that judgment without recourse to any consideration of the morality or immorality of killing insects.

Insecticides, as chemicals poisonous to living organisms, are more meaningful to me as concrete symbols of straight thinking than they are as mere physical substances to have around the house or garden. For they are the manifestations of a way of thinking that imagines hostile appearances of nature can be banished by direct applications of force. And, significantly, it is the force of death that is brought to bear. But, as any cell physiologist can testify, the ways in which our own cellular life processes differ from those of insects are much less important than the ways in which they are similar. Consequently, the application of cellular poisons to our houses and food must, in a very real way, be hurting ourselves, regardless of the amount of damage we can now measure. It cannot be good; the only question is, How bad? So the first strike against this way of dealing with insects is that it directly rebounds on us.

Moreover, does the method even achieve the desired objective? The goal is not really to get rid of particular individuals of the insect order but rather to make a negative manifestation of nature go away. Now, as vigorous selective agents, insecticides in our world are playing a significant role in the evolutionary development of all insect species. They neatly weed out the susceptible members of families, concentrating in insect gene pools all over the world the genetic factors conferring resistance to these chemicals. Thus the use of insecticides, by straightforward principles of natural selection, creates new races of insects, resistant to these substances and often more aggressive or tough in other ways. Already, we have gotten into fast-moving arms races with a number of species in which resistance has escalated to match escalations of toxicity. In some cases, the patterns of insect destruction of crops are now more devastating than before powerful insecticides were first used years ago. The method looks as if it works in the short run because it seems to dispose of all the visible pests immediately. But the long-range evaluation is unnerving. Not only does the method not make the hostile manifestation disappear; it directly makes it take worse forms.

Here we are at the last stop on the chain of false logic. The idea that we can make things we do not like go away by forcing them out of existence leads to action that harms us directly while making the things even less likable. Seen in retrospect, my way of solving the same problem was to accept insects as they were, to locate in my mind the source of negative interpretation of my perceptions of them, and then to disaffiliate my mind from that source (which meant the dissociation of consciousness from ego). As soon as I did that, insects were no longer the same. And they have been getting less the same ever since, in fact are turning into positive manifestations of nature. Meanwhile, the believer in insecticides must go on fighting a never-ending battle, his way of thinking leading him ever onward to frustration and despair.

2. The Use of Antibiotics

The parallel between antibiotics and insecticides is so striking that it requires little comment. In their importance as selective agents modifying the evolution of bacteria, antibiotics are strictly analogous to chemical poisons used to control insects. Their increasing use over the past thirty years correlates exactly with the appearance in greater and greater numbers of organisms that are more virulent in their parasitic relationships with man and terribly adept at developing resistance to the latest antibiotics out of the world's pharmaceutical laboratories. Hospital infections with these virulent strains have been rising sharply, as all medical personnel know. In my years of hospital work I saw many deaths of debilitated patients following recurrent hospital-borne infections, each bout following the application of the stronger antibiotic given to hold the last bout in check.

Predictably, the more powerful antibiotics are much more toxic to human cells and can be as dangerous to life as a generalized infection. Penicillin, the first true antibiotic to be discovered, interferes with the cell-wall formation of certain bacteria, and bacterial cells walls (the *outer surfaces* of the cell) are different in important ways from human cell walls. But many newer, more powerful antibiotics are toxic to basic cellular processes—processes we have in common with bacteria. Here again, the action suggested by straight thinking injures us directly and worsens the problem it was meant to solve.

But is there an alternative to killing bacteria? The analog of the process I used on insects may not suggest itself immediately. Yet it is available and is just as effective. To explain it, I must first point out the straightness of allopathy.

3. Allopathic Medicine

Allopathy is the system of medicine I was taught at Harvard. It is the system of medicine medical doctors are taught the world over. And few allopaths ever stop to consider that their system is only one possible way of doing it.

The unifying principle of allopathic practice is its philosophy of treating illness by counteracting the symptoms of illness. Thus if high blood pressure is a manifestation of disease, antihypertensive drugs are administered; if serious inflammation occurs on the surface of the body, antiinflammatory medications are applied. And so on and so on: this is the essence of the allopathic method. Now, "counteracting the symptoms of illness" has a very straight sound to it. *Counteract* suggests the use of force to make negative manifestations disappear, and *symptoms* suggests superficial appearance rather than inner reality. And, indeed, the·supposition that our dominant system of medicine is based in straight thinking is easy to confirm.

In what I am about to say I write as a man trained fully in general allopathic medicine. I undertook this training as a continuation of what

I saw as my general education, not as a step toward entering a particular profession. For the past two years I have been dissociated completely from the world of allopathic practice, during which time I have thought much about my experiences in it. My retrospective impression of allopathy is that it is unable to control well the phenomena of health and illness and that it is often unwillingly productive of methods that intensify manifestations of illness rather than ameliorate them. Such has been my own experience over the course of five years. I do not expect readers who are allopathic practitioners or patients to accept my view on faith any more than I expect law-enforcement agents or committed drug users to accept without proof my earlier views about the dangers of drugs. But I do ask all readers to give these arguments thought and to test them against their own experience. I must also say that I have met many intelligent, sensitive allopathic physicians who are genuinely dedicated to alleviating human suffering (some of whom unconsciously use non-allopathic methods to produce real cures). Furthermore, in rejecting allopathy as a theoretical system, I do not claim to have all the answers. There is much about health and illness I still do not understand, much knowledge I am still seeking. But I feel confident in making certain criticisms of the approach to disease that now predominates in our medical schools and hospitals.

Modern allopathic medicine is essentially materialistic. For example, the widely accepted germ theory of disease—a cornerstone of allopathic theory—states that certain microscopic entities (bacteria and viruses are the most important) whose appearance in space and time correlates well with other physical manifestations of illness are causative of illness. Therefore, the theory continues, infectious illness can profitably be treated by trying to force these entities out of existence. One of the great contributors to this theory was the German bacteriologist and Nobel laureate Robert Koch (1843-1910), author of a masterpiece of straight logic known to all allopaths as "Koch's Postulates." Medical students are required to accept these dogmas on faith, to recite them faithfully on examinations, and to interpret their observations of infectious disease through them. Here they are, as presented in the text I used in my microbiology course at Harvard:

> How can one prove that a given microorganism really causes a disease? Traditionally, the etiologic [i.e., causative] relationship between a microorganism and a disease is established by fulfilling "Koch's Postulates": (1) The microorganism must regularly be isolated from cases of the illness. (2) It must be grown in pure culture *in vitro* [i.e., in a test tube]. (3) When such a pure culture is inoculated into susceptible animal species, the typical disease

must result. (4) From such experimentally induced disease the microorganism must again be isolated.[6]

Actually, fulfillment of these postulates does no more than establish correlation between the presence of the germ in the body and the other physical manifestations of the illness as observed in animals. It does not prove that real-world patients get the same physical illness because they come into contact with the germ. You may ask, Doesn't fulfillment of Postulate Three prove cause? The animal was healthy before the germ was put into it and sick afterward. True. But inoculation of germs into animals (usually by injection) is a grossly unnatural procedure that obscures the relevance of any subsequent observations to the world beyond the laboratory.

In our consideration of research on drugs, we saw that experimental rigor obtained at the expense of relevance to the world at large is of questionable value because it increases the risk of formulating hypotheses that explain the data but are of no real use to us. We live in a world full of germs, some of which are correlated with physical symptoms of infectious disease. But only some of us get infectious diseases some of the time. Why? Because there are factors *in us* that determine what kind of a relationship we will have with those germs that are always out there—a relationship of balanced coexistence or one of unbalanced antagonism. Furthermore, outside of laboratories scientists do not (usually) go around inoculating us with potentially dangerous microorganisms. Fulfillment of the third of Koch's Postulates bypasses the whole system by which relationships with germs are internally determined. I admit that it looks as if germs cause disease, but remember: acceptance of appearance for reality is a distinguishing feature of straight thinking. It also looks as if drugs cause highs, and people who accept that proposition get into trouble.

My experiences in allopathic medicine, both as a patient and as a practitioner, have led me to conclude that all illness is psychosomatic. I do not use the word in the sense of "unreal" or "phony," as many allopaths do. Rather, I mean that all illness has both psychic and physical components, and it seems to me that the physical manifestations of illness (including the appearance of germs in tissues) are always effects, while the causes always lie within the realm of the mind, albeit the unconscious mind. In other words, the disease process seems to me to be initiated always by changes in consciousness. In the case of infectious illness, the initial causative change is not that germs appear to attack the body but that something happens in the person that permits a breakdown of the normal harmonious balance between the body and the microorganisms surrounding it.

For example, the staphylococci that seem to cause boils are normal inhabitants of our skins. Most of the time, their relationship to us is symbiotic—mutually beneficial. Occasionally, that balance breaks down and boils appear. The problem is to restore the balance, not to make the staph germs disappear. An allopath, thinking that the germs cause the boils, treats this condition by trying to make the germs go away, by giving antibiotics. But antibiotics merely kill off the germs that are most inclined to form harmonious relationships with us, leaving behind the more aggressive, tougher ones that are less inclined to enter into balanced existence with their hosts. Over the past thirty years, allopathic hospitals have become virtual factories for turning out new strains of staph that are not only highly resistant to several generations of antibiotics but also much more ruthless in their attacks on human beings.

Here is a familiar pattern. In attempting to control insects and germs by reliance on external, material substances, we meet with initial success and eventual failure. Sooner or later the substances fail us, and we find ourselves in a worse state than before. Many times, our use of materials becomes more and more desperate when we see them begin not to work and do not understand why they are not working. In our desperation, we often look for better or stronger substances. I can see no essential difference between this pattern and that of drug dependence. The user who depends on drugs to get into desirable states of consciousness becomes tolerant to them and cannot maintain his highs. If he fails to realize the nature of his problem, his use of drugs becomes more and more desperate, and he must search for something stronger. In other words, drug dependence—far from being an isolated phenomenon caused by particular substances—is simply a special case of a very general problem: reliance on external things to produce or maintain desired internal states (including highs, health, and freedom from anxiety about manifestations of nature). The name of this problem is materialism; its consequence is always the same; its cause is straight thinking.

In suggesting that infectious illness is actually initiated by psychic changes, I am not invoking mystical forces. Consciousness, as I have said repeatedly, is a real thing, and it has connections to every part of the body by way of the peripheral nerves. An unconscious impulse can easily be transmitted through the nervous system to the skin (or any other tissue), where it can cause changes resulting in the breakdown of equilibrium between us and the microorganisms we encounter.* Conversely, equilibrium can be restored by transmitting other impulses along the

---

* As an example of an area of my own ignorance, I might mention that I have no ready explanation for serious infectious illness in infants and young children, which is to say that I do not fully understand the development and workings of the unconscious mind.

same pathways, and this principle is the basis of nonallopathic healing. Unfortunately for allopaths, this kind of true healing (I have now seen a number of impressive cases) involves the transmission of consciousness through a branch of the nervous system—the autonomic nervous system—that allopathic medicine regards as "involuntary," that is, beyond the reach of consciousness. Thus, allopaths are prisoners of their own conceptions of the mind and body and will never discover this other sort of healing until they give up those conceptions. In medicine as elsewhere, straight thinking leads to an inability to describe, predict, or control external reality accurately and to an inability to see the reality of the direction in which the solution lies.

That there is a great deal wrong with the medical system of this country is no secret. We see all around us the manifestations of this wrongness: the impossible economics of the system, its inability to deliver medical care to those who need it most, the unwieldiness of its educational curriculums, and, most of all, its inability to make us a healthy society. The incidence of major killing diseases—heart disease, cancer, and stroke—continues to climb; the illnesses directly caused by allopathic methods and hospital practices get worse and worse; and the newest techniques of the system—I would single out organ transplants as a prime example—seem to be going in directions that are less and less natural. And because allopaths have no grip on the true causes of disease they cannot prevent us from getting sick; they can only treat our acute problems. I know a number of young physicians who see themselves as founders of a revolution in American medicine. They are very vocal about the curriculums of medical schools, the lack of good medical care, overcrowded hospitals, the rigidity of the profession, and so forth. But, like the allopaths they are, they fail to see that these symptoms of ill health of the system are but the superficial manifestations of something very wrong at the core. And as these young doctors fight to counteract those symptoms, they go on parroting and believing materialistic nonsense like Koch's Postulates, which are much more representative of the core problem. The real revolution in medicine, like all real revolutions, will go on at the level of conceptions.

4. The Allopathic Model in Psychiatry

I have already mentioned that I consider much of conventional psychiatry straight. Perhaps the best indication of its straightness has been its ready acceptance of the allopathic medical model in its approach to disturbances of the mind. Psychiatry today is a branch of allopathic medicine simply because psychiatrists themselves choose to be in that position. In the early years of this century psychiatrists imagined that affiliation with allopaths would make them more legitimate in the eyes of the public, and they themselves required medical training of students seeking entrance to their professional academies. This strategy has been disastrous because it has made most psychiatrists think of mental disturbances in straight terms.

For example, certain mental processes, like neuroses, which are normal phases of psychic development with strongly positive potential, are regarded negatively as manifestations of illness to be made to go away.* Now, the essence of neurosis is ambivalence—the simultaneous experience of opposite feelings. Ego consciousness cannot make sense of ambivalence because the ego, in its self/not-self classifications, thinks in terms of either/or. Consequently, ambivalence (a very real feeling) is threatening to the ego because it violates straight logic. The problem, then, is not the ambivalence but the way one looks at it. And if one looks at it only from the point of view of ego-centered waking consciousness, it looks so frightening that one can easily lapse into kinds of inaction and depression that seem to confirm the supposition that one is sick. All too often, this view is reinforced in treatment with conventional psychiatrists, many of whom see their function as strengthening the egos of their patients to resist neurotic conflicts. Like their medical counterparts, these allopathic psychiatrists use techniques that can make patients worse rather than better—the usual inverted consequence of action based on straight conceptions. In the next chapter I will suggest a very different way of conceiving of neurosis, one based on different premises and a positive viewpoint.

5. Political Action as a Means of Producing External Change

The use of political force, whether by those in power or those out of power, to effect changes in societies seems to me to be unmistakably analogous to all of the other variants of the straight model we have considered. And like them, it seems only to rebound on its users and make worse the very manifestations it is intended to improve. Americans have had an excellent chance to grasp this principle over the past few years, but to see it requires emotional detachment from *both* sides. As soon as one achieves this detachment, it is instantly clear that government repression directly increases the phenomena it is meant to suppress while antigovernment activity directly brings on further repression—an escalating cycle strictly parallel to those we have seen with insects and

---

* This attitude is particularly characteristic of modern psychotherapy. By contrast, classical psychoanalysis, in its deliberate ignoring of symptoms, is much more in the tradition of nonallopathic healing.

insecticides, bacteria and antibiotics. It is an invariable consequence of trying to effect changes in the world working from assumptions that are divergent from reality.

I hope the straightness of these examples is clear. In every case it arises from the confusion of our perceptions of reality with reality itself, from the formulation of erroneous hypotheses that do not conform to our own direct experience. I hope also that these examples convey something of the power of straight thinking in our world; at the moment it is the rule, not the exception.

REFERENCES

1. THOMAS R. BLACKBURN, "Sensuous-Intellectual Complementarity in Science," *Science* *172* (4 June 1971), p. 1003.
2. HUMPHREYS, C. *Concentration and Meditation*. Baltimore: Pelican Books, 1970, p. 83.
3. CARLOS CASTANEDA, *The Teachings of Don Juan: A Yaqui Way of Knowledge* (New York: Ballantine Books, 1969), pp. 127–132.
4. HEWITT, J. *A Practical Guide to Yoga*. New York: Funk & Wagnells, 1968, p. 114.
5. *Bhagavad-Gita*, translated by Swami Prabhavananda and Christopher Isherwood (New York: Mentor Books, 1944), p. 42.
6. E. JAWETZ, J. L. MELNICK, and E. A. ADELBERG, *Review of Medical Microbiology*, 6th ed. (Los Altos, California: Lange, 1964), p. 134.

Section II

PSYCHODYNAMICS OF ADDICTION

The term "psychodynamics" refers to the "science of the mind, its mental processes, and affective components that influence human behavior and motivations" (Freedman, Kaplan, & Sadock, 1975, p. 2601). That the phenomenon of drug use should have become an object of inquiry for this "science" was neither intuitive nor inevitable. Until early in the present century, the intemperate use of drugs was understood as one of the many manifestations of moral or spiritual weakness; individuals given to such activities were condemned, not treated.

Early American psychoanalysts gave some attention to the problems of the excessive use of alcohol, cocaine, and morphine, but not until the use of drugs came to be viewed as a social problem did the young disciplines of psychoanalysis, psychiatry, and psychology begin to inquire into its nature and origins.

Rado (1933) was the first psychoanalyst to suggest that, though destructive in its effects, drug use might represent an individual's attempt to cope with difficult emotional states. Prior to his work, the medical profession had viewed drug dependence as a toxicological manifestation of a drug's destructive actions on brain and body. Dismissing this conceptualization of the problem as ineffective, Rado argued that it was not the drug, but the individual's *impulse* to use it, that makes an addict. He viewed the craving of all drugs ("pharmacothymia") as a "psychologically-determined, artificially induced illness" arising from a specific psychological deficit, which he described as being "a special type of emotional alteration which might be designated 'tense depression'." This depression, characterized by painful tension and a high degree of intolerance to pain, sensitized the individual, he argued, to the drug's "pharmacogenic pleasure-effect."

Rado's work stimulated other psychoanalysts to think about the problem of drug use and provided a number of enduring motifs for future theory. Among these were (a) the centrality of the *impulse* to use a drug,

71

(b) the role of narcissism in addiction, (c) the adaptive function of drug use, and (d) the importance of the ego in the development of drug dependence. Finally, the most significant consequence of Rado's work was that it resulted in drug addiction being viewed as a psychological problem, and therefore within the purview of psychologists, psychiatrists, and the other mind science professionals to treat.

Chein, Gerard, Lee, and Rosenfeld (1964) in the main followed Rado's views of the role of pre-existing personality disturbance and consequent psychosocial maladjustment in the development of drug dependence. Whereas Rado cited "tense depression" as *the* specific emotional alteration that predisposed an individual to drug involvement, Chein et al. (1964), based on their experience with adolescent heroin users, argued that not only depression, but states of anxiety, bewilderment, panic, despair, self-rejection, and longing were likewise capable of giving rise to the impulse to use drugs. Beyond the precondition of "psychological deviancy" as the determining factor in liking opiate drugs, they argued for the necessity of specific social factors and the individual's experience of drug use as psychologically or socially helpful, useful, or adaptive.

Their psychological description of dependence, withdrawal, tolerance, "getting high," and other drug processes and experiences helped bridge the distance between pharmacological and psychological explanations of addiction. *The Road to H* (Chein et al., 1964) appeared at a time when drug use in America was increasing and rapidly spreading from the ghetto to the suburbs. Their book (a) helped practitioners dealing with clients from both areas to understand the development of drug involvement as a process, (b) suggested strategies for action for the emerging drug abuse prevention effort, and (c) offered a theoretical basis for comprehensive social planning, policy, and intervention aimed at eradicating the causes and "opportunities" for addiction.

Vaillant's (1975) brilliant reconsideration of "sociopathy" challenged existing characterizations and conceptualizations of the drug addict as "inhuman" and "untreatable." He argued that such views of the addict were the product of the frustration produced in the clinician by trying to treat the drug dependent individual in an outpatient setting, where control of the patient's self-destructive behavior was difficult or impossible, and where the addict's "immature defenses" (especially that of running away) could not be adequately confronted. He argued that the traditional view of the addict as one who experiences no anxiety, lacks motivation to change, and is incapable of feeling depression could not be maintained once he/she was "immobilized long enough . . . to be perceived as human" (p. 183).

Based on longitudinal studies of addicts in treatment (Glueck &

Glueck, 1943; Vaillant, 1966, 1973) and the similarity of the immature defenses of drug addicts and normal adolescents, Vaillant argued that "If we can wait 15 to 20 years, it becomes possible to demonstrate that intractable delinquents and addicts also remit" (1975, p. 183).

The implications of Vaillant's work for treatment were (and still are) significant and far-reaching. His prescriptions were for treatment practitioners to carefully assess the addict's ego functions, and then work to find a substitute for each disenabling immature defense, control self-destructive behavior, and provide a context for involvement and acceptance, e.g., the church, self-help residential treatment, "addiction" to a methadone clinic, a compulsory but real job, membership in various altruistic groups, or even marriage to an equally needy person. Vaillant's ideas have been widely quoted, discussed, and debated and have been influential in shaping the counseling strategies of methadone programs, increasing the use of residential treatment modalities, and enhancing the recognition and acceptance of self-help programs by drug treatment professionals. One can but speculate as to what might result were the entire drug treatment system dismantled and rebuilt along the lines that Vaillant has suggested.

In keeping with the psychoanalytic precedent established by Rado (1933), Wurmser's (1974) contribution cited the "compulsive" aspect of all addictive behavior. More so than Rado, he stressed the intrapsychically adaptive functions of drug use. Although the adaptive view of drug use did not originate with Wurmser (cf. Chein et al., 1964; Glover, 1932; Krystal & Raskin, 1970; Wieder & Kaplan, 1969; among others), his elegant reformulation of this view appeared at a critical moment in the history of the treatment field. Drug treatment was at that time dominated by approaches based on metabolic and physiologic theories (methadone maintenance) and various social learning models (therapeutic communities). Many methadone programs were beginning to realize that there were some of their clients whose drug use appeared to self-medicate specific psychiatric symptoms and conditions. Similarly, therapeutic communities began to identify a group of clients whose problems with compulsive drug use were not being responsibly addressed or successfully treated by the social learning model. As a result, in many of these programs there came to be an increased emphasis on formal counseling and more specific provisions for adjunctive psychiatric services for selected clients. Federal and state funding agencies soon began to mandate access to psychiatric, psychological, and counseling services for clients in both methadone maintenance and therapeutic community programs.

Emphasizing the heterogeneity of drug addicts, Wurmser proposed an hierarchical model of causation (after Freud) for drug dependence.

This model enabled workers in the addictions to appreciate and put into perspective the etiologic contributions of the various socioeconomic, cultural, and political factors which during the late 1960s and 1970s were more and more often being offered as simplistic explanations for the development of drug dependence in certain individuals and groups. By distinguishing between the "preconditional," "specific," "concurrent," and "precipitating" levels of causation, Wurmser's work established a theoretical basis for the empirical observation that *occasional* drug use did not invariably progress to *compulsive* drug use.

At the time that Khantzian's (1975) article on self-selection in drug dependence appeared, drug treatment programs, which until then had been treating opiate or alcohol dependent individuals, began to see increasing numbers of so-called "polydrug" clients, i.e., individuals using nonopiate drugs (sedative-hypnotics, psychostimulants, and hallucinogens) exclusively or in combination with opiates. Khantzian noted in the drug histories of program clients that most had experimented with a number of drugs of different pharmacological classes before "selecting" the one on which they subsequently became dependent. Without abandoning the traditional psychoanalytic emphasis on the unitary nature of the intrapsychic disorder in all of the addictions, he focused on how *specific drug effects*—energizing (amphetamines and cocaine), releasing (sedative-hypnotics), and controlling-stabilizing (opiates)—interact with *distinct personality factors and behavior patterns.* He suggested that an individual "selects" one as opposed to another drug in an attempt to cope with *specific problems* in the internal and external environments which without the drug effects would be unmanageable or unbearable.

Khantzian advanced the field's appreciation of the specific nature of the interaction of pharmacological and intrapersonal factors in the development of drug dependence. He thereby provided practitioners with a rationale for the differential treatment of the various drug dependencies.

Krystal and Raskin (1970) further specified the nature of the psychological precondition that disposed an individual to seek and become dependent upon drugs. Their analysis of the affective state characterized by Rado (1933) as "tense depression" emphasized its genetic determinants. Specifically, they suggested that the drug dependent person experiences an affective regression wherein previously differentiated states, particularly those of anxiety and depression, are dedifferentiated, becoming in form much like the all-or-nothing, highly somatized "Uraffect" characteristic of infancy. Their genetic view of this problem placed its origin in early infancy and in the defective development of the ego skills requisite for successful management of affective states.

Their elegant specification of the disorders of affect tolerance, object- and self-representation, and modification of consciousness that subserve the development of drug dependence provided a greater understanding of the nature, origin, and purpose of the painful psychosomatic states mediated by the drug effects.

Though thoroughly psychoanalytic in origin and expression, the ideas of Krystal and Raskin have found ready application in methadone treatment programs to problems of detoxification and maintenance. In particular, their clarification of the interrelationship of somatic distress and psychic pain has prompted practitioners to rethink and redefine existing protocols for short- and long-term opiate detoxification.

Zinberg was an early proponent (Zinberg, 1974; Zinberg & Robertson, 1972) of the idea that individual psychological factors (set), variables in the social context (setting), and drug effects (substance) must each be considered and balanced in order to adequately understand the motivation to use or continue to use an illicit psychoactive drug. In his paper (1975) on addiction and ego function, he critically reexamined the field from this perspective and concluded that despite the apparent wide acceptance of this triune concept the field still tended to view "the addicted state [simply] as the end point of a long personality process" (p. 567), and drug use as a form of self-medication. To counter these lingering notions, he reviewed the changing social definitions and patterns of use of several drugs, reemphasizing the effects of those aspects of "setting" on an individual's choice of drug and pattern of use, controlled or compulsive. His analysis of the ways in which cultural and social factors interact with elements of ego structure and function, though grounded in the post-Freudian, ego-psychological school of psychoanalysis, nonetheless offered a refreshingly new view of drug use.

More so perhaps than any other psychoanalytically-oriented theorist, Zinberg has been an outspoken, persuasive, and, above all, intelligible apologist for the adaptive, ego-functional view of drug use. His work has had broad appeal for theorists and practitioners of widely divergent persuasions, enabling many of them to understand, appreciate, and appropriate the insights available from the psychoanalytic perspective.

Gendreau and Gendreau (1970), after reviewing the body of empirical research done on "addiction-proneness," concluded that the significant personality differences between addicts and non-addicts reported in numerous previous studies and used as the basis for defining the "addictive personality" may well have been the result of methodological error. Thus, what had long been considered by psychologists to be a stable personality trait and, in parallel, by psychoanalysts as a characterological disorder common to all drug addicts was redefined as an artifact of experimental design and, hence, as a "nonobject." Their shattering of this enduring stereotype and undermining of its related trait-oriented theories of addiction facilitated the growing concern in the field with the identification and specification of the *situational* factors involved in drug use, an interest kindled some years earlier by emerging behavioral theories of addiction and its treatment.

REFERENCES

CHEIN, I., GERARD, D. L., LEE, R. S. & ROSENFELD, E. *The Road to H. Narcotics, delinquency and social policy.* New York: Basic Books, 1964.

FREEDMAN, A. M., KAPLAN, H. I. & SADOCK, B. J. *Comprehensive Textbook of Psychiatry—II.* Baltimore: Williams & Wilkins, 1975.

GENDREAU, P., & GENDREAU, L. P. The "addiction-prone" personality: A study of Canadian heroin addicts. *Canadian Journal of Behavioural Science.* 1970, *2*, 18-25.

GLOVER, E. On the etiology of drug addiction. In *On the early development of mind.* New York: International Universities Press, 1972.

GLUECK, S., & GLUECK, E. *Criminal Careers in Retrospect.* New York: Commonwealth Fund, 1943.

KHANTZIAN, E. J. Self selection and progression in drug dependence. *Psychiatry Digest,* 1975, *36*, 19-22.

KRYSTAL, H., & RASKIN, H. A. *Drug Dependence. Aspects of Ego Functions.* Detroit, Michigan: Wayne State University Press, 1970.

RADO, S. The psychoanalysis of pharmacothymia (drug addiction). *Psychoanalytic Quarterly,* 1933, *2*, 1-23.

VAILLANT, G. E. A 12-year follow-up of New York narcotic addicts: IV. Some characteristics and determinants of abstinence. *American Journal of Psychiatry,* 1966, *123*, 573-584.

VAILLANT, G. E. A 20-year follow-up of New York narcotics addicts. *Archives of General Psychiatry,* 1973, *29*, 237-241.

VAILLANT, G. E. Sociopathy as a human process. *Archives of General Psychiatry,* 1975, *32*, 178-183.

WIEDER, H., & KAPLAN, E. H. Drug use in adolescents: psychodynamic meaning and pharmacogenic effect. *Psychoanalytic Study of the Child,* 1969, *24*, 399-431.

WURMSER, L. Psychoanalytic considerations of the etiology of compulsive drug use. *Journal of the American Psychoanalytic Association,* 1974, *22*, 820-843.

ZINBERG, N. E. *High States: A Beginning Study.* Washington, D.C.: Drug Abuse Council, 1974.

ZINBERG, N. E. Addiction and ego function. *Psychoanalytic Study of the Child,* 1975, *30*, 567-588.

ZINBERG, N. E., & ROBERTSON, J. A. *Drugs and the Public.* New York: Simon and Schuster, 1972.

4

THE PSYCHOANALYSIS OF PHARMACOTHYMIA (DRUG ADDICTION)

Sandor Radó

1. THE CLINICAL PICTURE

Clinical psychiatry regards the disorders known as alcoholism, morphinism, cocainism, etc.—for which, as an inclusive designation, we may provisionally use the term "drug addiction"—as *somatic intoxications*, and places them in the classificatory group "mental disorders of exogenous origin." From this point of view, the process of mental dilapidation presented in the clinical picture of the addiction would appear to be the mental manifestation of the injury to the brain produced by the poisons. The investigation of the addictions has imposed upon it by this theory, as its first task, the determination in detail of the cerebral effect of the noxious substance. Ultimately, its goal would be the exact correlation of the course of the mental disorder with the toxic processes in the brain. But this investigation, especially in its experimental aspects, is disturbingly complicated by the fact that the poisons in question attack not only the brain but the rest of the organism as well; therefore, injurious effects may be exerted upon the brain by changes in other organs through an impairment of the general metabolism. The problem thus includes not

Reprinted with permission from *The Psychoanalytic Quarterly*, 1933, *2*, 1-23.
Authorized translation from the German manuscript by Bertram D. Lewin.
The first part of this article is the enlarged version of an address delivered before the Neurologic-Psychiatric Section of the New York Academy of Medicine, December 13, 1932.

only the direct influence of the poison on the brain, but also its indirect influence. It is, consequently, not remarkable that the notion that the problem of addiction is a problem of somatic intoxication has borne so little fruit.

How did it happen, then, that psychiatry became so wedded to this idea? The obvious answer is that the idea was developed because infectious diseases were used as paradigms. To be sure, one could not ignore the fact that alcohol, for example, does not "cause" alcoholism in the same sense as the spirochaete causes luetic infection. The pathogenic microörganisms attack a person quite regardless of what his wishes or purposes in the matter may be. But the drugs in question attack him only if he purposely introduces them into his body. This distinction, however, has not sufficiently affected psychiatric thinking. In psychiatry, the idea was promulgated that a certain type of "uninhibited," "weak-willed" or "psychopathic" individual happens to develop a passion for using these drugs—which means, to read between the lines, that how these substances get into the body is of no importance: the problem is scientific and worth touching only after they are inside. It must be admitted that after the drugs have made their entry, there is, unquestionably, a certain similarity to the infections. But in so far as psychological questions, such as the susceptibility of an individual to develop a craving for drugs, were broached at all, one was groping in the dark. The intoxication theory furnished no point of departure for any solution of this type of problem. Indeed, even if all the problems relating to somatic intoxication were solved, there would still be no answer to this type of question.

The psychoanalytic study of the problem of addiction begins at this point. It begins with the recognition of the fact that not the toxic agent, but the impulse to use it, makes an addict of a given individual. We see that this unprejudiced description focusses our attention on the very feature, which, under the influence of premature analogical reasoning, was permitted to fall by the wayside. The problem then presents a different appearance. The drug addictions are seen to be psychically determined, artificially induced illnesses; they can exist because drugs exist; and they are brought into being for psychic reasons.

With the adoption of the psychogenetic standpoint, the emphasis shifts from the manifoldness of the drugs used to the singleness of the impulse which unleashes the craving. The ease with which an addict exchanges one drug for another immediately comes to mind; so that we feel impelled to regard all types of drug cravings as varieties of *one single* disease. To crystallize this theory, let me introduce the term "pharmacothymia" to designate the illness characterized by the craving for drugs. We shall have occasion later to explain our selection of this term.

The older psychoanalytic literature contains many valuable contributions and references, particularly on alcoholism and morphinism, which attempt essentially to explain the relationship of these states to disturbances in the development of the libido function. Reports of this type we owe to Freud, Abraham, Tausk, Schilder, Hartmann and others in Europe; and in this country, Brill, Jelliffe, Oberndorf and others. Two definite conclusions could be drawn from these studies, namely, the etiological importance of the erotogenic oral zone and a close relationship to homosexuality. Several years ago, I outlined the beginnings of a psychoanalytic theory which aimed to include the whole scope of the problem of drug addiction.* Further, as yet unpublished, studies have led me to introduce the conception of pharmacothymia, to the preliminary description of which the present paper is devoted.

Since, for our purposes, suggestions derived from the theory of somatic intoxication are of no avail, we ourselves must select a suitable point of departure, taking our bearings from psychoanalysis. Our notion that despite the many drugs there is only one disease, suggests where we may begin. We must separate out of the abundant clinical findings those elements which are *constant* and determine their interrelationships empirically, and then from this material, formulate the general psychopathology, that is to say, the *schematic structure* of pharmacothymia. Generalizations which we can make in this way concerning the nature of the illness will discover for us the viewpoints and conceptions needed for the study of individual phenomena. If our outline is well founded, the more new details are added, the more will it reproduce living reality.

Pharmacothymia can occur because there are certain drugs, the "elatants," to give them an inclusive designation, which a human being in psychic distress can utilize to influence his emotional life. I have given a description of this influence in a previous communication *(loc. cit.)*. Here I need only say that there are two types of effects. First, the analgesic, sedative, hypnotic and narcotic effects—their function is easily characterized: they allay and *prevent* "*pain.*" Secondly, the stimulant and

---

* *The Psychic Effects of Intoxicants: An Attempt to Evolve a Psycho-Analytical Theory of Morbid Cravings.* Int. J. Ps-A. VII, 1926. Since this, I have reported the progress of my views in a number of addresses: "Drug Addiction" at the First Congress for Mental Hygiene, at Washington, D. C., May 1930; "Intoxication and 'The Morning After' " at a meeting of the German Psychoanalytic Society in Berlin, November 1930; "Depressive and Elated States in Neuroses and in Drug Addiction," a lecture course at the Berlin Psychoanalytic Institute, Spring 1931.

euphoria-producing effects—these promote or *generate pleasure*. Both types of effect, the pain-removing and the pleasure-giving, serve the pleasure principle; together they both constitute what may be called "the pharmacogenic pleasure-effect." The capriciousness of the pharmacogenic pleasure-effect is well known; it vitiates the best part of the experimental work of the pharmacologists. I have found that in addition to the pharmacological factors (nature, dose and mode of administration of the substance), the pleasure-effect depends essentially on a *psychological* factor—a certain active preparedness with which the individual approaches the pleasure-effect.

The thing which the pharmacothymic patient wishes the toxic agent to give him is the pleasure-effect. But this is not to be obtained without cost. The patient must pay for his enjoyment with severe suffering and self-injury—often, indeed, with self-destruction. These are assuredly not the effects desired. If, notwithstanding this fact, he clings to the use of drugs, it must be either because the pleasure gained is worth the sacrifice of suffering, or he is in a trap and is forced to act as he does.

Then we must ask: What is the nature of the psychic situation which makes acute the demand for elatants? What is the effect of this indulgence upon the mental life? What is there in it that makes the patient suffer? And why, in spite of the suffering, can he not cease from doing as he does?

The previous history of those individuals who take to the use of elatants in a general way reveals the following. There is a group of human beings who respond to frustrations in life with a special type of emotional alteration, which might be designated "tense depression." It sometimes happens, too, that the first reaction to the frustration takes the form of other types of neurotic symptoms, and that the "tense depression" appears only later. The intense, persistent suffering due to a severe physical illness may also lead to the same emotional state. The tense depression may change into other forms of depression; since pharmacothymia originates from the tense depression, let us designate it the "initial depression." It is marked by great "painful" tension and, at the same time, by a high degree of intolerance to pain. In this state of mind, psychic interest is concentrated upon the need for relief. If the patient finds relief in a drug, in this state he is properly prepared to be susceptible to its effects. The role of the initial depression, then, is to *sensitize* the patient for the pharmacogenic pleasure-effect. It is immaterial whether the drug comes into his hands by accident or whether it is prescribed by his physician for therapeutic purposes, whether he was induced to use it or made the experiment on his own responsibility; he experiences a pharmacogenic pleasure-effect, which is in proportion to his longing for relief, and this event frequently, therefore, determines his future fate. If the substance and the dose were well chosen, the first pharmacogenic pleasure-effect remains as a rule the most impressive event of its kind in the whole course of the illness.

We must consider the pharmacogenic pleasure-effect, particularly this maiden one, more intensively. That which makes it so outstanding, when viewed from without, is the sharp rise in self-regard and the elevation of the mood—that is to say, elation.* It is useful to distinguish conceptually between the pharmacogenic elation and the pharmacogenic pleasure-effect, although they merge in the course of the emotional process. The elation would then represent the reaction of the ego to the pleasure-effect. After therapeutic medication, we observe countless instances of the pharmacogenic pleasure-effect which do *not* set up an elation in the patient. It is evident that in the evolution of a pharmacothymia, it is essential that an elation should be developed. In our outline, we must confine ourselves to a description of the outspoken forms, yet we should like to emphasize that the pharmacogenic elation is a protean phenomenon. It may remain so inconspicuous, externally viewed, that a casual observer could overlook it, and nevertheless be an experience which is psychologically an elation. The elation also need not appear immediately after the first contact with the poison. The important thing is not, when it is experienced, but whether it is experienced.

What happens in a pharmacogenic elation can be understood only on the basis of further circumstantial discussion.

This individual's ego was not always so miserable a creature as we judge it to be when we encounter it in its "tense depression." Once it was a baby, radiant with self-esteem, full of belief in the omnipotence of its wishes, of its thoughts, gestures and words.** But the child's megalomania melted away under the inexorable pressure of experience. Its sense of its own sovereignty had to make room for a more modest self-evaluation. This process, first described by Freud,*** may be designated the reduction in size of the original ego; it is a painful procedure and one that is possibly never completely carried out. Now, to be sure, the path to achievement opens for the growing child: he can work and base his self-regard on his own achievements. Two things become evident. In the first place, self-regard is the expression of self-love—that is to say, of narcissistic gratification.† Secondly, narcissism, which at the start was

---

* "Elation" = *Rausch*. "Elatant" = *Rauschgift*. Tʀ.
** Ferenczi, S.: *Development of the Sense of Reality*. Trans. by Jones, in: *Contributions to PsA.*
*** Freud: *On Narcissism, an Introduction*. Coll. Papers IV.
† Cf. my article, *An Anxious Mother*. Int. J. Ps-A, IX, 1928.

gratified "at command" with no labor (thanks to the care of the infant by the adults), is later compelled to cope more and more laboriously with the environment. Or we might put it, the ego must make over its psychology from that of a supercilious parasite into that of a well adjusted self-sustaining creature. Therefore, a complete recognition of the necessity to fend for itself becomes the guiding principle of the mature ego in satisfying its narcissistic needs, that is to say, in maintaining its self-regard. This developmental stage of the "narcissistic system" we may call the "realistic regime of the ego."*

There is no complete certainty that one can attain one's objectives in life by means of this realistic regime; there is always such a thing as bad luck or adversity. It is even worse, certainly, if the functional capacity of the ego is reduced through disturbances in the development of the libido function, which never fail to impair the realistic regime of the ego. The maladapted libido can wrest a substitute satisfaction from the ego in the shape of a neurosis, but then the self-regard usually suffers. An ego whose narcissism insists on the best value in its satisfactions is not to be deceived in regard to the painfulness of real frustration. When it perceives the frustration, it reacts with the change in feeling we have described as "tense depression." Of interest to us in the deep psychology of this condition is the fact that the ego secretly compares its current helplessness with its original narcissistic stature,** which persists as an ideal for the ego, torments itself with self-reproaches and aspires to leave its tribulations and regain its old magnitude.

At this pass, as if from heaven, comes the miracle of the pharmacogenic pleasure-effect. Or rather, the important thing is that it does not come from heaven at all, but is *brought about by the ego itself.* A magical movement of the hand introduces a magical substance, and behold, pain and suffering are exorcized, the sense of misery disappears and the body is suffused by waves of pleasure. It is as though the distress and pettiness of the ego had been only a nightmare; for it now seems that the ego is, after all, the omnipotent giant it had always fundamentally thought it was.

In the pharmacogenic elation the ego regains its original narcissistic stature. Did not the ego obtain a tremendous *real* satisfaction by mere wishing, i.e., without effort, as only that narcissistic image can?

Furthermore, it is not only an infantile wish but an ancient dream of mankind which finds fulfilment in the state of elation. It is generally known that the ancient Greeks used the word "φαρμακον" to mean

---

* "Regime of the ego" = *Steuerung des Ichs.* TR.
** "Original narcissistic stature" = *narzisstische Urgestalt.* TR.

"drug" and "magical substance." This double meaning legitimates our designation; for the term "pharmacothymia," combining the significations of "craving for drugs" and "craving for magic," expresses aptly the nature of this illness.

At the height of the elation, interest in reality disappears, and with it any respect for reality. All the ego's devices which work in the service of reality—the ascertainment of the environment, mental elaboration of its data, instinctual inhibitions imposed by reality—are neglected; and there erupts the striving to bring to the surface and satisfy—either by fantasies or by floundering activity—all the unsatisfied instincts which are lurking in the background. Who could doubt that an experience of this sort leaves the deepest impression on the mental life?

It is generally said that a miracle never lasts longer than three days. The miracle of the elation lasts only a few hours. Then, in accordance with the laws of nature, comes sleep, and a gray and sober awakening, "the morning after." We are not so much referring to the possible discomfort due to symptoms from individual organs as to the *inevitable alteration of mood*. The emotional situation which obtained in the initial depression has again returned, but exacerbated, evidently by new factors. The elation had augmented the ego to gigantic dimensions and had almost eliminated reality; now just the reverse state appears, sharpened by the contrast. The ego is shrunken, and reality appears exaggerated in its dimenions. To turn again to real tasks would be the next step, but meanwhile this has become all the more difficult. In the previous depression there may have been remorse for having disregarded one's activities, but now there is in addition a sense of guilt for having been completely disdainful of real requirements, and an increased fear of reality. There is a storm of reproaches from all sides for the dereliction of duty toward family and work. But from yesterday comes the enticing memory of the elation. All in all, because of additional increments in "pain" the ego has become more irritable and, because of the increased anxiety and bad conscience, weaker; at the final accounting, there is an even greater deficit. What can be done, then? The ego grieves for its lost bliss and longs for its reappearance. This longing is destined to be victorious, for every argument is in its favor. What the pains of the pharmacogenic depression give birth to is, with the most rigorous psychological consistency, the craving for elation.

We obtain, thus, a certain insight into fundamental relationships. The transitoriness of the elation determines the return of the depression; the latter, the renewed craving for elation, and so on. We discover that there is a cyclic course, and its regularity demonstrates that the ego is now maintaining its self-regard by means of an artificial technique. This step involves an alteration in the individual's entire mode of life; it means a change from the "realistic regime" to a *pharmacothymic regime*" of the ego. A pharmacothymic, therefore, may be defined as an individual who has betaken himself to this type of regime; the ensuing consequences make up the scope of the manifestations of pharmacothymia. In other words, this illness is a narcissistic disorder, a destruction through artificial means of the natural ego organization.* Later we shall learn in what way the erotic pleasure function is involved in this process, and how the appreciation of its role changes the appearance of the pathological picture.

Comparing life under the pharmacothymic regime with life oriented towards reality, the impoverishment becomes evident. The pharmacothymic regime has a definite course and increasingly restricts the ego's freedom of action. This regime is interested in only one problem: depression, and in only one method of attacking it, the administration of the drug.

The insufficiency of this method, which the ego at first believes infallible, is soon demonstrated by sad experience. It is not at all the case that elation and depression always recur with unfailing regularity in a cyclic course. The part that puts in its appearance punctually is the depression; the elation becomes increasingly more undependable and in the end threatens complete non-appearance. It is a fact of great importance that the pharmacogenic pleasure-effect, and particularly the elation induced by repeated medication, rapidly wanes. Thus, we encounter here the phenomenon of "diminishing return" in terms of elation. I cannot promise to explain the dynamics of this fall. It is doubtless ultimately dependent on organic processes, which are referred to as the "development of a tolerance" but which cannot as yet be given an accurate physiological interpretation. During the past years an extensive study of this problem was initiated in this country. A comprehensive report of the results arrived at so far has been published recently by the pharmacologists A. L. Fatum and M. H. Seevers in *Physiological Reviews* (Vol. XI, no. 2. 1931). A reading of this report shows that such an explanation has not yet been found. I should like to contribute a point in relation to this problem from the psychological side; namely, the assurance that in the phenomenon of "diminishing return" in elation a *psychological* factor is involved: the patient's fear that the drug will be inefficacious. This fear is analogous to the fear of impotent persons, and, similarly, reduces the chances of success even more. We shall learn, below, which deeper sources give sustenance to this fear.

---

* In my article, *The Problem of Melancholia* (Int. J. Ps-A IX, 1928), I first alluded to the narcissistic nature of drug addictions.

The phenomenon of "diminishing return" intensifies the phase of depression, inasmuch as it adds to the tension the pain of disappointment and a new fear. The attempt to compensate the reduction of the effect by increasing the dosage proves to be worthwhile in the case of many drugs; a good example of this is morphine-pharmacothymia. With this develops the mad pursuit of the patients after the constantly increasing doses which become necessary. Moral obligations, life interests of other kinds are thrown to the winds, when it is a question of pursuing the satisfaction of this need,—a process of moral disintegration second to none.

Meanwhile, crucial alterations occur in the sexual life of the patient. In order to remain within the limits of this presentation, I must restrict my remarks to the most fundamental ones. All elatants poison sexual potency. After a transient augmentation of genital libido, the patient soon turns away from sexual activity and disregards more and more even his affectionate relationships. In lieu of genital pleasure appears the pharmacogenic pleasure-effect, which gradually comes to be the dominant sexual aim. From the ease with which this remarkable substitution is effected, we must conclude that pharmacogenic pleasure depends upon genetically preformed, elementary paths, and that old sensory material is utilized to create a new combination. This, however, is a problem which can be postponed. What is immediately evident is the fact that the pharmacogenic attainment of pleasure initiates an artificial sexual organization which is autoerotic and modeled on infantile masturbation. Objects of love are no longer needed but are retained for a time in fantasy. Later the activity of fantasy returns, regressively, to the emotional attachments of childhood, that is to say, to the oedipus complex. The pharmacogenic pleasure instigates a rich fantasy life; this feature seems especially characteristic of opium-pharmacothymia. Indeed, struck by this fact, the pharmacologist Lewin suggested that the "elatants" should be named "phantastica." The crux of the matter is that it is the pharmacogenic pleasure-effect which discharges the libidinal tension associated with these fantasies. The pharmacogenic pleasure process thus comes to replace the natural sexual executive. The genital apparatus with its extensive auxiliary ramifications in the erotogenic zones falls into desuetude and is overtaken by a sort of mental atrophy of disuse. The fire of life is gradually extinguished at that point where it should glow most intensely according to nature and is kindled at a site contrary to nature. Pharmacothymia destroys the psychic structure of the individual long before it inflicts any damage on the physical substrate.

The ego responds to this devaluation of the natural sexual organization with a fear of castration only too justifiable in this instance. This warning signal is due to the narcissistic investment of the genital; anxiety about the genital should then compel abstention from the dangerous practice, just as, at one time, it compelled abstention from masturbation. But the ego has sold itself to the elatant drugs and cannot heed this warning. The ego, to be sure, is not able to suppress the fear itself, but it perceives the fear consciously as a dread of pharmacogenic failure. This switching of the anxiety is, psychologically, entirely correct. Whoever secretly desires to fail because he is afraid of succeeding is quite right in being in dread of failure. The effect of the fear is naturally in accordance with its original intent; as we have learned, it reduces the pleasure-effect and the intensity of the elation.

By frivolously cutting itself off from its social and sexual activities the ego conjures up an instinctual danger, the extent of which it does not suspect. It delivers itself over to that antagonistic instinctual power within, which we call masochism, and following Freud, interpret as a death instinct. The ego had an opportunity to feel the dark power of this instinct in the initial depression; partly for fear of it then, the ego took flight into the pharmacothymic regime. The ego can defend itself successfully against the dangers of masochistic self-injury only by vigorously developing its vitality and thus entrenching its narcissism. What the pharmacothymic regime bestowed upon the ego, was, however, a valueless inflation of narcissism. The ego lives, then, in a period of pseudo-prosperity, and is not aware that it has played into the hands of its self-destruction. The ego, in every neurosis, is driven into harmful complications by masochism; but of all methods of combating masochism, the pharmacothymic regime is assuredly the most hopeless.

It is impossible for the patient not to perceive what is happening. His friends and relatives deluge him with warnings to "pull himself together" if he does not wish to ruin himself and his family. And at the same time, the elation diminishes in intensity continuously and the depression becomes more severe. Physical illnesses, unmistakably due to the use of the poison, afflict him with pains. Since the first temptation the picture has completely changed. Then, everything was in favor of the elation, whereas now the hopes set upon it have been revealed as deluding. It might be supposed that the patient would reflect on this and give up the drug—but, no; he continues on his way. I must admit that for many years I could not grasp the economics of this state of mind until a patient himself gave me the explanation. He said: "I know all the things that people say when they upbraid me. But, mark my words, doctor, *nothing* can happen to *me*." This, then, is the patient's position. The elation has reactivated his narcissistic belief in his *invulnerability*, and all of his better insight and all of his sense of guilt are shattered on this bulwark.

Benumbed by this illusion, the ego's adherence to the pharmacothymic regime is strengthened all the more. The pharmacothymic regime still seems to be *the* way out of all difficulties. One day, things have progressed so far that an elation can no longer be provided to combat the misery of the depression. The regime has collapsed, and we are confronted by the phenomenon of the *pharmacothymic crisis*.

There are three ways out of this crisis: flight into a free interval, suicide and psychosis.

By voluntarily submitting to withdrawal therapy, the patient undertakes a flight into a free interval. It is out of the question that he is actuated by any real desire to recover his health. In those rare instances in which the patient really wishes to be delivered from his pharmacothymia, as I have occasionally been able to observe in my analytic practice, he sets great store upon executing his resolve by himself, and it does not occur to him to seek aid from others. But, if he submits to a withdrawal cure, as a rule, he wishes only to rehabilitate the depreciated value of the poison. It may be that he can no longer afford the money for the enormous quantity of the drug that he needs; after the withdrawal treatment he can begin anew with much less expense.

Since the withdrawal of the drug divests the ego of its elation—its protection against masochism—the latter can now invade the ego. There it seizes upon the physical symptoms due to abstinence and exploits them, frequently to the point of a true masochistic orgy; naturally with the opposition of the ego, which is not grateful for this type of pleasure. As a result, we have the familiar scenes which patients produce during the withdrawal period.

Suicide is the work of self-destructive masochism. But to say that the patient kills himself because of a masochistic need for punishment would be too one sided a statement. The analysis of the suicidal fantasies and attempts of which our patients tell us, reveals the narcissistic aspect of the experience. The patient takes the lethal dose because he wishes to dispel the depression for good by an elation which will last *forever*. He does not kill himself; he believes in his *immortality*. Once the demon of infantile narcissism is unchained, he can send the ego to its death.

Furthermore, in suicide through drugs, masochism is victorious under the banner of a "feminine" instinctual demand. Remarkably enough, it is the deeply rooted high estimation which the male has for his sexual organ, his genital narcissism, which brings about this transformation and transmutes masochism into a feminine phenomenon. This sounds paradoxical but can readily be understood as a compromise. The ingestion of drugs, it is well known, in infantile archaic thinking represents an oral insemination; planning to die from poisoning is a cover for the wish to

become pregnant in this fashion. We see, therefore, that after the pharmacothymia has paralyzed the ego's virility, the hurt pride in genitality,
forced into passivity because of masochism, desires as a substitute the
satisfaction of child bearing. Freud recognized the replacement of the
wish to possess a penis by the wish to have a child as a turning point in
the normal sexual development of women. In the case we are discussing,
the male takes this female path in order to illude himself concerning his
masochistic self-destruction by appealing to his genital narcissism. It is
as though the ego, worried about the male genital, told itself: "Be com-
forted. You are getting a new genital." To this idea, inferred from empirical findings, we may add that impregnation biologically initiates a
new life cycle: the wish to be pregnant is a mute appeal to the function
of reproduction, to "divine Eros," to testify to the immortality of the
ego.

The *psychotic episode* as an outcome of the crisis is known to us
chiefly—though by no means exclusively—in alcohol-pharmacothymia.
This is a large chapter. I can only indicate the framework around which
its contents may be arranged.

The failure of the pharmacothymic regime has robbed the ego of its
protective elation. Masochism then crowds into the foreground. The
terrible hallucinations and deliria, in which the patient believes that he
is being persecuted, or threatened—particularly by the danger of castration or a sexual attack—and the like are fantasies that gratify masochistic wishes. The masochism desires to place the ego in a situation
where it will suffer, in order to obtain pleasure from the painful stimulation. The narcissistic ego offers opposition to this "pain-pleasure"; it
desires the pleasure *without* pain. The wishes of its masochism inspire
the ego with fear and horror. It can, to be sure, no longer prevent the
eruption of the masochistic fantasies, yet it looks upon them through its
own eyes. Thus, the latent *wish* fantasies of masochism are transformed
into the manifest *terror*-fantasies of the ego. Now it is as though the
danger proceeded from without; there, at least, it can be combated, and
the terrified patient attempts to do this in the imaginations of his psychosis.

It is even worse if the anxiety which protects the ego from masochism
breaks down. Then, the ego must accede to masochism. If the patient
has arrived at this point, he suddenly announces his intention of destroying his genital organ or—substitutively—inflicting some other injury upon himself. He actually takes measures towards the blind
execution of the biddings of his masochism; the patient's narcissism,
defeated, can only insure that he will literally act blindly. It dims his gaze
by means of delusion: the patient is not aware of the true nature of his

masochism and refuses to recognize it. Instead, he asserts that he must rid himself of his organ because this organ is a nuisance to him, or has been a source of harm, or the like. If we read, for this statement, "because this organ has sinned against him," a path opens for the clarification of the latent meaning of this delusion. We may now compare it with another type of delusion of self-injury, in which the patient is well aware that he is engaged in harming himself yet persists in his designs nonetheless. This variant of the delusion usually appears in the guise of the moral idea of sin; the ego believes that it must inflict a merited punishment upon itself, in order to purify its conscience. The central feature in this "moralizing" type of delusional state is self-reproach. It may be assumed that in the "unconcerned" type of delusional state, previously described, the ego institutes a displacement of the guilt and directs its reproaches, not against itself, but against its genital organ. Primitive thought finds displacements of this sort very easy. We often hear small children say: "I didn't do it. My hand did it." The life of primitive peoples is replete with instances of this sort. The patient, then, is incensed with his genital organ, dispossesses it of the esteem previously lavished upon it (its narcissistic investment), and wishes to part with it. It is as though the ego said to the genital organ, "You are to blame for it all. First you tempted me to sin." (Bad conscience for infantile masturbation.) "Then your inefficiency brought me disappointment." (Lowering of self-esteem through later disturbances of potency.) "And therefore you drove me into my ill-omened drug addiction. I do not love you any more; away with you!" The ego does not castrate itself; it wrecks vengeance on its genital.*

In the "unconcerned" form of delusion of self-injury, the ego obviously is still experiencing an after-effect of the continuous elation; it is still "beclouded by original narcissism." To masochism—that is, to knowledge that it wishes to injure itself and that this is its sole objective—the ego is blind and deaf. It is as though, in the ego's state of grandeur, whether or not it has a genital is of no moment. The genital offended the ego—away with it!

---

* In Ferenczi's ingenious theory of genitality (*Versuch einer Genitaltheorie*, 1923), the author calls attention to the fact that the relationship of the ego and the genital, in spite of all interests held in common, reflects profound biological antagonisms. The ego is, after all, the representative of the interests of the "soma"; and the genital, the representative of those of the "germ plasm." In so far as the ego feels itself at one with its genital libido, its genital organ impresses it as its most prolific source of pleasure; but for an ego that wishes peace, the genital becomes merely the bearer of oppressive tensions, which the ego wishes to shake off. From these and like premises, Ferenczi infers that—in the male—the act of procreation includes among its psychic qualities a "tendency towards autotomy of the genital."

The unconcerned type of delusion of self-injury occurs more frequently in schizophrenia than in pharmacothymia. In schizophrenia, the megalomania is responsible for the fact that the ego, under pressure of masochism, undertakes so easily to inflict the most horrible mutilations upon itself, such as amputations, enucleation of the eyeball, etc. The megalomania of schizophrenia and the megalomania of pharmacothymic elation are related manifestations of narcissistic regression. The former pursues a chronic course, the latter an acute, and they differ in regard to intellectual content and emotional tone; nevertheless, they both are based upon a regression to the "original narcissistic stature" of the ego.

Masochism in pharmacothymia may be attenuated into the passivity of a homosexual attitude. This fact gives us deep insight into the dynamics of homosexuality. The pharmacothymic regime has driven eroticism from its active positions and thereby, as a reaction, encouraged masochism. The genital eroticism which is on the retreat can then with the masochism enter into a compromise which will combine the genital aim of painless pleasure with the passive behavior of masochism, and the result of this combination, in men, is a homosexual choice of object.* The danger proceeding from the masochistic wish to be castrated, naturally remains extant. If it is of sufficient magnitude, the ego reacts to it with a fear of castration and represses the homosexual impulse, which afterwards in the psychosis may become manifest as a delusion of jealousy, or in the feminine erotic quality of the delusions of persecution.

The advantage of homosexuality as compared to masochism is its more ready acceptability to the ego. In overt homosexuality, the ego combats the masochistic danger of castration by denying the existence, in general, of any such thing as a danger of castration. Its position is: there is no such thing as castration, for there are no castrated persons; even the sexual partner possseses a penis. If the ego in pharmacothymia or after the withdrawal of the drug accepts homosexuality, this turn must be regarded as an attempt at autotherapy. The recrudescence of the genital function with a new aim, more readily attainable, psychologically speaking, permits the ego to return to, or fortify, the "realistic regime." After being reconciled to its homosexuality, the ego can subsequently take a new reparative step toward masculinity by progressing from a passive homosexual to an active homosexual attitude. Thus, male heterosexual normality is changed into active homosexuality by a three-stage process: (1) weakening of genital masculinity (because of intimidation due to threats of castration, diversion of the libido into the pharmacothymia,

---

* I shall discuss the conditions in women in another article.

etc.) and a corresponding reactive increase in the antagonistic masochism; (2) the confluence of genital pleasure and masochism in the compromise, passive homosexuality; and (3) the development of homosexuality
from the passive to the active form as the result of a vigorous reparative
action on the part of the ego. In corroboration of this idea is the finding,
hitherto neglected, that the homosexuality which the ego rejects and
combats by the formation of delusions (symptoms) is always passive homosexuality. These facts help to clarify clinical manifestations that appeared obscure and complex. Obviously, the ego may have become
homosexual, because of analogous circumstances, even before the pharmacothymia began.

These views, as I have presented them here, seem to me to throw new
light upon the problem of the relationship between homosexuality and
pharmacothymia. The homosexual background became evident to psychoanalysis, first in alcoholism, later in cocainism, and finally in morphinism. Since I attribute homosexuality to the influence of masochism,
and since, furthermore, every type of pharmacothymia attacks genitality
and by reaction strengthens masochism, the opportunity to effect this
compromise must naturally be present in every case of pharmacothymia.

The love life of pharmacothymics may present pathological features
other than homosexuality. These all derive from the basic situation described above, in my outline of the development of homosexuality, as
"stage (1)." The pharmacothymic whose potency is debilitated by masochism may find ways of preserving his heterosexuality. In the first
place, he may choose another compromise solution and become oriented
passively towards *women*. This erotic position is quite unstable; but it can
be reënforced, by an infusion of fetishism, to withstand the onslaught
of castration anxiety. With the aid of the fetishistic mechanism, the beloved woman is in imagination transmuted into the possessor of a penis
and elevated to take the place of the "phallic mother."* With this align-
ment of the instincts, the persons chosen as objects are, by preference,
women who have a prominent nose, large breasts, an imposing figure,
or, too, a good deal of money, and the like. Correlated with this, the
emotional tone in regard to the genital region of women is disturbed by
a sort of discomfort, and the patient assiduously avoids looking at it or
touching it. In mild cases of pharmacothymia, this passive orientation
towards women with its fetishistic ingredient often plays a major role,
but its distribution is by no means restricted to pharmacothymia. A
further intensification of the masochistic wish to be castrated, or better,
of the fear of castration aroused by this wish, then forces the patient

---

* Freud: *Fetishism*. Int. J. Ps-A. IX, 1928.

either to be abstinent or to follow the homosexual course and exchange the partner without a penis for one who possesses a penis. (See "stage (2)" described above.) In the second place, the ego may refuse to adopt as a solution the compromise of any passive orientation; it may respond to the danger proceeding from the masochistic instinct by a reaction formation. It is no easy task to divine what special conditions enable the ego to react in this way. But at any rate, the means used by the ego are the strained exertion of its pleasure in agression. Sadism is rushed to the rescue of imperiled masculinity, to shout down, by its vehemence, fear of castration and masochistic temptation. In this case, too, heterosexuality is preserved, but the ego must pay for this by entering the path of sadistic perversion. In the dynamics of the perversion of sadism, the *vis a tergo* of masochism is the crucial factor; in its construction, infantile and recent experiences are jointly effective, in the usual familiar manner. The appearance of this variant, that is, the production of a true sadistic perversion is not, to be sure, promoted by the pharmacothymia. I recognized this mechanism in non-pharmacothymic cases, and I have mentioned it here only because it may furnish us with the explanation of a conspicuous deformation of the character, which may be considered a counterpart of the perversion of sadism, and which often may be found in pharmacothymia. Particularly in drunkards, we are familiar with aggressive irritability, with unprovoked outbursts of hate or rage against women, and the like, which in apparently unpredictable fashion, alternate with states of touching mollification. We can now understand that the accesses of brutality are the substitutes of potency of the pharmacothymic who is fighting for his masculinity, and that his sentimental seizures are eruptions of the masochism which his pharmacothymia has reactively intensified.

Pharmacothymia is not ineluctably bound to this basic course with its terminal crisis. Many drugs, especially alcohol, admit of combating the recurrent depression by overlapping dosage. The patient takes a fresh dose before the effect of the previous one has ceased. If he does so, he renounces "elation" in the narrower sense of this word; for elation is a phenomenon dependent on contrast. Instead, he lives in a sort of "subdued continuous elation" which differs from simple stupefaction probably only because of its narcissistically pleasurable quality. This modified course leads through a progressive reduction of the ego to the terminal state of pharmacogenic stupor. A flaring up of the desire for a real elation or other reasons may at any time bring the patient back to the basic course with its critical complications.

This sketch of the theoretical picture of pharmacothymia roughly outlines the broad field of its symptomatology. One thing remains to be

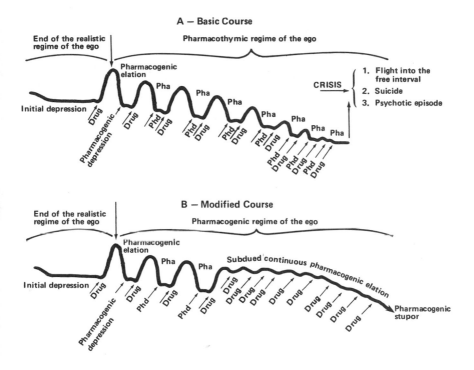

added. In more severe, advanced cases, symptoms appear which are the
result of cerebral damage, and which are consequently to be interpreted
with due consideration of the point of view of brain pathology. In this,
we may expediently make use of the psycho-physiological point of view
introduced into psychopathology by Schilder with the concept of "inroad
of the somatic" ("*somatischer Einbruch*").* If the poisons consumed have
damaged the brain substance, and permanently impaired cerebral activity, this is perceived in the mental sphere as a disturbance of the
elementary psychological functions. The psychic organization reacts with
an effort to adapt to this fact and correct the result. It is well to differentiate the phenomena which originate in this way, as the "secondary
symptoms" of pharmacothymia, from those "primary" ones which we
have been considering. The secondary symptoms are more characteristic
of the brain lesions which determine them than of the illness in which
they appear. This can be seen in the example of the Korsakoff syndrome,
which occurs in other conditions as well as in pharmacothymia.

---

* Schilder, Paul: *Über die kausale Bedeutung des durch Psychoanalyse gewonnenen Materials.*
Wiener klin. Wchschr. 1921.—The theory of general paralysis formulated by Hollos and
Ferenczi is based on a similar idea.

Finally, it might be pointed out that in addition to fullblown pharmacothymia there are obviously abortive forms of this illness. The patient may, generally speaking, retain the realistic regime, and use his pharmacothymic regime only as an auxiliary and corrective. He desires in this way to make up for the uncertainty in his realistic attitude and cover a deficit by means of counterfeit. By easy transitions we arrive at the normal person who makes daily use of stimulants in the form of coffee, tea, tobacco, and the like.

5

PERSONALITY AND ADDICTION: A DYNAMIC PERSPECTIVE

Isidor Chein, Donald L. Gerard, Robert S. Lee, and Eva Rosenfeld

Although the opiate addiction of the adolescents we have studied grew out of a long history of maladjustment in which those structural aspects of the personality discussed above were significant, neither maladjustment nor personality structure per se is sufficient to account for their becoming addicted. Two other sets of determinants are involved.

First, from an epidemiological standpoint, the social climate, attitudes, values, stresses, and gratifications current in his community and, of course, the availability of drugs significantly affect the likelihood that any particular youth with the personality characteristics described will experiment with drug use.

Second, from a psychiatric standpoint, the likelihood that he will become an addictive user of opiate drugs is most significantly affected by his experiences with drug use in the context of his current situation as this has been structured by his entire experience. This hypothesis, which we will attempt to illustrate in the following pages, may be formulated more clearly as follows: assuming that other conditions are favorable, *the probability of addiction is greater if the person experiences changes in his situation in connection with his use of opiate drugs which may be described as adaptive, functional, or ego-syntonic* and which he describes in terms which tell us that he regards the use of opiates as extremely worthwhile despite,

Reprinted with permission from *The Road to H: Narcotics, Delinquency, and Social Policy*, by I. Chein, D. L. Gerard, R. S. Lee and E. Rosenfeld, New York: Basic Books, Inc., 1964, 227-250.

or perhaps especially because of, the inconveniences and difficulties of being an addict in our society. We may think of these functional or adaptive changes in terms of forces operating at four levels within the individual: at the level of conscious experience; at the level of certain defenses; at the level of unconscious process; and at the level of psychophysiological reaction.

AT THE LEVEL OF CONSCIOUS EXPERIENCE

Closest to the surface, to the threshold of awareness and to communication, are certain common adaptive aspects of drug use. Though these are, in a sense, known to the users, they are not readily communicated by them because of problems of rapport, shame at confessing personal inadequacies, and their lack of experience in communicating subtle feelings and emotions. As they enter therapeutic relationships, they become more capable of formulating and communicating these phenomena.

One of the most striking of the phenomena is sympton relief. Heroin and morphine are efficient tranquilizing, or ataractic, drugs (at least they unquestionably are so for those individuals who become addicted). Overt symptoms of anxiety, obsessive thinking, and early delusional formations are modified or eliminated. Many individuals feel tense and restless before they begin to use opiates. When they use them they feel comfortable, relaxed, and peaceful. Apart from our own experience, some striking instances of symptom relief have been given by Wikler[1] and Lindesmith.[2]

An especially important and common instance of relief from symptoms is that opiate drugs are often helpful in quelling the anxiety and strain which addicts experience in a variety of interpersonal situations. Many feel shy, withdrawn, unacceptable, or socially inhibited. With opiates, they are able to participate more comfortably in the ordinary run of adolescent activities, e.g., dancing, dating, going out with the gang, or even in fighting. This is not to say that these are common activities of addicts, but that, when addicts do participate in them, they do so more effectively and with less malaise with the help of opiates than they would otherwise. This aspect of opiate use is analogous to the social use of alcohol. Paradoxically, this leads many young addicts into situations which they might otherwise avoid, but which, once entered, develop more-or-less inexorably into complex situations with which they cannot

[1] Abraham Wikler, *Opiate Addiction*, "Psychological and Neurophysiological Aspects in Relation to Clinical Problems" (Springfield, Ill.: Charles C Thomas, 1953).

[2] A. R. Lindesmith, *Opiate Addiction* (Bloomington, Ind.: Principia Press, 1947).

cope even with the help of drugs. Opiates can calm anticipatory anxiety, and they may sustain inadequate individuals through the trials of relatively superficial personal association, but the drugs cannot substitute for the basically adequate ego structure these individuals lack.

Many nonaddictive users of heroin may also take the drug for its helpful functions, just as many nonaddictive users of alcohol take an occasional "social drink." {We speculate that the individuals who are helped to deal with difficult situations for which they have adequate resources (i.e., the drug is helpful in easing the situation, but is not essential for an adequate performance) do not become addictive users. { Those who are helped to enter relatively enduring and demanding situations for which they lack adequate resources respond with increased anxiety as the situations develop and, hence, with a need for further ataraxia. Thus, they are led to the recurrent use of the drug, until they eventually learn to substitute the ataraxia for whatever they can get from coping with difficult situations.

Another important, consciously experienced, phenomenon is the intoxication experience itself, which the addict refers to as "being high." This experience is appreciated and enjoyed by the addict and by regular users, but by only a minority of experimental "normal" subjects. It is not, however, in any true sense, a euphoria—a feeling of stimulation, happiness, excitement.

The point at issue may perhaps be clarified by reference to two contrasting ideals of fulfillment: paradise and nirvana. Paradise represents an ideal situation in which all desires are easily satisfied. If one is hungry, one has but to reach out, and the means of satisfying hunger are at hand. Nirvana, by contrast, represents an ideal of fulfillment through absence of desire, and desire is itself viewed as an inherently frustrated state that cannot be compensated for through the pleasure of its gratification.

At least to the normal Western mind,[3] however, the prospect of endless

---

[3] That the issue may well transcend cultural differentiation is indicated by various experiments on rats described by Leon Festinger. In one experiment, for instance, it was established that hungry rats develop a preference for a box in which they are delayed on their way to food. "The Psychological Effects of Insufficient Rewards," *American Psychologist*, 16 (1961), 1-11.

It may also be noted that the same culture which produced the concept of nirvana also produced the most elaborate techniques for the continuance of sexual intercourse with the postponement of orgasm. If the absence of desire is the desideratum, then, short of eliminating desire altogether, the optimum condition should be to get rid of it with the utmost dispatch. The issue here is, however, complicated by one of the *mastery* of desire through its disciplined expression; the completely disciplined control of the expression of desire may be viewed as a more effective step in the direction of the *conquest* of desire than the attempt to suppress it. Closely related is the notion that pleasure itself is a snare and a delusion, not because it is sinful, but because its experience makes more difficult

fulfillment through an absence of desire is not a particularly attractive one. Normal men, for instance, do not look forward with great eagerness to the attainment of a maturation level in which they will find themselves beyond sexual desire; and, having attained an age characterized by a marked diminution of sexual desire, they do not typically look on this aspect of their attainment as an asset. Nor does the average person look forward to the day when he will be able to satisfy the nutritive needs of his body (and even to anticipate hunger) with a pill. The nirvana-like end state of gratification may be valued and enjoyed, but the pleasure is in the activity that goes into making the end state possible; the end state is itself, at least in part, enjoyable only in the security of the belief that it is not the final end, but that it will give way to remounting desire.

Human beings have devoted great ingenuity and planning to the development of means for intensifying desire and achieving an optimal protraction of the period of activity and of the investment and distribution of effort in achieving the end state.[4] Moreover, in the very vision

---

the passage to a state beyond desire. Hence, a major aspect of the disciplined expression of desire is the systematic cultivation of a sense of affective detachment from one's participation, an attitude remarkably akin to the high value placed by those of our youth who are attracted to narcotics on the capacity to remain "cool." In the latter terms, the most admirable performance, whether in sex, music, dancing, or whatever, is that of the virtuoso who displays no feeling whatsoever in the course of the performance. We may only be displaying our own culturocentrism when we express the suspicion that such a philosophy is attractive only to people who have been impelled by desire and tantalized by the vision of gratification, only to meet with frustration and disappointment.

[4] A great deal of confusion is generated by the failure to distinguish the pleasure of the activity leading to the end state from the pleasantness (to coin a verbal distinction, "pleasure" here signifying a turbulent, stirred-up, zestful enjoyment; "pleasantness," a serene, calm, passive enjoyment) of the end state. Even Freud, who was well aware of the significance of foreplay in sexual activity in building up the tension of desire and presumably also of the uneven crescendo of activity leading to the climax, failed to take account of this in his theoretical formulations and landed in serious theoretical difficulties as a result. Thus, in his characterization of an instinctual drive, Freud distinguished a source (a bodily state which leads to a continuous input of excitation), an object (with which it is necessary to interact in order to achieve the aim), and an aim (the elimination of the excitation). He identified the achievement of the aim with pleasure and so formulated the pleasure principle, a formulation that would in strict logic imply that aim-inhibited activity cannot be pleasurable—a conclusion inconsistent with other aspects of the theoretical system. At any rate, he recognized that he was in trouble when he realized that he had formulated the pleasure and nirvana (a basic striving to eliminate excitation) principles in identical terms. Since he must have known that the two principles referred to basically different aspects of behavior, he did not take the logical step of concluding that there was only one principle at work, but instead accepted the weak conclusion that there must be some qualitative difference in the fate of the energies involved in the two principles. Cf. Freud, "The Economic Problem in Masochism," *Collected Papers* (New York: Basic Books, 1959), II, 255-268.

It will be noted that Freud's basic characterization of an instinctual drive took no note whatever of the nature of the interaction with the object and, hence, of the potentially pleasurable (and sought) aspects of this interaction. In other contexts, however, he distin-

of paradise itself there was implanted an image of the unattainable; it is as if the creators of the myth could not tolerate the vision of the total satisfiability of all wants, some degree of frustration being necessary to the very ideal of fulfillment. And it was when they tore away this restriction that Adam and Eve lost their paradise, or perhaps they gained a deeper wisdom—that human beings do not belong in paradise, that their destiny can be achieved only through toil and pain. Adam and Eve could satisfy their wants in the Garden of Eden, but the satisfaction left little to enjoy.

At any rate, the addict's enjoyment of the "high" is not the enjoyment of a stirred-up, zestful state. It is not the enjoyment of intensified sensory input and orgastic excitement, not even on a hallucinatory or fantasied level. De Quincey and others to the contrary notwithstanding, it is not an enjoyment of enhanced creative experience or rich fantasies. It is, in fact, not an enjoyment of anything positive at all, and that it should be thought of as a "high" stands as mute testimony to the utter destitution of the life of the addict with respect to the achievement of positive pleasures and of its repletion with frustration and unresolvable tension. It is, in the main, an enjoyment of a nirvana-like state unpreceded and unenriched by the pleasure of getting there. It is an enjoyment of negatives. Awareness of tension and distress is markedly reduced. Contact with reality diminishes. Ideational and fantasy activity are decreased,

---

guished two kinds of pleasure in sexual activity. Thus, in his *Three Essays on the Theory of Sexuality* (New York: Basic Books, 1962) he wrote that the erogenous zones "are all used to provide a certain amount of pleasure by *being stimulated* in the way appropriate to them. This pleasure then leads to an increase in tension which in its turn is responsible for producing the necessary motor energy for the conclusion of the sexual act. The penultimate stage of that act is once again the appropriate *stimulation* of an erotogenic zone . . . by the appropriate object . . . ; and from *the pleasure yielded by this excitation* the motor energy is obtained . . . , which brings about the discharge of the sexual substances. This last pleasure is the highest in intensity. . . . It is wholly a pleasure of satisfaction and with it the tension of the libido is for the time being extinguished. . . . This distinction between the one kind of pleasure due to the *excitation* of erotogenic zones and the other kind due to the discharge of the sexual substances deserves . . . a difference in nomenclature. The former may be suitably described as 'fore-pleasure' in contrast to the 'end-pleasure . . .' " (pp. 76 ff.; italics added). It is likely that Freud somehow failed to distinguish in the "end-pleasure" the pleasure of the orgasm per se (a highly stirred-up state) and the pleasantness of the aftermath (the state of reduced tension), else it is difficult to see how he identified the pleasure principle with the reduction of tension. In any case, he did not think that the "end-pleasure" was available prior to puberty, which would imply that the prepubescent individual could not be governed by the pleasure principle, an obvious internal contradiction. Similarly, his notion that perversions arise from an excess of fore-pleasure with a resultant rejection of the "normal sexual aim"—i.e., the "end-pleasure"—would imply that sexual perverts are not governed by the pleasure principle.

In other major (and typically more rigorously formulated) psychological systems, one also finds difficulties that may be traced to the failure to make the distinction. Cf. Isidor Chein, "The Image of Man," *Journal of Social Issues*, XVIII (1962), 1-35.

often blotting out a disquieting and disturbing fantasy life that is characteristic of the unintoxicated state. Some addicts do manage unelaborated and unimaginative fantasies of wealth and status or masochistic fantasies of self-recrimination and the intention to reform. Addicts feel "out of this world" and content, as if all of their needs have been taken care of. Here, in "the junkie paradise," they experience what Wikler has described as a diminution of their "primary drives," of hunger, thirst, awareness of pain, and sexual tension. Their bodies are satisfied and sated.

There is a remarkable rhapsodic description of thumb-sucking by a grown girl (quoted by Freud in his *Three Essays on the Theory of Sexuality* [New York: Basic Books, 1962], p. 47), which could just as well illustrate the opiate high.

> It is impossible to describe what a lovely feeling goes through your whole body when you suck; you are right away from this world. You are absolutely satisfied, and happy beyond desire. It is a wonderful feeling; you long for nothing but peace—uninterrupted peace. It is just unspeakably lovely: you feel no pain and no sorrow, and ah! you are carried into another world.

The adolescent addict does not usually like to talk about the experience of the high, other than to commend it. First, it is difficult for him to find words to describe the experience. Second, he is ashamed, embarrassed, and secretive about it. In fact, some adolescent addicts attempt to deprecate the experience in the postwithdrawal phase of their addiction; they say that being high on heroin is nothing, marijuana is better, that they would be crazy to go back to an experience which gives them so little and costs them so much. Third, but this is more common among older and more experienced addicts, they often have a superior attitude to the nonaddict based on the idea that they possess a secret, magical, self-administrable source of pleasure which, in their estimation, is better than anything the nonaddict can have. The high is too good; verbalization at best degrades it. "If you want to know what the high is, take heroin and learn for yourself."

AT THE LEVEL OF CERTAIN DEFENSES

The general function of a psychic defense is to avoid anxiety. This may be accomplished by a subtle reordering of experience or by an alteration in the perception or in the manifestations of inner impulses

or outer events (projection, denial, reaction formation, etc.). The phenomena we have alluded to above (symptom relief, social facilitation,
and the experience of the high) are to a large measure expressions of
the opiate's capacity to inhibit or blunt the perception of inner anxiety
and outer strain. In this sense, the drug itself is a diffuse pharmacological
defense. However, there is another sense in which opiate addiction is
integrated into the psychological defenses of the adolescent addict. The
general structure of this integration is a mélange of projection, rationalization, and denial. The fact that he is an addict, despite the personal
and social implications of opiate addiction in our society, allays the anxiety he would experience if he were to face, express, or act out certain
impulses and wishes. He displaces the responsibility for his behavior
onto an auxiliary, executant ego about which, in effect, he can say: "Not
I, but the drug in me does these things. I am not responsible; it is the
monkey on my back."

That this is not conscious duplicity is attested by the genuine horror
and anxiety with which some of these "released" impulses and wishes
are recalled in the postwithdrawal phases of addiction. Of course, we do
not wish to imply that the opiates per se are "releasers," in some physiological sense, of repressed wishes or impulses of a specifically aggressive
or sexual nature. As one of the authors has pointed out in a comparison
of alcohol intoxication and opiate addiction,[5] the opiate addict to a large
measure "acts out" in the process of sustaining his addiction, and usually
not in the course of acute intoxication with the drug nor necessarily in
the actual physiological distress of the abstinence syndrome. It is sufficient for him to identify himself as *being an addict* to reap the benefit of
this auxiliary ego.

The wishes and impulses expressed through this auxiliary ego are
highly individualized. In the course of the addiction, the unspeakable
is spoken, and that which should never be done is done. This does not
occur in diffuse, patternless, or random misbehavior, but with remarkable precision of aim and aptness to the life situations and relationships
with important persons in the lives of the addicts. They do not, of course,
recognize the intentions of their behavior, however obvious these intentions may be to us. It requires months of work before a patient can
accept the integration of his behavior with ideas or feelings he fears to
perceive or communicate. Although there is no limit to the variety of
such integrations, there are a few general classes which occur frequently.

In the course of addiction, the addict may begin to express hostility

---

[5] Donald L. Gerard, "Intoxication and Addiction," *Quarterly Journal of Studies on Alcohol*,
16 (1955), 681-699.

toward parental figures—whom he regards as emasculating or control-ling—through theft from the parental home; overt anger (becoming "evil and nasty"); or through the spiteful, wasteful, or destructive use of parental furnishings, money, decorations, or clothing. Even his gen-eral delinquency and the use of narcotics itself may contain a strong component vector aimed at his parents. By becoming an addict, he can disappoint or frustrate those parents whose hopes or ambitions for their son are of the highest. Similarly, he may utilize his addiction for the expression of passive-dependent wishes, e.g., by giving up or avoiding employment; begging for money and gifts; soliciting loans without at-tempt to repay them; and withdrawing from activities, interests, and relationships outside his parental home.

The mother of an addict may want to take a lover or a new husband. This is not infrequent in the lives of the male adolescent addicts we have studied. Even though he regards his mother critically, he is likely to be extremely attached to, dependent on, and overidentified with her. Thus, he experiences his mother's intentions as a threat; he fears that he will lose her love and concern to this rival. His behavior in the course of his addiction then focuses on the rival. It is the rival's suits which are stolen and pawned; it just happens that the addict comes home "high" when his mother is entertaining this friend. In short, he persuades the rival through his behavior in sustaining his addiction that gaining a liaison with his mother is likely to be more trouble than it is worth.

The addict uses his addiction to express or act out repressed impulses and needs. From the standpoint of the discharge of psychic energy, this is probably pleasurable; in terms of eventual consequences, it can be disastrous. In terms of secondary reactions of guilt, such behavior can provoke tension and distress during abstinence which are alleviated, unfortunately too readily, by further indulgence in opiates.

AT THE LEVEL OF UNCONSCIOUS PROCESS

It is important to clarify the role of unconscious symbolism in ad-diction. Dreams, neurotic symptoms, wit, and the psychopathology of everyday life are enriched or burdened by their unconscious meanings. Similarly, many aspects of the addiction experience and process are linked with and emotionally colored by wishes, drives, and bodily ex-periences pertinent to the addict's early development and relationships. With exceptions, these tend to be communicated or expressed symbol-ically in the dreams and in the art work of the patients and in their responses to projective test material. For instance, dreams have the man-ifest content of a needle, fat, long, sticking into my body; being snowed under a mound of heroin; drinking heroin or being attacked by a monster with a huge syringe.

The exceptions, perhaps as important as the regularities, are those patients who tell us quite directly[6] that the syringe and needle ("the works," as they are called in the argot) are like a breast; when he is high, he feels that he is together with his mother, long ago, warm, comfortable, happy, at peace; when he injects the opiate solution, he mixes the solution with his blood and bounces the blood-opiate mixture back and forth from syringe to vein, and, as he does this, he has fantasies about intercourse.

By and large, those patients who directly associate their addiction experiences with these oral concepts have the most clinically evident ego disturbances; they suffer from anxiety verging on panic or are overtly psychotic. They are least able to repress or otherwise defend themselves against the perception of such ideas and images, and they are thus able to directly verbalize what may only be inferred from the symbolic communications of the others.

It is difficult to ignore the fact that unconscious symbolism of this sort occurs in addiction. The question is, "What role does it play in the genesis of addiction?" Addiction is a complex psychosocial behavior. Obviously, no one takes drugs for the first time with such ideas in mind as that the syringe is a breast or that, through taking opiates, he may regain a state of early infantile unity with his mother. No one becomes an addict simply because he is laden with unconscious oral fantasies and cravings for breasts, sustenance, or warmth. Rather, as he becomes an addict, the techniques and circumstances of drug use readily lend themselves as vehicles of expression for these facets of his unconscious mental processes. Though these unconscious symbolizations are less weighty in the motivations for becoming an addict than are the forces of conscious experience, especially the high, or the forces of the integration of the addiction in the psychic defenses, they probably do contribute importantly to the *appetite* for drug use in the same sense that spices, with their volatile oils and esters, may contribute to the appetite for otherwise prosaic foods. However, as the addiction progresses and the addict becomes increasingly involved with his addiction and correspondingly less

---

[6] Obviously, in a strict sense of the term "unconscious," such directly communicated meanings are not unconscious. The term is, however, also used in an extended sense to include that which is typically unconscious in the normal person under normal circumstances. We have elected to go along with such usage which is likely to have a familiar ring to most readers rather than enter into a discussion of such concepts as "primary" and "secondary" process and their relation to the concepts conscious—preconscious—unconscious, on the one hand, and to id—ego—superego, on the other.

involved in any attempt to deal with the world and current relationships, ever-larger portions of his psychic life are given over to this primitive level of gratification.

AT THE LEVEL OF PSYCHOPHYSIOLOGICAL REACTION

The concepts "craving," "dependence," and "tolerance" are usually found in textbooks of pharmacology in the section dealing with the opiate drugs. Our discussion here will emphasize the more psychological aspects of these psychophysiological forces.

Craving

"Craving" is, of course, merely a word. In common speech or in jest, we may say that we "crave" sweets or tobacco or love. We have no psychological lien on the term, no proprietary right to restrict its meaning to a particular reference. However, it is a useful rubric, in terms of which we may discuss certain attitudes and orientations. In the sense in which we wish to develop it, craving is a pathological phenomenon which entails recurrent states of liking, wanting, and seeking an entity or object but which differs from normal wanting, liking, and seeking in several important respects.

First, craving implies an abnormal intensity of desire.

Second, craving implies an abnormal intensification of the reaction to the failure to fulfill the desire. When a normal person cannot get what he wants, he may be sad and unhappy; one criterion of normality is that he seeks legitimate means to satisfy the desire, finds appropriate substitute gratifications, or waits until gratification becomes possible. But when a craving is not satisfied, there are intense emotional reactions of anger, rage, sulking, withdrawal, sullen resentment, or action aimed at getting that which is desired without regard to the consequences.

Third, craving implies an abnormal limitation in the modifiability of the desire (e.g., giving it up, lessening its intensity, accepting a substitute) as a result of experiences which emphasize the costs or the consequences of the satisfaction sought.

The development of craving for opiate drugs is an extremely important element in the addiction process. Addicts themselves distinguish varying degrees of craving for opiates. The intensity of craving is only partly related to the history of dependence on opiates. There are addicts who experience craving, in the defined sense, after very little experience with opiates, though in general the intensity of the craving is related to the duration of and the quantity of experience with opiates. We know that craving is not merely a consequence of the ability of the opiate to relieve organic distress. Postoperative and posttraumatic patients rarely become addicted to opiates. Alcoholics, whose general personality structure is remarkably similar to those of opiate addicts,[7] readily become addicted to opiates,[8] whether they receive opiates in the medical treatment of their alcoholism or illicitly. We know that the use of opiates is a necessary but not a sufficient condition of the development of craving. There are individuals who use heroin for the acute intoxication experience, for the alleviation of organic discomfort, or for the relief of anxiety without the development of craving. We know that craving is not inherent in the reactions to the opiate drugs.

It is extremely difficult to measure craving. We could attempt to measure the sacrifices an addict would accept to pay for a dose of opiates at a particular point in the history of his addiction (or in a particular cycle of addiction). However, such a measure would entail a rational, consistent weighing of price against commodity value (a phenomenon which occurs rarely enough in the purchase of socially approved commodities, e.g., automobiles); that is, it would assume the very kinds of ego activity which are foreign to craving. Complicating the issue, craving is not a constant in the individual. We have often noted sudden fluctuations in the extent of craving, either increasing or decreasing. Craving is not an isolated or automatic psychophysiological process. Nor is it highly correlated with degree of physiological dependence; indeed, it can occur in the truly addicted individual even when he has been completely relieved of physiological dependence on the drug. As the case histories we have cited indicate, the urge for opiate use occurs in complex interpersonal contexts, although they are often difficult to elucidate. Addicts have a considerable defensive stake in maintaining the anonymity and impersonality of their motivations, just as do persons with neurotic character problems who prefer to interpret their behavior as the most reasonable or only possible reactions to their circumstances or, as may be more fashionable today, in terms of psychogenetically formulated rationalizations.

Further complicating the issue is the distinction we have already drawn between craving and involvement. That is, some people find rewards in the use of narcotics, for the sake of which they suffer serious penalties, but which have nothing to do with the psychophysiological effects of the drug. Involvement with the drug and the drug-using subculture gives

---

[7] Donald L. Gerard, "Intoxication and Addiction," *op. cit.*

[8] Michael J. Pescor, "A Statistical Analysis of the Clinical Records of Hospitalized Drug Addicts," *U. S. Public Health Report Supplement* No. 143 (1943).

them a sense of a personal identity, a place in society, a commitment, personal associations based on a seemingly common purpose, a feeling of belonging to an in-group, a vocation and an avocation, and a means of filling the void in an otherwise empty life. Such people, too, may feel that they crave the drug; but this is not craving in the sense in which we are using the term. Craving is not a response to emptiness, but a characteristic mode of coping with even minor stresses of anxiety, frustration, and pain by an intense desire to revert to an intrauterine-like state of apparent self-sufficiency—a state that the drug can induce. In a sense, it is the direct opposite of involvement, although both craving and involvement may be found in the same individual. Involvement with narcotics is an expression of a need for a sense of being alive; craving is an expression of a need to withdraw from any semblance of active life.

Why do addicts develop a craving for opiate drugs? We have no final answer to this question. First, craving is conditional on valued personal experiences with the drugs. No one craves an experience that is wholly distasteful. The positive evaluation of the intoxication experience depends on the psychophysiological reactions to the drug; the situation in which the drug is used, which influences the evaluation of the intoxication experience; and the extent of experience with the drug as a source of satisfaction and as a means for the resolution of tension and distress.

Second, craving is an expression of the preferred modes of gratification adopted by the individual and, as such, is dependent on the individual's attitudes toward objects or sources of satisfaction independently of and preceding experience with opiate drugs. Whether an individual can or is likely to develop craving depends on the degree to which craving fits into his preferred modes of gratification and on the readiness with which (and the circumstances under which) he relapses into preference for modes of gratification into which craving fits. These are matters which are best viewed in the context of the psychosexual development of the individual.

We regard the strength of an individual's craving for opiates as a resultant of two groups of forces—those which have to do with personal experiences in relation to opiate drugs and those which have to do with the shaping of the individual's preferred modes of gratification. Consequently, we would expect to, and do, observe marked individual differences in the strength of craving. We would not expect these differences to be simple, nor would we expect simple relationships between intensity of craving and any one factor—the duration of opiate use, for instance. We would expect to observe individuals who sustain themselves for prolonged periods of their lives with small doses of opiates and others whose entire lives rapidly become dedicated to the intake of large quantities of these drugs.

The Psychophysiological Reaction to Opiate Drugs

Opiate intoxication is *not* an inherently delightful state;[9] neither, for that matter, is any kind or degree of intoxication. The pleasures of alcoholic beverages must be learned; they are learned in a context of beliefs and usages which support, modify, and interpret the individual's psychopharmacological reactions. Becker's study of marijuana use[10] documents the role of other users in support, modification, and interpretation of the effects of marijuana as a force in marijuana use in our culture. But it does not follow that the psychopharmacological effects of the opiates or their enjoyment are *merely* conditional on beliefs and usages. Indeed, it has been found that a minority of naïve subjects who are given opiates experimentally regard the effects as pleasant or desirable and that, by and large, this minority consists of the psychologically most disturbed of the subjects. Similarly, we believe that the prospective adolescent addict is to be found among the seriously disturbed adolescent population in those areas where drug use is endemic and among the even more seriously disturbed in those areas where it is not endemic, and we have found that, unlike naïve experimental subjects, the majority of prospective addicts enjoyed the effect of opiates from the beginning. This supports the hypothesis that psychological deviancy is a conditioning phenomenon for the liking of opiates. However, this need not be necessarily or entirely so.

There are a few apparently normal persons we have known who did enjoy their first experiences with experimental doses of opiates without apparent serious psychiatric illness. These, however, have not been naïve subjects; they knew that they were going to receive morphine, and they expected that the morphine would in some way influence their mood or ideational state. One colleague compared the experience with a day in a Turkish bath; he liked it, but had no inclination to repeat the experience. In short, it is possible that a "normal" subject would regard his first opiate intoxication as pleasant, but it is unlikely that he would begin to crave on the basis of this experience. It should also be remem-

---

[9] L. Lasagna, J. M. von Felsinger, and H. K. Beecher. "Drug-induced Mood Changes in Man," *Journal of the American Medical Association*, 157, (1955), 1006, 1113.

[10] H. S. Becker, "Becoming a Marijuana User," *American Journal of Sociology*, 59 (1953), 235-242.

bered that a substantial minority of regular users initially found the effects unpleasant. On the assumption that some of these were truly addicted, it follows that unpleasant effects on first experience are not incompatible with later addictive use.

What is enticing about the effects of opiates for those disturbed persons who do become addicts? Or, to put it differently, what are the relevant effects of the opiates on the emotional lives of these persons?

A major effect of opiates is that they reduce the awareness of sources of distress and increase the sense of detachment from or otherwise diminish the unpleasantness of the experience that would be associated with distress in less clouded states of consciousness. The pain threshold (i.e., the intensity of stimulation needed to produce pain), for example, is raised and the anxiety associated with pain is diminished so that normally painful stimulation becomes tolerable. Drive—hunger and sexual tension, for instance—is also reduced, so that there is relief from the discomforts of drive states which are blocked from normal channels of relief and from anxiety that may be associated with the unreduced drives. Opiates thus, in one way or another, give relief from distress. It is almost axiomatic that this relief-giving psychopharmacological property of opiates is a major factor in the development of craving. Conversely, a chronic need for such relief—whether because of an abnormally frequent recurrence of distress or because of an inability to tolerate relatively minor distress or to cope with sources of distress in more adaptive ways—is a necessary condition of the development of craving. Parenthetically, this is also a factor in the behavior of addicts who postpone their dose of opiates until they begin to have withdrawal symptoms; they do this to maximize the experience of relief.

Since the intensity of distress is a determinant of the quantity of relief (as impact is determined by the height from which an object falls), we would expect the degree of positive evaluation of opiate intoxication to be highly correlated with the initial level of distress. This is supported by the previously cited work of Lasagna et al. However, detailed research is still to be done. Moreover, although it is certain that opiates can influence anxiety and other distressing states, there may be important constitutional differences in responsiveness to these drugs and in the potential for relief from distress which they might afford.

There are psychopharmacological phenomena associated with intoxication with opiates apart from the "relief experience." To what extent these enter into the positive evaluation of the drug and the development of craving, it is difficult to say. For example, there is a feeling of "impact" in the stomach following intravenous injection of morphine or heroin which is characterized in addicts' terminology as "a bang." The addict may also enjoy sensations of bodily warmth, of tingling like "pins and needles," and pleasant eroticized scratching and itching. Some addicts talk of these visceral experiences as an aesthete or a gourmet talks of the objects of his special interest. However, since these visceral experiences occur at the threshold of the opiate intoxication experience and since they are most intense and evident in one particular means of opiate intoxication, particularly with the intravenous use of opiate drugs, we believe that they are of secondary importance in the development of craving.

Though it is partly feasible to discuss the psychopharmacological reaction to opiates apart from the situation in which they are used, in the reality of the addiction process this never occurs. In fact, at least in our society and in the social context in which we have studied addiction among adolescents, the life situation plays an important role in the positive evaluation of the intoxication experience.

Situation and the Positive Evaluation of Opiate Intoxication

Many adolescent addicts we have studied were able to tell us quite explicitly that they began their opiate use in a life situation rife with anxiety, tension, or disappointment and asserted that they experienced relief from these states in their initial intoxication. We know that the condition we have described for the development of craving—a high level of distress—is a common, probably a regular, phenomenon in the early addiction history of adolescent addicts. Since there are marked difficulties of communication with adolescent addicts, we do not learn easily about the level of emotional distress as a factor in the early establishment of a positive evaluation of the intoxication experience.

The situation is seemingly complicated by the fact that the relief experience may not occur in their initial opiate intoxication. The dosage may be inappropriate, e.g., too small to effect relief or so far above the individual's tolerance level that the appreciation of the distress-relief phenomenon may be blunted by the quick onset of coma or extreme somnolence. Moreover, these emotional states may not be consciously perceived or recognized. The adolescent addict may only recall or recognize, in the course of a therapeutic investigation, that he was highly perturbed by aspects of his life situation at the time when he began to use opiates. Then, too, the situation at the initial use of opiates need not be exceptionally anxious, tense, or depressive, even though, in fact, the prevalent level of malfunction of the novice is higher than of his peers who do not use opiates. Indeed, as has already been indicated, there may be long periods of opiate use without the development of craving.

Many cases can be cited of individuals who liked the effect of opiates from the beginning, but did not develop craving until a psychosexual crisis occurred. With the need for relief from anxiety verging on panic, their craving began.

Rado has hypothesized that a "tense depression" was the unique or special emotional state which was relieved by opiate intoxication.[11] In our experience, this has not been so; i.e., it is not the unique or particular emotional state in the prelude to addiction. Acute anxiety, bewilderment, incipient panic, increasing despair, and unhappiness born of a sequence of failures and disappointments are other common emotional states preceding addiction in the adolescent addicts we studied. There is another type of emotional state in the *Anlage* of addiction which is important, not so much for its frequency as for its bearing on the life situation; this is a state of longing, a distressing condition of unfilfillment pervasive of all the experience which is alleviated by opiate intoxication and may be conducive to craving.

There are some indications in the literature that something like craving may develop passively in experimental animals.[12] However, this obscures rather than clarifies the issue. Craving, as clinically observed, unquestionably develops in persons who liked and wanted opiates prior to any indications of pharmacological dependence on these drugs; craving much more typically leads to the pattern of use which establishes dependence than vice versa.

There are two other phenomena in the total situation of the person who becomes an addict which influence the positive evaluation of opiate intoxication. One is the fact that the current disturbed emotional state we have discussed above is an oustanding feature in a total situation which is grossly unsatisfactory. The "preaddict," if we may use this term, has been notoriously unsuccessful in his educational, occupational, sexual, or familial life. For those few exceptions who were able to manage without conspicuous failures in one or several of these areas, there are quite evident anxieties or psychiatric symptoms which contaminated, blunted, or negated whatever else was satisfactory in their lives. Since, by and large, they have not found satisfaction or achievement elsewhere in their lives, the opiate intoxication experience stands out with particular clarity and vividness; with opiate intoxication, they felt good as they had not felt good before and as they had not felt good with other sources of intoxication, e.g., marijuana or alcohol.

---

[11] S. Rado, "Psychoanalysis of Pharmacothymia," *Psychoanalytic Quarterly*, 21 (1933), 1-23.

[12] S. D. S. Spragg, "Morphine Addiction in Chimpanzees," *Comparative Psychology Monograph*, 15 (1940).

For a person who is not accustomed to the wine of success, any good feeling he creates for himself not only makes him feel good about the experience itself, but also makes him feel better about himself; in short, he has an experience of increased self-esteem or can prevent a decline in self-esteem. This is, of course, not due to the opiate itself; enhanced self-esteem is not observed in medical or surgical practice after the relief of pain by morphine. In part, it results from the achievement of a status and the provision of an alibi for failure. In addicts with strong craving, however, it is in large measure a psychic consequence of achieving a state of relaxation and relief from tension or distress through one's own activities, not through a physician's recommendation or prescription, but through an esoteric, illegal, and dangerous nostrum. We can observe an analogous phenomenon in people who win the Irish Sweepstakes; win on dice, cards, horses, or numbers; or even in persons who park in no-parking zones without getting a traffic ticket. They feel that their luck is running good; they feel important, worthwhile, and interesting; they feel a sense of pride and accomplishment. Such an illusory achievement is an important psychic phenomenon, particularly important when it stands out by contrast with the remainder of a person's life.

There is a telling Yiddish anecdote about two cockroaches who were swept out of a garbage heap in a barn. One fell onto a pile of horse manure; the other fell onto the bare ground. The one who fell in the horse manure became fat and glossy. The one who fell on the bare ground became thin and bedraggled. One day they met in the barnyard. The thin one was astonished by the appearance of his old companion and asked him, "Yankel, what is this? You are so fat and wealthy, and I am so skinny and poor." "My good fellow," Yankel replied, "my fortune is the inevitable consequence of superior industriousness, intelligently applied." The moral is that good fortune can be experienced as (belated) recognition of one's intrinsic worth. When self-esteem is meager, any satisfying experience may be a source of enhanced self-esteem, as well as of pleasure, and the means through which this experience is attained is cherished.

The other factor which conditions the positive evaluation of the opiate intoxication experience is of a social-psychological nature; it may be characterized as "looking for kicks." This phenomenon is related to widespread attitudes among contemporary adolescents, and particularly among those belonging to deprived urban groups. It is also related to the readiness for craving which we will discuss later in this chapter.

The search for kicks is a polar extreme of a valuable human and particularly adolescent phenomenon, that is, the search for new experience. Normally, the search for new experience leads to the broadening of one's intellectual and sensory horizons and to the pleasures of working at challenging and difficult situations and tasks which, despite anxiety and strain, are capped with some degree of mastery or even with non-disgraceful failure. In what strike us as the happiest lives, this is a never-ending process. In other instances, the outcome is not so fortunate. At one extreme, there is a total blunting of this complex drive; these are persons who live a life of stultifying routine. Indeed, some clever adolescents regard adult life as dull and unperceptive because they recognize that the tempo and intensity of this drive is lowered by increasing responsibilities. The search for kicks is, on the surface, at the other pole. It expresses a conscious search for new experience of a special kind; what is sought is fun, excitement, novelty, and new sensations, as though the experience of novelty per se were substituted for the confrontation and mastery of ever-new and challenging situations. The never-ending search for the essentially passive experience of novelty masquerades as a zest for living.

Any novel experience, legal or not, is regarded as worth trying, as an expression of joy, pride, and pleasure in living, provided that the venture is not fraught with the peril of evoking contempt or disgrace in the peer subculture. Though the opiate intoxication experience may be compared to other intoxications or to other experiences of release and relaxation, it is *sui generis*. The peculiar sequence of bodily sensations, of vascular and glandular responses, is undoubtedly a new experience, as is the partial disturbance of consciousness which accompanies this experience. In the argot of addicts: "Man, it's good, it's cool, it's gone." It is commendable as a kick in terms of the preaddict's values. Though we do not believe that the value of novelty per se is responsible for an inclination toward addictive use or toward craving, this is another force in the initial positive evaluation of the opiate's intoxication experience which encourage initial use and facilitates return to an experience which offered kicks.

There is a painful contrast between the theory of kicks and its manifestations in the lives of those adolescents who become addicts. In fact, looking for kicks is not a happy state of affairs or any kind of expression of joy in living. The kicks they seek are inseparably linked with trouble from the onset. Their kicks are usually highly mannered, group-oriented, and stereotyped. By and large, the new experiences they seek are limited to new ways of being intoxicated and new ways of affirming individuality through mannerisms of dress, hair style, speech, and gesture. Some have got their earlier kicks through gang membership and fighting; others, through the use of alcohol. Kicks, in effect, is a pleasure orientation by youngsters with an extraordinary lack of the capacity to feel happy; what they probably mean by the search for kicks is that they wish they could be happy and that they will try anything to achieve it. With opiates, they probably do not get what the word kicks seems to connote, but they do get relief, both from this complex drive and from other more simple drives, e.g., pain, sex, and hunger.

Dependence

"Dependence" means simply and literally that the addict comes to require, need, or lean on opiates for the maintenance of his normal or comfortable physiological functioning. We say that the addict becomes dependent on opiates in consequence of the regular use of these substances. The rate at which such dependence develops varies with the type of drugs and the quantity taken. For instance, he can become dependent on morphine through using the same small quantity once daily for a week. In order to become dependent on heroin in the dosages that are typically ingested, it must be taken at intervals closer to twelve hours than to twenty-four. One would, however, expect individual variability in this respect.

Dependence is not a conscious process, though its corollary, the acute abstinence syndrome, may be consciously experienced. When opiate drugs are taken with sufficient regularity, they insinuate themselves into the physiological processes (enzyme systems) of the central nervous system so that they become essential elements of its milieu. When this regular intake of opiate drugs is abruptly discontinued, a characteristic disturbance occurs; the intensity of this disturbance is a function of the duration of the regular use and the amount of drugs which are regularly ingested. Dependence is *not* related to psychological needs or motives; decerebrate dogs and newborn infants of addicted mothers can have an acute abstinence syndrome. Dependence is a biological process which entails the maintenance of a certain level of opiate drugs to maintain apparently normal bodily function, and, in this sense, the biological dependence on the opiates can be a force in the addiction process; without the opiate, the person indeed becomes physically ill.

The abstinence syndrome, however, unlike the fact of dependence, is much influenced and modified by psychosocial factors. It is true, in the novice addict, that the intensity of this self-limiting illness (nausea, goose flesh, restlessness, etc.) is far from unbearable. The intensity of these symptoms hardly justifies the illicit use of opiates to quell the symptoms, particularly since each evasion of the acute abstinence syndrome intensifies the ultimate experience of the abstinence syndrome. To the addict and the individual in the process of becoming an addict, however, even his relatively minor distress is intolerable; his inability to act in terms of long-range goals precludes consideration of the inevitable consequences of permitting the degree of dependence to build up.

In the case of the experienced addict, dependent on four or more injections of heroin a day to prevent the abstinence syndrome, abrupt withdrawal is an unquestionably severe physiological disturbance; he develops chills and fever, lacrimation, perspiration, vomiting, smooth and striated muscle cramps, diarrhea, tachycardia, insomnia, or restlessness. Despite this fact, even in an addict with signs of severe physiological disturbance at the withdrawal of opiates, the amount of distress is conditional on the setting in which the distress is experienced. Alone, it can be an almost unbearable experience. In a hospital ward, remarkably little medication often stills the distress associated with quite severe physiological disturbance, e.g., painful cramps and diarrhea. Conversely, patients with minor overt symptoms may be very demanding of medication. In this regard, Pfeffer has described the beneficial influence of group therapeutic interaction on a withdrawal ward.[13] Though dependence can be interpreted as a biological phenomenon, the patient's attitude toward the manifestations of dependence can only be understood psychosocially.

Lindesmith has placed considerable emphasis on this as the basic phenomenon in opiate addiction.[14] He has presented case material in support of the thesis that accepting the fact that one is "hooked" and that one must continue to rely on opiates in order to ensure freedom from withdrawal symptoms is central to identifying oneself as an addict. In part, he is correct; among adolescent addicts, the self-identification as addicts—i.e., as persons who require opiates for comfortable functioning—is an important phenomenon in their developing addiction, even though they may, in fact, at that time not yet be demonstrably dependent on opiates. The idea, "I need to have opiates," is certainly influenced by the phenomenon of dependence, but, indeed, is poorly correlated with the intensity of this biological phenomenon. An addict may experience some of the phenomena of withdrawal after a year of enforced abstinence as he enters a situation in which opiates may be obtained. By the same token, the diagnosis of withdrawal symptoms as evidence of true dependence is not a simple matter.

There is a minority of addicts who choose to endure withdrawal symptoms without medical help. They appear silent and sullen in the face of the severest symptoms. With persistence and interest, we can learn that

---

[13] A. Z. Pfeffer, personal communications.
[14] A. R. Lindesmith, *op. cit.*

they rationalize it as the most effective method of "kicking the habit" and, more fundamentally, that they are enacting a drama of sin and penance; they deserve to suffer for the misdeeds of their addiction, and through suffering they achieve catharsis. Generally speaking, these are the oldest and most experienced addicts, who are among the quickest to relapse after leaving a hospital, since they feel that suffering has undone their misbehavior and that they are free to sin again.

Tolerance

Tolerance is a concomitant of dependence. It occurs at a much slower rate than dependence; the body becomes dependent on a certain level of drug taken at a certain frequency much more readily than it acquires tolerance to that level. "Tolerance" refers to the fact that the body adapts—to varying degrees and at differing rates by the several organ systems of the body—to certain of the effects of the drug. The addict can, for instance, take quantities of opiates which would produce coma or death from respiratory inhibition in the nonaddict. Most germane to our discussion, tolerance is developed to the subtle emotional effects of the opiate which the addict craves. Though the addict can satisfy his need for normal bodily function without increasing his dosage, he must gradually raise his intake if he wishes to satisfy his craving. In the vernacular, he "can keep normal but can't get high." He no longer experiences a change of state. He is "tranquilized" so long as he can avoid withdrawal symptoms, but he gets no kicks, and he cannot "go on the nod," that is, he can no longer experience intensified relaxation and inwardness.

Interestingly, keeping normal even without getting high can for a short period be a valued experience for the addict who experiences craving. This depends on what is essentially a form or aspect of gratification through involvement. The addict holds off taking opiates as long as possible, so that he can experience the beginning of the abstinence syndrome; at this point, when he takes his usual or available dose, he experiences relief from a self-imposed physical distress. The rhythm of distress and relief, distress and relief again, becomes valued in itself. However, if his life situation is particularly difficult at this point in his addiction, he will not be satisfied with keeping normal; he will strive to get high again by increasing his dosage either in frequency or in quantity. Indeed, in general, when an addict reaches a point in a cycle of addiction where he cannot do more than keep normal either for economic reasons (the high cost and the poor quality of illicit drugs) or because he has become negatively adapted to the subtle emotional effects of the drugs, he usually "seeks a free period"[15]—withdrawal from the drug, acute abstinence, and at least a few weeks of detoxification—to be able to recapture the most valued experience of being high at a far lower level of dosage. Such patterns (postponement of drug-taking to enhance the effects, seeking a "free period," and discontent with dosage levels sufficient to merely ward off the abstinence syndrome), incidentally, may well provide diagnostic criteria of craving.

To review, the psychophysiological framework of opiate addiction may be generalized as follows: Insofar as psychophysiological factors play a role in addiction, the primary force in initiating and intensifying a cycle of addiction is craving. Dependence is a sustaining force, both physiologically and psychologically—relevant, but clearly secondary. Tolerance is a psychophysiological phenomenon which forces either increasing dosage or a free period, i.e., a period of abstinence to recapture certain of the satisfactions of opiate intoxication. Dependence is, of course, also relevant in the noncraving types of addiction, but is again secondary in importance to the underlying motivations in the development of the addiction. It may, however, play a major role in affecting the likelihood of getting into trouble. The development of tolerance is relatively unimportant in the involvement-without-craving type of addiction; in the noncraving, noninvolvement type, it plays a role in those searching for "kicks."

---

[15] S. Rado, *op. cit.*

6

SOCIOPATHY AS A HUMAN PROCESS: A VIEWPOINT

George E. Vaillant

Case histories of narcotic addicts who also were imprisoned for felony were selected to illustrate some underlying dynamics of Cleckley's so-called psychopath and some principles useful in their management. Often in outpatient settings, such individuals seem to be without anxiety, unable to experience depression, and without motivation for recovery; but in inpatient settings, such deficits appear illusory. Once such chronically sociopathic individuals are prevented from "running," their resemblance to individuals with severe but thoroughly "human" and comprehensible personality disorders becomes evident.

In treatment, external controls are important. It is vital both to appreciate the contagion of the psychopath's invisible anxiety and to provide such individuals with alternative defenses with which to mitigate their depression. Finally, sociopaths must be realistically, but not punitively, confronted with the consequences of their behavior.

The sociopathic character disorders are a confusing area of psychiatry. One reason for confusion is that in an outpatient setting the management

Reprinted with permission from the *Archives of General Psychiatry*, 1975, *32*, 178-183. Copyright 1975, American Medical Association.

This investigation was supported in part by the Grant Foundation, New York, and National Institute of Mental Health grants MH-10361 and MH-38798.

This report was published with permission from the *Massachusetts Journal of Mental Health*, Boston.

From the Department of Psychiatry, Harvard Medical School and Cambridge Hospital, Cambridge, Mass.

of these disorders produces therapeutic frustration. This frustration blurs our perception of important clinical realities, and the *defensive* maneuvers of the sociopath become wrongly interpreted as signs of that incurable entity, the *psychopath*. These signs include an apparent *absence of anxiety*, an apparent *lack of motivation for change*, and an apparent *inability to feel depression*.[1] This pejorative term, *psychopath*, is accurate only insofar as it describes the back of a patient fleeing therapy. If a psychiatrist sees the same patient in a prison hospital, he may doubt that such a disorder exists. For then he sees sociopaths face-to-face, and they are human. He is able to do what Edward Glover suggested 50 years ago; he can "apply to the special problems of anti-social behavior the principles established by Freud to mental function as a whole."[2]

What I am suggesting is that when the psychiatrist is protected from therapeutic frustration, when control is established and flight is not possible, the stigmata of psychopathy disappear. This report will be an effort to examine why in the eyes of most psychiatrists the outpatient sociopath may appear incorrigible, inhuman, unfeeling, guiltless, and unable to learn from experience; and yet in a prison hospital, the sociopath is fully human. I shall try to demonstrate that Cleckley's psychopath, immortalized in the *Mask of Sanity*,[3] is a mythical beast.

To illustrate that our textbook conceptions of the psychopath are illusions, I have chosen three narcotic addicts. All had extensive criminal records; all were sent against their will to the US Public Health Service Hospital at Lexington, Ky. All demonstrated an absence of anxiety, an absence of motivation to change, and an absence of overt depression. But, once immobilized, they became indistinguishable from Otto Kernberg's "borderline" patients and Elizabeth Zetzel's "primitive hysterics" that are familiar to most psychiatric teaching units. Such patients do not appear psychologically healthy, but they appear neither alien nor untreatable. Over a period of time, seemingly organic and immutable deficits emerge as dynamic and understandable defense mechanisms.

ABSENCE OF ANXIETY

An apparent absence of anxiety is a clinical hallmark that sets the *real* sociopath apart from most psychiatric outpatients. One reason that sociopaths conceal anxiety is that *their parents often experienced great difficulty tolerating tension in others.* They often used inappropriate means to relieve or to obscure anxiety in their children. The sociopath may confide to the psychiatrist that he had a "normal" family but that he was a "bad seed." He maintains that his parents (unlike the wicked fairy-tale stepparents who allegedly bring up neurotics) gave him "everything" he wanted. He often blames society for his behavior, but not his parents. His parents willingly corroborate the story. In the *Mask of Sanity*, Cleckley provides us with innumerable examples of wicked children and noble parents.[3] The psychopath seems the very antithesis of the fairy-tale hero.

An unsolicited letter from a woman whom I had never seen provided a vivid illustration of what may lie beneath parental innocence:

> Dear Sir: My son is a dope addict and because he no longer knows the truth himself, I don't know how long it has lasted. I do know that I cannot continue the way I've been doing; I have no resources left. . . . I have about 30 pawn tickets on which I cannot even pay the interest. Every time I renew things, he'd hock them again. He had been arrested a total of five times, dismissed from all cases. The lawyers and the bail cost me about $1,500. [*In short, she paid $1,500 to shield him from the normal consequences of his behavior.*] When he was working he made $60 a week. He was supposed to pay me $12 a week but I seldom got it. . . . Now he has started selling off my books, and, as I've already weeded these down to bare essentials in the interest of space, this makes me very nervous [*not angry but nervous*]. One example of how dissipated this is he says he sold his camera for $5. His camera was a Brownie and complete with case was a $10.50 Christmas gift from me. [*How difficult it was for her to decide to whom the camera really belonged!*]
>
> He is inarticulate and quarrels quickly and finds fault. He writes like a child and misspells words. He's losing his hair in front and has lost a tooth on the upper right. He is thin. I've lost my social career also. I have not had my hair fixed for a year—doing it myself. I have not bought any new clothes, and the getups I wear to school are a disgrace . . . no one even wants to walk to the door with me. I know I am an 'indulgent' mother, but what can I do? I don't want to let him go. I see these jungle addicts in the house, and I know that I am the buffer which is keeping him from looking like them.
>
> One example of how bad off I am is that every month I have one or two bounced checks, and the bank charges me $4 because of my poor record . . . what I am trying to say is that I have $288, that is all I have left until September 15 when we go back to school. [*The parents of sociopaths seem more in need of parental care than their children.*] Nevertheless, in one way or another, my son gets the money from me. . . . Last week he promised if I would give him $15 on Tuesday and Wednesday, he would go to the hospital on Thursday. I got up at 5:30 a.m. on Thursday and Friday, but he didn't want to go; and as we had such a terrible heat spell, I can't blame him. At night, I lock my door and barred

the door and jammed the lamp against it besides. Occasionally, he frightens me. [*Although reluctant to let her son experience anxiety, she subtly amplifies her own secret fears.*] Other times he seems so young and helpless. He is 22 and he is beautiful. Please tell me what to do.

The sociopath is supposed to be unable to postpone gratification; but in a family matrix intolerant of anxiety, postponement of gratification is difficult to learn. The letter demonstrates that it is never clear who is dependent on whom and who needs the help. The son's delinquency frightens his mother, but rather than oppose it, she conceals it. When she calls for help, she writes to a physician whom she has never seen and who is 700 miles away.

As the sociopath matures, he is not without anxiety; but it remains invisible to many observers—including judges and psychiatrists. Why? Neither the explanation that he cannot feel it nor the more sophisticated explanation that his anxiety is defended against by the ego mechanism of acting out is entirely satisfactory.

There are two other reasons that his anxiety is invisible. First, there are times that the sociopath makes his anxiety very clear to us; but at such times, our empathic response may blind us to it. By this I mean that the sociopath elicits from physicians and social workers the same response that he elicited from his parents. We behave as if to ask him to bear his anxiety would be too cruel, too disruptive, too sadistic, too authoritarian. Instead, we, too, respond by distorting the very reality that would help him to learn that anxiety is acceptable—both to himself and to others. Too seldom therapists are able to say to sociopaths, "I am sorry that you are feeling bad, but I think that you can manage the feeling."

Second, we are often blind to the sociopath's anxiety because we cannot bear it or because the sociopath has managed to transfer his anxiety to us. The resulting staff apprehension then serves to make the patient unreachable, unfeeling, incurable, and unaware that the staff anxiety that surrounds him was originally his own. (The situation is analogous to that of the well-defended Kraepelinian psychiatrist; he calls the acute schizophrenic's affect "flat" when, in fact, the affect is one of stark terror.) Consider the following example of concealed anxiety in a sociopath:

Case 1.—I was informed by several upset senior staff members that an unmanageable and notorious "psychopath" had returned to the US Public Health Service Hospital at Lexington, Ky, for the tenth time. He was reported to be on the admission ward out of control and holding the security staff at bay with a broom handle. It was with conscious fear that I learned that this unseen man was to be transferred to the psychiatric unit where I worked. I was anxious.

Once transfer was affected, I realized my fears were without substance. Confined to the isolation room and stripped to his shorts, he countered my anxiety with tranquility and charm. With injured innocence, he asked, "How can I regain my self-respect if I'm not given some clothes and let out of seclusion?" His behavior was beyond reproach; his privileges were soon returned, and so he left the unit.

A year later he returned. After having been refused medication, he had cut his wrists. It was at this point that I reviewed his chart, started to talk to him, and for the first time saw him in human dimensions. From suburban New York, he was the only child of middle-class, and apparently long-suffering parents. Only during his *fifth* admission to Lexington was it learned that his mother was secretly addicted to meperidine hydrochloride (Demerol) and that his father was an alcoholic. But his social history is not what is most pertinent. Rather more remarkable was the covert staff anxiety that was disclosed by his hospital record during this, his *tenth* admission. The Lexington medical staff was highly sophisticated to inappropriate demands for medication; but in one year, this known *psychopath* received the following results from laboratory procedures: six urinalyses—all normal; two urine cultures—no growth; ten different blood chemistry evaluations—all normal; an electrocardiogram; three roentgenograms of the chest and one of the skull; two gallbladder examinations; two gastrointestinal series; a barium enema; and a spinal tap—all of which were normal. At no time had he been organically ill.

Although he had never had a fever or evidence of an infection, he received penicillin. Although the patient was in a hospital that virtually never gave narcotics, even to patients with painful illness, he had received phenobarbital, codeine, pentobarbital (Nembutal), methadone hydrochloride, and chloral hydrate—all after his withdrawal period was completed. He also received 34 other medicines including meprobamate, imipramine hydrochloride, chlorpromazine, methamphetamine hydrochloride, chlordiazepoxide hydrochloride, and hydroxyzine hydrochloride.

There is little question that the staff response to this patient was unique. Nevertheless, he serves as an example of the difficulty that even sophisticated staff had in recognizing his anxiety; tolerating it or believing that he should tolerate it. The irrational therapeutic response he evoked had not become conscious in anyone's mind and, during the year, had been diffused among a large number of people.

Significantly, this tenth admission was his first imprisonment; it was the first time he ever had been made to stay in one place. Shortly after his second visit to the psychiatric unit, he built up a relationship in psychotherapy with one of the staff. Through this relationship, he learned to tell the physician on night duty, "I don't want any medicine—I just want to talk." (Admittedly, nonsociopathic patients can often learn to do this within a few days of hospitalization.) Once this lesson was learned, once his anxiety was conscious, he required—and received—no additional drugs. He caused the staff less anxiety; but he was able to show them more of his own. Previously, the patient had been unable to postpone gratification, but this was partly because nobody really tolerated his distress when he did so.

This man not only defended against anxiety with drug-seeking behavior, but he also manifested clear conversion symptoms. Psychiatrists, however, conceive of sociopathy and hysteria as two different syndromes and fail to recognize conversion in the sociopath. The hysteric is a woman; she is not out of control, and is immensely human. We see her conversion symptoms as a defensive process, and we perceive her distress behind these defenses. We believe her to be treatable. In contrast, the sociopath is usually a man and his physicians perceive him to be out of control. His defenses are invisible and his conversion symptoms are seen as conscious, hostile manipulation rather than unconscious efforts to conceal anxiety. Unfortunately, unrecognized defenses can seem to psychiatrists like deliberate offense; the psychiatrists defend themselves. Human beings are labeled "psychopaths."

LACK OF MOTIVATION

Sociopaths have a second hallmark that makes them appear inhuman: supposedly, they lack motivation for change. Sociopaths are supposed not to learn from experience. Often psychiatrists who have successfully banished the pejorative terms *psychopath* and *sociopath* from their vocabularies replace the terms with "passive-dependent" or "inadequate personality." In such cases, the psychiatrist perceives the distress but shrinks from the seemingly overwhelming oral, passive, and receptive qualities of these individuals. His own helplessness may be projected onto the patient. At this juncture, it is well to recall two things. First, adolescents sometimes seem unable to learn from experience, yet this is a temporary artifact of one stage of development. Second, if individuals respond to an unconscious fantasy or impulse, this is different from being unable to learn. Sociopaths are more adolescent than ineducable.

Case 2.—A 30-year-old black addict prisoner received the admission diagnosis of passive-dependent character disorder; his behavior over the preceding four years was consistent with the diagnosis. He had grown up in New Orleans. His father, a pullman porter, had always made an adequate living, but he was an extremely ineffectual man. At 8 years, the patient was a better carpenter than his father. In order that his father might resemble the fathers of his friends, he used to daydream that his father would spank him. His mother, the family disciplinarian, was also the patient's chief competitor in arguments and power struggles. But he could remember his mother forbidding him to do only one thing—to play the trumpet. When he reached adolescence, his uncle gave him a trumpet; he took it up with a vengeance. He experimented briefly with meperidine, but never became addicted.

He took five years of college training in music and band teaching. He also became a successful jazz musician. However, when he reached the point where he was performing well-applauded trumpet solos, he abruptly gave up the instrument. There was no reason except, "I was not as good as other people thought I was." For the same reason, he turned down a well-paying job with the Chicago Department of Education.

Two years after giving up the trumpet, he had an affair with a "flashy woman." After she had canceled a date, the patient, unaware of any resentment, developed an overwhelming, inexplicable urge to take meperidine. He rapidly became addicted and four years later came to Lexington as a prisoner. He had no insight into his problems and wanted psychotherapy to relieve his functional gastric bloating and, magically, to cure his addiction.

Many months later he began to speak about his love of the trumpet and said that he gave it up because, "I was afraid of becoming addicted to it. I was afraid that I would only be able to play the trumpet and be interested in nothing else." His fantasies about drugs became more explicit. He felt that marihuana was harmful. Although marihuana improved his trumpet playing, it made him think that he was too powerful. It might lead him to become "wild" and to drive his car too fast. In contrast, he felt that heroin was helpful to society and should be legalized. Heroin just made him drowsy and obtunded his sexual drive. When he got angry now, he got severe "ulcer" pains; these pains could be relieved with heroin. Only at the end of treatment was he able to talk tentatively about the anger he felt toward

whites—especially policemen. [Ten years before he had be-
longed to CORE, but after he gave up the trumpet, he had also
lost his interest in civil rights.] Any acknowledgment of negative
transference toward me or resentment of his mother was assiduously avoided.

Throughout, it was difficult to mobilize this man's motivation for treatment. Had he not been in prison, he would never have kept his appointments. Yet after a year of psychotherapy, it was clear that beneath
his "passive-dependent" camouflage there lurked a fairly competent individual who went to extraordinary pains lest some of his competence
become visible to others. It is not that sociopaths do not feel; they feel,
but fear lest they feel too much. For them recovery becomes synonymous
with unconsciously forbidden sexual and aggressive competence. It is
dangerous at 8 years to be a better carpenter than your father.

Case 3.—Another Lexington patient had wished two years
before her imprisonment to put her illegitimate baby up for
adoption. Instead, her mother insisted on keeping it. The patient
remembered watching in silent rage while her mother trium-
phantly passed her daughter's baby off to the mother's friends
as her own. A year later, the patient married a drug addict.
During this period she wrested her child away from her mother
and brought the child to live with her. The mother was furious
and the patient felt extremely guilty at depriving her mother of
the child. At this point she became addicted. When she was
imprisoned, her mother regained control of the child.
    Initially, the patient's anxiety over resumption of this struggle
once she left prison was invisible. Instead, the patient tried to
avoid help and preferred to deny herself parole than to return
to this conflict. The details of her dilemma and the fact that at
age 10 years her father had repeatedly sexually molested her
came out only after months in therapy that she, too, would have
fled had she not been in prison. In the setting of a prison hospital,
however, this woman's lack of interest in "getting well" became
dynamically understandable.

Perhaps the following vignette sums up the point of this section. Because the above patient deprecated her low self-image still further whenever her own strengths became evident, I asked her if she remembered
how the ugly duckling story had ended. Without hesitating, the patient
recounted the story as follows: The ugly duckling had been all black;
the other ducks went off and left the ugly duckling all alone—end of
story.

THE INABILITY TO EXPERIENCE DEPRESSION

The third hallmark of the sociopath is his apprent inability to experience depression and his inability to acknowledge that others matter to him. But it may be as preposterous to ignore depression in the sociopath who vehemently denies its existence, as it would be to ignore sexuality in the hysteric who feigns lack of interest in the subject.

Case 4.—A 25-year-old prostitute was sentenced to Lexington for five years for drug peddling. She was the daughter of a strict, middle-class, Christian Scientist family. Since age 16 years, the patient had been incorrigibly delinquent, and at first she seemed the very model of the classical psychopath.

Only after a year of imprisonment at Lexington and after many weeks of psychotherapy was depression more than an intellectual concept to this woman. Only gradually were another set of facts obtained. When the patient was an infant, her mother, unable to accept the responsibility of parenthood, had delegated her daughter's care to others. Like Arthur Miller's fatherless Willy Loman, the patient grew up feeling "kind of temporary" about herself. One day she finally protested to me, "You inject sadness into me." Until that time she had hidden behind a private rose-colored version of Christian Science or behind angry, child-like dissatisfactions that lifted too rapidly to resemble clinical depression.

After several months of therapy, and following a rather friendly hour the time before, she began to speak about her fears of intimacy; then, feeling anxious, she drew into herself and said, "I guess I am destined to be lonely." Two months later, on an occasion when she was denying that she felt any warmth or intimacy toward me, she spoke of herself as an IBM machine. She declared that I was seeing her only because "You were assigned to me." I wondered about her reluctance to consider the alternative formulation that she was human and that I might have chosen to work with her. She answered, "You are confusing and upsetting me. If you go on, I will stop therapy." During the next hour she was silent for the entire hour except to ask who solved the riddle of the sphinx; then, she described the sphinx as "a woman who ate everyone who was wrong." When I asked, "Do you mean that you're afraid of devouring people that you care about?" the patient retorted, "An astute observation, but what can you do about it?" During the next hour she spoke of getting close to her family; "I don't believe other people have feelings or emotions. When I see that they do, I push them away." On one occasion she became upset at a compliment and said, "The danger of intimacy with people is that people will depend on you; and, then, you may hurt them and let them down. . . . It is not nice to punish those who love you."

She handled separation in the following dissociative manner. She canceled the hour before I went away on vacation. She then wrote me an exceedingly cheerful postcard that ended with, "I have put my neurosis on the shelf till you get back." When I returned, like a good sociopath, she spent two appointments demanding tranquilizing drugs and then skipped the next appointment.

Near the expiration of her sentence, she said, "Of course, I'm fond of you. You listen like a parent and you're a good teacher." She skipped the next session. When she returned, she said, "Can you give me any reason why I should continue with therapy?" When I suggested that at this point one purpose of continuing was in order to say goodbye, she declared, "I never said goodbye to anybody!" She spent the next two sessions in angry manipulation and vituperation, and canceled all future appointments. She let a year go by; then, safely distant from me by several hundred miles, began to write. For five years she continued to write me sensible, warm, and often appropriately depressed letters. She did not return to drug use.

Glover has said of sociopaths:

> In addition to his incapacity to form deep personal attachments and his penchant to cause suffering to those who are attached to him, the psychopath is essentially a non-conformist, who in his reaction to society combines hostility with a sense of grievance.[2]

But the sociopath's "incapacity" represents defensive process, not inability. Close relationships arouse anxiety in them. Terrified of their own dependency, of their very real "grievances," and of their fantasies of mutual destruction, they either flee relationships or destroy them.

As the above case history illustrates, the depression of sociopaths resembles that of bereaved children. Bowlby has suggested that mourning in childhood is characterized by a persistent and unconscious yearning to recover the lost object.[6] The persistent crime and polydrug abuse of the sociopath represents a similar quest. Bowlby tells us that in lieu of depression, bereaved children, like sociopaths, exhibit intense and presistent anger that is expressed as reproach toward various objects including the self. However, Bowlby notes that such anger, if misunderstood, seems often "pointless enough to the outsider." Finally, sociopaths, like children, often employ "secret" anodynes to make loss unreal and overt grief unnecessary. Their need for secrecy is based on the fact that "to confess to another belief that the loved object is still alive is plainly to court the danger of disillusion." These defensive maneuvers then, serve to hide the child's and the sociopath's depression from our psychiatric view. The painstaking controlled studies of the Gluecks' have established beyond reasonable doubt that the sociopath usually was a neglected (i.e., bereaved) child[7] and that for this reason, serious delinquency (unlike most psychiatric conditions) can be prospectively predicted by age 6 years.[8]

In conclusion, I would like to recapitulate certain themes that were present in the above case histories. All had lacked a benevolent, sustained relationship with the same-sexed parent. All were afraid of intimacy and of assuming responsibility for it. None could believe that others could tolerate their anxiety, and all devoutly feared responsibility for achieving success by open competition. They could neither identify with authority nor accept its criticism. Finally, their persistent, seemingly mindless delinquencies made symbolic sense if interpreted dynamically—as one might interpret misbehavior in a dream or in a child's play therapy. In short, psychopaths are neither born that way nor incapable of change. I believe that their "incomprehensible" behavior is a product of a well-defended ego and of a strict, albeit primitive, conscience.

THE EGO MECHANISMS OF SOCIOPATHY

If the ego of the psychopath is not inadequate and if his superego is not absent, what are the underlying dynamics of the *psychopath* that make him or her seem so inhuman? Certainly, they employ very different styles of defense from neurotic outpatients. The classical defenses that underlie the neuroses are as distressing to the owner and as insignificant to the observer as a run in a stocking or a stone in one's shoe (i.e., repression, isolation, reaction formation, displacement, and dissociation).[9] The defense mechanisms that underlie sociopathy seem as harmless to the owner and as unbearably gross to the observer as a strong cigar in a crowded elevator (i.e., denial through fantasy, projection, turning against the self, hypochondriasis, and acting out). Because nobody likes them, these latter defenses are less well understood. Therapists have difficulty feeling sympathetic toward delinquent, prejudiced, passive-aggressive, and hypochondriacal individuals. Except in children, we are apt to call such defenses sins, not coping behavior.

Nevertheless, before the defensive armor of the sociopath is viewed as too different from our own, consider those hopeless character disorders—adolescents. They, too, make extensive use of the sociopath's defenses. They use mood-altering drugs without moderation and see others, not themselves, as out of step. Their physical complaints are often imaginary; so are many of their most passionate loves. No other age group is so passive-aggressive or so masochistic. Yet adolescence is a self-limiting disease! Thus, it becomes possible to view the ego mechanisms that underlie drug addiction, paranoia, hypochondriasis, eccentricity, and masochism as *immature defenses*.[9] True, we are unable to cajole, psychoanalyze, or beat somebody out of adolescence. They need to grow out of it slowly—with a little help from their peers. If we can wait 15 to 20 years, it becomes possible to demonstrate that intractable delinquents and addicts also remit.[10,11]

Although we build walls (concrete or social) to protect ourselves from sociopaths, our efforts to save ourselves are in vain. The more we punish them, the less they learn. This aspect of sociopaths is maddening and defies logic. However, Bowlby might remind us that it does not do much good to beat a bereaved child.[6]

There is also a second explanatory facet to the seeming illogic of sociopathy. Can you imagine a hypochondriac, an exhibitionist, or a paranoiac existing alone on a desert island? Of course not. These seemingly immutable character traits exist only in the presence of other people. In brief, immature defenses are not always the incurable bad habits that they appear on the surface. Sometimes, they are a means of making a painful truce with people whom we can neither live with or without.

If neurotic defenses are more often the modes with which we cope with instincts, immature defenses are most often the ways we cope with people.[12] In adult life, projection, hypochondriasis, fantasy, and masochism perpetuate a subtle process that we usually acknowledge only between mother and infant and perhaps between lovers—a loathed person may suddenly cause pain within a hypochondriac's body. In prejudice the obnoxious trait of a parent, inadvertently absorbed in childhood, may be projected onto some hapless minority group. The promiscuous daydreams of a minister become mysteriously acted out by his delinquent daughter. In *The Glass Menagerie* the fragile animals of Laura's fantasy came suddenly to life—inside her mind.

Put another way, if our inner worlds include relatively constant people toward whom we have relatively unambivalent feelings, in real life, our external relationships remain relatively assured, loving, autonomous, and well-demarcated. However, the interpersonal relationships of sociopaths remain perpetually murky and entangled. In an effort to preserve an illusion of interpersonal constancy, immature defenses permit ambivalent mental representations of other people—especially of parents—to be conveniently "split" (into good and bad) or moved about, and reapportioned. Just as neurotic mechanisms (e.g., displacement, isolation, and dissociation) transpose feelings, immature mechanisms magically maneuver feelings *and* their objects.

If we fail to understand the defensive process, we take the sociopath's defenses personally and condemn them. Perhaps one reason that we often label immature defenses perverse is that, once touched, we rarely can divorce ourselves completely. One reason immature defenses are so taboo is because they are contagious. In the presence of a drug addict, liberals become prejudiced; the masochist elicits our own latent sadism, and the malingerer our passive-aggression. When baited by their adolescent children, even the most reasonable and staid parents become hopelessly involved and utterly unreasonable. And yet the process by which this all happens is obscure and, if noticed, quite mysterious to an outsider. This phenomenon does much to account for the inhumanity of man to man that is seen throughout much of our criminal justice system. But there is no culprit. Only anticipation and understanding will allow therapists to disentangle themselves from the defenses of the sociopath.

TREATMENT

One conclusion of this report is that the dynamics of the so-called *psychopath* differ little from those of Kernberg's so-called *borderline*.[4] Nevertheless, conventional psychiatric management is not the answer to effective treatment.

1. Before treatment can begin with a sociopath, the therapist must find some way of dealing with the patient's self-destructive behavior. Be it via parole, commitment to a prison hospital, or the ideological grip of Synanon, real control over behavior is a *sine qua non* of treatment. Sociopaths *are* too immature for the therapist to suggest that a given behavior is self-detrimental and then to stand by helpless when they do it. Not only do sociopaths interpret such helplessness as lack of concern, but also unchecked, self-detrimental behavior scares the therapist. Although voluntary outpatient therapy may foster autonomy, this advantage is for naught if the therapist becomes so frightened that he is defensively blind to the human qualities of his patient. Therefore, it is no accident that we find the *borderline* imprisoned by suicide precautions in psychiatric teaching hospitals and the *psychopath* repeatedly locked up in maximum security institutions.

2. Control is important not only to prevent self-destruction but also to overcome the sociopath's fears of intimacy. His wish to run from the

pain of honest human encounter and from tenderness must be frustrated. He must be immobilized long enough for him to be perceived
as human. The challenge to psychiatry, however, is to separate control
from punishment and to separate help and confrontation from social
isolation and retribution. Possible models include sustained employment
enforced through parole, halfway house residence enforced by probation, "addiction" to methadone clinics, or the kind of therapeutic community behind bars that Kiger has devised for sociopaths at the Utah
State Hospital.[13] All seem vastly preferable to jails or psychiatric hospitalization, per se. In every case the hope of freedom is preferable to the
threat of imprisonment. Sociopaths should work for liberty, not pay for
past mistakes.

3. Too vigorous intervention or protection from harm can be as bad
as too little. Sociopaths are made worse by good defense lawyers. Their
anxiety should not be controlled. But it is not always easy to remember
that acute anxiety, like untreated insomnia, is a self-limiting, non-fatal
illness. The only way that the therapist can show the sociopath that
anxiety is bearable is by bearing it *with* him and by *not* trying to alleviate
it. The therapist must recognize that his wish to control the sociopath's
anxiety (whether by psychotropic drugs or by solitary confinement), is
countertransference. In fact, the therapist's own anxiety can be openly
acknowledged to the sociopathic patient. Brought up to believe that
anxiety is too dreadful to be borne and too awful to confess, the sociopath
is reasured that someone can be anxious and yet in control.

4. Sociopaths, like children, deny their depression and repress parental neglect. The therapist must learn to put little trust in their childhood histories as initially given.

5. From the start, the therapist must accurately assess each of the
sociopath's defenses. To relabel the "sociopath" as "borderline"—as is
currently fashionable—will obscure differential diagnosis and lead to
perceiving defenses as immutable or as attacks on the therapist. No
defense, however, can be abruptly altered or abandoned without an
acceptable substitute. Successful treatment demands that the therapist
try to help the patient develop a *substitute* for each defense. For example,
addicts give up addiction bit by bit; their abstinence is achieved via a
process analogous to mourning. Countless criminals have replaced acting
out with reaction formation and projection with altruism.

6. Interpretation of defenses like projection, denial through fantasy,
masochism, or major acting out is rarely effective. Besides substitution,
confrontation is the best way to breach immature defenses.

7. Finally, one-to-one therapeutic relationships are rarely adequate to
change the sociopath. A therapist—even five times a week—is not

enough to satisfy an orphan. At the start of the recovery process, only the church, self-help residential treatment, and addicting drugs provide relief for a sociopath's pain; they all work 24 hours a day. Conventional psychotherapy is most effective in helping people who have received too much or the wrong sort of parental attention. Only group membership or caring for others, or both, can eventually provide adults with parenting that they never received.

The paths out of sociopathy are like the paths out of drug addiction[14] and adolescence. These are usually quite independent of formal therapy and are derived from peer identifications. Membership in altruistic but revolutionary movements like Black Panthers, in self-help groups like Alcoholics Anonymous and Synanon, or even marriage to a person as needy as themselves are all more useful than intensive psychotherapy. A compulsory but real job, outside of prison, offers more than vocational counseling or prison trade schools.[14] The therapeutic community at the maximum security ward of the Utah State Hospital, where the inmates hold the keys both to the outside and to the seclusion rooms,[13] offers more than programs that try to transform *psychopaths* into *patients*.

Why? Sociopaths know only too well that they have harmed others; they can meaningfully identify only with people who feel as guilty as themselves. They can abandon their defenses against grief only in the presence of people equally bereaved. Only acceptance by peers can circumvent the sociopath's profound fear that he may be pitied. Only acceptance by "recovered" peers can restore his defective self-esteem. Finally, the psychopath needs to absorb more of other people than one person, no matter how loving, can ever provide. Sociopaths need to find groups to which they can belong with pride.

REFERENCES

1. CLECKLEY, H. M.: Psychopathic states, in Arieti S. (ed.): *American Handbook of Psychiatry*. New York, Basic Books, 1959, pp 567-588.
2. GLOVER, E.: *The Roots of Crime*. New York, International Universities Press, 1960.
3. CLECKLEY, H. M.: *Mask of Sanity*. St. Louis, C.V. Mosby Co., 1941.
4. KERNBERG, O.: The treatment of patients with borderline personality organization. *Int J Psychoanal* 49:600-619, 1968.
5. ZETZEL, E.: The so-called good hysteric, in *The Capacity for Emotional Growth*, London, Hogarth, 1970, pp 229-245.
6. BOWLBY, J.: Pathological mourning and childhood mourning. *J. Am. Psychoanal. Assoc.*, 11:500-541, 1963.
7. GLUECK, S., GLUECK E.: *Unraveling Juvenile Delinquency*. Cambridge, Mass, Harvard University Press, 1950.
8. GLUECK, S., GLUECK E.: *Toward a Typology of Juvenile Offenders*. New York, Grune & Stratton, Inc., 1970.
9. VAILLANT, G. E.: Theoretical hierarchy of adaptive ego mechanisms. *Arch. Gen. Psychiatry*, 24:107-118, 1971.

10. VAILLANT, G. E.: A 20-year follow-up of New York narcotic addicts. *Arch. Gen. Psychiatry,* 29:237-241, 1973.
11. GLUECK, S., GLUECK E.: *Criminal Careers in Retrospect,* New York, Commonwealth Fund, 1943.
12. FREUD, A.: *The Ego and the Mechanisms of Defense.* London, Hogarth Press, 1937.
13. KIGER, R. S.: Treatment of the psychopath in the therapeutic community, *Hosp. Community Psychiatry,* 18:191-196, 1967.
14. VAILLANT, G. E.: A 12-year follow-up of New York narcotic addicts: IV. Some characteristics and determinants of abstinence. *Am. J. Psychiatry,* 123:573-584, 1966.

7

PSYCHOANALYTIC CONSIDERATIONS OF THE ETIOLOGY OF COMPULSIVE DRUG USE

Leon Wurmser

Until now, there has been very little systematic exploration into the etiology of drug abuse. Glasscote et al. (1972) described the situation most aptly:

> It may be fruitless to make the effort to identify a group of universal causes of susceptibility. In any case, while there has been some interest in determining what drug users are *like*, by means of interviews and standardized tests, there has been little systematic effort to delineate and quantify causes. On the other hand, there has been much *hypothesizing* about the conditions, events, and circumstances that lead to drug abuse, most of which fall into three categories: the physical, the internal or intra-psychic, and the social and environmental (p. 19).

A study to fill at least part of the gap is envisioned here: viz., to *delineate*

Reprinted with permission from *The Journal of the American Psychoanalytic Association*, 1974, *22*, 820-843.

Presented at the 60th Annual Meeting of the American Psychoanalytic Association, Honolulu, 1973.

I should like to acknowledge the valuable suggestions I received from Drs. W. Arnold, H. Kniffin, D. Meers, N. Zinberg, and M. Gill.

in a systematic way the etiology of drug abuse on the basis of large-scale clinical experience with all types of this phenomenon.*

Inasmuch as most "drug abusers" are inaccessible to psychoanalysis proper, it is not surprising that, despite the huge upsurge over the last decade of drug abuse in general, and of intensive, compulsive drug use in particular, only a few psychoanalytic studies have appeared which could try to explore in depth the possible etiology of this illness. The contributions of Chein et al. (1964), Krystal and Raskin (1970), Wieder and Kaplan (1969), Dora Hartmann (1969), Savitt (1963), Panel (1970), Zinberg and Robertson (1972), and Khantzian et al. (1974) are notable examples. Earlier works—the essays of Rado (1926, 1933, 1963), Glover (1928, 1932), Savitt (1954), Limentani (1968), and the comments of Fenichel (1945), although still very interesting, seem outdated and barely applicable to most categories of drug abuse seen nowadays.

The question we intend to answer, then, is: What are the causes of drug abuse? This in turn raises the further question of what exactly is meant by "drug abuse." The term is so wide and imprecise, contains such a hodgepodge of clinical and social phenomena, and is so dependent on the bias of the observer, that a systematic study of its etiology would be as vast and comprehensive as an inquiry into the etiology of fever. It will therefore be necessary to define what we mean before embarking on our investigation.

SOME BASIC DISTINCTIONS AND DEFINITIONS

The usual definition of drug abuse is based simply on *sociolegal* criteria. According to Jaffe (1965), it is: "the use, usually by self-administration, of any drug in a manner that deviates from the approved medical or social patterns within a given culture" (p. 285). Jaffe narrows this broad definition by focusing on those "drugs that produce changes in mood and behavior." Similarly, Glasscote et al. (1972) apply the term drug abuse "to illegal, nonmedical use of a limited number of substances, most of them drugs, which have properties of altering the mental state in ways

---

*During the last nine years, I have seen about 40 patients in intensive, mostly psychoanalytically oriented psychotherapy, many for years and up to 400 hours; I have worked with about a dozen families of such patients, seen close to 1,000 patients (mainly narcotics addicts) in evaluations, group therapy, crisis intervention, while being clinically or administratively in charge of three drug abuse treatment programs (a program of compulsory abstinence from 1964 to 1968, a comprehensive treatment center with several modalities from 1969 to 1971, and a methadone maintenance program from 1971 to the present). For a time I had a small private practice devoted almost exclusively to this type of patient. Notes in shorthand were taken during all individual interviews and treatment sessions, and formed the essential basis for the following attempt to systematize these data.

that are considered by social norms and defined by statute to be inappropriate, undesirable, harmful, threatening, or, at a minimum, culture alien" (pp. 3-4).

Such sociolegal definitions obviously carry strong connotations of moral judgment and are based on specific ethical values. I believe a further delimitation can be made if the problem is viewed psychiatrically: drug abuse is the use of any mind-altering drug for the purpose of inner change, if it leads to any transitory or long-range interference with social, cognitive, or motor functioning or with physical health, regardless of the legal standing of the drug. Here, the judgment is based on impaired functioning and thus on an observable medical criterion, vague though it might still be.

For most purposes, however, even this definition is unsatisfactory because of its breadth. For a careful study of etiology, we had better set apart all those occasional or irregular drug users in whom the impairment is merely transitory; this latter group seems particularly heterogeneous and contingent. Our starting point is thus the discernment of two groups placed on the two extremes of a continuum. At the one end, we have the *experimenters* or casual users who represent the vast majority of participants in drug abuse (according to both definitions given above)—probably 90 percent. They present, medically and psychiatrically, very few and rare problems. Yet, much of the public's attention, the law's concerns and energies, the preventive efforts, are dedicated to these people. The experimenter takes a mind-altering drug a few times and feels he does not really need and require its effect. Out of curiosity, and just as much in order to avoid shame by not conforming with the adolescent peer group, he wants to prove that he has partaken of the initiation, that he knows what it is all about.

At the other end of the continuum, we have the *compulsive* drug abuser. He is the real problem. To him applies the statement that drug use is just a symptom of deep underlying problems. Only those relatively few experimenters proceed to compulsive drug abuse who carry the set of profound deficiencies and conflicts that we are going to explore in this study. It is the compulsive drug abuser who feels that the drug-induced state relieves him of what bothers him and gives him what he is missing, so that he feels unable to renounce the "high," regardless of dangers and threats he is usually fully cognizant of.

In the broad area between these two groups we encounter the so-called *recreational* user of drugs like alcohol or marijuana. For many recreational users the goal if merely relaxation, not intoxication; the amount of the active substance is so small that no interference with motor or mental functioning is noticeable. In many more so-called recreational users, the goal is indeed occasional or frequent intoxication. They usually claim that their temporary abdication of rational controls is an entirely free, noncompulsive activity. I have not reached any final conclusion about this group, but on the basis of my clinical experience, I would associate the first type of recreational users, the relaxers, with the experimenters, the second type, those striving to get "stoned," "high," or "down," with the compulsive users.*

COMPULSIVENESS

We turn now to this problem of "compulsive drug abuse" (cf. also Jaffe, 1965; Glasscote et al., 1972).

Of course, the question arises: how far is this compulsiveness of a physical nature? Is that not just what led to the prohibition of these drugs in the first place—that they induce inevitably or at least very often a physiologic dependence which henceforth cannot be broken?

If we carefully study, on the one side, history and treatment experience and, on the other side, the interesting observations in medically and psychiatrically induced addictions (e.g., when opiates were used to treat melancholics), we are forced to assign very little valence in the long range to this factor of physical dependence. In other words, as Hamlet said, "the readiness is all."

Those who work closely with compulsive drug users observe time and again that if their drug of predilection is taken away (or more precisely, if their drug effect of choice is removed), they sooner or later tend to substitute other symptoms. Neurotic depression and suicidal attempts, acts of violence, stealing, running away, severe attacks of anxiety, found prior to the use of drugs and sometimes accompanying the full-blown drug use, once the resorting to drugs is blocked, frequently reappear in exacerbated form and are often more destructive than drug use itself. Still more frequently, we encounter the replacement of a suddenly unavailable type of drug by a pharmacologically completely unrelated class: i.e., patients deprived of narcotics typically resort to alcohol and sedatives (especially barbiturates), which have no bearing on any physical withdrawal phenomena, but solely on the psychological need for a drug-induced relief. In other words, compulsive drug use is merely one symptom among others, the expression of an underlying disturbance, not the illness itself.

One implication of this observation is, of course, that the really difficult

---

*Similar considerations apply to the use of drugs for specific stressful situations: combat, examination, long-distance driving.

task in treating these patients is not the withdrawal from drugs, but the coping with the emotional need to use a drug, to use any drug, and to use many other equally harmful external means, to find relief. In other words: I have never yet seen a compulsive drug user who has not been emotionally deeply disturbed, who has not shown in his history the ravages of borderline, or even psychotic conflicts and defects. Only secondarily do we encounter the devastations caused by the drugs themselves. We may go one step farther: Not only do we encounter many other signs of pervasive severe psychopathology—most frequently of the borderline type—but the very criterion used to single out this group as compulsive drug users, namely "compulsiveness," leads us straight into the tangled thicket of how to define psychological health and illness, since this observable quality of compulsiveness or peremptoriness has been used by several psychoanalytic theoreticians (notably Waelder, 1936 and Kubie, 1954) to define illness:

"The essence of normality is flexibility in all of these vital ways. The essence of illness is the freezing of behavior into unalterable and insatiable patterns. It is this which characterizes every manifestation of psychopathology, whether in impulse, purpose, act, thought, or feelings" (Kubie, 1961, pp. 20-21). Our "habitués" are, without exception, paradigms for people overwhelmed with such "unalterable and insatiable patterns."

HIERARCHY OF CAUSES

Even if we select an apparently homogeneous group, e.g., narcotics addicts, we still are bewildered by the variety of causes and, correspondingly, the vast array of proffered, discussed, and disputed cause-and-effect relationships. We may try to discern layers of causes (or, to be more precise, layers of reasons [Schafer, 1973, p. 268]), ordered according to causative specificity, and start off with a superficial distinction between two factors that always appear to be present: The first is a psychological hunger or "craving" which we might describe as the *addictive search*—an entire group of activities, predating, accompanying, and following the compulsive drug use; they all are used to provide external relief for an internal urge of overpowering drivenness. We refer to activities such as irresistible violence, food addiction, gambling, alcohol use, indiscriminate "driven" sexual activity, or running away. The second factor is the more or less contingent, even accidental entrance of various drugs, in forms of both accessibility and seduction. This factor we shall call the *adventitious entrance of drugs*.

Behind this phenomenological distinction we can perceive a logical and historical structure of causes which we now examine, viewing them as a hierarchy of causes of various specificity. As is very often the case with such differentiations, what in this analysis is torn asunder into various groups and layers of reasons, is in reality a continuum, ranging from high to low specificity.

Freud (1895) distinguished four types of causes for an emotional disorder: (a) precondition; (b) specific cause; (c) concurrent cause; and (d) precipitating cause. This distinction seems to have been an original contribution of Freud to the philosophy of causation. With it, he tried to apply the basic concepts of accidental, necessary, and sufficient causes—which had originated with Aristotle and had been developed by d'Alembert, Leibnitz, and Schopenhauer—to the problems of motivation, in particular, to the causation of emotional illness. He used a precursor of this four-part model in Draft B (1893), replacing it later on by the concept of the complementary series (Sherwood, 1969).

I was not able to consider all the philosophical roots, merits, or weaknesses of this model as a basic logical concept, but I feel it may serve as heuristically better than other models of causation. Some of the following layers will be explored more in detail later on.

(a) A cardinal, indispensable, but broad layer of reasons is the precondition: "The factors which may be described as *preconditions* are those in whose absence the effect would never come about, but which are incapable of producing the effect by themselves alone, no matter in what amount the may be present" (Freud, 1895, p. 136). Applied to our problem, these inevitable preconditions can be located in a life history of massive narcissistic disturbances and in a rather specific pattern of family pathology. I describe this in more detail below (cf. also Wurmser, 1972a, 1972b). Here, it should be only stated that the narcissistic conflicts referred to pertain to massively overvalued images of self and others. The term narcissistic is used in the (precise) psychoanalytic sense of Freud (1914), Kohut (1971, 1972), Kernberg (1970), and Pulver (1970), namely, to denote an archaic overvaluation of the self or of others, a host of grandiose expectations, and the abyssmal sense of frustration and letdown if these hopes are shattered.

(b) "The *specific* cause is the one which is never missing in any case in which the effect takes place, and which moreover suffices, if present in the required quantity or intensity, to achieve the effect, provided only that the preconditions are also fulfilled" (Freud, 1895, p. 136).

Most people would now be inclined to seek the specific reason for compulsive drug use in the temptations by peers or pushers. I believe this would be misleading; it is, though semantically correct, clinically and theoretically wrong. We earlier differentiated "addictive illness" and "adventitious" appearance of the drug, and can now repeat that we find an emotional illness brewing independently, whether the drug enters or not. The specificity for its outbreak in manifest form lies in an experience of overwhelming *crisis*, accompanied by intense emotions like disillusionment and rage, depression, or anxiety, in an *actualization* of a lifelong massive conflict about omnipotence and grandiosity, meaning and trust—what we have just described as a narcissistic conflict. This actualization inevitably leads to massive emotional disruption and thus to the addictive search. In other words, if we focus on the *illness* "addictive syndrome," the specific reason is a more or less acute external and internal crisis bringing about an exacerbation of a narcissistic disturbance. We may call this a *"narcissistic crisis."* In contrast, if we focus on the *symptom* "drug abuse," we are wiser to talk about precipitating, rather than specific reasons, a category I shall mention shortly. Even without the advent of the drug itself, we still have the characteristic seeking for a way out, for an escape, a driven desperate attempt to find a crutch outside of oneself.

Much vaguer and several steps removed are the reasons ("causes") that litter the literature, all of which we can put in the next category. Their nature is very unspecific, broad, of little predictive value. They are shared by many who do not join in the illness, and vice versa. Yet, they indeed are the only reasons (and indeed "causes") which epidemiological and sociological studies are apt to find. The statistical methods employed by these disciplines tend to bring out the background factors leading to heightened incidence, but not the more specific correlations.

(c) "As *concurrent causes* we may regard such factors as are not necessarily present every time, nor able, whatever their amount, to produce the effect by themselves alone, but which operate alongside of the preconditions and the specific cause in satisfying the aetiological equation" (Freud, 1895, p. 136).

The most general of these concurrent reasons are widespread value conflicts in our culture and basic philosophical questions about the limitations of human existence. One crucial element is the conflict between democratic philosophies, postulating the dissolution of most external representatives of the superego, the increasing abolition of the restraining powers of authority and tradition, of external structures and restraints, and totalitarian philosophies, imposing the most tyrannical forms of such authority and power. Drugs are for many the shibboleth of liberation from authority, a symbol of protest and extreme privacy ("doing one's own thing").

A second element is the paradox with regard to mastery and domination of our outer and inner life: most of the ancient dreams of mankind about outer control have been fulfilled, whereas most of the techniques used in the past to gain an (albeit often spurious) sense of inner mastery and control have been discarded. Drugs provide a sense of magical domination and manipulation over one's inner life, analogous to that which science and technique appear to have over the outside.

Another socially more relevant value conflict is that between easy pleasure, immediate material gratification, and indulgence versus the often bizarre harshness of the responses by representatives of punitive and often corrupt authority (the death penalty for some small drug sales, sentences of 25 years for the giving away of one marijuana cigarette, entrapment and degradation of drug users by law enforcement officials). Thus, belonging to a drug-using countergroup can serve as protest against a profound inconsistency in the cultural fabric.

Another such factor may be the changed role of genital sexuality. For many, easily accessible sexuality is a source, not of anxiety, despair, and commitment, but of tedium and routine. The denied, split-off emotions involved in sexual yearnings are sought instead of other avenues, particularly with the help of pharmaca. Moreover, we might wonder how much the shallowness of, and presentation of shortcuts to, gratification by television, viewed for many hours daily from early childhood on and thus substituting a passive form of presentation for the development of an active fantasy life, may contribute to this search for easy stimulation (Grotjahn, 1971).

But most of all, we have to cite the social factors in the slums: social degradation, overcrowding, and overload in stimuli (especially noise and violence); the socially important role of the drug-using peer group as a substitute for the lacking family structure; and the even more relevant function of the drug traffic, and the black market needed to feed it, as an economic equalizer between ghetto and dominant middle-class society. All in all—these are unspecific broad factors—valid as much for occasional and recreational users (if indeed not more so) as for compulsive drug users.

Finally, we have to return to what I described phenomenologically as the "entrance of the drug" and labeled "*adventitious*":

(d) ". . . we may characterize as the *precipitating* or releasing cause the one which makes its appearance last in the equation, so that it immediately precedes the emergence of the effect. It is this chronological factor alone which constitutes the essential nature of a precipitating cause" (Freud, 1895, pp. 135-136).

We would assign the previously mentioned easy availability of drugs and the seduction by peers to this category ("social compliance" [cf. Hartmann, 1939]). The *advent* of the drug suddenly allows the previous desperate search to crystallize around the one object and activity that relieves the unbearable tension. In sum: there is no compulsive drug use without this trigger factor; but there is still an overriding emotional compulsiveness directed toward other activities and objects. It can be assumed that only the latter two sets of factors (concurrent and precipitating ones) are identical for experimenters and compulsive users alike.

CLINICAL OBSERVATIONS ABOUT PRECONDITIONS AND SPECIFIC REASONS

We turn now to a more detailed study of the first two sets of factors: what has been found so far in regard to the essential personality structure predisposing to, and the acute crisis immediately evoking drug use, and how these factors are matched by the pharmacological effect of various drugs.

The psychological factors of impulsiveness and low frustration tolerance are well known and undisputed. I should like to attempt an analysis that goes beyond these sweepingly general characterizations and may open the way to a deeper understanding of some actions and attitudes of these patients (perhaps of "sociopaths" in general?). Much is vague, tentative, even contradictory in what follows. Large gaps need to be filled. Careful longitudinal studies in depth, particularly in psychotherapy, psychoanalysis, and family research are needed to advance our knowledge.*

The Defect of Affect Defense

We start with what I believe to be the most important concept in a dynamic understanding of drug use. I consider all compulsive drug use an *attempt at self-treatment.*** The importance of the effect of the drug in the inner life of these patients can perhaps be best explained as an *artificial or surrogate defense against overwhelming affects.* Moreover, there evidently exists some specificity in the choice of the drug for this purpose. Patients prefer those drugs which specifically help them to cope with the affects that trouble them most.

---

*Explorations with the help of psychoanalytic or psychotherapeutic treatment are the only methods known today allowing a comprehensive recognition of the intrapsychic processes and, with that, an account of the motivational structure (cf. Waelder, 1962, 1970, Wurmser, 1972c). Yet, in this field, the exploration has been disappointingly scanty. The immediate reason is well known: that these patients are very poor candidates for psychotherapeutic approaches.

**Similarly, Krystal and Raskin (1970): ". . . the drug is not the problem, but is an attempt at a self-help that fails" (p. 11).

In the past, the satisfying, wish-fulfilling aspects of the drug effects have been emphasized. To put this in a catch phrase: drug use was seen as an expensive search for a cheap pleasure. This is certainly the popular and unreflective concept of why people take drugs. Earlier analytic theoreticians (Glover, 1932, Rado, 1926, 1933, 1963) subscribed to this idea, except that they saw in drug use, as in other symptoms, the satisfaction of unconscious wishes.

In other psychological studies of drug abuse, the focus was on the symbolic (again chiefly wish-fulfilling) meaning of drug intake as such (as oral supplies, illusory penis, or its self-destructive, self-punitive aspects) with little regard for the psychodynamic impact of the pharmacological effects themselves.

The view that drug use is an escape has also been popularly held, but largely with regard to intolerable external situations. The concept of the need for drugs as a defense against intolerable internal factors—and, more specifically, affects—has been described but scarcely until a very few years ago. Most tragically, legislation and public policy totally disregard this central factor.

Homer sang of Helena having "drugged the wine with an herb that overcomes all grief and anger and lets forget everything bad."

Freud (1930), too, described narcotics as a means of coping with pain and disillusionment. Glover (1932) was explicit with regard to "drug addiction" (referring to cocaine, paraldehyde, and presumably also to opiate addictions): "Its defensive function is to control sadistic charges, which, though less violent than those associated with paranoia, are more severe than the sadistic charges met with in obsessional formations" (p. 202) and: "Drug addiction acts as a protection against psychotic reaction in states of regression" (p. 203). In turn, he saw in unconscious homosexual fantasy systems "a restitutive or defensive system . . . [acting] as a protection against anxieties of the addiction type" (p. 203).

Rado (1963) named this aspect of affect defense "narcotic riddance" and opposed it to what he called "narcotic pleasure" and "narcotic intoxication" (a climactic sense of triumphant success). Fenichel (1945, p. 380) wrote: ". . . the addiction can be looked upon as a last means to avoid a depressive breakdown. . . ." Similarly, Chein et al. (1964) have described the "opiate's capacity to inhibit or blunt the perception of inner anxiety and outer strain. . . . In this sense, the drug itself is a diffuse pharmacological defense" (p. 233). Dora Hartmann (1969) pointed out that the conscious motivation for the use of drugs was in most cases "the wish to avoid painful affects (depression), alleviate symptoms, or a combination of these factors" (p. 389).

Wieder and Kaplan (1969) describe the drug of choice as "acting as a psychodynamic-pharmacogenic 'corrective' or 'prosthesis' " (p. 401). Their approach is almost identical to the one here suggested. They write:

> Chronic drug use, which we believe always occurs as a consequence of ego pathology, serves in a circular fashion to add to this pathology through an induced but unconsciously sought ego regression. The dominant conscious motive for drug use is not the seeking of 'kicks,' but the wish to produce pharmacologically a reduction in distress that the individual cannot achieve by his own psychic efforts (p. 403).

Krystal and Raskin (1970) emphasize the dedifferentiated, archaic, resomatized nature of the affect; because of the traumatic nature of affects in such persons, "drugs are used to avoid impending psychic trauma in circumstances which would not be potentially traumatic to other people" (p. 31).

The idea of defense against affects is also a well-known analytic concept and has been elaborated by Jones (1929), Anna Freud (1936), Fenichel (1934), and Rapaport (1953).

In all categories of compulsive drug use, the preeminence of archaic, chiefly narcissistic, conflicts is evident; what changes are some of the affects presenting the most immediate problem to the patient concerned. These affects are close to consciousness, are not really repressed, but cannot be articulated for a reason I shall subsequently describe.

Narcotics and barbiturates apparently calm intense feelings of rage, shame, and loneliness and the anxiety evoked by these overwhelming feelings.* In the words of a 22-year-old white heroin addict: "Everything in my life has to have its peak. I cannot accept things for what they are. The actual happening is a letdown compared to the anticipation. It seems then as if all of life comes down on me—in a sense of total despair. Then my first reaction is to get me some dope—not to forget, but to put me farther away from the loneliness, estrangement, and emptiness. I still feel empty and lonely when I am on dope, but it does not seem to matter as much. All is foggy and mixed up."

Heroin, for him, was a cure for disillusionment. He went so far as to say: "Heroin saved my life. I would have jumped out of the window—I felt so lonely." He wants to re-create the feeling of full acceptance and

---

*It is not certain how this pharmacogenic effect comes about. There are three possibilities: either the drug increases the thresholds of decompensation from narcissistic conflicts; or decreases the intensity of these conflicts; or functions as an artificial dampener on overwhelming affects, a kind of surrogate affect-defense in the narrow sense. Or the effect may consist of all three.

union, a fantasy whose reality he postulates as having characterized his early childhood; "I was given everything. I had a protector. Later, I realized I did not have it anymore: no protector, no shield—only myself" (Wurmser, 1972b).

This effect can be witnessed with particular clarity in patients who are put on methadone maintenance—especially if they are followed in psychotherapy both during periods of abstinence and while on the narcotic. I have seen 19 such patients in intensive psychotherapy, 14 of them for a prolonged period (several months to several years). A summary of these observations (Wurmser, 1972b) follows.

All the patients described feelings of loneliness, emptiness, and depression, of meaninglessness and pervasive boredom preceding drug use and following withdrawal. In all of them, very intense feelings of murderous rage and vengefulness; or of profound shame, embarrassment, and almost paranoid shyness; or of hurt, rejection, and abandonment, were discovered during psychotherapy. In all of them, these feelings of rage, shame, and hurt were reduced as soon as they were on methadone; in a few of them, they disappeared altogether; in some, they still occurred occasionally, but had a less overwhelming quality. Some of the patients said the drug made them feel normal and relaxed—implying that they felt those pervasive feelings states to be abnormal, sick, intolerable. Others said it helped them "not to think of the depression." Several said they felt bored, but that they preferred this to the overwhelming feelings before. The patient quoted above had this to say about methadone maintenance: "At least I do not *feel* that superlonely and excluded; I feel more at ease, although empty and bored. I still cannot be with people, but I can cope with the loneliness better. It keeps me from a showdown with myself; from the dilemma either to destroy myself completely or to move in a new direction without the aid of anything. . . . When I stop methadone, I cannot put up with any frustration. I cannot get enjoyment out of anything. I get frantic about every problem."

It was obvious that in none of these patients were the underlying inner problems resolved, but that the dampening of the mood disorder brought about by methadone was experienced as a great relief. Both the resulting boredom and the insufficient relief from the underlying conflicts led most of them to occasional or habitual use of other drugs while on methadone: mainly cocaine, Ritalin, or alcohol. (Since 1970, when most of these observations were made, the preference has shifted to Quaalude, Valium—and, still, alcohol.) One girl continued using barbiturates and eventually succeeded in killing herself with sedatives (albeit after discharge from methadone maintenance), quite in line, incidentally, with her mother's expectations, who had years before bought a cemetery plot for this, her youngest daughter, then in her late teens.

These patients try to re-establish an omnipotent position wherein either their self is grandiose and without limitations or where the other person ("the archaic self-object" of Kohut [1971]) is treated as all-giving and is required to live up to the highest ideals. As soon as limitations are imposed, the archaic emotions mentioned before emerge; they are uncontrollable and remind us much of those in psychotics. Rage is the most prominent one. Typically, this narcissistic rage is close to murderous or suicidal dimensions: when the ideal self or the ideal world has collapsed, only total devastation remains. Shame is the second one. It is the outcome of the conflict between the limited, disappointing self and the grandiose ideal self. Hurt, loneliness, rejection, abandonment, the third basic emotion in these patients, is the outcome of the experience that the other person (mother, father, girl friend, boy friend) is not as great and redeeming, as all-giving as expected; anthing short of total union with this person is experienced as total isolation and rejection. The importance of narcotics, including methadone, lies in their effect of reducing or even eliminating these basic three affects.

All patients describe states of craving after past or current withdrawal. The real content of this craving (after the physiologic symptoms have subsided) consists precisely in the upsurge of these most disturbing affects. The craving can be equated to a rapid narcissistic decompensation and the breakthrough of those archaic feelings evoked by a most massive sense of narcissistic frustration. In a few, this breakthrough is even experienced as fragmentation. The reinstatement of methadone leads to a prompt recompensation.

Psychedelic drugs counteract the emotional state of emptiness, boredom, and meaninglessness. The drug-induced illusion that the self is mystically boundless and grandiose and that the world becomes endowed with unlimited meaning seems to be a direct antidote to the pervasive sense of disillusionment in the ideal other person. It artificially re-creates ideals and values when they have been irreparably shattered inside and outside. It is important that this artificial ideal formation has a peculiarly passive-receptive ring, most like the identification with a hero in a movie or on TV. Indeed, there seems to be a remarkable similarity between the psychedelic experience and the turning on and tuning in to TV; several patients actually compare it to an inner movie.

Amphetamines and cocaine have superficially much in common with what I just described with regard to psychedelics in that they also eliminate boredom and emptiness. But these more or less conscious affects appear mostly to be caused by repression of feelings or rage, whereas with the compulsive users of psychedelics these moods are induced by the collapse of ideals without the same prominence of aggression. Accordingly, these stimulants provide a sense of aggressive mastery, control, invincibility, and grandeur, whereas the psychedelics impart a sense of passive merger through the senses. But there is more to it: The amphetamine effect serves as a defense against a massive depression or general feelings of unworthiness and weakness. In the few cases of compulsive amphetamine abuse which I was able to treat in intensive psychotherapy, long-term abstinence was accompanied by intense self-directed aggression, in some by suicidal rage and despair, in others by lethargy and self-degradation. Thus, amphetamine abuse can, at least in some patients, be called an artificial normalizing or even manic defense against the underlying affect of depression.

In all three categories, the intended functioning of the pharmacological effect itself as a *defense* against intense affects is quite certain and supported by statements from many other observers. Also, there is good clinical evidence to show some specificity in the correlation between drug choice and affect combatted. But the nature of this *pharmacogenic defense* is less clear. The affects themselves are of heterogeneous origin, but never just of "signal" nature; they are always of massive, "unneutralized," overwhelming character. Their connection with narcissistic conflicts is far more evident than with conflicts in object relations.

Just as the warded-off affects are of global and overwhelming nature, so is the pharmacogenic defense. I do not think that the latter can simply be identified with other well-known defense mechanisms, e.g., denial, or externalization. Yet, is it a defense *sui generis*? Is it a particular form of splitting? Or does it simply support a welter of well-known and individually varying defense mechanisms? The nature of this defense needs a separate, systematic study.

From this most cursory and tentative survey, we recognize the central role of *narcissistic conflicts* in all types of compulsive drug use. The choice of the drug of preference—often found only after long shopping around—is specifically related to the affects engendered by these conflicts: when the inner structures fail as defenses, the pharmacogenic effect has to serve this purpose of inner barrier.

If we suppress this attempt at self-treatment without massive support to the patient's ego, we often force him into more serious forms of decompensation: violent, even homicidal, rage in the narcotics addict, severe suicidal depression in the amphetamine user, a careless apathetic drifting in the user of psychedelics.

What has been described in these thoughts about the artificial defense is consonant with Kohut's (1971) statement: "The drug . . . serves not as a substitute for loved or loving objects, or for a relationship with them, but as a replacement for a defect in the psychological structure" (p. 46), although there are indications that drugs, drug effects, and ambience are not as devoid of object character as Kohut appears to state.

It should be noted, finally, that both defense and wish-fulfillment are relative concepts. Gill (1963) pointed out convincingly that every defense is simultaneously the fulfillment of a wish: ". . . a behavior is a defense in relation to a drive more primitive than itself, and a drive in relation to a defense more advanced than itself" (pp. 122-123).

Faulty Formation of Ego Ideal

Another aspect, implicit in some of what I have already described, is the *superego pathology*, the lack of meaning-giving, life-determining, life-guiding values and ideals, or, in their personified form, all-powerful myths. The affects just described usually emerge during or following a crisis wherein such central values, ideals, and myths have been shattered or when the need for such an ideal has become particularly prominent, its absence or unreliability particularly painful. And here the family pathology enters.

The following comments do not do justice to the importance of family pathology as etiological factors; a separate study is in preparation (cf. also Chein et al., 1964). The crucial factors in the family pathology appear, to date, to be consistency, setting of limits, and trustworthiness versus narcissistic indulgence and rage. Parents who did not provide a minimum of consistency, of reliability, of trustworthiness, of respon-siveness to the child, especially during his developmental crises, are not usable as inner beacons; instead they become targets of rebellious rage and disdain. Parents who vacillate between temper tantrums and in-dulgence, who allow themselves to live out their most primitive demands, parents who are more interested in their careers and their clubs and travels than in their children's needs to have them available, or parents who are absent for economic reasons and cannot impart the important combination of love and of firmness—all these parents, unless replaced in their crucial functions by capable substitutes, make it very difficult for their children to accept them as secure models for conscience and ego ideal, to internalize them, and to build them up as inner guardians against transgressions. It is my impression that the ego ideal in patients having such parents has remained archaic, unreliable, global; more ma-ture parts quickly collapse during adolescence or never emerge.

The "high," the relief and pleasure sought with the help of the drug, is a surrogate ideal, a substitute value, a chemical mythology, which normally would be supplied by the internal sense of meaning, goal-directedness, and value orientation. Moreover, peer group, drug culture and, most of all, the "hustling" itself, the whole chasing after the drug, and the ideal of the successful pusher who can beat the hated establishment (particularly in the ghetto), are powerfully determining models and values (cf. Preble & Casey, 1969).

The next aspect is the least secure and most presumptive one; yet, it may prove to be easier to observe and even quantify than the others.

Hyposymbolization

With this, I refer to the frequent observation of a general degradation, contraction, or rudimental development of the processes of symbolization and, with that, of the fantasy life. This curtailed ability or inability to symbolize pertains particularly to the patient's inner life, his emotions, his self-references. One example of this is the inability of most of these patients to articulate feelings. Many, if not all, relevant affects are translated into somatic complaints—e.g., craving and physical discomfort—or into social accusations—"It's all society's fault." They remain preverbal as affects. The same construction seems to hold true for the entire fantasy life. It is just this lacuna—whether it is a conflict-induced scotoma, or a genuine deficiency—which makes psychotherapy so particularly difficult and frustrating. After all, psychotherapy employs precisely the verbal band out of the spectrum of symbolic processes as its instrument. Tentatively, I dub this defect "hyposymbolization"; I consider it identical with what I found in Blos' (1971) concept of "concretization." Obviously, drugs do not function as a substitute for the lacking symbolization; nor do most enrich the impoverished fantasy life (except for what Louis Lewin [1924] called the Phantastica, i.e., the psychedelic drugs). Rather, their function lies in removing that vague discomfort and tension which replace the not perceived and not articulated affect and are experienced as "something wrong" in the body or the environment. Thus, the drugs are employed to alter body image and world image into a less unpleasant and more meaningful one.

Archaic Object Dependency

We have so far examined the psychodynamic role of the various pharmacological effects of these drugs. There is a further dynamic implication which is very important and far better known than these three: "Among *the unconscious motivations* (in addition to oral gratification and passive identification with a parent), the need to replace a lost object seemed to play a very important role" (D. Hartmann, 1969, p. 389). Many patients talk about their drug and the paraphernalia and circumstances surrounding it with a loving tenderness, as if it were a love partner. Obviously, it is the *object character* of the drug that assumes a central motivating power here rather than its pharmacological character. Actually, the very term, "drug dependency" reminds us of what we are dealing with, namely an *archaic passive dependency* on an all-giving, sempiternal, though narcissistically perceived—i.e., hugely inflated—object, as is evidenced by the singleminded devotedness and frenzy of the chase after the beloved, in the incorporative greed, the masturbatory and orgiastic aspects of the use, and in the mixture of ecstatic idealization and deprecation vis-à-vis the drug ("star dust," "blue heavens," "white lady" versus "shit," "sçag") (Wieder & Kaplan, 1969; Chein et al., 1964). Much of this reminds us of *fetishism*. Dynamic similarities and dissimilarities between these two syndromes need to be worked out: Do we find a similar split of the ego in addictive illness to the one described in fetishism? Glover implicitly raised this question in 1932; ". . . in the transition between paranoidal systems and a normal reaction to reality, drug addiction (and later on fetishism) represent not only continuations of the anxiety system within a contracted range, but the beginnings of an expanding reassurance system" (p. 211). He called fetishism the companion problem of addiction.

The problem raised by Kohut (1959, 1971) remains unsolved: Is this obvious relationship to archaic, easily replaceable part objects only secondary, and is it accurate to explain the dependence on drugs primarily not "as a substitute for object relations but as a substitute for psychological structure" (Kohut, 1959, p. 476)? In many cases this hypothesis seems to be borne out. Yet in others where a symbiotic relation or the dedication to a treatment community completely supplants a former drug dependence, I am quite inclined to see in the latter also an archaic, narcissistically experienced object relation.

Self-destructiveness

Very well known is the self-destructive, self-punitive aspect of drug abuse (Glover, 1932). In some cases, we may observe the direct equivalency of drug use with suicide. If we take the first away, the second become the menace. Drug abuse in itself can often (not always) be considered a tamed and protracted suicidal attempt, though we have to be cautious not to fall into the pitfall of the teleological fallacy (*post hoc, proper hoc*). In line with the other aspect of superego pathology, described above, where the faulty ideal formation was underlined, we may now add the important role of archaic forms of shame and guilt—as reflected (but not recognized) in many of the vindictive measures used at Synanon and other therapeutic communities, as well as in most of our legislation (Wurmser, 1973a, 1973b; Wurmser et al., 1973). There is no question that very primitive and global fears of humiliation and revenge play a dominant role in the social interaction of these patients; these are usually not simply the consequence of society's reaction, but part of the patient's make-up to begin with. The vindictiveness and corruptibility of the archaic superego is well known and is easily observed among our patients. This dynamic datum, however, is so frequent and general that I assign it a very low specificity for this type of pathology.

Regressive Gratification

This aim of drug use, also mentioned by Homer (Odyssey, Book IX, 90-97), has been studied most extensively. My previous emphasis, especially on the notion of the artificial affect defense, has been used to counterbalance the historical emphasis on this aspect. Both are obviously two sides of the same coin.

From all the forms of regressive gratifications attained with the help of the drug, it appears that the increase in self-esteem, the re-creation of a regressive *narcissistic state of self-satisfaction* is the most consistent one. This is particularly relevant when we see this aim of drug use as an integral part of the narcissistic crisis which typically marks the onset of compulsive drug use and to which we now turn.

Narcissistic Crisis

As discussed earlier, the specific reason for the onset of compulsive drug use lies in an acute crisis in which the underlying narcissistic conflicts are mobilized and the affects connected with these conflicts break in with overwhelming force and cannot be coped with without the help of an artificial affect defense.

Such a mobilization quite typically first occurs during adolescence, rarely earlier, and still more rarely later. Often the relapse from abstinence into drug use is regularly marked by the recurrence of such a crisis—which in turn is usually triggered by an external event's setting in motion the juggernaut of pervasive anxieties, rages, and narcissistic demands. This narcissistic crisis is thus the point at which the conflicts and defects converge with a particular external situation and with the availability of the seeming means of solution: the drug. By definition, a "narcissistic crisis" would have to entail a particularly intense disappointment in others, in oneself, or in both—so intense because of the exaggerated hopes, and so malignant because of its history's reaching back to very early times. Precipitating external events of such a crisis can most typically be found in family crises, coinciding with the maturational crisis of adolescence.

CONCLUSIONS: THE ETIOLOGICAL EQUATION

It appears very likely that it is the convergence of at least some, if not all, of six elements—massive defect of affect defense, the defect in value formation, the hyposymbolization, the desperate search for an object substitute, the intensely self-destructive qualities, and the search for regressive gratification—together with the intensity of the underlying narcissistic conflicts that forms the *predispositional* constellation for the "addictive illness" in general and for compulsive drug use in particular. It appears that the most specific of these predispositional factors are the need for affect defense and the compelling wish for regressive gratification; but only further research, including predictive studies, can elucidate the relative relevance of these six factors.

The *specific* reason is the mobilization of the underlying narcissistic conflict in what I called the narcissistic crisis.

The *precipitating* reason is the advent of the drug on stage, functioning only like the crucial though irrelevant messenger in the antique tragedy, a hapless catalyst: "I that do bring the news made not the match" (*Antony and Cleopatra*, II, V, 67).

Some or all of the six predispositional factors described may be *necessary reasons*. The *combination* of the *narcissistic crisis* (specific reason)—viz. a consequence of these predispositions, mobilized by maturational and environmental factors—with the *adventitious entrance* of the drug (precipitating reason) represents the *sufficient reason*.

It appears appropriate to end with two quotations that emphasize the necessity of etiological analysis. The first is from Vergil's Georgica II: "*Felix qui potuit rerum cognoscere causas*" (Fortunate is he who has been able to recognize the causes of things). The second is from Bacon's *Novum Organum*, I. (1620) and was in a sense the motto opening up the time of progress in science and technology: "*Scientia et potentia humana in idem coincidunt quia ignoratio causae destituit effectum*" (Human knowledge and power coincide in that regard that ignorance of cause prevents effective intervention).

REFERENCES

BLOS, P. (1971), Adolescent concretization: a contribution to the theory of delinquency. In: *Currents in Psychoanalysis*, ed. I. M. Marcus. New York: International Universities Press, pp. 66-88.

CHEIN, I., GERARD, D. L., LEE, R. S., & ROSENFELD, E. (1964), *The Road to H.* New York: Basic Books.

FENICHEL, O. (1934), Defense against anxiety, particularly by libidinalization. In: *Collected Papers*, First series, New York: Norton, 1953, pp. 303-317.

———(1945), *The Psychoanalytic Theory of Neurosis.* New York: Norton.

FREUD, A. (1936), *The Ego and the Mechanisms of Defense, The Writings of Anna Freud,* Vol. 2. New York: International Universities Press, 1968, pp. 31-34.

FREUD, S. (1895), A reply to criticism of my paper on anxiety neurosis, *Standard Edition,* 3:123-139. London: Hogarth Press, 1962.

———(1914), On narcissism: an introduction, *Standard Edition,* 14:69-102. London: Hogarth Press, 1957.

———(1930), Civilization and its discontents. *Standard Edition,* 21:59-145. London: Hogarth Press, 1961.

Gill, M. M. (1963), *Topography and Systems in Psychoanalytic Theory* [*Psychological Issues,* Monogr. 10]. New York: International Universities Press, pp. 122-123.

GLASSCOTE, R. M., SUSSEX, J. N., JAFFE, J. H., BALL, J., & BRILL, L. (1972), *The Treatment of Drug Abuse. Programs, Problems, Prospects.* Washington, D.C.: American Psychiatric Association and National Association on Mental Health.

GLOVER, E. (1928), The Etiology of Alcoholism. In: *On the Early Development of Mind.* New York: International Universities Press, 1956, pp. 81-90.

———(1932), On the Etiology of Drug Addiction. In: *On the Early Development of Mind.* New York: International Universities Press, 1956, pp. 187-215.

GROTJAHN, M. (1971), *The Voice of the Symbol.* Los Angeles: Mara Books, pp. 1-23.

HARTMANN, D. (1969), A study of drug-taking adolescents. *The Psychoanalytic Study of the Child.* New York: International Universities Press, 24:384-398.

HARTMANN, H. (1939), *Ego Psychology and the Problem of Adaptation.* New York: International Universities Press, 1960.

JAFFE, J. H. (1965), Drug addiction and drug abuse. In: *The Pharmacological Basis of Therapeutics,* ed. L. S. Goodman & A. Gilman. New York: Macmillan, pp. 285-311.

JONES, E. (1929), Fear, guilt and hate. In: *Papers on Psychoanalysis.* Boston: Beacon Press, 1967, pp. 314-319.

KERNBERG, O. F. (1970), Factors in the psychoanalytic treatment of narcissistic personalities. *Journal of the American Psychoanalytic Association,* 18:51-85.

KHANTZIAN, E. J., MACK, J. F., SCHATZBERG, A. F. (1974), Heroin use as an attempt to cope: clinical observations. *Amer. J. Psychiat.,* 131:160-164.

KOHUT, H. (1959), Introspection, empathy, and psychoanalysis. *Journal of the American Psychoanalytic Association,* 7:459-483.

———(1971), *The Analysis of the Self.* New York: International Universities Press.

———(1972), Thoughts on narcissism and narcissistic rage. *The Psychoanalytic Study of the Child,* 27:360-400. New York: Quadrangle Books.

KRYSTAL, H. & RASKIN, H. A. (1970), *Drug Dependence. Aspects of Ego Functions.* Detroit: Wayne State University Press.

KUBIE, L. S. (1954), The fundamental nature of the distinction between normality and neurosis. *Psychoanal. Quart.,* 23:167-204.

———(1961), *Neurotic Distortion of the Creative Process.* New York: The Noonday Press.

LEWIN, L. (1924), *Phantastica, Narcotic and Stimulating Drugs: Their Use and Abuse.* New York: Dutton, 1931; reprinted 1964, London: Routledge & Kegan.

LIMENTANI, A. (1968), On drug dependence: clinical appraisals of the predicaments of habituation and addiction to drugs. *Internat. J. Psycho-Anal.,* 49:578-590.

PANEL (1970), Psychoanalytic evaluation of addiction and habituation, W. Frosch, reporter.

Journal of the American Psychoanalytic Association, 18:209-218.

PREBLE, E. & CASEY, J. J. (1969), Taking care of business—the heroin user's life on the street. *Internat. J. Addictions,* 4:1-24.

PULVER, S. E. (1970), Narcissism: the term and the concept. *Journal of the American Psychoanalytic Association,* 18:319-341.

RADO, S. (1926), The psychic effects of intoxicants. *Internat. J. Psycho-Anal.,* 7:396-413.

———(1933), The psychoanalysis of pharmacothymia (drug addiction), *Psychoanal. Quart.* 2:1-23.

———(1963), Fighting narcotic bondage and other forms of narcotic disorders. *Comprehensive Psychiat.,* 4:160-167.

RAPAPORT, D. (1953), On the psychoanalytic theory of affects. In: *Collected Papers,* ed. M. M. Gill. New York: Basic Books, 1967, pp. 476-512.

SAVITT, R. A. (1954), Extramural psychoanalytic treatment of a case of narcotic addiction. *Journal of the American Psychoanalytic Association,* 2:494-502.

———(1963), Psychoanalytic studies on addiction: ego structure in narcotic addiction. *Psychoanal. Quart.,* 32:43-57.

SCHAFER, R. (1973), The idea of resistance. *Internat. J. Psycho-Anal,* 54:259-285.

SHERWOOD, M. (1969), *The Logic of Explanation in Psychoanalysis.* New York: Academic Press, pp. 172-174.

WAELDER, R. (1936), The problem of freedom in psychoanalysis and the problem of reality testing. *Internat. J. Psycho-Anal.,* 17:89-108.

———(1962), Psychoanalysis, scientific method and philosophy. *Journal of the American Psychoanalytic Association,* 10:617-637.

———(1970), Observation, historical reconstruction, and experiment: an epistemological study. In: *Psychoanalysis and Philosophy,* ed. C. Hanly & M. Lazerowitz. New York: International Universities Press, pp. 280-326.

WIEDER, H. & KAPLAN, E. H. (1969), Drug use in adolescents: psychodynamic meaning and pharmacogenic effect. *The Psychoanalytic Study of the Child,* 24:399-431. New York: International Universities Press.

WURMSER, L. (1972a), Drug abuse: nemesis of psychiatry. *Amer. Scholar,* 41:393-407.

——— (1972b), Methadone and the craving for narcotics: observations of patients on methadone maintenance in psychotherapy. San Francisco: Proceedings, Fourth National Conference on Methadone Treatment, pp. 525-528.

———(1972c), Author's reply. *Internat. J. Psychiat.,* 10:117-128.

———(1973a), Psychosocial aspects of drug abuse. *Maryland State Med. J.,* 22:78-83, 99-101.

———(1973b), Unpolitic thoughts about the politics of drug-abuse treatment. *J. Drug Issues,* 3:178-185.

———FLOWERS, E., & WELDON, C. (1973), *Methadone, Discipline and Revenge.* Washington: Proceedings, Fifth National Conference on Methadone Treatment.

ZINBERG, N. E. & ROBERTSON, J. A. (1972), *Drugs and the Public.* New York: Simon & Schuster.

8

SELF SELECTION AND PROGRESSION IN DRUG DEPENDENCE

Edward J. Khantzian

Many explanations have been advanced to explain why individuals become involved with drugs: They are "pleasure seekers"—their friends do it, or they do it, or "They are medicating themselves," or it is "suicide on the installment plan." If one turns to the scientific literature, one can find parallel sophisticated and technical elaborations on these themes. Early psychoanalytic formulations minimized the differences among various drugs (e.g., morphine, alcohol, cocaine, and depressants) and tended to emphasize the erotic, pleasurable aspects of drug-taking (1-3). Many of these and subsequent formulations stressed a regressive form of pleasure, the individual attempting to induce a regressive pleasurable state similar to an earlier phase of his development.

Although later formulations took into account the relief of tension and distress as a motive for taking drugs (4-6), surprisingly, there has continued to be an impressive emphasis placed on the pleasurable aspects of drug use to explain the compelling nature of drug dependence (7-11).

Glover, an exception to these trends, was one of the earlier psychoanalytic investigators who stressed the "progressive" and adaptive use of

Reprinted with permission from *Psychiatry Digest,* 1975, *36,* 19-22. Copyright 1975 by Medical Digest, Inc.

Dr. Khantzian is Director, Drug Treatment Services, The Cambridge-Somerville Mental Health and Retardation Center, Assistant Professor of Psychiatry at The Cambridge Hospital, Harvard Medical School.

drugs (12). He believed that the addict's involvement with drugs was akin to an obsessive involvement that protected the individual from more regressive, paranoid-sadistic tendencies and psychoses. Glover minimized the psychopharamacologic action of different drugs and emphasized their symbolic meaning to the addict.

Much emphasis has been placed recently on peer group pressures and the attitudes of the surrounding community as major etiologic influences in drug dependence. It is contended here that although peer group influences play a role, it is not a major role. Probably more important are attitudes in the surrounding community which view drug use and dependence as deviant. Zinberg has recently focused on the important part that the setting, including society's attitudes toward the addict as deviant, plays in determining the users' response to drugs (13-15). He maintains that the setting in good part accounts for the withdrawal from society and the regression that becomes so apparent in drug-dependent individuals. He believes that only a small fraction of people dependent on drugs use them as a function of personality or in response to painful affects.

Our own work and that of others has picked up on Glover's emphasis on the adaptive use of drugs, while incorporating a better appreciation of the psychopharmacologic action of the different drugs (16). Chein et al. affirmed that narcotic addiction was "adaptive and functional" and referred to opiates as effective "tranquilizing" or ataractic drugs (17). More recent works by others, emphasizing the use of drugs in the service of drive and affect defense, represent further specific elaborations on a point-of-view that considers the use of drugs as a way of coping with one's internal and external environment (18-20).

These more recent formulations have tried to take into account how the specific action of the drug interacts with internal psychological states and reactions. In the remainder of this discussion an attempt will be made to elaborate and focus upon how the personality organization and reactive patterns of an individual (hereafter referred to as the psychologic set) interact with various types of drugs upon which individuals become dependent in their attempts to cope. We will focus on the drug-set interaction from a psychoanalytic viewpoint in which dynamic (i.e., forces), economic (i.e., energy), structural, and adaptive factors are stressed.

DRUG-SET INTERACTION AND SELF SELECTION

People who have become involved with and dependent on drugs have frequently experimented with a wide variety and have become dependent on more than just one type. However, we and others have been impressed with the fact that many of these individuals self select and seem to have a predilection for a particular drug (8, 18-20). This self selection is related to the fact that the various drugs have distinctive psychoactive actions. In the course of experimenting with different drugs, an individual discovers that the action of one drug over another is preferred. In what follows we will explore how this preference results and is a function of the individual's discovering that a particular drug relieves internal dysphoric and distressful states and/or leads to improved functioning.

Energizing Drugs

The main drugs in this category are the amphetamines and cocaine. Although the two drugs are distinctly different in their mechanisms of action and metabolism, their energizing properties are well known. From our knowledge of catecholamine metabolism we know that both drugs produce a relative increase in the availability of norepinephrine at key neuro-receptor sites in the central nervous system, which in part accounts for the mood elevation or so-called high with the use of these drugs (21). Prior to the widespread use of these substances in the drug subculture of the late 1960's and early 1970's, many individuals had discovered the stimulating properties of amphetamines in the course of studying for exams or using "diet pills" to lose weight.

It has been our experience that these drugs are effective and take on a compelling quality for many users because they help to overcome the depletion and fatigue states associated with depression. Weider and Kaplan observed that the use of amphetamines leads to increased feelings of assertiveness, self-esteem, and frustration tolerance (8). Wurmser believes that the use of amphetamines helps to eliminate feelings of boredom and emptiness by producing a sense of "aggression mastery, control, invincibility, and grandiosity" by overcoming depression (18).

These reports seem to share in common and take into account the psychic and physical energy problems that are so commonly observed in depression and chronic depressive states. Conversely, but in support of the self-selection hypothesis, we have also been impressed with the fact that certain individuals have an aversion to amphetamines because they discover that in contrast to many depressive individuals, their hyper-anxious and/or hyper-aggressive tendencies are heightened and made worse by amphetamines. In the case of depression, much more energy is expended in the service of denial, guilt, and shame, with the result that the short-term energizing effects of the amphetamines and cocaine give a sense of relief by overcoming painful feelings of helplessness and passivity.

Releasing Drugs

Fenichel has referred to the quote, "the superego is that part of the mind that is soluble in alcohol" (6). This characterization could be applied equally well to the barbiturate and related sedative-hypnotic drugs, and effectively captures the basis for their appeal. Both alcohol and barbiturates in light to moderate doses have the effect of releasing the individual from his inhibitions. This in part is a function of a release of higher, regulatory centers, particularly in the frontal lobes (as demonstrated by EEG), and has been referred to by some as a reversible "chemical lobotomy." In a recent monograph, Smith and Wesson have used the term "disinhibition euphoria" to describe the action and effect of barbiturates (22).

Alcohol and sedative drugs seem to exert their influence in individuals by relieving internal distressful states associated with anxiety and conflicts. Although often the anxiety and conflict in drug-dependent individuals seem to be related to a classic neurotic constellation of inhibitions and defense in opposition to unacceptable impulses, it is probably more often the case that the anxiety and conflict are related to rigid defenses against more primitive and narcissistic longings. Krystal and Raskin have traced the problems in the object relations of many drug-dependent individuals, along the lines of Jacobson, to early phases of development where parental and environmental failures required the individual to rigidly wall off the self and object representations (20). They stress the enormous difficulties that the drug-dependent individual has with ambivalence and how he must deny and rigidly repress his aggression and need for love and forgiveness. They stress that aspect of the drug action, particularly with alcohol and short-acting barbiturates, which allows for brief and therefore tolerable fusion in the rigidly split-off self and object representations. That is, the person has an enormous stake in splitting off the "good" and "bad" parts (i.e., feelings, attitudes, ideas) of himself and others. This splitting is in the service of avoiding the ambivalence which is found by these individuals to be so intolerable. The use of such drugs are therefore less in the service of producing a "high" or euphoria, but more in the service of relief from dysphoria related to rigid and unstable defenses against painful affects and drives.

Controlling-Stabilizing Drugs

In our own work with narcotic addicts we have been particularly impressed with the muting and stabilizing action of narcotics. Previous formulations have stressed either the euphorogenic-pleasurable effect of narcotics and/or their ability to relieve a range of distressful or unpleasant affects as an explanation for the powerful tendency to induce and sustain an addiction. Although these formulations have merit, we have been more impressed with the specific muting action on the individual's rage and aggressive drives.

In previous reports, based on evaluation and treatment of over 200 addicts, we stressed developmental impairments and deficiencies in the egos of the narcotic addicts with whom we had worked (19). These deficiences were reflected in outbursts of rage, poor impulse control, and a general sense of dysphoria as a result of the threat they felt to themselves and others because of their violent feelings and impulses. We were repeatedly impressed with the addicts' subjective reports of their initial experience with opiates in which they discovered the immediate calming and stabilizing action of the drug. More specifically, we observed, ". . . in the course of responding to a carefully taken drug history, patients gave ample descriptions of dysphoric states of bodily tensions and restlessness, anger, rage, violent feelings, and depression that were relieved by heroin and other opiates. With an almost monotonous regularity, the patients used terms such as 'relaxed,' 'mellow,' 'calming,' and emphasized a total body reponse to describe the effects of opiates when they *first* began to use such drugs" (19). On the basis of these findings we hypothesized that individuals were predisposed and became addicted to opiates because they discovered the stabilizing action of these drugs on their egos. The drugs acted specifically (short-term) to reverse regressive states by attenuating and making more bearable painful drives and affects involving aggression, rage, and related depression.

IMPLICATIONS FOR PROGRESSION

Although our main thesis in this report has been to stress the predilection and self selection for certain drugs by different individuals, we have been equally impressed in our work with the tendency for addictions to progress and continue once an individual has heavily used a particular drug.

As we have already indicated, drugs of dependence can exert a powerful influence on various ego states and can induce alterations in functioning and in levels of distress that are more or less adaptive. However, in repeatedly resorting to a drug to obtain a desired state, the individual becomes less and less apt to come upon other human responses and solutions in coping with his internal life and the external world around him. It is in this respect that "an addiction takes on a life of its own." Consequently, there is an ever-increasing tendency for regression and withdrawal, which, as Zinberg has noted, is further compounded by society's inclination to consider such behavior as deviant and unacceptable (15). The regressed and withdrawn individual discovers that in the absence of other adaptive mechanisms, the distressing aspects of his condition can be relieved only by either increasing the use of his preferred drug or switching to other drugs to overcome the painful and disabling side effects of the original drug of dependence.

In short, the tragedy of drug dependence resides in the fact that heavy drug usage precludes the development of more ordinary human solutions to life problems. This is particularly true of adolescence, when high anxiety levels and tensions are the necessary ingredients for change, growth, and development. The emergence of drug and alcohol problems is notorious during this phase of life and personal development. Life's developmental challenges and crises extend beyond adolescence. The extent to which a person short-circuits and relieves his troubling emotions by resorting to drugs, the less he is apt to discover his own potential and capacities, and the more apt he is to perpetuate and progress in his dependence on chemical solutions in overcoming and muting his difficulties.

SUMMARY

This discussion has focused upon and emphasized the forces at work within individuals which cause them to seize upon the action of various drugs because they have been unable or unwilling to develop alternative ways to cope with dysphoric internal states. We have stressed that different psychologic sets predispose different individuals to a particular drug. We believe this emphasis is justified because we feel that the compelling nature of drug dependence cannot be sufficiently explained by simplistic formulations which stress pleasurable aspects of drug use, peer group pressures, or societal problems and attitudes, to the exclusion of in-depth psychological considerations.

REFERENCES

1. FREUD S., "Three Essays on the Theory of Sexuality (1905)," in *Stanford Edition*, Vol. 7, Hogarth Press, London, 1955.

2. ABRAHAM, K., "The Psychological Relation Between Sexuality and Alcoholism," in *Selected Papers of Karl Abraham*, Basic Books, New York, 1960.
3. RADO, S., *Psychoanal. Quart.*, 2:1, 1933.
4. RADO, S., *Am. J. Psychiatry*, 114:165, 1957.
5. WIKLER, A. A., & RASOR R. W., *Am. J. Med.*, 14:566, 1953.
6. FENICHEL O., *The Psychoanalytic Theory of Neurosis*, W. W. Norton, New York, 1945.
7. SAVIT, R. A., *Psychoanal. Quart.*, 32:43, 1954.
8. WIEDER, H., & KAPLAN, E., *Psychoanalytic Study of the Child*, 24:399, 1969.
9. WIKLER, A., *Behav. Sci.*, 16:92, 1971.
10. WIKLER, A., *Res. Publ. Assoc. Res. Nerv. Ment. Dis.*, 46:280, 1968.
11. GOLDSTEIN, A., *Arch. Gen. Psychiatry*, 26:291, 1972.
12. GLOVER, E., "On the Etiology of Drug Addicition," in *On the Early Development of Mind*, International Universities Press, New York, 1956.
13. ZINBERG, N. E., & ROBERTSON, J. A., *Drugs and the Public*, Simon & Schuster, New York, 1972. Pp. 44-102.
14. ZINBERG, N. E., "High States, A Beginning Study," *The Drug Abuse Council*, September, 1974.
15. ZINBERG. N.E., "Addiction and Ego Function," in *The Psychoanal. Study of the Child*, Vol. 30, Quadrangle/New York Times Press, 1975.
16. KHANTZIAN, E. J., et al., *Am. J. Psychiatry*, 131:160-164, 1974.
17. CHEIN, I., et al., *The Road to H*, Basic Books, New York, 1964.
18. WURMSER, L., "ethadone and the Craving for Narcotics: Observations of Patients on Methadone Maintenance in Psychotherapy," in *Proc. Fourth National Conference*, San Francisco, January, 1972.
19. KHANTZIAN, E. J., *Am. J. Psychother.*, 28:59;70, 1974.
20. KRYSTAL, H., & RASKIN, H. A., *Drug Dependence Aspects of Ego Functions*, Wayne State University Press, Detroit, 1970.
21. SCHILDKRAUT, J. J., *Am. J. Psychiat.*, 122:509, 1965.
22. SMITH, D. E., & WESSON, D. R., "Diagnosis and Treatment of Adverse Reactions to Sedative-Hypnotics," *National Institute on Drug Abuse*, Washington, 1974.

9

DRUG DEPENDENCE: ASPECTS OF EGO FUNCTION

Henry Krystal and Herbert A. Raskin

THEORY OF THE DEVELOPMENTAL HISTORY OF AFFECTS

Krystal's studies of drug withdrawal states led him to suggest that anxiety and depression evolve from a common precursor (Ur-affect) (1). In a drug dependent person there is a regression in regard to affects, anxiety and depression are again de-differentiated and show other attributes of primitivisation of affects, such as resomatization, deverbalization. The ideational component of the affect is isolated from its expressive aspects (glandular and muscular responses). The affects are experienced as threatening and therefore excluded from conscious awareness whenever possible. All of these characteristics, especially the regression to the "all or none" affective responses, impair their use as signals. We will presently attempt to discuss these in detail.

Prior to the "discovery" of the love object, the infant's response to distress takes a single form: totally somatic and uncontrollable. The establishment of the nuclei of self-representation and object-representation facilitates the separation of pain from the painful affects, which remain as a single, totally somatic reaction to the absence and threat of loss of the love object. In addition, the infant's physiological balance is so precarious, and lability so great, that affective disturbance produces immediate physical changes and pain. Anxiety in the infant may produce instant colic and hence be converted into severe pain. Other affects can

Reprinted with permission from *Drug Dependence: Aspects of Ego Function* by H. Krystal and H. A. Raskin, Detroit: Wayne State University Press, 1970, 20-35.

similarly be converted into painful physical symptoms, because the infant lacks the adult's protective ego functions and is more readily thrown into psychogenic shock which may be lethal. This type of reaction accounts for the child's confrontation with mortal fear; not fear of dying, but an enormous, overwhelming, deadly anxiety of being eaten up, swallowed, etc. This death anxiety is linked with the feeling of helplessness, immobility, suffocation, and remains the core of that overwhelming anxiety which in the adult we refer to as the "automatic anxiety" in trauma: castration anxiety, fear of dismemberment, losing one's mind (2). Perhaps it is also what Melanie Klein called "psychotic anxiety" linked with the ideational component of the fear of falling to bits. This feeling is unbearable, and is the thing that causes, or more properly, is the traumatic situation. It initiates a series of unconscious pathogenic reactions which represent the trauma syndrome.

Out of the infant's general state of distress, several states and feelings evolve. The "discovery" of the mother and her power to nurture and give relief shifts the ideational component of it from physical distress to the fear of the loss of the object. This shift establishes the basis for the object-representation in the child's mind.

With the increased acuity of perception and the maturation of the ego apparatuses of proprioception, the body image is gradually built up. Pain is separated from the general distress pattern, albeit it is never completely separated from anxiety. Still, the normal adult does not obtain automatic relief from physical pain by oral gratification. Some of this potential, however, is retained, as we shall demonstrate in our discussion of the placebo. This type of reaction is one of the remnants of infantile function which becomes important in drug dependence.

As to other affects, anxiety becomes separated from depression primarily in the fact that anxiety is the reaction to the expectation of danger, whereas depression represents a hopeless giving up and resignation. The "agitation" in anxiety serves an expressive function, and when the situation is hopeless, a flaccid or tense-immobile catatonoid, inhibited reaction develops (105). Depression and anxiety not only become separated but also become in a way antagonistic because of their physiologic association with opposing parts of the autonomic nervous system. Thus, it happens that sometimes either on order of physicians or in drug self-medication, people can stimulate the anxiety-agitation response (with amphetamine drugs or fear-producing thrills) as a way to combat the parasympathetic aspects of depression.

AFFECT DISTURBANCE IN DRUG DEPENDENCE

However, in many drug dependent persons we find an affect combining depression and anxiety, a disturbance in which the de-differentiation of anxiety and depression takes place or a state in which the differentiation was never successfully accomplished. Thus, in Krystal's studies of drug withdrawal states, the affect seemed to approximate the infantile "total" and somatic distress pattern rather than a clear-cut adult affect pattern (1). Rado was the first to describe this condition clinically, calling it "the anxious depression" of alcoholics (3). He did not, however, pursue in detail the nature and consequences of this regression. Engel considers "anxiety and depression withdrawal" to be the "primary affect of unpleasure" (2). His excellent and scholarly work traces the development of the Ur-affects in the infant in relation to drives and object representations, and confirms the expressive attitudes of anxiety ("flight or fight") and depression ("to give up") to be a psychological continuum, although they "represent two basic physiological states." He pointed out that depressions may become "maladaptive or unsuccessful in which case they seem to be potent provoking conditions for major psychic and somatic disorganizations, sometimes leading to death."

Perhaps Freud also hinted at this developmental history of the painful affects when he said about the infant's reaction to loss, in the "Problems of Anxiety," that "some things were fused together which later will be separated. He is not yet able to distinguish temporary absence from permanent loss" (4). Shur has come to similar conclusions about the development of affects and has drawn our attention to the fact that affects like other aspects of mental function, are subject to regression. Schur's work on the metapsychology of fear contributed the observation of a type of *physiological regression* in patients with dermatoses, which allows us to add another dimension to our knowledge of some drug dependent individuals. We gain an appreciation of a regression manifest in the words of Schur in "a regressive evaluation of danger and an ego which responds with deneutralized energy. This corresponds to the re-emerging somatic discharge phenomena." Upon observing that some patients developed symptoms representing anxiety equivalents instead of becoming conscious of their anxiety, Schur postulated that there was an "interdependence" between the ego's faculty to use secondary processes and neutralized energy, and the desomatization response (5). This implies an inverse relation between an individual's consciousness of his affect and the intensity of physiological (stress) responses and affect equivalents. The relevance of the *regression* vis-à-vis the problem of pain consists in the nature of pain, which is a complex conscious phenomenon composed of the perception of injury associated with disturbing affects. Commonly the affect involved is that of anxiety. However, in the regressed state the impact of the resomatized Ur-affect presents a complex danger. One of the results, which will be discussed in detail later, is the inability to tolerate even small amounts of anxiety, hence the failure of its signal function. This creates the threat of trauma, to which we shall return.

A reconsideration of the mode of development of the affect of anxiety from the infantile, that is, totally somatic, to the adult form suggests that the original pattern is modified by later experiences and developments. Verbalization and desomatization of affect represent one aspect of ego development (5). Learned responses to pain as the representative of danger represent another and important aspect. We will pursue the story of development of pain tolerance in the child, because it can serve us as a pattern and prototype for the development of individual resources for dealing with painful states and affects.

Pain is a perceptive process in which the possibility of injury is evaluated in terms of one's psychic reality. Anna Freud, in considering the effect of pain on children, observed:

> According to the child's interpretation of the event, young children react to pain not only with anxiety but with other affects appropriate to the contents of the unconscious phantasies, i.e., on the one hand with anger, rage and revenge feelings, on the other with masochistic submission, guilt or depression . . . and . . . where anxiety derived from phantasy plays a minor or no part, even severe pain is borne well and forgotten quickly. Pain augmented by anxiety, on the other hand, even if slight in itself, represents a major event in the child's life and is remembered long afterward, the memory being frequently accompanied by phobic defenses against its possible return (6).

Here, Anna Freud treats pain as an absolute perception, indicating that the child's responses to it are modified by the factors stated. We would maintain, however, that the very perception of pain, and hence its memory traces, are influenced by the child's interpretation of the experience. It is not really "pain" until the child, sometimes by looking at his parents and estimating their mood, decides whether he has received a spanking (been hurt) or a love-pat. Theresa Benedek discussed in some detail the child's need, upon perceiving pain, to appeal to his mother to find out whether he has been injured. She pointed out that the mother may respond to the child's need and reassure him by talking to him gently. The mother, responding to her own needs at the moment, may lose control of her own fears and express panic, or scold the child for getting hurt, adding guilt to fear—literally adding insult to injury (7). The child thus is deprived of an opportunity to observe, imitate and learn modes of behavior which he can use to increase his tolerance of anxiety and pain. He may be driven to repeat the pain in an attempt to master it and/or force magically a "better" response from his parent. In some drug dependent patients the drug represented a slightly improved version of the parent's response in regard to pain—the drug did give relief, but only postponed the anxiety *because it was itself experienced as dangerous.*

Identification and imitation of parental patterns of dealing with pain (physical and mental) are important. In some cultures patterns for dealing with pain are quite prominent. For instance, one may be expected to drink alcohol whenever one is upset, especially during the period of mourning, to the point of complete numbing. In other cultures the noisy expression of grief and pain is encouraged and accepted both as conscious experience and as a method of dealing with the feelings involved. In yet others, the males are required to tolerate pain, grief, and so forth, stoically, without even an outward resonse. The patterns for handling pain and unpleasant affects are usually the same for the given culture. Pain can be a part of depression or a substitute for it (8). We have had the opportunity to observe a number of so-called iatrogenic addicts who used narcotics primarily for the relief of physical pain (e.g., headaches or abdominal pains). With remarkable consistency we found a severe latent depression warded off by massive denial, hypomanic or obsessive-compulsive mechanism. Pain, like depression or anxiety, can be the direct symptom of intersystemic intrapsychic tension.

The relationship of this formulation to the state of drug dependence is well stated by Chessick (9). The drug dependent person frequently shows little awareness of his affects. Especially in the group of "medically addicted" individuals, there is a conspicuous absence of anxiety or depression, along with a great frequency of anxiety-equivalent symptoms. In psychoanalysis or psychotherapy with narcotic and alcohol dependent persons, the discovery and verbalization of the nature of affect is an important step toward making possible the giving up of regressive symptoms.

The perception of pain, or any discomfort, tension or stimulus, is a complex process of interpretation and association. The studies by Ostow on temporal lobe function suggest that the association paths of special importance are related to memory traces of an unpleasant nature concerned with avoidance patterns (10). Perhaps this fashion of perception of pain is predestined by the anatomical structure of pain fibers in such a way that we have a quick signal at first, via the unmyelinated pain fibers, and perception of the "pain" as such arrives only some time later, permitting an evaluation of it in the meantime. Sherrington, Livingston, and others, have concluded that pain is a conscious and complex process, rather than a primary perception (11-13).

Physiologists have found that higher brain centers can suppress or modify the perceptual quality of pain (14, 15). This seems to be the anatomical framework for the hysterical phenomena we discussed above. The time interval between the signal-perception and the full consciousness of pain can be utilized for the associative interpretation and modification of the pain experience. In the secure individual the infantile (total) fear response to pain is suppressed. This is attributable to the predominance of the secondary process, and the relatively lesser prevalence of destructive fantasies and wishes.

Inadequately understood is the mechanism by which the perception of pain is terminated psychically, as in the numbing which follows a crushing or cutting wound, or in the phenomenon of depersonalization. Our experience has been that depersonalization, *as a defense against anxiety or pain,* functions in a way exactly analogous to tissue-numbness. For instance, victims of Nazi torture very frequently became depersonalized when the torture became unbearable. Studies on convalescence by Krystal and Petty showed that either the onset of illness, development of pain, or the awareness of being ill or injured may be handled by depersonalization in normal subjects (16). One might say that either the depersonalization or the "numbing" represented a hysterical conversion symptom. Since it requires a quantity of counter-cathectic energy and ability to use it for a reversible splitting of the ego, we begin to appreciate the variety of ego functions involved in the mastery and tolerance of pain.

Of unusual research interest is the old method of managing pain by "counter-irritation." It acts as if pain tracts, a mental apparatus of perception, can be "overloaded" by other messages, such as heat or cold stimulation (from the same dermatomes), thus making the perception of pain indistinct. A host of pain relievers function on the basis of "overloading the lines" of an affected area with perception of heat, cold, sound, and so forth, thus muffling the conscious experience of pain.

Psychic pain can be handled in a similar manner. Freud has noted that counter-irritations or distractions are utilized to cope with physical and psychic pain, as in mourning. The mourner distracts himself, and only periodically returns to perceive the pain of loss, and to rework the loss piecemeal (17). The ability for such self-distraction, vis-à-vis pain of psychic or somatic origin, requires adequate energy and diversified object investments of the ego, which *clinically* can be seen to be impaired in many drug dependent persons. This is shown by the paucity and primitive nature of their object relations and gratifications. This is another mechanism involved in utilization and tolerance of pain. Tolerance for pain is a complex of ego functions which, when impaired, may create a greater than usual need of (and therefore a tendency to) drugs for the relief from pain of physical or psychic origin, in order to be able to tolerate the stresses of everyday living.

It is our contention that the very same ego-functions which are utilized in the reaction to physical pain become involved in the *handling of unpleasant (painful) affects*, and that these functions may be deficient, causing the organism to be less able to tolerate pain, anxiety, and so on, as signals. The individual who cannot deal with the unpleasant states becomes subject to stress and trauma. Szasz pointed out that anxiety is analogous in the ego-object orientation to the role of pain in self-perception in the ego-body plane of reference (18). Furthermore, there are parts of all those ego-functions which together are referred to as the "stimulus barrier." In the conscious experience of "pain," anxiety is an indispensable part of its urgent quality.

THE PROBLEM OF TRAUMA

Closely related to the subject of pain and painful affects, and perhaps even constituting only a variant of the same theme, is the concept of trauma. Freud stated that "the essence of a traumatic situation is an experience of helplessness on the part of the ego in the face of accumulation of excitation, whether of external or internal origin" (4). Dorsey indicates that the term trauma introduces an economic concept. "It means my inability to sustain and keep my mental balance when the exertion I am undergoing, the mental excitation I am suffering, is more than I can tolerate and, at the same moment, arouse my awareness for my identity" (19). The phenomenon of trauma includes "paralysing, immobilizing, or rendering to a state of helplessness, ranging from numbness to an emotional storm in affect behavior"; also "disorganization of feelings, thoughts and behavior, as well as physical symptoms reflecting autonomic dysfunction" (20). We would prefer to emphasize that this autonomic overaction is actually part of overwhelming and overflowing affect and that the affect disorganization represents a regression in which the affects are de-differentiated and discharged in a total excitation pattern like the infant. By definition, once the traumatic process is initiated, it represents a chain of unconscious reactions, which may result in a variety of specific and lasting psychopathological states.

Among these, increased susceptibility to future traumatization and decreased ability to tolerate affects, and to utilize them as signals, are virtually unavoidable (21).

Raskin, Petty, and Warren related the question of trauma to drug dependence (addiction) in the following manner:

> Through every stage of the development of the addiction the person we are dealing with is helpless to make an adequate adjustment by himself. His personality is characterized by serious defects in its development and pathological tendencies inherent in its structure. He is intolerant of anxiety. He avoids or escapes experiencing it through impulsive action. Before discovering the effect of drugs, his sense of security and well-being are dependent upon the immediate gratification of his needs and wants. The ordinary delays and inconveniences of daily living are experienced by him as intolerable frustrations. He cannot escape them. Unbearable tensions are experienced which he feels the environment should relieve. When the relief is not forthcoming, he feels that his inalienable right to happiness as a human being has been abrogated. Thus, simultaneously confronted with the irresistible need for immediate gratification and an ungratifying environment, it is inevitable that he will feel justified in employing any measure to rectify his deprivation (22).

The drug dependent personality as such does not exist. There are a variety of factors and influences, however, which make drug use, abuse, and dependence more likely. Among the factors discussed so far, several suggest that drugs are used to avoid impending psychic trauma in circumstances which would not be potentially traumatic to other people. Such potential sources are regression vis-à-vis affect, the inability to utilize anxiety or affects as a signal, and the inability to tolerate pain and painful affects, especially the Ur-affects or predecessors of depression and anxiety. Since this Ur-affect is conceptualized as the infant's reaction to loss, it begs the question of object relations, which will be taken up later.

The point to be made is that the resistance to trauma, the stimulus barrier, is defective in drug dependent persons.

THE STIMULUS BARRIER

The stimulus barrier has usually been visualized as a wall, or as Freud put it, a "crust" or "protective shield," analogous to the hornified layer of the skin:

It acquires the shield in this way: its outmost surface ceases to have structure proper to living matter, becomes to some degree inorganic and thenceforward functions as a special envelope or membrane resistant to stimuli. In consequence, the energies of the external world are able to pass into the next underlying layers which have remained living, with only a fragment of their original intensity; and these layers can devote themselves behind the protective shield to the reception of the amounts of stimulus which have been allowed through it. By its death, the outer layer has saved all the deeper ones from a similar fate, unless, that is to say, stimuli reach it which are so strong that they break through the protective shield (23).

This model of the stimulus barrier, derived from the function of the skin and the sensory organs, is inadequate in that it does not acknowledge that dealing with stimuli and affects is an active process. This analogy does not view the protection of the organism against trauma as an active ego function but as a sort of sieve or dam which performs entirely passively, unselectively, and whose function is not subject to variation. We would prefer to define the stimulus barrier as the sum total of all the individual's resources which prevent or work toward the prevention of the syndrome of traumatization.

STIMULUS BARRIER AND AFFECT TOLERANCE

In meeting and coping with perceptions, affects, and ideas, many methods and ego functions are employed. The development of a crust might be effective in raising the stimulus threshold, but not the stimulus tolerance. Especially in relation to painful states, it is essential to distinguish between the acuity of perception of the stimulus and the affects arising from dealing with the perception. We are concerned with pain tolerance and not pain threshold. We wish to make explicit our view that the mastery of affects involves the same problems as that of external stimuli, and that the failure to master, to keep within bounds of tolerance, or to ward off affects can produce psychic trauma. Similarly, memories and unconscious memory traces pose a danger of overwhelming the ego with the intensity of stimulation related to previous perceptions, (including those understood only later), memories of trauma in the past, and traumatic screens (20, 24). We conceptualize the drug dependent patient's plight as living in the dread of being overwhelmed with the primary unpleasure affects as a result of the after affects of trauma in infancy. These persons function as though they had an unconscious memory of this danger of trauma by being overwhelmed with the Ur-affect of anxiety-depression, and must ward it off by the mechanism of denial and their dependence upon drug effects.

An interesting correlate at this point is a clinical observation so frequently experienced in meeting with opiate dependent persons. The deficit in the integrity of their psychic stimulus barrier almost seems to be unconsciously perceived by these persons. Their inability to deal adequately and effectively with the stimulus and its provoked affectual response is eloquently expressed by their consciously stated desire and aim to gain a status of "oblivion" through the use of the drug. This same goal in relation to dealing with potential traumatizing affects is reflected by Chein (25, p. 229) in his considerations of drug dependence and Nirvana. The opiate dependent person is stated to be seeking Nirvana rather than Paradise. The latter represents an ideal situation in which all desires are easily and immediately satisfied; Nirvana constitutes the ideal of fulfillment through the absence of desire, and desire itself is viewed as an inherently frustrated state that cannot be compensated for through the pleasure of its gratification.

USE OF DRUGS IN AUGMENTING STIMULUS BARRIER

The traumatic situation, however, is difficult to recognize because of the multiplicity of functions involved. For one, the threat is not exactly from the intensity of stimuli but, as Murphy pointed out, "the specific intensity of meaning" (26). In fact, the absence of stimuli can be just as disturbing. Also, intense stimulation or affect may be preferred, sought by drug users in warding off that which is threatening. This might be the way the amphetamine and other stimulant drug users prefer to tolerate excitement, hypomania, sensory hyperacuity, and the physiological aspects of anxiety (jitters, etc.) rather than the threatening depression or boredom. One might say that the stimulus barrier in this instance is augmented by drugs, exciting perceptions and affects against the specific threatening perception. The analogy that fits this picture better is the "living" action at cell membranes selectively absorbing some ions and using the exertion of others in the process, and at the same time the balance between the two for maintaining the pH, and the electrochemical charge at the surface—and who knows how many other functions at the same time?

Even the function of perception is subject to modification. Petrie showed that experimental subjects consistently decreased or increased the quantity of perceptions. The former also "reduced" the amount of pain they experienced, while under the same circumstances they later "augmented" it. Among the groups tested, alcoholics were consistently "average augmenters" and none were "reducers." Alcohol, aspirin, or placebos decreased the degree to which they augmented their perception, including pain (27). At the same time, we have commented on the drug dependent person's selective lack of or awareness of the one Ur-affect for the relief of which they take the drug. This is a selective "numbing" and blocking.

The ego functions that guard the integrity of the psyche (and therefore the organism) are complex and interrelated. Keiser has pointed out:

> The loss of any one function must necessarily affect all the functions of the ego, since the ego must compensate, or find other means of satisfaction, for those drives or partial drives that can no longer be discharged or gratified through their accustomed pathways. Furthermore energy must be expended on the alteration of the ego function. Hence, it can be postulated that whenever the barrier surrounding a specific ego function is threatened with extinction, a feeling of psychic helplessness is generated. The clinical results of this feeling of helplessness may then be manifest primarily in the area of the damaged ego function (28).

What we are observing with drug dependent individuals in regard to ego functions may have a prehistory in terms of disturbances of drives and affects (1), a resulting disturbance of the ability to deal with the affects, and consequently all the variety of abnormalities of ego functions we are describing here. Finally, drugs themselves are used to produce yet other (temporary) changes in ego functions and consciousness as a means of dealing with or relieving the dysphoric states produced by the disturbed functions.

REFERENCES

1. Krystal, H. "The Study of Withdrawal from Narcotics as a State of Stress." *Psych. Quart. Suppl.* 36: 53-65, 1962.
2. Engel, G. L., "Anxiety and Depression—Withdrawal the Primary Affect of Unpleasure." *Int. J. Psychoan.* 43: 89-98, 1962.
3. Rado, S., "The Psychoanalysis of Pharmacothymia." *Psych. Quart.* 2: 2-23, 1935.
4. Freud, S., *Inhibitions, Symptoms and Anxiety.* S.E.20, 1926.
5. Schur, M., "Comments on the Metapsychology of Somatization." *Psychoan. St. Child* 10: 119-64, 1955.
6. Freud, A., "The Role of Bodily Illness in the Mental Life of Children." *Psychoan. St. Child* 7: 69-81, 1952.
7. Benedek, T., "Towards a Biology of a Depressive Constellation." *J. Am. Psychoan. Assn.* 4: 389-427, 1956.
8. Bradley, J. J., "Pain Associated with Depression." *Brit. J. Psych.* 109: 741-45, 1963.
9. Chessick, R. D., "The Pharmacogenic Orgasm in Drug Addicts." *Arch. Gen. Psych.* 3: 545-56, 1960.
10. Ostow, M., "Psychic Function of Temporal Lobes as Inferred from Seizure Phenom-

ena." *Arch. Neur. & Psych.* 77: 79—5, 1957.
11. KRYSTAL, H., (ed.), *Massive Psychic Trauma*. N.Y., Int. U. Press, 1968.
12. LIVINGSTON, W. K., "What is Pain?" *Sc. Amer.* 407: 3-9, 1953.
13. MELZACK, R., "The Perception of Pain." *Sc. Amer.* 457: 3-12, 1961.
14. BEECHER, H. K., "The Relationship of Wounds to Pain Experienced." *J.A.M.A.* 197: 1609-13, 1956.
15. BEECHER, H. K., "The Subjective Response and Reaction to Sensation." *Am. J. Med.* 20: 107-13, 1956.
16. KRYSTAL, H., & T. A. PETTY, "The Psychological Aspects of Normal Convalescence." *Psychosomatics* 2: 1-7, 1961.
17. FREUD, S., *Mourning and Melancholia*. S.E.14: 245, 1917.
18. SZASZ, T., *Pain and Pleasure*. London, Tavistock, p. 77, 1957.
19. DORSEY, J. M., Opening Remarks to Second Workshop in *Massive Psychic Trauma*, ed. H. Krystal. N.Y., Int. U. Press, p. 48, 1969.
20. RANGELL, L., "The Metapsychology of Trauma," in S. Furst's *Psychic Trauma*. N.Y., Basic Books, pp. 51-85, 1967.
21. SOLNIT, A., & M. KRIS, "Trauma and Infantile Experiences: a Longitudinal Perspective," in S. Furst's *Psychic Trauma*. N.Y., Basic Books, pp. 175-221, 1967.
22. ——, T. A. PETTY, & M. WARREN, "A Suggested Approach to the Problem of Narcotic Addiction." *Am. J. Psych.* 113: 1089-94, 1957.
23. FREUD, S., *Beyond the Pleasure Principle*. S.E.18: 27, 1920.
24. GLOVER, E., "The Screening Function of Traumatic Memories." *Int. J. Psychoan.* 10: 90-93, 1929.
25. CHEIN, I., D. L. GERALD, R. S. LEE, & S. ROSENFELD, *The Road to H.* N.Y., Basic Books, 1964.
26. —— "Trauma and Loss." *J. Am. Psychoan. Assn.* 9: 519-32, 1961.
27. PETRIE, A., *Individuality in Pain and Suffering*. Chicago, U. of Chicago Press, 1967.
28. KEISER, S., "Freud's Concept of Trauma and a Specific Ego Function." *J. Am. Psychoan. Assn.* 15: 781-94, 1967.

10

ADDICTION AND EGO FUNCTION

Norman E. Zinberg

Slowly but definitely there is a growing acceptance of the idea that in order to understand what motivates someone to use illicit drugs and what effect these drugs will have on him, one must take drug, set, and setting into account (Brecher, 1972; *Drug Use in America*, 1973; Edwards, 1973; Khantzian et al., 1974; Weil, 1972; Zinberg and Robertson, 1972; Zinberg and DeLong, 1974). That is, for such understanding the pharmacological action of the drug, how a person approaches the experience, which includes an assessment of his entire personality structure, and the physical and social setting in which the use takes place must all be considered and balanced. A not unusual paradox has begun to develop: the concept of drug effect being a product of these three variables is becoming a commonplace among mental health professionals before the implications of the notion for psychoanalytic theory, in particular, and personality theories, in general, have been worked through (Eddy et al., 1963; Jaffe, 1970; Khantzian, 1974; Wurmser, 1973; Yorke, 1970). Thus, existing misconceptions about a one-to-one relationship between personality maladjustment and drug use and addiction continue unabated.

In this essay, building on the work of several psychoanalytic theorists (Gill and Brenman, 1959; Hartmann, 1939; Klein, 1959; Rapaport, 1958; Zinberg, 1963), especially that of David Rapaport, I shall present

Reprinted with permission from *The Psychoanalytic Study of the Child*, 1975, *30*, 567-588.

Dr. Zinberg is a Faculty Member of Harvard Medical School at The Cambridge Hospital and of The Boston Psychoanalytic Institute. The material for this paper was gathered as part of a study of the social basis of drug abuse prevention funded by The Drug Abuse Council, Inc., 1828 L Street, N.W., Washington, D.C. The work of Richard C. Jacobson and Wayne M. Harding on that project was invaluable to this essay.

clinical studies of compulsive drug use, describe how the users' responses to drugs have changed over time, review Rapaport's positions and show how these apply to the clinical states described, and, finally, discuss the implications of all this for dynamic theory and therapy.

THE INFLUENCE OF SOCIAL SETTING ON DRUG USE

Before turning to the clinical studies of compulsive drug use and users, I shall briefly consider the belief that such use almost invariably stems from severe personality maladjustment or from the individual's being overwhelmed by a powerful chemical. It is true that people described as oral dependent (Rado, 1958), unable to tolerate anxiety (Goldstein, 1972) or aggression (Khantzian, 1974; Wurmser, 1973), or borderline schizophrenics (Radford et al., 1972), do use various illicit drugs to help them deal with their painful affects. Their histories reveal that following the discovery of their drug or drugs of choice, a quick and insistent dependence develops. But it is my contention that these people make up only a fraction, and probably a small one, of even the addict population, let alone the general drug-using population. The idea that certain personality types seek out drug experience because of a specific, early, unresolved developmental conflict, and that such people predominate in the addict group or in the much larger group of controlled users, is based on retrospective falsification. That is, looking at drug users and especially addicts, after they have become preoccupied with their drug experience, authorities assume that these attitudes and this personality state are similar to those the user had before the drug experience, and thus led to it. Then "evidence" from the user's developmental history and previous object relationships is marshaled to show that the addicted state was the end point of a long-term personality process.

This is *not* to say that internal factors are not involved in the decision to use drugs, in the effects of the drugs on the individual, on the rapidity and extent of the increase in drug use, and on the addiction itself and its psychological and social concomitants. But it is to say that there are no psychological profiles or consistent patterns of internal conflicts or phase-specific developmental sequences that can be put forward as the determining factor in the history of drug use and addiction.

Yet, this reasoning persists despite our cultural historical experience with alcohol (Chafetz and Demone, 1962). In the eighteenth century this powerful drug was used very much as heroin is today (Harrison, 1964): 75 or 80 percent of drinkers were alcoholics. Today while there may be 6 to 8 million alcoholics, there are 100 million controlled drinkers of every personality type. Our relative control over alcohol stems from the inculcation of social maxims and rituals (Zinberg and Jacobson, 1974a). "Don't start until sundown," "Know your limit," "Don't drink alone" all serve to minimize excess consumption. There is no consistent effort to select out susceptible personality types, and growing evidence suggests that not even those who do become alcoholics represent specific personality types (McCord and McCord, 1960; Wilkinson, 1970). Hence, it is surprising that there continues to be so much emphasis on the personality of the drug user when there is growing evidence of the power of the social setting to sustain controlled use of a powerful drug among many different personality types (Chafetz and Demone, 1962; Powell, 1973; Zinberg and Jacobson, 1974b).

While the bulk of the clinical work to be presented here will be concerned with the compulsive use of heroin, the history of LSD use over the last decade makes a nice beginning. From about 1965 to 1969 both professionals and the public were terrified by occasional and compulsive use of LSD (Smith, 1969; Tarshis, 1972). Mental hospitals such as Bellevue and Massachusetts Mental Health Center reported that 25 to 35 percent of their admissions resulted from bad trips (Brecher, 1972). The general feeling at that time was that even a single dose of LSD could tip someone who was either seriously disturbed or at a particularly vulnerable life moment, while continued, heavy use, according to this view, would inevitably wear away an individual's psychological capacity to function. Statistics which cited these frequent admissions to mental hospitals, along with lurid accounts in the media of suicides, homicides, and generally bizarre behavior, seemed to justify the fears.

With the passage of just a few years the situation looks quite different. McGlothlin and Arnold (1971) studied 256 subjects who had taken a psychedelic drug before 1962, that is, before the enormous publicity of the "Leary era" with its incredible hopes for enlightenment and insight, and the anxiety that inevitably accompanies an act believed to be so daring and potentially disappointing. Although McGlothlin and Arnold's subjects acknowledged that taking these drugs was a powerful experience—indeed some of the subjects thought it had deeply affected their lives—there were no bad trips reported of the kind that lead to mental hospitalization. And today when, according to the 1973 Report of the President's Commission on Marihuana and Drug Abuse, psychedelic drug use is the fastest growing drug use in the United States (*Drug Use in America*, 1973), mental hospitals no longer report bad trips as a factor in admissions. As of July 1974 the Massachusetts Mental Health Center did not know when they last had such an admission, but they were sure that it had been years rather than months ago (Grinspoon, 1974).

Clearly, the pattern of use has changed. The individual taking 200 to

250 trips in one year in a furious search for mystic enlightenment has given way to the two- or three-times-a-year tripper who closely follows countercultural maxims designed to minimize anxiety. To "only trip in a good place at a good time with good people" makes sense with a drug which increases certain perceptual responses. The fact is that the same strong drug is used today by an increasingly wide variety of personality types. Thus the evidence indicates that it was the social setting that got out of hand; before those wild years of the 60s and since, users in a calmer social setting could adapt to and tolerate the experience.

Another excellent piece of work offers further support for this position. The Barr et al. study (1972), which gave LSD to subjects before 1962, strongly suggests that one cannot assume that those people ordinarily diagnosed as significantly disturbed react more severely to these drugs than those considered "healthier." This work shows that a typology of responses to the drug can be constructed, but that they would not be directly determined by the degree of emotional disturbance. Thus personality is a factor in the drug response, just as the drug itself produces unquestioned strong effects, but without a careful understanding of the powerful, and in the case of LSD, almost determining, influence of social setting, many authorities could and did misinterpret what happened in the 60s.

Another example of the power of the social setting to determine drug use and, in this case, the development of drug dependency and addiction comes from our sad experience in Vietnam. Hundreds of thousands of American youths found themselves among people who hated them, fighting a terrifying war they neither understood nor approved, with illicit drugs readily available (Wilbur, 1972, 1974; Washington Post, 1971). The Army's misunderstanding of marihuana use led to an "educational" campaign against that drug and the enforcement of penalties. Enlisted men quickly found in heroin an odorless, far less bulky replacement which had the unique property of making time seem to disappear. As almost every enlisted man in Vietnam desired nothing so ardently as to have the year to DEROS (Date of Expected Return from Overseas) pass, many thousands used great quantities of that pure, cheap white powder (Zinberg, 1971, 1972a, 1972b). Data from the rehabilitation centers and from camps processing men returning from overseas leave no doubt that a great many of those using heroin were physiologically addicted. Also, final Army data make it possible to say assuredly (despite the Army's early claims that only those who were heavy drug users before service became addicted) that these young men displayed a wide variety of personality types, that they came from diverse social, ethnic, geographic, and religious backgrounds, and that few were drug users before they went to Vietnam (Robins, 1974). When authorities and professionals alike realized the extent of heroin use in Vietnam, consternation and surprise were expressed that such a variety of people who did not conform to addict stereotypes could become addicts, and fear about what would happen in the United States when these people returned dominated most discussions (Wilbur, 1974). These concerns rested on the traditional view that heroin was so powerful a drug that once one was in its thrall there was no escape. Also, the underlying suspicion remained that, despite the evidence of a variety of personality types using the drug, the users were potential drug-dependents who would have been saved in the United States by the lack of availability of heroin.

Studies of returned Vietnam veterans have shown that for a fraction (under 10 percent) of those who had become drug dependent these fears of continued addiction were realized, but that the vast majority (over 90 percent) gave up heroin upon return to the United States. The determining factor in their heroin use had been the intolerable setting of Vietnam, and once they returned to the United States neither the power of the drug nor a susceptible personality proved to be decisive in keeping them drug dependent (Robins, 1974).

DESCRIPTION OF ADDICTS

The sample of U.S. addicts was obtained from a large detoxification center and two psychological-treatment-oriented methadone clinics. Over a period of 16 months 54 addicts were interviewed for approximately two hours each. They ranged in age from 19 to 34; 35 were male and 14 black. Addicts were chosen solely on the basis of their having applied to the methadone clinic or having gone into the fourth day of detoxification on a day when the investigator had time available. Although each of the addicts studied was as sharply different from the next in presentation and general superficial personality as any other members of the population, a psychodynamic formulation showed them to be remarkably alike in their psychological difficulties.

To begin with, junkies look a lot alike: they are usually thin, their clothing shabby, and their person somewhat unkempt. Initial conversations reveal their almost total preoccupation with heroin or its replacements and the life style that surrounds its compulsive use. Drug effect, drug availability, drug necessity—getting off, copping, hustling—and a concern with the legal, physical, and psychological hazards that go with those interests preoccupy them. As a result of their addiction they see themselves as deviants with little sense of relatedness to the straight world. Their sense of themselves seems to derive from their negative social and psychological responses such as antisocial activities, rebellion, expressed aggression against the "bastards," and from their own victimization. In Erikson's (1959) terms, they depend on a negative identity for a measure of self-esteem and self-definition.

In our conversations the subjects revealed a direct belief in magic, often centering around the drug and its use, but extending to other areas as well. Junkies frequently tell of how their lives have been starcrossed, with ordinary events being given the power to save or destroy. In these stories frank primary process thinking seems available to consciousness. These thoughts come out as distorted ideas: "I knew if my parents told my grandfather about my sister's marriage, it would kill him, and I was the only one who could stop them." "I knew the train would be late that day before I got on it. There was an aura around the whole station." Or they show an indistinct differentiation between objective reality and a fantasy or magical view: "All it takes is for me to get my shit together, then I can handle all that." The defenses of projection, introjection, and denial are consistently prominent, as is repression, which will be considered separately. As their associations tend to be loose anyway, the combination gives an almost bizarre flavor to most interactions: "I never give in. I'm always fighting the dope and those bastards in the clinic gave me the wrong dope. I know that it doesn't work on me in liquid form and they won't help me cut down by getting the pills."

It must be remembered that despite this presentation of themselves junkies are rarely schizophrenic. Vaillant's 12-year follow-up (1966a, 1966b) found few addicts in mental hospitals, and the clinical impressions of other investigators since then support his work. Since the growth of heroin use in the late 60s, undoubtedly more borderline or schizophrenic people have used heroin as an effort at self-medication, but they remain a small minority—which strikes me as remarkable every time I finish another interview, for it is hard to believe that all addicts are not crazy after talking with them.

There is a general conscious deterioration of the superego. Junkies will tell you fairly frankly that they do what they have to do to survive and get drugs. They know that they cannot be trusted to follow the usual rules, ethics, and codes of social behavior. Tales of stealing from and lying to friends and family abound. Usually there is little real acceptance of responsibility. Their anger and blame for all sorts of troubles are reserved for those circumstances or people that spoiled the perfect deal, the neat setup—often authorities in some form. But always the drug is the basic preoccupation. Their readiness to blame those who interfere with their using the drug so that it works magically is unending. The hours given over in methadone clinics to discussing dosage and whether they are getting enough of the drug, in the right form, by the right person, at the right time, in the right way are literally uncountable. These expressions, while they seem paranoid in flavor and content and carry bitterness and conviction, are nonetheless not paranoid in a paranoid schizophrenic way. The addicts permit their ideas to be more or less susceptible to reality testing if the tester is willing to be subtle, forceful, and extremely patient.

And, as one might expect, while the junkies accept their own unwillingness to play by the rules, they deeply and passionately feel that others, particularly authorities, must. In a way there is no paradox here because their primitive unconscious superego never rests. Junkies are not only self-destructive in the sense that they are incredibly accident prone and constantly arranging to be hurt, but they also manage almost never to do well for themselves in the simplest life transactions. They do lose laundry slips and money, choose the wrong alternative at each instance, and are invariably being gypped at the very moment they think they are slyest. These experiences ostensibly result in an increase in blame for "them" and a feeling that the big strong ones, the doctors, counselors, probation officers, should be more helpful to and more responsible for the poor addict; but this position is invariably accompanied by rigorous and overwhelming self-loathing.

As a result they are argumentative, particularly in a methadone clinic, about matters affecting their precious substance, but very ineffectually so. This need to be unpleasant and to set up struggles that are doomed to defeat arises directly from their insistence on putting and keeping themselves in a weak position. But often if one pushes further into the arcane thought processes surrounding each instance of trouble, fantasy fears that have developed into phobias become apparent. For example, a methadone clinic regulation requires a physical examination; two appointments in a row were missed by several patients, putting them in jeopardy of dismissal from the clinic. Careful questioning revealed that a baseless rumor was circulating that anyone who didn't "pass" the physical would be hospitalized, and since addicts' response to hospitals is truly phobic, they didn't show up for the exam. The development of similar overwhelming fears among junkies is quite common and somehow exaggerated when juxtaposed against the superficial tough (but done in) guy/gal image they try to project.

The breakdown in logical thinking, the disorganization of the ordinary cognitive process above and beyond the difficulty in reality testing is so severe that the inexperienced interviewer fails to understand their educational and vocational accomplishments. Their memories, for example, are terrible, and there seems to be no psychodynamic rhyme or reason to the lacunae. Thinking of repression simply as a defense and an aid to denial and projection does not help one to achieve a dynamic formulation. Neither can one rely for an explanation on conscious dissembling. Certainly the interviewer knows that there is much overt lying to hide real or fancied transgressions and to protect secret pockets of potential gratification. But the forgetting of both significant and insignificant life events and activities often acts more to the addict's detriment on his own terms. Hard as it is to imagine, some even forget a stash of drugs, and they easily manage not to remember addresses, appointments, relevant history, and so on, which could help get them a welfare check or other disability assistance. Running through all this cognitive deterioration is a disorientation of the time sense, which may well be related to the drug experience. Heroin seems to "make time go away," and compensating for that experience may be difficult.

Taken overall, then, this study of addicts shows people whose everyday psychological state seems compatible with a diagnosis of borderline schizophrenia or worse, but who are not schizophrenic; whose current ego functions and cognitive capacities make past accomplishments inexplicable, but who are at times remarkably capable and intellectually able; and who, from this dynamic perspective, appear a lot alike. It is easy to understand the temptation to use this sort of material to work out formulations that would "explain" their seeking drugs and drug dependency. It must be remembered, however, that compared to psychoanalysis or intensive dynamic therapy, these interviews are brief and superficial. Further and more intensive interviewing might disclose more subtle and pervasive evidence of early gross family and individual psychiatric impairment. However, within the severe limitations of this study, the families of these patients were described as consistently different from each other. Only four cases presented frank early histories of emotional disturbance, early school difficulty, and the general sense of oddness associated with early borderline schizophrenia or early severe character disorders.*

ADDICTION AND RELATIVE EGO AUTONOMY

Rapaport (1958) delineated the factors that maintain relative ego au-

---

*There is some further preliminary evidence that tends to point in the same direction but stems from interviews that were even more cursory, done by social workers and with a different intent. Within this sample, 30 families were interviewed by a social worker to decide upon admission to a methadone clinic. Although there were great differences in the family structure and the degrees of difficulty within the family, the workers found that only two of the families thought that the principal disturbances between the addict subjects and their significant others began before serious drug use.

tonomy. He began by observing that nonliving matter cannot escape the impact of the environment and thus the results of the interaction are invariant and statistically predictable. This is not true of living matter. At times psychoanalytic theory has tried to pretend that inner forces are strong enough to develop some sort of predictability despite the uncounted variables acting through the physical and social environment, but this has not worked out. Using the Berkeleyian and Cartesian positions to develop a dialectic, Rapaport points out that in the Berkeleyian view man is totally independent of the environment and totally dependent on inner forces and drives. He need have little concern for the external world since it is "created" by inherent forces. The cartoon psychiatrist who is shown asking someone who has been hit by a car, "How did you cause this to happen to you?" is an exaggerated clinical version of this position.

Descartes, on the other hand, saw man as a clean slate upon which experience writes. He is totally dependent upon and thus in harmony with the outside world, and totally independent of, autonomous from, internal desires. In essence, Cartesians, like behaviorists, view such drives and the unconscious supposedly containing them as nonexistent. This may well account for the failure of learning machines. Human conflicts over success and failure turned out to be more dominant than the desire for M&Ms.

Rapaport reasons that neither of these totally divergent positions speaks to man's experience: that to understand how the ego, whose functions determine and delineate a sense of self, remains relatively autonomous and copes with the demands of the external environment and of the basic, inborn forces Freud termed "instinctual drives" requires consideration of both and their interactions. The autonomy Rapaport postulated is always relative, and the inside drives and the outside environment carefully balance each other. Drives prevent man from becoming a stimulus-response slave,* while the constant stream of stimulus nutriment from the environment mediates and moderates the primitive drives** by sustaining primary ego apparatuses such as motor capacity, thinking, memory, perceptual and discharge thresholds, and the capacity for logical communication. In addition, external reality nurtures those secondary ego apparatuses—such as competence, cognitive organization,

---

*Rapaport tells the story of the man who did not march in step to an enthralling military band because he was pondering, and points out how falling in love saved Orwell's Protagonist of *1984*, at least temporarily, from the press of that overwhelming environment.
**Here, Rapaport uses the story of Moses and the great king who had been told by his seers and phrenologist that Moses was cruel, vain, and greedy. Upon finding Moses gentle, wise, and compassionate, the king planned to put his wise men to death. Moses demurred, saying, "They say truly what I am. What they could not see was what I have made of it."

values, ideals, and a mature conscience, determined by each particular culture as adaptive—and allows these characteristics to become successfully estranged from original drive functions.

Thus the relationship between the ego's relative autonomy from the id and the ego's relative autonomy from the environment is one of interdependence. When drives are at peak tension, as in puberty, the ego's autonomy from the id is in jeopardy. Adolescents try to combat their tendency to subjectivity, seclusiveness, and rebellion by the external reality-related converse of these—intellectualization, distance from primary objects, and efforts at total companionship. But it is an unequal and often painful struggle.

The ego's autonomy from the id can also be disrupted by minimizing the balancing input from external reality. Experiments with stimulus deprivation (Bexton et al., 1954; Heron et al., 1953, 1956; Lilly, 1956) showed how susceptible individuals became autistic and suffered from magical fantasies, disordered thought sequences, disturbed reality testing, primitive defenses, and poor memory under such conditions.

Similarly, conditions which permit only restricted and frightening forms of stimulus nutriment impair the ego's relative autonomy from the external environment. When, as in a concentration camp, external conditions maximize the individual's sense of danger and arouse fears and neediness, the drives no longer act as guarantors of autonomy from the environment but prompt surrender. The deprivation of varied stimulus nutriment and its replacement by insistent streams of instructions in the stimulus-deprivation experiments gave those instructions power and engendered belief. In order to maintain a sense of separate identity, values, ideologies, and orderly thought structures, people require support for existing verbal and memory structures. Not surprisingly, Rapaport used George Orwell's *1984* as a text—one which described in exact and clinical detail how this interdependence functioned under environmental conditions intended to turn the individual into a stimulus-response slave.

Throughout his discussion Rapaport insists that the superego in particular is dependent on consistent stimulus nutriment. The convention, or American Legionnaire, syndrome—when moderate, respectable men and women remove themselves from their usual routines and social relationships and behave in an impulsive and uncontrolled manner—makes it very clear how heavily the strictures of conscience depend on social structure.

The junkies described earlier have lost varied sources of stimulus nutriment. Families have been alienated and previous social relationships severed; or, if contact remains, it consists usually of acrimonious or pleading discussions about giving up drugs. Addicts are declared deviant by the larger society and are referred to as an epidemic, a plague, and the "number one problem" of the country. The social input available to them is thus either a negative view of themselves or the ceaseless patter of their compulsive drug-using groups. Have you copped? When? Where? Was it good? What do I need to cop? What if I can't? Who got busted? Will I get busted? These are conditions, albeit self-arranged, which meet the conditions of stimulus-deprivation experiments. At the same time the addict's desire for gratification from the drug itself, and the memory of the result, a withdrawal syndrome, if the drug is unavailable, keeps drive structures at peak tension.

According to Rapaport's formulation, a regressive state should develop when the ego is unable to maintain its relative autonomy from either the id or the external environment. In such a state the barriers differentiating ego and id processes become fluid. Images, ideas, and fantasies based on primary process thinking rise to consciousness, and there develops a reliance on more and more primitive defenses. The sense of voluntariness and of having inner control of one's actions in relation to oneself and to the external environment disappears. Is that not exactly what I have described as the general clinical picture of the junkie?

The necessity to cop, which excessively increases the addict's dependence on the environment, impairs his ego's autonomy from the id. At the same time, being labeled deviant decreases varied contacts with the usual environmental supports and thus also impairs his ego's autonomy from the id. The addicts' efforts to continue some coherent relationships with whatever objects are left to them make them dependent on external cues. They suffer constantly from doubts about their ability to maintain such relationships, and they cling to stereotyped views of themselves. This clinging to what remains of the external environment maximizes the ego's autonomy from the id, but at the cost of minimizing the conscious input of and trust in affective and ideational signals that usually regulate judgment and decision—that is, at the cost of impairing the ego's autonomy from the environment.

Thus the addicts' relative autonomy from both id and external environment is impaired. They are isolated from their own useful emotions and those views of the world which permit a coherent and integrated sense of self. They are at the mercy of primitive impulses and an overwhelming sense of neediness that invades, or more nearly blocks out, a capacity to perceive and integrate "objective" reality. Filled with doubts, they gullibly respond to those in the external environment who offer schemes or promises that might bring magical succor.

As a result of these impaired autonomies the ego must make do with insufficient or distorted input from both id and external environment. The ego must modify its structures to conform to this new, more restricted, and primitive pattern. It is my clinical impression that the addict's ego fights to retain whatever level of ego functioning can be saved. It is this very struggle to retain some measure of ego functions which is a principal source of the rigidity that therapists working with the addicts, in and out of methadone clinics, find so trying. As long as addicts are classified by the larger culture as deviants, it is hard to imagine that they can see themselves as anything else. And as long as their relationships with the external world continue to supply only restricted stimulus nutriment, the blocking of most affective input not oriented to direct gratification *probably* will continue. Whatever new ego homeostasis the individual has achieved, is likely to be rigid and to have a slow rate of change. When threatened, as these people's egos constantly are, by changeable but insistent demands for gratification from drive structures, the new homeostasis of ego functioning cannot easily integrate fresh stimulus nutriment, not even input that is as neutral and sustaining as a therapeutic relationship. Or perhaps it would be more accurate to say: *particularly* the input of a therapeutic relationship because these interactions are *intended* to be at variance with the addicts' usual interpersonal interactions and to make their usual reliance on selective perception, quick repression, projection, and denial more difficult.

There are two other points which stress the importance of the social setting. In showing how the labeling of the addict as a deviant becomes a key factor in impairing his relative ego autonomy I described the extent to which primary process ideation such as interest in magic, belief in animism, generalized unfounded suspiciousness, and acceptance of extremely childish rhetoric become regressively active in regular ego functioning. Junkies often seem to me to be vaguely aware of their own primitive response. But they cannot integrate such thinking sufficiently to make it part of a conscious way of questioning the world, i.e., secondary process, first because the primitive feelings much of the time seem so real. A second interrelated issue is the unconscious effort to retain existing capacity to function no matter how unsatisfactory. In the 60s users of LSD had a similar problem. They too regarded their "trip" as exceptional and at that point found few points of reference between the trip experience and their previous social and psychological experiences. But by the 70s, as a recent study contends (Zinberg, 1974), occasional psychedelic drug users have the same unusual psychic experiences that their counterparts of the 60s had. However, the accumulated and widely dispersed knowledge about the experience prepared them for it. They think about their experiences and discuss them with friends in order to separate out drug effect from essential and usual self-perspectives. Thus the experience is secondary process oriented.

PROSPECTIVE STUDY OF ADDICTION

In 1967-68 I engaged in a large-scale interviewing process to select candidates for a controlled experiment giving marihuana to human subjects (Zinberg and Weil, 1970). Three of those interviewed but not selected for the experiment, who had not used heroin at that time, have gone on to become compulsive heroin users. One is included in the sample of 54 described above, and I have had some lengthy conversations with the other two. They are reluctant to be followed, so I cannot make a full report. Suffice it to say that although all three had many individual quirks and peculiarities in 1967, none was at all like the prototypical junkie then and all three are now. In 1967 the man included in the present sample was rebellious and active in radical politics, intensely intellectual, harshly self-searching, with high standards for himself and others. He had a wide circle of friends and acquaintances which was beginning to narrow at the time I knew him as a result of political disagreements. Nevertheless, his sense of objective reality was not in doubt, his memory was excellent, and his capacity for logical thinking was of the highest order. At that time he had begun to be estranged from his parents, particularly his father, although they too were committed to the political left, and their disagreement was more on method than principle. Previously, despite a lifetime of arguing and concern about economic instability, their relationship had been an enduring one, and he had been quite close to two of his three siblings.

In 1973, while being detoxified for the third time, he had not seen or heard from a family member in over two years. His thought processes were slow and jumpy, and his associations loose. Although he remembered me, he had difficulty in sticking to the subject of the interview, wandering to questions about my hospital function, his medications, and his chances of recovering. When he returned to the subject, his memory was poor, his recall distorted, and his acceptance of responsibility for himself *nil*. At that moment he was on probation for two offenses and had another charge of possession with intent to sell narcotics pending. He gave every evidence of being an impulsive, poorly controlled person. Physically it was hard to recognize him as the same man, and he too said, "I'm not the same person you talked to then."

Both here and in England I have interviewed (Zinberg and Robertson, 1972) many heroin addicts of up to 30 years' standing who showed no emotional or intellectual deterioration. Hence, I do not believe the drug itself was responsible for this man's deterioration, nor can I, on the basis of my previous knowledge of this man, accept the explanation of preexisting addictive personality. I do not at this writing understand what pushed him into addiction. He claims it was fortuity. Following many severe political disappointments and a marked reduction in his social group, he found himself with people whose regular polydrug use, including heroin, was far heavier than his previous standard. They were heavy users of downers (barbiturates), which he had never liked. When they took downers, he used heroin. After a year and a half of chipping (occasional use), he woke up one morning after not using and recognized that the severe stomach cramps, gooseflesh, and sweating meant that he was strung out. He made many efforts to kick, but after that it was essentially downhill all the way.

No doubt somewhere in his psyche the conflicts concerning responsibility, self-sufficiency, and rebellion existed in 1967. But as Freud (1937) argues so persuasively, latent conflicts of all sorts may exist, but whether they will ever become manifest is determined by the subject's life experiences. It is my impression—and I hope to be able to study these three men more thoroughly—that just as with the Vietnam heroin users, it was the changed social setting that was instrumental in impairing their relative ego autonomy.

TREATMENT OF ADDICTS

Mental health workers of all sorts in methadone clinics, detoxification centers, and the like, already have discovered that therapy must be oriented around current reality. Basically it is important for the therapist to point out again and again what his job is. He wants to work with addicts in ways that will help them to find out how their heads work and how they consistently manage to do the worst for themselves. The therapist is friendly, but he is not there to love them, and anyway his love has no special magical healing property. Neither is he a boss, a job counselor, a dispenser of drugs, or the arbiter of dose increases; he has no prescriptions for living with or without drugs. What stops the addicts from using him appropriately, from trying to make sense of what is going on in their lives? How is it that they want him to be anything but a therapist and want so much to bamboozle, provoke, or seduce him? These are the sorts of questions the therapists find themselves asking.

They are keenly aware of the disappointments, deprivations, and social and psychological isolation of a junkie's life, just as therapists are aware of the high excitement to be found in hustling, copping, and shooting up, compared with which a straight life is seen as a conscience-oriented gray straitjacket, and they try to convey their ability to understand this conflict. Therapists point out how the longings for authoritarianism and the clear-cut concepts of what's right and wrong, at least for others, are based on the junkies' lost trust in their own controls, judgment, and awareness of their own wishes. In effect, the therapy aims at understanding how those ego functions which operate do so; how those that might don't; and what makes such ego functioning difficult; also, how the primitive unconscious superego is active but not helpful. The therapy further intends to show how the remaining ego capacity which at times attempts realistically to modify and moderate behavior is ignored.

This therapeutic approach is well known and intended to help restore the lost relative ego autonomy by using the therapist, clinic, and hospital as a source of fresh, diverse stimulus nutriment. These significant social relationships also act to help the subject's embattled ego be less fearful of his drives. Usually, the theory of technique lags behind the formation of a general theory even if individual practitioners learn how to use theoretical concepts intuitively. This essay is intended to add an understanding of what happens to the ego as a result of the changed social condition of the addict and of how this theoretical position can be extended into technique. Hence, if this theoretical view of the patient's problems is accepted, a therapist would not often or forcefully interpret projection or confront denial. It would be useless and actually psychonoxious to point out that the junkie's feeling that the staff of a clinic is hostile and wants to degrade and deprecate him stems from his own destructive preoccupations with himself and others. Rather the staff members consistently explain what they are there for and ask what troubles the addict about their function; that is, therapists provide him with constant, gentle reaffirmation of reality and show how unnecessary much of his difficulty with it is. Thus, the need for the projection and denial becomes less urgent.

Although some discussion of the addict's past and of his or her family relationships may have occasional usefulness, generally speaking this area is of less interest when working with the addict group than in more usual dynamic therapies. For one thing, such discussions often turn into an interest in the motives and interrelationships that may have led the addict to drug use and drug dependency, and this, if the formulations derived in this paper are accurate, is a fruitless area. At least, when one considers the complexity of drug, set, and setting interactions, it is not one that can be worked on until the addict is in better psychological condition. Incidentally, a further complication with most of the 54 addicts studied—and this is again part of the social setting—is that they are "treatment wise." Almost all of them have had experiences in concept houses and with confrontation groups of all sorts. Although they have rarely followed through with these programs, they have developed a patter about what they are feeling and why they are the way they are that serves as armor against reasonable conversation. A therapist following the theory of technique offered here, rather than showing interest in the motivation for drug use and being drawn into discussions of dependency, neediness, anxiety, aggression, and aspects of early development and early family life, would allow that the addict might have had to do many things *then* but could *now* stop and recognize that this or that action might not be as necessary as he experiences it.

It is around therapeutic interactions such as these that this theory of technique becomes important. At times, dynamic therapists who know that they must work toward reestablishing relative ego autonomy and relieving the pressure of the archaic superego feel that unless they uncover and help the patients understand the initial motivations for the behavior, they are not doing their job. When therapists have a concern that they must do both, it creates a duality in the therapy. With people as embattled and desperate as the addicts, it is a subtle and difficult therapeutic problem to remain constant in outlining the therapeutic context and the reduced fields of relationship both to drive structures and to the external environment. Bringing in long-term motivational conflicts is seductive. Maintaining the awareness that such clarifications are both too confusing to the addicts and too frustrating for the therapist is very difficult. The therapist should remember that junkies do not do well for themselves, and the higher the therapeutic hopes of the therapist, if they are excessive, the greater the disappointment. It is no accident that from Synanon on many "therapies" for junkies involved punishing, authoritarian regimens. Most addicts are provocative. They ask to be contained in a way that could easily be translated into a wish to be punished. It is my impression that, whether the addict asks for punishment or not, fulfilling such a wish sets up a vicious cycle. Punishment is followed by a sense of entitlement, followed by guilt, followed by a fresh, unconscious desire to be punished. A therapy that questions the current premises of the addict's behavior and indicates that he has choices and has to accept responsibility for them is containing and limit-setting; and if it is carried out with respect for the dignity of the patient and a precise understanding of his premises, it is neither punishing nor gimmicky.

To sustain such a therapy requires an awareness of the crucial role of the social setting in the current ego state of the addict. And for many professionals that means a shift in their assessment of what has happened to the individual who has become drug dependent. Without that shift the tendency to focus on motivations and unconscious conflicts which could have led to the dependency would be well-nigh irresistible. These factors remain important, as set is as integral a variable as setting, but personality conflict is no longer seen as *the* direct cause of the addict's deterioration.

REFERENCES

BRECHER E. M. & EDITORS OF CONSUMER REPORTS (1972), *Licit and Illicit Drugs.* Boston: Little Brown.
BARR H. L., LANGS, R. J., HALL, R. R. et al. (1972), *LSD: Personality and Experience.* New York: Wiley Interscience.
BEXTON, W. H., HERON, W., & SCOTT, T. H. (1954), Effects of Decreased Variation in the Sensory Environment. *Canad. J. Psychol.,* 8:70-76.
CHAFETZ. M. E. & DEMONE, H. W., JR. (1962), *Alcoholism and Society.* New York: Oxford Univ. Press.
Drug Use in America: Problem in Perspective (1973). Second Report of the National Commission on Marihuana and Drug Abuse. Washington, D.C.: U.S. Government Printing Office.
EDDY, N. B., HALBACH, H., ISBELL, H. ET AL. (1963), Drug Dependence. *Bull. W.H.O.* 2:721-733.
EDWARDS, G. (1973), *The Plasticity of Human Response.* London: Maudsley Hospital (mimeograph).
ERIKSON, E. H. (1959), *Identity and the Life Cycle [Psychol. Issues,* Monogr. 1]. New York: Int. Univ. Press.
FREUD, S. (1937), Analysis Terminable and Interminable. *S.E.,* 23:209-253.
GILL, M. M. & BRENMAN, M. (1959), *Hypnosis and Related States.* New York: Int. Univ. Press.
GOLDSTEIN, A. (1972), Heroin Addiction and the Role of Methadone in Its Treatment. *Arch. Gen. Psychiat.,* 26:291-298.
GRINSPOON, L. (1974), Personal communication.
HARRISON, B. (1964), *English Drinking in the Eighteenth Century.* New York/London: Oxford Univ. Press.
HARTMANN, H. (1939), *Ego Psychology and the Problem of Adaptation.* New York: Int. Univ. Press, 1958.
HERON, W., BEXTON, W. H., & HEBB, D. O. (1953), Cognitive Effects of a Decreased Variation in the Sensory Environment. *Amer. Psychologist,* 8:366-372.
—— DOONE, B. K., & SCOTT, T. H. (1956), Visual Disturbances After Prolonged Perceptual Isolation. *Canad. J. Psychol.,* 10:13-18.
JAFFE, J. H. (1970), Drug Addiction and Drug Abuse. In: *The Pharmacological Bases of Therapeutics,* ed. L. S. Goodman & A. Gilman. New York: Macmillan.
KHANTZIAN, E. J. (1974), Opiate Addiction. *Amer. J. Psychother.,* 28:59-70.
—— MACK, J. E., & SCHATZBERG, A. F. (1974), Heroin Use as an Attempt to Cope. *Amer. J. Psychiat.,* 131:160-164.
KLEIN G. S. (1959), Consciousness in Psychoanalytic Theory. *J. Amer. Psychoanal. Assn.,* 7:5-34.
LILLY, J. C. (1956), Mental Effects of Reduction of Ordinary Levels of Visual Stimuli on Intact Healthy Persons. *Psychiat. Res. Rep.,* 5:1-9.
McCORD, J. & McCORD, W. (1960), *Origins of Alcoholism.* Stanford: Stanford Univ. Press.
McGLOTHLIN, W. H. & ARNOLD, D. O. (1971), LSD Revisited. *Arch. Gen. Psychiat.,* 24:35-49.
ORWELL, G. (1949), *1984.* New York: Harcourt Brace.
POWELL, D. H. (1973), Occasional Heroin Users. *Arch. Gen. Psychiat.,* 28:586-594.
RADFORD, P., WISEBERG, S., & YORKE, C. (1972), A Study of "Main-Line" Heroin Addiction.

The Psychoanalytic Study of the Child, 27:156-180.

RADO, S. (1958), Narcotic Bondage. In: *Problems of Addiction and Habituation*, ed. P. H. Hoch & J. Zubin. New York: Grune & Stratton, pp. 27-36.

RAPAPORT, D. (1958), The Theory of Ego Autonomy. In: *The Collected Papers of David Rapaport*, ed. M. M. Gill. New York: Basic Books, 1967, pp. 722-744.

ROBINS, L. (1974), A Followup Study of Vietnam Veterans' Drug Use. *J. Drug Issues*, 4:62-81.

SMITH, D. E. (1969), Lysergic Acid Diethylamide. *J. Psychedel. Drugs*, 1:3-7.

TARSHIS, M. S. (1972), *The LSD Controversy*. Springfield, Ill.: Thomas.

VAILLANT, G. E. (1966a), A 12-Year Followup of New York Narcotic Addicts: I. *Amer. J. Psychiat.*, 122:727-737.

———— (1966b) A 12-Year Followup of New York Narcotic Addicts: III. *Arch. Gen. Psychiat.*, 15:599-609.

Washington Post (1971), The U.S. Army: Battle for Survival, 8-part Series, September 12-20.

WEIL, A. T. (1972), *The Natural Mind*. New York: Houghton Mifflin.

WILBUR, R. S. (1972), How to Stamp Out a Heroin Epidemic. *Today's Health*, July, pp. 9-13.

———— (1974), The Battle Against Drug Dependency within the Military. *J. Drug Issues*, 4:27-33.

WILKINSON, R. (1970), *The Prevention of Drinking Problems*. New York: Oxford Univ. Press.

WURMSER, L. (1973), Psychoanalytic Considerations of the Etiology of Compulsive Drug Use. Presented at the 60th Annual Meeting of the American Psychoanalytic Association, Honolulu, Hawaii.

YORKE, C. (1970), A Critical Review of Some Psychoanalytic Literature on Drug Addiction, *Brit. J. Med. Psychol.*, 43:141-159.

ZINBERG, N. E. (1963), The Relationship of Regressive Phenomena to the Aging Process. In: *The Normal Psychology of the Aging Process*, ed. N. E. Zinberg & I. Kaufman. New York: Int. Univ. Press.

———— (1971), GI's and OJ's in Vietnam. *N.Y. Times Mag.*, December 5.

———— (1972a), Heroin Use in Vietnam and the United States. *Arch. Gen. Psychiat.*, 26:486-488.

———— (1972b), Rehabilitation of Heroin Users in Vietnam. *Contemp. Drug Prob.*, 1:263-294.

———— (1974), *"High" States*. Washington, D.C.: Drug Abuse Council Special Studies Series, SS-3.

———— & DELONG, J. V. (1974), Research and the Drug Issue. *Contemp. Drug Prob.*, 3:71-100.

———— & JACOBSON, R. C. (1974a), The Social Basis of Drug Abuse Prevention (unpublished).

———— ———— (1974b), The Natural History of Chipping (unpublished).

———— & ROBERTSON, J. A. (1972), *Drugs and the Public*. New York: Simon & Schuster.

———— & WEIL, A. T. (1970), A Comparison of Marihuana Users and Non-Users. *Nature*, 226:719-723.

11

THE "ADDICTION-PRONE" PERSONALITY: A STUDY OF CANADIAN HEROIN ADDICTS

Paul Gendreau and L. P. Gendreau

Evidence supporting the "addiction-prone" personality theory of narcotic addiction was reviewed. A non-addict control sample was selected that incorporated several parameters found to be lacking in previous studies comparing addicts and non-addicts. The results on the MMPI of the non-addict sample were compared to those of an addict group. Contrary to the "addiction-prone" theory, the results of the addict and non-addict groups were not reliably different. The results were discussed in terms of the "addiction-prone" theory, and an alternative to the "addiction prone" theory was suggested.

Nyswander (1956) has stated: "If there is no significant difference between the personality structure of addicts and non-addicts drug addiction would seem to be primarily due to the action of drugs," or if "the addict has a specific unique accommodation of psychological factors then those factors would be truly meaningful" (p. 64) in explaining why a person becomes addicted.

The major emphasis to date on research on narcotic addiction has

Reprinted with permission from the *Canadian Journal of Behavioral Science*, 1970, *2*, 18-25. Copyright 1970, Canadian Psychological Association.

The authors express thanks to officials of Kingston Penitentiary for allowing testing of addicts, and to Drs. L. A. Gendreau, G. Scott, D. Andrews, and M. Eveson for their advice on the research project.

supported the addiction-prone personality theory—i.e., that persons who have taken narcotics had specific psychological weaknesses, which were satisfied by heroin (other substitutes are codeine and Demerol). The "addiction-prone" personality has been variously described as being (a) inadequate and passive, with associated neurotic traits (Ausubel, 1958; Eveson, 1963; Gerard & Kornetsky, 1955; Gilbert & Lombardi, 1967; Hill, Haertzen, & Davis, 1962; Nyswander, 1956; Savitt, 1963; Scott, 1963; Wikler, 1952; Wikler & Rasor, 1953; Yahraes, 1963; Zimmering, 1952); (b) psychopathic (Felix, 1944; Gilbert & Lombardi, 1967; Hill, Haertzen, & Glaser, 1960; Olson, 1964; Stanton, 1956); (c) less psychopathic than non-addict control groups (Gerard & Kornetsky, 1955; Hill et al., 1962; Zimmering, 1952); (d) sexually maladjusted (Hoffman, 1964; Letendresse, 1968; Nyswander, 1956; Wikler, 1952; Zimmering, 1952); and (e) prone to anxiety and depressive traits (Ausubel, 1958; Eveson, 1963; Gilbert & Lombardi, 1967; Hill et al., 1962; Van Kaam, 1968; Wikler & Rasor, 1953).

Of the above studies, Gerard and Kornestsky (1955), Hill et al. (1962), Gilbert and Lombardi (1967), and Zimmering (1952) reported that their addict groups differed from non-addict control groups. However, each of the studies had certain problems in design. Gerard and Kornetsky (1955) paid their control subjects to complete the projective tests, whereas the addict group was not paid. Secondly, the projective tests were not scored blindly (blind scoring of protocols by a psychologist other than the authors failed to find significant differences). The two groups of subjects differed significantly as to IQ, and, of the original 91 controls, selected data were reported on only 23 of these subjects. Zimmering (1952), again using projective tests, based his conclusions on a small sample of 12 hospitalized non-addicts. There were 22 subjects in the addict group. Zimmering did not include statistical evidence for concluding that the drug-addict sample demonstrated far more pathology than the non-addict sample. Hill et al. (1962) selected his controls from a U.S. maximum security prison.

They found that the addicts differed from the criminals on the depression (D), masculinity-femininity (Mf) and hypomania (Hy) scales of the MMPI. The control sample was suspect, for, in Canada at least, maximum security inmates generally are older, have longer records, and are classed as having little rehabilitative potential. Hill also used factor analysis on the MMPI items to identify specific addict traits; but, according to Shure and Rogers (1965), factor analysis of the MMPI has led to spurious combinations of results or factors. Secondly, Hill's two groups varied as to IQ, and this variable has, along with age differences, been found to influence results if penal samples were used (Stanton, 1956). Gilbert and

Lombardi (1967) reported that their addicts scored more highly on the depression (D), Hy, Pd and Pt (psychasthenia) scales of the MMPI as compared with their non-addict sample. Non-addicts were selected from a socio-economic level similar to that of the drug addicts; however, there was no indication as to the degree of criminal activity engaged in by the control group. In Canada, Stevenson, Lewis, Lingley, Trasov, and Stanfield (1956) reported that Canadian drug addicts engaged in criminal activity prior to ever having received their first narcotics conviction. Thus, previous evidence that has suggested an "addiction-prone" personality may have been in part due to inadequate control-group samples, at least in those cases where controls were used. In order to ensure that differences exist between addicts and non-addicts, an adequate control group compared to drug addicts had to meet the following criteria: (a) subjects came not only from the same socio economic level, but also had opportunities to obtain narcotics, but failed to become addicted; (b) the control group had a criminal record; and (c) age and IQ differences were minimized between the two groups. The sample was derived from a penal population, and the MMPI was the measuring instrument.

Assessment of addicts by means of the MMPI avoided the subjectivity involved in interpreting projective tests and afforded comparisons with those studies that have found specific differences between addicts and non-addicts on the MMPI. The present investigation compared MMPI personality profiles of incarcerated drug addicts to those of a non-addict control group that conformed to the criteria outlined above.

METHOD

Subjects

The addict and non-addict Ss had all received penitentiary sentences of two years of more. The crimes of the 51 Ss that composed the addict group were breaking and entering, possession of drugs, theft, robbery, and fraud. Seven of these Ss had brief records of only two or three convictions. Eighteen of the Ss had a least 10 convictions each and were classified as habitual recidivists. The addict group inhabited the Toronto area, occasionally travelling to Montreal for drug supplies.

The non-addict sample was composed of 82 inmates all of whom had lived in and around Toronto. All control Ss case histories indicated that these Ss had opportunities to have come in contact with narcotics. Ten of these inmates were narcotics pushers; never having been addicted to opiates. Sixteen Ss had records of fraudulent crimes. Their case histories revealed that they had been involved in various criminal rackets and had been exposed to drugs. Twenty-two Ss had records of predominantly breaking and entering. They did not have long criminal records. Eighteen Ss were habitual recidivists with a wide variety of crimes. Most of them were heavy drinkers and had used various stimulants. Finally, 17 Ss had records of physical violence and armed robbery.

Ages of both groups ranged from 17 to 63 years and intelligence scores ranged from Beta classification of dull normal to very superior. The mean age and IQ scores of addicts were 30.5 and 104.0, respectively. The mean age and IQ scores of non-addicts were 29.5 and 103.2, respectively.

Psychological Tests

The Beta IQ test and the Minnesota Multiphasic Personality Inventory (MMPI) formed the testing battery.

Procedure

The non-addict control group was selected before Ss were classified in any manner by prison authorities. The control group was chosen using the previously outlined criteria. The drug addicts were incarcerated at Kingston Penitentiary, the main housing institution for drug addicts in Ontario.

The MMPI and IQ testing of Ss took place at Kingston, Ontario, Federal Penitentiary for the period from January 1962 to January 1965 * with the following exceptions: for part of 1962 and 1963 recidivists were not being tested and, thus, some data were lost. The non-addict sample was selected from test scores taken for the period from 1 January 1962 to 1 January 1965. All Ss were tested by trained clerks or the senior author within two weeks after arrival at the penitentiary. A total of 51 addict profiles were completed in the three-year period. Seven addicts were not tested as they were recidivists, and seven others refused testing. A total of 1,500 non-addict profiles were completed in the twenty-month span. From the 1,500 non-addict profiles, 200 non-addict test profiles were selected at random. From this smaller sample, 82 non-addict profiles were found to fit the non-addict criteria.

---

*During the last three years the majority of Ontario addicts have been sent to Matsqui, B.C.; thus, the inclusion of data only up to 1965.

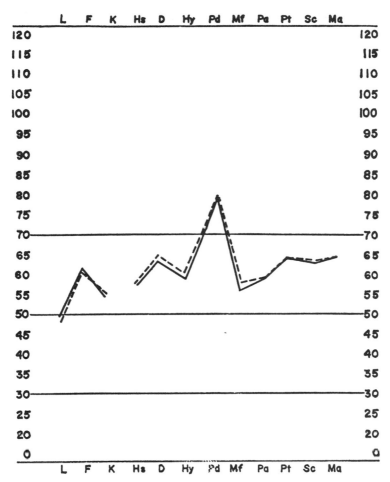

FIGURE I
An MMPI *profile of incarcerated addicts (--) and incarcerated non-addicts (—) on a standard* MMPI *profile sheet.*

RESULTS

Figure 1 summarizes the MMPI-scale scores of addicts and non-addicts. All MMPI scales were scored except the *Si* scale. No significant differences were found using two-tailed *t*-test comparisons. Only two scales, the *Mf* ($t = 1.34$, $df = 131$) and *Hy* ($t = 1.46$. $df = 131$) were slightly elevated in favour of the addict group. The MMPI scores on the *F, Hs, Pd, Pa, Pt,* and *Ma* scales were almost identical for the two groups (all *t* values less than one).

Typically a normal MMPI profile lies within *T*-30 to *T*-70. Only the *Pd* scale, for both groups, was elevated above *T*-70.

DISCUSSION

The negative results suggest that significant differences between addicts and non-addicts reported in previous studies may have been in part due to failure in sampling techniques. If the control subjects come from a similar socio-economic level as addicts and have a prior criminal record, they produce a personality profile markedly similar to addicts.

Previous comparisons of addicts and non-addicts on the MMPI (Hill et al., 1962; Gilbert & Lombardi, 1967) reported significant differences between the two groups on the *D, Hy, Pd, Mf, Pt,* and *Ma* scales. The present study confirmed none of those findings; indeed, it would be expected by chance that one of the 12 *t*-test comparisons would be significant. The addict profile with its high *Pd* and elevated *Ma* scale (a 4-9 profile) was much like MMPI profiles of criminals (Dahlstrom & Welsh, 1960).

Hill et al. (1960), Olson (1964), and Stanton (1956) have also found similar (4-9) MMPI profiles on narcotic-addict samples. Also of interest is that a sociological comparison (Stevenson et al., 1956) of addicts and non-addicts in Vancouver failed to distinguish between the two groups on variables such as type of childhood, family life history, education, employment record, use of alcohol and tobacco, previous criminal records prior to addiction, and variety of sexual behaviour. It must be noted that the addicts studied are classed as criminal addicts. In 1964 (statistics supplied by the Federal Solicitor General's Dept., Penitentiaries Division, Ottawa) there were an estimated 3,355 addicts, 90 per cent of them labelled criminal addicts. The 1968 census was 3,805, 91 per cent criminal, 6 per cent medical, and 3 per cent nurses and pharmacists. Little is known at present about the non-criminal addict category.

The importance of psychological factors in the addiction process are not denied. However, to ascribe distinct traits to addicts is discouraged. Although the MMPI in itself is a restricted test of personality, other tests, whether they be projective, self-concept, or personal construct tests, have distinct restrictions in themselves and the principle of an appropriate control sample still adheres.

One alternative to the "addiction-prone" theory has been proposed by Lindesmith (1968). He has argued that opiate addiction was due to the addict making a cognitive connection (in terms of linguistic symbols and cultural patterns) between withdrawal stress and the absence of opiates. Although Lindesmith's own evidence for his theory remains controversial (Miller, 1969), some recent animal work has provided some support for his view. Nichols (1965) has successfully conditioned rats to morphine and concluded that "opiate-directed" behaviour in rats depended upon an association being built up between drinking morphine and withdrawal. Those animals trained to drink morphine unpaired with withdrawal symptoms failed to initiate opiate-taking behaviour. The "hook" in morphine seemed to come from using the drug to alleviate withdrawal stress rather than from euphoric effects. Weeks (1964) and Wikler (1965) have also reported similar data. This approach may prove more useful in examining the etiology of addiction than the "addiction-prone" theory.

This latter methodology is emphasized in contrast to an "addiction-prone" theory concerning heroin addiction, so that, with the occurrence of increased usage of stimulants and hallucinogenics, research resources may be used optimally, rather than attempting to discover an "amphetamine personality," etc. Hopefully, 30 years of failing to identify an addict personality will generalize caution to research carried out on drug-dependent subjects who use drugs other than heroin derivatives.

REFERENCES

AUSUBEL, D. P. *Drug addiction; physiological, psychological and sociological aspects.* New York: Random House, 1958.

DAHLSTROM, W. G., & WELSH, G. S. *An* MMPI *handbook—a guide to use in clinical practice and research.* Minneapolis: Minneapolis University Press, 1960.

EVESON, M. Drug addiction: a hypothesis for experimental test. *Canadian Journal of Corrections,* 1963, 5, 110-19.

FELIX, R. M. An appraisal of the personality types of addicts. *American Journal of Psychiatry,* 1944, 100, 462-7.

GERARD, D. L., & KORNETSKY, C. Adolescent opiate addiction: a study of control and addict subjects. *Psychiatric Quarterly,* 1955, 10, 457-86.

GILBERT, J. G., & LOMBARDI, D. N. Personality characteristics of young male narcotic addicts. *Journal of Consulting Psychology,* 1967, 31, 536-8.

HILL, H. E. The soical deviant and initial addiction to narcotics and alcohol. *Quarterly Journal of Studies on Alcohol,* 1962, 23, 562-82.

HILL, H. E., HAERTZEN, C. A., & DAVIS, H. An MMPI factor analytic study of alcoholics, narcotic addicts and criminals. *Quarterly Journal of Studies on Alcohol,* 1962, 23, 411-31.

HILL, H. E., HAERTZEN, C. A., & GLASER, R. Personality characteristics of narcotic addicts as indicated by the MMPI. *Journal of General Psychology,* 1960, 62, 127-39.

HOFFMAN, M. Drug addiction and hypersexuality: related modes of mastery. *Comprehensive Psychiatry,* 1964, 5, 262-70.

LETENDRESSE, J. D. Masturbation and its relation to addiction. *Review of Existential Psychology and Psychiatry,* 1968, 8, 16-27.

LINDESMITH, A. R. *Addiction and Opiates.* Chicago: Aldine, 1968.

MILLER, J. S. Addiction, a persistent cognition? *Contemporary Psychology,* 1969, 14, 301-2.

NICHOLS, J. R. How opiates change behavior. *Scientific American*, 1965, 212, 80-8.

NYSWANDER, M. *The drug addict as a patient*. New York: Grune and Stratton, 1956.

OLSON, R. MMPI sex differences in narcotic addicts. *Journal of General Psychology*, 1964, 71, 257-66.

SAVITT, R. A. Psychoanalytic studies on addiction. *Psychoanalytic Quarterly*, 1963, 32, 43-57.

SCOTT, G. D. Classification and offense characteristics of criminal behavior. A paper presented to Forensic Psychiatric Seminar, Queen's University, 1963.

SHURE, G. H., & ROGERS, M. S. Note of caution on the factor analysis of the MMPI. *Psychological Bulletin*, 1965, 63, 14-19.

STANTON, J. M. Group personality profile related to aspects of antisocial behavior. *Journal of Criminal Law, Criminology and Police Science*, 1956, 47, 340-9.

STEVENSON, G. H., LEWIS, G., LINGLEY, R., TRASOV, G., & STANFIELD, H. *Drug addiction in British Columbia, a research survey*. Vol. I, II, Federal Department of Justice, 1956.

VAN KAAM, A. Addiction and existence. *Review of Existential Psychology and Psychiatry*, 1968, 8, 54-64.

WEEKS, J. R. Experimental narcotic addiction. *Scientific American*, 1964, 210, 46-52.

WIKLER, A. A psychodynamic study of a patient during experimental self-regulated readdiction to morphine. *Psychiatric Quarterly*, 1952, 76, 270-93.

WIKLER, A. Conditioning factors in opiate addiction and relapse. In D. M. Wilner and G. G. Kasselbaum (Eds.), *Narcotics*. New York: McGraw-Hill, 1965.

WIKLER, A., & RASOR, R. Psychiatric upsets of drug addiction. *American Journal of Medicine*, 1953, 14, 556-70.

YAHRAES, H. Narcotic drug addiction. *Mental Health Monograph*, U. S. Department of Health, Education and Welfare, 1963, 2 (Whole No. 1021).

ZIMMERING, P. Drug addiction in relation to problems of adolescence. *American Journal of Psychiatry*, 1952, 109, 272-8.

Section III

PSYCHOSOCIAL PERSPECTIVES ON ADDICTION

As we discussed earlier, authors often reflect the ideological frame of reference of their respective disciplines. Ideas are creatively combined on occasion and integrated even more rarely. Be that as it may, the following selections have been organized around the theme of psychosocial perspectives in the addictions—a multitheoretical area that represents a diversity of interests. For example, Lindesmith (1938) suggests that addiction is primarily the result of an individual making the association—vis-à-vis his cultural milieu—that the withdrawal syndrome accompanies the cessation of opiates. Lindesmith proposes, therefore, that the social environment mediates psychological mechanisms that process drug use information. Becker (1967) and Zinberg (1974) make similar suggestions; their emphasis is different however.

Becker emphasizes the sociocultural personal influence and, therefore, power obtained by an experienced user; such experience minimizes the subjective anxiety that naive users often associate with the temporary symptoms that result from drug use. As a result, Becker hypothesizes that "drug psychoses" (a function of drug experience) varies as a consequence of the historical development of a subculture. More recently, Bunce (1979) has gathered important evidence in support of the earlier ideas of Becker. Zinberg (1974) further clarifies the relationship between psychological processes (set), social influence (setting), and psychoactive drug (substance) by examining the interactive roles of these factors in producing certain "effects." In addition, Zinberg, Harding, and Winkeller (1977) demonstrate that long-term, moderate illicit drug use is primarily supported by social sanctions and rituals developed by segments of the drug subculture; these regulatory mechanisms are factors mitigating against *compulsive* drug use.

Ausubel's work (1961) is more fundamental. He suggests that there are multiple causes for addiction: external precipitating factors (e.g., availability of drugs, cultural tolerance, etc.) and internal predisposing factors (e.g., motivational immaturity, adjustive value that a drug possesses, etc.). It is on the basis of the relative prominence of these various factors that chronic and reactive addiction can be distinguished.

The self-help movement has been concerned with addiction from a more personal perspective than the helping professions. Jones (1957) developed the therapeutic community (TC) concept for psychiatric hospitals through the "deprofessionalization" of his staff and by questioning basic assumptions about treatment, roles, role relationships, and values. To this end, daily community meetings were implemented; these meetings served as the nucleus of a social organization that became more important than its constituent components or its individual members. Knowledge of therapeutic communities spread rapidly throughout the psychiatric field; Charles Dederich adopted and adapted much of Jones' thinking when he applied the TC concept to drug addiction and founded the Synanon Foundation in 1958. The Synanon Foundation opened its first house in Santa Monica, California, with 50 residents. Cherkas (1965) suggests that Synanon is successful because of Dederich's charismatic and exhibitionist nature.

The Synanon Foundation prohibits drug use of any sort among its members; it therefore offers the opportunity for members to develop a sense of self-esteem, personal involvement, and responsibility within a drug-free environment. Cherkas indicates that there is no expectation to "cure" the addict while at Synanon, any more than a realistic psychotherapist expects to cure schizophrenia.

The goals of Synanon are to (a) help addicts understand the nature of being, and (b) assist them in developing adequate coping skills so that they can find satisfying roles within a drug-free community. Synanon makes no claim to reduce the addict's dependent lifestyle; critics believe that this model of treatment replaces drug dependency with group dependency. These critics find a measure of support since there is little emphasis by the program for participants to extend the Synanon philosophy to an addiction-free life *in the general community*.

The aim of Synanon is to develop a professional "Synonite" who is a trained leader and will establish new branches of Synanon. As a result of this philosophy, it is often found that members of Synanon are unable to leave their therapeutic environment and make the transition back to the general community. From the Synanon point of view, this problem cannot be considered as evidence of failure since the program's ultimate goal is to enable the addict to remain drug-free. Synanon represents the still present ideology that one can only survive in a drug-free state. This drug treatment model precipitates and sustains the present day controversy between those treatment providers who work in drug-free therapeutic communities and those who work within drug-substitution or drug-antagonist treatment environments.

Regardless of the controversial nature of the Synanon philosophy, it served as the model for many other drug treatment programs. For example, the Synanon concept, a drug-free therapeutic community, was the precursor to programs such as Daytop Village, Phoenix House, Odyssey House, and Project Turnabout. Although these programs differed significantly from Synanon and from each other, these developed from a mutually shared concept. In fact, many treatment programs and providers still refer to the "concept" house model or philosophy, i.e., a therapeutic program whose philosophy, is consistent with the original treatment concept at the Synanon Foundation. It was the therapeutic community and the Synanon model in particular that was responsible for transforming addiction, a "medical" phenomenon, into a sociopolitical problem and for bringing treatment out of the institution and into the community.

Peele and Brodsky (1975) are responsible for transforming addiction from an intrapersonal, sociopolitical problem to an interpersonal phenomenon—an experience they compare and contrast with "love." Although they warn that love and addiction ideally have nothing to do with one another, Peele and Brodsky suggest that the concept of love is often misused to describe interpersonal dependency—an addiction. Their position is creative and provocative. Although *Love and Addiction* has not yet fulfilled its heuristic potential, this work paves the way for new conceptualizations of addiction and, perhaps, a clue to more successful treatment interventions.

REFERENCES

Ausubel, D. P. Causes and types of narcotic addition: A psychosocial view. *Psychiatric Quarterly*, 1961, *35*, 523-536.

Becker, H. History, culture, and subjective experience. An exploration of the social basis of drug-induced experiences. *Journal of Health and Social Behavior*, 1967, *8*, 163-176.

Bunce, R. Social and political sources of drug effects: The case of bad trips on psychedelics. *Journal of Drug Issues*, 1979, *9*(2), 213-233.

Cherkas, M. S. Synanon: A radical approach to the problem of addiction. *American Journal of Psychiatry*, 1965, *121*, 1065-1068.

Jones, M. The treatment of personality disorders in a therapeutic community. *Psychiatry*, 1957, *20*, 211-220.

Lindesmith, A. R. A sociological theory of drug addiction. *American Journal of Sociology*, 1938, 43, 593-613.

Peele, S., & Brodsky, A. Introduction, *Love and Addiction*. New York: Taplinger, 1975, 1-8.

ZINBERG, N. *"High" States, A Beginning Study.* A publication of the National Drug Abuse Council, September 1974, 1-50.

ZINBERG, N., HARDING, W., & WINKELLER, M. A study of social regulatory mechanisms in controlled illicit drug users. *Journal of Drug Issues,* Spring 1977, 7, 117-133.

12

A SOCIOLOGICAL THEORY OF DRUG ADDICTION

Alfred R. Lindesmith

Current theories of drug addiction tend to be moralistic rather than scientific. Any satisfactory theory must attempt to account for the fact that the repeated administration of opiates sometimes is followed by addiction and sometimes is not. The factor which accounts for this differential effect appears to be the person's knowledge or belief, supplied him by his cultural milieu, concerning the nature of the distress that accompanies the sudden cessation of the opiate. If he fails to realize the connection between this distress and the opiate he escapes addiction, whereas if he attributes the discomfort to the opiate and thereafter uses the opiate to alleviate it he invariably becomes addicted. Addiction is generated in the process of using the drug consciously to alleviate withdrawal distress. No exceptions to this theory could be found. It is confirmed by analysis of certain aspects of addict argot and by the consideration of certain types of crucial cases. The theory provides a simple means of accounting for many aspects of the habit. It is methodologically significant in that it is based upon case data and is at the same time universal in form and subject to definite verification or disproof.

The problem of drug addiction has been an important one in this country for several decades and has proved to be a difficult one to handle

Reprinted with permission from *American Journal of Sociology*, 1938, *43*, 593-613.

The study on which this paper is based was carried out at the University of Chicago under the direction of Dr. Herbert Blumer.

from a theoretical as well as from a therapeutic standpoint. In spite of more than a half-century of experimentation with "cures," the drug addict has continued to relapse and thereby aroused the wonder and ire of those who have attempted to treat him. It has frequently been said that the drug user cannot be cured "if he doesn't want to be cured"; but this appears to beg the question, for it is the very essence of addiction that the victim desires to use the drug—and also at the same time desires to be free of it. An indication of the strength of the addict's attachment to his drug is furnished by the fact that when the Japanese government in 1929 permitted unregistered opium-smokers in Formosa to register and gave them the choice of applying for either a cure or a license, only thirty out of approximately twenty-five thousand asked for the cure.[1]

Current explanations of the drug habit appear to center about a few general conceptions and modes of approach, none of which have led to convincing results. Psychiatrists have often regarded the use of opiates as an escape from life and have viewed addicts as defective persons seeking to compensate for, or avoid, their inferiorities and mental conflicts.[2] As would be expected, addicts have been labeled as "psychopaths" with the assumption that the attachment of this ambiguous label in some mysterious way explained the phenomenon. Various statements as to the percentage of defective persons among addicts have not been accompanied by any comparison with the percentage of defective persons in the general nonaddicted population. In fact, the need or desirability of this sort of comparison does not seem to have occurred to the majority of these writers.

This point of view contrasts the "psychopath," who is assumed to be susceptible to addiction, with "normal" persons who are presumed by implication to be immune, or, if they accidentally become addicted, they are said to quit and remain free. No evidence has been produced, however, which indicates that any but an exceedingly small percentage of

---

[1] Report to the Council of the League of Nations by the Committee of Enquiry into the Control of Opium Smoking in the Far East, II (1930), 420.

[2] This general view is not only widespread among psychiatrists but is popularly held as well. The great majority of writers in medical journals on this subject assume it. It may be found elaborated in a typical form in the following articles by L. Kolb: "Pleasure and Deterioration from Narcotic Addiction," *Jour. Ment. Hyg.*, Vol. IX (October, 1925); "Drug Addiction in Relation to Crime," *ibid.*, (January, 1925); "The Struggle for Cure and the Conscious Reasons for Relapse," *Jour. Nerv. and Ment. Dis.*, Vol. LXVI (July, 1927); and "Drug Addiction—a Study of Some Medical Cases," *Arch. Neurol. and Psychiat.*, Vol XX (1928). It is also developed by Dr. Schultz in "Rep. of the Comm. on Drug Addicts to Hon. R. C. Patterson, etc.," as reported in *Amer. Jour. Psychiat.*, Vol. X (1930-31).

addicts ever remain free of the drug for long periods of years,[3] and no "normal" person has ever been shown to be immune to the subtle influence of the drug. It appears from an examination of the literature that all "normal" persons who have been foolhardy enough to imagine themselves immune and have consequently experimented upon themselves and taken the drug steadily for any length of time have become addicts, or "junkers," as they usually style themselves.[4] The contention that any type of person can be readily cured of the drug habit in a permanent sense is without any support in terms of actual evidence. We have found that narcotic agents and others who are in close contact with the actual problem ordinarily acquire a wholesome fear of the drug and do not delude themselves concerning their own capacity to resist its influence.

A French medical student[5] in the course of writing a thesis on morphine decided to experiment upon himself. For five consecutive days he took an injection each evening at about nine o'clock. He reported that after three or four injections he began to desire the next ones, and that it cost him a decided effort to refrain from using it the sixth night. He managed to carry out his plan, but clearly implied that if he had continued the experiment for a short time longer he believed that he would have become addicted. The addict, in his opinion, is *un homme perdu* who is rarely able ever again to retain his freedom. This account constitutes an interesting document for the individual who believes that he or anyone else is immune to addiction by reason of a superabundance of willpower or because of an absence of psychopathy. In 1894 Mattison advised the physician as follows:

> Let him not be blinded by an under estimate of the poppy's power to ensnare. Let him not be deluded by an over confidence in his own strength to resist; for along this line history has repeated itself with sorrowful frequency, and,—as my experience will well attest—on these two treacherous rocks hundreds of promising lives have gone awreck.[6]

---

[3]Dansauer and Rieth ("Über Morphinismus bei Kriegsbeschädigten," in *Arbeit und Gesundheit- Schriftenreihe zum Reichsarbeitsblatt*, Vol XVIII [1931]), found that 96.7 per cent of 799 addicts had relapsed within five years after taking a cure. Relapse after more than ten years is sometimes mentioned. We ourselves were acquainted with an addict who stated that he had abstained for fifteen years before resuming the drug. We have never encountered or read an authentic account of any so-called cured addict who did not show by his attitudes toward the drug that the impulse to relapse was actively present.

[4]It is characteristic of practically all addicts prior to their own addiction that they do not expect or intend to become addicts.

[5]L. Faucher, *Contribution à l'étude du rêve morphinique et de la morphinomanie* (Thèse de Montpellier, No. 8 [1910-11]).

[6]*JAMA*, Vol XXIII.

Sir William Willcox states:

> We know people who say: "I am a man, and one having a strong will. Morphine or heroin will not affect me; I can take it as long as I like without becoming an addict." I have known people—sometimes medical men—who have made that boast, and without exception they have come to grief.[7]

The conception of opiates as affording an escape from life also does not appear to be satisfactory or correct in view of the well-known fact that the addict invariably claims that all the drug does is to cause him to feel "normal." It is generally conceded that the euphoria associated with the use of opiates is highly transitory in character, and while it is true that during the initial few weeks of use the drug may cause pleasure in some cases and may function as a means of escape, still, when addiction is established, this no longer holds true. The drug addict who is supposed to derive some mysterious and uncanny pleasure from the drug not only fails to do so as a rule but is also keenly aware of the curse of addiction and struggles to escape it. Far from being freed from his problems, he is actually one of the most obviously worried and miserable creatures in our society.

Finally, we may call attention to the fact that the current conception of the addict as a "psychopath" escaping from his own defects by the use of the drug has the serious defect of being admittedly inapplicable to a certain percentage of cases. L. Kolb, for example, finds that 86 per cent of the addicts included in a study of his had defects antedating, and presumably explaining, the addiction. One may therefore inquire how addiction is to be explained in the other 14 per cent of the cases. Are these persons addicts because they are free from defects? The assumption is sometimes made that those in whom defects cannot be found have secret defects which explain the addiction. Such an assumption obviously places the whole matter beyond the realm of actual research. Moreover, one may ask, who among us does not have defects of one kind or another, secret or obvious?

In general, it appears that the conception of the drug addict as a defective psychopath prior to addiction is more in the nature of an attempt to place blame than it is an explanation of the matter. It is easy and cheap to designate as "inferior" or "weak" or "psychopathic" persons whose vices are different from our own and whom we consequently do

---

[7]*Brit. Jour. Inebriety*, XXXI, 132.

not understand.[8] Similarly, the "causes" of addiction as they are often advanced—"curiosity," "bad associates," and the "willingness to try anything once"—suffer from the same moralistic taint. Undoubtedly these same factors "cause" venereal disease, yet science has ceased to be concerned with them. In the case of drug addiction we still are more interested in proving that it is the addict's "own fault" that he is an addict than we are in understanding the mechanisms of addiction.

It was noted long ago that not all persons to whom opiate drugs were administered for sufficiently long periods of time to produce the withdrawal symptoms became addicts. It frequently occurs in medical practice that severe and chronic pain makes the regular administration of opiates a necessity.[9] Some of the persons who are so treated show no signs of the typical reactions of addicts and may even be totally ignorant of what they are being given. Others to whom the drug is administered in this way return to it when it has been withdrawn and become confirmed addicts. This fact caused German and French students of the problem to adopt distinct terms for the two conditions—those who received the drug for therapeutic reasons and who showed none of the symptoms of the typical "craving" of addicts were spoken of as cases of "chronic morphine poisoning," or "morphinism," whereas addicts in the ordinarily accepted sense of the word were called "morphinomanes" or, in German, *Morphiumsüchtiger*.[10] Attempts have been made to introduce such a usage in this country, though without success, and it is consequently awkward to try to refer to these two conditions. In this paper the term "habituated" will be used to refer to the development of the mere physiological tolerance, whereas the term "addiction" will be reserved for application to cases in which there is added to the physiological or pharmacological tolerance a psychic addiction which is marked by the appearance of an imperious desire for the drug and leads to the development of the other characteristic modes of behavior of the drug addict as he is known in our society. For persons who are merely habituated

---

[8]The aim of this paper is to present a sociological theory of opiate addiction which appears to offer possibilities for a rational and objective understanding of the problem without any element of moralization. This theory is based upon informal and intimate contact over a long period of time with approximately fifty drug addicts. The main points of the theory have been tested in the material available in the literature of the problem, and no conclusions have been drawn from case materials collected unless these materials were clearly corroborated by case materials in the literature.

[9]Dansauer and Rieth (*op. cit.*) cite two hundred and forty such cases. Many of these cases had used the drug for five or more years without becoming addicts.

[10]See e.g., Levinstein, *Die Morphiumsucht* (1877); F. McKelvey Bell, "Morphinism and Morphinomania," *N.Y. Med. Jour.*, Vol. XCIII (1911); and Daniel Jouet, *Etude sur le morphinisme chronique* (Thèse de Paris [1883]).

to the drug without being addicted there is no need for special conceptual treatment any more than persons who have had operations need to be set off as a distinct class. Once the drug has been removed, these persons show no craving for it or any tendency to resume its use, unless, perhaps, the disease for which the opiate was originally given reappears.

Any explanation of the causation of drug addiction must attempt to account for this fact that not all persons who are given opiates become addicts. What are the factors which cause one man to escape while the next, under what appear to be the same physiological conditions, becomes an incurable addict? Obviously the factor of the patient's knowledge of what he is being given is an important one, for clearly if he is ignorant of the name of the drug he will be unable to ask for it or consciously to desire it. The recognition of the importance of keeping the patient in ignorance of what drugs he is being given is quite general. Various devices which serve this end, such as giving the drug orally rather than hypodermically, keeping it out of the hands of the patient and permitting no self-administration, mixing the dosage of opiates with other drugs whose effects are not so pleasant and which serve to disguise the effects of the opiate, etc., have been advocated and have become more or less routine practice. But in some cases individuals who are fully aware that they are receiving morphine (or some other opium alkaloid), may also not become addicted, even after prolonged administration.[11] Other factors besides ignorance of the drug administered must therefore operate to prevent the occurrence of addiction in such cases. What seems to account for this variability—and this is the crux of the theory being advanced—is not the knowledge of the drug administered, but the knowledge of the true significance of the withdrawal symptoms when they appear and the use of the drug thereafter for the consciously understood motive of avoiding these symptoms.[12] As far as can be determined, there is no account in the literature of anyone's ever having experienced the full severity of the withdrawal symptoms in complete knowledge of their connection with the absence of the opiate drug, who has not also become an addict. Addiction begins when the person suffering from withdrawal symptoms realizes that a dose of the drug will dissipate all his discomfort and misery. If he then tries it out and actually feels the almost magical relief that is afforded, he is on the way to confirmed

---

[11]The case of Dr. H., cited later in this paper, is such a case.

[12] Withdrawal distress begins to appear after a few days of regular administration but does not ordinarily become severe until after two, three, or more weeks, when its severity appears to increase at an accelerated rate. In its severe form it involves acute distress from persistent nausea, general weakness, aching joints and pains in the legs, diarrhea, and extreme insomnia. In isolated cases death may result from abrupt withdrawal of the drug.

addiction. The desire for the drug, and the impression that it is necessary, apparently become fixed with almost incredible rapidity once this process of using the drug to avoid the abstinence symptoms has begun. Among confirmed addicts it appears to be the general rule also that those who have the greatest difficulty in obtaining regular supplies of narcotics ("boot and shoe dope fiends") are precisely those who develop the most intense craving for it and use it to excess when the opportunity presents itself. In other words, deprivation is the essential factor both in the origin of the craving and in its growth.

In order to prove the correctness of the theory advanced it is necessary to consider, first, its applicability to the general run of cases—that is, to determine whether or not addicts become addicted in any other way than through the experience with withdrawal and whether there are nonaddicts in whom all of the conditions or causes of addiction have occurred without actually producing addiction. We do not have the space here to go into an extended analysis and explanation of any large number of cases. We can only state that from our analysis of the cases that have come to our attention, both directly and in the literature, it appears to be true without exception that addicts do, in fact, become addicted in this manner and that addiction does invariably follow whenever the drug is used for the conscious purpose of alleviating withdrawal distress. That this is the case is strikingly brought out by the addict's own argot. The term "hooked" is used by drug-users to indicate the fact that a person has used the drug long enough so that if he attempts to quit withdrawal distress will force him to want to go on using the drug. At the same time, "to be hooked" means to be addicted, and anyone who has ever been "hooked" is forever after classified by himself as well as by other addicts as belonging to the in-group, as an addict, a "user" or "junker," regardless of whether he is using the drug at the moment or not.[13] Similarly, a person who has not been "hooked," regardless of whether he is using the drug or not, is not classified as an addict.[14] It is a contradiction in terms of addict argot, therefore, to speak of "a junker who has never

---

[13]We have checked this point with addicts who had voluntarily abstained for as long as six years. They unhesitatingly declared themselves to be addicts who happened not to be using drugs at the time—i.e., "junkers" or "users" who were "off stuff."

[14]A type of individual who uses the drug without being hooked is the one who uses it, say once a week, and thus avoids the withdrawal distress. Such a person is called a "joy-popper" or "pleasure-user" and is not regarded as an addict until he has used the drug steadily for a time, experienced withdrawal distress, and become hooked. He then permanently loses his status as a "pleasure-user" and becomes a "junker." An addict who has abstained for a time and then begins to use it a little bit now and then is not a "pleasure-user"—he is just "playing around." See D. W. Maurer's article in the April, 1936, issue of American Speech.

been hooked" or of an individual who has been "hooked" without becoming an addict. Addict argot admits no exceptions to this rule. We
found that drug users invariably regard any query about a hypothetical
addict who has not been compelled to use the drug by the withdrawal
distress, or about a hypothetical nonaddict who has, as incomprehensible
nonsense. To them it is self-evident that to be "hooked" and to be an
addict are synonymous.[15]

As we have indicated, our own experience is in entire accord with this
view of the addict as it is crystallized in his vernacular. In addition we
have found certain types of cases which bear more directly upon the
theory and which offer conclusive, and, we may say, experimental, verification of the theory. It is upon cases of this type which we wish to
concentrate our attention.

Crucial instances which strongly corroborate the hypothesis are those
cases in which the same person has first become habituated to the use
of the drug over a period of time and then had the drug withdrawn
without becoming addicted; and then, later in life, under other circumstances, become a confirmed addict. Erwin Strauss[16] records the case of
a woman

> who received morphine injections twice daily for six months,
> from February to July of 1907, on account of gall stones. After
> her operation in July the drug was removed and the patient did
> not become an addict[17] but went about her duties as before, until
> 1916, nine years later, when her only son was killed at the Front.
> She was prostrated by her grief, and after intense anguish and
> thoughts of suicide, she thought of the morphine which had
> been administered to her nine years before. She began to use
> it, found it helpful, and soon was addicted. *What is particularly
> noteworthy is that when asked if she had suffered any withdrawal symp-
> toms when the drug was withdrawn the first time, in 1907, she stated
> that she could not recall any.* [Italics are mine.]

---

[15] As the other evidence which indicates how central and how taken for granted the role
of withdrawal distress in addiction is, we may mention that the addict's word "yen" refers
simultaneously to withdrawal distress *and* to the desire for the drug. Also, "to feel one's
habit" means to feel the withdrawal distress. Addicts call cocaine non-habit-forming because
it does not cause withdrawal distress when stopped.

[16] "Zur Pathogenese des chronischen Morphinismus," *Monatschr. für Psychiat. und Neurol.,*
Vol. XLVII (1920).

[17] As defined, e.g., in the *Report of the Departmental Committee on Morphin and Heroin
Addiction* to the British Ministry of Health: "A person who, not requiring the continued
use of a drug for the relief of the symptoms of organic disease, has acquired as a result
of repeated administration an overwhelming desire for its continuance, and in whom
withdrawal of the drug leads to definite symptoms of mental or physical distress or disorder."

Another case of the same kind was interviewed by the writer.

> A man, Dr. H., was given morphine regularly for a considerable period of time when he underwent three operations for appendicitis with complications. He was not expected to live. As he recovered, the dosage of morphine was gradually reduced and completely withdrawn without any difficulty. Although the patient suffered some discomfort during the process and knew that he had been receiving morphine, he attributed this discomfort to the processes of convalescence. Dr. H. had had occasion to see drug addicts in his medical practice and had always felt a horror of addiction and had sometimes thought he would rather shoot himself than be one. This attitude of horror remained unaltered during the hospital experience just related. Several years later, Dr. H. contracted gall stone trouble and was told that an operation would be necessary. Opiates were administered, and Dr. H., who wished to avoid another operation at all costs, administered opiates to himself, hoping that the operation might not be necessary. He began to use the drug for pains of less and less significance until he found himself using it every day. He became apprehensive during this process, but reasoned with himself that there was nothing to be alarmed about, inasmuch as drug addiction was certainly not the horrible thing it was supposed to be and he was certain that he would have no difficulty in quitting. His horror of addiction disappeared. When he attempted to quit he found that it was more difficult than he had supposed. He, of course, noticed the regular recurrence of the withdrawal illness and *then realized in retrospect that he had experienced the same symptoms, without recognizing them, several years before.* [Italics are mine.]

A third case of the same kind is briefly mentioned by Dansauer and Rieth,[18] and two others have come to the attention of the writer. Obviously the number of instances in which a coincidence of this kind is likely to occur is very small, but those that have been found, unequivocally and without exception, indicate that if morphine is withdrawn carefully, without the patient's recognizing or noticing the symptoms of abstinence, no craving for the drug develops. The typical phenomena which signalize addiction, such as the tendency to increase the dose inordinately, to exhibit and feel a powerful desire to obtain the drug at any cost, and to be unhappy without it—these phenomena do not put in their appearance until the patient has discovered that there are with-

---

[18] *Op. cit.*, p. 103.

drawal symptoms of a persistent severe character and has used the drug for a time, solely or chiefly to prevent these symptoms from appearing. In the argot of the addict, when this has occurred the person is "hooked"; he "has a habit." If he quits before it occurs or if he resolutely refrains from using the drug to alleviate the abstinence symptoms the first time he experiences them, he may still escape. If the symptoms occur in their full intensity, however, the impulse to seek relief in the drug, when it is known that only the drug will give relief, is irresistible—especially since the patient is not likely to realize that the danger of addiction is present. He thinks only of the fact that he can obtain relief from those terrible symptoms, which, to the uninitiated, may be genuinely terrifying.

As an illustration of the process of the establishment of addiction which we are attempting to isolate, another case of a man who became addicted in medical practice may be cited.

> Mr. G. was severely lacerated and internally injured as the result of an accident. He spent thirteen weeks in a hospital during which time he received frequent does of morphine, some hypodermically and some orally. He paid no attention to what it was that was being used on him and felt no effects of any unusual character except that the medicine to some extent relieved him of pain. He was discharged from the hospital, and after several hours began to develop considerable discomfort and irritability and the other symptoms of morphine withdrawal. He had no idea what was the matter. In about twelve hours he was violently nauseated and during his first night at home called his family physician in at two o'clock in the morning, fearing that he was about to die. The physician also was not certain what was wrong, but gave him some mild sedatives and attempted to encourage him. The violence of the symptoms increased during the next day to such an extent that Mr. G. began to wish that he would die. During the course of the second night the family physician decided that he was perhaps suffering from withdrawal of opiates and gave Mr. G. an injection of morphine to find out. The effect was immediate; in about twenty minutes Mr. G. fell asleep and slept on in perfect comfort for many hours. He still did not know what he had been given, but when he woke up the next day the doctor told him, and said, "Now we are going to have a time getting you off!" The dosage was reduced and in a week or two the drug was entirely removed, but Mr. G., during this short time, had become addicted. After the drug had been removed for a few days, he bought himself a hypodermic syringe and began to use it by himself.[19]

---

[19]Interviewed by the writer.

It may seem surprising at first glance that many addicts do not know what is wrong with them the first time that the abstinence symptoms occur. This is not difficult to understand when one realizes that many persons seem to think that withdrawal symptoms are purely imaginative or hysterical in character. Even in spite of the occurrence of these symptoms in animals which have been subjected to the prolonged administration of opiates, and in spite of their occurrence in patients who have no idea what opiates are or that they have been given any, students of drug addiction have sometimes asserted that these symptoms have no physiological basis. In view of this belief among the instructed, it is easy to understand the layman who believes the same thing when he begins to experiment with the drug. Furthermore, there is nothing whatever in the initial effects of the drug to furnish the slightest clue as to what happens later. As the use of the drug is continued, in the same proportion that tolerance appears and the positive effects diminish the withdrawal symptoms increase until they obtrude themselves upon the attention of the individual and finally become dominant. In most cases of confirmed addiction the drug appears to serve almost no other function than that of preventing the appearance of these symptoms.

One of the most difficult features of addiction to account for by means of any explanation of the drug habit in terms of the positive effects, or euphoria, supposed to be produced by it, is the fact that during the initial period of use there takes place a gradual reversal of effect so that the effects of the drug upon an addict are not only not the same as their effects upon a nonaddicted person but they are actually, in many respects, the precise opposite.[20] This is true both of the physiological and of the psychological effects. The initial dose causes one to feel other than normal, whereas in the case of the addict the usual dose causes him to feel normal when he would feel below normal without it. The euphoria intially produced by the drug has often been emphasized as a causative factor, but inasmuch as this euphoria, or "kick," disappears in addiction, the continuation of the drug habit cannot be explained in this way.[21] Moreover, when administered therapeutically to allay pain, there is often absolutely no euphoria produced even in the initial period, and the patient may nevertheless become addicted. In fact it is possible for a person to be unconscious during the entire initial stage when tolerance

---

[20]This has been partially emphasized by Erlenmeyer, as quoted by C. E. Terry and Mildred Pellens, *The Opium Problem* (1928), pp. 600 ff., and it has been noted in one way or another, in much of the physiological research that has been done on morphine effects.

[21]The English Departmental Committee in 1926 (*op. cit.*) stated that whatever may have been the original motive, the use of the drug is continued not so much from that original motive as "because of the craving created by the use" (quoted in Terry and Pellens, *ibid.*, pp. 164-65).

is established and still become addicted, as a consideration of the implications of the case of Mr. G. shows. It is this reversal of effect which accounts at one and the same time for the seductive aspect of opiates as well as for their insidiousness. As they cease to produce pleasure they become a necessity and produce pain if removed. The euphoria produced by the drug at first makes it easy to become addicted but does not account for the continuance of the habit when the euphoria is gone. A theory which makes the withdrawal distress central in addiction takes account of this reversal of effects.

It follows, if one believes that the drug habit is to be accounted for on the basis of the extraordinary or uncanny state of mind it is sometimes supposed to produce, that addicts should be able to recognize such effects immediately and easily. It is a notorious fact, however, and one that baffles the addicts as well as those who study them, that under certain conditions the drug user may be completely deceived for varying periods of time into believing that he is receiving opiates when he actually is not, or that he is not receiving any when as a matter of fact he is. We shall not elaborate this point any more than to call attention to the fact that it has been put into practice as a principle in a number of gradual reduction cures wherein, without the addict's knowledge, the amount of the drug was gradually reduced and finally withdrawn entirely while injections of water or a saline solution were continued.[22] Then when the addict had been free of opiates for several days, or a week, or even more, he was told that he had not been getting any of his drug for some time and usually discharged, sometimes in the vain hope that this experience might prove to him that it was only his "imagination" which led him to think he needed his drug! The fact that such a thing is possible is evidence that the direct positive effects per se are not sufficiently extraordinary to make addiction intelligible.

The tendency of the addict to relapse may be readily explained in terms of the viewpoint outlined, as arising from the impression that is made upon him when he observes the remarkable and immediate effects the drug has in dissipating unpleasant physical or mental states. What the addict misses when he is off the drug is not so much the hypothetical euphoria as the element of control. On the drug he could regulate his feeling tone; when he is not using it, it appears to him that he is the passive victim of his environment or of his changing moods. During the initial period of use the only effects of an injection to which attention

---

[22]*Ibid.*, pp. 577 ff. quoting C. C. Wholey; *ibid.*, pp. 572 ff., quoting M. R. Dupouy. A number of addicts have somewhat sheepishly admitted to us that they had been deceived in this manner for as long as ten days.

is paid are ordinarily the immediate ones lasting but a few minutes or, at most, a half-hour or an hour or so. This episodic significance of injections changes into a continuous twenty-four-hour-a-day sense of dependence upon the drug only after the addict has learned from the recurrence of the beginnings of withdrawal symptoms, as the effects of each shot wore off, that the drug was necessary to the continuance of his well-being. He learns to attribute effects to the "stuff" which are in part imaginary—or rather, projections of the need for it which he feels. When he is off, every vicissitude of life tends to remind him of his drug and he misses the supporting and sustaining sense of its presence. And so the ordinary pleasures of life are dulled, something seems to be amiss, and the unhappy addict eventually relapses—either deliberately or otherwise. If he does not relapse it appears that he nevertheless remains susceptible to it for long periods of years. Cases of relapse after as long as ten or more years of abstinence are recorded.[23]

The thesis of the paper is that addiction to opiate drugs is essentially based upon the abstinence symptoms which occur when the effects of the drug are beginning to wear off rather than upon any positive effects or uncanny or extraordinarily pleasurable state of mind erroneously supposed to be produced by the drug in continued use. Addiction is established in the first instance in a process involving

1. The interpretation of the withdrawal symptoms as being caused by the absence of opiates,[24] followed by
2. The use of the drug for the consciously understood purpose of alleviating these symptoms or of keeping them suppressed.

As a result of this process there is established in the addict the typical desire for the drug, a constant sense of dependence upon it, and the other attendant features of addiction. The attitudes which arise in this experience persist when the drug has been removed and predispose toward relapse. When the point is reached at which withdrawal symptoms intrude themselves upon the attention of the individual and compel him to go on using the drug, he also has forced upon him the unwelcome definition of himself as a "dope fiend." He realizes then what the craving for drugs means and, applying to his own conduct the symbols which the group applies to it, he is compelled to readjust his conception of himself to the implications of this collective viewpoint. He struggles

---

[23]Kolb, "Drug Addicts—a Study of Some Medical Cases," *loc. cit.*

[24]It is significant to note that this belief that withdrawal distress is caused by the absence of the opiate is not adequate or correct from the standpoint of physiological theory.

against the habit and then eventually accepts his fate and becomes "just another junker." Obviously when the withdrawal distress has entered into the conscious motives of the person and he realizes that he must anticipate the recurrence of these terrible symptoms if he does not assure himself of a supply of the drug, and when the definition of self as an addict has occurred, the drug user becomes ripe for assimilation into the culture of drug addiction as it exists chiefly in our underworld.

The proposed theory has advantages and implications beyond those already mentioned. It is applicable in form to all cases and, as indicated, an extensive exploration of the literature as well as many interviews with addicts has so far failed to uncover a single negative case, even of a hearsay type. Moreover, it harmonizes and rationalizes various aspects of the habit which have often been regarded as paradoxical or contradictory in character—as, for example, the fact that addicts claim they do not obtain pleasure from the drug, the initial reversal of effects, and the strange tendency of addicts to relapse when, from a medical standpoint, they appear to be cured.

A number of further implications of the point of view presented seem to have important bearings on certain theories of social psychology and of sociology. Thus students of the writings of George H. Mead will notice that the hypothesis follows the lines of his theory of the "significant symbol" and its role in human life. According to the view presented, the physiological effects of the drug do not become effective in influencing the psychic and social life of the person until he has applied to them the "significant symbols" (or, perhaps, in Durkheimian language, "collective representations") which are employed by the group to describe the nature of these effects. Addiction, in other words, appears as a process which goes on, on the level of "significant symbols"—it is, in other words, peculiar to man living in organized society in communication with his fellows.[25]

[25]Very young children, the feeble-minded, and the insane would not be expected to have the necessary sophisticated conception of causality or the ability to manipulate "significant symbols" which, as we have indicated, are necessary preconditions of addiction.

Dr. Charles Schultz in a study of 318 cases found only 14 patients, or less than 5 per cent, who were "probably high-grade morons, and even these gave the impression of having their dull wits sharpened by the use of drugs" (*loc. cit.*). Regarding insanity—it has been noted that it confers immunity to addiction and that insanity appears to occur less frequently among the blood relations of addicts than among the blood relatives of samples of the general population. O. Wuth, "Zur Erbanlage der Süchtigen," *Z. für die Ges. Neur. und Psychiat.*, CLIII (1935), 495 ff.; Alexander Pilcz, "Zur Konstitution der Süchtigen," *Jahrb. für Psychiat.*, LI (1935), 169 ff.; Jouet, *op. cit.;* Sceleth and Kuh, *JAMA*, LXXXII, 679; P. Wolff, *Deutsche medizinische Wochenschrift*, Vol. LVII, in his report on the results of a questionnarie, etc. Note the testimony by Gaupp. Bratz, and Bonhoeffer.

On the immunity of children see R. N. Chopra *et al.*, "Administration of Opiates to Infants in India," *Indian Med. Gaz.*, LXIX (1934), 489 ff., "Opium Habit in India," *Indian Jour. Med. Research,* Vol. XV (1927); "Drug Addiction in India and Its Treatment," *Indian Med. Gaz.*, LXX (1935), 121 ff.

This theory rationalizes and explains the reasons for the ordinary rules-of-thumb employed in the therapeutic administration of morphine to prevent addiction. Some of these rules and practices include (1) keeping the patient in ignorance of the drug being used, (2) mixing other drugs with different and less pleasing effects with the opiate, (3) varying the model of administration and disguising the drug in various kinds of medicines. The significance of these practices appears to be that they prevent the patient from attributing to morphine the effects which it in fact produces—in other words, they prevent the patient from applying certain collective symbols to his own subjective states, prevent the whole experience from being associated with the patient's preconceptions of drug addiction, and so prevent addiction.

The proposed hypothesis has the further advantage of being essentially experimental in character in the sense that it is open to disproof, as, for example, by anyone who doubts it and is willing or foolhardy enough to experiment on himself with the drug. As has been indicated, the writer has been unable to find any record in the literature of an experiment of this character which, prolonged enough to be a test—that is, which lasted long enough so that the withdrawal distress upon stoppage of the drug was pronounced—did not result in addiction. This appears to constitute an exception to what is often assumed to be true of knowledge in the field of the social sciences—namely, that it confers, *ipso facto*, the ability to control. It is in accord with the well-known fact that addiction to narcotic drugs is peculiarly prevalent in those legitimate professions in which theoretical knowledge of these drugs is most general—that is, in the medical and allied professions.

A further significant implication of the viewpoint presented is that it offers a means of relating phenomena of a purely physiological variety to cultural or sociological phenomena. The interpretation of withdrawal distress, which we have emphasized as a basic factor in the beginning of addiction, is, it should be emphasized, a cultural pattern, a social interpretation present in a formulated fashion in the social milieu exactly like other knowledge or beliefs. When the organic disturbances produced by the withdrawal of the drug intrude themselves upon the attention of a person, they impede his functioning and assume the nature of a problem demanding some sort of rationalization and treatment. The culture of the group supplies this rationalization by defining the situation for the individual and in so doing introduces into the motives and conceptions which determine his conduct other factors which lead to addiction whenever the drug is continued beyond the point at which this insight occurs.

Finally, we should like to emphasize again the methodological implications of the study. A great deal of argumentation has taken place in sociology on the matter of methodology—whether universal generalizations are possible or not, concerning the role of statistical generalizations and of quantification generally, and concerning the so-called case method. Most of these arguments have tended to take place on an abstract level, whereas it would seem that in the final analysis they can be settled only in terms of actual results of research. We therefore regard it as significant that the theory advanced in this study is not quantitative in form, nor is it a purely intuitive generalization which is not subject to proof, but that it is experimental in form in spite of the fact that it is based upon the analysis of data secured largely in personal interviews. It is, moreover, stated in universal form and is therefore not dependent upon or relative to a particular culture or a particular time. As such it provides the possibility of its own continuous reconstruction and refinement in terms of more extended experience and of more elaborated instances. It other words, it provides a place for the exceptional or crucial case which George H. Mead has described as the "growing point of science."[26]

---

[26]In an essay, "Scientific Method and Individual Thinker," in *Creative Intelligence* (1917).

13

HISTORY, CULTURE AND SUBJECTIVE EXPERIENCE: AN EXPLORATION OF THE SOCIAL BASES OF DRUG-INDUCED EXPERIENCES

Howard S. Becker

So-called "drug psychoses" can be interpreted as the anxiety reaction of a naïve user occasioned by his fear that the temporary symptoms of drug use represent a permanent derangement of his mind. Participation in a drug-using subculture tends to minimize such occurrences, because other users present the person with alternative explanations of his experience that minimize its lasting effects. A comparison of LSD and marihuana use suggests that the number of drug-induced psychoses varies historically, being a function of the historical development of a subculture.

In 1938, Albert Hoffman discovered the peculiar effects of lysergic acid dieythlamide (LSD-25) on the mind. He synthesized the drug in 1943 and, following the end of World War II, it came into use in psychiatry, both as a method of simulating psychosis for clinical study and as a means of therapy.[1] In the early 1960's, Timothy Leary, Richard

Reprinted with permission from the *Journal of Health and Social Behavior*, 1967, *8*, 163-176.
[1] See "D-lysergic Acid Diethylamide—LSD," *Sandoz Excerpta*, 1 (1955), pp. 1-2, quoted in Sanford M. Unger, "Mescaline, LSD, Psilocybin and Personality Change," in David Solomon, editor, *LSD: The Consciousness-Expanding Drug*, New York: Berkley Publishing Corp., 1966, p. 206.

Alpert and others began using it with normal subjects as a means of "consciousness expansion." Their work received a great deal of publicity, particularly after a dispute with Harvard authorities over its potential danger. Simultaneously, LSD-25 became available on the underground market and, although no one has accurate figures, the number of people who have used or continue to use it is clearly very large.

The publicity continues and a great controversy now surrounds LSD use. At one extreme, Leary considers its use so beneficial that he has founded a new religion in which it is the major sacrament. At the other extreme, psychiatrists, police and journalists allege that LSD is extremely dangerous, that it produces psychosis, and that persons under its influence are likely to commit actions dangerous to themselves and others that they would not otherwise have committed. Opponents of the drug have persuaded the Congress and some state legislatures to classify it as a narcotic or dangerous drug and to attach penal sanctions to its sale, possession, or use.

In spite of the great interest in the drug, I think is is fair to say that the evidence of its danger is by no means decisive.[2] If the drug does prove to be the cause of a bona fide psychosis, it will be the only case in which anyone can state with authority that they have found *the* unique cause of any such phenomenon; a similar statement applies to causes of crime and suicide. Whatever the ultimate findings of pharmacologists and others now studying the drug, sociologists are unlikely to accept such an asocial and unicausal explanation of any form of complex social behavior. But if we refuse to accept the explanations of others we are obligated to provide one of our own. In what follows, I consider the reports of LSD-induced psychoses and try to relate them to what is known of the social psychology and sociology of drug use. By this means I hope to add both to our understanding of the current controversy

[2]On this point, to which I return later, the major references are: Sydney Cohen, "Lysergic Acid Diethylamide: Side Effects and Complications," *Journal of Nervous and Mental Diseases*, 130 (January, 1960), pp. 30-40; Sydney Cohen and Keith S. Ditman, "Prolonged Adverse Reactions to Lysergic Acid Diethylamide," *Archives of General Psychiatry*, 8 (1963), pp. 475-480; Sydney Cohen and Keith S. Ditman, "Complications Associated with Lysergic Acid Diethylamide (LSD-25)," *Journal of the American Medical Association*, 181 (July 14, 1962), pp. 161-162; William A. Frosch, Edwin S. Robbins and Marvin Stern, "Untoward Reactions to Lysergic Acid Diethylamide (LSD) Resulting in Hospitalization," *New England Journal of Medicine*, 273 (December 2, 1965), pp. 1235-1239; A. Hoffer, "D-Lysergic Acid Diethylamide (LSD): A Review of its Present Status," *Clinical Pharmacology and Therapeutics*, 6 (March, 1965), pp. 183-255; S. H. Rosenthal, "Persistent Hallucinosis Following Repeated Administration of Hallucinogenic Drugs," *American Journal of Psychiatry*, 121 (1964), pp. 238-244; and J. Thomas Ungerleider, Duke D. Fisher and Marielle Fuller, "The Dangers of LSD: Analysis of Seven Months' experience in a University Hospital's Psychiatric Service," *Journal of the American Medical Association*, 197 (August 8, 1966), pp. 389-392.

over LSD and to our general knowledge of the social character of drug use.

In particular, I will make use of a comparison between LSD use and marihuana use, suggested by the early history of marihuana in this country. That history contains the same reports of "psychotic episodes" now current with respect to LSD. But reports of such episodes disappeared at the same time as the number of marihuana users increased greatly. This suggests the utility of considering the historical dimension of drug use.

I must add a cautionary disclaimer. I have not examined thoroughly the literature on LSD, which increases at an alarming rate.[3] What I have to say about it is necessarily speculative with respect to its effects; what I have to say about the conditions under which it is used is also speculative, but is based in part on interviews with a few users. I present no documented conclusions, but do hope that the perspective outlined may help orient research toward generalizations that will fit into the corpus of sociological and social psychological theory on related matters.

THE SUBJECTIVE EFFECTS OF DRUGS

The physiological effects of drugs can be ascertained by standard techniques of physiological and pharmacological research. Scientists measure and have explanations for the actions of many drugs on such observable indices as the heart and respiratory rates, the level of various chemicals in the blood, and the secretion of enzymes and hormones. In contrast, the subjective changes produced by a drug can be ascertained only by asking the subject, in one way or another, how he feels. (To be sure, one can measure the drug's effect on certain measures of psychological functioning—the ability to perform some standardized task, such as placing pegs in a board or remembering nonsense syllables—but this does not tell us what the drug experience is like.)[4]

We take medically prescribed drugs because we believe they will cure or control a disease from which we are suffering; the subjective effects they produce are either ignored or defined as noxious side effects. But some people take some drugs precisely because they want to experience these subjective effects; they take them, to put it colloquially, because

---

[3]Hoffer's recent review of this literature, for which he disclaims completeness, cites 411 references (Hoffer, *op. cit.*).

[4]See, for instance: New York City Mayor's Committee on Marihuana, *The Marihuana Problem in the City of New York*, Lancaster: Jacques Cattell Press, 1944, pp. 69-77; and C. Knight Aldrich, "The Effect of a Synthetic Marihuana-Like Compound on Musical Talent as Measured by the Seashore Test," *Public Health Reports*, 59 (1944), pp. 431-433.

they want to get "high." These recreationally used drugs have become the focus of sociological research because the goal of an artificially induced change in consciousness seems to many immoral, and those who so believe have been able to transform their belief into law. Drug users thus come to sociological attention as lawbreakers, and the problems typically investigated have to do with explaining their lawbreaking.

Nevertheless, some sociologists, anthropologists and social psychologists have investigated the problem of drug-induced subjective experience in its own right. Taking their findings together, the following conclusions seem justified.[5] First, many drugs, including those used to produce changes in subjective experience, have a great variety of effects and the user may single out many of them, one of them, or none of them as definite experiences he is undergoing. He may be totally unaware of some of the drug's effects, even when they are physiologically gross, although in general the grosser the effects the harder they are to ignore. When he does perceive the effects, he may not attribute them to drug use but dismiss them as due to some other cause, such as fatigue or a cold. Marihuana users, for example, may not even be aware of the drug's effects when they first use it, even though it is obvious to others that they are experiencing them.[6]

Second, and in consequence, the effects of the same drug may be experienced quite differently by different people or by the same people at different times. Even if physiologically observable effects are substantially the same in all members of the species, individuals can vary widely in those to which they choose to pay attention. Thus, Aberle remarks on the quite different experiences Indians and experimental subjects have with peyote[7] and Blum reports a wide variety of experiences with

---

[5]I rely largely on the following reports: Howard S. Becker, *Outsiders*, New York: The Free Press, 1963, pp. 41-58 (marihuana); Alfred R. Lindesmith, *Opiate Addiction*, Bloomington: Principia Press, 1947 (opiates); Richard Blum and associates. *Utopiates*, New York: Atherton Press, 1964 (LSD); Ralph Metzner, George Litwin and Gunther M. Weil, "The Relation of Expectation and Mood to Psilocybin Reactions: A Questionnaire Study," *Psychedelic Review*, No. 5, 1965, pp. 3-39 (psilocybin); David F. Aberle, *The Peyote Religion Among the Navaho*, Chicago: Aldine Publishing Co., 1966, pp. 5-11 (peyote); Stanley Schacter and Jerome E. Singer, "Cognitive, Social and Physiological Determinants of Emotional State," *Psychological Review*, 69 (September, 1962), pp. 379-399 (adrenalin); and Vincent Newlis and Helen H. Newlis, "The Description and Analysis of Mood," *Annals of the New York Academy of Science*, 65 (1956), pp. 345-355 (benzedrine, seconal and dramamine).

Schacter and Singer propose a similar approach to mine to the study of drug experiences, stressing the importance of the label the person attaches to the experience he is having.

[6]Becker, *op. cit.*

[7]Aberle, *op. cit.*, and Anthony F. C. Wallace, "Cultural Determinants of Response to Hallucinatory Experience," *Archives of General Psychiatry*, 1 (July, 1959), pp. 58-69 (especially Table 2 on p. 62). Wallace argues that ". . . both the subjective feeling tone and the specific content of the hallucination are heavily influenced by . . . the cultural milieu in which hallucination, and particularly the voluntary hallucination, takes place." (p. 62.)

LSD, depending on the circumstances under which it was taken.[8]

Third, since recreational users take drugs in order to achieve some subjective state not ordinarily available to them, it follows that they will expect and be most likely to experience those effects which produce a deviation from conventional perceptions and interpretations of internal and external experience. Thus, distortions in perception of time and space and shifts in judgments of the importance and meaning of ordinary events constitute the most common reported effects.

Fourth, any of a great variety of effects may be singled out by the user as desirable or pleasurable, as the effects for which he has taken the drug. Even effects which seem to the uninitiated to be uncomfortable, unpleasant or frightening—perceptual distortions or visual and auditory hallucinations—can be defined by users as a goal to be sought.[9]

Fifth, how a person experiences the effects of a drug depends greatly on the way others define those effects for him.[10] The total effect of a drug is likely to be a melange of differing physical and psychological sensations. If others whom the user believes to be knowledgeable single out certain effects as characteristic and dismiss others, he is likely to notice those they single out as characteristic of his own experience. If they define certain effects as transitory, he is likely to believe that those effects will go away. All this supposes, of course, that the definition offered the user can be validated in his own experience, that something contained in the drug-induced melange of sensations corresponds to it.

Such a conception of the character of the drug experience has its roots, obviously, in Mead's theory of the self and the relation of objects to the self.[11] In that theory, objects (including the self) have meaning for the person only as he imputes that meaning to them in the course of his interaction with them. The meaning is not given in the object, but is lodged there as the person acquires a conception of the kind of action that can be taken with, toward, by and for it. Meanings arise in the course of social interaction, deriving their character from the consensus participants develop about the object in question. The findings of research on the character of drug-induced experience are therefore predictable from Mead's theory.

---

[8]Blum, et al., op. cit., p. 42.

[9]See the case cited by Becker, op. cit., pp. 55-56.

[10]The studies cited in footnote 5, supra, generally make this point.

[11]See George Herbert Mead, Mind, Self and Society, Chicago: University of Chicago Press, 1934, and Herbert Blumer, "Sociological Implications of the Thought of George Herbert Mead," American Journal of Sociology, 71 (March, 1966), pp. 535-544.

DRUG PSYCHOSES

The scientific literature and, even more, the popular press frequently state that recreational drug use produces a psychosis. The nature of "psychosis" is seldom defined, as though it were intuitively clear. Writers usually seem to mean a mental disturbance of some unspecified kind, involving auditory and visual hallucinations, an inability to control one's stream of thought, and a tendency to engage in socially inappropriate behavior, either because one has lost the sense that it is inappropriate or because one cannot stop oneself. In addition, and perhaps most important, psychosis is thought to be a state that will last long beyond the specific event that provoked it. However it occurred, it is thought to mark a more-or-less permanent change in the psyche and this, after all, is why we usually think of it as such a bad thing. Overindulgence in alcohol produces many of the symptoms cited but this frightens no one because we understand that they will soon go away.

Verified reports of drug-induced psychoses are scarcer than one might think.[12] Nevertheless, let us assume that these reports have not been fabricated, but represent an interpretation by the reporter of something that really happened. In the light of the findings just cited, what kind of event can we imagine to have occurred that might have been interpreted as a "psychotic episode"? (I use the word "imagine" advisedly, for the available case reports usually do not furnish sufficient material to allow us to do more than imagine what might have happened.)

The most likely sequence of events is this. The inexperienced user has certain unusual subjective experiences, which he may or may not attribute to having taken the drug. He may find his perception of space distorted, so that he has difficulty climbing a flight of stairs. He may find his train of thought so confused that he is unable to carry on a normal conversation and hears himself making totally inappropriate remarks. He may see or hear things in a way that he suspects is quite different from the way others see and hear them.

Whether or not he attributes what is happening to the drug, the experiences are likely to be upsetting. One of the ways we know that we are normal human beings is that our perceptual world, on the evidence available to us, seems to be pretty much the same as other people's. We

---

[12]See the studies cited in footnote 2, *supra*, and the following reports of marihuana psychoses: Walter Bromberg, "Marihuana: A Psychiatric Study," *Journal of the American Medical Association*, 113 (July 1, 1939), pp. 4-12; Howard C. Curtis, "Psychosis Following the Use of Marihuana with Report of Cases," *Journal of the Kansas Medical Society*, 40 (1959), pp. 515-517; and Marjorie Nesbitt, "Psychosis Due to Exogenous Poisons," *Illinois Medical Journal*, 77 (1940), 278-281.

see and hear the same things, make the same kind of sense out of them and, where perceptions differ, can explain the difference by a difference in situation or perspective.[13] We may take for granted that the inexperienced drug user, though he wanted to get "high," did not expect an experience so radical as to call into question that common sense set of assumptions.

In any society whose culture contains notions of sanity and insanity, the person who finds his subjective state altered in the way described may think he has become insane. We learn at a young age that a person who "acts funny," "see things," "hears things," or has other bizarre and unusual experiences may have become "crazy," "nuts," "loony" or a host of other synonyms.[14] When a drug user identifies some of these untoward events occurring in his own experience, he may decide that he merits one of those titles—that he has lost his grip on reality, his control of himself, and has in fact "gone crazy." The interpretation implies the corollary that the change is irreversible or, at least, that things are not going to be changed back very easily. The drug experience, perhaps originally intended as a momentary entertainment, now looms as a momentous event which will disrupt one's life, possibly permanently. Faced with this conclusion, the person develops a full-blown anxiety attack, but it is an anxiety caused by his reaction to the drug experience rather than a direct consequence of drug use itself. (In this connection, it is interesting that, in the published reports of LSD psychoses, acute anxiety attacks appear as the largest category of untoward reactions.)[15]

It is perhaps easier to grasp what this must feel like if we imagine that, having taken several social drinks at a party, we were suddenly to see varicolored snakes peering out at us from behind the furniture. We would instantly recognize this as a sign of delirium tremens, and would no doubt become severely anxious at the prospect of having developed such a serious mental illness. Some such panic is likely to grip the rec-

---

[13]See Alfred Schutz, *Collected Papers*, vols. I and II, The Hague: Martinus Nijhoff, 1962 and 1964, and Harold Garfinkel, "A Conception of and Experiments with 'Trust' as a Condition of Stable Concerted Actions," in O. J. Harvey, editor, *Motivation and Social Interaction*, New York: Ronald Press Co., 1963, pp. 187-238.

[14]See Thomas J. Scheff, *Being Mentally Ill: A Sociological Theory*, Chicago: Aldine Publishing Co., 1966.

[15]See Frosch, *et al., op. cit.*, Cohen and Ditman, "Prolonged Adverse Reactions . . . ," *op. cit.*, and Ungerleider, *et al., op. cit.* It is not always easy to make a judgment, due to the scanty presentation of the material, and some of the reactions I count as anxiety are placed in these sources under different headings. Bromberg, *op. cit.*, makes a good case that practically all adverse reactions to marihuana can be traced to this kind of anxiety, and I think it likely that the same reasoning could be applied to the LSD reports, so that such reactions as "hallucination," "depression" and "confused" (to use Ungerleider's categories) are probably reactions to anxiety.

reational user of drugs who interprets his experience as a sign of insanity.

Though I have put the argument with respect to the inexperienced user, long-time users of recreational drugs sometimes have similar experiences. They may experiment with a higher dosage than they are used to and experience effects unlike anything they have known before. This can easily occur when using drugs purchased in the illicit market, where quality may vary greatly, so that the user inadvertently gets more than he can handle.

The scientific literature does not report any verified cases of people acting on their distorted perceptions so as to harm themselves and others, but such cases have been reported in the press. Press reports of drug-related events are very unreliable, but it may be that users have, for instance, stepped out of a second story window, deluded by the drug into thinking it only a few feet to the ground.[16] If such cases have occurred, they too may be interpreted as examples of psychosis, but a different mechanism than the one just discussed would be involved. The person, presumably, would have failed to make the necessary correction for the drug-induced distortion, a correction, however, that experienced users assert can be made. Thus, a novice marihuana user will find it difficult to drive while "high," but experienced users have no difficulty. Similarly, novices find it difficult to manage their relations with people who are not also under the influence of drugs, but experienced users can control their thinking and actions so as to behave appropriately.[17] Although it is commonly assumed that a person under the influence of LSD must avoid ordinary social situations for 12 or more hours, I have been told[18] of at least one user who takes the drug and then goes to work; she explained that once you learn "how to handle it" (i.e., make the necessary corrections for distortions caused by the drug) there is no problem.

In short, the most likely interpretation we can make of the drug-induced psychoses reported is that they are either severe anxiety reactions to an event interpreted and experienced as insanity, or failures by the user to correct, in carrying out some ordinary action, for the perceptual distortions caused by the drug. If the interpretation is correct, then untoward mental effects produced by drugs depend in some part

---

[16]Although LSD is often said to provoke suicide, there is very little evidence of this. Cohen, *op. cit.*, after surveying 44 investigators who had used LSD with over 5,000 patients, says that the few cases reported all occurred among extremely disturbed patients who might have done it anyway; Hoffer, *op. cit.*, remarks that the number is so low that it might be argued that LSD actually lowers the rate among mental patients. Ungerleider reports that 10 of 70 cases were suicidal or suicide attempts, but gives no further data.

[17]See Becker, *op. cit.*, pp. 66-72.

[18]By David Oppenheim.

on its physiological action, but to a much larger degree find their origin in the definitions and conceptions the user applies to that action. These can vary with the individual's personal makeup, a possibility psychiatrists are most alive to, or with the groups he participates in, the trail I shall pursue here.

THE INFLUENCE OF DRUG-USING CULTURES

While there are no reliable figures, it is obvious that a very large number of people use recreational drugs, primarily marihuana and LSD. From the previous analysis one might suppose that, therefore, a great many people would have disquieting symptoms and, given the ubiquity in our society of the concept of insanity, that many would decide they had gone crazy and thus have a drug-induced anxiety attack. But very few such reactions occur. Although there must be more than are reported in the professional literature, it is unlikely that drugs have this effect in any large number of cases. If they did there would necessarily be many more verified accounts than are presently available. Since the psychotic reaction stems from a definition of the drug-induced experience, the explanation of this paradox must lie in the availability of competing definitons of the subjective states produced by drugs.

Competing definitions come to the user from other users who, to his knowledge, have had sufficient experience with the drug to speak with authority. He knows that the drug does not produce permanent disabling damage in all cases, for he can see that these other users do not suffer from it. The question, of course, remains whether it may not produce damage in some cases and whether his is one of them, no matter how rare.

When someone experiences disturbing effects, other users typically assure him that the change in his subjective experience is neither rare nor dangerous. They have seen similar reactions before, and may even have experienced them themselves with no lasting harm. In any event, they have some folk knowledge about how to handle the problem.

They may, for instance, know of an antidote for the frightening effects; thus, marihuana users, confronted with someone who has gotten "too high," encourage him to eat, an apparently effective countermeasure.[19] They talk reassuringly about their own experiences, "normaliz-

---

[19]Cf. the New York City Mayor's Committee on Marihuana, *op. cit.,* p. 13: "The smoker determines for himself the point of being 'high,' and is over-conscious of preventing himself from becoming 'too high.' This fear of being 'too high' must be associated with some form of anxiety which causes the smoker, should he accidentally reach that point, immediately to institute measures so that he can 'come down.' It has been found that the use of beverages such as beer, or a sweet soda pop, is an affective measure. A cold shower will also have the effect of bringing the person 'down.' "

ing" the frightening symptom by treating it, matter-of-factly, as temporary. They maintain surveillance over the affected person, preventing any physically or socially dangerous activity. They may, for instance, keep him from driving or from making a public display that will bring him to the attention of the police or others who would disapprove of his drug use. They show him how to allow for the perceptual distortion the drug causes and teach him how to manage interaction with nonusers.

They redefine the experience he is having as desirable rather than frightening, as the end for which the drug is taken.[20] What they tell him carries conviction, because he can see that it is not some idiosyncratic belief but is instead culturally shared. It is what "everyone" who uses the drug knows. In all these ways, experienced users prevent the episode from having lasting effects and reassure the novice that whatever he feels will come to a timely and harmless end.

The anxious novice thus has an alternative to defining his experience as "going crazy." He may redefine the event immediately or, having been watched over by others throughout the anxiety attack, decide that it was not so bad after all and not fear its reoccurrence. He "learns" that his original definition was "incorrect" and that the alternative offered by other users more nearly describes what he has experienced.

Available knowledge does not tell us how often this mechanism comes into play or how effective it is in preventing untoward psychological reactions; no research has been addressed to this point. In the case of marihuana, at least, the paucity of reported cases of permanent damage coupled with the undoubted increase in use suggests that it may be an effective mechanism.

For such a mechanism to operate, a number of conditions must be met. First, the drug must not produce, quite apart from the user's interpretations, permanent damage to the mind. No amount of social redefinition can undo the damage done by toxic alcohols, or the effects of a lethal dose of an opiate or barbiturate. This analysis, therefore, does not apply to drugs known to have such effects.

Second, users of the drug must share a set of understandings—a culture—which includes, in addition to material on how to obtain and ingest the drug, definitions of the typical effects, the typical course of the experience, the permanence of the effects, and a description of methods for dealing with someone who suffers an anxiety attack because of drug use or attempts to act on the basis of distorted perceptions. Users should have available to them, largely through face-to-face participation with

---

[20]*Ibid.*, and Becker, *op. cit.*

other users but possibly in such other ways as reading as well, the definitions contained in that culture, which they can apply in place of the common-sense definitions available to the inexperienced man in the street.

Third, the drug should ordinarily be used in group settings, where other users can present the definitions of the drug-using culture to the person whose inner experience is so unusual as to provoke use of the common-sense category of insanity. Drugs for which technology and custom promote group use should produce a lower incidence of "psychotic episodes."

The last two conditions suggest, as is the case, that marihuana, surrounded by an elaborate culture and ordinarily used in group settings, should produce few "psychotic" episodes [21] At the same time, they suggest the prediction that drugs which have not spawned a culture and are ordinarily used in private, such as barbiturates, will produce more such episodes. I suggest possible research along these lines below.

NON-USER INTERPRETATIONS

A user suffering from drug-induced anxiety may also come into contact with non-users who will offer him definitions, depending on their own perspectives and experiences, that may validate the diagnosis of "going crazy" and thus prolong the episode, possibly producing relatively permanent disability. These non-users include family members and police, but most important among them are psychiatrists and psychiatrically oriented physicians. (Remember that when we speak of reported cases of psychosis, the report is ordinarily made by a physician, though police may also use the term in reporting a case to the press.)

Medical knowledge about the recreational use of drugs is spotty. Little research has been done, and its results are not at the fingertips of physicians who do not specialize in the area. (In the case of LSD, or course, there has been a good deal of research, but its conclusions are not clear and, in any case, have not yet been spread throughout the profession.) Psychiatrists are not anxious to treat drug users, so few of them have accumulated any clinical experience with the phenomenon. Nevertheless, a user who develops severe and uncontrollable anxiety will probably be brought, if he is brought anywhere, to a physician for treatment. Most probably, he will be brought to a psychiatric hospital, if one is available; if not, to a hospital emergency room, where a psychiatric resident will

---

[21] I discuss the evidence on this point below.

be called once the connection with drugs is established, or to a private psychiatrist.[22]

Physicians, confronted with a case of drug-induced anxiety and lacking specific knowledge of its character or proper treatment, rely on a kind of generalized diagnosis. They reason that people probably do not use drugs unless they are suffering from a severe underlying personality disturbance; that use of the drug may allow repressed conflicts to come into the open where they will prove unmanageable; that the drug in this way provokes a true psychosis; and, therefore, that the patient confronting them is psychotic. Furthermore, even though the effects of the drug wear off, the psychosis may not, for the repressed psychological problems it has brought to the surface may not recede as it is metabolized and excreted from the body.

Given such a diagnosis, the physician knows what to do. He hospitalizes the patient for observation and prepares, where possible, for long-term therapy designed to repair the damage done to the psychic defenses or to deal with the conflict unmasked by the drug. Both hospitalization and therapy are likely to reinforce the definition of the drug experience as insanity, for in both the patient will be required to "understand" that he is mentally ill as a precondition for return to the world.[23]

The physician then, does *not* treat the anxiety attack as a localized phenomenon, to be treated in a symptomatic way, but as an outbreak of a serious disease heretofore hidden. He may thus prolong the serious effects beyond the time they might have lasted had the user instead come into contact with other users. This analysis, of course, is frankly speculative; what is required is study of the way physicians treat cases of the kind described and, especially, comparative study of the effects of treatment of drug-induced anxiety attacks by physicians and by drug users.

Another category of non-users deserves mention. Literary men and journalists publicize definitions of drug experiences, either of their own invention or those borrowed from users, psychiatrists or police. (Some members of this category use drugs themselves, so it may be a little confusing to classify them as non-users; in any case, the definitions are provided outside the ordinary channels of communication in the drug-using world.) The definitions of literary men—novelists, essayists and poets—grow out of a long professional tradition, beginning with De Quincey's *Confessions*, and are likely to be colored by that tradition. Lit-

---

[22]It may be that a disproportionate number of cases will be brought to certain facilities. Ungerleider, *et al.*, *op. cit.*, say (p. 392): "A larger number of admissions, both relative and real, than in other facilities in the Los Angeles area suggests the prevalence of a rumor that 'UCLA takes care of acid heads,' as several of our patients have told us."

[23]See Thomas Szasz, *The Myth of Mental Illness*, New York: Paul B. Hoeber, Inc., 1961.

erary descriptions dwell on the fantasy component of the experience, on its cosmic and ineffable character, and on the threat of madness.[24] Such widely available defintions furnish some of the substance out of which a user may develop his own definition, in the absence of defintions from the drug-using culture.

Journalists use any of a number of approaches conventional in their craft; what they write is greatly influenced by their own professional needs. They must write about "news," about events which have occurred recently and require reporting and interpretation. Furthermore, they need "sources," persons to whom authoritative statements can be attributed. Both needs dispose them to reproduce the line taken by law enforcement officials and physicians, for news is often made by the passage of a law or by a public statement in the wake of an alarming event, such as a bizarre murder or suicide. So journalistic reports frequently dwell on the theme of madness or suicide, a tendency intensified by the newsman's desire to tell a dramatic story.[25] Some journalists, of course, will take the other side in the argument, but even then, because they argue against the theme of madness, the emphasis on that theme is maintained. Public discussion of drug use thus tends to strengthen those stereotypes that would lead users who suffer disturbing effects to interpret their experience as "going crazy."

AN HISTORICAL DIMENSION

A number of variables, then, affect the character of drug-induced experiences. It remains to show that the experiences themselves are likely to vary according to when they occur in the history of use of a given drug in a society. In particular, it seems likely that the experience of acute anxiety caused by drug use will so vary.

Consider the following sequence of possible events, which may be regarded as a natural history of the assimilation of an intoxicating drug by a society. Someone in the society discovers, rediscovers or invents a drug which has the properties described earlier. The ability of the drug to alter subjective experience in desirable ways becomes known to increasing numbers of people, and the drug itself simultaneously becomes available, along with the information needed to make its use effective.

---

[24]For a classic in the genre, see Fitzhugh Ludlow, *The Hasheesh Eater,* New York: Harper and Brothers, 1857. A more modern example is Alan Harrington, "A Visit to Inner Space," in Solomon, *op. cit.,* pp. 72-102.

[25]Examples are J. Kobler, "Don't Fool Around with LSD," *Saturday Evening Post,* 236 (November 2, 1963), pp. 30-32, and Noah Gordon, "The Hallucinogenic Drug Cult," *The Reporter,* 29 (August 15, 1963), pp. 35-43.

Use increases, but users do not have a sufficient amount of experience with the drug to form a stable conception of it as an object. They do not know what it can do to the mind, have no firm idea of the variety of effects it can produce, and are not sure how permanent or dangerous the effects are. They do not know if the effects can be controlled or how. No drug-using culture exists, and there is thus no authoritative alternative with which to counter the possible definition, when and if it comes to mind, of the drug experience as madness. "Psychotic episodes" occur frequently.

But individuals accumulate experience with the drug and communicate their experiences to one another. Consensus develops about the drug's subjective effects, their duration, proper dosages, predictable dangers and how they may be avoided; all these points become matters of common knowledge, validated by their acceptance in a world of users. A culture exists. When a user experiences bewildering or frightening effects, he has available to him an authoritative alternative to the lay notion that he has gone mad. Every time he uses cultural conceptions to interpret drug experiences and control his response to them, he strengthens his belief that the culture is indeed a reliable source of knowledge. "Psychotic episodes" occur less frequently in proportion to the growth of the culture to cover the range of possible effects and its spread to a greater proportion of users. Novice users, to whom the effects are most unfamiliar and who therefore might be expected to suffer most from drug-induced anxiety, learn the culture from older users in casual conversation and in more serious teaching sessions and are thus protected from the dangers of "panicking" or "flipping out."

The incidence of "psychoses," then, is a function of the stage of development of a drug-using culture. Individual experience varies with historical stages and the kinds of cultural and social organization associated with them.

Is this model a useful guide to reality? The only drug for which there is sufficient evidence to attempt an evaluation is marihuana; even there the evidence is equivocal, but it is consistent with the model. On this interpretation, the early history of marihuana use in the United States should be marked by reports of marihuana-induced psychoses. In the absence of a fully formed drug-using culture, some users would experience disquieting symptoms and have no alternative to the idea that they were losing their minds. They would turn up at psychiatric facilities in acute states of anxiety and doctors, eliciting a history of marihuana use, would interpret the episode as a psychotic breakdown. When, however, the culture reached full flower and spread throughout the user population, the number of psychoses should have dropped even though (as a variety of evidence suggests) the number of users increased greatly. Using the definitions made available by the culture, users who had unexpectedly severe symptoms could interpret them in such a way as to reduce or control anxiety and would thus no longer come to the attention of those likely to report them as cases of psychosis.

Marihuana first came into use in the United States in the 1920's and early '30's, and all reports of psychosis associated with its use date from approximately that period.[26] A search of both *Psychological Abstracts* and the *Cummulative Index Medicus* (and its predecessors, the *Current List of Medical Literature* and the *Quarterly Index Medicus*) revealed no cases after 1940. The disappearance of reports of psychosis thus fits the model. It is, of course, a shaky index, for it depends as much on the reporting habits of physicians as on the true incidence of cases, but it is the only thing available.

The psychoses described also fit the model, insofar as there is any clear indication of a drug-induced effect. (The murder, suicide and death in an automobile accident reported by Curtis, for instance, are equivocal in this respect; in no case is any connection with marihuana use demonstrated other than that the people involved used it.) [27] The best evidence comes from the 31 cases reported by Bromberg. Where the detail given allows judgment, it appears that all but one stemmed from the person's inability to deal with either the perceptual distortion caused by the drug or with the panic at the thought of losing one's mind it created.[28] Bromberg's own interpretation supports this:

> In occasional instances, and these are the cases which are apt to come to medical attention, the anxiety with regard to death, insanity, bodily deformity and bodily dissolution is startling. The patient is tense, nervous, frightened; a state of panic may develop. Often suicide or assaultive acts are the result [of the panic]. The anxiety state is so common . . . that it can be considered a part of the intoxication syndrome.[29]

> The inner relationship between cannabis [marihuana] and the onset of a functional psychotic state is not always clear. The inner reaction to somatic sensation seems vital. Such reactions consisted of panic states which disappeared as soon as the stimulus (effects of the drug) faded.[30]

---

[26]Bromberg, *op. cit.*, Curtis, *op. cit.*, *and Nesbitt, op. cit.*
[27]Curtis, *op. cit.*
[28]See Table 1 in Bromberg, *op. cit.*, pp. 6-7.
[29]*Ibid.*, p. 5.
[30]*Ibid.*, pp. 7-8.

Even though Bromberg distinguishes between pure panic reactions and those in which some underlying mental disturbance was present (the "functional psychotic state" he refers to), he finds, as our model leads us to expect, that the episode is provoked by the user's interpretation of the drug effects in terms other than those contained in the drug-using culture.

The evidence cited is extremely scanty. We do not know the role of elements of the drug-using culture in any of these cases or whether the decrease in incidence is a true one. But we are not likely to do any better and, in the absence of conflicting evidence, it seems justified to take the model as an accurate representation of the history of marihuana use in the United States.

The final question, then, is whether the model can be used to interpret current reports of LSD-induced psychosis. Are these episodes the consequence of an early stage in the development of an LSD-using culture? Will the number of episodes decrease while the number of users rises, as the model leads us to predict?

LSD

We cannot predict the history of LSD by direct analogy to the history of marihuana, for a number of important conditions may vary. We must first ask whether the drug has, apart from the definitions users impose on their experience, any demonstrated causal relation to psychosis. There is a great deal of controversy on this point, and any reading of the evidence must be tentative. My own opinion is that LSD has essentially the same characteristics as those described in the first part of this paper; its effects may be more powerful than those of other drugs that have been studied, but they too are subject to differing interpretations by users[31] so that the mechanisms I have described can come into play.

The cases reported in the literature are, like those reported for marihuana, mostly panic reactions to the drug experience, occasioned by the user's interpretation that he has lost his mind, or further disturbance among people already quite disturbed.[32] There are no cases of permanent derangement directly traceable to the drug, with one puzzling exception (puzzling to those who report it as well as to me). In a few cases the visual and auditory distortions produced by the drug reoccur weeks or months after it was last ingested; this sometimes produces severe upset among those who experience it. Observers are at a loss to explain

---

[31]Blum, *et al.*, *op. cit.*, p. 42.
[32]See footnote 2, *supra*.

the phenomenon, except for Rosenthal, who proposes that the drug may have a specific effect on the nerve pathways involved in vision; but this theory, should it prove correct, is a long way from dealing with questions of possible psychosis.[33]

The whole question is confused by the extraordinary assertions about the effects of LSD made by both proponents and opponents of its use. Both sides agree that it has a very strong effect on the mind, disagreeing only as to whether this powerful effect is benign or malignant. Leary, for example, argues that we must "go out of our minds in order to use our heads,"[34] and that this can be accomplished by using LSD. Opponents[35] agree that it can drive you out of your mind, but do not share Leary's view that this is a desirable goal. In any case, we need not accept the premise simply because both parties to the controversy do.

Let us assume then, in the absence of more definitive evidence, that the drug does not in itself produce lasting derangement, that such psychotic episodes as are now reported are largely a result of panic at the possible meaning of the experience, that users who "freak out" do so because they fear they have permanently damaged their minds. Is there an LSD-using culture? In what stage of development is it? Are the reported episodes of psychosis congruent with what our model would predict, given that stage of development?

Here again my discussion must be speculative, for no serious study of this culture is yet available.[36] It appears likely, however, that such a culture is in an early stage of development. Several conceptions of the drug and its possible effects exist, but no stable consensus has arisen. Radio, television and the popular press present a variety of interpretations, many of them contradictory. There is widespread disagreement, even among users, about possible dangers. Some certainly believe that use (or injudicious use) can lead to severe mental difficulty.

At the same time, my preliminary inquiries and observations hinted at the development (or at least the beginnings) of a culture similar to that surrounding marihuana use. Users with some experience discuss their symptoms and translate from one idiosyncratic description into another, developing a common conception of effects as they talk. The notion that a "bad trip" can be brought to a speedy conclusion by taking thorazine by mouth (or, when immediate action is required, intravenously) has spread. Users are also beginning to develop a set of safe-

---

[33]Rosenthal, *op. cit.*
[34]Timothy Leary, "Introduction" to Solomon, *op. cit.*, p. 13.
[35]Frosch, *et al., op. cit.* and Ungerleider, *et al., op. cit.*
[36]The book by Blum, *et al., op. cit.*, attempts this, but leaves many important questions untouched.

guards against committing irrational acts while under the drug's influence. Many feel, for instance, that one should take one's "trip" in the company of experienced users who are not under the drug's influence at the time; they will be able to see you through bad times and restrain you when necessary. A conception of the appropriate dose is rapidly becoming common knowledge. Users understand that they may have to "sit up with" people who have panicked as a result of the drug's effects, and they talk of techniques that have proved useful in this enterprise.[37] All this suggests that a common conception of the drug is developing which will eventually see it defined as pleasurable and desirable, with possible untoward effects that can however be controlled.

Insofar as this emergent culture spreads so that most or all users share the belief that LSD does not cause insanity, and the other understandings just listed, the incidence of "psychoses" should drop markedly or disappear. Just as with marihuana, the interpretation of the experience as one likely to produce madness will disappear and, having other definitions available to use in coping with the experience, users will treat the experience as self-limiting and not as a cause for panic.

The technology of LSD use, however, has features which will work in the opposite direction. In the first place, it is very easily taken; one need learn no special technique (as one must with marihuana) to produce the characteristic effects, for a sugar cube can be swallowed without instruction. This means that anyone who gets hold of the drug can take it in a setting where there are no experienced users around to redefine frightening effects and "normalize" them. He may also have acquired the drug without acquiring any of the presently developing cultural understandings so that, when frightening effects occur, he is left with nothing but current lay conceptions as plausible definitions. In this connection, it is important that a large amount of the published material by journalists and literary men places heavy emphasis on the dangers of psychosis.[38] It is also important that various medical facilities have become alerted

---

[37]Ungerleider, *et al.*, deny the efficacy of these techniques (pp. 391-392): "How do we know that persons taking LSD in a relaxed friendly environment with an experienced guide or 'sitter' will have serious side effects? We have no statistical data to answer this, but our impression (from our weekly group sessions) is that bad experiences were common with or without sitters and with or without 'the right environment.' This does not minimize the importance of suggestion in the LSD experience."

[39]For journalistic accounts, see Kobler, *op. cit.*, Gordon, *op. cit.*: R. Coughlan, "Chemical Mind-Changers," *Life*, 54 (March 15, 1963); and H. Asher, "They Split My Personality," *Saturday Review*, 46 (June 1, 1963), pp. 39-43. See also two recent novels in which LSD plays a major role: B. H. Friedman, *Yarborough*, New York: Knopf, 1964; and Alan Harrington, *The Secret Swinger*, New York: World Publishing Co., 1966.

to the possiblity of patients (particularly college students and teenagers) coming in with LSD-induced psychoses. All these factors will tend to increase the incidence of "psychotic episodes," perhaps sufficiently to offset the dampening effect of the developing culture.

A second feature of LSD which works in the opposite direction is that it can be administered to someone without his knowledge, since it is colorless, tasteless and odorless. (This possibility is recognized in recent state legislation which specifies *knowing* use as a crime; no such distinction has been found necessary in laws about marihuana, heroin, peyote or similar drugs.) It is reported, for instance, that LSD has been put in a party punchbowl, so that large numbers of people have suffered substantial changes in their subjective experience without even knowing they had been given a drug that might account for the change. Under such circumstances, the tendency to interpret the experience as a sudden attack of insanity might be very strong.[39] If LSD continues to be available on the underground market without much difficulty, such events are likely to continue to occur. (A few apocalyptic types speak of introducing LSD into a city water supply—not at all impossible, since a small amount will affect enormous quantities of water—and thus "turning a whole city on." This might provoke a vast number of "psychoses," should it ever happen.)

In addition to these technological features, many of the new users of LSD, unlike the users of most illicit recreational drugs, will be people who, in addition to never having used any drug to alter their subjective experience before, will have had little or nothing to do with others who have used drugs in that way. LSD, after all, was introduced into the United States under very reputable auspices and has had testimonials from many reputable and conventional persons. In addition, there has been a great deal of favorable publicity to accompany the less favorable—the possibility that the drug can do good as well as harm has been spread in a fashion that never occurred with marihuana. Finally, LSD has appeared at a time when the mores governing illicit drug use among young people seem to be changing radically, so that youth no longer reject drugs out of hand. Those who try LSD may thus not even have had the preliminary instruction in being "high" that most novice marihuana users have before first using it. They will, consequently, be even less prepared for the experience they have. (This suggests the prediction

---

[39]Cf. Cohen and Ditman, "Complications. . . . ," *op. cit.*, p. 161: "Accidental ingestion of the drug by individuals who are unaware of its nature has already occurred. This represents a maximally stressful event because the perceptual and ideational distortions then occur without the saving knowledge that they were drug induced and temporary."

that marihuana users who experiment with LSD will show fewer untoward reactions than those who have had no such experience.)[40]

These features of the drug make it difficult to predict the number of
mental upsets likely to be "caused" by LSD. If use grows, the number
of people exposed to the possibility will grow. As an LSD-using culture
develops, the proportion of those exposed who interpret their experience as one of insanity will decrease. But people may use the drug
without being indoctrinated with the new cultural definitions, either
because of the ease with which the drug can be taken or because it has
been given to them without their knowledge, in which case the number
of episodes will rise. The actual figure will be a vector made up of these
several components.

A NOTE ON THE OPIATES

The opiate drugs present an interesting paradox. In the drugs we
have been considering, the development of a drug-using culture causes
a decrease in rates of morbidity associated with drug use, for greater
knowledge of the true character of the drug's effects lessens the likelihood that users will respond to those effects with uncontrolled anxiety.
In the case of opiates, however, the greater one's knowledge of the drug's
effects, the more likely it is that one will suffer its worst effect, addiction.
As Lindesmith has shown,[41] one can only be addicted when he experiences physiological withdrawal symptoms, recognizes them as due to a
need for drugs, and relieves them by taking another dose. The crucial
step of recognition is most likely to occur when the user participates in
a culture in which the signs of withdrawal are interpreted for what they
are. When a person is ignorant of the nature of withdrawal sickness, and
has some other cause to which he can attribute his discomfort (such as
a medical problem), he may misinterpret the symptoms and thus escape
addiction, as some of Lindesmith's cases demonstrate.[42]

This example makes clear how important the actual physiology of the
drug response is in the model I have developed. The culture contains
interpretations of the drug experience, but these must be congruent
with the drug's actual effects. Where the effects are varied and ambiguous, as with marihuana and LSD, a great variety of interpretations is
possible. Where the effects are clear and unmistakable, as with opiates,

---

[40]Negative evidence is found in Ungerleider, *et al., op. cit.* Twenty-five of their 70 cases
had previously used marihuana.

[41]Lindesmith, *op. cit.*

[42]*Ibid.*, cases 3, 5 & 6 (pp. 68-69, 71, 72).

the culture is limited in the possible interpretations it can provide. Where the cultural interpretation is so constrained, and the effect to be interpreted leads, in its most likely interpretation, to morbidity, the spread of a drug-using culture will increase morbidity rates.

CONCLUSION

The preceding analysis, to repeat, is supported at only a few points by available research; most of what has been said is speculative. The theory, however, gains credibility in several ways. Many of its features follow directly from a Meadian social psychology and the general plausibility of that scheme lends it weight. Furthermore, it is consistent with much of what social scientists have discovered about the nature of drug-induced experiences. In addition, the theory makes sense of some commonly reported and otherwise inexplicable phenomena, such as variations in the number of "psychotic" episodes attributable to recreational drug use. Finally, and much the least important, it is in accord with my haphazard and informal observations of LSD use.

The theory also has the virtue of suggesting a number of specific lines of research. With respect to the emerging "social problem" of LSD use, it marks out the following areas for investigation: the relation between social settings of use, the definitions of the drug's effects available to the user, and the subjective experiences produced by the drug; the mechanisms by which an LSD-using culture arises and spreads; the difference in experiences of participants and non-participants in that culture; the influence of each of the several factors described on the number of harmful effects attributable to the drug; and the typical response of physicians to LSD-induced anxiety states and the effect of that response as compared to the response made by experienced drug culture participants.

The theory indicates useful lines of research with respect to other common drugs as well. Large numbers of people take tranquilizers, barbiturates and amphetamines. Some frankly take them for "kicks" and are participants in drug-using cultures built around those drugs, while others are respectable middleclass citizens who probably do not participate in any "hip" user culture. Do these "square" users have some shared cultural understandings of their own with respect to use of these drugs? What are the differential effects of the drugs—both on subjective experience and on rates of morbidity associated with drug use—among the two classes of users? How do physicians handle the pathological effects of these drugs, with which they are relatively familiar, as compared to their handling of drugs which are only available illicitly?

The theory may have implications for the study of drugs not ordinarily used recreationally as well. Some drugs used in ordinary medical practice (such as the adrenocortical steroids) are said to carry a risk of provoking psychosis. It may be that this danger arises when the drug produces changes in subjective experience which the user does not anticipate, does not connect with the drug, and thus interprets as signs of insanity. Should the physician confirm this by diagnosing a "drug psychosis," a vicious circle of increasing validation of the diagnosis may ensue. The theory suggests that the physician using such drugs might do well to inquire carefully into the feelings that produce such anxiety reactions, interpret them to the patient as common, transient and essentially harmless side effects, and see whether such action would not control the phenomenon. Drugs that have been incriminated in this fashion would make good subjects for research designed to explore some of the premises of the argument made here.

The sociologist may find most interesting the postulated connection between historical stages in the development of a culture and the nature of individual subjective experience. Similar linkages might be discovered in the study of political and religious movements. For example, at what stages in the development of such movements are individuals likely to experience euphoric and ecstatic feelings? How are these related to shifts in the culture and organization of social relations within the movement? The three-way link between history, culture and social organization, and the person's subjective state may point the way to a better understanding than we now have of the social bases of individual experience.

14

"HIGH" STATES: A BEGINNING STUDY

Norman E. Zinberg

1. INTRODUCTION

While everyone knows what it is to be "high," whether on drugs, on an experience, or on life in general, almost everyone has great difficulty describing a particular high state in a way that makes sense to a person who has not experienced it. And to an outside observer who tries to learn by observing people who are high, the state appears maddeningly amorphous. These epistemological difficulties have deterred efforts to develop coherent phenomenological studies of the area. To complicate the topic further, many of the studies that do exist have been colored by the researcher's need morally to condemn or to support those who seek highs. It is not surprising that the voluminous material on both drug and non-drug highs that has appeared over the last decade neglects one absolutely fundamental question: What is the person experiencing that is worth the risks, the trouble, and potentially the costs?

This essay addresses the question and considers the phenomenology of changes in consciousness colloquially known as "high states."

Since consciousness change is the subject to be studied, a theoretical framework for the concept of consciousness is needed. I will use the general concepts and usual terminology of psychoanalytic theory, but I intend to avoid speculative, theoretical, metapsychological generali-

---

Reprinted with permission from the National Drug Abuse Council, 1974, 1-50.

zations and to stay close to clinical observations.* The experimental section focuses solely on descriptive generalizations of opiate- and psychedelic-drug-induced states. These particular high states have been selected for reasons of research strategy and also because they are sufficiently prominent to justify my emphasis on what has prevented us from progressing further in such studies.

The most important single concept about drug-induced states to emerge in the last decade is this—to understand the subject's response one must consider drug, set, and setting as a basic whole (1, 3, 4). "Set" refers to the person's attitude toward the experience and includes his personality structure. "Setting" refers to the influence of the physical and social environment in which the drug use takes place. To understand an individual's decision to use a drug and his response to the experience at any effective dose below toxic levels, one must consider all three factors. Hence, the social attitudes toward the experience being studied directly affect the experience itself. The drug-set-setting conceptual model indicates that while we cannot change influences, we can delineate what the influences are.

My insistence on the set/setting interaction means that I place less emphasis on the irremediable basic influence of early psychic development. While I do not ignore this early aspect of set, I see the effects of persistent social attitudes, particularly when magnified by the mass media and accepted by the public as a social crisis, as a factor influencing the continuing personality development of the individual (4).

2. MORALITY

The current controversy about consciousness-change grew out of the Timothy Leary "Turn On, Tune In, and Drop Out" movement of the early sixties. Leary's knack for publicity and the provocative phrase encouraged partisanship. Sides were chosen, and although many of the players have changed, the fors and againsts play and replay the match. This is not to say that public and professional condemnation of drug use began at that time—an American crusade against drugs going back one hundred years has been abundantly documented (7)—but before

---

*In formal terms, thus I will note that consistent, latent (i.e., unconscious) themes reverberate through different manifest contents and that both conscious and unconscious processes are contained within a dynamic equilibrium. This equilibrium is seen as encompassing varying and conflicting motives and defenses such as the differentiation between primary and secondary process (5). But I will not take up more abstract concepts such as cathexis-countercathexis of drive gratification in its relation to energetic and structural points of view (6).

the sixties the issue created little moral struggle. Early drug users, such as the bohemians, blacks, and musicians who used marihuana, the addicts on heroin, generally accepted themselves as bad or weak and might be called "repentant deviants" (8). When caught, they accepted their punishment without a murmur, and there was no Friends of the Addict civil liberties group in existence to help them.

Leary's enthusiasm for the wonders of psychedelic drugs hit the right note in the United States of the sixties; and a horde of mostly young people began to try LSD. They also began to defend the right to use it and to dispute the right of social institutions, that is the Establishment, to prevent them. Despite growing efforts at sane and rational consideration of the subject (4, 9, 10, 11, 12), like the 1973 Smithsonian conference, the fight still goes on. The Establishment's counterattack consists first of legal strictures: all the psychedelic drugs are classified by the federal drug laws as Group I, which means one to five years in jail for possession. Next, although much of the experimental work intended to prove the physical harm of these drugs has come to little (13, 14), mention continues to be made in the media and in scientific papers of chromosome breaks (15, 16, 17), drug-induced psychoses (18), and the like, nowadays usually phrased ambiguously. This phrasing keeps the spectre of the drugs' potential harm vivid, while the writer avoids any outright contention that there is much evidence for it. Most persistent have been attacks on the acid-induced psychological state in terms of "schizoid response," "regression," "distorted body image," "dissociation," "loss of ego boundaries," "apathy" and so on. All of these phrases are much used by professionals when discussing severe emotional disorders, but they would not ordinarily be used to describe an intoxication, a high, or an alternate state of consciousness,* unless they were intended to be pejorative.

The other side has been equally verbose. The League for Spiritual Discovery and its descendants speak of "transcendence of body and mind," "supracosmic unity," "macro spirit," "rebirth," and so on. All these mystical and religious phenomena are ostensibly experienced on a "trip" and are not what the public usually associates with intoxication or highs.

Thus the battle was joined—one side convinced of the badness and harm of high states and the other declaring them to be "renewing." The users, no longer "repentant" deviants, had become "enemy" deviants (8).

---

*The word "altered" is popularly used to describe these states. I prefer "alternate" in order to avoid the idea that the change alters consciousness from the way it *shoud* be.

The heavy use of marihuana which began in the mid-sixties stirred up the same ideological debates. And when heroin use increased and methadone was publicized as a more socially acceptable alternative, methadone too provoked ideological controversy.†

Today many young people have rediscovered alcohol, a socially acceptable drug (without giving up marihuana and controlled use of psychedelics, I might add), but they use the terminology garnered from psychedelia. They do the same with Sopors (methaqualone), a new favorite similar to barbiturates. Members of a high school group described sitting around after ingesting ethanol and asking each other, "Are you high yet?" "Where is it taking you?," for all the world like an LSD "trip," a word they often retain. The struggle that began with Leary now encompasses in its rhetoric and its concern with morality almost all efforts to get high with or without drugs. Meditation and other non-drug highs, the attainment of which was also usually cloaked in the most righteous, religious metaphor, entered the picture as cures for drug using. But it was conveniently overlooked that the drugs were ostensibly taken to get to the same place meditation might take you. Such a struggle for some sort of moral hegemony inhibits objective study of the states themselves.

This was not always so. The attempt to study the drug experience itself has sturdy roots. The best phenomenological descriptions so far are the work of Havelock Ellis (19). In 1902, writing in the *Popular Science Monthly,* Ellis described his experiences and experiments with mescal. He recorded his responses in detail (a remarkable capacity for control was needed to do so) and concluded that the drug affected neither emotional nor intellectual centers but rather concentrated its effect on the sensory system. Ellis thoroughly enjoyed his experience, although he doubted that it could have therapeutic value. To test the possibilities of the drug he varied set and setting. He varied set by giving the drug to an artist friend and then to others whose sensibility he thought would be different from his own. He experimented with setting by arranging to have different lighting effects when he next took the drug and to have a friend play unknown piano pieces so that he could avoid a stereotyped response. One comparison that occurred to him, and is evocative of my interest in this paper on the continuum of high states with or without drugs, was his interest in comparing drug effects with those

---

†This may have historical precedents. Grinspoon (10) points out that Baudelaire and members of Le Club des Hachichins, when discussing their remarkable highs on hashish, may at times have been taking opium and treating their response to this depressant as if it were a euphoriant high.

feelings ordinarily experienced in that borderland between waking and sleeping, a notion he unfortunately failed to pursue. The article concluded by his accepting with relish a friend's suggestion that at the next medical congress one half of the membership should take mescal and the other half should observe them.

This remarkable paper, with its clarity, objectivity, and easy acceptance of a nonphysicalistic scientific approach, has been largely forgotten, along with other discussions from the same period. The experimenters with psilocybin and LSD in the fifties and early sixties also noted their experiences without the cant that developed in the post-Leary decade beginning in 1963, but these have also largely been ignored (20, 21, 22). For several years psychiatrists in training at the Massachusetts Mental Health Clinic routinely volunteered to try LSD. The experimenters gave it to the trainees in order to see if the drug effects indeed mimicked schizophrenia, so that they could learn about the disease. This was the beginning of the stereotyped model that connects an unusual high with a disease. The scientists had a preconceived notion about the drug's effects. They were disappointed when they found little connection with schizophrenia, and this was a principal reason why many researchers were willing to abandon the field after the drugs came into popular illicit use. The researchers' interest in mental "disease" to a certain extent contaminated their phenomenological observations, but they had another interesting reason for choosing psychiatric residents. Observations of the drug's effects had indicated that one result was increased empathy. The modestly stated contentions of the experimenters were a far cry from those of the flower/love children of the Haight that came later, but the researchers did think that these doctors in training, after the drug trip, were more in tune with their patients and more understanding of them. Other studies reported similar findings. A group of psychiatrists at Chestnut Lodge took the drug and afterward noted a number of specific and general changes in their therapeutic response (23, 24), all toward greater empathy.

This pre-Leary body of literature is particularly noteworthy because there was little concern expressed or reported about untoward drug effects. A recent study by McGlothlin and Arnold (25) collected 267 cases of people who took LSD or psilocybin before 1961, either experimentally or for therapeutic purposes; although several were deeply affected by their experience, no bad trips were reported. The bad trip as a frequent phenomenon (18) apparently grew out of the *sturm und drang* of the Leary era and it has subsided since then. We don't really know why this occurred. Perhaps the hypersensory reaction noted by

Ellis included hypersuggestibility; perhaps the sensitivity to setting made the bad trip and the accompanying psychotic symptoms of the sixties an understandable result of so much conflict.

In any case, there were many such reactions. By 1967 the Massachusetts Mental Health Center and Bellevue believed that 20 to 25 percent of admissions were directly or indirectly related to the ingestion of psychedelic drugs (18). Today the bad trip as a reason for hospital admission has virtually disappeared, but not because the number of people trying the drugs has declined. The second report of the President's Commission on Marihuana and Drug Abuse (26) states that the number of people trying psychedelic drugs was up 133 percent in 1972, the largest increase of any drug category. But use has undergone a change. The 100- or 200-times-a-year tripper is now an extremely rare bird. A different pattern has emerged. Today, two or three times a year a small selected group of experimenters will carefully choose a special setting and rediscover Ellis' hyperesthesia. With set and setting thus controlled, there are few bad trips. And the illicit users have evolved social rituals that make this drug use relatively stable. The development of social rituals and mores by some young people as a way of controlling drug use and preventing drug abuse may be demonstrating to the larger culture and to students of drug use a profound truth about drug control (27).

3. DRUG, SET, AND SETTING

Griffith Edwards, Director of the Maudsley Hospital Drug Research Unit in London, has proposed in a recent paper (28) the use of a concept of plasticity to describe a drug's potential for varying effect. His paper is an effort to standardize and potentially quantify the extent to which a drug's effect can be modified by set and setting. In addition to the potential importance of the concept of plasticity, this English paper agrees in several areas with my work, an indication of some cross-national applicability in this research. For instance. I have difficulty with that body of work that assumes that some specific neuroticism or unconscious conflict preexisted in those individuals who become addicts or who have a serious emotional disturbance as a result of drug use. According to this view, inability to deal with aggression or anxiety or love has driven these individuals to opiates as a tranquilizer, pacifier, or replacement. Besides the tendency to tautological reasoning in much of this work (they must have been sick to do this or they wouldn't have done it), there is a playing down of the impact of the experience of drug taking on personality. Anyone who has lived the life of an addict in the United States for any period of time is changed by the experience. The required life style of hustling and "copping," always on the verge of what for the addicts is a total frustration and deprivation, seems to result in their having more personality similarities than differences. Whether these apparent similarities stem from preexisting traits or whether they are the result of shared experience is hard to know.

The same uncertainty exists about who will have a bad psychedelic trip. Obviously some people like the experience more than others, so we must conclude that some personality factor is at work, but Edwards and I agree that it is not as direct and specific as has often been believed. Some very neurotic and schizophrenic people apparently enjoy different drug experiences without untoward effects. A recent original book by Barr *et al.* (29) (also cited by Edwards) suggests that more holistic aspects of personality organization shape the LSD experience. Thus set would be more dominated by the total ego organization of the person than by a specific, unconscious conflict or psychopathological syndrome. Edwards devotes just a paragraph to the direct influence of personality on drug choice or response. But the extent to which the environment exerts plastic influences on drug-related behaviors, and the devices by which it does so, occupy about one-third of his longish paper. (He describes the paper as appealing to those with a taste for three-volume Victorian novels, which is another similarity to this work.) He carefully selects anthropological accounts to show how the same doses of a drug, used in very similar ways, result in entirely different responses. In one tribe alcohol leads to wild activity; another tribe reacts with exaggerated decorum. Reports of psychedelic drug use in non-Western cultures tell of facilitation of individual integration into the total society and its values. Such reports sharply contrast with many observers' views of how this drug experience works in England and the United States. Thus the plasticity of the drug response across different personalities is thoroughly demonstrated. What is not easy to specify is the way setting accomplishes its modification and determination of the drug's effect.

Straightforward suggestion is an oversimplification. Ellis (19), for instance, points out how, before giving the drug to a friend, he had told in detail of his experience, only to find that his friend had quite a different tale to tell afterwards. In our society the very idea of taking "a drug" sets up a conflict of hopes and anxieties which affect the experience. These responses vary from society to society and from individual to individual. Once the individual experiences the psychoactive effects of the drug itself, he will select explanatory constructs out of the range of cognitive and emotional percepts *available to him*. His response will follow from his available explanations of his situation. Edwards points out how fallacious it is to try to remove the specific incident, drug taking, from its social matrix. "One could not hope to understand the English country gentleman's fox-hunting simply by exploring his attitude towards the fox" (28), in his beautiful analogy.

Hence all efforts at phenomenological study must be qualified. I can only study what is experienced at this time in the United States; what I describe may turn out to be universal aspects of particular drugs or only reflections of local historical perspectives. However, as long as the reader and I keep this relativism in mind, as well as the cultural limitations on my powers of observation and objectivity, it is a beginning.

4. THEORETICAL FRAMEWORK

As early as 1904, Manfred Bleuler of Switzerland took Freud to task for his relative lack of interest in consciousness as compared with his enormous interest in unconsciousness. In fact, Freud did give some attention to the concept of consciousness (30, 31) in his earliest writings,* but of course not nearly so much as he gave to his discoveries of the unconscious, conflict, and defense. Although these discoveries led him to formulations that attempted a total theory of human psychology, his basic work was clinical and concerned with the roots of human malfunction. Thus it was the process of ideas and affects attaining or being barred from consciousness and how this process impaired functioning that preoccupied him and his followers. Freud considered the ideas and affects that attained consciousness to be relatively superficial and merely an end point that must be traced back in order to understand the important underlying conflict. The dynamics of consciousness *per se* were either overlooked or discussed in terms of repression and other mechanisms essentially concerned with the interactions of consciousness and unconsciousness.

Freud's original concept of consciousness, which was stated as early as *The Project for a Scientific Psychology* (30) and *Studies in Hysteria* (31), simply meant the special function of attention, that is, consciousness that was attending to something. In *The Project* he notices the altering of this state, but generally speaking he discusses the altering as part of psychic difficulty. His other use of the term consciousness refers to the total state of the organism, that is, the organism is conscious in the sense of being aware—aware of its existence and so on.

Freud thus used consciousness to define those functions which were within the scope of a person's awareness. In his early topographical

---

*The best and most comprehensive summary by far of *The Psychoanalytic Theory of Consciousness* is Appendix I of *LSD: Personality and Experience*, by Barr et al. (29)

theory of mentation (32), contents outside of awareness were in the system Ucs (unconscious). One major flaw in the topographical theory (which Freud began to abandon after the turn of the century) was the difficulty of explaining the topographical position of the forces barring material from consciousness. The forces of defense were automatic and technically unconscious but were not part of that which was being repressed. Thus they had to be related to consciousness.

To the extent that Freud saw the function of consciousness as having a quantitative aspect, that is, of operating with forces of energy, these forces could be shifted around and were regulated by the needs of attention or defense. Consciousness, in other words, could attend to a variety of perceptions at different times, depending on the quality of the perception, the strength of it, or the needs of the individual at that moment.

Breuer (31), by way of his great interest in the case of Anna O., argued for the existence of ideas which were outside the main core of the personality but could remain there in a relatively fixed or static condition. His formulation in *Studies in Hysteria* can be paraphrased like this: certain ideas can exist in consciousness; although the individual is at that moment not entirely aware of their existence, no specific resistance is met when an attempt is made to bring the dissociated contents into consciousness. This formulation suggests that what can become conscious at a given moment represents, albeit in part, a pattern of deployment of the capacity to attend (33) and is not solely a product of the relaxation of repression. I will return to this later.

What Freud thought of this formulation at the time is not known, but he strongly rejected it subsequently (33, 34), on the grounds that it was not dynamic. His pursuit of the active role of the defenses left little room for the explicit notion of an altered state of consciousness that was neither directly available to attention nor directly barred from it.

In retrospect, however, we see that the drift of the development of psychoanalytic theory was compatible with such an idea. The replacement of the topographical view of the mind with the structural concepts of id, ego, and superego led to increasing emphasis on the regulatory functions of the ego. The detailing of the place of perceptual thresholds, logical thinking, and other cognitive organizations expands the theoretical possibilities for a dynamics of consciousness. This pursuit has continued to occupy psychoanalytic theorists. Freud, however, followed his interest in the one area where he was preoccupied with consciousness change, the dream state.

In *The Interpretation of Dreams* (32) he speaks of consciousness as "a sense organ for the apprehension of psychical qualities." In this altered state, that is, the dream state, there is a lowering of barriers between consciousness and unconsciousness. Besides this actual lowering of barriers there are shifts in the investment of attention in various available mental and emotional systems. Some form of this conceptual foundation has dominated the view of alternate states of consciousness ever since. Even Barr *et al.*, whose work is enormously sophisticated, point out in their concluding chapter that "LSD does not work merely by lifting repression, any more than alcohol really works by dissolving the superego, but many of the effects do seem to be attributable to alterations in important defenses. If this is the case, it is to be expected that most of the time what emerges into awareness will be frightening—since it has been held back precisely because it arouses anxiety" (29).

The tenacious correlation between the dream and the drug- or non-drug-induced alternate state of consciousness provokes several questions. To what extent is the drug-induced state similar to the non-drug-induced state, for example, meditation, the dream state, the hypnogogic state, a stress reaction, or other regularly occurring psychological phenomena? Are the responses of accentuation of imagery, release of imagination and fantasy, and reworking of personal interactions in the psychedelic drug state similar to the condensation, symbolization, and displacement characteristic of dreaming? Often in remembered dreams forbidden ideas and acts are depicted and thus make their way into consciousness. They then either fade or are distorted. Is the same process at work when the musings stimulated during a "trip" are recalled at later times?

I will discuss these questions in reverse order. The work of the psychologist David Rapaport (35, 39) attempts to explore more thoroughly the function of consciousness so as to integrate psychoanalytic concepts that are dominated by an interest in primitive motivation, such as dream work, and ego psychology. Rapaport sees consciousness as both organized and selective; states of consciousness deal with structures, so that memory organization, cognitive style, ordering of perceptions, even a generative grammar are all functions of consciousness. Thus consciousness becomes a distinctive pattern of experience which reflects the existing balance among all the other aspects of personality, such as drive, defense, conscience, perceptual thresholds, and so on. Awareness itself becomes a way of dispersing the different kinds of energies available in consciousness.

Freud played with similar ideas in an early and neglected paper (40) which is important to the development of this argument. Consciousness may receive impressions, Freud noted, but not retain them in the same way that the mystic pad game allows the erasure of writing on the outer surface of the pad. Thus for the impressions retained on the under surface of the pad to show themselves on the superficial removable skin requires a break in the skin, that is, a shift in the defense structure. Conversely, to return to Rapaport's formulation, these impressions once registered on consciousness could be retained if they were integrated —rewritten if we are to follow our analogy—into other conscious systems such as those of logic and rationality. Rapaport went further (36) and assigned to varieties and forms of consciousness the function of striking a balance between internal and external perceptions of reality and of differentiating between them. The ultimate purpose of this growing capacity to select among differentiated perceptions is the development of a form of thought which encourages socialization.

With the introduction of socialization, alternate states of consciousness can be seen to be differentiated from the Freudian view of dream states. Dream states are drive-dominated and partake not only of the mechanisms of condensation, symbolization, and displacement, but also of timeless, concrete, magical, and idiosyncratic thinking. This primary process type of thinking allows opposite affects to exist without efforts of synthesis. Thus the products of this sort of thinking are unacceptable and are specifically barred by the system of defenses from consciousness. Were the material from these states to be unerasable, then the balancing and differentiating functions of consciousness described by Rapaport would be upset, and social adaptation interfered with.

However, Rapaport does not explicitly discuss the selection process by which internal and external perceptions are sorted out for this balancing process. If the aim is socialization, it is logical to assume that the percepts of reality made most readily conscious would be those whose function in the average expectable environment (41) has been prepared for. Is it not equally logical to assume that there are percepts that are more or less "left out," not because they need to be specifically repressed but because they have not been prepared for socially and thus have a lower priority for social adaptation? This argument takes us back to the formulation derived from *Studies in Hysteria*, which suggested that certain ideas could exist out of awareness but without having generated specific resistance to their entry into consciousness.

The imagery, fantasy formation, and intra- and interpersonal responses which follow psychedelic drug use could then be very different from a dream state. Much of the material I will present in the next section seems to me, despite considerable individual differences, compatible with secondary-process rather than primary-process thinking. The ideation has been socially prepared for, at least to a certain extent, and to that extent can be integrated into existing cognitive structures.

No doubt this is not 100 percent true; certain elements of a "trip" survive to be synthesized better than others. But the reports of many of my subjects and much of what has been written by responsible and apparently objective subjects who have themselves taken a psychedelic drug (as opposed to describing a patient or a friend who does so) support the notion that the mechanisms of the psychedelic drug response are different from those of a dream state and more susceptible to synthesis. Havelock Ellis (19), as a result of his varying set and setting, achieved what he reports as a lasting capacity to visualize colors differently. Kafka and Gaarder (23) indicate that the changes in their therapeutic technique and understanding were lasting. In the present climate of social opinion I must add that those early experiences reported by LSD experimenters in the professions seem to be mainly positive. This, in my opinion, only means that those are the experiences people troubled to report. There is no reason to doubt that some individuals experienced negative responses just as easily as positive ones.

My conclusion from all this is that endowing an idea with importance is a function of attention and that usual modes of perceiving limit attention (42). Various cognitive processes, which are themselves part of and bound to existing psychic structures, endow an idea with importance. That these processes are bound to psychic structures indicates that they are available to consciousness, are relatively autonomous in relation to primitive motivations, and are reality-oriented, thus secondary-process. As a mode of psychic functioning this sort of secondary-process thinking is opposed to the easily displaceable, readily symbolized, primary-process states, such as dreams, which are not bound and are heavily invested with primitive motivation. Perceiving, under secondary-process circumstances of binding, becomes automatized. For ideas and objects to be endowed not simply with importance but with the capacity to be perceived differently requires an ability to attain a different perceptual vantage point. This perceptual shift allows them to be *not* familiar and hence not part of the automatized process; they are fresh, which *per se* implies importance. For these fresh percepts to be worth reexamining requires de-automatization, which is exactly—whether positive or negative, enlightening or anxiety-provoking—how subjects describe their drug experiences.

If all of this sounds a great deal like what happens theoretically in psychoanalysis, it is *not* my intention to compare the two. Certainly the aim of a psychoanalysis is to-de-automatize certain modes of perception which limit attention and support self-deceit. However, in the analytic experience a careful and organized redirection of attention or a reconstruction of the inhibition of perception and the contributing mechanisms and motives involved follows the perceptual shift. All of this consistent, structural attention to inhibitions is a far cry from the few hours of relatively directionless shifting that occurs after drug ingestion. Nevertheless, there may be one fundamental aspect of psychoanalytic theory and technique from which we can understand these two experiences which are quantitatively and qualitatively so different.

Psychoanalysis, too, argues that whatever may originally act as an inhibition against bringing an impression into consciousness, whether specific defense or automatized perception, may after a time no longer be necessary. Nonetheless, the mechanisms of defense, once activated, continue to function. This automaticity is usually derived not so much from the specific impression barred from consciousness, for example, a man's strong feelings of empathy and tenderness for another man, but from the way in which that specific impression fits into the more holistic personality, or rather ego organization, developed by that person, for example, to be a controlled, independent, careful responder to others' feelings. If explanatory constructs are provided, a particular notion of man-to-man tenderness need not be barred; a time of mourning or a tragedy could permit the ideas and affects to reach and remain in consciousness. But sometimes similar but gratuitous tenderness, which contains few elements demanding specific repression (for example, powerful sexual urges), will not achieve awareness because of its place in the hierarchy of ego organization. In a psychedelic drug state such empathic responses are frequently experienced and sometimes retained. This particular shift in the hierarchy of what attains awareness in our example may have been carefully prepared for socially in the contemporary United States by the peace-not-war counterculture and the like, especially among those choosing to take a psychedelic drug. My argument assumes that any such potential shift in the holistic personality must necessarily already have been underway, but some de-automatizing experience activated the change.

The indistinct and unsatisfactory part of the comparison of this process to psychoanalysis is the analogy with the process of working through. Here a clarification of the same mechanism is made to the patient in different words at different times and in different areas of his life to show the continuity of personality and the consistency and strength of the inhibiting forces. The patient may see a concept as irrational—his difficulty in separating thought from act, for example—but not become aware of it the next time because he experiences his formulation as a natural connection, until it is pointed out. Then at some point in the psychoanalysis it is as if, after one more such clarification, he gets the whole concept "all of a sudden" and "accepts" the idea that thoughts don't kill, and he will be unlikely to mix that up again (at least for a while). The last clarification was no more succinct or convincing than many of the others, but at that point the preparation is sufficient for it to serve as an activating agent.

The experience of a high may well de-automatize some rigid modes of perception, but the subject does not have the opportunity systematically to integrate the resulting awareness into his ego organization. As a result, it must often fade or exist somewhere in consciousness as an interesting psychological artifact *unless,* by way of his changing social and psychological interests, a process similar to working through already has taken place. Then the drug or any other high experience might serve as that final clarification. It seems possible that the phenomenon of people taking hundreds of "trips" a year was an attempt to work through elusive glimpses of insight achieved with perceptual shifts. The tantalizing glimpses of insight may not have been prepared for by any sort of working-through process. Thus the efforts to "know" were efforts to breach the unprepared defense structure without recognizing that defenses are not "bad" but are salient parts of the ego organization whose functioning is central to our well-being or homeostasis. Such efforts easily could result in considerable personality disorganization, and under those conditions of ego disruption true primary-process thinking might well emerge.

So far, in response to the three questions raised on page 250, I have discussed the difference between the dream state and the psychedelic-drug-induced state and the potential for greater availability of the impressions raised during a drug experience. I have not taken up the similarities and dissimilarities of drug-induced and non-drug-induced consciousness changes. Certain aspects of this question are covered in the previous discussion. Consciousness change of all sorts is described as a normative function of the ego apparatus. Impressions from such changes can partake of primary process as in dream states or from secondary process when the potential cognitive structures are available. The development of such structures is dependent on the input of the social setting. Hence an idea that might be frightening and unacceptable at one time—for example, the nineteenth-century American Indian's peyote rites express an interest in man becoming God—might be the idle musing of another generation.

Despite these beginnings, it is difficult to differentiate among different alternate states of consciousness. It seems safe to assume that everyone has experienced non-drug-induced consciousness changes even if we put dream states and hypnosis aside. The hypnogogic state between waking and sleeping fulfills the criteria of an alternate state. When preparing this paper late on a Saturday afternoon I got sleepy and lay down to take a nap. Twice within five minutes the phone rang and I was called to answer it. After giving explicit and irritated instructions not to be disturbed, I again tried to sleep. A few minutes later I jumped awake to the sound of a telephone. Only this time the phone had not rung. Delusional and hallucinatory experiences of this sort are extremely common if not universal. Not many of us have attempted deep meditative states, but we have experienced intense reveries where the qualities of the mental processes seem different from everyday consciousness. Thus it is easy to suggest that all alternate states of consciousness have basic similarities and exist on a sort of continuum, with the drug-induced state perhaps being just a little further along than the meditative state.

While there is considerable logic to this idea of a continuum, it also leaves much unexplained. Non-drug-induced states have more specific and definable continuities with usual consciousness. The telephone-ringing hypnogogic experience described above allowed for a very different mental experience, in which internal reality overwhelmed the ordinary ability to differentiate between internal and external reality. To attain deep meditative states apparently requires practice and concentration. Effort and commitment of this intensity generate cognitive and ego structures that prepare for the meditative consciousness change. I have argued that drug-induced changes are also not haphazard but are subject to social preparation. These preparations are unconscious and are not dedicated specifically to achieving the particular experience that occurs when the drug is taken. In that sense the drug experience is discontinuous. Although the individual plans to take the drug, once it is ingested the consciousness controls are shifted chemically. Yet even here some individuals at least can enforce control over a high or alternate state. I have seen—and Daniel X. Freedman reports an identical case (43)—an extremely controlled, compulsive man take a large dose (250 mg) of LSD and then feel virtually nothing. Besides a slight buzzing at the back of his head this man somehow overcame the chemical and retained at all times his usual state of consciousness. This example indicates that control must be surrendered to the chemical.* The process of making that decision means some awareness of regularities, continuities, and logical consistencies.

Nevertheless, this is like the example of working through. Although

---

*Although the matter is incidental to this study, the capacity of experienced users to control highs has received far too little attention. For example, I have interviewed heroin dependents who consciously use the drug as an energizer, in direct contradiction to its pharmacological action, and I can document the same variations of response to all the high-evoking drugs.

we may find theoretical similarities between a drug-induced high and psychoanalysis, our essential capacity to perceive reality tells us that they are so basically different as to make the comparison inapplicable. Most subjects who are not ideologically committed to a position on drugs versus non-drugs and have experienced both drug-induced and non-drug-induced consciousness changes contend that they are different, although they cannot always articulate how. Also, many of us who have watched and worked with people trying high states observe that they are having apparently different experiences. The observable physiological responses and the ways in which they express themselves have quite dissimilar qualitites. Discussions of meditation in particular reflect a faddish quality, but that might be a necessary step toward perceptual receptivity.

Fortunately this is a paper on beginnings. The question of how high states are or are not congruent needs much closer attention, starting with a study of the experience under conditions that are free of cant. We should attempt a method that intends to establish communication and intends to develop a generalized explanation of how these states fit into human functioning.

5. THE DRUG STATES

Who is observed, where, and under what conditions determines much of what one can find out about the experience of consciousness change. Each choice limits the quantity and quality of the information obtained. As long as that is recognized and researchers attempt to describe as accurately as they can how they went about getting the information reported, a body of information from different perspectives can be amassed and eventually correlated for consistencies and inconsistencies (1).

I decided to interview experienced users when high in "natural" settings, and, in the case of some heroin users, again just after they came down. The second interview was conducted with all but four of the heroin users right after they came down, because the high lasted only one to three hours at the most after the initial interview.

Those four not interviewed then were reinterviewed at a later time. Because a psychedelic high continues for eight to ten hours, waiting around for a second immediate interview was impractical. But all of the subjects who took MDA were reinterviewed at a later date. The sample is biased, not only because all the subjects were experienced users but also because they were willing to talk to me while they were high. I set out to see what in the drug-induced consciousness-change experience was central, repetitious, and consistent among these subjects. My previous experience with psychedelic drug users had convinced me that reactions to the drugs were continuous with individual personality differences, and I accepted the likelihood that a typology of responses could be developed (29). However, in this section I want to describe reactions that most or all of the participants experienced, albeit to different degrees.

The sample consists of 11 heroin users of average age twenty-six years interviewed in apartments, parks, and other public places, and 23 MDA users of average age twenty-five interviewed in parks, houses, and on beaches. Although five of the heroin users originally came from middle-class backgrounds, all were now living marginal existence supported either by welfare, itinerant menial labor, or illegal activities. All but four of the MDA users were of middle-class backgrounds, and all had either a job or a specific creative activity (painting, writing), or were students. Six of the heroin users were interviewed as couples and the other five singly. MDA was taken in groups as large as six and as small as three, but it was usually easy to detach one person and talk to him or her in relative privacy. I knew personally many of them in one capacity or another (social acquaintance, student, psychiatric consultee, methadone clinic patient, Vietnam veteran, colleague), and the others were directly connected to someone known (friend, "roommate," colleague, spouse). Drugs *per se* were not taken as an experiment. Rather, I asked people I knew who used heroin or occasionally tripped if they would notify me of the event so that I could spend some time with them trying to understand what they were experiencing. Thus all subjects were prepared for my non-high participation in their high experience.

All of the heroin users had used at one time or another a wide variety of drugs (marihuana, psychedelics, other opiates, barbiturates, amphetamines, Valium, methaqualone, alcohol), although three had not tried psychedelics, and all agreed that heroin was far and away their drug of choice. Obviously as a group they were people who would take what they could get, but their opinions about marihuana ranged from the five cases of overt dislike, "it makes me paranoid and disorganized," to "Well, man, it will put you down if you can't get anything else." Only one of the heroin users particularly liked his psychedelic experience, which as in all the cases occurred as part of a wide flurry of drug use. Fairly heavy to heavy alocohol use, either current or in the recent past, was reported by all subjects. All regarded themselves as addicts ("strung out") and reported shooting up heroin of undetermined strength from three to eleven times a day.

It is hard to be sure just how LSD, mescaline, psilocybin, MDA, DMT, and the other psychedelic drugs differ from each other. MDA use was selected because users report it as "milder" ("You don't get all the chemical noise of LSD") and steadier. Also, the MDA around—and it could be demonstrated that all the subjects' drugs came from the same original source—had been assayed and found pure—a rather unusual event on the black market. MDA is known on the street as "the love drug" because its effects are particularly evident in interpersonal relationships. That suited me well, because my greatest area of understanding is just there and not in color-form perception or other areas possibly affected by the drug. This effect also made it likely that users would be interested in talking while tripping. All MDA subjects regarded themselves as experienced and had tripped before, from two to fifteen times; all used marihuana an average of once or twice a week. Several had tried other drugs—4 cocaine one to three times: 2 heroin once; 5, amphetamines one to five times—but none was really experienced with any other drugs than marihuana, psychedelics, and alcohol. And, although all drank, they expressed the classical preference of marihuana users for beer and wine. Only one subject classified himself as a moderate drinker; the rest described themselves as light imbibers.

Mostly my questions about the experience were open-ended: "What does it feel like?" "Can you compare it to anything?" Then I would take off on some response to try to keep a smooth conversation going and still be sure to explore the kinds of fantasy and imagery experienced, the degree of anxiety, general response to commotion and physical activity, the availability of early and primitive motivation, the availability of early memories, the accessibility of paranoid ideation and awareness of potential for cataclysmic events, concerns about loss of control, response to time, sound, color, and form, changes in body imagery, and investment in aggressive and hostile feelings, response to pain, sexual interest, and the quality of feelings about other people. The interviewees might lapse at times into reverie. At that point I would wait and resume when it seemed appropriate. Often subjects would fill me in on what they had been thinking in the interim. A few times I was asked to "get lost" because my questions were annoying (2 heroin) or interfering with the trip (4 MDA), but these interruptions came after considerable conversation.

Heroin seemed to have a more specific and consistent effect. The response right after injection is described as one of great relief. Tension runs out of the body, and bones and muscles feel fluid and relaxed. (At no time did anyone mention orgiastic sexual imagery; as a result of this experiment and many other interviews I have come to regard this as a myth.) Then comes the lightheaded dizziness described as a high. The sensation of dizziness is pleasant and not severe; the user has no trouble walking, for instance, in contrast to the experience with the same level of high with alcohol.

The leading response, along with the relaxation, seems to be a dampening down of stimuli from both within and without. This consciousness change affects the user's relationship with himself so that he feels distant. "It's as if I'm all the way down a long tunnel. I see you and her and I can listen to what you ask me but it would be just as easy not to. You seem to be moving around too quickly to be worth the effort of keeping up. I'm not much interested in what I'm saying either." The tunnel or cave image occurred often when subjects attempted to describe the sense of distance from stimuli apparently characteristic of this group's response to the drug. Their descriptions are entirely compatible with experiments that show that someone on morphine, though he feels no pain, knows whether he has been brushed by a feather or stuck lightly or deeply with a needle. My subjects knew when an act or a conversation might be painful or anxiety-provoking, but their consciousness was simply not invested in that response. They weren't interested.

Whatever the response was that I have described as lack of interest, it covered most of the other issues on my interview agenda. Fantasy production was low. No self-produced visual imagery was reported, and response to visual suggestions on my part was virtually *nil*. Music was played in a couple of places where I did the interviews and got some foot-tapping and other signs of interest, but I thought that came more through the force of personality continuity than as a drug-stimulated response. My occasional questions about time led me to realize that time went very quickly for them. I checked on this repeatedly, because the time of these interviews went very slowly for me. After an hour one man thought ten minutes had elapsed, while the woman who had shot up at the same moment thought only five.

Conversations about family background stimulated some interest, but no special early memories were elicited and no anxiety was reported. In response to my questions about angry or hostile feelings: "Man, I feel good and I want everybody else to feel good. If he [the police] knew how good I felt, he just couldn't want to do me harm." Paranoid ideation could be stimulated but without much drive behind it. No specific changes in body image seemed to occur, but in response to questions in this area all subjects thought they must actually look different when they go about their everyday activities, and they feel themselves, at least at times, to be "uptight."

One woman responded to my question about sexual interest: "I'd like him to be doing me right now but it's a lot of trouble to get started. By the time I get around to doing something to get him with it, I don't think I'll be that interested any more." That about summed it up. Eating also often seemed to be too much trouble.

Despite the feelings of lassitude, activity was possible, and people moved around and began activities not long after shooting up, if there seemed to be an important enough reason for doing so. As stated, most of what they said indicated how good they felt. But to the best of my capacity to be objective, these expressions were simply not convincing to me. The feelings of distance described, while relieving, carried with them an underlying sadness. This is not the place to argue whether depression leads to heroin addiction or whether the life of an addict guarantees depression. That affect, however, dominated the interview as it wore on and certainly dominated the further conversation as the subjects came down. I tried out a metaphor on some subjects, asking them if they imagined heroin thickened their skins (both literally and symbolically), or if they felt like they were wrapped in cotton batting. "Yeah, man, you can't get through my skin now, no one can get to me. And I can't get to you either."

Such remarks occurred during our discussions of interpersonal relationships. I had the sense that in this altered state the heroin users lost considerable judgment about the effects of personal interactions on themselves and on others. Just as their resistance to pain is increased, so, they imagine, is others'. They know what rules of conduct as well as laws are, but the more delicate ability to empathize and be sensitive to people needs a thin skin and a concern about effects that my sample of heroin addicts did not wish to call upon.*

MDA is taken by mouth: the form is usually 100 mgm of a white powder which comes in a thin gelatine capsule. If the powder is taken out of the capsule and dissolved in water it begins to work faster. Either way there is a certain restlessness as people wait the one-half hour to one hour it takes to work on an empty stomach.

On each occasion when I observed this event someone made a joke about the drug not working and maybe it was a placebo. Then, after what did seem a long time waiting, one person after another would say "Oh!" and in answer to my questions would describe seeing the sky with sudden clarity, and a feeling of ease and benevolence. Along with this initial "vast tranquilizer" effect came some nausea. Three subjects retched briefly and several described some muscle tightening, especially around the jaw, which also passed after a few minutes.

---

*It should be remembered that this sample all had had the debilitating and ego-subordinating experience of being a junkie in this culture. The above description of the high state may well not apply to people in this culture who are not opiate dependent.

Once high, there is an ability to concentrate attention on a specific area. Ordinarily, people apparently attend to a large volume of stimuli and devote considerable effort to integrating these stimuli into a gestalt. This constant effort at integration shifts focus when the person concentrates on one or another stimulus, but steady concentration always occurs within an awareness of the whole. The drug effects allow one to focus on a reduced field of attention so that a particular item stands out. Many of the large volume of stimuli are regarded as extraneous, and the item replaces the gestalt. It is as if when a subject focuses on the sky for a time the blue of the sky and the white of a cloud occupy all of his attention and everything else is screened out. Thus, when he says that he is really seeing the sky for the first time, he means that he is able to focus just on that without being distracted either by other stimuli, for example, the sea, earth, other sounds, etc., or, probably more important, by the task of integrating stimuli so that he can perceive and respond to them within a familiar gestalt.

As nearly as I could learn, no real perceptual changes occur. Rather, what happens is a de-automatization of repetitive, usual modes of responding. Subjects reported on color, sound, and form, when asked, with complete accuracy, invariably, however, pointing out details that seemed more pertinent now than before. This seemed especially true for color and the blending and mixing of colors. At times, when subjects were asked to focus on them, forms and shapes received the same total attention and sense of discovery as did color. In contrast to the impatience with which the subjects waited the hour for the drug to take effect, they now felt almost unaware of time's passage. It was hard to get an answer to the question, "How long have we been here?" When they did answer they usually thought it to have been longer than it was. This slowing of time continued through the eight to twelve hours of the drug's effects.

The capacity to focus on specific items seemed to explain much of what the subjects experienced. They could concentrate on inner processes as well as outer perceptions. It was not that particular fantasies were any different, that is, more primitive or connected to basic motivation, but that one fantasy or idea was noticed in great detail. It could be thoroughly explored so that the connected affects and ideation which would ordinarily be swept past in the rush of stimuli could receive attention. The introspection thus achieved seems fresh. Subjects could find things unpleasant, such as sand, flies, cold, or even the noise of a fellow traveler, but no one reported angry or aggressive feelings during the drugged period. However, there was considerable internal interest in previous aggression and meanness that appeared in fantasies or in reveries about personal interactions.

As near as I could piece it together, it was during these reveries that attention might shift to another participant. The groups that invited me to be with them had been very careful to choose only participants who were friendly, even—to mention a much-used word—loving. They believed in the counterculture maxim developed during the sixties that you only trip at a good time in a good place with good people. Hence, when the focus of the group shifted to their interest in each other or to some friend who was not present, there was prior preparation for the expression of positive feelings during the so-called "sentimental phase." People did speak openly of caring for each other and, I had the impression, used the drug experience to say things usually barred from conversation. Despite much talk about origins and memories, no early memories were reported that seemed to have been specially recovered at this time. One person told how he felt when he first met his present girlfriend and how, out of a mixture of anxiety, annoyance, and liking, he had picked out the traits and responses he now loved. A young woman talked about the last time she had seen her mother and of how, out of a mixture of disappointment and longing, she had behaved distantly and now recognized that she did the same thing with her boyfriend. She pointed out how his mouth tightened and his eyebrows came together in an unusual way when she behaved that way, but he never did say he was hurt. He responded by saying that he knew she had been thinking of that interaction and that he really knew she loved him and wished that he could break through his own withdrawal at times like that and tell her what he had been feeling.

This sort of dialogue was typical. The insights described did not seem so earthshaking, although they were spelled out in convincing detail, but it was the repeated insistence on empathic awareness of what the other was thinking that most fascinated me. It was usually at about this point that I would try to split off one individual in order to investigate further and more confidentially both the degree of insight and the extent of the empathy. In general, once apart, subjects elaborated with more explicit and personal details about their own motivation and what they thought the person they were addressing experienced. If I asked what some other person in the group was feeling, the interviewee might say that he didn't feel with that other person at the moment, or he might respond, or he might go off onto someone else. Not only were subjects able to describe what others felt, for example, he is thinking about sex with X or I think he is lost in his childhood or his relationship with Y, but they were also able to say something about the cues that led to these conclusions. The way somebody's body was now gripping the sand, the way the lines formed around his mouth or the way he looked over there and then looked away. These cues were ones I had not noticed until they were pointed out to me. However, the intermediate steps of how the cues led to the final empathic awareness could not be articulated. I would then drift over to the person we had been talking about and ask what he had been thinking. Eighty percent of the time my original respondent was correct down to quite fine details. It was remarkable, and it gave me some sense of why some psychedelic users of my acquaintance had become so interested in ESP. I asked particularly if this empathy was based on unusual closeness to a particular individual and usually was told no. And in fact it seemed to operate as effectively with people who were not close friends. Certainly it was not bound by sexual interest. While couples who were going together might show particular interest in each other, each could respond to others across sexual lines.

Naturally I asked about myself and suggested that any time a subject noticed something about me I would appreciate his mentioning it. There were no occasions, even with the group that specified my presence as "a pain in the ass," when this invitation was not accepted. With only one exception the comments were remarkably accurate and on one occasion embarrassingly so. Some were obvious, such as pointing out when I had relaxed and felt comfortable with them or when I was envious and wished I too had taken the drug or fearful and glad I hadn't. But others were more subtle, noticing my disappointments, stimulation, or annoyance with individuals and myself before I was aware of them.

Questions about sexual response while on the drug were surprisingly uniform. Sexual relationships were possible especially as the drug waned, but during the height of the high people described a greater interest in a general, diffuse, sensualism than in specific sexuality such as intercourse or masturbation (although two subjects told me that when they had taken the drug alone, and only then, did they become sexually preoccupied and masturbate frequently). This sensualism showed itself in a wish to touch others or to feel the sand, grass, water, flowers, or the like. Again the desire to touch and pleasure in touching was specifically pan-sexual and often not connected to everyday closeness. Although one of the drug's most potent, consistent effects is the inhibition of the desire to eat, late in the day a single grape or bite of certain foods or liquids was described as a sensual experience.

Much has been made of body image change during the drug experience, and so I was surprised at how little material I got in this area. People often reported noticing the color of various body parts as different from what they thought, as being now suffused with violet, purple, or blue. The size and shape of body parts—for instance, when urinating—were rediscovered and concentrated upon. But there was little I could classify as genuine distortion of body image.

While no one in any of these groups reported any special anxious feelings, every once in a while someone would say, "Knock it off, it's spoiling my trip." However, my questions about paranoid thoughts or potential concerns about cataclysmic events got the frequent response: "See that cloud over there. If I let myself go that way I could see it as wild and threatening, as part of what I have to face when I go back. I could get into something really strange but I don't want to. I'll go off in my head somewhere else." Discussions about police and arrests brought similar comments. My impression was that anxiety-provoking responses were readily available in the drug state, but that these subjects felt they had control over them. I wondered aloud once what would happen if one person lost that control. Would the empathy result in everyone's panicking? They reassured me and said that someone could and would use his or her empathy to talk that person down. I couldn't push this subject under the circumstances, as I didn't want to spoil the experience for people, but I felt the subject was unresolved. Four people said they had become anxious for a little while during other trips but got over it rather quickly. None of my subjects had ever had a bad trip. During my observations there were no periods of panic or hallucinations in my terms. Several subjects said that when they closed their eyes or stared at a particular object delightful visual panoramas emerged that they called hallucinations. These were always reported as pleasant and seemed to me to be an exploitation of the subjects' capacity to fix an image and play tricks with their unwavering concentration rather than a hallucination.

6. DISCUSSION

Any effort to convey a composite picture of how a drug affects a person is faulty because it neglects the richness of individual difference. I thought it justified in this case not only because I wanted to begin to build a large collection of descriptions of drug experiences but also because my collection of "experimental" subjects reflected no orderly plan. Hence, as this effort represented no formal research design, it seemed most worthwhile to find out whatever I could, in the time I had, in the way easiest for me. My effort was not really random, however, for I had interviewed many users of all sort of drugs before I attempted to formalize the procedure even this much.

Increasingly I find this informal kind of experiment at least as productive as the more formal procedures (1). When doing other experiments with marihuana, a much milder consciousness-altering drug, I worked in a laboratory setting under double-blind conditions (44, 45, 46). There seemed to be certain advantages to a uniform setting when the experimenter doesn't know whether a subject has received a placebo or an active substance. The assumption was that the setting is the same for both groups of subjects. However, when a subject is "straight," many of his perceptions and the attitudes resulting from those perceptions are automatized. This group of subjects is more likely to have consistent reactions to a laboratory before and after receiving a placebo. But the subjects receiving an active substance react to the setting as it becomes part of their changed perceptual responses. For some of the subjects the laboratory setting may become a focus of interest, and many of their responses will be influenced by the setting. Others may focus on something else, and the interaction of set and setting, which may be operative, will be hard to understand or to notice. In a deep sense, with a perceptual shift the meaning of the setting changes for the drug-receiving group, and the laboratory is not in that sense the same place that it is for the control group. If the experimenter believes that the setting is the "same," he may be introducing a subtle error in his reasoning. My use of a natural setting and no control group avoids this issue entirely.

In those previous experiments, naive subjects were selected with the hope that we would get a purer, that is, not preconditioned, response to the drug's effect. However, some subjects experienced anxiety about this odd thing happening to them that they didn't understand, and as each subject had preexisting concerns about odd things happening to him, we got many responses that were individually idiosyncratic but had little to do with the drug experience *per se*. Again, this could lead the experimenter to think of these as responses specifically to marihuana. In the interviews described in this paper all subjects were prepared for the experience and "knew" what to expect. This certainly opened the way for suggestible people to have happen to them what they knew in advance was going to happen to them. Either way, this difficulty in finding appropriate controls illustrates how hard it is to do experimental work in this area: it is always a trade-off of one difficulty for another.

The two groups of subjects studied in this paper couldn't be more different—in choice of drug, life style, class backgrounds, present occupations, and so on. Hence, it is fortunate that there is no interest in specifically comparing their experiences but only in thinking through what our observations tell us is new or at least different from conventional wisdom. It will come as a surprise to no one that I conclude that, while these two drugs have consistent effects which are quite different from each other, one must think of both in terms of the interaction of drug, set, and setting in order to understand the reasons for taking the drug, the results of taking it, and the experience itself. Further, this interaction cannot be viewed cross-sectionally but requires a longitudinal perspective. That is, it is not sufficient to decide about or to categorize a person's personality structure and/or the influence of a particular physical or social setting as if the personality structure was immutable and the settings could be standardized. I contend that a dynamic interaction is set up in which the person's experiences in settings influence and probably actually change certain aspects of his personality which, in turn, affects the setting, and so on. This interaction requires consistent reassessment of the effects of each element, and this is of special importance where the issue, drug use, is seen as a critical social matter and receives enormous and affect-provoking attention from the mass media.

Whether personality does or does not change as a result of either drug use or changes in contemporary culture is a key question. Generally speaking, psychoanalytic theory has dismissed such changes as relatively superficial compared to the basic development of intrinsic, and perhaps even psychobiological, intrapsychic structures. I accept drives, essential ego and superego functions, and capacity for object relations as the roots of the motivational and the developmental tree. It is my conviction that a study of each of the 34 individuals observed would show a continuity of basic personality structure before, during, and after drug use.

That there is a continuity of the essential personality does not mean, however, that some personality change might not be of great importance in that person's life and extended psychological development. Of all people, psychoanalysts should not make light of the importance of small shifts in personality reorientation. Remember Freud's often quoted comment that for psychoanalysis to change neurotic suffering to ordinary human misery is no small event. Erik Erikson (47), among others, points up the importance of contemporary culture when he shows how different historical moments encourage different resolutions of the same conflict. For example, a girl or a man fearful of sex could become rigidly conventional and sexually unresponsive during one cultural epoch. In another era the same person might behave promiscuously and yet be expressing the same conflict. But one can see that the consequences of these differing responses to the person's life and to his or her interpersonal relationships and thus to eventual personality development are considerable, even though at a basic level there is personality continuity and consistency.

Another example, which presents a closer analogy to drug use, is that of a teacher I have followed closely as part of another project, also studying the impact of critical social issues on attitude and then on personality (48). During the course of a fifteen-session dynamic group experience concerned with integrating black and white students into the same classes, this woman professed conviction that her previous position against busing children was wrong *without* any underlying change in her feelings about the issue. As a result of her "conversion" she made new friends at school and was elected a teachers' representative. In a short time the superficial change in attitude, intended only to be pleasing to her group, deepened and became a driving force in her life, opening up new vistas. As a result of these new activities she confronted old fears and noticeably changed her approach to the world. I see this as a lasting personality change, and the sequence as one which has received too little attention from psychoanalytic theorists.

Let us take our sample of heroin users. In my interviews with them I was particularly struck by their insensitivity to pain and by how this insensititvity made it difficult for them to be concerned about others' pain. I understood something of what scares people about junkies. I understood, too, how easy it would be to describe them as severe narcissistic personality disorders and to find deep, underlying conflicts about hostility or sexuality which one might imagine led them to this powerful drug. Heroin seems to turn them back on themselves, to obliviate depression—at least for a short time—and to calm the most savage of inner beasts.

However, in thinking about their histories and current lives, I found too many discrepancies and inconsistencies to fit those theories. I was reminded of two other clinical experiences. Between 1950 and 1952 I studied a number of displaced people from Germany, most of whom had had concentration camp experiences. They described in painful detail what it meant suddenly to find the social structure, which you accepted without much question and of which you were a part, utterly hostile. Police were no longer guardians but enemies; neighbors of years speak of you as filth. Many of the displaced people so treated reported a major shift in their views of themselves. Self-doubts became overwhelming and developed to a point at which Orwellian confessions out of a conviction of guilt—we all have enough more or less unconscious guilts, however blameless our lives—were not out of the question. The amount of time spent in this atmosphere was critical to the long-reaching effect of the experience on personality, as was the preexisting personality structure. But what preexisting personality structure tolerated these chaotic social events with the least disruption? Grete L. Bibring (49) and others suggest that it was not *our* model of maturity with a flexible ego and superego, viable object relations, and an emotional investment in a useful function, but rather those with severe narcissistic character disorders who put survival in personal terms first.

To put the same proposition in individual terms, consider a child who is aggressive, curious, intelligent, manually dextrous, from a stable, middle-class family. Such a child often experiments with pain, his own and other beings', and may well pull a wing off an occasional fly. At a certain point in his education he decides that he wants to be a surgeon. Whatever the influence of primitive sadistic drives on his early experimentation, they are not what continues to fuel his ambition. Over the years he has interacted with parents, teachers, and others who recognized his intellectual capacity, manual dexterity, and perhaps noticed his ability to visualize successfully in a three-dimensional context. They encouraged his interests.

Gradually these interests, except in cases of severe emotional disturbance, become relatively autonomous. As this young man progresses through medical school and into a surgical residency, he learns how to stick knives into people. It is emotionally a very difficult thing to do. For him to do it comfortably he needs the full support of his peers, the law, social institutions, and the recipient. With all that reassurance, the neophyte surgeon has few doubts that what he does is a good and not a bad thing. Should all this support be withdrawn *in toto*, should he be called a sadistic monster by all those socially significant others at any point in his training, his continued ability confidently to perform surgical procedures would be sharply impaired. Perhaps later, after years of practice and a fuller knowledge of his ability to deal with himself and his skill, such an assault could be withstood. But not earlier. The social disapproval and resultant self-doubt would disturb his relative ego autonomy, cause questioning of the motivation for each act, and permit primitive conflicts long dormant to reassert themselves.

This disruption of cultural context and medical education occurred in 1936 in the life of the German Jews I studied and stands as a metaphor for what happens to some drug users in our society. In many ways the comparison is as apt for the MDA sample or for the marihuana users of the mid-sixties (4) as for our heroin users, because it presents a picture of what happens to a nonmedical drug user in our society under current laws. Although doing something which he initially regards as a minor legal infraction—and by the late sixties trying heroin seemed so to many—at some point he must recognize that he has committed a felony. This recognition comes to many marihuana users when they stop using friends' grass and go out and buy their own; it comes to heroin users when they feel that they want to use it because they miss the effect and not just for a kick. If the user is middle-class, should a parent discover the use, he is rushed to a psychiatrist. If he is low-skilled/working-class, he is beaten up or in 50 percent of the cases (according to a Harris poll of parents) turned in to the police to "save" him. The law and our social institutions are ready to punish him more severely than for almost any crime, including murder in many states. The newspapers refer to him as a crisis, an epidemic, and a social disease.

This insistence that someone is socially and destructively deviant and unacceptable for ordinary social relationships with key individuals and social institutions is a powerful force, particularly with the young. It is my contention that the decision to try a drug in certain situations of set and setting need not have deep, complex, or emotionally disturbed motivational structures behind the decision. Obviously there are those whose decision to choose heroin is powerfully self-destructive and antisocial. But I have now had the opportunity, in the United States and in Vietnam (50, 51, 52), to know people both before and after they have used heroin, and I am sure that those motives are not the only ones. Once defined as deviant, removed from usual social supports, thrust into an increasingly less diverse group for social stimuli, drawn into constant real and imagined conflict with the police and the law, personality changes occur. When all this is aided by the persistent use of a drug that, at least in the United States of 1974, furthers this social process, is it a surprise that heroin users can be diagnosed as severe narcissistic character disorders? Whatever they may have been before starting to use heroin, they will certainly fulfill that diagnosis after a prolonged period of heroin addiction.

Another of my underlying assumptions throughout this beginning study is that, whatever eventually happens to people who use a drug, whether alcohol, marihuana, psychedelics, or heroin, an interest in consciousness change and intoxicants is normative. All known cultures except the Eskimos, who have a number of rituals that involve hyperventilation, have used one intoxicant or another. The trick apparently is to develop control over use, and that seems to be true almost regardless of the chosen drug. Richard Schultes (53) documents the enormous sophistication and control with which some primitive cultures use very powerful drugs and the terrible abuse and results of the same drugs used in other cultures. Our own society still has the major problem of alcohol control with a sizable fraction of users (6 to 8 percent). But this is a long way from two centuries ago, when you were either alcoholic (80 to 90 percent) or you were a teetotaler, and when the United States government was paying the builders of the Erie Canal one dollar and one quart of whiskey a day, beginning with four-ounce portions at 6 A.M. The eighteenth-and nineteenth-century alcohol addiction, which certainly be compared to the heroin addiction of today, receded not because of strengthened personality structure (perhaps some of my readers may have a more positive view of the ennoblement of mankind than I do and will disagree here) or more punitive laws. Prohibition failed in countries other than the United States just as miserably as it did here. What did slowly emerge, and has been partially or even largely successful, is the internalization of social mores (27). "Being drunk is unattractive," took hold in contrast to the eighteenth-century conviction that whiskey made you stronger, wiser, and a better lover. "Too many calories in booze" replaced the social premium put on robustness.

At this point in my discussion I must take time for the obligatory, but nonetheless important, declaration that a belief in the efficacy of social control as opposed to personal or legal controls does *not* mean that I view any of these drugs as harmless or that I am espousing their use. It does mean that I think that people will try to change consciousness with or without drugs, but for the foreseeable future in our culture more often with drugs, and that one function of this study of the experience is to understand how *use* of drugs for consciousness change differs from *abuse*. They are not the same, although it is conceivable that some drugs are sufficiently powerful to make that difference academic. Thus we study what happens, but I repeat that for this to be meaningful the user, the researcher, and the society need to be studied along with the drug.

From what I have presented so far I think it fair to say that each pattern of drug use constitutes a distinctive mode or quality of experiencing. It was my impression that MDA was a fairly strong drug. Even so, the MDA users studied could experiment with the drug without too much anxiety. They felt sufficiently in control to search for a personal response in which an interesting experience from the use of the drug was maximized and the potential trauma from the effects of the drug itself and from its illegality were proportionally less. This is not an endorsement of MDA or any other psychedelic drug use. In my discussion of the experience I was impressed by the effects of the drug on awareness and sensitivity. I was not impressed by the insight potential of that extremely interesting experience for the person's lasting relationship with himself and others. Much of the greater awareness of personal motivation, which was felt quite directly and was neither dreamlike nor ephemeral at the time, seemed relatively superficial and in retrospect even trite. The ability to perceive others' responses correctly was empathic and sensitive. However, its chief interest seemed to lie less in the subjects' greater lasting appreciation or closeness to that other person than in his fascination with what went on in his own head. He could preoccupy himself not just with his own thought and emotional processes but with how his thought and emotional processes responded to those of someone else. This was clearly for some of my subjects a bewitching game, but just as I do not see that enchantment as permanent and destructive, neither do I find much credence in the hope of its opening a new vista to human relationships.

There have been some social consequences of psychedelic drug use, or more accurately of the expectations aroused by such use. Probably most have been fads, such as the widespread use of "psychedelic" colors and music. It is easy to dismiss any single fad as having little social consequence, but when several such relatively transient social movements appear at the same time it is hard for me to dismiss the possibility that these "far out" or deviant groups are not performing a testing service for the larger culture (54). I have followed the formation and fate of several communes since the middle sixties. It is my impression that in several instances the psychedelic drug experience precipitated the effort at group living. The close empathic group experience of the drug gave rise to the rather naive hope that people could establish the same sort of closeness in a special everyday living arrangement. This closeness would be group-oriented and the group empathy was supposed to override the intensity and exclusive sexuality of one-to-one relationships, leading to a greater sharing with more people and a reduction of competition, jealousy, and greed. Some of these communes ended miserably; some in their efforts at community child care, shared living facilities, and alternate work patterns were worthy of more study than they got. Many leading respectable social theorists contend that all of us may need to think about changing family structures which call for shared kitchens, child care, and other amenities. In the communes these experiments went on, but because the participants were seen as deviants, the lessons they had for the larger culture were generally overlooked.

This is exactly my point about the MDA use I studied. Instead of constantly comparing the users' experience to standards of the larger culture, why not consider it on its own terms? Experiments giving subjects a psychedelic drug under laboratory conditions invariably obtain physiological and psychological tests. The test results use the subjects as their own controls or compare their results to others when abstinent ("straight"). Then it is found that on these measures the drugged subjects show *impaired* attention. Barr *et al.* demonstrate that subjects after taking LSD show greater reliance on color than form, which the experimenters describe as regression and maladaptation. There is little effort to ascertain how one best adapts to the drug state.* The ability to organize the impressions of the changed color perception in the drug state rather than attempt to continue the usual color/form ratio would seem to be highly functional rather than regressive.

Adequate intellectual, emotional, and physical control in the alternate state needs to be thought through in the terms of the alternate state and not compared to the standards of ordinary consciousness. This is equiv-

---

*Although they do see those who insist on relying more heavily on form as rigid.

alent to differentiating activity proper from ego activity (55, 56). A soldier charges and captures a machine gun nest, defeating a dozen enemy in the process. When asked how he decided to attempt this feat, he says he was only following orders. Thus he was physically active but accepted a passive ego state. Conversely a scholar struggling with a knotty problem or a business manager deciding to risk capital on a new venture may not move a muscle, but his internal strivings qualify as ego activity.

The subjects on MDA varied considerably on their capacity to organize impressions and on the activity proper versus ego activity scale, and although there were predominant modes, individuals handled the experience differently during different parts of the day. Some, particularly those with more drug experience (but it also varied by personality), were quite active physically. They moved around, did exercises, swam, and so on, while others clearly hated to move but could if they had to. Some, and several of the physically active ones were among these, showed one form of ego (or superego) activity by struggling with the drug experience itself. They questioned what they were feeling at each moment, often comparing it to their straight state and attempting to determine if their consciousness had changed, and if so, how much. Others tried to get into the experience. They focused their attention on the new perspectives that emerged and recognized the de-automatization as an opportunity to see some things differently. It seemed to me that this group relied less on frequent comparisons with their usual state of consciousness and did not worry about it as an impairment. Nor did they begin immediately to idealize it. The idea that there is a "correct" way of attending which applies at all times is not the sole property of experimenters. Subjects, too, seem to believe this, although often they reverse the procedure and insist that it is the altered state that is correct. To my mind, the group of my subjects who knew they would achieve this state in advance and then did so were ego passive; they followed orders, like the charging soldier.

So far, my studies of these consciousness-changing experiences have not indicated that usual ideas need be thrown out, such as the strength of continuing personality and the notion that there is a range of human responses to all stimuli no matter how esoteric. But I will close by expressing doubts about one of my most cherished ideas. I have long insisted that to understand much about another person's experience I need not have undergone each event. While there are limits to a sensitive person's capacity to empathize—for example, I am not sure most grown-up white people can fully grasp the intricacy of growing up black in this culture—the range of fantasy and mutual identification is remarkably wide. As a male psychoanalyst I think I have worked successfully with, for example, pregnant women and people of different faiths, back-grounds, and temperaments. However, I must note that one reason for the tradition of a training analysis is to give the neophyte a chance to experience what it is like to be a patient. In this work I think I should have heeded the advice of my MDA subjects, that my experimental capacity would have improved had I taken the drug with them. I feel exactly the same way about the heroin part of the experiment, although only two of those subjects made the suggestion.

As this decision goes against much of what I have previously stood for, I have had to decide why I have this preference for the shared experience here and not in any other aspect of my work. One reason came to light after I began to discuss this issue with a number of respected colleagues in the drug field. Almost none of them, it turned out, had tried the drugs whose effects and whose users they were so assiduously studying. They were frightened. Again and again, stable, competent colleagues told me, "I wouldn't take the chance. I don't want to mess myself up." Sometimes they vaguely said it was illegal, but I would point out that Dr. Grof and others at Spring Grove Hospital could arrange for them to be legal experimental subjects themselves and try a psychedelic drug, and, if not heroin, certainly they could arrange for morphine. They then would say it was too risky personally.

Leaving aside the extent to which these conversations revealed the shakiness many of us feel about our emotional stability, the talks irra-tionally stood out against a long medical tradition of auto-experimen-tation and against the known facts about these drugs. A recent article in the *New England Journal of Medicine* (57) discussed the time-honored practice of physicians trying drugs on themselves. Although there were occasional tragedies, the article emphasized the general success and safety of the procedure. Doctor and patient both felt more secure with medications so tested, and much was learned about the limits of pre-scribing. Above all, there was a human scale for what was going on. The article lamented the passing of this tradition.

The other reason for sharing the experience is more serious. Most of the people I talked to were actively engaged in countering the exagger-ated and lurid publicity accorded nonmedical drug use; they were work-ing toward a sound knowledge of these drugs and toward rationality in the legal and medical approach to them. At the same time they shared an overriding fear of the drugs. No wonder there has been so little interest in the experience of consciousness change. No wonder experi-mental work has been done at such a great distance from the actual experiences that one often thinks "so what?" after the findings are pre-sented. Most researchers have seen the drug experience as completely discontinuous from their own lives and have wanted to keep it this way. Rather than persuading society toward scientific considerations of drugs, they have been influenced by the social setting toward distance and irrationality.

I do not mean to suggest that the personal experience of the experimenter who takes these drugs with his subjects will necessarily itself supply interesting data. The story of Timothy Leary is proof enough of the unreliability of this method as a source of primary data. But I suspect that objective people could be trained to work with others and at least collect a different level of data from that obtained by nondrugged experimenters. Also, it would certainly indicate in the most powerful possible way that these are experiences to be worked with and that they are not destructive fearsome forces. Until the experimenter feels free to do it either way, depending on the exigencies of the experiment, I can't imagine the scientist exploring this important area of research successfully.

In time, as drug experiences come to be socially accepted and socially controlled (58), a person like myself could readily empathize with this experience without undergoing it. I can work with experiences that I can never have, as I could never become pregnant or grow up in the Middle West, or experiences I choose not to have because I know what I'm like: I do not choose to play golf or undergo experiences that I rationally conceive to be frightening such as skydiving or drag-racing.

The removal of a consciousness-change experience from the realm of the mystical and religious might make it possible for someone like myself to make a *rational* choice whether to try it or not. Then and only then can we more fully exploit this remarkable research tool. There is a current disillusion with social science and a fear of closed horizons. I do not like to bring this up in connection with altered consciousness states because so much of the language surrounding the issue has been apocalyptic. But the possibilities of studying the processes of perception and attention in this area are certainly sufficiently significant for me to declare that we may have been neglecting something of great importance.

REFERENCES

1. TART, C. T. (1972). States of Consciousness and State-Specific Sciences. *Science* 176:1203-10.
2. VOLKERT, E. H., ed. (1951). *Social Behavior and Personality Contributions of William I. Thomas to Theory and Social Research*. New York: Social Science Research Council.
3. WEIL, A. T. (1972). *The Natural Mind*, pp. 12-90. New York: Houghton Mifflin.
4. ZINBERG, N. E., & ROBERTSON, J. A. (1972). *Drugs and the Public*, pp. 44-102. New York: Simon and Schuster.
5. FREUD, S. (1933). New Introductory Lectures on Psychoanalysis. *Standard Edition*, XXII, 3-182. London: Hogarth Press, 1964.

6. KLEIN, G. S. (1968). Psychoanalysis, II. Ego Psychology. In *International Encyclopedia of the Social Sciences*, ed. D. L. Sills, vol. XIII. New York: Macmillan and The Free Press.
7. MUSTO, D. (1973). *The American Disease*. New Haven and London: Yale University Press.
8. GUSFIELD, J. (1968). On Legislating Morals: The Symbolic Process of Deviant Designation. *50 California Law Review 61*.
9. KAPLAN, J. (1970). *Marihuana: The New Prohibition*. New York and Cleveland: World Publishing Co.
10. GRINSPOON, L. (1971). *Marihuana Reconsidered*. Cambridge: Harvard University Press.
11. BRECHER, E. M., *et al.* (1972). *Licit and Illicit Drugs*. Boston: Little, Brown and Company.
12. TART, C. T. (1971). *On Being Stoned*. Palo Alto, Calif.: Science and Behavior Books.
13. TJIO, J., PAHNKE, W. N., & KURLAND, A. A. (1969). LSD and Chromosomes: A Controlled Experiment. *Journal of the American Medical Association* 210:849-56.
14. WEIL, A. T. (1970). Adverse Reactions to Marihuana: Classification and Suggested Treatment. *New England Journal of Medicine* 282:997-1000.
15. COHEN, M. M., MARINELLO, M., & BACH, N. (1967). Chromosomal Damage in Human Leukocytes Induced by Lysergic Acid Diethylamide. *Science* 155:1417-19.
16. COHEN, M. M., HIRSCHHORN, K., & FROSCH, W. A. (1967). In Vivo and In Vitro Chromosomal Damage Induced by LSD-25. *New England Journal of Medicine* 277:1043-49.
17. COHEN, M. M., HIRSCHHORN, K., VERBO, S., FROSCH, W. A., and GROESCHEL, M. (1968). The Effect of LSD-25 on the Chromosomes of Children Exposed in Utero. *Pediatric Research* 2:486-92.
18. ROBBINS, E. S., FROSCH, W. A., & STERN, M. (1967). Further Observations on Untoward Reactions to LSD. *American Journal of Psychiatry* 124:393-95.
19. ELLIS, H. (1902). Mescal, A Study of a Divine Plant. *Popular Science Monthly* 41:52-71. See pp. 53ff. for specific references to John Mooney, Indian agent; Hernandez and Sahagum, travelers; and the missionary, Father Ortega; see also Diguet, L. (1899). *Nouvelles Archives des Missions Scientifiques* IX:621-25.
20. HYDE, R. W. (1960). Psychological and Social Determinants of Drug Action. In *The Dynamics of Psychiatric Drug Therapy*, ed. G. J. Sarwer-Foner, Springfield, Ill.: Charles Thomas.
21. SAVAGE, C. (1952). Lysergic Acid Diethylamide (LSD): A Clinical-Psychological Study. *American Journal of Psychiatry* 108:896-900.
22. MOGAR, R. E., and SAVAGE, C. (1954). Personality Change Associated with Psychedelic (LSD) Therapy: A Preliminary Report. *Psychotherapy: Theory, Research and Practice* 1:154-62.
23. KAFKA, J. S., and GAARDER, K. R. (1964). Some Effects of the Therapist's LSD Experience in his Therapeutic Work. *American Journal of Psychotherapy* XVIII:236-43.
24. KAFKA, J. S. (1964). Technical Applications of a Concept of Multiple Reality. *International Journal of Psycho-Analysis* XLV:575-78.
25. McGLOTHLIN, W. H., and ARNOLD, D. O. (1971). LSD Revisited—A Ten-Year-Old Followup of Medical LSD Use. *Archives of General Psychiatry* XXIV:35-49.
26. *Drug Use in America: Problem in Perspective* (1973). Washington, D.C.: Government Printing Office.
27. ZINBERG, N. E., and JACOBSON, R. C. (1974). The Social Basis of Drug Abuse Prevention. Unpublished manuscript.
28. EDWARDS, G. F. (1973). *The Plasticity of Human Response*. Maudsley Hospital, London (mimeographed).
29. BARR H. L., LANGS R. J., HOLT, R. R., GOLDBERGER, L., and KLEIN, G. S. (1972). *LSD: Personality and Experience*. New York: Wiley Interscience.
30. FREUD, S. (1895a). Project for a Scientific Psychology. *Standard Edition*, I, 281-397. London: Hogarth Press, 1966.
31. BREUER, J. and FREUD, S. (1895b). Studies in Hysteria. *Standard Edition*, II, 3-305. London: Hogarth Press, 1955.

32. FREUD, S. (1900). The Interpretation of Dreams. *Standard Edition*, vols. IV and V. London: Hogarth Press, 1953.

33. ——— (1925). A Note on the Unconscious in Psycho-Analysis. *Standard Edition*, XII, 255-66. London: Hogarth Press, 1958.

34. ——— (1915). The Unconscious. *Standard Edition*, XIV, 159-215. London: Hogarth Press, 1957.

35. RAPAPORT, D. (1942). *Emotions and Memory*. 2d ed. New York: International Universities Press, 1959.

36. ——— (1951). States of Consciousness: A Psychopathological and Psychodynamic View. In *The Collected Papers of David R. Rapaport*, ed. M. M. Gill, pp. 385-404. New York: Basic Books, 1967.

37. ——— (1957). Cognitive Structures. In *The Collected Papers of David R. Rapaport*, ed. M. M. Gill, pp. 631-44. New York: Basic Books, 1967.

38. ——— (1958). The Theory of Ego Autonomy: A Generalization. In *The Collected Papers of David R. Rapaport*, ed. M. M. Gill, pp. 722-44. New York: Basic Books, 1967.

39. ——— (1960). On the Psychoanalytic Theory of Motivation. In *The Collected Papers of David R. Rapaport*, ed. M. M. Gill, pp. 853-915. New York: Basic Books, 1967.

40. FREUD, S. (1925). A Note on the "Mystic Writing Pad." *Standard Edition*, XIX, 227-32. London: Hogarth Press, 1961.

41. HARTMANN, H. (1939), *Ego Psychology and the Problem of Adaptation*. New York: International Universities Press, 1958.

42. KLEIN, G. S. (1959). Consciousness in Psychoanalytic Theory: Some Implications for Current Research in Perception. *Journal of the American Psychoanalytic Association* 7:5-34.

43. FREEDMAN, DANIEL X. Personal communication.

44. WEIL, A. T., ZINBERG, N. E., and NELSEN, J. (1968). Clinical and Psychological Effects of Marihuana in Man. *Science* 162:1234-42.

45. WEIL, A. T., and ZINBERG, N. E. (1969). Acute Effects of Marihuana on Speech. *Nature* 222:434-37.

46. ZINBERG N. E., and WEIL, A. T. (1970). A Comparison of Marihuana Users and Non-Users. *Nature* 226:719-23.

47. ERIKSON, E. (1958). *Young Man Luther*. New York: W. W. Norton.

48. ZINBERG, N. E., BORIS, H. N., and BORIS, M. (1973). Are Piano Lessons Different from the Appreciation of Music? Baltimore: Johns Hopkins University Press.

49. BIBRING, G. L. (1954). The Displaced Person in an American Psychiatric Clinic. *Bulletin of World Association for Mental Health* II:20-24.

50. ZINBERG, N. E. (1971). GI's and OJ's in Vietnam. *New York Times Magazine*, December 5, 1971.

51. ——— (1972). Heroin Use in Vietnam and the United States: A Contrast and a Critique. *Archives of General Psychiatry* 26:486-88.

52. ——— (1972). Rehabilitation of Heroin Users in Vietnam. *Contemporary Drug Problems* 1:263-94.

53. SCHULTES, RICHARD. Presentation at Conference on Altered States of Consciousness. April 1973.

54. ERICKSON, K. (1966). *The Wayward Puritan*. New York: Wiley.

55. ZINBERG, N. E. (1967). Psycho-Analytic Training and Psycho-Analytic Values. *International Journal of Psycho-Analysis* 48:88-96.

56. ——— (1972). Value Conflict and the Psychoanalyst's Role. In *Moral Values and the Superego Concept in Psychoanalysis*, ed. S. C. Post. New York: International Universities Press.

57. ALTMAN, L. K. (1972). Auto-experimentation. *New England Journal of Medicine* 286:346-52.

58. FREEDMAN, D. X. (1971). Drugs and Culture. *Triangle*, vol. 10, no. 3.

15

A STUDY OF SOCIAL REGULATORY MECHANISMS IN CONTROLLED ILLICIT DRUG USERS

Norman E. Zinberg, Wayne M. Harding and Miriam Winkeller

An ongoing study of controlled marihuana, psychedelic, and opiate users shows that long-term, moderate illicit drug use is primarily supported by rituals and social sanctions. These guidelines for use, developed by segments of the drug subculture, militate against compulsive use. This work demonstrates the necessity of viewing quality of drug use as a function of sociocultural as well as pharamacological and psychological factors. Findings suggest that a system of social controls similar to that operating for alcohol use could be a more reasonable means of preventing compulsive use than the present prohibition of any and all illicit drug use.

The level of hysteria and irrationality which characterized the cultural response to the explosion of illicit drug use in the 1960s has greatly diminished. Along with this emotional change, policy positions and strat-

Reprinted with permission from the *Journal of Drug Issues*, Spring 1977, 7(2), 117-133. Copyright © 1977 by JDI, Inc.

Dr. Zinberg is Associate Clinical Professor of Psychiatry at the Harvard Medical School. Mr. Harding and Ms. Winkeller are respectively Research Associate and Research Coordinator at the Cambridge Hospital. This study was supported by a grant from The Drug Abuse Council, Inc., 1828 L Street, N.W., Washington, D.C. 20036 and was carried out at the Cambridge Hospital, Department of Psychiatry (A Central Facility of the Cambridge-Somerville Mental Health and Retardation Center), Cambridge, Mass. 02139.

egies which were then accepted as virtual articles of faith are now being questioned. Maintenance treatment programs for opiate addicts have become socially more acceptable as an alternative to abstinence, and universal drug education in the schools, once looked to as a panacea to prevent drug abuse, has become suspect as a stimulator of drug use. At the same time, the national policy toward the use of certain drugs—legal prohibition—has resulted in such high costs, both financial and psychological, that "drug abuse is coming to be seen not as a disease to be 'wiped out' but as a chronic ailment to be managed" (Vogl, 1973). And according to a recent Harris poll (Harris, 1976), 86 percent of the public now opposes sending a marihuana smoker to jail, a major reversal from 1969 when 42 percent of parents indicated they would turn their own children over to the police for using marihuana (Zinberg and Robertson, 1972).

Despite these changes in outlook, however, the public and professional discussion of drug use remains centered on one aspect—the harmful pharmacological properties of the illicit substances being taken by significant numbers of people. A more important and more promising dimension—that of the quality of drug use, including the diversity in drug-using styles and the corresponding differences in the consequences of use, ranging from beneficial to deadly—has been all but ignored, except, possibly, in connection with marihuana.[1] The belief that the social policy regarding drugs, including marihuana, flows logically from their chemical goodness or badness seems to have obscured the important fact that the way in which a drug is used may mitigate or potentiate its pharmacological properties.

In 1972 The Drug Abuse Council, Inc., of Washington, D.C., began to sponsor a study of controlled drug use which was undertaken by the authors—a study designed to locate and investigate users of marihuana, the psychedelics, and the opiates who, like most social drinkers, have managed to maintain regular, moderate using patterns that do not interfere with effective functioning. From the longitudinal interview data collected up to this time, we have been able to draw one clear conclusion: that achieving controlled use depends chiefly on developing and assimilating social sanctions and social rituals (Jacobson and Zinberg, 1975; Zinberg, 1975; Zinberg, Jacobson, and Harding, 1975; Zinberg and Jacobson, 1976; Harding and Zinberg, 1977).

---

[1]Harris (1976) found that "the American people see more dangers in the use of alcoholic beverages than in use of marihuana . . . a complete reversal of public attitude since 1969." However, dissatisfaction with Draconian penalties which did not stop widespread use and other less rational factors may be equally important components of the softening attitude toward marihuana use and the greater interest in the way it is used.

This paper begins with a review of other work in which occasional use is mentioned, and then it describes our study method and assesses the validity of our data. Next it presents a profile of the sample, describes the nature of controlled use, and defines social rituals and sanctions. Finally, it emphasizes the need to consider various patterns of drug use in terms of the sociocultural context as well as the pharmacological and psychological context. The paper refers to current alcohol use because the controlled use of alcohol offers a model for other drug use which would be preferable to the present costly and punishing model of total prohibition.

REVIEW OF PREVIOUS RESEARCH

The research literature on drug use tends to reflect the reigning cultural outlook on illicit drugs in three related ways: by failing to differentiate between use and excessive use; by focusing on extreme using patterns and overlooking moderate use; and, if non-compulsive using styles are acknowledged, by concentrating on marihuana and excluding the psychedelics and heroin.

Many if not most investigators simply do not bother to differentiate between use and excessive use. In her review of 35 different studies, Heller (1972) states that their most serious flaw is that "they have lumped together all drug users without considering the extent of their use."

Second, extreme using patterns—heroin addiction being the prime example—have been singled out for intensive study, but very little attention has been paid to delineating those patterns of use which lie between abstinence and compulsive use. A typology has not yet been developed which adequately represents the range of drug-using behavior. Terms intended to indicate frequency or quality of use—chipper, experimenter, addict, neophyte user, experienced, casual, habitual, chronic, recreational—are often used in quite different ways by different investigators, sometimes without definition. This situation caused the Shafer Commission to conclude that "it is often difficult to ascertain who is being described, what kind of behavior is being evaluated . . . or what actual or potential risks of such behavior are likely" (National Commission on Marihuana and Drug Abuse, 1973).

Third, to the extent that the existence of regular non-compulsive using styles has been acknowledged, marihuana use has received almost all of the attention, whereas little interest has been shown in non-compulsive psychedelic and heroin use. This difference could, of course, be in accord with the actual ratio of non-compulsive to compulsive users in the three drug categories. But until quite recently there were no definitive statistical data on this ratio.[2] Thus the difference in emphasis probably also reflects the pervasive belief that chemical differences between drugs are the main determinant of the outcome of their use. For example, Blumer, Sutter, Hamed, et al. (1967) note the possibility of continued non-compulsive use of marihuana, but they suppose that heroin cannot be used on an occasional basis because it develops greater dependency than does marihuana.

There is no direct equivalent in the research literature for the pattern of drug consumption which we call controlled use, though the terms "occasional use" and "chipping" (in the case of heroin) come close. A careful search, including use of the computerized Medline file[3] and covering a 47-month period (January 1969 through November 1972), revealed only one research article specifically concerned with the occasional use of *any* illicit drug.

That article describes a study conducted by Douglas Powell in 1973. Powell interviewed subjects who had been occasional users of heroin for at least three years without becoming physically addicted. Many of the using patterns described in Powell's report appear so unstable or so damaging that they lie outside the patterns of controlled use we are investigating. Nevertheless, his study supports our efforts in that he has established the existence of occasional heroin users and has found that such users "are responsive to research and can be studied reliably with relatively simple techniques."

Although only Powell's article deals specifically with occasional drug use, this subject is mentioned in books and articles whose essential thrust is on other matters. The dates of publication of the following thirteen examples range from 1961 to 1976, and they are concerned with marihuana, psychedelics, or opiates.

Becker (1963) discusses occasional marihuana use as a stage in which "the individual smokes sporadically and irregularly" because he has not yet established a reliable source for the drug. Robins and Helzer (1975) found that Vietnam veterans and non-veteran control subjects reported that occasional marihuana use did not interfere with their work or health; in addition, some veterans as well as some non-veterans used heroin

---

[2]A careful epidemiological study by Bourne, Hunt, and Vogt (1975) and a review and reworking of studies by Hunt and Chambers (1976) strongly suggest that the number of non-compulsive heroin users is in fact several times larger than the number of addicts. This represents a radical departure from the longstanding belief that the number of non-compulsive heroin users is small.

[3]The Medline file contains citations from 1,100 of the journals indexed for Index Medicus.

occasionally and did not become addicted. Goode (1969a) defines the occasional marihuana smoker as "someone comparable to the social drinker, to whom marihuana is a pleasant but largely dispensable and not particularly important aspect of life," and he asserts that such benign using patterns predominate. Gordon (1974) alludes to "occasional" versus "chronic" marihuana users but fails to define either. The term "taster" (Keniston, 1969) and "experimenter" (Kaplan, 1971) have been applied to both marihuana and psychedelic users. McGlothlin (1974) finds that psychedelic use is usually infrequent and self-limiting—that most users discontinue use after several years. Scher (1961, 1966) discusses controlled heroin use in work done through the Cook County Narcotic Project and claims to be the first to make public mention of it as a discrete phenomenon. Chein, Gerard, Lee, et al. (1964) found youths who use heroin on a weekend or party basis; the authors characterize such use as the "honeymoon stage," as if it were an inevitable prelude to addiction. Dobbs (1975) warns that not all applicants to methadone programs who are using heroin may be drug-dependent. Crawford (1976) contrasts addicted users with certain friends of theirs who had used heroin for a year but had not become addicted. Newmeyer (1974) located users who he believed should not be regarded as representative of a junkie population because they "could sample heroin without becoming addicted." While these and other authors have recognized the existence of non-compulsive drug use, none have followed through with a systematic study either because they found it of insufficient importance or because they were deterred by the inherent difficulty of such work.

STUDY METHODS

The major goals of our Drug Abuse Council study are to: (1) locate controlled users of marihuana, the psychedelics, and the opiates; (2) describe such users and their various patterns of use; and (3) identify the factors which stabilize and destabilize controlled use.

Potential subjects for the study were initially solicited through universities, advertisements in the underground press, and a variety of social service agencies, such as halfway houses, drug treatment centers, and counseling centers. (Most subjects located through agencies were staff members or friends of clients.) Although these methods yielded some subjects, it proved very difficult to locate controlled heroin users. As might be expected, controlled users of heroin, to a greater extent than users of other drugs, fear that disclosure may damage their relations with employers and friends. Fortunately, once our project was underway, we found (as Powell did) that after subjects had completed the screening and interview procedure, they were often willing to refer drug-using friends and acquaintances to us. We also recruited six indigenous data gathers (members of the drug-using subculture) to assist in locating and interviewing subjects.[4] Seventy percent of the subjects have become involved in the study through personal contact with another subject, with an indigenous data gatherer, or with a staff member.

The following four criteria were developed for selecting participants. (1) A subject had to have used marihuana, a psychedelic, or an opiate for at least one year. (2) He had to be willing to participate in follow-up interviews. (3) He had to have used the drug frequently enough to be considered a regular user, but not so frequently that he was physically addicted to it (in the case of opiates), or that his level of use was likely to interfere with effective personal and social functioning. No precise cutoff points for frequency of use were established (see Zinberg, Harding, and Apsler, 1976 for a discussion of this decision). In practice, a marihuana user who had used only a dozen times in the previous year was not selected because his use seemed too infrequent to be regarded as regular; contrariwise, a weekly user of psychedelics was not selected because this level of use seemed to indicate a compulsive relation to the drug. (4) When subjects were polydrug users, all of the drugs (including alcohol) had to be used non-compulsively. A moderate biweekly heroin user who was physiologically addicted to barbiturates was therefore not eligible to participate.[5]

Interviews lasted at least an hour and a half and sometimes more than two hours. Subjects were paid approximately $10 per interview. A flexible interview schedule was adopted to allow the interviewers to pursue interesting issues as they arose. But data were gathered on each subject's history of drug use (including alcohol); his relations to work and school, as well as to family and mates; his relations with drug-using and non-drug-using peers; his physical health and emotional stability; the details of drug-using situations; and basic demographic variables.

---

[4]Indigenous data gatherers were trained in our interviewing techniques. Since all interviews were tape-recorded, the research staff could monitor the work. The three data gathers who were recruited from within the sample—two women and one man—proved extremely capable and reliable. They contributed the bulk of the data not gathered by the research staff.

[5]At this stage of the research these criteria still seem reasonable, although they arbitrarily exclude large groups of people whose illicit drug use may in no way be deleterious. Perhaps the most interesting group we have excluded comprises "conventional addicts" (McAuliffe and Gordon, 1975). The classical example of this kind of user is the physician who can easily obtain a regular supply of opiates of known quality, has access to sterile syringes, and knows how to inject the drug properly. Although physiologically addicted, the physician can control his dosage and can continue ordinary functioning.

VALIDITY OF THE DATA

In addition to the interviewer's subjective impressions of a subject's veracity, four opportunities existed to crosscheck the data. First, in the course of a single interview several similar questions about a given topic were asked in order to test the consistency of the subject's responses. Second, consistency was tested in later interviews by means of core questions identical to those used in preceding interviews. Third, indigenous data gatherers added a quasi-ethnographic perspective to the research. When possible, they observed subjects in drug-using and other life situations, and thus were often able to check the accuracy of interview data. Fourth, 40 percent of the subjects were in some way related to another subject or to a person outside the sample who was also interviewed. Relationships included mates, spouses, friends, roommates, and siblings. These relationships allowed us to corroborate many of the details that subjects reported about their life styles and levels of drug use.

PROFILE OF THE SAMPLE

Because a random sample of controlled drug users could not be drawn for this study, a brief description of our subjects should be given. A profile of the sample reveals that despite some limitations the subjects are diverse in terms of basic demographic variables.

To date, interviews have been conducted with 99 controlled users.[6] Follow-up interviews have been conducted with 31 subjects and are still in progress. Subjects range in age from 14 to 70 years, with a median age of 23 years. If one divides the sample into age groups that correspond roughly to adolescence (14-20 years), early adulthood (21-30), and maturity (over 30), 35 subjects fall into the adolescent group, 43 into the adult group, and 21 into the mature group. There are 61 white males, 23 white females, seven black males, and three black females.

The disproportionate representation of whites in the project resulted from the need to select indigenous interviewers from among the occasional users who seemed competent, in order to uncover more users. At the beginning of the project the first few subjects studied were white, and as it was questionable at that time whether we would be able to find many subjects at all, we eagerly recruited indigenous interviewers with-

---

[6]Interviews were also conducted with 21 subjects whose drug use was either compulsive or so infrequent or so recent that they could not be included in the sample. These interviews, which provided valuable comparative data, were used to refine the interview schedule and sometimes (as indicated above) to verify data on controlled subjects.

out taking into account the fact that they necessarily would develop a sample from their own social group. But now that we know that occasional users are numerous and cut across racial, ethnic, age, and sex boundaries, we could systematically develop a more balanced sample from any group simply by finding the appropriate indigenous interviewer.

Similarly, the predominance of middle-class and lower-middle-class interviewers reflects the social class distribution of the sample. Only seven subjects are upper class; 38 have been ranked middle-middle; 25 lower-middle; and 29 lower. Seventy-two of the subjects have completed a high school education or better; 13 have not finished high school; and 14 are still in high school. Excluding those subjects currently involved in a post-high-school education (27), seven have B.A.'s, 13 have M.A.'s, and three have Ph.D.'s. Fifteen subjects are married and 15 are living with a mate. Eleven subjects have been separated or divorced. Nineteen subjects have children. Of those subjects who are employed full-time, two are professional (e.g., physicians); 21 are white-collar managerial (e.g., high school teacher, counselor, middle-level management); two are white-collar clerical (e.g., secretary); nine are blue-collar skilled (e.g., plumber, electrician); and nine blue-collar manual (e.g., waitress, sales clerk).

Ninety-six of the subjects use (or have used) marihuana in a controlled way, 52 use (have used) psychedelics, and 47 use (have used) opiates. (Because the categories overlap, these totals exceed the total number of subjects.) For analytical purposes, subjects have also been grouped according to their primary drug—the illicit drug they prefer to use and which they use with sufficient frequency to be classified as regular users. Such grouping by primary drug yields 35 marihuana users, 21 psychedelic users, and 43 opiate users.

THE NATURE OF CONTROLLED USE

Our sample of 99 controlled users can be distinguished from compulsive users in a number of ways. All subjects tend to maintain regular ties to social institutions, such as work-place, school, and family. At the time of their last interview, 27 subjects were in school (two of them part-time); 43 were working full-time; eight were working part-time; one had retired; and four who had regular work histories had recently become unemployed. Of the remaining subjects, only six fell into a "hustling/hanging out" category; others were involved in child care, housekeeping, and so forth. Controlled users maintained ordinary social relationships with non-drug users. None of the subjects manifested demonstrable physiological or psychological impairment attributable to their controlled use.

Drug use is of course important to controlled users. Our subjects have clearly stated that they would miss their primary drug if it were no longer available. Significantly—and this finding contrasts with the results of studies of compulsive users—our subjects demonstrate an ability to keep drugs on hand for some time without using them, and to continue their leisure activities. Controlled heroin users in our sample wait for "good" circumstances to use the drug (a social sanction), as opposed to compulsive users, who generally restrict use only when the drug is unavailable. Most subjects are deviant only by virtue of their drug use. Some have an earlier history of criminal activity or school disciplinary problems, but generally this has not overlapped with their current period of controlled use.

The data from our study challenge the prevailing tendency to regard regular, non-compulsive use (particularly heroin use) as simply a brief transition stage between abstinence and serious drug-related problems. The mean length of time of controlled use for our subjects is 4.0 years, and with heroin users alone it is 3.6 years.[7] With some subjects (including heroin users) controlled use has exceeded ten years. But more important than the duration of controlled use is evidence indicating the stability of these using patterns. None of our subjects has shifted toward significantly more frequent use even through such crises as divorce and job loss. On the contrary, any long-term shifts have tended to be in the direction of less drug involvement.

The sample comprises a wide variety of controlled use patterns. Some subjects use heroin only on weekends. Marihuana use may be confined to two evenings during the week and increase slightly on weekends, or use may be limited to special occasions and activities, such as going to the movies or to a concert. Some subjects are spree users: they take a drug on a daily basis over a short period—perhaps during a vacation—but virtually abstain at other times. These examples and others have led us to conclude that frequency of use is an unreliable measure of control. Only at the extremes of the using spectrum (for example, when psychedelics are used on a daily basis over an extended period) does frequency alone differentiate between compulsive use and controlled use (Zinberg, Harding, and Apsler, 1976).

---

[7]The mean period of controlled use is lowered by our including some subjects with histories of controlled use of slightly over one year (to help clarify the question of how controlled use is first established). Long-term follow-up will reveal how long these early controlled use patterns persist.

Assessment of control, therefore, requires evaluation of the meaning the subject attaches to drug use, the circumstances under which drugs are used, evidence of any limiting effects on performance, and other variables which are value-laden and therefore difficult to quantify. In fact, controlled use is best demonstrated by presenting detailed case material that illustrates a typical pattern, such as the case of Linda D.[8]

Linda D, a small, attractive, 26-year-old woman, who has been an occasional heroin user for five years, lives in a working-class neighborhood near Boston with her five-year-old daughter, Sara. Although there have been no formal legal arrangements, she has been separated from her husband, Michael, for approximately five years. They remain friendly, and he contributes to Sara's support from his earnings as a commercial artist as well as caring for her two or three days per week. He lives nearby with another woman.

Linda grew up in New York City. She remembers little about her father, who died when she was four years old and her brother, David, was two. After her father's death, her mother began to work part-time. Family relations were strained and there was little money. When Linda was ten, her mother remarried but was divorced one year later. Despite the briefness of that formal relationship Linda describes her stepfather as a "good friend." She continued to see him with her mother's approval until his death when Linda was 20.

Linda's mother now lives alone in New York and earns a comfortable living supervising hospital social workers. Over the last five years Linda's relationship with her mother has become "smoother . . . more cordial," but it remains more a matter of "mutual respect" than "love." They visit each other several times a year: "She wants to see her granddaughter, but she really hates kids; just wants to see her, not touch her." Linda mentions contact with her brother, David, who now attends graduate school in the Midwest. Most recently she attended David's wedding. She feels close to him although they cannot seem to "communicate, especially about our childhood."

There is no history of alcoholism or compulsive drug use in Linda's immediate family. Her mother has always smoked but has not used alcohol. After her father's death, her mother used sedatives under a doctor's prescription for several months and then appropriately discontinued use. Her stepfather drank socially. On a visit home after one year of college, Linda learned from David that he had taken drugs while on

---

[8]For other brief case descriptions of controlled opiate users, see Zinberg and Jacobson (1976).

a trip to Mexico. He appeared to have experimented with psychedelics and marihuana, but he did not describe his experiences precisely even though Linda made it clear that she also used drugs.

Linda began to use tobacco occasionally at age 16, and soon received her mother's permission to smoke. Regular smoking, which did not begin until Linda was 20, now continues at less than a pack a day. Her first use of alcohol occurred with friends when she was 16. Because she did not like the taste of alcohol, use remained very infrequent—"an occasional sloe gin fizz"—until she reached age 23 and began working in a bar/restaurant. Initial regular alcohol use was rather heavy—two to three drinks per day for several months—but then it tapered off to a drink or two occasionally, and now continues at that pace, with occasional periods of abstinence of two or three weeks due to dieting.

At age 16 Linda with several girlfriends became aware that boys in the private high school they attended were using marihuana. Initially "horrified" by their discovery, they placed an anonymous call to a government agency for information about marihuana and read several pamphlets about drug use. The "research" convinced them that marihuana "wasn't really terrible," a view that was confirmed by the boys' accounts of the drug. Shortly thereafter Linda and three girlfriends were "turned on" by the boys. She found the high pleasant and became "infatuated" with marihuana, using two to four times a week, primarily on weekends. Use declined to twice a week at the end of the eleventh grade, was always social, and continued at that rate through Linda's first year at college in the Midwest. She "dealt" marihuana to friends for "kicks" and "for the excitement," turning very little profit.

Though Linda had done very well in high school, she found her first year at college academically "boring." She took a full-time job as a waitress, which detached her from fellow freshmen, but soon became friendly with a group of seniors who were interested in psychedelics. They read about LSD and asked more experienced users about it. As Linda explained, "There were all these rumors going around about what you should do, what you should't do," and accordingly the group selected a pleasant setting and arranged to be introduced to LSD by an experienced user who served as a guide. Linda undertook the experience feeling "like I was doing something incredibly brave," with many fears of a bad trip or lasting psychosis. The "trip" turned out to be "lovely," and the group continued to use every weekend for six months.

Linda completed her freshman year satisfactorily but had already resolved not to return to college. After a brief visit home she hitch-hiked to California with the conscious goal of becoming a "junkie." Despite the fact that she "had no sense what it was to be a junkie" and "didn't know any junkies," she "wanted to do junk" because she had heard "it was the best high in the world."

Upon her arrival in California, Linda "crashed" in a house with a group of several young males and two older men. This group had an intense commitment to drug use. Linda immediately began frequent use of a variety of drugs, chiefly psychedelics and methedrine (injected). After a few months her attachment to the group waned and she met an outsider, Michael, who was dealing heroin. He introduced her to heroin and was, incidentally, her first sexual partner. She moved in with him, and her use of psychedelics, amphetamines, and marihuana markedly declined as she began using heroin regularly.

Linda and Michael dealt heroin together, and within five months she had become a daily user, always, however, using less than he did. She describes herself in retrospect as a "half-assed junkie," usually injecting once a day but sometimes as often as three times a day. Dealing proved lucrative. She and Michael sold large quantities to just a few customers, keeping risks low. After several months their supply of heroin was interrupted. Michael experienced considerable physical discomfort while Linda had only moderate stomach cramps; she was sufficiently naive to attribute their illness to food poisoning. Only after several phone calls to a physician friend did Linda finally realize that Michael and she were experiencing withdrawal. When their heroin supply was restored, she cut back her heroin use to only once a day, and after two or three days would "purposely abstain for a day." She allied herself with another woman who had a similar pattern of controlled use and attempted to exert some control over Michael's use.

Michael, however, resumed dealing both marihuana and heroin, and returned to his earlier heavy use. Soon he was arrested on a marihuana charge, and faced jail. Linda, whose previous brushes with the law had been only for hitch-hiking, became frightened and depressed. She decided to "flee" the deteriorating situation for New York. Ignoring his legal problems, Michael followed her. Both resolved to stop all drug use. Michael began working as an apprentice to an artist; Linda attended college and worked part-time in a travel agency. They were married. A few months later Linda met a couple who were "chipping." After some hesitation she introduced them to Michael and the four began social and restrained weekend use of heroin. Linda, who had always injected heroin, now "snorted" (inhaled heroin into the nose) for the first time and only used the drug in this social situation. Michael, however, quickly began injecting heroin with compulsive users outside the group. He attempted to hide this extra use from Linda.

Becoming pregnant, Linda discontinued all drug use, including tobacco and alcohol, out of concern for her unborn child. Two weeks after giving to birth to Sara, and in the face of Michael's growing addiction, Linda announced that she was leaving and made immediate arrangements to move. Michael again promised to reform. He went through withdrawal without much difficulty and accompanied her to Boston. But in a short time he resumed compulsive use and Linda left him. Since their separation in 1970 Michael's drug use has moderated, which has permitted a continued relationship if not a full reconciliation.

Currently Linda uses heroin, usually snorting, about once a week or less. Use is always social, partly because the human interaction surrounding use contributes to her pleasure and partly because she feels that solitary use, especially by vein, is unsafe. Linda has adopted a number of additional rules for use. By keeping two sets of "works" (the apparatus used for injecting) on hand, one reserved for herself and the other to be shared by guests, she guards against hepatitis. Dosage is tested by injecting a portion of her share and waiting to gauge its effects before injecting the remainder. Use is planned carefully so as not to interfere with her responsibilites to her daughter. She waits to use, for example, until her daughter is with Michael, feeling that "it would not be good to be high if I had to deal with her." She does not go out "in public" when she is high and will not use if it might interfere with her work.

During her almost six years of controlled heroin use, Linda's additional regular drug use has been confined to alcohol and tobacco, and to occasional use of Valium for therapeutic purposes. Marihuana use has become rare—perhaps four times a year. She finds that marihuana makes her feel "uncomfortable" and "inhibited," and while many of her friends use regularly, she declines to join them. During this period she has had several part-time jobs as a waitress or bartender; for three years she was also co-director of a local day-care center. Her lifelong love of travel takes her to California or the West Indies whenever such trips are financially feasible. Her active social life includes several distinct circles of friends: one from the neighborhood in which she has lived during this entire period; one from work; one from the day-care center; and others elsewhere. Except for her actual using companions, her friends do not know that she has used or is using heroin.

Linda has no definite plans for the future. Her daughter has begun kindergarten, leaving her more time for work, but she is increasingly dissatisfied with waitressing. She has had several serious sexual relationships with men, but nothing permanent has emerged, and she is cautious about living with someone just for financial convenience and security. She expects her use of heroin to continue.

Linda is representative of our sample and of the problems of analysis of our data. Enough detail of her early life is presented to show that there are no gross psychic difficulties either in her personal development or in her family. On the other hand, if one should want to account for problems in her later life, one could find in Linda's background—as in most life histories—sufficient factors, such as the death of her father and separation from her stepfather, to do so. But from our point of view, what we know about her background does not explain her journey to California to become a junkie. Neither does her psychological profile explain her later ability to move away from heroin use so compulsive as to cause a withdrawal syndrome or her continuing infatuation with heroin. What seems clear is that when in a social situation with another compulsive user, Linda is prone to compulsive use; and conversely, she can maintain controlled use of this powerful drug when she can find a social group that supports such a pattern of use. At this point the research team believes that Linda has developed internal controls that would mitigate against compulsive use in almost any social situation. But could she have developed such internalized psychological structures without the peer group control experience? In the subsequent sections we will explore those sanctions and rituals developed by social groups to prevent compulsive use (Zinberg, 1975). Further statements on the relationship between individual personality structure and the receptiveness to social structures that permits limited use are in preparation.

RITUALS AND SOCIAL SANCTIONS

When the 99 subjects in our sample are viewed individually, a variety of variables, including personality, family background, and availability of the drug, can be identified as influencing their controlled drug use. One crucial variable, however, applies to all members of the sample—the acquisition of rituals and social sanctions that reinforce but limit use.

The term ritual refers to the stylized, prescribed *behavior* surrounding the use of a drug. This behavior may include methods of procuring and administering the drug, selection of a particular social and physical setting for use, and special activities undertaken after the drug has been administered. The term social sanction refers to the precepts and rules regarding the circumstances which permit use but prescribe limits.[9]

In our culture the paradigm for controlled drug use is the use of

---

[9]Our use of the terms rituals and social sanctions does not conform precisely to either general anthropological use (Goody, 1961) or sociological use (Gibbs, 1965). We, for example, use social sanctions to refer to those rules of conduct which sociologists label norms, while they use the term sanctions to refer to the measures taken to enforce the norms.

alcohol, a psychoactive drug which has as great a potential for producing profound physiological and psychological harm as any illicit drug. The seriousness of alcoholism, while not denied, is placed in a new light when the number of alcoholics in the United States—some 6 to 8 million—is compared to the number of Americans who drink but avoid compulsive use—some 105 million (New York Times, 1973). Clearly, the vast majority of people who drink alcohol succeed in controlling their use of this powerful drug.

The widespread, *non-compulsive* use of alcohol in the United States can best be explained in terms of its sociocultural context—the rituals and social sanctions which the culture has developed. Alcohol-using rituals define acceptable use: having a beer with the boys after work, a few martinis at a cocktail party, a highball before dinner, wine with dinner, a drink at a business luncheon. This is not to say that use cannot and does not occur at other times but when it does, the users are aware that they are taking special exception to the social sanctions which govern use. Having a bloody Mary with breakfast is acceptable behavior on an occasional basis—a Sunday brunch with friends, for example—but having vodka with breakfast every morning would violate the social sanction that drinking should not interfere with work. Sanctions permit and even encourage drinking, but they condemn promiscuous use and drunkenness. The maxims are familiar: "Know your limit," "Don't drink and drive," "Don't drink before sundown," "A few beers on the way home from work or while watching TV are fine, but don't drink on the job."

The laws and regulations which apply to the manufacture, distribution, and consumption of alcohol also play a part in preventing compulsive use and thus, properly speaking, constitute social sanctions. But the informal and internalized rituals and social sanctions exert even greater influence. We avoid drunkenness more because we feel it is unseemly—and drunken driving more because we have learned it is unsafe—than because of the possible legal consequences.

The internalization of these social sanctions and rituals begins in early childhood. The child sees his parents and other adults drinking. He also learns the possibilities of excess as well as the varieties of acceptable drinking patterns from newspapers, movies, magazines, and television. In some cases this socialization process is more direct—children sip wine at religious rituals and celebrations, or taste their parents' drinks. Many authorities believe that a gradual and careful early introduction to alcohol by parents contributes to restrained adult use (Chafetz and Demone, 1962; Wilkinson, 1970).

True, adolescents often test the limits of the social sanctions and rituals by getting drunk and nauseated. Yet, in contrast to the anxiety aroused when parents are faced with an adolescent's illicit drug use, neither the adolescent nor his parents need have much fear that such occasional experimentation with alcohol will seriously or permanently disrupt social relationships and performance at school or work. The adolescent sees numerous adult examples of controlled use and can easily find friends who share his interest in drinking as well as his commitment to social sanctions which limit use. As the new user begins to drink in public with the direct or tacit approval of adults, the general culture's rituals and social sanctions and his previous learning meld into an individualized but socially acceptable pattern of alcohol use. And social reinforcement for controlled use continues throughout his adult life.

SOURCES AND FUNCTIONS OF CONTROLLING RITUALS AND SOCIAL SANCTIONS

The rituals and social sanctions for the use of all drugs—not just alcohol—operate at several different levels; in small groups (for example, using only in a certain room, assigning one group member to secure the premises); among collections or classes of people (cocktail parties, beer at ball games, drug use at rock concerts, wine with dinner in Italian households); and in the culture as a whole (coffee drinking and alcohol use). Various segments of society may develop and observe either complementary or opposing rituals and social sanctions, although even when they are opposing, each segment is to some extent cognizant of and influenced by the other. Although illicit drug users do not observe the mainstream culture's sanctions, they are aware of these sanctions and stand in jeopardy of being punished for violations, they are restricted in the way they can use the drugs, and some feel "guilty" about violating them. The Drug Abuse Council (DAC) data indicate that controlled users adhere to those specific rituals and social sanctions which each group develops for itself, and that the peer using group is the prime mechanism by which these guidelines for controlled use are developed.

It is true that, within the subculture of drug users, rituals exist which do not contribute to control. In some heroin addict subcultures, for example, bragging about the size of one's heroin habit or the ability to hustle glorifies compulsive use (Feldman, 1968; Preble and Casey, 1969; Stephens and Levine, 1971; Young, 1971). Injecting oneself with septic needles, driving a car when intoxicated with alcohol, and experimenting to see how large a dose of LSD one can withstand—all these practices increase the risks to the user. Some rituals, such as sharing "works," may have been intended originally to facilitate control of use. But without viable social sanctions which define limited use and are accepted by the group, the rituals either become empty, obsessive rites with no power to control use or, worse, become actual supports for compulsive use. Other types of rituals do not contribute to control because they are unrelated to the consequences of drug use. For example, "booting" (drawing blood into the syringe and reinjecting, perhaps several times) does not seem to contribute either to control or to increased risk, although it is probably more common among compulsive than among non-compulsive users.

The controlling rituals and social sanctions to which the subjects of the DAC study subscribe function in five overlapping ways.

1. They define moderate use and condemn compulsive use. For instance, several subjects use heroin with friends every weekend but condemn use at other times as "junkie"-like.

2. The rituals and sanctions limit use to physical and social settings which are conducive to a positive or safe drug experience. A maxim shared by virtually all psychedelic-using subjects is, "Use in a good place at a good time with good people."

3. Rituals and sanctions reinforce the principle that dependence or addiction should be avoided. Subjects who use heroin are acutely aware that they can become addicted, and they interpret increasing tolerance to drug effects as a signal to cut back on use.

4. The sanctions and rituals assist the user in interpreting and controlling the drug high itself. Passing a joint around provides an opportunity to gauge the effect of the drug after each "toke" and thus to titrate dosage accordingly.

5. Rituals and sanctions support the user's non-drug-related obligations and relationships. For example, some subjects do not use opiates on Sunday evening because this would leave them too tired to work effectively on Monday.

The subjects of the DAC study acquired rituals and social sanctions gradually during the course of their illicit-drug-using careers. The details of this process varied from subject to subject. Some had been controlled users from the outset; others, like Linda, went through one or more periods of compulsive use before firmly establishing control. Virtually all subjects, however, required the assistance of other controlled users to construct appropriate rituals and social sanctions out of the folklore and practices of the diverse subculture of drug-takers.

It is this association (often fortuitous) among controlled users which provides the necessary reinforcement for avoiding compulsive use. Virtually all DAC subjects are or have been connected with a controlled use group. Subjects rarely use drugs alone; over 80 percent of their use takes place with other controlled users. One of the most important sanctions, independently developed and subscribed to by almost all of our sample, restricts close contact with heroin addicts to the buying of heroin, and particularly discourages "shooting up" with addict-suppliers.

Thus the controlled use group redefines what is considered a highly deviant activity by the larger culture as an acceptable social behavior within the group. As Goode (1969b) observed concerning marihuana use, the using group reifies social sanctions and rituals, and institutionalizes controlled use. This conclusion is also consistent with Young's (1971) study of drug use in London, where Young found that some groups "contain lore of administration, dosage and use which tend to keep . . . lack of control in check, plus of course informal sanctions against the person who goes beyond these bounds."

While controlled use groups are the main source of rituals and social sanctions, there also appear to be at least four secondary sources. First, some of the precepts learned in the course of culture-based socialization in the controlled use of alcohol may be successfully adapted to the use of illicit drugs. Second, the lessons learned about controlling one illicit drug may be applicable to another. If this is so, one might expect to find, for example, that early controlled marihuana use is predictive of later controlled psychedelic use. Third, control over one drug, in the narrow sense of ability to deal with a drug high, may be transferred to another drug experience when the drugs are pharmacologically similar. For example, a user who had achieved some control over a barbiturate high might be better prepared to cope with a heroin high. Fourth, direct exposure to compulsive users who are obviously suffering from adverse drug effects may sometimes be helpful to controlled users. Such exposure may strengthen the sanctions the controlled users have already adopted by consciously or unconsciously delineating the differences between the two groups: differences in their relationships to the drug itself, in their integration of drug use into a personal and social context, and, of course, in the consequences of use.

DRUG USE AND THE SOCIOCULTURAL CONTEXT

Underlying the social and legal taboos against illicit use of the psychedelics, heroin, and, to a lesser extent, marihuana, is the conviction that because of their pharmacological properties these drugs cannot be taken on a long-term, regular basis without causing serious problems. The unfortunate condition of heroin addicts and other compulsive users is regularly invoked as "proof" of this "pharmacomythology" (Szasz, 1975). In contrast, our DAC study demonstrates that regular use of these substances on a controlled basis is possible. Moreover, the data indicate that peer group influences, which are usually considered to contribute only to the "bad" use of drugs, can provide the necessary support, in the form of rituals and sanctions, for avoiding compulsive use. These findings suggest that the management of illicit drug use by means of elaborate, culturally based, controlling social sanctions and rituals needs to be investigated as a realistic and more humane way of preventing drug "abuse" than the present method of total prohibition.

Our culture does not yet recognize, much less support, controlled use. Users are declared deviant, or "sick" and in need of help, or "criminal" and deserving of punishment. Family-centered socialization for use is not available. Parents, even if they were willing to help, would be unable to provide guidance either by example (as with alcohol) or in a factual, non-moralistic manner.

If parents tell a youngster not to use drugs because they are harmful, he can disregard the advice because his experience proves otherwise. Having already tried marihuana or the psychedelics, he knows to some degree what the use of drugs involves. The using group and the drug culture also reinforce his discovery that drug use, in and of itself, is not bad or evil and that the warnings coming from the adult world are a hoax. If parents try a different tack and tell the young person that some drugs are all right but others, such as the opiates, have a high risk component and should be avoided, their position again is vulnerable. "They still don't know what they're talking about," thinks the youngster. "Not having tried marihuana or the psychedelics, how can they know anything about the opiates?" Parents, moreover, by counseling their children that some illicit drugs are "more all right" than others, are placed in the position of approving an illegal activity. Thus their role as conveyors of the public morality becomes glaringly inconsistent.

If the parents try to obtain firsthand knowledge of the drug experience by smoking marihuana, taking a psychedelic, or shooting heroin, similar difficulties result. At the very least, they not only are sanctioning but are themselves engaging in a deviant act. This problem pales, however, before those that arise when the parents try to find out where to get the drug and then how to interpret the high. If they ask the children to get them the drug or to be with them while they are experiencing the high, the traditional roles of instructor and pupil are reversed. While the youngsters may enjoy this novel authority, such a situation creates enormous anxiety for the parents. Our findings show (Jacobson and Zinberg, 1975) that many parents never achieve a high because of the dynamics of the social situation, or, worse, that they are thrust into a major panic reaction which convinces them that the drug is bad and their children are on the road to destruction. The youngster is also placed in an extremely difficult caretaking role. If the parents try to avoid this pitfall by obtaining the drug in question from their own peers, they are again participating in an illegal activity. In short, illicit drug use is a no-win situation for everyone.

Culturally approved information on drug use usually comes to the adolescent through a drug education course in school or through the mass media. Such courses warn adolescents about the dangers and problems of drug use. While current courses tend to be more factual and less openly moralistic than those of the sixties, they rarely consider the social and psychological contexts in which use takes place; and thus they cannot approach the question of what differentiates controlled use from compulsive use. It may be wise to postpone drug use until late adolescence or early adulthood, but in the ambiance of the school no teacher can condone even limited experimentation with illicit drugs by anyone at any age. Hence the courses do not deal with the complexities of buying drugs and checking quality, administering safely, titrating dosage, or controlling the high state. Generally speaking, the messages from the mass media are even more disapproving. Heroin use is viewed as a plague, a social disease. Stories about bad psychedelic trips resulting in psychosis or suicide have served for years as media staples. And in the current climate of extreme carefulness lest offence be given to ethnic groups, it seems that drug users or peddlers, along with hopeless psychotics, are the only villains left to be featured in the innumerable "cops and robbers" serials and movies shown on television.

Therefore, the task of educating people about controlled use rests squarely with the peer group—an utterly inadequate substitute for cross-generation, long-term socialization. To a large degree, association with controlled users is a matter of chance rather than of deliberate personal choice. Because illicit drug use must be a covert activity, newcomers are not presented with an array of using groups from which to choose. (Even Linda, who is more comfortable and assured about her controlled use than most other heroin users, hides it from non-using friends.) Early in their using careers, many DAC subjects, like Linda, became involved with groups in which members were not well schooled in controlled use, or with groups in which compulsive use and risk-taking were the rule. Such subjects went through periods when drug use interfered with their ability to function and when they frequently experienced untoward drug effects. Eventually these subjects became controlled users, but only after they had realigned themselves with new companions—a difficult and uncertain process. Unfortunately, many adolescent users are unable to make this shift.

Cultural opposition also complicates the development of controlled use by creating a black market in which the drugs being sold are of uncertain quality. With marihuana, variations in the content do not present a significant problem since dosage can be easily titrated and adulterants are not harmful. At the worst, the neophyte user pays more than he should for a poor product. But for other drugs there are wide variations in strength and purity which make the task of controlling dosage and effect more difficult. Psychedelics are at times misrepresented: LSD, PCP, or the amphetamines, for example, may be sold as mescaline. With heroin, purity is unknown and the risk of an overdose is thus increased; at the same time, if adulterants are used when the drug is injected, the risk of infection may be heightened.

Ideally, the present policy of prohibition of drug use by legal means is justifiable if it persuades some people never to use drugs and influences others to abandon them. There is no doubt that prohibition does discourage excessive use—a goal with which we sympathize—but there is simply no way of knowing how much "abuse" the policy of prohibition prevents. It is unclear how many people would choose to use illicit drugs if prohibition were suspended, and it is also unclear how many who had tried drugs would go on to become compulsive users in the absence of prohibition. Moreover, the data presented here indicate that the prohibition policy actively contributes to the prevailing dichotomy between abstinence and compulsive use. While it prevents some people from using drugs at all, it may make it extremely difficult for anyone who wishes to use them to select a moderate using pattern. This outcome may have been acceptable before the 1960s when there were few potential drug experimenters, but it may well prove catastrophic in an age when adolescent experimentation approaches statistically normal behavior.

Present policies may even be interfering with our well entrenched cultural control over the use of alcohol. The DAC data suggest that today many teenagers have adopted alcohol as part of their drug culture. After using marihuana they often try to assuage the "munchies" (the hunger that may occur after marihuana use) with sweet pop wines. They may pass around a bottle and ask one another, "Are you off yet?"—treating alcohol as a "head drug" rather than as an intoxicant that can promote gregariousness. In view of the fact that adolescent alcohol use is often associated with illicit drug use, legal prohibition, which builds a wall between generations, threatens to disrupt the transmission of controlling rituals and social sanctions concerning the use of alcohol. Adolescents who reject parental advice about drugs may simultaneously reject the culture's controlling social sanctions and rituals in regard to alcohol, thus setting for themselves the enormous task of re-inventing these guidelines.

The chief difficulty in achieving social control over drugs is that significant changes will be required in both public attitudes and social policy before effective rituals and social sanctions can develop. These social controls are not the work of a moment; they develop slowly over time in ways that fit the culture. Griffith Edwards (1973), who calls this kind of response "cultural plasticity," describes how the use of a drug can be slowly evolved by different tribes. One tribe may use the same drug as an energizer that another tribe uses as a tranquilizer, depending on how the drug fits each group's controlling rituals and sanctions. We certainly do not recommend the wholesale, immediate legalization of marihuana, psychedelics, and opiates, for such an abrupt shift in policy would make impossible the natural development of the elaborate social support and carefully defined social context of use which are needed to prevent abuse.

Three steps, however, can be taken now to develop familiarity with the drugs in frequent use and thus to lay the basis for social controls. First, the laws can be changed to encourage legitimate areas of drug research and experimentation. Second, more comprehensive and value-neutral information about licit and illicit drugs can be given to the general population. Third, distinctions can be drawn among the various degrees of drug use, thus allowing knowledge about the controlling conventions to be disseminated. All these actions will help to strengthen the existing subcultural rituals and social sanctions and to remove prevailing misconceptions about the power and danger of these drugs.

In the first area, decriminalization of marihuana should be extended beyond those few states which have already adopted it, and federal penalties for use should be dropped. More extensive research on the possible medical applications of marihuana and the psychedelics should be supported. The progress of research should be publicized so that the public image of these drugs as "bad," to the extent that they are unworthy of such study, will be dissipated. In Europe and England heroin is known as a superior analgesic and antitussive, and it should gradually be made available for such uses in the United States. Experimentation with various models of heroin maintenance clinics and induction clinics for the treatment of addicts should also begin.

Specific actions to begin to implement the second and third steps are also needed. Drug education programs which are no more than disguised campaigns to eliminate use should be replaced with genuine efforts to provide users and non-users with rudimentary pharmacological data and, more important, with detailed information about the consequences of the *various* patterns of use. Doctors, teachers, counselors, and others who encounter actual and potential drug users and who now routinely condemn any use as abuse should be taught the distinction between use and abuse. Surely it makes no sense to alienate and undermine those segments of the population of drug-takers that are attempting to stand against abuse. Another important step would be the greater availability to users of low-cost laboratories providing complete confidential analyses of street drugs. A few of these are now in existence and it has become clear that they can help users know what they are taking and thus contribute to a notion of quality control.

These recommendations represent only the first of many changes which would be required before coherent social sanctions could develop around illicit drug use and before more realistic legal controls could evolve. It is not possible to specify the sequence of changes with any confidence, for to do so would be to ignore the essential fact that using patterns will shift in response to these changes and to other new factors. When such shifts have begun, intensive research aimed at measuring them will be needed in order to provide data upon which to base further constructive steps.

REFERENCES

BECKER, H. S. (1963) Outsiders: Studies in the Sociology of Deviance, Free Press of Glencoe, Glencoe, Illinois.

BLUMER, H., SUTTER, A., HAMED, S. et al. (1967) Becoming hard core narcotic addicts, The World of Youthful Drug Use, University of California, School of Criminology, Berkeley, p. 73-75.

BOURNE, P., HUNT, L., and VOGT, J. (1975) A Study of Heroin Use in the State of Wyoming. Foundation for International Resources, Washington, D.C.

CHAFETZ, M. E. and DEMONE, H. W., Jr. (1962) Alcoholism and Society, Oxford University Press, New York.

CHEIN, I., GERARD, D. L., LEE, R. S. et al. (1964) The Road to H, Basic Books, New York.

CRAWFORD, G. A. (1976) Precursors to Heroin: A Comparison of Heroin Addicts and their Non-addicted Friends. Presented at National Drug Abuse Conference, New York, March 25-29.

DOBBS, W. H. (1971) Methadone treatment of heroin addicts, JAMA 218:1536-1541.

EDWARDS, G. F. (1973) The Plasticity of Human Response. Maudsley Hospital, London. (mimeograph)

FELDMAN, H. (1968) Ideological supports to becoming and remaining a heroin addict, J. Health and Social Behav., 9:131-139.

GIBBS, J P. (1965) Norms: the problem of definition and classification, Am. J. Sociol. 70:586-594.

GOODE, E. (ed.) (1969a) Marihuana, Atherton Press, New York.

GOODE, E. (1969b) Multiple drug use among marihuana smokers, Social Problems 17:48-64.

GOODY, J. (1961) Religion and ritual: the definitional problem, Brit. J. Sociol. 12:142-164.

GORDON, P. H. (1974) Toward the resolution of the controversy surrounding the effects and social health implications of marihuana use, J. Drug Education 4:13-24.

HARDING, W. M. and ZINBERG, N. E. (1977) The effectiveness of the subculture in developing rituals and social sanctions for controlled use, Drugs, Rituals and Altered States of Consciousness (Ed. B.M. du Toit). A.A. Balkema, Rotterdam, Netherlands.

HARRIS, L. (1976) A lenient attitude on pot fines, Chicago Tribune, January 26, 1976.

HELLER, M. (1972) The Sources of Drug Abuse. Addiction Services Agency Report, New York, June.

HUNT, L. G. and CHAMBERS, C. D. (1976) The Heroin Epidemics: A Study of Heroin Use in the United States, 1965-1975, Spectrum Publications, Inc., New York.

JACOBSON, R. and ZINBERG, N. E. (1975) The Social Basis of Drug Abuse Prevention, Drug Abuse Council Monograph Series SS-5, Drug Abuse Council, Washington, D.C.

KAPLAN, J. (1971) The New Prohibition, The World Publishing Company, New York.

KENISTON, K. (1969) Heads and seekers: drugs on campus, countercultures and American society. Am. Scholar, 38, 1968-1969.

MCAULIFFE, W. E. and GORDON, R. A. (1975) A test of Lindesmith's theory of addiction: the frequency of euphoria among long-term addicts. Am. J. Sociol. 79:795-840.

MCGLOTHLIN, W. H. (1974) The epidemiology of hallucinogenic drug use, Drug Use Epidemiological and Sociological Approaches, John Wiley and Sons, New York, p. 279-301.

National Commission on Marihuana and Drug Abuse, Second Report (1973) Drug Use in America: Problem in Perspective, Government Printing Office, Washington, D.C.

NEWMEYER, J. (1974) Five years after: drug use and exposure to heroin among the Haight-Ashbury free medical clinic clientele, J. Psychedelic Drugs 6:61-65.

New York Times (1973) April 9.

POWELL, D. H. (1973) Occasional heroin users: a pilot study, Arch. Gen. Psychiatry 23:536-594.

PREBLE, E. and CASEY, J. J., Jr. (1969) Taking care of business—the heroin users' life on the street, Int. J. Addictions 4:1-24.

ROBINS, L. N. and HELZER, J. E. (1975) Drug use among Vietnam veterans—three years later, Med. World News—Psychiatry, p. 44-49, October 27.

SCHER, J. (1961) Group structure and narcotics addiction: notes for a natural history, Int. J. Grp. Psychotherapy 11:81-93.

SCHER, J. (1966) Patterns and profiles of addiction and drug abuse, Arch. Gen. Psychiatry 15:539-551.

STEPHENS, R. and LEVINE, S. (1971) The "street addict role": implications for treatment, Psychiatry: J. for the Study of Interpersonal Processes 34:351-357.

SZASZ, T. (1975) Ceremonial Chemistry: The Ritual Persecution of Drugs, Addicts and Pushers. Anchor Press/Doubleday, Garden City, New York.

VOGL, A. J. (1973) Drug abuse: is the tide turning? Med. Econ. p. 82-99, May 28.

WILKINSON, R. (1970) The Prevention of Drinking Problems. Oxford University Press, New York.

YOUNG, J. (1971) The Drugtakers: The Social Meaning of Drug Use, MacGibbon and Kee, Ltd., London.

ZINBERG, N. E. (1975) Addiction and ego function, Psychoanal. St. Ch. 30:567-588.

ZINBERG, N. E., HARDING, W. M., and APSLER, R. (1976) What Is Drug Abuse? Unpublished manuscript.

ZINBERG, N. E. and JACOBSON, R. C. (1976) The natural history of chipping, Am. J. psychiatry 133:37-40.

ZINBERG, N. E., JACOBSON, R. C., and HARDING, W. M. (1975) Social sanctions and rituals as a basis of drug abuse prevention, Am. J. Drug and Alcohol Abuse 2:165-182.

ZINBERG, N. E. and ROBERTSON, J. A. (1972) Drugs and the Public, Simon and Schuster, New York.

16

CAUSES AND TYPES OF NARCOTIC ADDICTION: A PSYCHOSOCIAL VIEW

David P. Ausubel

Addiction to narcotic drugs is one of the most serious but least understood medico-social problems of our time. The grievous lack of public enlightenment about this problem reflects in part its inherent complexity as well as the paucity of definitive research findings dealing with physiological, psychological, and social aspects of addiction. But an even more important cause, perhaps, of both lay and professional misunderstanding of the drug addiction problem is the continuous stream of lurid and sensational misinformation about this topic which appears in the various mass media.

THE ADDICT'S VIEW

Let us examine first the addict's own view of the cause of drug addiction. According to him, all human beings are equally susceptible to addiction. The unlucky victim need only have the misfortune to be introduced to the drug as a result of abnormal curiosity, chance encounters with addicts and narcotic peddlers, or prolonged illness. Then, once he is caught in the "iron grip" of physical dependence on the drug he is allegedly powerless to help himself. He is obliged to continue using more narcotics "just to stay normal," that is, to avoid the "unbearable" symptoms that ensue when the drug is discontinued.

This dangerously distorted account of the causes of drug addiction is a great comfort to the addict. It puts his illness in the most favorable

Reprinted with permission from *Psychiatric Quarterly*, 1961, 35, 523-531. Copyright 1961, Human Sciences Press, New York.

possible light and also absolves him of all responsibility. Unfortunately, however, he has not only successfully deluded himself, but has also managed, with the unwitting co-operation of the mass media, to foist his understandably biased view on a credulous American public. Physical dependence and withdrawal symptoms are genuine physiological phenomena, and association with confirmed addicts or drug peddlers *is* the typical way in which candidate addicts are introduced to narcotics. But neither factor explains *why* an individual becomes a drug addict.

Physical Dependence

How credible is the physical dependence explanation? In the first place, although the symptoms of withdrawal are distressing, they are generally no worse than a bad case of gastro-intestinal influenza, and, in any event, largely disappear within 10 days. Thus, unless other potent satisfactions were derived from the narcotic habit, it is difficult to believe that any individual would be willing to pay the fantastic price of the drug and risk imprisonment and social ostracism merely to avoid a moderately severe 10-day illness. Second, every year thousands of persons with serious fractures, burns and surgical conditions receive opiates long enough to develop physiological dependence, but are nevertheless able to break this dependence quite easily. Third, the dosage of morphine (or equivalent) required to prevent withdrawal symptoms is never more than one to two grains daily. Hence, why will drug addicts take up to 20 grains a day if they take the drug, as they claim to, "just to feel normal"? Fourth, withdrawal symptoms can be adequately prevented and relieved if morphine is taken hypodermically. Therefore, why will addicts run the risk of thrombophlebitis and septicemia by injecting the drug "main-line"—or directly into their veins—with crude, homemade syringes? The answer to both third and fourth questions is that the large dose and the "main-line" route increase the "kick" or euphoric effect. Fifth, new, synthetic opiate-like drugs have been developed which have all of the analgesic and euphoric properties of opiates, but for which withdrawal symptoms are minimal. Nevertheless, the evidence is conclusive that addiction develops just as rapidly for these drugs as for other opiates (1).

Last, if physical dependence were a significant causal factor in drug addiction, how could we explain the fact that at least 75 per cent of all addicts discharged from federal hospitals start using the drug almost immediately after release (2)? By the time of release, it is at least a year since physical dependence was broken. If addicts are really so terrified by withdrawal symptoms, why should they start developing the habit all over again after suffering the symptoms once and then escaping their clutches?

MULTIPLE CAUSALITY IN DISEASE

Generally speaking, research on drug addiction has been hampered by the same type of faulty thinking that has plagued the investigation of the causes of such other complex disorders as cancer, tuberculosis and juvenile delinquency. This is the error of assuming that since the disorder in question *appears* to be identical in all individuals, it must necessarily have the same *single* cause in all instances. Actually, there are many different kinds of drug addicts, and the causes of drug addiction are multiple and additive in their impact rather than mutually exclusive. As in most other diseases, the causes of drug addiction include both *internal* factors originating within the affected individual (e.g., hereditary susceptibility) and *external* factors originating within the environment. Each type of factor may be further categorized with respect to whether its impact occurs immediately prior to, and is essential for, the appearance of the disease (*precipitating*), or is operative over a longer period of time and merely contributory (*predisposing*). In tuberculosis, for example, hereditary susceptibility to the inroads of tubercle bacilli is the predisposing internal cause, and temporary lowering of general resistance (as in overexertion or exposure to extremes of temperature) is the precipitating internal cause. Comparable external causes would include overcrowded living conditions, on the one hand, and actual exposure to an adequately large dose of tubercle bacilli, on the other.

It makes little sense, therefore, to talk about *the* cause of tuberculosis. Exposure to a reasonably large dose of virulent organisms is a necessary causal factor but is rarely a sufficient cause in the absence of particular hereditary susceptibility to tuberculosis, depressed standards of living, and transitory lapses in general resistance to disease. In any given case, one particular factor may overshadow all others and thus provide a spurious appearance of single causality; but this neither guarantees that this same factor will be equally prominent in other cases nor excludes the operation of other factors in the same case. All we can say in this regard is that if any one of the relevant causes is especially salient, the other contributory factors are less necessary to bring about the disease. If one individual, for example, by virtue of his heredity, happened to be highly susceptible to tuberculosis, whereas his neighbor happened to be highly resistant to this disease, the former would obviously succumb to a much smaller dose of tubercle bacilli than would be necessary to strike down the latter. It also follows that both the severity of the disease and the outlook for recovery would vary in accordance with the relative prominence of the various casual factors.

MULTIPLE CAUSALITY IN DRUG ADDICTION

The causal picture in drug addiction is quite analogous to that just described for tuberculosis. Availability of narcotics (that is, exposure to addicts and drug peddlers, or, in the case of physicians and others, even more direct access to the drug) is the *external precipitating* factor. No matter how great an individual's susceptibility, he obviously cannot become a drug addict unless he has regular access to narcotics. The factor of relative availability explains why the rate of addiction is so much higher in slum areas and among members of the medical and allied professions than in middle-class neighborhoods and among other occupational groups. To account for the higher Puerto Rican addiction rate in comparably exposed Negro and Puerto Rican sections of New York City's Harlem slum area (3), and for the much higher addiction rate in China than in Japan (4), one must invoke a major predisposing factor, also of environmental origin, namely, degree of community or cultural tolerance for the practice.

But *external* factors alone cannot explain all of the known facts about the incidence and distribution of drug addiction. In a given slum area of uniformly high exposure to and tolerance for the drug addiction habit, why is the practice limited to a relatively small minority of the residents, and why do male adolescents constitute such a disproportionately large percentage of the affected group? Why do some addicts originate in middle-class neighborhoods despite little exposure to narcotics and strong community disapproval of the habit? To explain these facts, we must turn to the important internal factor of differential susceptibility. In the same sense that individuals are not equally susceptible to tuberculosis, they are not equally susceptible to drug addiction.

TYPE OF ADDICTION

Maturational Deficiency. The most serious, and prognostically least hopeful, variety of drug addiction occurs among individuals who fail to undergo adult personality maturation, that is who fail to develop the long-term drives and corresponding motivational traits characteristic of normally mature adults in our society. Such motivationally immature persons are typically passive, dependent, irresponsible, lacking in perseverance and self-discipline, and preoccupied with achieving immediate, pleasurable self-gratification. They are unconcerned about marriage, raising a family, socially useful employment, vocational achievement, financial independence, and constructive service to the community (5). The euphoria (objectively unwarranted feelings of ecstasy, well-being and self-confidence) induced by narcotics has uniquely efficient adjustive value for them. It provides immediate and effortless pleasure and dulls their self-critical faculties, thereby enabling them to feel supremely contented with their immature and inadequate adjustment to life's problems. Hence, since few other adjustive mechanisms are able to compete with drugs in attractiveness to persons possessing this type of personality structure, the disorder tends to be chronic, and the outlook for recovery is poor.

What are the sources of the motivational immaturity that constitutes the internal predisposing factor in drug addiction? Apart from hereditary proclivities toward such personality traits as passivity, self-indulgence, and excessive need for pleasurable self-gratification, the principal causes of motivational immaturity are particular kinds of unsatisfactory parent-child relationships. Considerations of space do not permit a full discussion of this topic. But examination of the kinds of relationships that drug addicts as children and adolescents have had with their parents reveals several typical patterns: 1) the extremely *overprotecting* parent, who shields the child from all independent experience and all possibility of failure so that he never gets the opportunity to set mature goals for himself or to act independently; 2) the extremely *underdominating* parent, who makes no demands on the child for mature behavior and leads him to believe that he is a specially privileged person whose needs will always be satisfied by others; and 3) the extremely *overdominating* parent, who imposes excessively high goals on the child, thereby inviting complete sabotage of the goals of adult maturation as soon as the child can escape from parental control (6).

Reactive Addiction

Reactive addiction is the most common type of addiction found in the United States today, having increased spectacularly since the end of World War II. It is a transitory, developmental phenomenon, occurring principally among slum-dwelling adolescents with essentially normal personalities. The adjustive value of drugs for these individuals is simply that they provide an outlet both for the exaggerated rebelliousness and defiance of conventional norms (which is not uncommon among American adolescents generally), and for the particular aggressive attitudes associated with membership in an underprivileged and often ethnically stigmatized segment of the urban population. These precipitating internal factors are further compounded by such external factors as the ready availability of drugs, high community tolerance for addiction, and coercive pressures from addict associates in the closely-knit predatory gangs of the urban slum. Dabbling or experimenting with drugs has no unique adjustive value for the tensions and attitudes operative in this context. It is just one of many possible nonspecific ways of expressing aggression, hostility, nonconformity, and identification with deviant age-mates. Like juvenile delinquency, therefore, this type of addiction gradually diminishes and is eventually discarded by most of the reactive drug users, with the approach of adult life, as normally mature family and vocational interests assert themselves and as adolescent identification with deviant norms correspondingly declines.

A difficult problem in differential diagnosis is posed by the fact that the motivationally immature type of addict is found most commonly (although by no means as exclusively as is the reactive type of addict) among adolescent and young adult males in urban slum areas. This is hardly surprising, when one considers that motivational immaturity is no more rare in such areas than elsewhere, and that the actual development of addiction in highly susceptible individuals is further abetted by adolescent stresses, gang influences, racial and social class tensions, social demoralization, high availability of narcotics, and high community tolerance for the drug habit. How then does one distinguish between these two basically different types of addicts, both of whom are often represented in the same gang?

Data collected by the Research Center for Human Relations of New York University (7) suggest several feasible criteria for differential diagnosis. Motivationally immature addicts tend to use narcotics more regularly, in larger quantities, and more for their adjustive values than "for kicks." They also tend to manifest more serious and deep-seated personality problems, to be peripheral rather than active members of delinquent gangs, and to participate more in the remunerative, criminal ventures of the gangs than in their athletic, heterosexual and gang warfare activities. Reactive users, on the other hand, are typically week-end "joy-poppers" who much more rarely take the drug regularly enough or in sufficient quantity to develop physical dependence. They are more likely to be delinquent before addiction, to come from the economically more depressed homes in the neighborhood, and to use drugs either to conform to age-mate standards or as just another nonspecific means of expressing antisocial attitudes. After the age of 18, the reactive drug user tends to abandon both his active, predatory gang interests and his casual use of drugs in favor of more mature, conventional concerns with vocation and family; but the motivationally immature habitual user retreats further from normal adult adjustment into drug-induced euphoria.

Miscellaneous Varieties of Drug Addiction

A relatively rare form of narcotic addiction is found sometimes among individuals suffering from neurotic anxiety and depression. These addicts, usually professional persons who have easy access to the drug, tend to use small, stabilized doses of opiates for the *sedative* rather than euphoric effects. Possessing strong achievement drives and normally mature motivational traits, they value the drug solely for its anxiety-reducing properties and for its ability to soften the unreasonably harsh and critical view that anxious and depressed individuals take of themselves. But since many other adjustive mechanisms (e.g., rationalization, compensation, delusion, fantasy, phobia, compulsion) are available, and since the barbiturates and tranquilizers are, in any case, both more efficient and legally accessible for the desired purposes, this type of addiction is becoming increasingly more rare. Drug addiction also occurs occasionally among certain vicious, remorseless criminals, the aggressive antisocial psychopaths, who use the addiction habit merely as a nonspecific means of expressing hostile and destructive personality trends.

SUMMARY

The addict's dependence on continued use of narcotics to avoid withdrawal symptoms is not a significant factor in causing drug addiction, even though the drug addict has been amazingly successful in deluding both himself and the American public into believing that it is primary causal consideration. Physical dependence cannot account convincingly for the surplus dosage and intravenous route habitually taken by the confirmed addict, or for the latter's willingness to risk social ostracism and incarceration just to avoid a moderately severe 10-day illness. Neither does it adequately explain the recurrence of addiction long after physical dependence is lost, nor the strong addicting-potential of new opiate-like drugs which give rise to only minimal degrees of physical dependence, nor the ease with which normal persons are able to overcome the physical dependence on narcotics which they may inadvertently acquire during the course of prolonged illness. All of these facts suggest that susceptibility to drug addiction is variable rather than uniform, and that addicts use opiates primarily for their euphoric properties.

The causes of drug addiction are both multiple and additive in their impact. As in most other diseases, they include factors orginating both within the person (internal) and within his environment (external), and each category in turn may be further divided into predisposing and precipitating causes. The major external and necessary precipitating factor is the ready availability of the drug, a factor which is reinforced by the predisposing environmental factor of high community or cultural tolerance for the pratice. These external factors are sufficient to induce the disorder in individuals who are highly susceptible to addiction.

Susceptibility to drug addiction (the internal factor) is largely a reflection of the relatively great adjustive value which narcotic drugs possess for potential addicts. This adjustive value is most specific and efficient in the case of those individuals for whom the euphoric properties of opiates are most attractive. These are persons who manifest the internal predisposing factor (failure to develop the drives and motivational traits characteristic of normally mature persons in our society). This internal predisposing factor (motivational immaturity) is itself largely an outcome of particular kinds of unsatisfactory parent-child relationships, as well as partly a reflection of various temperamental traits of hereditary origin.

Susceptibility to drug addiction is less marked when the euphoric effects of opiates have less specific and efficient adjustive potential. This occurs when the susceptibility reflects internal precipitating factors of a more transitory nature, such as adolescent revolt against conventional norms, gang pressures, and attitudes associated with residence in a socially demoralized urban slum or membership in a racial minority group.

On the basis of the relative prominence of these various causal factors, it is both possible and diagnostically important to distinguish between two major and essentially different types of drug addicts. In instances where increased susceptibility to addiction is indicative of long-standing motivational immaturity (the internal predisposing factor), the highly specific and efficient adjustive value of the drug makes for a chronic type of disorder with a very poor prognosis. Where external causal factors are more prominent and internal factors are of a more temporary (precipitating) nature, the adjustive value of the drug is less specific and efficient, and the resulting (reactive) type of addiction accordingly tends to be a transitory aberration similar to juvenile delinquency. Both types of addiction, however, the motivationally immature as well as the reactive, are found most commonly among adolescent males in the urban slums. This is because motivational immaturity occurs just as frequently there as elsewhere, and because all of the other internal and external causal factors (the various developmental and social stresses, the high availability of the drug, the high community tolerance) tend to converge on teen-age boys who reside in such areas.

REFERENCES

1. WIKLER, A.: Opiate Addiction. p. 50. Thomas, Springfield, Ill. 1953.
2. PESCOR, M. J.: Follow-up study of treated narcotic drug addicts. Public Health Report, Supplement No. 170, 1943.
3. Committee on Public Health Relations, New York Academy of Medicine: Conference on Drug Addiction among Adolescents. p. 64. Blakiston. New York, 1953.
4. MERRILL, F. T.: Japan and the Opium Menace, Institute of Pacific Relations, and the Foreign Policy Association. New York, 1942.
5. PESCOR, M. J.: A statistical analysis of the clinical records of hospitalized drug addicts. Public Health Report, Supplement No. 143, 1938.
6. AUSUBEL, D. P.: Drug Addiction: Physiological, Psychological and Sociological Aspects. pp. 43-44. Random House, New York, 1958.
7. Research Center for Human Relations of New York University: Report No. II, Personal Background of Drug Users, Delinquents, and Controls. New York, 1957.

17

THE TREATMENT OF PERSONALITY DISORDERS IN A THERAPEUTIC COMMUNITY

Maxwell Jones

In this paper, I shall describe a community treatment approach, with particular reference to patients with personality disorders, being utilized in Belmont Hospital, near London. This approach was not specifically developed for the treatment of personality disorders; and I am inclined to think that it could, with certain modifications, be used in the treatment of most, if not all, types of psychiatric cases.[1] Nevertheless, I shall here refer chiefly to patients with personality disorders, both because the majority of patients in the unit under discussion fall into this category, and because the treatment of personality disorders, although it presents a serious challenge to psychiatry, is today probably less well organized than that of the two other large diagnostic categories—the psychoses and the neuroses.

Reprinted with permission from *Psychiatry*, 1957, *20*, 211-220. Copyright © 1957; by the William Alanson White Psychiatric Foundation, Inc.

Maxwell Jones, M.B., Ch.B., Univ. of Edinburgh 31; M.R.C.P. (Edin.) 35; D.P.M. (Lond.) 35; M.D. (Gold Medal Thesis) 47; Lecturer in Psychiat., Univ. of Edinburgh 35-36; Commonwealth Fund Fellow, Univ. of Pennsylvania and Columbia Univ. 36-38; Specialist in Psychiat., Mill Hill Emergency Hospital (Maudsley Hospital 39-45; Consultant Psychiat., Postgraduate Medical School of London 47-51; Consultant in Mental Health, World Health Organization, Geneva, 50-51; Director, Social Rehabilitation Unit, Belmont Hospital, Sutton, Surrey, England 46-.

I would like to thank Dr. Louis Minski, Physician Superintendent at Belmont Hospital, Sutton, Surrey, England, for his cooperation in the work described here.

[1]Maxwell Jones and R. A. Matthews, "The Application of the Therapeutic Community Principle to a State Mental Health Programme," *Brit. J. Med. Psychol.* (1956) 29:57-62.

A century ago psychotic patients presented many of the problems which today are associated with the treatment of personality disorders; they were little understood and, while arousing a certain degree of compassion, also aroused considerable fear. The public conscience was satisfied if they could be segregated and people could be found who were willing to look after them. Since then the general public has become much more informed about the psychotic, and the fact that the psychiatrist himself believes that he has a better understanding of the subject and even claims to successfully treat some of these patients is no doubt reassuring to the outsider. No one questions that these people are really "ill," and consciously, at least, few people still think of them as "bad."

The neurotic, who is more familiar and therefore easier to understand, arouses relatively less anxiety in the public mind; his symptoms have come to have a respectability which would have appeared impossible to the objective observer of 100 years ago, and the need for treatment is recognized. Private psychiatric practice, like any competent big business, has not been slow in meeting the demand—at a price! The situation for the non fee-paying neurotic is much less satisfactory.

The situation concerning the personality disorders is much more chaotic. In the areas of diagnosis and treatment less is known. More important, however, is the less favorable climate of public opinion, compared with the psychoses and the neuroses. What can one offer disturbed people with antisocial personality problems who urgently need help? If they have money, it may be possible to treat them privately or to arrange for their admission to a suitable clinic. For most cases, however, admission to a state hospital will have to be considered. Most psychiatrists agree that such cases do not fit *successfully* into the ordinary wards of a state institution; they cannot tolerate discipline and soon disrupt the ward by their antisocial behavior. Yet little or nothing seems to be done to bring about a more satisfactory treatment environment. Can it be that the psychiatrists themselves reflect something of the public prejudice toward these people?

It is, I think, reasonable to postulate that the emotionally unstable personality, the passive-aggressive personality, and the sociopathic personality[2] arouse negative responses not only in the general public but also in the very people whose understanding they must depend on if they are ever to be helped. This difficulty is, of course, related to the fact that people with personality problems not infrequently get into trouble with the law and are therefore seen as potentially dangerous.

---

[2] I am here following the American Psychiatric Association classification of mental disorders.

The psychiatrist, whose training must presumably help him to guard against social pressures which favor punishment and segregation rather than treatment, has a responsibility to improve the hopelessly inadequate treatment facilities so far available for such persons. It is against this background that I suggest the therapeutic community as a rational treatment approach to cases whose personality disturbance is of sufficient severity to result in their being sent to the hospital or to prison. Such therapeutic communities might be located either in an existing psychiatric hospital or prison or be housed separately. In any case, they would call for an entirely new social organization and specially trained medical staff who would need to assume roles differing in many respects from those which they traditionally follow.

BACKGROUND

While, as far as I know, the Social Rehabilitation Unit at Belmont Hospital represents the first attempt to treat adult personality disorders of the antisocial type in a community setting, similar approaches have been used with other types of disorders. For instance, there have been several attempts to treat adolescent behavior disorders in a community setting.[3]

My own experience with the idea of a therapeutic community began in 1940 at Mill Hill Emergency Hospital (Maudsley Hospital) near London, where I had charge of a unit of 100 beds set aside for the study and treatment of cases of neurocirculatory asthenia (effort syndrome) occurring in the British armed forces. At the Hospital, after careful physiological studies on these men, we came to have a fairly clear understanding of the mechanism of symptom formation.[4] We were able to show that patients complaining of severe left chest pain had a significantly diminished diaphragmatic excursion, compared with those who lacked this symptom; that the left chest pain could be alleviated temporarily by root block or injection of local anesthetic into the appropriate muscles of the chest wall, and so on. In time we came to have a considerable degree of understanding of the other common symptoms found

---

[3]A. Aichhorn, *Wayward Youth;* New York, Viking, 1935. Bruno Bettelheim, *Love Is Not Enough;* Glencoe, Ill., Free Press, 1950. Fritz Redl and David Wineman, *Controls From Within: Techniques for the Treatment of the Aggressive Child;* Glencoe, Ill., Free Press, 1952.

[4]Maxwell Jones, "Physiological and Psychological Responses to Stress in Neurotic Patients." *J. Mental Sci.* (1948) 94:392-427. P. Wood, "Da Costa's Syndrome (Or Effort Syndrome)," *British Med. J.* (1941) 1:767-772; "Da Costa's Syndrome (Or Effort Syndrome); Mechanism of Somatic Manifestations," *British Med. J.* (1941) 805-811; "Aetiology of Da Costa's Syndrome," *British Med. J.* (1941) 1:845-851.

in neurocirculatory asthenia, such as breathlessness, headache, postural giddiness, and fainting.

We began to have frequent meetings of all patients and staff, and the results of our studies were fed back to the patients. They were deeply interested, for all hundred men had the same syndrome of symptoms, and many of them had been experimental subjects in our studies of exercise physiology. They began to understand the meaning of their symptoms in terms of physiological mechanisms—for example, why they tended to faint *after* exercise and not during it, why the left chest pain was caused by tension and fatigue of the muscles of the chest wall and not, as they had originally supposed, by the heart, and so on.[5] The nature of their symptoms, their own lay ideas about illness, and their experiences at the hands of the medical profession had all tended to focus their attention on their hearts. Thus, while right chest pain was common, it was rarely commented on unless the patient was questioned specifically on this point; even a case of previously unrecognized dextrocardia referred his pain to the left chest region!

The community discussions and feedback of our research findings began to bring about a change in the patients' attitudes toward their symptoms. They began to view them more objectively, being helped in this by the free use of models and diagrams of the central nervous system, circulatory system, and so on. We even created a character called "Nervy Ned" whose symptoms were portrayed in a series of cartoons hung around the walls of the meeting room.

By the end of the war the culture in the Neurocirculatory Asthenia Unit had changed in several fundamental ways. The treatment focus had moved from individual interviews in the doctor's office to community meetings with all patients and staff present. Discussion of symptoms was carried on largely by the patients themselves, the older patients teaching the new arrivals, and there was little need for staff intervention. In a limited sense, the treatment was being carried on by the patients in collaboration with the staff. The attitude of the patients toward their symptoms had changed remarkably. New admissions quickly accepted the belief expressed by their peers that there was no question of heart disease and that the symptoms were mainly due to emotional conflict. They readily accepted the idea that further treatment must be directed to the cause of the conflict and that the symptoms themselves were not of much importance.

Despite the fact that each patient was in the hospital for a period of

---

[5]The patients had all been seen by cardiologists before being sent to us and had been fully investigated by electrocardiography and other means.

only six to eight weeks and that our treatment goal was the very humble one of changing the patient's attitude toward his symptoms, the results, judged clinically, were surprisingly good. In 1941, 49 percent of neurocirculatory asthenia cases were returned to the army, and by 1944 the figure had risen to 66 percent. By the end of the war we had begun to achieve a therapeutic culture in which the sharing of much of the treatment procedure with the patients was helping a common ideology to emerge.

In 1945 I continued the development of community methods of treatment in a different setting—a 300-bed unit in another hospital for the treatment of some of the most neurotic cases from among the 100,000 ex-prisoners of war repatriated from Europe and the Far East. The results of treatment, as judged by a follow-up study, were considered to be good.[6] Repatriated ex-prisoners of war who did not appear severely neurotic were rehabilitated in the 17 Civilian Resettlement Units run by the army authorities, and here also the therapeutic community principle was utilized.[7] These experiences led to the establishment of the Industrial Neurosis Unit—later renamed the Social Rehabilitation Unit—at Belmont Hospital in 1947. This was intended primarily for the treatment and rehabilitation of chronically unemployed people with various types of psychiatric diagnosis, but excluding the overt psychotic and mentally defective. My colleagues and I soon found that the majority of our cases had personality problems, and over the ten years of the Unit's existence, there has been a growing tendency for psychiatrists and the courts to send us this type of case.

I have sketched in the background of the present Social Rehabilitation Unit in order to make it clear that we have come to use a community treatment approach for various reasons and while treating different types of psychiatric cases. We have tried to adapt this approach to the problem of treating personality disorders and have come to feel that it may well serve as a pattern for further units for the treatment of such cases in hospitals.[8] There is a similar need for special treatment units

---

[6]Maxwell Jones and J. M. Tanner, "Clinical Characteristics, Treatment, and Rehabilitation of Repatriated Prisoners of War with Neurosis," *J. Neurol. Neurosurg. and Psychiat.* (1948) 11:53-60. Maxwell Jones, *The Therapeutic Community;* New York, Basic Books, 1953.

[7]A. T. M. Wilson, Martin Doyle, and John Kelnar, "Group Techniques in a Transitional Community," *Lancet* (1947) 252:735-738.

[8]A recommendation on these lines has been made by the Royal Medico-Psychological Association in submitting its evidence to the Royal Commission on the Law Relating to Mental Illness and Mental Deficiency currently sitting in London. See "The Royal Commission on the Law Relating to Mental Illness and Mental Deficiency," *J. Ment. Sci.* (1954) 100:994-1020.

Since this article was written the report, "Royal Commission on the Law Relating to Mental Illness and Mental Deficiency, 1954-1957," Her Majesty's Stationery Office, Lon-

for antisocial personality disorders in prisons.[9]

DESCRIPTION OF THE SOCIAL REHABILITATION UNIT

The Social Rehabilitation Unit at Belmont Hospital is a semi-experimental unit of 100 patients and 30 staff comprising about one-quarter of the larger hospital. Belmont Hospital itself is a psychiatric hospital for the inpatient treatment of neurotic and early psychotic patients coming from all parts of England. It is an open hospital, admitting patients without any legal formalities whatsoever, and is run by the National Health Service. The Unit patients are a heterogeneous group, defined largely by exclusion as somewhere short of frank psychosis in the degree of illness, and somewhere above the minimal range of 'normal' intelligence. For the most part, they would be described clinically as having personality problems or acting-out disorders, although their symptomatology may include a wide range of neurotic and mild psychotic manifestations.

The staff, like the patients, are formally much like those of other psychiatric centers of this type. There are four psychiatrists, a psychiatric social worker, a clinical psychologist, and a total nursing staff of seventeen. In addition, there are two full-time Disablement Resettlement Officers, seconded to us by the Ministry of Labour to help in the placement of patients in jobs and vocational training schemes when they leave the hospital. Finally the staff includes six social scientists working on a grant from the Nuffield Foundation and two Fulbright fellows.

Patients stay in the hospital for periods ranging up to a year, the average length of stay being four to six months. There are no locked wards, and most of the patients have come voluntarily. A small minority have been referred by the courts, and have been put on probation with the stipulation that they accept treatment for a period of up to a year, the actual time being left to the discretion of the psychiatrist. The latter patients could easily abscond, although they seldom do so; they would

---

don, has appeared and in this three main groups of patients are recommended for legal and administrative purposes: mentally ill patients, psychopathic patients, and patients of severely subnormal personality. The Report deals at some length with the need for special treatment facilities and legislation to deal with social problems resulting from psychopathy. If implemented, the recommendations will make for much more careful study of the problems of treatment, segregation, and rehabilitation of antisocial personality disorders.

[9]In Europe, a start along these lines is being made by Professor Peter Baan in Utrecht. The much older center at Hersdtvester near Copenghagen is employing some of the concepts of a therapeutic community and Georg Stürup claims good results in the treatment of criminal psychopaths. See S. Taylor, "The Psychopath in Our Midst: A Danish Solution," *Lancet* (1949) 256:32-36.

then, however, be liable to arrest by the police. The patients are free to leave the hospital daily from 4 P.M. to 7 P.M. and on weekends.

Approximately six new patients arrive in the Unit every Monday; only in case of emergency do new patients arrive at other times. On arrival, a new patient is introduced to the Unit by a reception committee of older patients and does not see any staff members for an hour or more. He tends to form a temporary group with the other new patients who have arrived on the same day, and this group is deliberately organized around the reception committee for the first 48 hours, after which time it is hoped that they will be assimilated into the Unit. Patients are, on admission, assigned to three formal groups—a ward, a doctor's group, and a workshop. Through the daily round of meetings and socials they also come to participate in numerous other formal and informal groupings.

There are four wards, three for the men and one for the women patients. The patients are distributed randomly to the four doctors, each of whom assumes medical responsibility for his patients, although treatment is done mostly in the groups. There are four workshops—painting and decorating, furniture repair, tailoring, and the domestic group—each with an instructor in charge; these are designed to simulate as much as possible the conditions of workshops in the outside world. In addition, perhaps paradoxically, the workshops are intended to foster social identifications by engaging in work for the general benefit of the Unit community, without providing personal profit for the workers. Since the functioning of workshops, like that of other groupings and activities in the Unit, is the essence of treatment, the motivation to participate is assumed to be a measure of the willingness to participate in treatment.

The 100 patients and 30 staff meet collectively for 75 minutes on the five weekdays from 8:30 A.M. to 9:45 A.M. This is referred to as a community meeting, whereas a group meeting involves only a part of the total population. After the community meeting the patients go to their doctor's group or to work therapy. Every patient is in a doctor's group four days a week and in a ward group meeting and a workshop meeting once a week. The staff meet separately for 30 minutes daily and have 3 one-hour meetings every week. In addition, the social therapists (or nurses) have seminars with the permanent staff seven days a week. There is also a meeting on Saturday morning for all those among the patients or staff who care to attend, and a weekly family group which anyone may attend and to which patients are invited to bring their relatives. Finally there is a weekly instructors' group attended by most of the staff, and a visitors' group every Friday morning, at which time 8 volunteer patients and most of the staff meet with interested outsiders. There are approximately 1,000 visitors a year, mostly from the fields of social science and psychiatry.

In the community meetings there is an opportunity for information of all kinds to be fed back, and spontaneous expression of feeling is welcomed. This information may be purely factual, but more often relates to some controversial issue and indicates something of the feelings and personalities of the informants. It is one of the characteristics of the Unit culture that it is considered desirable to talk about one's feelings and to share these confidences with everyone. Privileged communications, even between patients and staff, are discouraged, the preference being for communication to the group. The communication of feelings is not, as in most therapeutic groups, limited to the patients, but the staff are also free to express their own feelings; for example, I would feel free to express my anxiety about a group of patients who, by their antisocial behavior, appeared to be threatening our good relations with the society outside. Thus in the main the discussion centers around the current tensions in the Unit, and around an attempt to understand these and to resolve them.

One indication of the growth of the therapeutic culture is the fact that communications are much freer now than they were a few years ago. At one time we used psychodrama and other projection techniques as a warming-up process, but we have dropped such methods as the community has seemed to become sufficiently uninhibited to do without them. However, the use of communication in a community meeting is extremely complex, and we do not, as yet, know how much the patients tend to select what to communicate and what to hold back. It is probable that there are still many subjects which they talk about in the privacy of their wards or of informal groups, which they do not communicate directly in the meeting. Nevertheless, we have reason to think that we have moved a relatively long way in the direction of open communication.[10]

Communications are not only at a verbal level, for much acting-out occurs in the meetings. This is an important point, since most of our patients have had little education and are relatively incapable of conceptual thinking.[11] Preoccupation with psychoanalytic methodology has tended to overemphasize conceptual thinking at the expense of simpler forms of communication. A community meeting affords an opportunity for the appreciation of the differences in values and meanings between

---

[10]William Caudill, Fredrick C. Redlich, Helen R. Gilmore, and Eugene B. Brody, "Social Structure and Interaction Processes on a Psychiatric Ward," *Amer. J. Orthopsychiatry* (1952) 22:314-334.

[11]Redlich and his colleagues at Yale have pointed to the need for techniques by which relatively uneducated patients can be enabled to communicate with their doctors. See F. C. Redlich, A. B. Hollingshead, and Elizabeth Bellis, "Social Class Differences in Attitudes toward Psychiatry," *Amer. J. Orthopsychiatry* (1955) 25:60-70.

psychiatrists and their patients; and our experience has shown that the psychiatrist can be taught to speak the patient's language.

Nevertheless, the constant verbalization of problems and working-through in daily group and community meetings leads to the development of a rather sophisticated and articulate community, and visitors are constantly surprised by the understanding and insight which patients show in handling their problems in collaboration with the staff. Many of the patients come to have some awareness of the problems of sorting out relevant and therapeutic communications from irrelevant and harmful ones—although there are times when the patients seem to accept "wrong" interpretations from other patients and resist what appear to be "right" interpretations from other patients or staff.

Social attitudes come in for frequent discussion. For example, there is discussion of such problems as informing and discipline, which have sinister associations to many patients, particularly those who have been in prison, yet have obvious importance in relation to the establishment of free communication. Also important are the various attitudes which patients adopt toward the general topic of "treatment." How many patients in psychiatric hospitals have clear ideas on this subject? One is tempted to ask the same question in relation to hospital staffs—and I can recommend, to staff members who are prepared to recognize this problem, the advantages of discussing the topic in community with the patients, for a surprising amount of mutual education can result. The trained staff member is forced to review some of his traditional attitudes and is unable to retreat to his safe position of omnipotent silence.

An instance of this has been our discontinuing the use of sedatives as a result of community discussions—even though they are used in large amounts in most psychiatric hospitals. Stimulated by the frequently occurring problem of drug addiction and the tensions produced by the acting-out patients in demanding sedatives from the night staff, this topic was raised for discussion on many occasions. The community slowly changed its attitude toward this aspect of treatment, until it is now accepted by everyone that our previous practice of giving sedatives was in the main a defense against difficulties—on the part of both patients and staff—which were much better dealt with by verbalization or other forms of acting-out in the group or community meetings. While little distinction is made by the patients between the use of sedatives and of alcohol, the latter can be seen, in the main, as a regressive symptom of the patient, whereas sedation can be frequently seen as a symptom of both the patient and the staff. That is, the staff's need to give sedatives often reflects their anxieties, and is not always a specific therapeutic procedure designed to meet the treatment needs of the patient. I know of only one other hospital where the use of sedatives has been discontinued, and this again was the result, in part, of a careful analysis of the staff motivations in prescribing drugs.

THE DYNAMICS OF THE THERAPEUTIC COMMUNITY

At the Unit, we believe that the cases of personality disorder which we see have resulted in the main from adverse environmental factors which have prevented personality growth from occurring in the ordinary way. Although we are dealing exclusively with adult patients of both sexes, we feel that it is logical, even at this late stage, to create a permissive and understanding environment, where the patient is afforded the opportunity of gaining some awareness of his personality as other people see it, and of getting help in modifying his behavior and way of relating to other people, if he wishes to do so. It is for this reason that we have gone to great pains to develop a democratic social organization where permissiveness and a spirit of inquiry and helpfulness predominate. In such an environment the antisocial patient finds it difficult to reproduce the responses from society which he has come to anticipate. For example, if he behaves provocatively and aggressively, he is not met with the same anger and rejection. Instead of being faced by a tangible authority against whom he can react, he is faced by his peers, who show an interest in the meaning of his behavior and expect him to discuss it with them collectively. In a case like this, the familiar or the expected does not happen, and one result is that the antisocial patient has little or no opportunity to rationalize his behavior. It is difficult for him to blame his environment, which instead of punishing him and rejecting him, as he has anticipated, has shown a desire to help him. It is not easy for even an antisocial isolate to continue his usual behavior when he is daily reminded of the effect of his behavior on the people with whom he lives, and who are, or have been, in difficulties with society just as much as he has.

He may, however, find some means of re-establishing his familiar pattern—for instance, by identifying himself with a rebel group. Such a group may be made up of new patients who re-enforce each other's beliefs, despite reassurance to the contrary, that the majority of the staff and patients are just pretending to be interested, while behind this facade they, like everyone else, are critical and punitive. Such a situation, however, is just as prone to be discussed by the community as is the case of deviant behavior by a single person.

All this presupposes that the majority of patients and staff have identified themselves with the unit ideology and are prepared to see deviant behavior as a symptom of illness calling for treatment rather than punishment. Needless to say, this state of affairs varies considerably in accordance with numerous factors, such as the rate of intake of new patients, the simultaneous arrival of a number of very destructive patients, the predominance of withdrawn and relatively nonparticipant patients, the experience and state of emotional equilibrium in the staff, and so on. At times, the social climate in the Unit has been such that satisfactory treatment was impossible, and we seriously considered stopping new admissions until the community had been able to deal with some of its outstanding problems. Moreover, a familiar social phenomenon in the Unit—as Robert Rapoport, one of our social anthropologists, has noted—is a tendency to cycles of destruction and repair.[12]

Nevertheless, we feel that most patients come to accept in some degree the willingness of the community to help. The patient sees the small community, which concerns itself continuously with the most intimate aspects of his life, as something tangible—as a society probably more real than any previous outside society has ever been to him. He finds that this community contains a number of highly trained people who share with the patients the burden of responsibility relating to all current problems and work with him in trying to bring about the resolution of tensions and the understanding of the motivations of behavior.

Reality testing is an important aspect of Unit life. The small society of the Unit strives, to a greater extent than is true in most hospitals, to be a microcosm of outside society. In the daily discussions of deviant behavior, the meaning of such behavior is analyzed as far as possible, but no attempt is made to escape from an awareness of the bad effects of such behavior on others. Patients who have been in frequent conflict with the law often remark that this procedure is much more distressing to them than punishment by the law, which usually represents a hated authority and not, as here, a group made up of their fellows.

Although we do not fully understand the learning process involved, we observe in the Unit that some patients show an increase in the capacity to empathize. We are beginning to think that in the broad field of personality disorders patients may be seen in terms of their lack of capacity to empathize—to place themselves in another person's shoes. This restriction of the normal capacity to feel oneself into another person's life situations clearly limits social interaction, from the point of view of both emotional understanding and capacity to predict the responses of other people. The person cannot know how others will respond to him, since he cannot fully comprehend their attitudes and feelings. The same difficulty in empathy leads to limited capacity for social communication.

---

[12]Robert N. Rapoport, "Oscillations in Sociotherapy," *Human Relations* (1956) 9:357-374.

The person may understand intellectually the meaning of what is being said or the significance of actions, but since he cannot feel himself into the situation, he does not have understanding, in the fullest sense of the term.

To quote my colleague Seymour Parker,

> A lack of capacity to empathise will also lead to relative inability to be self-critical. The individual cannot see himself as others see him. In fact it is doubtful if these patients have more than a rudimentary concept of self since this term may be defined as an incorporation and organisation of the appraisals of oneself, derived from interaction with significant others.[13]

Harrison Gough states,

> When confronted with disapproval, the psychopath often expresses surprise and resentment. He cannot understand the reasons for the observer's objection and deprivation because this involves an evaluation of his behavior from the standpoint of the other . . . or society. He will violate others' wishes and desires because he does not conceive of his own actions as inimical to their wants.[14]

The increase in empathy which we observe seems to be part of a general tendency to identification with the Unit—which the majority of patients develop, in some degree, at least. This is probably the most significant change that occurs in treatment by community methods of the kind that we are using. This identification, which implies that the person has some positive feelings for other members of the community, seems to coincide with an increase in feelings of anxiety and guilt. It would seem that the patient no longer acts out his conflicts on an alien society from which he is largely isolated, both by his feelings of hostility and by his inability to empathize. Up to now he has felt free to satisfy his emotional needs with something like the freedom of a child of two. This is no longer possible when he begins to have a feeling relationship with the people who suffer as a result of his uninhibited behavior. He becomes anxious to retain their support and understanding and feels guilty about harming them.

The development or modification of what might be called the social

---

[13]Seymour Parker, "Role Theory and the Treatment of the Anti-Social Acting Out Disorders," *Brit. J. Delinquency* (1957) 7:285-300.

[14]H. G. Gough, "A Sociological Theory of Psychopathy," *Amer. J. Sociology* (1949) 53:359-366.

conscience would certainly seem to be an important aspect of the treatment process. At this point we believe that we should provide ample opportunity for patients to play socially useful roles.

The participation of patients in the administration of the Unit and in treatment gives them a highly significant role in the community and is of major importance in this context. While not all patients avail themselves of this opportunity in an overt way, even the silent members may be affected by this state of affairs, and administrative decisions and the like are taken in their name, since they are members of the community.

The community has a relatively clearly defined culture, which is always being examined and modified. This examination, testing, and elaboration of certain basic attitudes and beliefs has a specific significance for the community, and if the members adopt these values as their own, this has probably considerable therapeutic value. The same might be said of the code of beliefs held by Alcoholics Anonymous. However, many of the basic assumptions inherent in our concept of a therapeutic culture require much closer scrutiny than they have yet received. It is generally held in the Unit that it is a good thing to talk in the community, that authority is delegated by the doctors to the community, and so on; but we have, as yet, no certainty about the validity of these beliefs. Experience indicates that these beliefs are at least partly valid, but the careful refinement and sorting out of the aspects that are most essential and effective in dealing with particular cases are still far from realized.

Thus while our growth so far has been largely intuitive, we are now in a position to begin to test some of our basic assumptions. We certainly do not claim to have any treatment theory as yet, and we borrow freely from current methods of psychotherapy and particularly from group therapy. Social and environmental factors in treatment are seen as complementary to more specific treatment methods. What is to us the most interesting and fruitful part of our work is the opportunity for mutual education and treatment. Because of the type of case, the freedom to alter the social environment, and the treatment ideology of the staff, it has become possible to participate freely with the patients in the day-to-day treatment procedures.[15]

---

[15]In this paper I have tended to stress the more hopeful aspects of the therapeutic community, mainly because of the predominant feeling of pessimism regarding the treatment of severe personality problems. There is, however, another side to the question which has not been developed and would need another paper to explain. I have talked as though the hospital authorities and society generally were favorable to our treatment approach. In the main, this has been so, but as the Unit's culture has become progressively more on the democratic-equalitarian model it has become difficult to live in the same building with the rest of the hospital run on a hierarchical model. Moreover, our permissive attitude to the treatment of delinquency has led to a certain amount of criticism from outside.

We do not as yet know the complete specifications of the type of patient which can best be treated in a therapeutic community such as ours. As I have already stated, the method developed in treating different types of patients, and I feel that small semi-autonomous units of approximately 100 patients, given a considerable degree of freedom to develop their own social organization, would be the best pattern for even large mental hospitals.[16] Our growth has many points in common with the findings of the workers associated with the Washington School of Psychiatry,[17] and more recently Boston Psychopathic Hospital.[18] It is almost by chance—or, more accurately, as a result of social pressure—that we have come to treat a population largely composed of personality problems. In a sense, it could be said that we are putting society to work to treat a condition which society has been largely responsible for; or, alternatively, it could be said that personality problems represent anomalies of growth resulting from adverse environmental factors, and that we are concerned with the establishment of an environment which affords a second opportunity for growth—this time toward, rather than against, ordinary society. In spite of our lack of knowledge, we feel that therapeutic communities of the kind we have described represent a treatment milieu where other perhaps more specific methods of treating personality problems could be developed. In such an environment, there is at least a chance that the unwilling patient can be induced to stay voluntarily and to accept treatment.

What are the results of treatment by the methods we use? We have only done one follow-up study to date;[19] the results, although now rather out of date, were encouraging and showed that there was a significant change in the social attitudes of the majority of patients which persisted after they left the hospital.

Finally, I would like to stress the tremendous stimulation of working in collaboration with the type of patient I have described. Far from being negativistic, hostile, and destructive, as one might expect, they have taught the Unit staff new perspectives in treatment. They have helped us to understand the limits of treating in isolation one member of a disturbed family, and we now frequently treat two members of the same family in the hospital at the same time. They have also taught us to

[16]World Health Organization, Technical Report Series No. 73; Geneva, 1953.

[17]Harry Stack Sullivan, *The Interpersonal Theory of Psychiatry;* New York, Norton, 1953. Alfred H. Stanton and M. S. Schwartz, *The Mental Hospital;* New York, Basic Books, 1954.

[18]R. W. Hyde, *Experiencing the Patients' Day; A Manual for Psychiatric Hospital Personnel;* New York, Putnam, 1955. Milton Greenblatt, Richard H. York, and Esther L. Brown, *From Custodial to Therapeutic Patient Care in Mental Hospitals;* New York, Russell Sage Foundation, 1955.

[19]Maxwell Jones, *The Therapeutic Community;* New York, Basic Books, 1953.

question many of our notions of treatment goals; what appears to be an appropriate social adjustment in the milieu of the hospital may unfit the person for life when he returns to his own culture, and so on. It is a stimulating, exciting, and at times frightening environment to work in, but on the whole immensely therapeutic and educative for all of us.

18

SYNANON FOUNDATION—A RADICAL APPROACH TO THE PROBLEM OF ADDICTION

Marshall S. Cherkas

The finite mind does not require to grasp the infinitude of truth,
but only to go forward from light to light.

P. Bayne

This simple statement must reflect our attitude toward the complex problem of narcotics addiction. Although there has been much written about the subject, there have been very few encouraging words, nor has there been satisfaction with the present state of knowledge. During my psychiatric training, I became interested in the growth of an unusual organization involved with the mastery of the hopelessness that encompasses the addict and those who deal with him. The organization, Synanon, was receptive to my interest, and cooperated in the last one and one half years mutually to explore the nature of the organization's goals, effects, techniques and attitudes relating to narcotics addiction.

Synanon Foundation, Inc., is a non-profit national organization providing residential treatment for the basic character problems of the narcotics addict. It was founded in Santa Monica, California, in 1959 as a result of the sustained relationship between a number of former nar-

Reprinted with permission from the *American Journal of Psychiatry*, 1965, *121*, 1065-1068. Copyright © 1965, the American Psychiatric Association.

Read at the 120th annual meeting of the American Psychiatric Association, Los Angeles, Ca., May 4-8, 1964.

Dr. Cherkas is Consulting Psychiatrist, Los Angeles County Dept. of Mental Health.

cotics addicts and Charles Dederich, an inspired leader, ex-alcoholic and colorful man of struggle. Synanon grew from a small cult which flourished on the basis of the surprising recognition that its members somehow were able to stay "clean" (free of narcotics) simply because of their attachment to the group. Many articles have been written in magazines for public consumption (*Manas, Time, etc.*) with some description of the early dramatic history. As of December 1, 1963, there were 205 men, 67 women and 24 young children located in the 5 centers across the country, including Reno, Nevada; Westport, Connecticut; San Diego and San Francisco, as well as Santa Monica, California. The rate of growth in population continues to increase.

A highly controversial agency, Synanon has developed a unique program which offers remarkable advantages to the addict. Run almost entirely by former addicts who have stayed on in the program as administrators, laborers, "therapists" and general staff, the program offers the addict an opportunity to become part of an ex-addict community where there is daily evidence that persistence of effort and continuous self-appraisal will provide media for promoting the self-esteem that has been foreign to the addict except under the influence of narcotics.

There is no expectation to "cure" the addict any more than a realistic psychotherapist *expects* to cure schizophrenia. The goals of Synanon are rather to understand the addict, provide him with adequate biological supplies (as with modest standards of food, clothing, shelter and medical care), and to help him find need-satisfying roles in a drug-free, unique community. It is to be especially noted that there is little interest in extending this addiction-free existence into the general community by "cure"; rather there is emphasis on the proliferation of more "clean-man-days" (drug-free days × number of people) for each individual within Synanon. Further, the goals of Synanon are to expand its services so as to provide for the many addicts who now remain in the community-at-large.

There are also hopes of developing a kind of professional Synanite who is trained as a leader for setting up new branches or to assume considerable responsibility within the established centers. Further, there are some wishes to improve modestly upon their creature comforts, so as to approach those of the general public.

The techniques associated with the setting have sprung from a kind of pragmatic experience without much theoretical basis. That innovations are frequent points out the fluidity of the program, best exemplified in the admission procedure. Starting out, the new member is tested for motivation by "experts" who speak his language and are intimately familiar with his background of the streets. In reality, very few have been turned down by the "reception committee." Synanon accepts almost any addict, regardless of financial status, and largely is limited by the actual physical plant's potential. It is an inexpensive therapy since the members live modestly and provide most of their necessary food and supplies through teams that "hustle" items from the local community that would otherwise be wasted or destroyed.

Once admitted, the new member breaks his habit "cold turkey" (without the assistance of drugs), and seemingly responds quite swiftly to the emotional support of his fellow members. After a few days of initial adjustment, the members are assigned work projects and become seriously involved in their daily chores under close supervision from senior members.

The process of self appraisal is intensive and encompasses all residents excluding the children. Besides attending daily luncheon sessions, which largely resemble philosophical discussion groups, the members are all required to engage in a therapeutic design, the "synanon" session. This is *leaderless* group therapy held 3 times weekly with frequent exchange of members from one group to another. Composition of the groups is determined by a senior member of Synanon. The kinds of interaction in these groups are shocking to the neophyte observer, for there is no leader to dispel the tremendously hostile assaults on individuals from some of the participants. Yet, in spite of this, or perhaps because of this, there appears to be evidence of maturation in most individuals as they continuously succeed in defending themselves over the space of time. Another important therapeutic device is the use of tape recordings regularly played for various groups within the organization. They may consist of simple doctrine from administration, play-backs of highly charged synanon sessions, or perhaps some poignant debate extracted from a high level policy meeting. Thus, in spite of the growing size of the organization, each individual somehow has frequent contact with the senior leaders and the director, as well as the policies of the organization.

It is difficult to evaluate appropriately the importance of the founder, Charles Dederich, and his principal aides. Undoubtedly, Dederich's successful battle with prejudice and political and legal obstacles has shown that he is no mere well-intentioned spiritual reformer. He is intelligent, resourceful, and a man of conviction. As well, he can be obstinate, naive and defensive. He draws information from a few professional consultants in law, psychiatry and sociology, but there is no question that the final authority for decisions rests in Dederich. Perhaps his most outstanding characteristic is his pride of accomplishment, which at times borders on grandiosity. His assistants (all ex-addicts) have strongly identified with him and are intensely loyal.

An interesting facet to the methodology of Synanon is its exhibitionistic nature. Not only has Synanon used the press and theater to educate the public and to defend itself from sincere and irrational attackers, but it has made use of the need for public contact through hundreds of speaking engagements to promote a sense of adequacy and hope into the Synanon speakers themselves. Thus, a recent former addict may soon find himself conversing with the public as an invited guest speaker, a man of achievement, rather than a pitied prisoner or "patient."

The relationship between Synanon and professionals is worthy of note. For several years there was little contact with professionals except for casual visitors. Dr. Lewis Yablonsky, a sociologist, became deeply interested and involved in Synanon as Director of Research and has become a staunch supporter. Dr. Dan Casriel was one of the first psychiatrists to probe Synanon, and his recent fascinating book, "So Fair A House," elucidates and expands on many more characteristics of Synanon. After studying Synanon through my third year of residency training with guidance from Dr. Frank Tallman, chairman of the department of social psychiatry, UCLA, I have remained to consult on a part-time basis under the auspices of the Los Angeles County Department of Mental Health. Dr. Elliot Markoff, a UCLA psychiatry resident, is also intensively involved at Synanon. Thus, there is clear evidence that interest from professionals is reciprocated to some degree. Where there was considerable initial mistrust, there is now a cautious receptivity.

Amongst the many struggles of Synanon are the legal and financial ones. Still fighting zoning restrictions in several cities, Synanon is continuously struggling for permanent property. Initial hopes for U.S. governmental land have largely been destroyed. There have been several attempts to gain NIMH research grants, but this has failed to date probably partly because of governmental conservatism and Synanon's lack of experience in application methods. There still remains the vital question as to where the financial responsibility lies for this kind of organization.

Some support has come from various states. Nevada has participated in an experiment with Synanon as a means of studying the effect of Synanon on rehabilitation of criminals. In the minds of some at Synanon there has crept a feeling that Synanon may have value in other types of antisocial behavior problems.

In a state of constant financial crisis, Synanon has reached a point where its current annual budget will approach or exceed one million dollars. Of this amount, approximately 75% comes from donated goods and services. The actual expenses are such that cash receipts of approximately three dollars will support one person for one day. To meet financial obligations, Synanon has recently undertaken several business ventures which may be profitable.

What has been achieved to date by these efforts? Of the people in residence as of January 1, 1964, there has been a total of 140,227 "clean-man-days," or 61,357 from 1963 alone. From the census of December, 1963, the following table gives a breakdown of length of residence of the members:

1 person— over 5 years	19 persons— 9-12 months
13 persons— 4-5 years	31 persons— 6-9 months
10 persons— 3-4 years	59 persons— 3-6 months
17 persons— 2-3 years	89 persons— 0-3 months
33 persons— 1-2 years	TOTAL—272

These figures do not reflect the frequency of recidivism, which is common. There have also been about 250 members who have left and never returned and presumably are back on drugs. Of course, this group would be valuable for study at some time in the future. Although always encouraged to remain within the foundation, 20 people have left Synanon as "third-stagers" (those who live and work outside of Synanon but maintain a close affiliation). This step is usually taken after one to two years of residency.

SUMMARY

Synanon is a relatively new, voluntary, private and non-profit experimental organization which has created a therapeutic program for narcotic addicts with limited goals. In a sense, a kind of unique, separate and transient society is provided for the addict wherein he can live and mature free from drugs. Struggling for existence and status, it has nevertheless provided some interesting concepts and techniques for dealing with the problems of narcotics addiction. Although Synanon has sought to maintain its identity by sometimes overlooking the efforts of other researchers in this area, it nevertheless merits considerable attention for its own methods and theoretical constructions which may hopefully evolve through scientific research.

ADDENDUM

The statistics herein have been obtained from Dr. Elliot Markoff, a coworker, who is at the Neuropsychiatric Institute, UCLA Center for the Health Sciences, Los Angeles, Calif.

From 9/1/58 to 4/1/64 Synanon has had 844 admissions, of whom 359 were still in residence at the latter date. Another 26 were in "third stage" (living and working outside of Synanon although maintaining some affiliation—but clearly "clean" of drug use). Although there has been no formal follow-up, it is felt that most who left prematurely (459) returned to drug use. This is based on the fact that practically all who left for brief periods and returned admitted drug use on the outside.

Of those who have remained, many have left prematurely for brief periods and returned to stay. In 1963, 193 "split" (2/3 of whom had less than 3 months in Synanon) but 147 of these reentered in that same year.

All those in residence are definitely "clean" during their stay. More than 25% of those who could have been eligible for 2 years in residence actually remained for at least that period.

19

INTRODUCTION TO
LOVE AND ADDICTION

Stanton Peele with Archie Brodsky

Love" and "addiction": the juxtaposition seems strange. Yet it shouldn't, for addiction has as much to do with love as it does with drugs. Many of us are addicts, only we don't know it. We turn to each other out of the same needs that drive some people to drink and others to heroin. And this kind of addiction is just as self-destructive as—and a lot more common than—those other kinds.

Ideally, love and addiction do not have anything at all to do with one another. They are polar opposites. Nothing could be further removed from genuine love—conceived as a commitment to mutual growth and fullfillment—than the desperate self-seeking dependency which, with drugs, we call addiction. Yet in practice, we tend to get them confused. We often say "love" when we really mean, and are acting out, an addiction—a sterile, ingrown dependency relationship, with another person serving as the object of our need for security. This interpersonal dependency is not *like* an addiction, not something analogous to addiction; it *is* an addiction. It is every bit as much an addiction as drug dependency.

This is in some ways a personal book. I began to write it when I observed the destructive consequences, psychological and moral, of many love relationships. I concluded that these relationships did not measure up either to the lovers' self-proclaimed ideal of love, or to what I understood love to be. As the book has broadened in scope, I have

---

developed the theme wherever possible in the form of psychological vignettes. These are fictional accounts, inspired not so much by clinical observation as by normal experience. Although fictional, the characters in these accounts are in a sense familiar to us all. As composite portrait of commonly observed patterns of behavior, they do not represent actual living individuals but instead are images of people who are trapped in addictive relationships, and people who are growing mature enough to love out of strength rather than need.

These stories depict the experience of being young in post-World War II America. They are about how the insularity of our family lives in childhood—along with the mania of our era for finding boyfriends and girlfriends, husbands and wives—conditions us to be dependent on other people. Such is the fate of mainstream Americans. True, poverty may be a cause of addiction but in the middle-class young we see that material comfort, too, may contribute to addiction. Addiction can be inescapable, when a person is denied the means to resolve his problems. It can also stem from the protection from reality that an overly supportive environment provides. In this regard, it is not accidental that many of the stories in these pages are about relatively privileged people whose maturation was delayed by long years of schooling. As much as anything else, this is a book about growing up.

In today's uncertain world, there are many people who can identify with the experience of unwise or desperate love. And there are many people who can identify with the experiences of aimlessness and self-doubt, fear and escapism. Some of these readers may find that this broadened concept of addiction gives them a concrete way to interpret their experiences. In this sense, too, *Love and Addiction* is a personal book, one whose relevance can only be accurately interpreted by each individual.

This is a book about addiction which focuses on interpersonal relationships. Its main purpose is to explore what addiction really is, psychologically, socially, and culturally. It does this in two ways—first, by showing what really happens when a person becomes dependent (or resists becoming dependent) on a drug; second, by showing how the same process may occur in other areas of our everyday lives, especially our relationships with those with whom we are most intimately involved.

The first part of this exploration is relatively straightforward, since much of it has already been done. Drug researchers like Isidor Chein, Charles Winick, and Norman Zinberg have shown convincingly that it is not drugs that addict people, but people who addict themselves. Heroin and morphine do not always produce the "physical" symptoms that we associate with addiction, while these symptoms can and do occur with other drugs such as cigarettes and coffee, depending on the user's cultural background, expectations, mood, and emotional needs. Once we have reviewed this research, all that remains is to interpret the addiction process to bring out its relevance to love and other human involvements.

For if addiction is now known *not* to be primarily a matter of drug chemistry or body chemistry, and if we therefore have to broaden our conception of dependency-treating objects to include a wider range of drugs, then why stop with drugs? Why not look at the whole range of things, activities, and even people to which we can and do become addicted? We must, in fact, do this if addiction is to be made a viable concept once again. At present, addiction as a scientific notion is falling into disuse because of the mass of contradictory data about drugs and their effects. Since people who take narcotics often do not get addicted, scientists are beginning to think that addiction does not exist. Yet, more casually, we find the word being used in an increasing number of contexts—"addicted to work," "addicted to gambling"—because it describes something real that happens to people.

Addiction does exist, and it is a large issue in human psychology. An understanding of addiction will help answer the question of why we repeatedly return to things we have done before—the question of habit. Addiction can be considered a pathological habit. It occurs with human necessities, such as food and love, as well as with things which people can do without, such as heroin and nicotine.

In other words, addiction is not something mysterious, something about which our ordinary experience has nothing to say. It is a malignant outgrowth, an extreme, unhealthy manifestation, of normal human inclinations. We can recognize examples of addiction in ourselves even when we would not characterize ourselves entirely, or even basically, as addicts. This is why the ideal of addiction can be an important tool in our self-understanding. But for its value to be realized, it must be redefined. There has to be a fundamental change in the way we think about addiction.

If we want to reformulate the concept of addiction we have to start where the concept is commonly and traditionally applied—that is, with drugs. This is a very different kind of book from, say, Wayne Oates's *Confessions of a Workaholic*, which accepts a conventional theory of drug addiction and goes on to draw an informal, semihumorous analogy to compulsive work patterns. Such a book is useful, if for no other reason than that it shows that people are beginning to use the notion of addiction to explain diverse areas of their experience. But Oates does not examine the implications of the analogy he draws. What we want to do here is not to apply an existing concept of addiction to love relationshps, but to *change* the concept. This means starting by showing how drugs really work. If we seek to establish that addiction is just as real, just as concrete when a person is the object as when a drug is the object, then we must first confront the old stereotypes of "physical addiction" and "drug addiction" that are so deeply ingrained in our thinking.

As a social psychologist dealing mainly with human relations, I first became interested in drugs when I began to see how people were misconstruing human problems as physical or biochemical problems. It soon became clear to me that our attitudes about drugs are very revealing about ourselves. This is an area where our society's uneasiness about individual autonomy is most plainly expressed. A fear of external control over people's minds and souls is at the center of our anxieties. This fear is present in all Western countries where drug use is viewed as a social problem. But America has exhibited a more extreme response to drugs, especially the opiates, than any other country in the world, precisely because it feels the severest conflict over the impossibility of living out a traditional ideal of personal initiative.

What we think drugs do influences what they can do, and so by studying drugs we learn about our attitudes toward ourselves. Questions of self-mastery and mastery over the environment provide the key to the susceptibility to addiction; when we think of drugs as overpowering, it is because we doubt our own psychological strength. The social history of American's evolving reactions to mind-altering drugs, even drugs such as marijuana and LSD which are not regarded as "addictive," tells us a lot about how we view our own strength as individuals and as a society. It tells us, in other words, about our predisposition to give ourselves over to addiction—to drugs, to people, to anything.

Interpersonal addiction—love addiction—is just about the most common, yet least recognized, form of addiction. Highlighting it helps us break down the stereotype of the "drug addict" and arrive at a better understanding of the way addiction affects us all. On the other side, the antithesis of addiction is a true relatedness to the world, and there is no more powerful expression of that relatedness than love, or true responsiveness to another person.

The issue of love versus addiction is one that is very close to our lives, and thus one that we can do something about as individuals.

The environment that is most important to us is the human one. This is why, when we get addicted, we tend to get addicted to people. Similarly, our best hope of breaking out of addiction is by learning better ways of dealing with people. This is true not only for romantic involvements but also for family ties and friendships.

Our families have a tremendous impact on our addictive, or nonaddictive, potential, since they teach us either self-confidence or helplessness, self-sufficiency or dependency. Outside the family, much of our modern social environment takes the form of organizations, such as schools. Our experiences with such institutions can instill in us serious doubts about our capacity to manage our own lives, let alone to interact creatively with the rest of the world. And in reality, they may keep us from developing that capacity to the fullest. Here is where the impulse toward escape and dependency arises. One of the best things we can do to safeguard ourselves against addiction, therefore, is to understand how our social environment affects us and to develop the internal strength to become something more than creatures of society.

Addiction is not a chemical reaction. Addiction is an *experience*—one which grows out of an individual's routinized subjective response to something that has special meaning for him—something, anything, that he finds so safe and reassuring that he cannot be without it. If we want to come to terms with addiction, we have to stop blaming drugs and start looking at people, at ourselves, and at what makes us dependent. We still find that we learn habits of dependence by growing up in a culture which teaches a sense of personal inadequacy, a reliance on external bulwarks, and a preoccupation with the negative or painful rather than the positive or joyous.

Addiction is not an abnormality in our society. It is not an aberration from the norm; it is itself the norm. The dependency which is addiction is a mirror-image of more basic dependencies that we learn at home and in school. The addict's search for a superficial, external resolution of life (whether through drugs or so-called "love") follows directly from the superficial, external relationships we are led to have with each other, with our own minds and bodies, with the physical world, with learning and work and play. Those young people who suddenly repudiate convention and seek solace in drugs, or a religious commune, are only expressing tendencies that were always present in acceptable guises in their home and school lives.

Excessive parental supervision, artificial criteria for learning, and a reverential attiude toward established institutions, such as organized medicine—along with other cultural influences—combine to leave us without moorings in our direct daily experience. What can be done to combat this widespread addictive drift? We can start by gathering tools of self-analysis, developing criteria for assessing our personal involvements, and raising questions that may not ordinarily occur to us. Asking whether a certain kind of "love" may in fact be an addiction can be the first step toward reexamining and restructuring a life.

The progression of this book moves outward from the small to the large: from the effects of drugs to a portrait of the addict as a person, then to relationships between two people, then to the social causes of addiction, and finally to the possibilities for personal growth and social change. Our aim is greater self-awareness and self-realization. By its very nature, addiction is easier to diagnose than to cure. Since a reliance on simple, universal solutions to life is the problem we are dealing with, any resort to a similar program for curing it would just amount to replacing one addiction with another, something addicts do all the time. Since the problem stems from a lack of secure underpinnings in life—from a paucity of life experience, contentment, and self-fulfillment—any real solution will of necessity be a complex one. Such a solution will certainly entail the development of internal capacities—interests, joys, competencies—to counteract the desire for escape and self-obliteration. It means wanting and having, something to offer another person. For love is made possible by an integrity of being in two individuals who come together to share, not out of passive dependence but out of surety and strength.

Section IV

BEHAVIORAL APPROACHES TO ADDICTION

During the early 1960s, an alternative model of psychopathology was gaining acceptance and popularity. This behavioral approach viewed psychopathology as a learned set of dysfunctional behaviors rather than as a result of deep-seated psychological trauma or physical illness. Behavioral treatment involves applying procedures and techniques derived from known principles of learning to modify, reduce, or eliminate maladaptive behavior and foster the acquisition of more adaptive behavior patterns. Within this *Zeitgeist,* Wikler's 1965 chapter on conditioning factors in opiate addiction and relapse emerged. This paper was the first to consider the roles of instrumental and classical conditioning in addiction; also, Wikler preceded contemporary cognitive-behavior modification theorists and practitioners by analyzing the relationship between cognitive and behavioral phenomena. Wikler carefully examined and considered the mediating role of cognitions in the acquisition and maintenance of addictive behavior patterns. Consequently, Wikler's view of the addict was one of an active, self-determining individual who was not simply a victim of circumstance or conditioning. Addicts were human beings with feelings, thoughts, motives, and ideas, all of which were considered to come into play during the acquisition, maintenance, and extinction of addictive behavior.

Specifically, Wikler's position foreshadowed contemporary research by indicating that euphoria and fear of withdrawal were not sufficient to account for heroin addiction. Wikler also made the distinction between reinforcement which is a result of the reinforcing properties of the drug (pharmacological reinforcement) and reinforcement which is indirect, i.e., not contingent upon drug usage.

Wikler's papers are supported by data obtained in the animal laboratory. Since the generalization of this type of data to humans can be considered equivocal, at best, Wikler's propositions are in need of additional empirical support. Nevertheless, by considering addiction as a

337

"learned phenomenon," Wikler's formulations permit the development and implementation of precise treatment techniques, e.g., extinguishing specific conditioned responses which maintain addictive behavior patterns. Interestingly, however, few practitioners have implemented treatment programs based on the sophisticated theoretical perspectives provided by Wikler. It may be that his formulations were too complex for most practitioners to utilize within the typical treatment setting. Wikler's consideration and theoretical inclusion of the perceptual, cognitive, and internal events which mediate behavior placed his "conditioning approach" twenty years ahead of its contemporary counterparts in cognitive-behavioral psychological theory.

Crowley's paper carefully examines the role of "reinforcer" during the use of a variety of drugs. In particular, he clarifies the differences between (1) primary positive and negative reinforcement and (2) secondary positive and negative reinforcement. Further, he distinguishes the concept of negative reinforcement from punishment—two often confused concepts. Crowley does not emphasize the cognitive or neural mechanisms underlying the conditioning process to the extent that Wikler does; however, Crowley's work illustrates the differential reinforcing properties of a variety of drug classes.

Gilbert's work differs dramatically from Crowley's since Gilbert postulates that drug abuse may not have much to do with pharmacology. Moreover, Gilbert's position is more traditionally behavioristic because he persuasively offers a rationale and framework within which drug abuse can be considered to be rooted in the development of excessive behaviors, like any other excessive behavior, without having to infer psychopathology and disease.

Reviews of the behavioral literature (Callner, 1975; Krasnegor, 1980) have found that treatment approaches based on this perspective have mixed efficacy. Specifically, aversive conditioning approaches (e.g., electric shock, chemical aversion, covert sensitization) have had some mixed success but concurrently generate major ethical and medical risk concerns for potential patients. Conversely, the social learning approaches (e.g., stimulus control, contingency management, controlled use, multicomponent programs) appear to be the most promising in a wide variety of applications and appear "to be the direction to take, given the encouraging results" (Krasnegor, 1980, p. 48).

REFERENCES

CALLNER, D. A. Behavioral treatment approaches to drug abuse: A critical review of the research. *Psychological Bulletin*, 1975, *82*, 143-164.
KRASNEGOR, N. A. Analysis and modification of substance abuse: A behavioral overview. *Behavior Modification*, 1980, *4*, 35-56.

20

CONDITIONING FACTORS IN OPIATE ADDICTION AND RELAPSE

Abraham Wikler

THEORETICAL CONSIDERATIONS

In achieving an impressive degree of mastery over the world about us, the growth of the natural sciences has been characterized by an ever-increasing supplementation of "private operations" (sensing, feeling, inducing, deducing) with "public" ones (control and manipulation of measurable variables). As one result, even our "private" ways of perceiving the world have changed from those of our prescientific ancestors, so that at sunset, we no longer "see" the sun sinking into the sea, but "see" it disappearing beneath the horizon.

Such subtle but far-reaching changes have also occurred in our dealings with our hearts, livers, and kidneys, but in dealing with our own and other people's behaviors, most of us are still content with mentalistic explanations, the terms of which, "private" as they are, remain undefined though they may be quantified in the sense of counting the frequency of their occurrence in one or another situation. This mentalistic orientation has characterized most attempts to describe and explain drug (including opiate) addiction and relapse no less than other forms of deviant human behavior. In consequence, the clinician has tended to accept his patient's mentalistic interpretation of his addiction and his frequent relapses to drugs as a valid one—for who else would know better what his feelings are than the patient himself? And does not one

Reprinted with permission from *Narcotics*, edited by D. I. Wilner and G. G. Kassebaum, New York: McGraw-Hill, 1965, 85-100.

behave in accordance with one's feelings? To be sure, the psychoanalysts have often answered both questions in the negative, designating the patient's verbally expressed feelings as "conscious," and their own dissenting conscious feelings about the patient's feelings as "unconscious" ones of the patient. This certainly represents a commendable attempt to break out of the solipsistic straitjacket which, had it been allowed to restrain Columbus, would have left us convinced that the earth is flat because we "see" it that way. Unfortunately, however, the psychoanalyst's explanations of human behavior, including drug addiction and relapse, are also couched in mentalistic terms and hence cannot be tested for validity in the accepted manner of the natural sciences—i.e., by use of "public" operations, at least directly.

Possibly for these reasons, the clinician's interests in the problem of drug addiction and relapse have been focused on the occurrence of drug-induced "euphoria." It has been debated whether or not morphine, heroin, and other narcotic drugs (henceforth, morphine will be used as a prototype) produce euphoria in all persons or only in atypical or deviant ones (16, 21), but few have ventured to question the decisive importance of euphoria as the main determinant of the addict's behavior, both in his initial addiction and in his subsequent relapses—for this is also the addict's explanation. Likewise in agreement with the addict, clinicians have generally regarded morphine-induced physical dependence merely as an unpleasant complication, serving as a deterrent rather than as a motivating factor in relapse, for who but a masochist would see any virtue in those properties of a drug that produced "the agonies of the damned" when withheld after long-continued use?

The present writer would not deny that certain effects of single doses of morphine may be decisive in determining the initial *choice* of that drug from among many other "euphorogenic" agents for continued use by some persons. Indeed, in collaboration with several colleagues (9, 10, 15, 11, 7, 8) he has presented data acquired by "public" operations indicating one class of effects of morphine on nontolerant postaddicts, which theoretically at least may play such a role—namely, reduction of the influence on behavior of motivating variables in general, and of nociceptive ones in particular, but whether or not such effects have anything to do with euphoria is indeterminable and, in this writer's opinion, quite irrelevant. Of more importance would be the development of methods for testing the hypothesis that, other factors being equal, any drug possessing such effects, regardless of whether or not it also produces euphoria, would be chosen for repeated use by the same kind of person who uses morphine in this manner.

Be this as it may, however, the writer has stated reasons for doubting the prevailing opinion that the quest for euphoria and the fear of abstinence distress are responsible for self-maintenance of addiction to morphine (25, 27). Mainly, these are three: (1) tolerance to the euphoric effect of morphine develops quickly and is not achieved again in anything like the intensity of the initial effect despite progressive increase in dosage; (2) even with unlimited supplies of the drug and the privilege of self-injection in amounts and at intervals ad libitum, the addict, at least under experimental conditions, is a miserable creature, beset by remorse, guilt, and anxiety; and finally (3) there appears to be no adequate reason why experienced addicts cannot withdraw themselves in a relatively painless manner either by gradual reduction of dosage or substitution and subsequent withdrawal of methadone. In mentalistic terms, the conclusion drawn from these considerations and other subjective data gathered in a study of a patient during self-regulated readdiction to morphine (25) was that the motivations for self-maintenance of addiction in man are largely unconscious ones, above all the gratification by each dose of morphine of the need for the drug engendered by physical dependence. Furthermore, it was suggested (27) that "being hooked" furnishes the addict with a motivational basis for sustained activity ("hustling for drugs") directed to recurring but attainable goals, thereby preventing boredom and also securing approval from his peers, i.e., "addict society."

Likewise, the writer has doubted that the quest for euphoria constitutes the only, or even the major, motivation to relapse, in spite of the addict's conscious insistence thereon, for the acceptance of such an explanation would entail acceptance of the improbable assumption that the addict "remembers" only the euphoric effects of the first few doses of morphine and "forgets" the months or years of misery experienced during addiction. Rather, statements occasionally made by postaddicts to the effect that they have experienced symptoms resembling those of acute abstinence from morphine long after withdrawal of the drug (26) led the author to hypothesize that physical dependence may become conditioned to environmental situations specifically associated with availability of morphine, and hence "abstinence distress," or something very much like it, may be reactivated long after "cure" when the postaddict finds himself in a similar situation, thus providing an unconscious motivation to relapse and renewed self-maintenance of addiction as described above (24).

Another way in which relapse might come about as a result of conditioning was suggested by Kolb (14) in the following terms:

> The addict, even if he has sufficient narcotics, becomes uncomfortable several times a day when the last dose wears down.

If another dose is not available, he suffers acute distress in about 18 hours. Over a period of years, he relieves such discomfort or distress thousands of times by injection of morphine. During this same period he enjoys the drug in pleasurable association with friends and by taking it to get the effect that many of them describe by the statement, "It makes my troubles roll off my mind." By thus building up a strong association between pleasure and pain and the taking of a narcotic he becomes conditioned to taking one in response to most any situation that may arise.

Expressed for the most part in mentalistic terms, the validity of such speculations is difficult, if not impossible, to test directly, but to those who are familiar with behavioristic-conditioning theory, their similarity to certain concepts definable in terms of "public" operations should be apparent. Restating the writer's views in such terms (28, 29), relapse may be attributed at least in part to two factors operating during previous episodes of addiction: (1) classical conditioning of physical dependence through repeated temporal contiguities between a specific environment and the occurrence of morphine-abstinence phenomena; and (2) reinforcement of instrumental activity (morphine-acquisitory behavior) through repeated reduction by the drug of such abstinence phenomena as developed during intervals between doses. This "two-factor learning theory" of relapse could be expanded further by introduction of some additional concepts such as "secondary reinforcement," "drive (or stimulus) generalization," and "scheduling" of reinforcement for the purpose of redefining and testing other factors in the genesis of relapse already described in mentalistic terms, but only brief allusions to these concepts will be made in this paper because actual research to date has been confined to investigation of factors 1 and 2.

EXPERIMENTAL INVESTIGATIONS

Though some of the consequences of the two-factor learning theory of relapse may eventually be testable in man, both ethical and practical considerations require the use of animals for direct testing of the conditionability of physical dependence and the putatively reinforcing processes operating during addiction. With regard to the latter, similar hypotheses and data bearing upon them have been reported by Nichols et al. (19), Nichols and Davis (18), and Davis and Nichols (2), who employed forced drinking of dilute (0.5 mg per ml) aqueous solutions of morphine under water-deprivation conditions for reinforcement of "choice" drinking of the same solution by morphine-abstinent rats; by

Headlee et al. (6), who reinforced head turning in a particular direction by making intraperitoneal injection of morphine contingent upon this operant in morphine-abstinent rats; by Beach (1), who reinforced running of rats to one arm of a Y maze by establishing temporal contiguity between "residence" in that arm and presumed reduction of morphine-abstinence phenomena there by prior intraperitoneal injection of morphine; by Weeks (22) and Weeks and Collins (23), who developed a technique for self-maintenance of addiction through intravenous (intra-cardiac) self-injection of morphine in rats; and by Yanagita et al. (32) and by Schuster and Thompson (20), who utilized a similar method for reinforcing intravenous self-injection of morphine in monkeys.

In our own investigations (carried out exclusively in the rat so far) we circumvented difficulties encountered with forced drinking of morphine solutions or parenteral injections of morphine *for reinforcement* by use of a relatively new drug, etonitazene [1-(beta-diethylaminoethyl)-2-(*p*-ethoxybenzyl)-5-nitrobenzimidazole methane sulfonate] in very dilute aqueous solution for drinking. Though structurally unrelated to morphine (13) it has been shown to be 1,000 times as potent as morphine by parenteral injection for analgesia in the rat (5) and to have morphine-like effects not only in this species but also in monkey and man, in both of which it has been shown to suppress morphine-abstinence phenomena as well (3, 4). Preliminary studies (30) revealed that water-deprived rats would drink a 5 mcg per ml concentration of etonitazene in distilled water as avidly as tap water and that within 4 to 7 min after starting to drink, normal rats would show typical morphinelike effects (tail rigidity, exophthalmos, and stupor alternating with quick, jerky movements). This was also true for rats acutely (18 hr) abstinent from morphine, in which drinking of this solution also abolished an easily observable sign of abstinence, namely, increased frequency of "wet-dog" shakes (so-called because of their resemblance to those of a dog shaking water off its back). Later it was found that rats, morphine-addicted or not, will readily drink such dilute aqueous solutions of etonitazene even without any prior water deprivation, thus eliminating the necessity of introducing that condition as a complicating variable in the design of experiments on conditioning and reinforcement.

Because of these promising early results, more systematic investigations (17, 31) were then undertaken to characterize as precisely as possible the phenomena of the morphine abstinence syndrome in the rat, and the effects thereon of drinking dilute aqueous solutions of etonitazene, without prior water deprivation. Those results bearing most directly on the conditioning and reinforcement studies to be described later may be summarized as follows:

1. Elevated wet-dog frequencies are reliable indicators of early morphine abstinence in the rat, roughly paralleling other signs of early abstinence such as increased activity, hypothermia, loss of body weight, and increased defecation, urination, and hostility—all compared with observations made concurrently on normal control rats.

2. In rats maintained on single intraperitoneal injections of morphine at 8 A.M. daily (E's),* increased wet-dog frequencies, as well as other early abstinence phenomena, become manifest at least as early as 22 to 24 hr after the last previous injection of morphine.

3. When E's are permitted to drink a 10 mcg per ml aqueous solution of etonitazene instead of water over the preceding 17-hr period, no significant differences from normal rats receiving single intraperitoneal injections of saline at 8 A.M. daily (C's)* can be found on comparison 22 to 24 hours after the last previous injections.

4. Whereas E's drink very much larger volumes of 5 or 10 mcg per ml aqueous solutions of etonitazene than they do of water when only one or the other fluid is available from 3 P.M. to 8 A.M. next morning (during the latter part of which period E's are morphine-abstinent), the volumes of water or etonitazene consumed by C's during the same period under the same conditions are not significantly different (though one of a group of 4 C's died after drinking the 10 mcg per ml drug solution).

In light of this information, the studies on conditioning of physical dependence and reinforcement of drug-acquisitory behavior were designed in the following manner. Experimental conditions were arranged in such a way that over a 6-week "training" period, the occurrence of nocturnal morphine-abstinence phenomena in E's ($N = 7$) was repeatedly associated with "residence" in one (preferred) end of a three-compartment linear maze, where only distilled water was available for drinking, and relief from nocturnal morphine-abstinence phenomena was associated with "residence" in the other (nonpreferred) end, where only a 10 mcg per ml aqueous solution of etonitazene was available for drinking, the drug solution being also "tagged" with anise flavor to provide additional discriminative cues (food was available ad libitum in both ends at all times). Another group of E's ($N = 7$) was "trained" in exactly the same manner except that the drinking fluid in the nonpreferred end consisted only of anise-flavored water, and both training schedules were replicated concurrently for two groups of C's ($N = 7$ each) except that for the first of these two groups, the anise-flavored etonitazene solution contained 5 mcg per ml of that drug. For convenience, the four groups will be designated in the order described as ET, ENT, CT, and CNT.

_____

*E, "experimental animals"; C, "control animals."

Following the training period, all injections were terminated, and all rats were transferred to home cages (food and tap water ad libitum), where they remained thenceforth except on "relapse" and other test days conducted at intervals up to 155 days after termination of injections. On the morning of each relapse test day (9, 23, 44, 58, 72, 87, 94, and 142 days after termination of injections) wet-dog frequencies for each rat were measured immediately after removal from home cage, weighing, and returning to home cage, and also immediately after removal from home cage, weighing, and placing in the linear maze (preferred end), in alternate order from rat to rat; from 8 P.M. the same day to 8 A.M. next morning, each rat was afforded "free choice" between distilled water in the preferred and an anise-flavored, 5 mcg per ml aqueous solution of etonitazene in the nonpreferred end of its linear maze. Between the seventh (94th day of abstinence) and eighth (142d day) relapse tests, two successive extinction procedures were carried out. In the first free choice was permitted between distilled water in the preferred and anise-flavored water in the nonpreferred end, and in the second, between distilled water in both ends. In addition, six tests on forced drinking, without prior water deprivation, were made on all rats from 8 P.M. to 8 A.M. at intervals throughout the study—four on forced drinking of the anise-flavored 5 mcg per ml aqueous solution of etonitazene, one of the anise-flavored water, and one of the distilled water, each in the nonpreferred end. The purpose of these tests was to provide comparative data on how much each rat would drink of each of the fluids mentioned "by constraint" (forced-drinking tests) and "by choice" (relapse tests). Finally, a supplementary study was also carried out on four new E's and four new C's in which both groups were trained over a 9-day period in a manner similar to that already described for ENT and CNT, and then subjected, 9 and 23 days after termination of injections, to relapse tests conducted exactly as described above, except that the fluid in the nonpreferred end was only anise-flavored water, to determine whether or not previous addiction to morphine results in an increased affinity of rats for the anise flavor per se.

Considered in relation to the theory, the results were as follows:

1. Classical Conditioning of Physical Dependence. On every relapse test, wet-dog frequencies of E's (ET + ENT) were higher in the linear mazes than in the home cages, and although on some tests wet-dog frequencies of C's (CT + CNT) changed in the same direction, the magnitude of change was less. A mixed type of analysis of variance revealed that on the second relapse test (23 days abstinent from injections), F ratios for variances due to previous treatment (E's vs. C's), test conditions (linear maze vs. home cage), and "interactions" (E's vs. C's linear maze vs. home cage) were all significant. On the first relapse test

(9 days) only one, but on the third (44 days), fourth (58 days), and fifth (72 days), two of the three F ratios were significant. All three F ratios were again significant when the analysis was made on means obtained for each rat on twelve tests (including the sixth, seventh, and eighth relapse tests as well as the single-day tests during the extinction procedures) from the 84th through the 155th days of abstinence.

Especially significant theoretically is that such presumptive evidence of "conditioned abstinence" was manifested by E's long after "cure"—i.e., after body weight, 24-hr tap-water consumption (home cage), and wet-dog frequencies *in the home cage* had returned to the levels of C's (from the 23d day of abstinence onward, although through the 72nd day, wet-dog frequencies of E's were generally slightly higher than in C's). As between ET and ENT, or between CT and CNT, no significant differences in wet-dog frequencies were found.

2. Reinforcement of Instrumental Activity (Drug-acquisitory Behavior). In each of the first four relapse tests (through the 58th day of abstinence) and again on the eighth (142d day) relapse test (after completion of the extinction procedures), the percentage of fluids consumed in the form of anise-flavored etonitazene solution (5 mcg per ml) by choice was significantly greater for E's (ET + ENT) than for C's (CT + CNT) by the Mann-Whitney "U" test. The ratios, volumes of the anise-flavored etonitazene solution consumed by constraint to those consumed by choice, were about 8:3 for E's and 5:1 for C's at 9 to 10 days, and about 2:1 for E's and approaching infinity (almost zero consumption of the drug solution) for C's at 142 to 155 days of abstinence. In the supplementary study, the percentage of fluids consumed in the form of anise-flavored water on the two relapse tests (9 and 23 days abstinent) was *less* for E's than for C's, though the difference was significant only on the first test. These results indicate that the greater intake of anise-flavored etonitazene solution by E's than by C's in the first four and in the eighth relapse tests cannot be explained merely as a reflection of "residual cross-tolerance" (between morphine and etonitazene) in E's or of a greater affinity of E's for anise flavor per se. Rather, the data suggest that relative to C's, etonitazene solution is less negatively (or more positively) reinforcing for E's, even long after cure. Not predicted by theory, however, were the findings that the etonitazene solution was reinforcing to equal degrees for ET and ENT on the first relapse test, and that whereas such reinforcement continued with little change for the ENT group, it fell progressively for the ET group over the next four relapse tests. These observations suggest that such "self-training" as the ENT rats may have undergone during the 12-hr (8 P.M. to 8 A.M.) free choice drinking period in the first relapse test could have been sufficient for

maximal positive reinforcement; whereas the forced drinking of the anise-flavored drug solution which the ET group underwent in the programmed training period could have produced, in addition, some negative reinforcement based on pharmacologic properties of etonitazene other than morphine-abstinence reducing ones. Presumably, the negatively reinforcing properties of etonitazene were even more pronounced for the CT and CNT groups, since they were resistant to the extinction procedures, whereas the latter were effective for the ET and for the ENT group as well, which likewise exhibited evidence of negative reinforcement on the sixth and seventh relapse tests.

DISCUSSION

Though the data are consistent with the two-factor learning theory of relapse, this conclusion must be a tentative one at present, because the experiments described have not ruled out with assurance the possibility that the differences between E's and C's in the relapse tests were due to latent but long-enduring hyperirritability in the former as a result of previous addiction to morphine, rather than to the putative interactions between morphine abstinence and the specified stimulus arrangements in the linear mazes during training. While the low frequencies of wet dogs in the home cage on the relapse tests would seem to rule out such a possibility, they were somewhat higher in E's than in C's through the 72d day of abstinence as already noted, and in an earlier study (17) rats withdrawn from morphine at a final "stabilization" dose level of 360 mg/kg per day showed small but consistent differences from control rats for 4 to 6 months. Conceivably, therefore, the duration of time over which relapse tests in the present study were made may not have been sufficient to reveal the effects of conditioning and reinforcement during training as such.

These two interpretations (alternative or combined) of the data have a number of different consequences for further research and therapy in man. Thus, if the behavior of E's (compared with C's) in relapse tests was due only to residual hyperirritability, then the method of morphine withdrawal in the treatment of human addicts is not a crucial issue, provided it is sufficiently painless to ensure the addict's cooperation. Rather, the problem is to determine the exact physiological nature and the duration of such residual hyperirritability and to devise methods of treatment to shorten or control it by pharmacologic or other means. By use of the cold pressor test, Himmelsbach (12) was able to show that the autonomic reactivity of postaddicts is slightly greater than that of normal subjects for over 6 months after withdrawal of morphine. It is conceivable that with more refined techniques, differences of this sort would be revealed for even longer periods. If such proves to be the case, currently prevailing methods of treatment—withdrawal of morphine by substitution and subsequent withdrawal of methadone, supervised abstention from drugs of all kinds in a drug-free environment for as long a period of time as is practicable combined with institutional and postinstitutional psychotherapy and social rehabilitative measures—would need to be modified only in details, not in principle.

If, on the other hand, the behavior of E's relative to C's in the relapse tests was due to conditioning and reinforcing procedures employed during training, then the implications of the experimental results for the drug-withdrawal phase of treatment in man are quite far-reaching, for methods would have to be devised for extinguishing "conditioned abstinence" and reinforced drug-acquisitory behavior. This is not accomplished by *passive* withdrawal of, and prolonged abstention from, morphine in a "drug-free environment" with or without nonspecific psychotherapy, any more than satiating a rat with food and keeping it away from the Skinner box for a period of time will "cure" it of its lever-pressing "habit," previously reinforced by food rewards under conditions of food deprivation. Rather, true extinction of both processes would require an attack on each separately in reverse order under very different conditions. Thus, extinction of morphine-acquisitory behavior would require maintenance of the state of morphine deprivation, i.e. prolongation of the abstinence syndrome by some means passively, coupled with non-reinforcement of instrumental *activity* directed toward (unsuccessful) acquisition of the drug. Practical realization of such an extinction procedure would depend on the development of at least two new drugs, namely, one which if substituted for morphine would produce on abrupt withdrawal a prolonged, though not necessarily severe, abstinence syndrome, and another which, though not effective in suppressing abstinence phenomena produced by withdrawal of the first drug, would be sufficiently reinforcing on other grounds so that the addict would "work" for it on some schedule of reinforcement proven to be optimal by experiment. Of necessity, this phase of treatment would have to be carried out in an institution where, after its completion and withdrawal of the abstinence-maintaining drug, therapy could be directed toward elimination of the hypothetical residual hyperirritability discussed above.

In addition, some elementary principles of reinforcement therapy could be applied to what may be called "positive reconditioning" of the patient while he is still in the institution. This refers to scheduling of rewards for "work therapy." Monetary payment for socially useful work in crafts and industries within the institution would serve more effectively than verbal reinforcement for supplanting physical dependence on narcotic drugs as a motivational basis for "hustling" especially if such payment is made on a piecework (fixed ratio) schedule, and opportunities are provided for spending part of the wages for objects (other than drugs) that are immediately satisfying to the patient.

Ideally, however, extinction of conditioned physical dependence should be carried out in the addict's natural "drug-available" environment, so that he could be exposed to that conditioned stimulus and the secondary reinforcers (addict society) repeatedly, provided that the hoped-for extinction of drug-acquisitory behavior previously carried out in the institution, coupled with close surveillance and, if necessary, appropriate nonnarcotic pharmacologic therapy and psychotherapy for suppression of conditioned abstinence and reduction of anxieties probably involving the same physiologic systems (stimulus or drive generalization) is sufficiently effective to ensure against reexposure to the unconditioned response, namely morphine-abstinence phenomena generated by readdiction.

These speculations have been presented not for the purpose of recommending immediate changes in our treatment programs for addicts but to illustrate how restatement of some mentalistic concepts about drug addiction and relapse in behavioristic terms may enable us to test their validity by experiment. Though, as stated, the role of conditioning factors in morphine addiction and relapse is not yet fully elucidated, the "public" operations by which they may be are quite readily discernible, and further research along the lines indicated may yet enable us to deal with these clinical problems more effectively than heretofore.

REFERENCES

1. BEACH, H. D.: Morphine Addiction in Rats, *Can. J. Psychol.*, 11:104 (1957).
2. DAVIS, W. M. & NICHOLS, J. R.: Physical Dependence and Sustained Opiate-directed Behavior in the Rat: A Preliminary Report, *Psychopharmacologia*, 3:139 (1962).
3. DENEAU, G. A., MCCARTHY, D. A., & SEEVERS, M. H.: Physical Dependence Liability Studies in the Monkey, Add. I, Min. 20th Meeting, Committee on Drug Addiction and Narcotics, National Research Council, Washington, D.C., National Academy of Sciences, 10-11 January, 1959.
4. FRASER, H. F., ISBELL, H., & WOLBACH, A. B., Jr.: Addictiveness of New Synthetic Analgesics, Add. 2, Min. 21st Meeting, Committee on Drug Addiction and Narcotics, National Research Council, Washington, D.C., National Academy of Sciences, 11-12 January, 1960.
5. GROSS, R., & TURRIAN, H.: Ueber Benzimidazolderivate mit starker analgetischer Wirkung, *Experientia*, 13:401 (1957).
6. HEADLEE, C. P., COPPOCK, H. W., & NICHOLS, J. R.: Apparatus and Technique Involved in a Laboratory Method of Detecting Addictiveness of Drugs, *J. Am. Pharm. Assoc., Sci. Ed.*, 44:229 (1955).

7. HILL, H. E., BELLEVILLE, R. E., & WIKLER, A.: Studies on Anxiety Associated with Anticipation of Pain: II. Comparative Effects of Pentobarbital and Morphine, *A.M.A. Arch. Neurol. Psychiat.*, 73:602 (1955).
8. HILL, H. E., BELLEVILLE, R. E., & WIKLER, A.: Motivational Determinants in Modification of Behavior by Morphine and Pentobartibal, *A.M.A. Arch. Neurol. Psychiat.*, 77:28 (1957).
9. HILL, H. E., FLANARY, H. G., KORNETSKY, C. H., & WIKLER, A.: Relationship of Electrically Induced Pain to the Amperage and the Wattage of Shock Stimuli, *J. Clin. Invest.*, 31:464 (1952).
10. HILL, H. E. KORNETSKY, C. H., FLANARY, H. G., & WIKLER, A.: Studies on Anxiety Associated with Anticipation of Pain: I. Effects of Morphine, *A.M.A. Arch. Neurol. Psychiat.*, 67:612 (1952).
12. HIMMELSBACH, C. K.: Studies on the Relation of Drug Addiction to the Autonomic Nervous System: Results of Cold Pressor Tests, *J. Pharmacol. Exp. Therap.*, 73:91 (1941).
13. HUNGER, A. J., KEHRLE, J., ROSSI, A., & HOFFMAN, H.: Synthese basisch substituirter, analgetisch wirksamer Benzimidazolderivate, *Experientia*, 13:401 (1957).
14. KOLB, L.: Drug Addiction As a Public Health Problem, *Sci. Monthly*, 48:391 (1939).
15. KORNETSKY, C. H.: Effects of Anxiety and Morphine on the Anticipation and Perception of Painful Radiant Thermal Stimuli, *J. Comp. and Physiol. Psychol.*, 47:130 (1954).
16. LASAGNA, L., VON FELSINGER, J. M., & BEECHER, H. K.: Drug Induced Changes in Man: I. Observations on Healthy Subjects, Chronically Ill Patients and "Post-addicts," *J. Am. Med. Assoc.*, 157:1006 (1955).
17. MARTIN, W. R., WIKLER, A., EADES, C. G., & PESCOR, F. T.: Tolerance to and Physical Dependence on Morphine in Rats (abstract), *Pharmacologist*, 4:154 (1962).
18. NICHOLS, J. R. and DAVIS, W. M.: Drug Addiction: II. Variation of Addiction, *J. Am. Pharm. Assoc., Sci. Ed.*, 48:259 (1959).
19. NICHOLS, J. R., HEADLEE, C. P., & COPPOCK, H. W.: Drug Addiction: I. Addiction by Escape Training, *J. Am. Pharm. Assoc., Sci. Ed.*, 44:229 (1955).
20. SCHUSTER, C. R., & THOMPSON, T.: A Technique for Studying Self-administration of opiates in Rhesus Monkeys, presented at 25th Meeting, Committee on Drug Addiction and Narcotics, National Academy of Sciences, National Research Council, Ann Arbor, Mich., 16 February, 1963.
21. VON FELSINGER, J. M., LASAGNA, L., & BEECHER, H. K.: Drug Induced Changes in Man: 2. Personality and Reactions to Drugs, *J. Am. Med. Assoc.*, 157:1113 (1955).
22. WEEKS, J. R.: Experimental Morphine Addiction: Method for Automatic Intravenous Injections in Unrestrained Rats, *Science*, 138:143 (1962).
23. WEEKS, J. R., & COLLINS, R. J.: Some Factors Affecting Performance of Self-maintained Addict Rats, presented at 25th Meeting, Committee on Drug Addiction and Narcotics, National Research Council, National Academy of Sciences, Ann Arbor, Mich., 16 February, 1963.
24. WIKLER, A.: Recent Progress in Research on the Neurophysiological Basis of Morphine Addiction, *Am. J. Psychiat.*, 105:329 (1948).
25. WIKLER, A.: A Psychodynamic Study of a Patient during Self-regulated Readdiction to Morphine, *Psychiat. Quart.*, 26:270 (1952).
26. WIKLER, A.: "Opiate Addiction: Psychological and Neurophysiological Aspects in Relation to Clinical Problems," Charles C. Thomas, Publisher, Springfield, Ill., 1953.
27. WIKLER, A.: Rationale of the Diagnosis and Treatment of Addiction, *Conn. State Med. J.*, 19:560 (1955).
28. WIKLER, A.: Mechanisms of Action of Opiates and Opiate Antagonists, Public Health Monograph, no. 52, Government Printing Office, Washington, D.C., 1958.
29. WIKLER, A.: On the Nature of Addiction and Habituation, *Brit. J. Addict.*, 57:73 (1961).
30. WIKLER, A., GREEN, P. C., SMITH, H. D., & PESCOR, F. T.: Use of a Dilute Aqueous Solution (5 mcg/ml) of a Benzimidazole Derivative with Potent Morphine-like Actions Orally As a Presumptive Reinforcing Agent in Conditioning of Drug-seeking Behavior in Rats (abstract), *Federation Proc.*, 19:22 (1960).

31. WIKLER, A., MARTIN, W. R., PESCOR, F. T., & EADES, C. G.: Factors Regulating Oral Consumption of Etonitazene Solution by Morphine-addicted Rats (abstract), *Pharmacologist*, 4:154 (1962).
32. YANAGITA, T., DENEAU, G. A., & SEEVERS, M. H.: Physical Dependence to Opiates in the Monkey, with Demonstration, Presented at 25th Meeting, Committee on Drug Addiction and Narcotics, National Research Council, National Academy of Sciences, Ann Arbor, Mich., 16 February, 1963.

21

DYNAMICS OF DRUG DEPENDENCE: IMPLICATIONS OF A CONDITIONING THEORY FOR RESEARCH AND TREATMENT

Abraham Wikler

Though usually initiated through social reinforcement, self-administration of psychoactive drugs (SAPD) is soon reinforced pharmacologically through suppression (by each successive dose) of a homeostatic need generated by successive central counteradaptive changes (CCCs) that develop unconditionally in response to the initial (receptor site) actions of such drugs and their "reflex" consequences (signs of drug effects). Temporal contiguity between pharmacological reinforcement and recurring exteroceptive and interceptive stimuli (CSs) results in increasing probability of occurrence of both CCCs and SAPD in the presence of the CSs (appetitive conditioning), even long after detoxification (DTX). To prevent relapse, both conditioned CCCs (conditioned abstinence, CA) and conditioned SAPD should be actively extinguished after DTX by elicitation of CA

Reprinted with permission from *Archives of General Psychiatry*, 1973, *28*, 611-616. Copyright 1973, the American Medical Association, Inc.

From the Department of Psychiatry, University of Kentucky Medical Center, Lexington.

This paper was presented as the first Daniel H. Efron memorial lecture at the 11th annual meeting of the American College of Neuropsychopharmacology in San Juan, Puerto Rico, 12-15 December 1972.

Preparation of this paper was supported, in part, by Research Grant Nos. MH 13194 and MH 17748 from the National Institute of Mental Health.

and programmed SAPD under conditions preventing pharmacological reinforcement. Associated psychopathologies and previous state-dependent learning may pose problems in rehabilitation.

In successive formulations of the definition of drug dependence, the World Health Organization (WHO) has stressed, to an increasing degree, a feature common to all types of drug dependence:

> A particular state of mind that is termed *psychic dependence*. In this situation, there is feeling of satisfaction and a psychic drive that require periodic or continuous administration of the drug to produce pleasure or avoid discomfort. Indeed, this mental state is the most powerful of all of the factors involved in chronic intoxication with psychotropic drugs, and with certain types of drugs it may be the only factor involved, even in the most intense craving and perpetuation of compulsive abuse . . . physical dependence is a powerful factor in reinforcing the influence of psychic dependence upon continuing drug use or relapse to drug use after attempted withdrawal (1, p. 263).

Defined in this manner, the concept of psychic dependence has a strong common sense appeal in as much as it is consonant with the pain-pleasure principle that has been taken for granted as sufficient explanation for behavior by the man in the street, idealist philosophers, and introspectively inclined psychiatrists and psychologists. The pain-pleasure pinciple, however, is empty tautology, for its perfect circularity becomes apparent after a moment's reflection. Nor can one infer from its WHO definition alone just what the tangible variables are of which psychic (as oppose to physical) and dependence are functions.

Analysis of a more detailed description of psychic dependence (2) suggests that this term refers to reinforcement of drug-using behavior as a consequence of interactions between certain pharmacological (i.e., physical) actions of a drug with certain organismic variables that had *not* been engendered by previous doses of that drug. This term also refers to reinforcement of drug-using behavior dependent on social reinforcement in which a "need to belong," rather than the pharmacological actions of the drug, plays the dominant role.

In contrast, physical dependence clearly refers to reinforcement of drug-using behavior as a consequence of interactions between certain pharmacological actions of a drug with organismic variables that *had been* engendered by previous doses of the drug. Implied further is that for each kind of interaction there is a corresponding subjective state which drives the user to renewed self-administration of the drug. Thus, in a psychically dependent person each self-administered dose of the drug is said to alter in a "pleasurable" direction, of course, an unpleasant mood state that was the consequence, not of the effects of previous doses of the drug, but of antecedent anxiety, depression, boredom, and the like. At the same time, such drug use (together with affirmation of popular beliefs about drug-produced highs, thrills, rushes, etc) gains for the user acceptance into a dominant or deviant social group that provides him with many other kinds of reinforcement.

In the tolerant and physically dependent user, however, each dose of the drug is said merely to stave off or suppress the "pain and suffering" associated with abstinence phenomena. Finally, the WHO definitions imply that relapse, even long after drug withdrawal, is due to craving aroused by the memory of the "pleasures" experienced formerly in the state of psychic dependence; presumably, the pain and suffering associated previously with physical dependence are somehow forgotten, even though the literature is replete with accounts of the "agonies of the damned" reported retrospectively by former drug-users themselves.

CONDITIONING FACTORS IN OPIOID DEPENDENCE

In an attempt to devise an operationally definable conceptual framework for research that would provide cells for all of the known and putative variables of which drug dependence may be a function, I have elected to use a conditioning theory of opioid dependence as a model (3-5). Drug dependence is defined as ". . . habitual, non-medically indicated drug-seeking and drug-using behavior which is contingent for its maintenance upon pharmacological and usually, but not necessarily, upon social reinforcement" (6). So defined, the strength of drug dependence may be measured by its resistance to extinction or suppression.

Pharmacological reinforcement is viewed as the result of interactions between certain pharmacological effects of the drug and sources of reinforcement, i.e., organismic variables upon which the reinforcing properties of the drug are contingent. Pharmacological reinforcement is said to be direct if such sources of reinforcement had not been engendered by the drug itself, or indirect if the contrary is true. Furthermore, sources of direct pharmacological reinforcement may be intrinsic (built into the central nervous system) or developmental (acquired in the course of personality development or otherwise). In our present state of knowledge, the only examples of a source of indirect pharmacological reinforcement are the changes in the central nervous system that are adduced to explain physical dependence (7). But the concept is meant to include

Reinforcing Processes in Opioid Dependence*

Reinforcing Processes	Sources of Reinforcement	Reinforcing Events	Behavior
I. Social Street corner society; slum big shots; cultist rituals and beliefs	Need to belong; boredom; anomie; hostility to establishment	Acceptance by deviant sub-culture	Drug-taking in accordance with rituals; affirmation of cultist beliefs
II. Primary Pharmacological A. Direct (nondrug engendered = psychic dependence)	1. Intrinsic (cerebral drug-sensitive reward systems?) 2. Developmental (personality): anxiety in particular situations	1. Relatively nonspecific drug effects (release or blockade of NE, DA, ACh, etc, in brain) 2. Specific pattern of agonistic actions of opioid drugs	1. Subjective: high; thrills (intravenous only) Objective: elated behavior 2. Subjective: content; coasting Objective: nodding; leveling of performance
B. Indirect (drug-engendered = physical dependence)	Early abstinence changes (manifest or detectable by subject's cerebral sensors); restlessness, etc	Suppression of early abstinence by next dose of opioid (NB, tolerance has developed to directly reinforcing effects of opioids)	Subjective: craving and satisfaction of craving Objective: hustling for opioids; increasing dose and frequency of opioid taking (appetitive reinforcement)
III. Secondary Pharmacological (conditioning of reinforcing processes to exteroceptive and interoceptive stimuli) A. Direct B. Indirect	Classically conditioned CNS changes (counteradaptive to agonistic effects of opioids A. Conditioned inhibition of CNS reward systems B. Conditioned abstinence changes	Agonistic effects of opioids as in IIA & B, but after IIA and B, suppression of conditioned abstinence is more reinforcing	Subjective A. "Low;" "disgusted" B. "Sick;" "got the flu;" "need a fix" Objective A. Depressive behavior B. Signs of opioid abstinence (conditioned); renewed hustling; RELAPSE

* Reinforcement is the consequence of interaction between sources of reinforcement and reinforcing events.
(Table reprinted from Wikler A: Sources of reinforcement for drug using behavior: A theoretical formulation, in *Pharmacology and the Future of Man, Proceedings of the 5th International Congress of Pharmacology, San Francisco 1972*. Basel, Switzerland, Karger, to be published, 1973, vol 1.)

other, yet to be discovered kinds of drug-engendered organismic variables which, interacting with the drug, may be found to be reinforcing. Also, direct or indirect pharmacological reinforcement may be primary (unconditioned) or secondary (conditioned).

THEORY OF RELAPSE

Details of this conceptual scheme are presented in the Table. It should be noted that craving (indicated also by the equivalent phrase, "need a fix") and relapse long after detoxification are attributed to reactivation by previously conditioned exteroceptive or interoceptive stimuli (or both) of classically conditioned central counteradaptations to the original, agonistic effects of opioids as well as reactivation of whatever the neural processes may be that underlie operant conditioning of drug-seeking behavior.

That morphine-abstinence phenomena in animals can be conditioned has been demonstrated by two methods: (1) pairing a specific environment with the relatively slow onset and progression to peak intensity of the abstinence syndrome that follows abrupt withdrawal of morphine, the method used in our laboratory (8, 9); and (2) pairing a discrete stimulus with the nalorphine-precipitated morphine-abstinence syndrome, the method used by Goldberg and Schuster (10, 11).

I might add that some evidence of the conditionability of the nalorphine-precipitated abstinence syndrome in man (unpublished observations) was obtained some 20 years ago in my original studies (with H. Isbell, MD, and H. F. Fraser, MD) on the precipitation of abstinence syndromes by nalorphine in experimental subjects receiving multiple daily doses of morphine, methadone, or heroin (12). In five subjects partially tolerant to morphine or methadone administered subcutaneously on a fixed four-times daily schedule by ward aides, single doses of nalorphine given on an irregular schedule always provoked typical opioid-abstinence phenomena within two to three minutes after subcutaneous injection. Later in the course of the study, saline trials occasionally substituted for nalorphine also evoked (during the first 2 to 3 weeks of such trials) complaints of "hot and cold all over," "cramps," "nausea" or "gagging" (or both), and, frequently, objective responses including yawning, lacrimation, rhinorrhea, and mydriasis within 30 minutes after subcutaneous injection. Then such responses to saline rapidly declined and personal inquiry by myself revealed that the subjects, all of them highly experienced hustlers, had been watching each other and had come to the (correct) conclusion that if the first one to receive the injection on a given day did not get sick within two to three minutes, the shot for that day was a "blank." At the time, I castigated myself for not having employed a more sophisticated experimental design. In retrospect, the observation that decoding of the experimental design by these subjects altered the properties of the conditioned stimulus attests to the power of cognitive labeling in man and suggests that verbal psychotherapy, if properly employed, might be useful in facilitating extinction of conditioned abstinence in conjunction with behavioral extinction procedures.

Returning to the animal data, a most important point is that in rats the conditioned abstinence sign studied, increased frequency of wet-dog shakes in the conditional environment, persisted for 155 days (five months) after withdrawal of morphine. In monkeys studied by Goldberg and Schuster (11), the conditioned nalorphine-precipitated abstinence phenomena, transitory suppression of lever-pressing for food, vomiting, salivation, and bradycardia could be elicited for up to 120 days after withdrawal of morphine.

As for operant conditioning of drug self-administration in animals, this has been demonstrated by many investigators and, with both the drinking and self-injection techniques, it has been shown that such operantly trained animals will relapse (13-16). However, these studies do not settle the question of whether such relapse is related to previous *indirect* pharmacological reinforcement (physical dependence) or to previous *direct* pharmacological reinforcement (one of the meanings of psychic dependence), an example of which is the self-maintenance on very small intravenously administered doses of morphine by naive monkeys (17). Jones and Prada (18) found that while most dogs will not initiate self-injection of morphine, such animals will maintain their addiction by self-injection after they have been made physically dependent by passive injections of morphine and will relapse promptly after morphine withdrawal and removal from the operant chamber for as long as six months.

All that can be said presently is that previous physical dependence can be a powerful factor in facilitating relapse. Whether such facilitation is due to protracted abstinence (19-21), to conditioning processes, or to a combination of both, is a problem for future investigation. In my own studies, rats with previous physical dependence relapsed in choice drinking tests (etonitazene solution vs water) at intervals of one to three weeks over a period of about one year after withdrawal of morphine, even without formal operant conditioning (22). However, the persistent potency (for at least 137 days after morphine withdrawal) of a secondary (conditioned) exteroceptive reinforcer generated by previous temporal contiguity between such a stimulus and suppression of early morphine-abstinence phenomena suggests the possibility that even without ob-server-manipulated operant training, opioid-seeking behavior can be-come interoceptively conditioned in subjects who undergo the continuous cycle of early opioid abstinence and its suppression by the next dose of the drug (23).

IMPLICATIONS FOR RESEARCH AND TREATMENT

Allusion has already been made to two problems that require further investigation: the rules of protracted abstinence and of conditioning factors in the genesis of relapse. The latter, however, is part of a more general problem of conditioning of drug effects, both classical and op-erant. Emboldened by the data and ideas of Konorski (24), Miller and DiCara (25), and Miller (26), I venture to propose (27), at least for simplification of the problem of drug conditioning, that the neural mech-anisms of classical and operant conditioning are the same, the phenom-enological differences being due to the differences in what is reinforced: a reflexly elicited unconditioned response (UR) in the case of classical conditioning or an emitted UR in the case of operant conditioning. The reinforcing event in *both* cases is the delayed activation of rewarding or punishing limbic structures that follows presentation of the uncondi-tioned stimulus (US, in operant terms, the reinforcer) and the UR which the US elicits.

If this assumption is correct, then two behaviors are conditioned in operant conditioning: the emitted behavior in which the experimenter is interested and the UR elicited by the reinforcer (US) in which he is not interested (except for people like Shapiro (28) who recorded not only lever presses but also parotid salivary secretion during acquisition of food-reinforced responding by dogs). Stein has offered an interesting suggestion how delayed activation of limbic structures may be the critical reinforcing event:

> Pairing an operant response with reward may be viewed as an instance of Pavlovian conditioning. Response-related stimuli (environmental as well as internal) are the conditioned stimulus and reward is the unconditioned stimulus. By virtue of the pair-ing, the medial forebrain 'go' mechanism is conditioned to re-sponse-related stimuli. Thus, on future occasions, any tendency to engage in the previously rewarded behavior initiates facili-tatory feedback by activaton of the 'go' mechanism, and thereby increases the probability that the response will run off to com-pletion. In the case of punishment, periventricular activity is conditioned to stimuli associated with the punished operant.

This decreases the probability that the operant will be emitted in the future because feedback from the 'stop' mechanism will tend to inhibit the behavior (29, p. 94).

In the special case of those behaviors we call "drug effects," I have suggested (27) that what becomes conditioned are central processing events following the initial (agonistic) effects of drugs at neuronal receptor sites in the afferent arms of reflex circuits. These are broadly conceived to include not only the familiar bulbospinal reflexes, but also complex afferent-processing-efferent and feedback networks, the afferent neurons of which may lie outside the pia mater (exteroceptors and interoceptors such as baroreceptors and chemoreceptors) or at various loci in the brain (chemoreceptors, osmoreceptors, thermoreceptors). In this view, certain drug effects are reflex or adaptive responses to their initial effects as afferent receptor sites (e.g., morphine emesis [30, 31]) while other drug effects represent compensatory (feedback) responses to initial effects of such drugs at peripheral effector sites (32). In these cases, pairing a neutral stimulus (CS) with administration of the drug on repeated occasions results in conditioned responses that mimic the URs (32-34).

In other cases, such as those of drugs acting on post-synaptic receptors in autonomic ganglia, compensatory centrally processed responses are developed after repeated pairings of the CS and US. The CRs that emerge are opposite in direction to the URs. For example, repeated pairing of a CS with subcutaneously administered atropine (in dogs and cats) eventually results in profuse salivation on presentation of the CS that can be blocked by atropine, piperidyl benzilate (Ditran), or propranolol (3, 35, 36). It is still not clear whether this paradoxical CR represents unconditioned potentiation (by supersensitization of the chronically atropinized salivary glands to acetylcholine and catecholamines [37]) of a specific, conditioned, central adaptation to peripheral blockade of salivary secretion, or a nonspecific, conditioned, central adaptive response to noxious stimulation. In either case, the phenomenon illustrates that in the cases of drugs acting at effector sites, it is an unconditionally acquired adaptive response that becomes conditioned.

Conditioning of unconditionally acquired adaptive responses is also illustrated by the conditioning of hypoglycemic responses to saccharine in man as reported by Kun and Horvath (38) and by the remarkable experiments of Roffman and Lal (39) who found that in mice, after repeated pairing of a CS with reduced oxygen tension that unconditionally produced hypothermia and prolongation of hexobarbital narcosis, presentation of the CS alone evoked hyperthermia and shortening of hexobarbital narcosis.

Apparently, however, not all unconditionally acquired feedback circuits are adaptive, at least from a teleological perspective. In the rat, Woods and his co-workers (40) were able to condition the hypoglycemic effects of subcutaneously administered insulin and found evidence of insulin-like activity in the blood just before the appearance of conditioned hypoglycemia. Also, Woods et al. (41) reported that after repeated subcutaneous administrations of tolbutamide, injection of the tolbutamide vehicle alone evoked conditioned insulin secretion and hypoglycemia. Interestingly, they mention that, "Since conditioned hypoglycemia has been found to require intact vagus nerves and to be eliminated with atropine . . . , the implication is that the animals can be made to neurally increase their insulin output" (42, p. 231).

In any case, adaptive or not, these data likewise indicate that in the cases of the USs insulin and tolbutamide, what becomes conditioned is not, respectively, the transport of glucose across membranes of glucose-utilizing cells or the direct stimulation of pancreatic islet beta cells, but a central processing event mediated to the pancreatic islets by the vagus nerve. This results in secretion of more insulin and hence, in conditioned hypoglycemia—for what purpose, we cannot say (at least presently).

Applying these concepts to the problem of drug dependence, it is further postulated that as drug administrations are continued in frequent temporal contiguity with certain exteroceptive or interoceptive stimuli, or both, these CSs come to elicit, as CRs, successive unconditioned adaptations and counteradaptations to the initial (agonistic) actions of the drug at receptor sites in afferent arms of neutral reflex (broad sense) circuits (27). In this view, the CRs that develop in the allegedly nontolerant and nonphysically dependent joy-popper (occasional opioid user) can be expected to be different from those that develop in the tolerant and physically dependent addict, but in both cases the consequences of this view are that the CRs are opposite in direction to the initial reflex responses to the agonistic effects of the drug and are experienced as dysphoria (Table). In as much as in self-injectors such behavior had also become operantly conditioned, evocation of such classically conditioned counteradaptive responses by the CSs, even long after detoxification, can be expected to result in relapse.

Another consequence of this view is that the sharp distinction that is usually made between psychic dependence (direct pharmacological reinforcement) and physical dependence (indirect pharmacological reinforcement) becomes untenable. Thus, it may be questioned whether after the first few doses of any of the drugs of abuse, including those said not to produce physical dependence (amphetamines, cocaine, cannabis products), the drug-reinforcing processes remain direct (i.e., non-drug engendered). In the case of morphine it has been demonstrated that in naive chronic spinal dogs, hindlimb abstinence phenomena can be precipitated by nalorphine given one hour after a single dose of morphine (42); in man, clear-cut abstinence phenomena can be evoked by nalorphine hydrochloride (15 mg), or heroin (15 mg) four times daily for as little as two or three days (12).

The interactions between opioids and neurotransmitters are still obscure, but it is known that many psychoactive drugs release, block reuptake of, or otherwise alter the effects of neurotransmitters at their receptor sites and that the central nervous system is equipped with elaborate neural, positive and negative feedback circuits (43) that serve to counteract such direct drug effects. Perhaps such neural feedback circuits tend to overshoot and thereby generate new sources of reinforcement with or without those abstinence signs we have learned to recognize (e.g., the abstinence syndromes that follow abrupt withdrawal of opioids, barbiturates, or ethanol after chronic intoxication with these drugs). Certainly in the case of amphetamine, long considered to be a drug that does not produce physical dependence, the prolonged rebound REM sleep that ensues after its abrupt withdrawal (44, 45), as well as the succeeding transitory bulimia followed by affective depression, are abstinence phenomena that were not recognized as such for so long because the patient, being asleep, did not complain.

In terms of the pain-pleasure principle, is the speed-freak impelled to self-inject methamphetamine in closely spaced doses and to relapse in the Haight-Ashbury environment after crashing there because of the memories of the highs produced by the first dose or of the lows that followed? Similar questions may be asked about cocaine self-administration and marihuana smoking. However, answers to these questions in terms of the pain-pleasure principle will not be meaningful; rather, the answers should be sought in terms of the biochemical-neurophysiological mechanisms that are involved in the development of successive counteradaptations to the initial receptor actions of such drugs and in reinforcement.

Some implications of this conditioning theory for treatment of drug-dependent persons in general (46) and of opioid-dependent persons in particular (47) have been discussed extensively elsewhere. Suffice it here to point out that mere detoxification with or without conventional psychotherapy and prolonged retention in a drug-free environment does not result in extinction of the conditioned responses any more than satiating a rat with food (i.e., reducing its hunger drive) and keeping it away from the operant cage for a period of time will cure it of the lever-pressing habit acquired previously under conditions of food deprivation

(9). Rather, what is needed in post-detoxification treatment are repeated elicitation of the conditioned responses by appropriate conditional stimuli and *active* extinction of them by programmed self-injection of the drug of dependence under conditions that preclude its reinforcing effects.

As has been pointed out already, verbal psychotherapy might be utilized effectively to hasten extinction if it is directed toward cognitive relabeling of the conditioned responses instead of toward resolution of alleged oral fixations and the like. In the particular case of detoxified opioid-dependent persons, a promising means of achieving extinction is afforded by the availability of long-lasting orally effective narcotic antagonists (48) that not only prevent opioid euphoria but also, and more importantly, prevent suppression of opioid abstinence phenomena by opioids and the renewed development of physical dependence even after repeated doses of opioids (i.e., they prevent reinforcement of conditioned abstinence and of conditioned opioid-seeking behavior).

In the practical application of these principles, the detoxified and narcotic antagonist-maintained patient, while still in the hospital, should be exposed to "laboratory" facsimiles of his "bad associates," and to anxiety-producing situations that, mimicking the stimuli to which he had been exposed while hustling for opioids previously, are likely to evoke conditioned abstinence. The patient should be required to self-inject genuine, guaranteed pure heroin repeatedly, with all the rituals to which he had been accustomed, in doses which are greater than those he would be likely to obtain on the street, but which are insufficient to overcome the narcotic antagonist blockade. It can be expected that eventually the patient will refuse to self-inject heroin further and the laboratory facsimiles of his presumed exteroceptive and interoceptive conditioned stimuli will cease to evoke signs of conditioned abstinence. Then the patient may be discharged from the hospital, but he should continue to be maintained on the antagonist in his home environment with its real-life conditioned stimuli (including secondary reinforcers).

Very likely in responding to these conditioned stimuli the patient will resort to self-injection of bags of heroin, but it can be expected that such spontaneous recovery from extinction will be short-lived because of previous active extinction in the hospital and continued narcotic antagonist blockade. It is difficult to estimate how long narcotic-antagonist blockade should be maintained, but inasmuch as protracted abstinence can last for approximately ten months after abrupt withdrawal of morphine following experimental chronic morphine intoxication in man (20), one year would seem reasonable provided that randomly taken urine samples remain drug-free during the last few months.

Equally important is the problem of retraining the detoxified patient to hustle for socially approved reinforcers in the drug-free internal state after having successfully deprived him both of the reinforcers (both primary and secondary) and the opioid internal state generated during years of opioid dependency. To this end more serious consideration should be given than has been to the fact, recently confirmed (49), that the vast majority of opioid postaddicts are people with various forms of psychopathology, the most common being psychopathy or, more politely, sociopathy. Among other characteristics, psychopaths are unable to delay gratification (i.e., to emit sustained, goal-directed activity under conditions of delayed reinforcement and consummation). Theoretically, an ideal vocation for such a person would be one that paid off immediately on successful completion of a task, but it is difficult to think of such occupations in our society other than illegal or shady ones.

Perhaps behavior-modification therapies could be devised for training postaddict "psychopaths" to work for reinforcements delivered at progressively longer fixed intervals and to delay their consumption for progressively longer periods. Also, cognizance should be taken of the possibility that, as in the rat (50, 51), some socially useful behaviors that the patient had acquired in the opioid internal state are rapidly extinguished in the drug-free internal state. Should research demonstrate that state-dependent learning (dissociated learning) applies to the opioid-dependent state in man, then such socially useful behaviors may have to be relearned through appropriate therapy.

PREVENTION OF DRUG DEPENDENCE

From all of the foregoing, it is apparent that drug dependence is largely a consequence of certain rather subtle pharmacological actions of drugs of abuse coupled with equally subtle conditioning processes. Therefore, control of drug-availability, to the extent that this is possible practically, is essential for prevention of drug dependence. However, the historical association between the development of mythologies about drug effects (from the allegedly nonaddicting properties of heroin [52] and meperidine [53] to the contemporary psychedelic preoccupations of so many of our youth and their older apologists) and the spread of drug abuse and drug dependence in the United States indicates that social reinforcement plays a significant role in bringing the host and the agent together.

Dealing with this factor in the cause of drug dependence takes us beyond the confines of scientific discourse since value judgments enter here—do we envisage with equanimity a society, say in 1984, whose members find their major primary reinforcers in psychotropic drugs and their secondary reinforcers in drug-cult beliefs and practices (46)? If not, then as psychopharmacologists we should do what we can to dispel the magical thinking about drug effects that permeate our society. At the very least, we can refrain from falling in line with the popular argot that refers to drug effects in such seductive but meretricious terms as highs or psychedelic experiences. We can also be honest enough to say that drugs which alter the mind do so by altering the brain—a difference that should make a difference to any thoughtful person—and that even drugs which do not produce gross evidence of organic brain damage (like heroin or marihuana) can, nevertheless, produce serious behavioral damage after long-term use. To be sure, social reinforcement of drug use is a function not only of mythologies about drug effects, but also of cultural, political, and economic conditions. In these areas, however, our roles as psychopharmacologists do not particularly qualify us to express other than personal value judgments. Hence, this is a good time to conclude this lecture.

REFERENCES

1. EDDY, N. B., et al: Drug dependence: Its significance and characteristics, in Blachly P. H. (ed): *Drug Abuse: Data and Debate.* Springfield, Charles C Thomas Publishers, 1970, pp. 259-282.
2. CAMERON, D. C.: Abuse of alcohol and drugs: Concepts and planning, *WHO Chron* 25:8-16, 1971.
3. WIKLER, A.: Recent progress in research on the neurophysiological basis of morphine addiction. *Am. J. Psychiatry* 105:329-338, 1948.
4. WIKLER, A.: On the nature of addiction and habituation. *Br. J. Addict.* 57:73-80, 1961.
5. WIKLER, A.: Sources of reinforcement for drug using behavior: A theoretical formulation, in *Proceedings of the Fifth International Congress on Pharmacology*, Basle, Karger, to be published, pp. 135-136.
6. WIKLER, A.: Present status of the concept of drug dependence. *Psychol. Med.* 1:377-380, 1971.
7. WIKLER, A.: Theories related to physical dependence, in Mulé, S. J., Brill, A. (eds): *The Chemical and Biological Aspects of Drug Dependence.* Cleveland, Chemical Rubber Co Press, 1972, pp. 359-377.
8. WIKLER, A.: Conditioning factors in opiate addiction and relapse, in Wilner D. I., Kassebaum, G. G. (eds): *Narcotics*, New York, McGraw-Hill Book Co Inc, 1965, pp. 85-100.
9. WIKLER, A., PESCOR, F. T.: Classical conditioning of a morphine abstinence phenomenon, reinforcement of opioid-drinking behavior and "relapse": In morphine-addicted rats. *Psychopharmacologia* 10:255-284, 1967.
10. GOLDBERG, S. R., SCHUSTER, C. R.: Conditioned suppression by a stimulus associated with nalorphine in morphine-dependent monkeys. *J. Exp. Anal. Behav.* 14:235-242, 1967.
11. GOLDBERG, S. R., SCHUSTER, C. R.: Conditioned nalorphine-induced abstinence changes: persistence in post-dependent monkeys. *J. Exp. Anal. Behav.* 14:33-46, 1970.
12. WIKLER, A., FRASER, H. F., ISBELL, H.: N-allylnormorphine: Effects of single doses and

precipitation of acute "abstinence syndromes" during addiction to morphine, methadone or heroin in man (post-addicts). *J. Pharmacol. Exp. Ther.* 109:8-20, 1953.

13. KUMAR, R., STOLERMAN, I. P.: Resumption of morphine self-administration by ex-addict rats: An attempt to modify tendencies to relapse. *J. Comp. Physiol. Psychol.* 78:457-465, 192.

14. NICHOLS, J. R., HEADLEE, C. P., COPPOCK, H. W.: Drug Addiction: I. Addiction by escape training. *J. Am. Pharm. Assoc.* 45:788-791, 1956.

15. THOMPSON, T., OSTLUND, W.: Susceptibility to re-addiction as a function of the addiction and withdrawal environment. *J. Comp. Physiol. Psychol.* 59:388-392, 1965.

16. WEEKS, J. R., COLLINS, R. J.: Patterns of intravenous self-injection by morphine-addicted rats, in Wikler A. (ed): *The Addictive State: Proceedings of the Association for Research in Nervous and Mental Disease.* Baltimore, Williams & Wilkins Co., 1968, vol 46, pp. 288-298.

17. WOODS, J. H., SCHUSTER, C. R.: Reinforcement properties of morphine, cocaine, and SPA as a function of unit dose. *Int. J. Addict.* 3:231-237, 1968.

18. JONES, B. E., PRADA, J. A.: Relapse to morphine (M) use in dog, abstracted. *Fed. Proc.* 31:551, 1972.

19. HIMMELSBACH, C. K.: Clinical studies of drug addiction: Physical dependence, withdrawal and recovery. *Arch. Intern. Med.* 69:766 772, 1942.

20. MARTIN, W. R., JASINSKI, D. R.: Physiological parameters of morphine dependence in man: Tolerance, early abstinence, protracted abstinence. *J. Psychiatr. Res.* 7:9-17, 1969.

21. MARTIN, W. R., et al: Tolerance to and physical dependence on morphine in the rat. *Psychopharmacologia* 4:247-260, 1963.

22. WIKLER, A., PESCOR, F. T.: Persistence of "relapse-tendencies" of rats previously made physically dependent on morphine. *Psychopharmacologia* 16:375-384, 1970.

23. WIKLER, A., et al: Persistent potency of a secondary (conditioned) reinforcer following withdrawal of morphine from physically dependent rats. *Psychopharmacologia* 20:103-117, 1971.

24. KONORSKI, J.: *Integrative Activity of the Brain: An Interdisciplinary Approach.* Chicago, University of Chicago Press, 1967.

25. MILLER, N. E., DiCARA, L. V.: Instrumental learning of urine formation by rats: Changes in renal blood flow. *Am. J. Physiol.* 215:677 683, 1968.

26. MILLER, N. E.: Learning of visceral and glandular responses. *Science* 163:434-445, 1969.

27. WIKLER, A.: Conditioning of successive adaptive responses to the initial effects of drugs. *Cond. Reflex,* to be published.

28. SHAPIRO, M. M.: Respondent salivary conditioning during operant lever pressing in dogs. *Science* 132:619-620, 1960.

29. STEIN, L.: Amphetamine and neural reward mechanism, in Steinberg, H., de Reuck, A. V. S., Knight, J. (eds): *Ciba Foundation Symposium on Animal Behaviour and Drug Action.* London, J. & A. Churchill, 1964, pp. 91-118.

30. WANG, S. C., BORISON, H. L.: The vomiting center: A critical experimental analysis. *Arch. Neurol. Psychiatry* 63:928-941, 1950.

31. WANG, S. C., GLAVIANO, V. V.: Locus of emetic action of morphine and hydergine in dogs. *J. Pharmacol. Exp. Ther.* 111:329-334, 1954.

32. LANG, W. J., ROSS, P., GLOVER, A.: Conditional responses induced by hypotensive drugs. *Eur. J. Pharmacol.* 2:169-174, 1967.

33. PAVLOV, I. P.: *Conditioned Reflexes: An Investigation of the Physiological Activity of the Cerebral Cortex.* Anrep, G. V. (trans-ed), New York, Dover Publications Inc, 1960, pp. 34-35.

34. KLEITMAN, N., CRISLER, G.: A quantitative study of a salivary conditioned reflex. *Am. J. Physiol.* 79:571-614, 1927.

35. KOROL, B., SLETTEN, I. W., BROWN, M. L.: Conditioned physiological adaptation to anticholinergic drugs. *Am. J. Physiol.* 211:911-914, 1966.

36. LANG, W. J., et al: Classical and physiologic adaptive conditioned responses to anti-

cholinergic drugs in conscious dogs. *Int. J. Neuropharmacol.* 6:311-315, 1966.
37. EMMELIN, N.: Supersensitivity following "pharmacological denervation." *Pharmacol. Rev.* 13:17-37, 1961.
38. KUN, E., HORVATH, I.: The influence of oral saccharin on blood sugar. *Proc. Soc. Exp. Biol. Med.* 66:175-177, 1947.
39. ROFFMAN, N., LAL, H.: Voluntary control of hepatic drug metabolism: A case of behavioral drug tolerance, in *Proceedings of the Fifth International Congress on Pharmacology.* Basle, Karger, to be published, p. 195.
40. WOODS, S. C., HUTTON, R. A., MAKOUS, W.: Conditioned insulin secretion in the albino rat. *Proc. Soc. Exp. Biol. Med.* 133:964-968, 1970.
41. WOODS, S. C., ALEXANDER, K. R., PORTE, D. Jr.: Conditioned insulin secretion and hypoglycemia following repeated injections of tolbutamide in rats. *Endocrinology* 90:227-231, 1972.
42. WIKLER, A., CARTER, R. L.: Effects of single doses of N-allylnormorphine on hindlimb reflexes of chronic spinal dogs during cycles of morphine addiction. *J. Pharmacol. Exp. Ther.* 109:92-101, 1953.
43. AXELROD, J.: Neural and hormonal control of catecholamine synthesis, in Kopin, I. J. (ed): *Neurotransmitters: Proceedings of the Association For Research in Nervous and Mental Disease.* Baltimore, Williams & Wilkins Co, 1972, vol 50, pp 229-240.
44. OSWALD, I.: Effects on sleep of amphetamine and its derivatives, in Costa, E., Garattini, S. (eds): *International Symposium on Amphetamine and Related Compounds.* New York, Raven Press, 1970, pp. 865-871.
45. OSWALD, I., THACORE, V. R.: Amphetamine and phenmetrazine addiction: Physical abnormalities in the abstinence syndrome. *Br. Med. J.* 2:427-431, 1963.
46. WIKLER, A.: Some implications of conditioning theory for problems of drug abuse, in Blachly, P. (ed): *Drug Abuse: Data and Debate.* Springfield, Charles C Thomas Publishers, 1970. (Reprinted in *Behav. Sci.* 16:92-97, 1971.)
47. WIKLER, A.: Requirements for extinction of relapse-facilitating variables in a narcotic antagonist treatment program, in Villareal, J. (ed): *Proceedings of the First International Conference on Narcotic Antagonists, Warrenton, Va, Nov. 26:29, 1972.* New York, Raven Press, to be published.
48. MARTIN, W. R., GORODETZKY, C. W., McCLANE, T. K.: An experimental study in the treatment of narcotic addicts with cyclazocine. *Clin. Pharmacol. Ther.* 7:455-465, 1966.
49. MONROE, J. J., ROSS, W. F., BERZINS, J. I.: The decline of the addict as "psychopath": Implications for community care. *Int. J. Addict.* 6:601-608, 1971.
50. BELLEVILLE, R. E.: Control of behavior by drug-produced internal stimuli, *Psychopharmacologia* 5:95-105, 1964.
51. HILL, H. E., JONES, B. E., BELL, E. C.: State dependent control of discrimination by morphine and pentobarbital. *Psychopharmacologia* 22:305-313, 1971.
52. TAYLOR, W. J. R., CHAMBERS, C. D., BOWLING, C. E.: Addiction and the community (narcotic substitution therapy). *Int. J. Pharmacol.* 6:28-39, 1972.
53. ISBELL, H., WHITE, W. M.: Clinical characteristics of addiction. *Am. J. Med.* 14:558-565, 1953.

22

THE REINFORCERS FOR DRUG
ABUSE: WHY PEOPLE TAKE DRUGS

Thomas J. Crowley

Learning can be defined as behavioral change through experience, and drug abuse behavior, which develops with experience, is therefore one kind of learned behavior. If a particular behavior is regularly reinforced, organisms learn to generate that behavior with increasing frequence. This is *operant learning* in which the organism operates upon the environment to obtain reinforcements; such learning probably contributes heavily to drug abuse behavior. Relying on learning theory, this paper will attempt to synthesize available information on the reinforcers for drug abuse behavior into a clinical approach to drug-abusing patients.

CLASSES OF REINFORCEMENT

Drugs in Primary Positive Reinforcement

Primary reinforcers are inherently reinforcing; by themselves they can reinforce behavior. Examples of primary reinforcers include food, sex,

Reprinted with permission of Grune & Stratton, Inc. from *Comprehensive Psychiatry*, 1972, *13*, 51-62.

The author thanks Dr. C. O. Rutledge, Dr. Fred Todd, Dr. Robert Kelly, and Dr. John Kelly for their valuable comments on this manuscript.

From the University of Colorado Medical Center and V.A. Hospital, Denver, Colo.

Presented at the Colorado Psychiatric Society Midwinter Meeting, January 30, 1971, Vail, Colo.

Supported in part by NIMH Grant I-R03-MH 18208-01.

water, and electrical stimulation in certain brain loci. Secondary reinforcers are learned reinforcers. For instance, money has no inherent
reinforcing value, but it becomes a powerful reinforcer when one learns
that it can be used to obtain primary reinforcers.

Clinical reports indicate primary reinforcement from certain drugs.
The intravenous administration of methamphetamine immediately produces intense physical pleasure described as "a whole body orgasm" and
named the "flash" or "rush" (1). Intravenous heroin administration
causes a similar sensation. The reports of users leave little doubt that
these sensations are highly reinforcing at the first exposure.

Animal studies have confirmed the clinical impression that certain
drugs are primary reinforcers, while others are not. Monkeys with in-
dwelling cannulae press levers to obtain injections of morphine, codeine,
cocaine, amphetamine, pentobarbital, ethanol, and caffeine (2). They do
not press to receive nalorphine, nalorphine-morphine mixtures, chlorpromazine, mescaline, or saline. Schuster and Thompson's thorough
review (3) concludes that certain drugs are primary reinforcers for self-
administration in several species.

Reinforcement presented immediately after a behavior is more effective in increasing the frequency of the behavior. Intravenous narcotic
and stimulant administration is reinforced almost instantly by the drug
flash, and, as expected, the rapid reinforcement of i.v. administration
produces a more persistent and pernicious drug habit. Similarly, even
orally, self-administration behaviors develop more frequently with rapid-
acting barbiturates than with the slow-acting ones (4).

Assumedly, a dose of intravenous methamphetamine would be physically pleasurable to anyone. Why then do some subjects continue to use
drugs, while others do not? Users in impoverished environments, with
few other reinforcers available, will probably seek drug reinforcement
more actively. This is likely the case with restrained, isolated, experimental monkeys; with heroin users in American black ghettoes; and with
cocaine users in the Andes (5). Similarly, long experience with disturbed,
unloving parents seems to convince many young people that they can
never achieve respect or love from others. These people have not learned
to expect reinforcement from their environment, and so they may more
actively seek the predictable, regular reinforcement of drug abuse.

Drugs in Primary Negative Reinforcement

In popular jargon, "negative reinforcement" is equated with "punishment." But technically, a negative reinforcer is a stimulus, the termination of which reinforces behavior (6). Such stimuli are aversive, and

negative reinforcement is the reinforcement resulting from the cessation of these aversive (punishing) stimuli. For example, one may open the window when the room becomes too hot; the termination of the aversive stimulus, heat, negatively reinforces the window-opening behavior.

Physical dependence follows the continued use of narcotics, sedative-hypnotics, and alcohol. When abstinent from these drugs, the chronic user becomes anxious, tremulous, and physically ill. The termination of this aversive, abstinence state by self-administration of the drug negatively reinforces the drug-taking behavior.

Negative reinforcement may help determine temporal patterns of drug abuse. Users of methamphetamine do not develop the extreme withdrawal symptoms of narcotic, alcohol, or barbiturate users. Since their immediate withdrawal discomfort is limited, methamphetamine abusers can frequently interrupt their "runs" of drug administration with "crashes" of abstinence (1, 7, 8). Stimulant self-administration by monkeys and rats is also intermittent (2, 8, 9). Conversely, human narcotic addicts (10), and monkeys (2) lever-pressing for narcotics or barbiturates, steadily administer their drugs. Monkeys are only somewhat less regular in working for alcohol. Apparently, any drug affording primary positive reinforcement may be abused, but the habit's constancy in both animals and men is a function of whether developing dependence produces a withdrawal state, the termination of which negatively reinforces drug administration.

Mello (11) suggests that alcohol may impair one's ability to attend to or distinguish aversive elements of the environment. Even without physical dependence on alcohol, this "blotto" effect may negatively reinforce alcohol abuse by reducing the user's perception of aversive stimuli, and the same would probably be true with narcotics and sedative-hypnotics.

Drugs in Secondary Positive Reinforcement

As noted earlier, objects or situations develop secondary reinforcement properties through regular association with the obtaining of primary reinforcers. Thus, the past reinforcement history is very important. Some secondary reinforcers for self-administration seem unrelated to the pharmacologic effect of the drug, while others appear to be directly related to the drug's behavioral effects.

The "mellow yellow" fad exemplified secondary reinforcement *unrelated to drug effects*. Stories that the smoking of dried banana peels produced an hallucinogenic drug experience led to "banana rallies" in Greenwich Village and widespread banana smoking. One third of users interviewed described a variety of "psychedelic" experiences, changes in mood, etc., from the smoke, but two thirds found little or no effect (12). Most drug users have now apparently decided that "banana grass" was a hoax and have dropped it from the drug scene. This apparently inert placebo probably produced neither primary positive nor primary negative reinforcement. But the formation of social groups sharing banana rallies, banana music, and a joint defiance of authority could provide strong, secondary, non-drug-related reinforcement for banana smoking behavior in certain people. Mellow yellow use was probably reinforced only by these group activities.

Social grouping also seems to reinforce drug use in the methamphetamine colonies of large cities, permiting entry into a unique subculture (7). But unlike mellow yellow, methamphetamine abuse also obtains potent primary positive reinforcement, contributing to the persistence of methamphetamine abuse as mellow yellow smoking disappears.

Other secondary reinforcement probably *is related* to the behavioral effects of the drugs. Three variables interact here: differential drug effects, differential dose effects, and the previous reinforcement history of the user.

First, different abused drugs have different behavioral effects. For example, placebo, morphine, pentobarbital, chlorpromazine, LSD-25, pyrohexyl, amphetamine, and alcohol each characteristically alter question-answering behavior in a psychological test (13). As another example, while narcotics appear to induce passivity, alcohol and barbiturates may promote aggressive behavior. "The alcoholic takes a drink, goes home, and beats his wife; the narcotic addict takes a 'shot,' goes home, and his wife beats him" (10). Narcotic addicts receiving maintenance doses of opiates are rarely aggressive or antisocial, whereas these same patients become pugnacious, hostile, and sexually uncontrolled when receiving barbiturates (14).

Second, variations in behavioral effects are not only drug-dependent, but are probably *dose-dependent* as well. Small doses of alcohol can facilitate sexual or aggressive behaviors (release of inhibition), while large doses cause behavioral suppression and coma. Similarly, when the "stimulant," methamphetamine, and the "sedative," phenobarbital, are administered to pairs of fighting rats, smaller doses of each drug increase fighting, while larger doses of each decrease it (15, 16).

A user may find that his own behavior after a certain dose of a certain drug alters the behavior of others toward him. If that alteration proves reinforcing to the user (which would be a function of the third factor here, the *previous reinforcement history*), the drug-taking behavior itself would be reinforced. "The choice of a particular class of drugs may be explained on the basis of the assumption that a given agent facilitates or hinders specific patterns of behavior that are acceptable to the user" (14). Wieder and Kaplan observed that "when an individual finds an agent that faciliates his preexisting preferential mode of conflict solution, it becomes his drug of choice" (17).

Differential reinforcement accruing from the differential behavioral effects of various drugs appears critical to drug choice. "The common reaction given by narcotic addicts when asked why they have not used stimulants is that they do not like the effect. [A group of stimulant users] unanimously declared just the opposite. They wanted to speed up, act, accomplish" (18). One amphetamine-abusing patient (17) rejected heroin because "I don't want to withdraw, to sit back and nod, or get away from feeling. . . . I take a drug to cope with life, to be productive, and get recognition. I'm a shy extrovert, and people come to me when I'm on dex because I look happy, I'm not uptight, and my persecution complex is gone. I get inspired and enthusiastic, I can dream up and write term papers, I can think and concentrate." Finding reinforcement in the social effects of drug-induced activity, this patient chose stimulants over narcotics.

Another possible example of secondary positive reinforcement from drug-induced behavioral changes comes from the Lexington Hospital (19). Amphetamine abusers there had markedly elevated 874 MMPI profiles, which were significantly different from the profiles of the general addict population. Although the MMPI is not standardized for this unique group, and so must be cautiously interpreted, this profile usually indicates insecurity, lack of self-reliance, passive-dependence, an inability to think for oneself, and a failure to assume a dominant role in interactions with others (20). The drug effects reported by the Lexington abusers almost exactly reverse this description. Amphetamine increased their loquaciousness, alertness, and energy, produced a sense of cleverness, "crystal-clear thinking," and "invigorating aggressiveness," while it decreased their ambivalence. Thus, a specific drug effect on assertiveness may transiently "correct" a specific personality defect in assertiveness. Such behavioral changes could contribute heavily to drug choice.

Chaining may also produce secondary positive reinforcement related to drug effects. A whole series of previously neutral objects or events may develop reinforcement characteristics through association with a primary reinforcer. For example, depressing a syringe plunger is intimately associated with the heroin "flash." Plunger-depressing is thereby reinforced and it may also become a reinforcer itself, capable of reinforcing closely associated acts, such as inserting the needle. Needle-insertion could in turn come to be a reinforcer for applying the tourniquet, etc. Theoretically, chaining could be carried all the way back, e.g., to associating with a pusher. It is difficult to assess just how effective remote chaining is in maintaining drug-abuse behavior, but it may contribute something to recidivism. Through chaining, mere association with pushers might become mildly reinforcing. Seeking only that reinforcement, an exuser would be exposed to pressure to use drugs again.

Drugs in Secondary Negative Reinforcement

In the absence of true drug withdrawal, syndromes like withdrawal have been elicited in animals by neutral stimuli that had previously accompanied genuine withdrawal. For example, nalorphine injections induce acute withdrawal in morphine-dependent monkeys, and if a buzzer is regularly paired with nalorphine, eventually the buzzer alone induces some withdrawal symptoms—heart rate change, salivation, and emesis (21). Comparable phenomena do occur in rats (22) and might occur in humans (23). For instance, a man who had frequently undergone genuine (unconditioned) withdrawal in his parents' home might undergo conditioned withdrawal upon subsequently entering their home. This would be a form of Pavlovian conditioning, in which objects or events regularly associated with an unconditioned aversive state would develop conditioned aversive properties. The user might then take drugs to terminate the *conditioned* withdrawal, and the termination would reinforce the drug-using behavior. This process can be termed secondary (or learned) negative reinforcement of drug-using behavior.

REINFORCERS OBTAINABLE FROM DIFFERENT DRUG CLASSES

Evaluating a drug-abuser lies in asking the question, "Why does this patient at this time take this drug?" "Why this patient?" and "Why at this time?" involve issues of the past reinforcement history and the current environment, which are beyond the scope of this discussion. But different classes of reinforcement may accrue from the use of different drugs, and "Why this drug?" may be answered by those differences, which are summarized in Table 1 and are discussed below. The table may prove useful in evaluating drug choice and planning treatment, but it obviously cannot be applied blindly as a cookbook; its use depends on a thorough understanding of each patient's past history and current circumstances.

Table 1.—Potential Reinforcers for Abuse of Various Classes of Drugs

Reinforcement	Narcotics	Stimulants	Sedative-Hypnotics and Alcohol	Hallucinogens and Marijuana	Multiple Drug Use	Mellow Yellow (Placebo)
Primary positive	+	+	+	+/0	+	0
Primary negative						
Termination of withdrawal	+	0	+/0	0	0	0
Reduced attention to, or discrimination of, aversive stimuli	+	0	+	+	+/0	0
Secondary positive						
Social, unrelated to drug effects	+	+	+	+	+	+
Social, related to drug effects on behavior	+	+	+	+	0	0
Chaining	+	?	?	?	?	0
Secondary negative	+	0	+/0	0	0	0

+, reinforcement present; 0, reinforcement absent; +/0, weak reinforcement probable; ?, data inadequate to form conclusion

Narcotics

Primary positive reinforcement is considerable, especially when the drugs are used intravenously. Apparently, however, since many occasional users spontaneously discontinue narcotics (24), this reinforcement must be weighed against others that the user has learned are available to him. One might eschew drugs, e.g., if they cost him the love of his girl friend; whereas, another user, whose past experience led him to believe that he could not be loved, might seek continuing reinforcement from drugs.

Negative reinforcement for narcotic administration is also powerful. The withdrawal syndrome is particularly uncomfortable, and relief comes very rapidly after drug use. Negative reinforcement from diminished attention to aversive stimuli in the environment (the "blotto effect" or "going on the nod") also follows narcotic administration. Narcotics thus chemically induce social isolation for people seeking it on the basis of past unhappy experiences.

The abuse of heroin and its relatives certainly obtains secondary positive reinforcement. The drugs facilitate entrance into a gang. For people who find rebellion against authority to be reinforcing, narcotic abuse places them in conflict with the law and with social mores. Thus, unrelated to drug effects, reinforcing social relations are established through narcotic use.

As noted earlier, narcotics may reduce aggressiveness. This direct drug effect on behavior might increase the reinforcement some users could obtain from certain environments. Chaining, in which each element of the chain of drug abuse behaviors develops reinforcing properties for preceding elements, is difficult to assess but may contribute to recidivism, as discussed above.

Secondary negative reinforcement with narcotics occurs in the laboratory and probably develops in humans who have been withdrawn repeatedly under similar circumstances.

Stimulants

The amphetamines, cocaine, and related compounds are stimulants. As noted above, their abuse results in strong primary positive reinforcement. Primary negative reinforcement apparently does not occur with the amphetamines because the withdrawal syndrome is mild or absent, and, rather than decreasing attention, these drugs actually increase attention to aversive stimuli, eventuating in a paranoid psychotic state.

Secondary positive reinforcement unrelated to drug effects is probably considerable for young "speed freaks" in methamphetamine colonies. Drug use makes them part of a subculture, joining them with others rebelling against law and society.

Amphetamine abuse is probably the clearest case for secondary positive reinforcement from a drug-induced change in behavior. As noted above, the drug may be used by those who wish to increase their assertiveness.

Chaining might occur with stimulants, but the absence of a serious withdrawal syndrome makes it unlikely that secondary negative reinforcement could be important.

Sedative-hypnotics and Alcohol

The barbiturates and alcohol produce primary positive reinforcement (2), and probably so do a number of commonly abused sedative-hypnotics (meprobamate, ethchlorvynol, glutethimide, etc.).

Although the withdrawal syndrome from these drugs is extremely severe, the sedative-hypnotics relieve withdrawal symptoms very slowly.

In one study (25), a patient in barbiturate withdrawal required 2 days of continuing drug administration to alleviate his symptoms; whereas, narcotic withdrawal is relieved almost immediately by narcotic administration. Since the strongest primary negative reinforcement for behavior occurs when the aversive state terminates immediately upon completion of the behavior, primary negative reinforcement with alcohol or barbiturate withdrawal is probably weaker than with the narcotics. Indeed, monkeys sometimes spontaneously stop alcohol self-administration, weathering marked withdrawal symptoms before beginning again (2). This pattern is not seen in monkeys taking pentobarbital, which may be more rapid-acting than alcohol.

On the other hand alcohol and the sedative hypnotics exert a potent blotto effect. This may produce major negative reinforcement in states of severe intoxication.

Secondary positive reinforcers unrelated to the pharmacologic effects of sedative-hypnotics probably vary considerably with different patients. High dose amphetamine abusers sometimes mix barbiturates in the syringe, and they apparently take great pride in discussing their various recipes. The social reaction to such boasting is undoubtedly reinforcing for many users. For the housewife abusing sleeping drugs alone at home, "getting away with something" may be reinforcing, being a clandestine antagonistic action toward her husband or others.

The direct behavioral effects of different doses of sedative-hypnotics are complex and poorly understood. For example, when phenobarbital is acutely administered to rats, high and low doses affect aggression oppositely. Chronically administered, the drug has no effect on unlearned aggression, but impairs the learning of new aggressive behavior (15). We are thus limited in assessing what secondary reinforcement may accrue from the direct behavioral effects of these drugs. However, clinicians have long suspected that one reason for the abuse of alcohol and sedative-hypnotic drugs is the expression of hostility. The aggression of the intoxicated husband may be a powerful aversive stimulus for his wife, and if spouse-punishing reinforces him, he may use intoxicants to punish her.

Chaining could occur with these drugs, and given the severity of the withdrawal syndrome, secondary negative reinforcement might take place.

Hallucinogens and Marijuana

There is very little information available on hallucinogen and marijuana reinforcement. But for 2000 years the Indians have used marijuana as a euphoriant (26), suggesting some primary positive reinforcement for the use of hemp derivatives. In naive users, this effect is probably small, for they cannot distinguish the experiences of smoking marijuana or placebo (27). Some other hallucinogens may produce primary positive reinforcement. In subhallucinogenic doses DOM ("STP", 2,5-dimethoxy-4-methyl amphetamine) and DOET (2,5-dimethoxy-4-ethyl amphetamine) made human subjects euphoric (28). However, monkeys will not self-administer mescaline even after 1 month of free, priming injections (2). Users sometimes describe an LSD flash, but it is probably induced by the other drugs which contaminate 90% of "street samples" (29).

"Pronounced physical and mental discomfort" reportedly occur upon withdrawal from high-dose hemp abuse as practiced in India (26), but withdrawal symptoms are not common at the lower doses used in Western societies. This obviously limits primary negative reinforcement from the termination of withdrawal.

These drugs may reduce the aversiveness of the user's environment by altering, rather than reducing his perception of aversive stimuli, producing another kind of primary negative reinforcement. By analogy, a laboratory rat which is regularly shocked in a chamber will crouch, defecate, urinate, and look "frightened" whenever it is in the chamber. If the walls are painted in patterns, the light brightened, and a tone is introduced, the chamber will be less aversive to the rat when he next enters it. Altering the stimulus parameters of a previously aversive environment makes it less aversive. The ability of the hallucinogens to alter one's perception of environmental stimuli may provide negative reinforcement to users who find the unchanged stimuli aversive. One of my patients recently said to another, "Maybe you take acid to make the world beautiful when it really isn't." Perhaps the users' "need to feel" (30) is just a need to feel different.

Powerful secondary reinforcement unrelated to drug effects unquestionably promotes the use of marijuana and the hallucinogens. A cult of abuse has arisen around them, and membership is obtained through drug use. One becomes a member of an "in-group" by smoking marijuana or "dropping acid." Again, the element of rebellion in this drug use may be very reinforcing to certain people.

Smith (31) writes that LSD "produces an inhibition of aggression and an orientation toward nonviolence," and Blacker's group (32) noted "profound nonaggressive attitudes" among users. The LSD experience is highly aversive (a "bad trip") if the user is angry at the time, Baker reports, and he speculates that chronic use might suppress anger through this repeated aversive conditoning. If verified, this would be a unique example of a direct drug effect being used in autoconditioning of emotional responses. There is no evidence for chaining or secondary negative reinforcement from the hallucinogens or marijuana.

Multiple Drug Abuse

Some people indiscriminately abuse numerous drugs, obtaining primary positive reinforcement from any drug with that capacity. Certain drug combinations could be more reinforcing than either constituent alone, one drug altering the the biochemical response to another. For instance, we find that amphetamine's release of norepinephrine from rat brain tissue is significantly reduced if the animals have been chronically maintained on phenobarbital (Azzaro, Rutledge, and Crowley, in preparation).

Primary negative reinforcement through withdrawal is unlikely since most indiscriminant users probably do not take any one drug frequently enough to develop physical dependence.

Secondary positive reinforcement unrelated to drug effects may follow multiple drug use. The now-familiar reinforcement of social grouping again emerges from newspaper reports of partying youths drawing blindly from a bowl containing various pills.

Primary negative reinforcement through altered attention and secondary positive reinforcement from the behavioral effects of a particular drug must be relatively unimportant to people who randomly mix drugs. If the user's "mixed bag" includes alcohol, sedative-hypnotics, or narcotics, there would be some primary negative reinforcement through the blotto effect. But these users do not habitually seek speed, go on the nod, nor get blotto. Such behavioral effects, as noted above, probably contribute to drug-selection, and the chief characteristic of this syndrome is nonselection. Of course, this would not apply to those users who habitually and carefully combine only certain drugs in certain proportions.

Again, there is no direct evidence for chaining in multiple drug abuse, and in the absence of a withdrawal syndrome there could be no secondary negative reinforcement.

Mellow Yellow

As discussed earlier, it appears that the only reinforcements maintaining banana-smoking are secondary positive and unrelated to drug effects.

DIFFERENT TREATMENTS AFFECT DIFFERENT REINFORCEMENTS

Table 1 points up the seriousness of narcotic abuse—all types of reinforcement may help to maintain the behavior. The self-administration of no other drug class is reinforced in so many ways. Since various treatments are addressed to different reinforcers, treatment planning depends first upon evaluating which reinforcers are significant in a particular case, and then applying the appropriate treatment. Let us use narcotic abuse as an example of the effects of various treatments on different reinforcers.

Methadone maintenance eliminates primary positive reinforcement. Methadone, a long-acting narcotic, is given in such high doses that the user becomes tolerant to the common street-dose of heroin. This tolerance, by blocking the "narcotic high" (the primary positive reinforcement), permits *extinction* of heroin-administration behavior through nonreinforcement: repeated injections produce no reinforcing "high," and the behavior gradually ceases. By contrast, disulfiram (Antabuse) *punishes* alcohol self-administration, producing physical illness after drinking. Extinction by nonreinforcement is generally more successful than punishment in eliminating a habit, and indeed methadone appears to be more effective in reducing heroin abuse than is disulfiram in reducing alcohol abuse. By eliminating primary positive reinforcement, methadone maintenance also deconditions chaining, for only continued association with a primary reinforcer maintains reinforcing properties in the elements of the chain.

Methadone maintenance also interferes with primary negative reinforcement. Through tolerance it blocks the blotto effect of heroin in street doses; neither is heroin needed any longer to terminate withdrawal, because methadone is sufficiently long-acting that, taken once daily, it prevents withdrawal.

Since methadone maintenance prevents physiological withdrawal, it would help decondition the conditioned withdrawal state that permits secondary negative reinforcement. Users may undergo withdrawal in certain places, or with certain people, so frequently that the mere appearance of those places or people begins to precipitate withdrawal through Pavlovian conditioning. As long as the user stays on methadone, true physiological withdrawal would never again be paired with the precipitating stimuli, gradually deconditioning their association to withdrawal. Thus methadone maintenance removes the opportunity for secondary negative reinforcement, which accrues when a conditioned withdrawal state is terminated by drug-taking.

As noted above certain users may be able to obtain more social reinforcement through the narcotics' suspected ability to reduce aggressiveness. Assumedly, methadone would also have this property, which might provide some reinforcement for patients to continue on methadone.

Methadone maintenance attacks so many reinforcers for narcotic abuse that in most cases no other treatment is needed (33, 35), and similar blockers for other drug classes are being sought (36). Dole and Nyswander believe that methadone's success may indicate a metabolic origin in addiction (37), but the drug's interference with the reinforcement for narcotic abuse argues as strongly for a behavioristic basis to the disorder.

Detoxification (the withdraw-and-dry-out treatment) only affects primary negative reinforcement. The user who is forcibly withdrawn from heroin will no longer have withdrawal symptoms, the termination of which could reinforce drug use. But high relapse rates after detoxification demonstrate the importance of other reinforcers to which the treatment is not addressed.

Psychotherapy might aim at secondary positive reinforcers by examining the user's typical ways of relating to people, how drug-induced changes in his behavior obtain reinforcements for him, and why he finds reinforcement in association with rebellious groups. Psychotherapy might examine how the user came to doubt his capacity to achieve reinforcements other than drugs and might be used to demonstrate to him, through the relationship with the therapist, that he can obtain other major reinforcers. Experience, however, has shown that traditional psychotherapy alone for drug abuse tends to be unsuccessful, probably because it leaves untouched so many other important reinforcers.

Clinicians commonly apply one or another of the above treatments, saying of treatment failures, "He wasn't motivated to change." Careful consideration of the multiple reinforcers involved might indicate the motivation for a particular patient to continue his drug abuse, leading to a more comprehensive program of therapy tailored to the needs of the individual addict. For some, this might mean only hospitalization and withdrawal; for most, perhaps, methadone maintenance; and for some others, methadone maintenance plus psychotherapy. The key to this kind of treatment planning lies in a detailed analysis of what reinforcers most actively maintain the self-administration habit in each patient.

SUMMARY

Drug-abuse behavior may be maintained by reinforcement of the following types: (1) primary positive; (2) primary negative (a) by termination of withdrawal; (b) by reducing attention to, or discrimination of, aversive stimuli; (3) secondary positive (a) social and unrelated to drug effects; (b) social and related to drug effects; (c) chaining; and (4) secondary negative.

Which type of reinforcement functions to maintain drug-abuse behavior appears to depend partly upon the class of drugs employed. The following drug classes are discussed in terms of reinforcers maintaining their abuse: narcotics, stimulants, sedative-hypnotics and alcohol, hallucinogens and marijuana, and placebo.

Different treatment modalities are aimed at different types of reinforcement. Using narcotic abuse as an example, methadone maintenance, detoxification, and traditional psychotherapy are discussed in terms of their effect on each of the types of reinforcement maintaining the drug habit.

REFERENCES

1. SMITH, D. E.: The characteristics of dependence in high-dose methamphetamine abuse. Int. J. Addictions 4:453, 1969.
2. DENEAU, G., YANAGITA, T., and SEEVERS, M. H.: Self-administration of psychoactive substances by the monkey. Psychopharmacologia (Berlin) 16:30, 1969.
3. SCHUSTER, C. R., and THOMPSON, T.: Self-administration of and behavioral dependence on drugs. Ann. Rev. Pharmacol. 9:483, 1969.
4. JAFFE, J. H.: Drug addiction and drug abuse. In Goodman, L. S., and Gilman, A. (Eds.): The Pharmacologic Basis of Therapeutics (ed. 4). New York, Macmillan, 1970.
5. GODDARD, D., deGODDARD, S. N., and WHITEHEAD, P. C.: Social factors associated with coca use in the Andean region. Int. J. Addictions 4:577, 1969.
6. HOLLAND, J. C., and SKINNER, B. F.: The Analysis of Behavior. New York, McGraw-Hill, 1961, p. 53.
7. SMITH, R.: The world of the Haight-Ashbury speed freak. J. Psychedel. Drugs 2: 172, 1969.
8. THOMPHSON, T., and PICKENS, R.: Stimulant self-administration by animals: Some comparisons with opiate self-administration. Fed. Proc. 29:6, 1970.
9. PICKENS, R., and HARRIS, W. C.: Self-administration of d-amphetamine by rats. Psychopharmacologia (Berlin) 12:158, 1968.
10. WIKLER, A.: A psychodynamic study of a patient during experimental self-regulated re-addiction to morphine. Psychiat. Quart. 26:270, 1952.
11. MELLO, N. K.: Some aspects of the behavioral pharmacology of alcohol. In Efron. D. H. (Ed.): Psychopharmacology: A Review of Progress 1957-1967. Washington, U.S. Government Printing Office, 1968.
12. ANGRIST, B. M., SCHWEITZER, J., FRIEDHOFF, A. J., and GERSHON, S.: Banana smoking: Chromatographic analysis of baked skins. New York J. Med. 67:2983, 1967.
13. HILL, H. E., HAERTZEN, C. A., WOLBACH, A. B., and MINER, E. J.: The Addiction Research Center Inventory: Standardization of scales which evaluate subjective effects of morphine, amphetamine, pentobarbital, alcohol, LSD-25, pyrohexyl, and chlorpromazine. Psychopharmacologia (Berlin) 4:167, 1963.
14. WIKLER, A., and RASOR, R. W.: Psychiatric aspects of drug addiction. Amer. J. Med. 14:566, 1953.

15. CROWLEY, T. J., and RUTLEDGE, C. O.: Aggressive behavior in phenobarbital-treated rats. *In* Scientific Proceedings in Summary Form, Annual Meeting of the American Psychiatric Association, Washington, American Psychiatric Association, 1971.
16. —: Chronic vs. acute methamphetamine or imipramine in rats: fighting and motor activity. Fed. Proc. 30:503, 1971.
17. WIEDER, H., and KAPLAN, E. H.: Drug use in adolescents. Psychoanal. Stud. Child 24:399, 1969.
18. FISCHMAN, V. S.: Stimulant users in the California Rehabilitation Center. Int. J. Addictions 3:113, 1968.
19. ELLINGWOOD, E. H.: Amphetamine psychosis: I. Description of the individuals and process. J. Nerv. Ment. Dis. 144:273, 1967.
20. DAHLSTROM, W. G., and WELSH, G. S.: An MMPI Handbook. Minneapolis, University of Minnesota Press, 1960, p. 203.
21. GOLDBERG, S., and SCHUSTER, C. R.: Conditioned suppression by a stimulus associated with nalorphine in morphine-dependent monkeys. J. Exp. Anal. Behav. 10:235, 1967.
22. WIKLER, A., and PESCOR, F. T.: Classical conditioning of a morphine-abstinence phenomenon, reinforcement of opioid drinking behavior, and "relapse" in morphine-addicted rats. Psychopharmacologia (Berlin) 10:255, 1967.
23. —: On the nature of addiction and habituation. Brit. J. Addict. 57:73, 1961.
24. CHEIN, I., GERARD, D. L., LEE, R. S., and ROSENFELD, E.: The Road to H. New York, Basic Books, 1964, p. 159.
25. ISBELL, H., ALTSCHUL, S. KORNETSKY, C. H., EISENMAN, A. J., FLANARY, H. G., and FRASER, H. F.: Chronic barbiturate intoxication, Arch. Neurol. (Chicago) 64:1, 1950.
26. CHOPRA, G. S.: Man and marijuana. Int. J. Addictions. 4:215, 1969.
27. WEIL, A. T., ZINBERG, N. E., and NELSON, J. M.: Clinical and psychological effects of marijuana in man. Int. J. Addictions. 4:426, 1969.
28. SNYDER, S. H., FAILLACE, L. A., and WEINGARTNER, H.: DOM (STP), a new hallucinogenic drug, and DOET: effects in normal subjects. Amer. J. Psychiat. 125:356, 1968.
29. SMITH, D. E.: Editor's note. J. Psychedelic Drugs 3:5, 1970.
30. FREEDMAN, D. X.: On the use and abuse of LSD. Arch. Gen. Psychiat. (Chicago) 18:330, 1968.
31. SMITH, D. E.: LSD, violence, and radical religious beliefs. J. Psychedelic Drugs 3:38, 1970.
32. BLACKER, K. H., JONES, R. T., STONE, G. C., and PFEFFERBAUM, D.: Chronic users of LSD: The "acidheads." Amer. J. Psychiat. 125:341, 1968.
33. Methadone Maintenance Evaluation Committee: Progress report of evaluation of methadone maintenance treatment program as of March 31, 1968. JAMA 206:2712, 1968.
34. DOLE, V. P., NYSWANDER, M. E., and WARNER, A.: Successful treatment of 750 criminal addicts. JAMA 206:2708, 1968.
35. —, ROBINSON, W., ORRACA, J., TOWNS, E., SEARCY, P., and CAINE, E.: Methadone treatment of randomly selected criminal addicts. New Eng. J. Med. 280:1372, 1969.
36. JAFFE, J. H.: Psychopharmacology and opiate dependence. *In* Effron, D. H. (Ed.): Psychopharmacology: A Review of Progress 1957-1967. Washington, U.S. Government Printing Office, 1968.
37. DOLE, P., and NYSWANDER, M. E.: Methadone maintenance and its implication for theories of narcotic addiction. Res. Publ. Ass. Res. Nerv. Ment. Dis. 46:359, 1968.

23

DRUG ABUSE AS EXCESSIVE BEHAVIOR

R. M. Gilbert

Four things are proposed in this paper. The first is that pharmacology may not have very much to do with drug abuse. The second is that drug taking in itself is, generally speaking, neither harmful nor undesirable. Drug taking need pose a problem only when it is excessive, that is to say, when it occurs with frequency sufficient to disrupt the effective functioning of an organism. Thirdly, because it is the excessive nature of the drug-taking behaviour that is the problem, just as much as the fact that drugs are involved, it is probably as wise to search for the causes of drug abuse among the causes of all kinds of excessive behaviour as it is to focus upon the peculiarly pharmacological aspects of the drug-taking situation. For example, alcoholism may have as much in common with overeating as it has with social drinking. The fourth proposal is that a recently discovered experimental procedure known as schedule induction, which is capable of generating vast amounts of apparently unadaptive behaviour, may provide a useful model for excessive human behaviour generally, and drug abuse in particular.

WHY DO ORGANISMS TAKE PSYCHOTROPIC DRUGS?

The obvious answer is that these drugs are taken for the desirable pharmacological effects that they provide. Alcohol is consumed to sedate

Reprinted with permission from *Canadian Psychological Review*, 1976, *17*, 231-240.
Based on an invited lecture given at Université Laval and elsewhere during 1975.

and to release inhibitions. Heroin is injected to relieve pain and to achieve euphoria. Caffeine is taken to aid wakefulness. LSD-25 is used to promote hallucinations. In addition, chronic use of psychotropic drugs causes dependence, and a drug may be taken more for its ability to relieve abstinence symptoms than for its other effects.

The problem with the obvious answer is that there is much evidence to suggest that drug use has quite different causes, and indeed that some drugs may be taken in spite of rather than because of their pharmacological effects. What follows is a very brief and selective review of some of the evidence against the importance of pharmacology.

To begin with nicotine: Cigarette smoking is a prevalent and dangerous habit that is difficult to discard and generally thought to be maintained by dependence on nicotine. If people smoke in order to achieve or maintain a nicotine blood level one would expect that reducing the nicotine content of cigarettes would produce a compensating increase in the number of cigarettes smoked. The results of many studies indicate that, at best, there is only partial compensation. For example, Russell, Wilson, Patel, Cole, and Feyerabend (1973) examined the effect of substituting high- or low-nicotine cigarettes for regular cigarettes during 5-hr. portions of the working day. They found that the 10 subjects did not compensate for the changes in nicotine content. Goldfarb, Jarvik, and Glick (1970) asked heavy smokers to switch for 3 weeks to lettuce-leaf cigarettes to which varying amounts of nicotine had been added. Subjects smoked fewer lettuce cigarettes than regular cigarettes (a mean of 15.6 per day as opposed to 23.1 per day), but consumption of lettuce cigarettes was quite independent of their nicotine content, which ranged from 0.0 to 2.25 mg per cigarette (the usual range is 1.2-1.6 mg). Experience with the stronger tasting and generally less acceptable lettuce cigarettes reduced subsequent consumption of their regular cigarettes to a mean of 17.0 per day, at least for one week. Administration of nicotine by capsule, independently of smoking, has been shown to produce only a slight reduction in cigarette use, a reduction that nowhere near compensated for the ingested nicotine (Jarvik, Glick, and Nakamura, 1970). A study that may be very significant in its elucidation of the controlling variables in cigarette smoking is one conducted by Goldfarb and Jarvik (1972). They gave 18 smokers halved regular cigarettes for one week and told them to smoke only as far as a half-way line on full-size cigarettes for another week. Subjects smoked pretty much the same number whether they were smoking cut, lined or regular cigarettes, suggesting that lighting a cigarette may be more important than smoking one. The data from all of these experiments indicate that nicotine is not an important factor in the regulation of cigarette consumption.

I have dwelt at length on supposed nicotine dependence for two reasons. One reason is that some of the best experiments on the role of pharmacology in drug dependence have been done on nicotine's role in smoking. The other reason is that smoking may be the strongest of drug habits, even stronger than heroin use. Russell (1974) reported a study of 278 London, England opiate users who were asked to rank drugs according to their "need" for them. Cigarettes were the most needed drug, ahead of alcohol, coffee, tea, barbiturates, amphetamines, hallucinogens, and even opiates, including heroin. Russell also observed that 3 out of 4 smokers want to or have tried to stop smoking, that only 15 per cent do stop, and that only 2 per cent can engage in occasional smoking. Even this most powerful of drug habits, as I have indicated earlier, is not clearly dependent on the pharmacological properties of the ingested compound.

Caffeine is probably the most widely used drug. According to the results of a survey of drinking practices conducted for the Addiction Research Foundation, well over 90 per cent of Ontario's adult population use it. Goldstein, Kaiser, and Whitby (1969) have shown experimentally that physical dependence on caffeine is associated with the use of 5 or more cups of coffee a day. In Ontario, it would appear that about 25 per cent of the adult population is physically dependent on caffeine. (Gilbert, 1976b). Do heavy coffee drinkers drink coffee because they are physically dependent on caffeine? Our survey data suggest that there are other sources of control; that there are very different patterns of tea and coffee use in spite of the pharmacological similarity of these two caffeine-containing beverages. What varies chiefly between heavy and moderate users of caffeine is the amount drunk, and I shall suggest later that control over the quantities consumed could also be non-pharmacological.

In the same survey, a strong correlation was discovered between cigarette smoking and coffee consumption but not tea consumption. The difference is probably related to the patterning of the two beverages. Tea is drunk at meals, coffee between meals—when cigarettes are usually smoked. People who drink a lot of coffee and smoke a lot may experience environments that cause them to overbehave between meals. Conversely, people who drink a lot of tea may be caused to overbehave at meals.

Situation dependency also seems to be a conspicuous feature of heroin and alcohol use. Heavy users often cease excessive drug use when the environment is changed—often too without apparent withdrawal symptoms. The expected avalanche of heroin addicts among returning Vietnam veterans did not materialize. Of a sample of 492 enlistees whose urine was positive for opiates at the time of departure from Vietnam, three-quarters claimed that while in Vietnam they had been dependent on heroin. On their return to the U.S.A. most ceased using opiates, and 8-12 months later only 7 per cent showed signs of dependence (Robins, Davis, and Goodwin, 1974).

The Addiction Research Foundation runs a farm community for skid-row alcoholics. They are taken off skid-row and subjected to a period of enforced abstinence that is imposed on their arrival at the farm. In this very different environment they just stop drinking—it seems to be as simple as that. Subsequently, a majority of residents engage in moderate social drinking, maintaining voluntary abstinence on most days (Oki, 1974). The lack of withdrawal symptoms on arrival at the farm, and the subsequent ability to drink moderately, both suggest that the former alcoholism was maintained largely by features of the skid-row environment rather than by physical dependence on alcohol. Likewise, heroin use in Vietnam was maintained by the soldiers' environment there rather than by physical dependence on heroin.

One of my favourite studies on the role of certain non-pharmacological factors in alcohol consumption employed a group of non-abstinent alcoholics and a group of social drinkers who were both given a fake taste test that involved the consumption of vodka and tonic or tonic alone when they were led to believe that either drink could be vodka and tonic or tonic alone (Marlatt, Demming, and Reid, 1973). Neither group of subjects was able to tell the difference between the two drinks: estimates of alcohol content were based on what they were told they were drinking, rather than on what they were actually drinking. To me, the most interesting features of their data, however, are the amounts consumed. Subjects could drink as much as they pleased during the tests. Both groups drank much more when they were told that the drink contained alcohol than when they were told that it did not contain alcohol, whether or not the drink actually contained alcohol. Alcoholics distinguished themselves by drinking more than the social drinkers under all four conditions. They consumed their greater quantities making fewer sips than social drinkers, but the sips, of course, were considerably larger. One might conclude from these data that alcoholics drink a lot of alcohol because they drink a lot of all fluids, and because, like most people, they drink more of a fluid when they believe it to contain alcohol.

Doubts can also be cast on the basis for the consumption of drugs available on the illicit market. Of the 817 samples of alleged psychotropic "street" drugs received for analysis by the laboratories of the Addiction Research Foundation during the period April 1971-March 1973, 160, or just over 20 per cent, contained no known psychotropic drug. Of the 624 samples that were alleged to be a particular drug (as opposed to just a psychotropic drug), 364 (58 per cent) did not contain the alleged ingredient. In particular, only 1 of 113 samples of alleged mescaline actually contained mescaline; only 8 of 25 samples of alleged heroin actually contained heroin; only 10 of 21 samples of alleged cocaine actually contained cocaine; and only 38 of 69 samples of an alleged amphetamine drug actually contained amphetamine (Dr. J. A. Marshman—personal communication). This analysis is continuing. It indicates that, if anything, the proportion of psychoactive street drugs without a psychoactive component may be increasing, possibly a consequence of increasing general austerity, but perhaps too representing a growing realization on the part of dealers of the lack of importance of pharmacology in drug abuse.

The selection of evidence just presented borders on the polemical in an attempt to belabour a point that has been made often. The point is simply this: Because a substance *can* have a pharmacological effect, it does not automatically follow that use of the substance is caused by or maintained by that effect. None of the evidence I have cited rules out a role for pharmacology. For example, it is conceivable that the non-pharmacological determinants of smoking owe their origin and even their continuing effectiveness to the reinforcing properties of nicotine, and that extinction of the effectiveness would require a longer period than has been employed in the reported experiments. Nevertheless, it appears to me to be the case that the more one investigates drug use the more important seems to be the role of non-pharmacological factors.

WHEN SHOULD DRUG USE BE A PROBLEM?

Drug use becomes a problem, generally speaking, when it occurs to excess. Historical quirks produce situations in which some psychoactive drugs are banned altogether, but the selection of drugs for proscription by a community usually bears little relation to the actual harm caused by using the drug. Heroin is an obvious example. Because of the hysteria associated with this drug, it is not realized that moderate use occurs extensively. Such use was noted in the study of Vietnam veterans, whose authors concluded ". . . the occasional use of narcotics without becoming addicted appears to be possible even for men who have previously been dependent on narcotics" (Robins et al., 1974). When drug use is sanctioned, there are invariably some who claim that all use of a particular drug is harmful. However, drug use in moderation is usually tolerated with equanimity. Often it is believed to make a positive contribution to society. Drug use to excess is rarely applauded, especially when it is seen to interfere with the effective functioning of an individual or those around her. The problem is often that of defining excess. If social drinkers always took one or two drinks a day, and alcoholics always more than six drinks a day, there would be no problem in drawing the line. In reality there is a continuum of consumption, as has been shown in many studies, particular by de Lint and Schmidt (1968) who examined the alcohol buying behaviour of a large sample of Ontario's adult population. (In case it seems strange that buying should be given as evidence of consumption, it should be noted that observation of actual consumption is impractical, and that interrogation about drinking practices leads to severe underestimation and possible distortion of consumption levels (Pernanen, 1974). Distortion probably occurs with respect to the reporting of food consumption: according to a national survey by Nutrition Canada (1973), overweight people eat less than average amounts of food (Table 5-13, P. 84).) The data we have about use of other drugs suggest too that there is a continuum of consumption between moderate and excessive users. Thus, any attempt to define the limits of excessive use must seem arbitrary.

The problem of defining excessive use should not deter us from appreciating that excessive use is the problem. Diseases associated with the use of alcohol, caffeine, and tobacco all increase in incidence with increased use of the drug. Interference with normal functioning increases with excessive use because of these diseases, because of intoxication, and because of the inordinate amount of time spent in seeking, preparing, and consuming the substance.

Let us compare drug use with eating. They differ in that one is necessary and the other is not. However, this may serve only to locate the distribution function at a different point on the scale. I am confident that, if data were available, one would find that the frequency distribution of amounts eaten would be distributed in much the same way as the frequency distributions of drug consumption. Defining excessive eating is not so much of a problem, because calorific balance provides a fairly clear borderline, but the hazards of behaving excessively can be very similar. The incidence of various diseases increases with obesity. Obesity, which can be regarded as chronic food intoxication, interferes with normal functioning, as does the inordinate amount of time spent in seeking, preparing, and consuming the food. Obesity and alcoholism may be similar in other respects. During fake taste tests alcoholics drink more than other people, as indicated earlier (Marlatt, et al., 1973). Obese people eat more than other people under similar conditions (Hill and McCutcheon, 1975). Moreover, as the alcoholics drink more by taking fewer but larger sips, so do the obese eat more by taking fewer but larger bites, in both cases achieving a higher rate of consumption.

So-called compulsive behaviours, for example, book-buying, hand-washing, and lip-licking, are probably distributed in a similar manner. It is their excessive nature that is the problem, not their mere occurrence. Handwashing becomes a problem only when it occurs so frequently that skin is diseased, hands are disabled, and little time is left to do anything else.

THE CAUSES OF DRUG ABUSE

If drug use is a problem because it is excessive, rather than because it occurs, it seems reasonable to search for the causes of drug abuse among the causes of excessive behaviour rather than among the causes of drug use. Thus one would ask questions about an alcoholic in this order:

1. Why is she behaving to excess?
2. Why is alcohol drinking her excessive behaviour?

rather than in this order:

1. Why does he drink alcohol?
2. Why does he drink alcohol excessively?

The second order is the conventional one. It assumes that the causes of drug *use* somehow act more strongly to produce drug *abuse*; that if you know why the person drinks alcohol, you can more easily find out why the person drinks alcohol excessively. The first order of questions assumes that there are two sets of predisposing conditions: one that causes excessive behaviour, and another that causes the excessive behaviour to be alcohol drinking. In pursuing the implications of the two orders of questions one soon sees a difference in the potential consequences of a strategy to reduce alcohol drinking. If the second order is appropriate, reducing alcohol drinking would not have any particular effect on other behaviour, except that the former alcoholic would have to be doing *something* at the times when he used to drink alcohol. If the first question is appropriate, one is left with the conclusion that merely reducing an alcoholic's alcohol drinking would cause her to behave excessively in other, possibly equally harmful ways. Proper treatment in this case should involve attacking the causes of excessive behaviour.

There is no substantial evidence that substitution of one excessive behaviour for another occurs when a particular excessive behaviour is reduced in frequency or eliminated. There is a little evidence, however; some of it anecdotal. Members of Alcoholics Anonymous are said to drink inordinate amounts of coffee. There is better evidence that eating replaces smoking as excessive behaviour. For example, British middle-aged males tend to be about 30 lbs. over their ideal weights if they are non-smokers and only 15 lbs. overweight if they are smokers. The weights of ex-smokers catch up with those who have never smoked after only a few years of abstinence (Khosla and Lowe, 1971). (Incidentally, middle-aged ex-smokers may be even more likely to have heart trouble than either smokers or those who have never smoked (Khosla and Lowe, 1973), possibly a consequence of the accelerated weight-gain on quitting.)

Other evidence that might point to the importance of excessive behaviour comes from studies of multiple drug use. Alcohol consumption is positively correlated with both cigarette and coffee consumption (Friedman, Siegelaub, and Seltzer, 1974), although our own data show that the correlation between alcohol and coffee consumption breaks down at the highest levels: presumably, beyond a certain point, consumption of the one physically excludes excessive consumption of the other. Alcoholics, especially young alcoholics, appear also to use and abuse drugs other than caffeine and nicotine more than non-alcoholics (Freed, 1973). Thus there is an indication that overbehaving by one person may take a variety of forms. However, it is also possible that use of one drug has a special relationship to the use of one or more other drugs that obviates the need to postulate a common, independent etiology for the excessive use of both drugs. For example, I have found that caffeine consumption by poorly nourished rats may cause alcohol consumption (Gilbert, 1976a).

If indeed there are two sets of conditions that predispose excessive behaviour, it is entirely possible that each is a behaviour-environment interaction, one determining that excessive behaviour will occur, the other that a particular behaviour will occur to excess. Are there behaviour processes that are known to generate excessive behaviour?

SCHEDULE INDUCTION OF EXCESSIVE BEHAVIOUR

There is one procedure, first reported by Falk (1961), that reliably generates quite extraordinary amounts of behaviour. Most of the data concerning this procedure have been gained with rats and other infra-humans, although there is evidence too that it can generate excessive behaviour in humans (Kachanoff, Leveille, McLelland and Wayner, 1973). Most of the excessive behaviour that has been generated by this procedure has been water drinking, but there is evidence too, as I shall indicate later, that it can generate inordinate consumption of drugs. Falk's original study consisted of training hungry rats to press a bar for small pellets of food that could be gained, on the average, once every minute. Each pellet was about one-three hundredth of the regular daily ration. A water bottle was continuously available. Falk observed that, while working for the small, intermittently available pellets, the rats drank an average of 3.43 times their regular *daily* intake in each 190-minute session (Falk, 1961). (To put this increase in perspective: adult humans typically drink about 3 pints of fluid a day, although there is wide variation. Thus, translated into human terms, which is not always advisable, Falk's rats were drinking the equivalent of 17 12-ounce bottles of beer in the three-hour session.) The pattern of the induced drinking was quite predictable. When a pellet was earned it was immediately consumed, and a draught of water was taken to "wash it down," so to speak. The excessive drinking, or polydipsia, generated by this procedure was given the name *schedule-induced polydipsia,* "schedule-induced" because the excessive drinking is caused by the schedule of presentation of the food pellets. It was discovered later that if the pellets are presented more frequently than about once every 30 seconds, or less frequently than about once every 4 minutes, then polydipsia is not induced to any marked degree. The number of pellets presented on each occasion is also an important variable. For a given interval there is generally more polydipsia but less drinking per pellet with an increase in the number of pellets. Falk (1966) introduced the term "adjunctive behaviour" to describe the behaviour generated by such schedules. It is an apt term, neutral with respect to the origin of the behaviour, but descriptive of the behaviour's supernumerary relationship to the schedule that maintains it.

Much valuable work has been done on scehdule-induced behaviour since 1961 (see Falk, 1972; and Segal, 1972 for reviews). The salient findings have been:

(i) Whenever reinforcers are doled out to a deprived animal in small portions and within a certain range of delivery rates, the animal is likely to engage in excessive behaviour that is not obviously related to the reinforcer.

(ii) The type of excessive behaviour that occurs depends on what is possible. Polydipsia is most commonly studied, but polyphagia and pica have also been induced, as have excessive aggression, tail gnawing, hair licking, and wheel running. Schedule-induced excessive behaviour has been observed in species as different as pigeon, rat, and man.

(iii) It is not necessary for the animal to work for the spaced reinforcers. For example, intermittent feeding induces polydipsia in the rat whether or not barpressing or any other kind of behaviour is required for food presentation.

(iv) If it can, schedule-induced behaviour occurs shortly after presentation of each of the spaced reinforcers, rather than elsewhere in the inter-reinforcer interval. However, schedule-induced behaviour will occur at any chosen point of the interval if it is possible for a brief period only at that point. Thus schedule induction is not necessarily a post-reinforcer phenomenon. It can occur whenever it is possible to emit the behaviour, although it is more likely to occur at some times than others.

(v) It is possible to prevent the development of a particular schedule-induced behaviour by preloading (e.g., with water in the case of drinking) or by providing strongly competing behaviour. It is difficult to eliminate established schedule-induced behaviour by pre-loading, although it can be eliminated by provision of strongly competing behaviour. Generally speaking, adjunctive behaviour disappears as soon as the conditions of its maintenance no longer exist (i.e., as soon as reinforcement is no longer intermittent).

(vi) The opportunity to emit an induced behaviour can serve as a reinforcer for other behaviour. Furthermore, inducing conditions where excessive behaviour is readily available are likely to be chosen over inducing conditions that do not easily allow occurrence of excessive behaviour.

Mechanisms of adjunctive behaviour remain obscure. Assertions that schedule-induced drinking is some kind of post-prandial artifact (Lotter, Woods, and Vasselli, 1973), are inconsistent with the data on meal-size (Millenson, 1975), and with demonstrations that such drinking can be readily separated from eating (Gilbert 1974a, b). Claims that adjunctive behaviour is a response to the thwarting conditions of the spaced reinforcement (Falk, 1972), while intituitively intriguing, do no more than describe the conditions of occurrence of this kind of behaviour. The suggestion that suitable spacing of reinforcing events causes a non-specific increase in motor excitability is also intriguing (Wayner, Singer, Cimino, Stein, and Dwoskin, 1975): it may be a sufficient behavioural explanation of the production of excessive behaviour, as opposed to the production of a particular excessive behaviour, which would depend in addition on the availability of appropriate stimuli and other factors.

As well as the work on adjunctive water polydipsia, there have also been many demonstrations of schedule-induced oral drug consumption, including solutions of alcohol, barbiturates, caffeine, and morphine. Consumption of alcohol under this procedure has been studied more than consumption of other drugs. Alcohol polydipsia is substantially similar to water polydipsia, but the following differences may be noted: (1) Under similar inducing conditions, alcohol polydipsia is usually less than water polydipsia; (2) Alcohol polydipsia declines during extended sessions, but water polydipsia persists; (3) Alcohol polydipsia may continue when the conditions for schedule induction are removed, whereas water polydipsia always ceases; (4) Alcohol polydipsia may be less sensitive to attenuation by stressors such as non-contingent electric shock.

The schedule-induction procedure has been found to be extremely useful as a means of making delivery of a concentrated solution of alcohol act as a reinforcer (Meisch, Henningfield, and Thompson, 1975). However, its value as a potential model of alcoholism is best exemplified by the fact that it is the only available experimental procedure that causes physical dependence on alcohol without relying on injection, intubation or forced oral consumption. As indicated earlier, drug abuse does not imply physical dependence. It should be added here that physical dependence could be a by-product of drug abuse without being in any way a cause of the excessive drug taking. In fact, as long as consumption is maintained, there might be no indication of physical dependence. Only when consumption stops, for whatever reason, and a withdrawal syndrome appears, would physical dependence be noticed. Nevertheless, its ability to cause rats to drink sufficient alcohol to make them physically dependent is an indicator of the possible importance of the process of schedule-induction in drug abuse.

Alcohol drinking sufficient to cause physical dependence has been induced during a number of experiments in which many sessions are given daily for many days (Ogata, Ogata, Mendelson, and Mello, 1972; Falk, Samson, and Winger, 1972; Samson and Falk, 1974). Two kinds of intermittency seem to be required for the production of physical dependence on alcohol, although definitive experiments remain to be done. In all these experiments, 6 daily one-hour sessions were given, each separated from the next by 3 hours. Also, pellets were presented at 2-minute intervals during the one-hour sessions. Physiologically, the net result was to maintain a constant high blood-alcohol level, averaging about 150 mg/100 ml. Pathologically, the net result was to produce tremors, spasticity, seizures, and even death when keys were shaken near rats that had been living under this regimen for 3 months, but that had been deprived of alcohol for 5-10 hours.

An extraordinarily interesting feature of the most recent of these studies (Samson and Falk, 1974) is that the very high alcohol consumption induced by the spaced feeding procedure declined when a more preferred fluid was available. In fact, when 0.25% saccharin was the alternative fluid, and the food allowance was reduced to 10 g per day, i.e., even less than required to maintain 80 percent of free-feeding body weight, some rats starved and died rather than switch back to the alcohol solution whose calories would have kept them alive. Saccharin solution intake meanwhile was of the order of 300 ml per day. This study illustrates the importance of palatability in alcohol consumption, and reinforces the point that which behaviour occurs to excess depends crucially on the immediate environmental situation in which the schedule-inducing conditions obtain. Heintzelman, Best, and Sinclair (1976) criticized the work on schedule-induced alcohol dependence because of their finding that rats did not maintain their consumption when withdrawn from the drug and then given free access to both alcohol and water without the conditions of schedule-induction being in effect. In view of Samson and Falk's data, they should have expected that alcohol might be forsaken for another fluid. Moreover, an observation that animals no longer drink a lot of alcohol when the conditions of schedule induction are removed may do no more than reinforce the view, expressed above, that excessive drug use is situation-dependent.

I mentioned earlier that there is a little evidence that this procedure can be used to generate excessive behaviour in humans. Such work is at an early stage, but will surely increase in quantity and become more sophisticated. In one of the few reports so far Kachanoff et al. (1973) described how unusual amounts of drinking from a water fountain could be induced in hospitalized patients diagnosed as schizophrenic when opportunities to earn pennies for pulling a cord were intermittently spaced. Other behaviour occurred to excess under the same conditions. Pacing was recorded but the authors also reported an increase in verbalization, jumping, and grooming as a function of the schedule of availability of the coins. In addition to this kind of demonstration, schedule-induction may have been a factor in the experimental elicitation of aggressive behaviour in nursery-school children by Frederiksen and Petersen (1974), and in other such studies.

In conclusion, I would like to stress that the role of schedule-induction in human drug abuse is at present merely a matter for speculation, although it is clear to me that the notion of drug abuse as excessive behaviour provides an exceedingly provocative and useful approach that is consistent with much that we know about the abuse of drugs, and about excessive behaviour generally. If the speculation about the role of schedule induction is to be taken seriously, an attempt must be made to identify, at least at an intuitive level, the conditions of everyday life that can induce excessive behaviour. One approach might be to explore the possibly relevant, common features of the environment-behaviour interactions of people that engage in conspicuous excessive behaviour, and to compare them with the interactions of people that do not appear to behave excessively. If speculation is to be elevated to the status of hypothesis, the comparison should reveal different patterns of interaction. The environment-behaviour interactions of overbehavers should correspond to the conditions for inducing excessive behaviour, whereas the interactions involving normal people should not.

REFERENCES

DE LINT, J. and SCHMIDT, W. The distribution of alcohol consumption in Ontario. *Quarterly Journal of Studies on Alcohol*, 1968, *29*, 968-973.

FALK, J. L. Production of polydipsia in normal rats by an intermittent food schedule. *Science*, 1961, *133*, 195-196.

FALK, J. L. Schedule-induced polydipsia as a function of fixed-interval length. *Journal of the Experimental Analysis of Behavior*, 1966, *9*, 37-39.

FALK, J. L. The nature and determinants of adjunctive behaviour. In R. M. Gilbert and J. D. Keehn (Eds.), *Schedule effects: drugs, drinking, and aggression.* Toronto: University of Toronto Press, 1972, Pp. 148-173.

FALK, J. L., SAMSON, H. H., and WINGER, G. Behavioral maintenance of high concentrations of blood ethanol and physical dependence in the rat. *Science*, 1972, *177*, 811-813.

FREDERIKSEN, L. W., and PETERSON, G. L. Schedule-induced aggression in nursery school children. *Psychological Record*, 1974, *24*, 343-351.

FREED, E. X. Drug abuse by alcoholics: a review. *International Journal of the Addictions*, 1973, *8*, 451-473.

FRIEDMAN, G. D., SIEGELAUB, A. B., and SELTZER, C. C. Cigarettes, alcohol, coffee and peptic ulcer. *New England Journal of Medicine*, 1974, *290*, 469-473.

GILBERT, R. M. Ubiquity of schedule-induced polydipsia. *Journal of the Experimental Analysis of Behavior*, 1974, *21*, 277-284.

GILBERT, R. M. Schedule-induced ethanol polydipsia in rats under conditions of restricted fluid availability. *Psychopharmacologia*, 1974, *38*, 151-157.

GILBERT, R. M. Dietary caffeine and alcohol consumption in rats. *Journal of Studies on Alcohol*, 1976, *37*, 11-18. (a)

GILBERT, R. M. Caffeine as a drug of abuse. In R. J. Gibbins, Y. Israel, H. Kalant, R. E. Popham, W. Schmidt, R. G. Smart, *Research Advances in Alcohol and Drug Problems.* (Vol. III). New York: Wiley, 1976. Pp. 49-176. (b)

GOLDFARB, T. L., and JARVIK, M. E. Accommodation to restricted tobacco smoke intake in cigarette smokers. *International Journal of the Addictions*, 1972, *7*, 559-565.

GOLDFARB, T. L., JARVIK, M. E., and GLICK, S. D. Cigarette nicotine content as a determinant of human smoking behavior. *Psychopharmacologia*, 1970, *17*, 89-93.

GOLDSTEIN, A., KAISER, S., and WHITBY, O. Psychotropic effects of caffeine in man. IV. Quantitative and qualitative differences associated with habituation to coffee. *Clinical Pharmacology and Therapeutics*, 1969, *10*, 489-497.

HEINTZELMAN, M. E., BEST, J., and SENTER, R. J. Polydipsia-induced alcohol dependency in rats: a re-examination. *Science*, 1976, *191*, 482-483.

HILL, S. W., and McCUTCHEON, N. B. Eating responses of obese and nonobese humans, *Psychosomatic Medicine*, 1975, *37*, 395-401.

JARVIK, M. E., GLICK, S. D., and NAKAMURA, R. K. Inhibition of cigarette smoking by orally administered nicotine. *Clinical Pharmacology and Therapeutics*, 1970, *11*, 574-576.

KACHANOFF, R., LEVEILLE, R., McCELLAND, J. P., and WAYNER, M. S. Schedule-induced behavior in humans. *Physiology and Behavior*, 1973, *11*, 395-398.

KHOSLA, T., and LOWE, C. R. Obesity and smoking habits. *British Medical Journal*, 1974, *4*, 10-13.

KHOSLA, T., and LOWE, C. R. Relative risks of obesity and smoking. *British Medical Journal,* 1973, *4,* 106.

LOTTER, E. C. WOODS, S. C., and VASSELLI, J. R. Schedule-induced polydipsia: an artifact. *Journal of Comparative and Physiological Psychology,* 1973, *83,* 478-484.

MARLATT, G. A., DEMMING, B., and REID, J. B. Loss of control drinking in alcoholics. *Journal of Abnormal Psychology,* 1973, *81,* 233-241.

MEISCH, R. A., HENNINGFIELD, J. E., and THOMPSON, T. Establishment of ethanol as a reinforcer for rhesus monkeys by the oral route: initial results. In M. M. Gross (Ed.), *Alcohol Intoxication and Withdrawal* (Advances in Experimental Medicine and Biology; v. 59). New York: Plenum Press, 1975. Pp. 323-342.

MILLENSON, J. R. The facts of schedule-induced polydipsia, *Behavior Research Methods and Instrumentation,* 1975, *5,* 257-259.

Nutrition Canada, *National survey.* Ottawa: Information Canada, 1973.

OGATA, H., OGATA, F., MENDELSON, J. H., and MELLO, N. K. Evaluation of a technique to induce alcohol dependence and tolerance in the mouse by the use of schedule-induced polydipsia. *Japanese Journal of Studies on Alcohol,* 1972, *7,* 27-35.

OKI, G. Alcohol use by Skid Row alcoholics: Part I. Drinking at Bon Accord. Addiction Research Foundation Substudy No. 612, 1974.

PERNANEN, K. Validity of survey of data on alcohol use. In R. J. Gibbins, Y. Israel, H. Kalant, R. E. Popham, W. Schmidt, and R. G. Smart (Eds.), *Research advances in alcohol and drug problems.* (Vol. I). New York: Wiley and Sons, 1974. Pp. 355-374.

ROBINS, L. N., DAVIS, D. H., and GOODWIN, D. W. Drug use by U.S. Army enlisted men in Vietnam: a follow-up on their return home. *American Journal of Epidemiology,* 1974, *99,* 235-249.

RUSSELL, M. A. H. The smoking habit and its classification. *The Practitioner,* 1974, *212,* 791-800.

RUSSELL, M. A. H., WILSON, C., PATEL, U. A., COLE, P. V., and FEYERABEND, C. Comparison of effect of tobacco consumption and carbon monoxide absorption of changing to high and low nicotine cigarettes. *British Medical Journal,* 1973, *4,* 512-516.

SAMSON, H. H., and FALK, J. L. Alteration of fluid preference in ethanol-dependent animals. *Journal of Pharmacology and Experimental Therapeutics,* 1974, *190,* 365-376.

SEGAL, E. F. Induction and the provenance of operants. In R. M. Gilbert and J. R. Millenson (Eds.) *Reinforcement: behavioral analyses.* New York: Academic Press, 1972, P. 1 34.

WAYNER, M. J., SINGER, G., CIMINO, K., STEIN, J., and DWOSKIN, L. Adjunctive behavior induced by different conditions of wheel running. *Physiology and Behavior,* 1975, *14,* 507-510.

Section V

PHYSIOLOGICAL FORMULATIONS OF ADDICTION

Explanation of psychoactive drug effects at the physiological level is now the norm in psychiatry and pharmacology. Physiological descriptions of the *processes* of drug tolerance, dependence, and withdrawal have likewise long been accepted. (See Platt & Labate, 1976, Chap. 5, for a review of such theories for heroin.) It was not until the 1960s, however, that the first physiological theory of the *etiology* of drug addiction was advanced. Based upon their "success" in treating out-patient heroin addicts with methadone, an orally-effective, long-acting opiate analgesic, Dole and Nyswander (1965, 1966, 1967) proposed the idea of a "metabolic deficiency" as the cause for heroin addiction. Although they did not specify the nature of this deficiency, it was postulated to cause the afflicted individual to experience intensely euphoric, as opposed to the usual dysphoric, effects from the first dose of heroin. Thereafter, craving for the drug would be overwhelming, disruption of the normal routines of daily living would follow, and thus lead inevitably to a life of crime.

On the basis of the reported success of the Dole and Nyswander program in New York City, the use of methadone maintenance as a treatment modality rapidly spread across the nation. Whereas Dole and Nyswander had defined heroin addiction as a *medical* problem of the individual, the municipal, state, and federal governments gradually came to view it as a *public health* problem of society. Methadone seemed to be the answer. As noted by Platt and Labate (1976), "methadone programs have received the heaviest government support in the history of the drug abuse treatment effort" (p. 288). Somehow, enhancing the quality of the life of the drug dependent individual became less important than providing a solution to society's putative public health problem of drug addiction. (See Corman, Johnson, Khantzian, & Long, 1973, for a comparison of these two emphases.)

Methadone maintenance has been criticized on many grounds. According to Szasz, it is equivalent to "maintaining the prisoners of pharmacracy on dope and the victimizers on dollars" (1976, p. 102), and "treating addiction to heroin with methadone is like treating addiction to scotch with bourbon" (1974, p. 72). It has been decried for its emphasis on drug-oriented instead of human solutions to social problems (Lennard, Epstein, & Rosenthal, 1972).

Although undeniably controversial on a number of levels, methadone maintenance continues to be seen as an at least partial "cure" for some of the destructive behaviors associated with heroin addiction. Whereas it does not resolve the many personal problems of heroin dependence, it does offer the addict an opportunity to do something else in life besides seek drugs (Cohen, 1974). Perhaps, then, it should be properly viewed as a specific treatment for the behavioral state of *addiction*, and not for the psychophysiological condition of *dependence*. From the perspective of the treatment practitioner, methadone maintenance does provide a means to get the addict out of the street and into the clinic, where, hopefully, the *real* treatment may be able to get the street out of the addict.

In light of the enormous interest and speculation kindled by the discovery of the endorphins, the decision to include something about these substances in this section was an easy one. Finding a suitable article, however, was not so easy. First, the discovery of the endorphins was not the work of any one individual. Second, endorphin research is a biochemical field; its research findings are therefore communicated in the difficult and unfamiliar languages of biochemistry and psychopharmacology. Third, the field is so new that its literature cannot yet contain any truly classic contributions. After reviewing the scientific and popular endorphin literature, we selected the articles by Goldstein (1978a, 1978b, 1978c)—one of the major figures in the field—on the basis of their extreme readability.

After years of work by a number of researchers, Pert and Snyder (1973) demonstrated the presence of stereospecific opiate-binding sites in the brain. These opiate receptors were found to be selectively distributed within the brain (and later, along the spinal cord and in the intestines as well), with most located in areas in or associated with the limbic system, which is that portion of the brain thought to modulate emotional responses (Kuhar, Pert & Snyder, 1973). It was hypothesized that the opiate receptor might be part of a neurotransmitter or neuromodulator system mediated by some naturally occurring or endogenous substance acting as a morphine-like compound. This hypothesis was subsequently proved with the identification (Hughes, Smith, Kosterlitz, Fothergill, Morgan, & Morris, 1975) of an opiate-like substance—thereafter referred to as "enkephalin." Work with enkephalin led to the further specification of the brain's internal opiates, and today all of these endogenous morphine-like substances are collectively referred to as the endorphins.

Endorphins have been implicated in the mechanisms of acupuncture which produce analgesia and block opiate withdrawal (Pomeranz, 1977). The possible role of endorphins in schizophrenia and the affective disorders is presently under study by Kline's group (1977) and Lindstrom and his colleagues (1978), respectively. Although the endorphins have not yet been implicated in the development of opiate dependence, the idea that an endorphin-mediated biochemical defect might predispose a person to opiate dependence is an intriguing one.

Employing methods based upon those used in endorphin research, Mohler and Okada (1977) have recently demonstrated the existence of an exquisitely specific benzodiazepine receptor in the brain, and the search is now on for an endogenous benzodiazepine-like substance (Skolnick, 1979). It will be very interesting to follow developments in this area. The implications of the presence of an endogenous substance capable of mediating sedative and anti-convulsant effects would indeed be far-reaching. In the Epilogue to this volume we consider some of the implications of this pharmacology of the future.

The reader interested in the psychological or behavioral aspects of endorphin research should be prepared to review and digest a formidable body of technical, biochemical and pharmacological literature in order to find those studies or conclusions which may have direct clinical applicability. The following references are offered as possible points of entry to the literature of this highly volatile research area: Bunney, 1979; Guillemin, 1978, Snyder, Childers, and Creese, 1979.

REFERENCES

BERLE, B. B., & NYSWANDER, M. Ambulatory withdrawal treatment of heroin addicts. *New York State Journal of Medicine*, 1964, *64*, 1846-1848.

BUNNEY, W. E. (moderator) Basic and clinical studies of endorphins. *Annals of Internal Medicine*, 1979, *91*, 239-250.

COHEN, S. Methadone maintenance: A decade later. *Journal of Drug Issues*, 1974, *4*, 327-331.

CORMAN, A. G., JOHNSON, B., KHANTZIAN, E. J., & LONG, J. Rehabilitation of narcotics addicts with methadone: The public health approach versus the individual perspective. *Contemporary Drug Problems*, 1973, *2*, 565-578.

DOLE, V. P., & NYSWANDER, M. A medical treatment for diacetylmorphine (heroin) addiction. A clinical trial with methadone hydrochloride. *Journal of the American Medical Association*, 1965, *193*, 80-84.

DOLE, V. P., & NYSWANDER, M. E. Rehabilitation of heroin addicts after blockade with methadone. *New York State Journal of Medicine*, 1966, *66*, 2011-2016.

DOLE, V. P., & NYSWANDER, M. E. Rehabilitation of the street addict. *Archives of Environ-*

mental Health, 1967, *14,* 477-480.

DOLE, V. P., NYSWANDER, M. E., & KREEK, M. J. Narcotic blockade. *Archives of Internal Medicine,* 1966, *118,* 304-309.

DOLE, V. P., NYSWANDER, M. E., & WARNER, A. Successful treatment of 750 criminal addicts. *Journal of the American Medical Association,* 1968, *206,* 2708-2711.

GOLDSTEIN, A. The endorphins—their discovery and significance. In *Current Concepts in Postoperative Pain.* (a special report) New York: *Hospital Practice,* 1978. (a)

GOLDSTEIN, A. The endorphins and pain—what we have learned. In *Current Concepts in Postoperative Pain.* (a special report) New York: *Hospital Practice,* 1978. (b)

GOLDSTEIN, A. The endorphins—their physiologic and pathologic potentials. In *Current Concepts of Postoperative Pain.* (a special report). New York: *Hospital Practice,* 1978. (c)

GUILLEMIN, R. Peptides in the brain: The new endocrinology of the neuron. *Science,* 1978, *202,* 390-402.

HUGHES, J., SMITH, T. W., KOSTERLITZ, H. W., FOTHERGILL, L. A., MORGAN, B. A., & MORRIS, H. R. Identification of two related pentapeptides from the brain with potent opiate agonist activity. *Nature,* 1975, *258,* 577-579.

KLINE, N. S., LI, C. H., LEHMANN, H. E., LAITHA, A., LASKI, E., & COOPER, T. Beta-endorphin-induced changes in schizophrenic and depressed patients. *Archives of General Psychiatry,* 1977, *34,* 1111-1113.

KUHAR, M. J., PERT, C. B., & SNYDER, J. H. Regional distribution of opiate receptor binding in monkey and human brain. *Nature,* 1973, *245,* 447-451.

LENNARD, H. L., EPSTEIN, L. J., & ROSENTHAL, M. S. The methadone illusion. *Science,* 1972, *176,* 881-884.

LINDSTROM, L. H., WIDERLOV, E., GUNNE, L-M., WAHLSTROM, A., & TERENIUS, L. Endorphins in human cerebrospinal fluid: Clinical correlations to some psychotic states. *Acta Psychiatrica Scandinavica,* 1978, *57,* 153-164.

MOHLER, H., & OKADA, T. Benzodiazepine receptor: Demonstration in the central nervous system. *Science,* 1977, *198,* 849-851.

PERT, C. B., & SNYDER, S. H. Opiate receptor: demonstration in nervous tissue. *Science,* 1973, *179,* 1011-1014.

PLATT, J. J., & LABATE, C. *Heroin Addiction. Theory, Research and Treatment.* New York: Wiley, 1976.

POMERANZ, B. The brain's opiates at work in acupuncture. *New Scientist,* 1977, *73,* 12.

SKOLNICK, P. CNS benzodiazepine receptors: Physiological studies and putative endogenous ligands. *Pharmacology, Biochemistry and Behavior,* 1979, *10,* 815-823.

SNYDER, S. H., CHILDERS, S. R., & CREESE, I. Molecular actions of opiates: Historical overview and new findings on opiate receptor interactions with enkephalins and guanyl nucleotides. In H. H. Loh & D. H. Ross (Eds.), *Neurochemical mechanisms of opiates and endorphins (Advances in biochemical psychopharmacology,* Vol. 20). New York: Raven Press, 1979.

SZASZ, T. S. *The Second Sin.* New York: Anchor Books/Doubleday, 1974.

SZASZ, T. S. *Heresies.* New York: Anchor Books/Doubleday, 1976.

24

A MEDICAL TREATMENT FOR DIACETYLMORPHINE (HEROIN) ADDICTION

Vincent P. Dole and Marie Nyswander

A group of 22 patients, previously addicted to diacetylmorphine (heroin), have been stabilized with oral methadone hydrochloride. This medication appears to have two useful effects: (1) relief of narcotic hunger, and (2) induction of sufficient tolerance to block the euphoric effect of an average illegal dose of diacetylmorphine. With this medication, and a comprehensive program of rehabilitation, patients have shown marked improvement; they have returned to school, obtained jobs, and have become reconciled with their families. Medical and psychometric tests have disclosed no signs of toxicity, apart from constipation. This treatment requires careful medical supervision and many social services. In our opinion, both the medication and the supporting program are essential.

Reprinted with permission from the *Journal of the American Medical Association*, 1965, *193*, 80-84. Copyright © 1965, American Medical Association.

This study was supported by the Health Research Council grant U-1501 of New York city, and by the National Association for Prevention of Addiction to Narcotics.

Major contributions to this investigation were made by the following: Mary Jeanne Kreek, MD, bone marrow biopsies and tests of narcotic tolerance; Joyce Lowinson, MD, and George Lowen, MD, expansion of the program at Manhattan General Hospital; Nathan Poker, MD, measurements of intestinal motivity; David Becker, MD, and Eugene Furth, MD, tests for thyroid function; and Norman Gordon, MD, Alan Warner, and Ann Henderson, measurements of motor skills of patients, and ratings with intelligence tests and mood scales.

From the Rockefeller Institute, and Manhattan General Division of Beth Israel Hospital, New York.

The question of "maintenance treatment" of addicts is one that is often argued but seldom clearly defined. If this procedure is conceived as no more than an unsupervised distribution of narcotic drugs to addicts for self-administration of doses and at times of their choosing, then few physicians could accept it as proper medical practice. An uncontrolled supply of drugs would trap confirmed addicts in a closed world of drug taking, and tend to spread addiction. This procedure certainly would not qualify as "maintenance" in a medical sense. Uncontrolled distribution is mentioned here only to reject it, and to emphasize the distinction between distribution and medical prescription. The question at issue in the present study was whether a narcotic medicine, prescribed by physicians as part of a treatment program, could help in the return of addict patients to normal society.

No definitive study of medical maintenance has yet been reported. The Council on Mental Health of the American Medical Association, after a thorough review of evidence available in 1957 (1), concluded that "the advisability of establishing clinics or some equivalent system to dispense opiates to addicts cannot be settled on the basis of objective facts. Any position taken is necessarily based in part on opinion, and on this question opinions are divided." With respect to previous trials of maintenance treatment, the Council found that "Assessment of the operations of the narcotic dispensaries between 1919 and 1923 is difficult because of the paucity of published material. Much of the small amount of data that is available is not sufficiently objective to be of great value in formulating any clear-cut opinion of the purpose of the clinics, the way in which they operated, or the results attained." No new studies bearing on the question of maintenance treatment have appeared in the eight years since this report was published. Meanwhile, various medical and legal committees have called for additional research (2-6).

The present study, conducted under the auspices of the departments of health and hospitals, New York city, has yielded encouraging results; patients who before treatment appeared hopelessly addicted are now engaged in useful occupations and are not using diacetylmorphine (heroin). As measured by social performance, these patients have ceased to be addicts. It must be emphasized that this paper is only a progress report, based on treatment of 22 patients for periods of 1 to 15 months. Such limited study obviously does not establish a new treatment for general application. The results, however, appear sufficiently promising to justify further trial of the procedure on a larger scale.

PROCEDURE

The patients admitted to the program to date were men, aged 19 to

37, "mainline" diacetylmorphine users for several years with a history of failures of withdrawal treatment. They have reported no substantial addictions to other agents (although most of them had used barbiturates or tranquilizers when narcotic drugs were unavailable), and they were not psychotic. Patients came from the streets, from drug withdrawal units, from referrals by social agencies and physicians who had heard of the program, and from recruitment of addicted friends by patients under treatment. Further details of their history are given in the Table.

Division of Program Into Three Phases.—PHASE 1.—The addict patients were stabilized with methadone hydrochloride in an unlocked hospital ward, given a complete medical workup, psychiatric evaluation, a review of family and housing problems, and job-placement study. After the first week of hospitalization, they were free to leave the ward for school, libraries, shopping, and various amusements—usually, but not always, with one of the staff. Patients lacking a high school diploma started in classes that prepare students for a high school equivalency certificate. For the present study the time in this initial phase was arbitrarily set at six weeks.

During this phase of hospitalization, the treatment unit was kept small (four to nine patients). This was felt necessary because most patients started the treatment with serious anxieties and doubts. The limitation of patient load allowed the staff to individualize the daily ward activities and deal with the special problems of each patient.

PHASE 2.—This began when subjects left the hospital and became outpatients, returning every day for methadone medication. They were asked to drink their medication in the presence of a clinic nurse, and to leave a daily urine specimen for analysis. When indicated, this rule has been relaxed; reliable patients who have been on the program for several months have been given enough medication for a weekend at home or a short trip. Continued contact with the hospital staff was provided as required. The most important services needed during this phase of treatment were help in obtaining jobs, housing, and education.

PHASE 3.—This phase is the goal of treatment, the stage in which an ex-addict has become a socially normal, self-supporting person. The two patients who are considered to have arrived at this phase are still receiving maintenance medication since the physicians in charge of their treatment feel that withdrawal at this time would be premature. Supervision of their medication is as careful as in phase 2; the only distinction between patients in phases 2 and 3 is in the degree of social advancement.

PHASE 1A.—This phase designates a special group of four patients who are being maintained on high doses under close and continuing observation to reveal any delayed toxic effects of methadone (Table). So far, none have been found. These patients live on a metabolic ward, and

Maintenance Therapy of Ex-Addicts With Methadone Hydrochloride, Summary of First 15 Months (February 1964 to May 1965)

	Status Before Admission to Program										Status Since Admission			
Ethnic Group*	Age,† Years FD	A	Previous Treatments‡ F	S	M	P	Arrests	Education	Best Job§	Military Service Years	Time on Program, Months	D¶	P#	HS**	Present Activity
E	16	22	–	3	3	–	6	8th grade	Truck driver	–	15	150	1a	Cert	Preparing for college (Sept 1965)
E	18	31	3	3	2	–	8	1 year high school	Odd jobs (few months each)	–	15	180	1a	Cert	Horticulture school
P	21	33	2	–	4	–	14	2 years high school	Office clerk	–	10	100	1a	Cert	Employed (rehabilitation work)
E	20	30	1	2	3	1	1	Graduated high school	Store manager	A3	10	180	1a	–	Employed (usher cashier in theater)
E	17	22	–	–	6	–	4	2 years high school	Shipping clerk	–	11	100	3	–	Employed (parking lot foreman)
E	21	25	–	–	–	12	1	2 years college	Musician	––	10	100	3	–	Employed intermittently (musician)
E	18	25	–	–	2	–	6	Graduated high school	Radio operator in military service	N4	3	100	2	–	Employed (office work)
N	17	32	1	–	2	–	9	2 years high school	Clothes presser	–	1½	100	1	NS	Seeking employment
N	22	37	–	1	1	–	3	2 years high school	Truck driver	A4	1½	80	1	NS	Seeking employment
P	15	23	–	–	–	–	1	2 years high school	Head usher	A3	1½	90	2	Cert Army	Working as waiter
N	16	27	–	–	4	–	1	3 years high school	Stock clerk	A5	1½	130	1	NS	Seeking employment
E	18	22	3	–	3	2	4	1 year college	Mason	–	1	100	1	–	Seeking employment
P	25	35	1	–	2	–	3	1 year	Paint sprayer	–	½	110	1	–	Employed

Group*	FD†	A†	F‡	S‡	M‡	P‡	Adm	Education	Job§	Military‖	Dose¶	No.	Phase#	Cert**	Employment
N	18	30	2	—	—	—	6	3 years high school	Shipping clerk	AF4	½	70	1	NS	Seeking employment
E	18	24	—	10	—	—	0	8th grade	Installing window screens	—	3	115	2	NS	Employed
P	14	30	—	—	—	—	2	2 years high school	Office clerk	M3	3	70	2	NS	Welfare (seeking employment)
P	19	25	—	16	—	—	10	2 years high school	Office clerk	AF2½	3	110	2	NS	Employed (hospital record room)
E	17	19	—	—	1	1	0	Graduated high school	None	—	3	120	2	—	Vocational school (barber)
P	13	20	—	—	1	—	2	3 years high school	Stock boy	—	3	50	2	NS	Employed (hospital laundry)
E	19	26	—	—	2	—	8	2 years high school	Construction laborer	—	1½	100	2	NS	Seeking employment
N	14	30	—	—	—	—	2	8th grade	Shipping clerk	AF4	1½	10	2	Cert	Leather goods company interpreter

*For comparison with other treatment series, patients classified into three groups: Western European ancestry (E), Puerto Rican and Cuban (P), and Negro (N).

†Age first used diacetylmorphine (FD); age at admission (A).

‡Number of admissions to Federal Hospital—Lexington, Ky (F), state hospitals—Manhattan State, Central Islip (S), municipal hospital—Manhattan General, Metropolitan, Riverside (M), private clinics and groups, including Synanon (P).

§All but two patients were employed at time of admission. Job indicated is best position ever held.

‖Time in Army (A), Navy (N), Marines (M), or Air Force (AF).

¶Dose methadone hydrochloride given orally, mg/day.

#Phases of treatment 1a—four patients, residents on metabolic ward of Rockefeller Institute; 1—new patients, being stabilized on methadone therapy, they sleep in hospital but may leave during day for school, shopping, or job; 2—patients newly discharged, living at home or rooming house, needing social support; 3—ambulatory patients who are self-supporting.

**High school equivalency status. If not a high school graduate, each patient was encouraged to enroll in night school to prepare for high school equivalency certificate. Those who have completed this course, passed examination, and received certificate are indicated by "Cert"; those now in night school indicated by "NS."

so are still classified in phase 1, but as measured by social adjustment they have progressed to phase 2 or 3, since all are either employed or going to school. The ward serves mainly as their residence, which they are free to leave as they wish subject only to the general routine of hospital activities.

Narcotic Medication.—Patients have differed markedly in tolerance to narcotics at the beginning of treatment, and in the rate with which they have adapted to increasing doses of medication. Individualization of treatment thus has been necessary. A rough estimate of initial tolerance was made from each new patient's history of drug usage, with allowance for exaggeration since addicts coming to a maintenance program usually fear that physicians will not prescribe enough medication, and with recognition of the fact that the number of "bags" used by an addict is not a reliable measure of narcotic tolerance. The diacetylmorphine content of a "bag" obtained on the street today is low and variable. This estimate provided a guide to initial dosage, but the only sure way to measure tolerance is to observe the reaction to test doses of narcotic drugs. The schedule, therefore, differed for each patient.

On admission patients usually have shown mild or moderately severe symptoms of abstinence, the last shot of diacetylmorphine having been taken some hours before. These patients were relieved promptly by one or two doses of morphine sulfate (10 mg) or dihydromorphione (Dilaudid) hydrochloride (4 mg), given intramuscularly, and then started on oral methadone hydrochloride therapy (10 to 20 mg. twice daily). Patients coming to treatment without symptoms were started on a regimen of methadone without other medication, but were watched carefully for appearance of symptoms after admission. After the first 24 hours most patients could be maintained comfortably on the oral medication alone. The dose of methadone hydrochloride was increased gradually over the next four weeks to stabilization level (50 to 150 mg/day). Two patients in whom tolerance at the expected rate failed to develop have been held at lower doses (Table). With some patients, treated early in the study, the buildup of dosage was too rapid; they became overly sedated for a few days, and two of them had transient episodes of urinary retention and abdominal distention. Other patients, given too little, have become abstinent, exhibiting malaise, nausea, sweating, lacrimation, and restlessness. With more accurate prescription, patients have not become euphoric, sedated, or sick from abstinence at any stage of treatment. They have simply felt normal, and have not asked for more medication.

After the patients reached maintenance level, the morning and evening doses were combined by progressive reduction of the evening medication with an equal addition to the methadone taken in the morning.

After discharge from the hospital patients could thus be maintained by a single daily visit to the outpatient clinic. The patients who have had difficulty in spanning a 24-hour period with a single dose have been given medication to take at home; this has been a minor problem, limited to those who could visit the clinic only in the evening. In all cases it has been made clear to the patients (and accepted by them as a condition of treatment) that the amount of medication and the dosage schedule were the responsibility of the medical staff. Physicians did not discuss dosage with the patients, although of course they listened carefully to any report of symptoms that might suggest excess or lack of medication.

Laboratory Control.—The urine of every patient was collected daily in the hospital and at each clinic visit, to be analyzed for methadone, morphine (the chief metabolite of diacetylmorphine), and quinine (a regular constituent of the street "bag"). The thin layer chromatographic method of Cochin and Daly (7) was used, after preliminary extraction of the alkaloids from urine with cation exchange resin. The sensitivity of the procedure was such that it would give a definite positive if a patient had taken an average "bag" of diacetylmorphine during the preceding 24 hours.

RESULTS

The most dramatic effect of this treatment has been the disappearance of narcotic hunger. All of the patients previously had made efforts to remain drug-free after withdrawal, but were unable to resist the craving. Drug hunger became intolerable for most of them shortly after discharge from a withdrawal unit and return to their neighborhood. It became especially severe when they were exposed to emotional stress. With methadone maintenance, however, patients found that they could meet addict friends, and even watch them inject diacetylmorphine, without great difficulty. They have tolerated frustrating episodes without feeling a need for diacetylmorphine. They have stopped dreaming about drugs, and seldom talk about drugs when together. Patients have even become so indifferent to narcotics as to forget to take a scheduled dose of medication when busy at home.

The extent to which the patients have ceased to behave as addicts, and their reliability in reporting illegal drug use, were verified by the results of urinanalysis. Negative results in almost all analyses showed that use of diacetylmorphine has been rare and sporadic, although the patients have had ample exposure to addict friends and pushers. Remarkably, the episodes of drug taking were reported by the patients spontaneously, and their reports have correlated with the laboratory evidence.

An interesting phenomenon, which has been seen in several patients, was the production of symptoms typical of drug deficiency by acute emotional stress. Anxiety in some susceptible patients caused malaise, nausea, yawning, and sweating, indistinguishable from the effects of abstinence, even though the patients were being maintained on large doses of medication. After experiencing relief with reassurance but without additional medication, susceptible patients have become less alarmed by these symptoms, and the episodes have occurred less frequently. In two other patients symptoms suggesting abstinence have appeared in the course of mild respiratory-tract infections. These symptoms, not associated with anxiety, were difficult to evaluate, but in any event disappeared in a few days without need for increase in medication. These observations suggest that the effectiveness of methadone can vary with changes in psychological and metabolic state.

The degree of tolerance established by methadone was titrated in six patients by giving diacetylmorphine, morphine, dilaudid, or methadone intravenously in a double-blind study. The drugs were given in randomized order and various doses six hours after the last administration of methadone. Stabilization with methadone, as here described, was found to make patients refractory to 40 to 80 mg diacetylmorphine (which would cost $10 to $25 if purchased on the street). Larger amounts were not systematically tested; probably blocking would extend to greater doses since two patients with high tolerance showed little reaction to intravenous injection of 200 mg of diacetylmorphine—a huge amount, possibly enough to kill a nontolerant individual.

Unscheduled, but perhaps necessary, experiments in drug usage were made by four patients. These subjects found that they did not "get high" when "shooting" diacetylmorphine with addict friends on the street. Both the patients and their friends were astounded at their lack of reaction to the drug. They discontinued these unrewarding experiments without need for disciplinary measures, and have discouraged other patients from repeating the experiment. So long as patients take methadone as scheduled, they apparently cannot feel the euphoria of an addict taking a street bag of diacetylmorphine.

Complications.—The chief medical problem has been constipation. The tonus of the sigmoid and the defecation reflex remain depressed even in patients with high tolerance to the narcotic effects of methadone, while the motility of the upper gastrointestinal tract appears to be unaffected. Five patients, given a barium sulfate meal and followed with daily x-ray examinations for a week, showed normal or only slightly delayed passage of barium through the small intestine, but in three of the five, the evacuation of barium from the colon was abnormally slow.

Fecal impaction has occurred when patients have made no effort to defecate for several days. Patients therefore were instructed to take a hydrophilic colloid every day, and a supplementary laxative or enema if bowels have not moved for three days. With these precautions patients have had no further difficulty.

Apart from constipation, patients have shown no major ill effects ascribable to use of methadone. The tendency of addicts to leukocytosis (9,000 to 14,000 white blood cells/cu mm with 60% to 80% polymorphonuclear cells [10]) continued, apparently unaffected by this medication. Bone marrow biopsies in four patients after eight months of treatment were normal. No effect of methadone on renal function was disclosed by repeated urinanalyses. Liver-function tests, when originally normal, remained so. Results of basal metabolic rate, thyroid uptake of sodium iodide I 131, red blood cell uptake of labelled triiodothyronine, and plasma protein-bound iodine were normal in three patients who had been stabilized on methadone hydrochloride (100 to 150 mg/day) for four to six months. Some patients have reported excess sweating in hot weather, but no one has been unable to work for this reason.

Mental and neuromuscular functions appear unaffected. Patients have performed well in school and at various jobs. Studies of motor skill (accuracy in tracking moving targets) showed normal coordination. We have not yet been able to find a medical or psychological test capable of distinguishing patients on methadone therapy from normal controls. They can, of course, be distinguished by urinanalysis.

There has been no problem so far in holding patients. Only two of the patients who started treatment have been discharged. These uncooperative and disruptive psychopaths were transferred to withdrawal units. Two others who were admitted specifically for tolerance tests at an early stage of the study were returned (as originally planned) to the withdrawal unit from which they came; both subsequently have asked to return to the program. A fifth patient signed out after only four days on the ward, and also asked to return.

COMMENT

Previous efforts to treat addict patients with narcotic medication have been handicapped by lack of sufficiently long-acting agents. The Council's report (1) noted that in 1919 to 1923 experience, "in all instances it was eventually found necessary to give drugs to addicts for self-administration." This is inherent in the pharmacology of parenterally administered morphine, which was used in these clinics and would probably apply to other agents with short periods of action such as diacetylmorphine, dihydromorphine, or meperidine. If addict patients are to be maintained with any of these drugs, they would need several injections per day; otherwise they would return to the street for additional drugs.

Projected into large-scale treatment, a medical use of short-acting narcotic drugs would require dispensaries staffed to give thousands of injections per day, with rooms or park benches in the neighborhood for addicts to wait between shots. Alternatively, physicians would have to yield control of drug administration to the addicts themselves. Neither alternative is acceptable. With methadone (9), however, the situation is much different since patients can be stabilized with a single daily dose, taken orally, under medical control. Maintenance of patients with methadone is no more difficult than maintaining diabetics with oral hypoglycemic agents, and in both cases the patient should be able to live a normal life.

We believe that methadone has contributed in an essential way to the favorable results, although it is quite clear that giving of medicine has been only part of the program. This drug appears to relieve narcotic hunger, and thus free the patient for other interests, as well as protect him against readdiction to diacetylmorphine by establishing a pharmacological block. A previous attempt by one of us (M.N.) to treat addict patients without narcotic medication ended in failure (10). Other clinics, attempting to rehabilitate patients after withdrawal, have had equally poor results. These, however, are indirect arguments. When the treatment program is sufficiently well established, the necessary control studies with social support, but without medication, must be made.

REFERENCES

1. COUNCIL ON MENTAL HEALTH: Report on Narcotic Addiction, *JAMA* 165:1707-1713 (Nov 30); 1834-1841 (Dec 7); 1968-1974 (Dec 14) 1957.
2. Joint Committee of American Bar Association and American Medical Association of Narcotic Drugs, Interim and Final Reports: *Drug Addiction: Crime or Disease?* Bloomington, Ind: Indiana University Press, 1961.
3. President's Advisory Commission on Narcotic and Drug Abuse, Appendix 1. Final Report, U.S. Government Printing Office, Nov. 1963.
4. New York Academy of Medicine, Committee on Public Health: Report on Drug Addiction: II, *Bull. NY. Acad. Med.* 39: 417-473 (July) 1963.
5. ELDRIDGE, W. B.: *Narcotics and Law*, Chicago: American Bar Foundation, 1962.
6. National Council on Crime and Delinquency. Advisory Council of Judges. Narcotics Law Violations: Policy Statement. New York, 1964.
7. COCHIN, J., and DALY, J.: Rapid Identification of Analgesic Drugs in Urine With Thin-Layer Chromatography, *Experientia* 18:294-295 (June 15) 1962.
8. LIGHT, A. B., and TORRANCE, E. G.: Opium Addiction: VI. Effects of Abrupt Withdrawal Followed by Readministration of Morphine in Human Addicts With Special Reference to Composition of Blood, Circulation, and Metabolism, *Arch. Intern. Med.* 44:1-16 (July) 1929.
9. ISBELL, H., et al: Liability of Addiction of 6-Dimethylamino 4-4-diphenyl-3-heptanone

(Methadon, "Amidone" or "10820") in Man. *Arch. Intern. Med.* 82:362-392 (Oct) 1948.

10. BERLE, B., and NYSWANDER, M.: Ambulatory Withdrawal Treatment of Heroin Addicts, *New York J. Med.* 64:1846-1848 (July) 1964.

25

SUCCESSFUL TREATMENT OF 750 CRIMINAL ADDICTS

Vincent P. Dole, Marie E. Nyswander and Alan Warner

A four year trial of methadone blockade treatment has shown 94% success in ending the criminal activity of former heroin addicts. The majority of these patients are now productively employed, living as responsible citizens, and supporting families. The results show unequivocally that criminal addicts can be rehabilitated by a well-supervised maintenance program.

In November 1963, on the initiative of the Health Research Council of New York city, a study of heroin addiction was started at Rockefeller University Hospital. The council recognized the need for new methods of treatment. Thousands of heroin addicts were filling the jails of New York city. It seemed reasonable to ask whether some medication might control the drug hunger of these criminal addicts, and enable them to live in the community as decent citizens.

Clinical studies conducted in the metabolic ward during 1964 and extended to Beth Israel Medical Center in 1965 suggested that this result might be achieved by using the familiar drug methadone hydrochloride

Reprinted with permission from the *Journal of the American Medical Association*, 1968, *206*, 2708-2711. Copyright 1968, American Medical Association.

From Rockefeller University and Beth Israel Medical Center, New York.

Read before the Section on Preventive Medicine at the 117th annual convention of the American Medical Association, San Francisco, June 19, 1968.

This investigation was supported by grants from the Health Research Council (City of New York Department of Health) and the New York State Narcotic Addiction Control Commission.

in a new way. By establishing tolerance to methadone, and subsequently maintaining the tolerant state with a constant daily oral dose, we found it possible to block the action of heroin, and eliminate the hunger for narcotic drugs (1). Patients, thus blockaded, felt no narcotic effects, but lost their compulsive desire for heroin. They stopped being criminals, and in the majority of cases became productive members of society. A preliminary report of the clinical findings was published in 1965 (2).

At the time of this report, the potential value of treatment for large scale use remained indeterminate. The results, although encouraging, were limited to the treatment of a few patients for a few months. The present report summarizes the much more extensive experience of the past four years (Fig 1). The number of criminal addicts who have been rehabilitated with methadone treatment is large enough to empty a moderate sized jail, and there are at least 1,000 more addicts waiting for treatment. Detailed records of medical and social status have been kept for all patients, and analyses of urine for narcotic drugs, barbiturates, and amphetamines have been made at least weekly (3).

All patients admitted to treatment from the beginning of the research (January 1964) to the time of this report (June 1968) are included in the statistics, except for a special group of patients who received combined treatment for addiction and tuberculosis, and a few patients who had been started on methadone therapy elsewhere and were accepted as transfers. For some analyses, such as measures of social stability and productivity, the tabulation has been limited to patients who have been in treatment for more than three months.

A notable feature of the treatment program has been the absence of compulsion or confinement. It has not been found necessary in the methadone program to apply prison techniques for control of behavior. Some addicts who had been notorious troublemakers in prison-type programs have become ordinary patients with methadone treatment. Not all have responded favorably, of course; some patients have been discharged for disruptive behavior, or because of nonnarcotic drug abuses. All of these failures—including patients who had been in treatment for only one day—are included in the statistics (Table 1).

PROCEDURE

Addicts with a history of at least four years of mainline heroin use and repeated failures of withdrawal treatment were admitted to treatment in the order that they applied, subject to the following conditions: age 20 to 40 (upper limit raised to 50 in the third year of the study), no legal compulsion (i.e., methadone treatment not a condition of probation

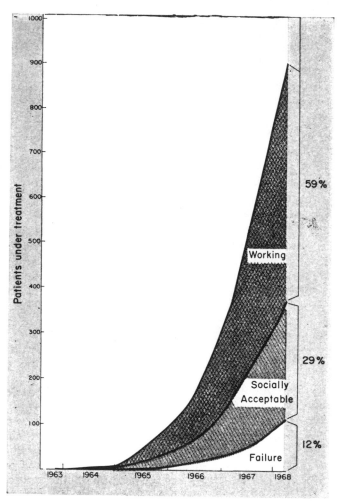

1. Growth of the methadone maintenance treatment program. In addition to patients in treatment, approximately 1,000 addicts are awaiting admission to program.

or parole), no major medical complication (e.g., severe alcoholism, epilepsy, schizophrenia), and resident of New York city. During the first 18 months only men were admitted to the program; subsequently a woman's unit has been in operation, with admission by the same procedure except that the intake office attempts to bring in married couples to the two units at approximately the same time.

The treatment program is divided into three phases, related to the

Table 1.—Discharges From January 1964 to May 1968*

Cause	Time on Program, mo				
	<1	1-6	6-12	>12	
Behavior	5	23	13	13	(50%)
Drug abuse					
Heroin	0	0	0	0	(0%)
Nonheroin	2	2	0	5	(8%)
Medical					
Disability	4	8	7	8	(25%)
Death	2	1	5	1	(8%)
Voluntary	2	2	1	5	(9%)
	(14%)	(33%)	(24%)	(29%)	

*There were 863 total admissions and 109 total discharges (13% of admissions).

progress of rehabilitation with methadone maintenance continuing throughout. During phase 1, a six week period of hospitalization on an open medical ward, the patients are brought to a blockading level of methadone. The new patient should be given this medication in relatively small, divided orally administered doses (e.g., 10 mg twice daily), and brought to maintenance level (80 to 120 mg/day) gradually, over a period of four to six weeks. Some experience in regulation of dose is necessary: if the medication is increased too rapidly, the patient will become over-sedated during the first few weeks, and may experience urinary retention and constipation, whereas if the dose is inadequate, a patient who had been using a large amount of heroin will have unnecessary withdrawal symptoms. There appears to be a wide margin of safety in administration of methadone to patients who have been heroin addicts, but of course the physician must avoid giving an excessive dose to a new patient. When in doubt, the safe rule is to give the medication in divided doses and observe the effects over the first 24 hours.

As the dose is gradually increased over a period of four to six weeks, the medication makes the patient refractory to narcotic drugs and eliminates (or greatly reduces) any narcotic drug hunger, presumably by maintaining a blockade of the sites of narcotic drug action. There should be no euphoria or other undesirable side effects (except mild constipation) if the medication is given in proper dosage. If the patient appears to be sedated during this induction phase the dose of methadone should be held constant or reduced until further tolerance is developed.

More recently, we have been testing a strictly ambulatory treatment, and have obtained favorable results, confirming the previous reports of Brill and Jaffe (4) and of Wieland (5). New patients are started on small doses of methadone and are gradually brought up to stabilization level, as closely supervised outpatients. This is much less expensive than hospitalization and, with proper supervision, equally successful.

Phase 2 begins for the patients when they are discharged to the outpatient clinic, and continues for at least a year. The newly discharged patients return for medication to the outpatient clinic each weekday, and are given medication to take home for the weekends. Later, as justified by good conduct, the patients are permitted to come at less frequent intervals, taking out doses of medication for the intervening days. At least once per week (with rare exception) each patient is required to drink a full dose of the medication in the clinic, and thus demonstrate that he has maintained his tolerance by taking medication during the intervals. Each time that a patient comes to the clinic he is required to leave a urine specimen for analysis.

Phase 3 is reached when the subject has become a stable and socially productive member of the community, and can be treated as an ordinary medical patient. To be classified in this category, he must be acceptably employed (either in a job or at school, or if a woman, as a homemaker), and have no further problems with drugs or alcohol. The stability of rehabilitation must be proven by one year of normal life in the community. Medically the treatment of these patients remains the same as the treatment of patients in phase 2; they also take at least one dose of medication in the clinic each week, and leave a urine specimen.

Patients who have been discharged for misconduct, or who have been asked to leave the program, have been withdrawn from medication by gradual reduction in dose over a period of about a month. This is done easily and without discomfort. We have not, however, considered it desirable to withdraw medication from patients who are to remain in the program, since those who have been discharged have experienced a return to narcotic drug hunger after removal of the blockade, and most of them have promptly reverted to the use of heroin. It is possible that a very gradual removal of methadone from patients with several years of stable living in phase 3 might succeed, but this procedure has not yet been adequately tested.

The supportive services provided by the methadone program and community agencies have been related to the needs of the patients. Some patients, when freed from the burden of heroin addiction, have ceased all antisocial activity; they obtained jobs without further assistance and began to support their families. These exceptional individuals needed nothing from the program except medical supervision. More frequently, the slum-born, minority group criminal addict needed help to become a productive member of society. Many of these individuals came to us from jail with no vocational skills, no family, and no financial resources. They were further handicapped by racial discrimination and by their police records.

RESULTS

Drug-related crime has been sharply reduced by the blockade of narcotic drug hunger. Prior to treatment 91% of the patients had been in jail, and all of them had been more or less continuously involved in criminal activities. Many of them had simply alternated between jail and the slum neighborhoods of New York city. The crimes committed by these patients prior to treatment had resulted in at least 4,500 convictions (for felonies, misdemeanors, and offenses), a rate of 52 convictions per 100 man-years of addiction. The figure is obviously a minimum estimate of their pretreatment criminal activity since convictions measure only the number of times an addict has been caught. For every conviction, the usual addict has committed hundreds of criminal acts for which he was not apprehended.

Since entering the treatment program, 88% of the patients show arrest-free records. The remainder have had difficulties with the law. Some of these individuals, however, were arrested merely on suspicion, on charges such as loitering, or by inclusion in a group arrest. In such cases, if the charges were subsequently dismissed, the episode has not been considered a criminal offense in our statistics. The remainder, 5.6% of the patients, were guilty of criminal offenses, and were convicted. In all, there have been 51 convictions in 880 man-years of treatment experience (a rate of 5.8 convictions per 100 man-years). Table 2 shows a more detailed analysis of these data.

We believe that the record of convictions of patients in treatment is essentially complete since a patient receiving methadone cannot absent himself for longer than a week without being missed. Moreover, legal representation is available for arrested patients. It provides both an accurate definition of the charge, and an incentive for the arrested person to report his difficulty. As to the estimate of arrests and convictions

Table 2.—Convictions* of 912 Patients on Methadone
Therapy, January 1964 to May 1968 (939 Patient-Years)

	Felony	Misdemeanor	Lesser Offenses
Narcotics	3	10	0
Dangerous drugs	0	4	0
Nondrug crimes	0	27	7
Rate per 100 patient-years	0.3	4.4	0.7

*Convictions for offenses committed while patients were receiving treatment. Pretreatment conviction rate (all offenses) was 52 per 100 patient-years.

of patients before treatment, we have only a minimal and incomplete figure. The reduction in crime, therefore, is at least 90% (Fig 2).

All patients convicted of crimes and removed from treatment by imprisonment were discharged from the program. Some of them have been, or will be, readmitted on completion of their jail sentences. A few other patients were discharged voluntarily. Of a total of 863 admitted to treatment, ten (1.2%) were discharged from methadone treatment at their own request because they wished to leave New York; these patients are not considered either successes or failures since their outcome is not

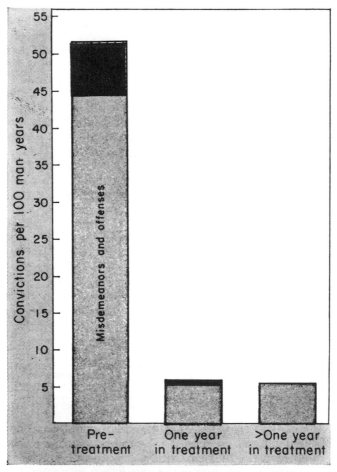

2. Reduction in criminality of 912 former heroin addicts, as measured by 90% drop in rate of convictions.

definitely known. The remainder (12%), all of whom we report as failures of the program, can be classified both by the length of time in treatment and the reason for discharge (Table 1). In most cases the misconduct that led to discharge involved uncooperative or antisocial behavior, or nonnarcotic drug abuse (including alcoholism). For these individuals—fortunately the minority—stopping heroin use with blockade treatment was not enough to open the way for rehabilitation. Possibly more elaborate programs, combining blockade treatment with psychotherapy and sheltered environment, might have succeeded.

Since blockade with methadone makes heroin relatively ineffective, a patient cannot use heroin for the usual euphoria, nor will he experience abstinence symptoms after an experiment with the drug. He can, however, remain drug-oriented in his thinking, and be tempted to return to heroin. Many patients have made sporadic attempts to use heroin again, especially during the first six months of treatment. Their habits of association with addicts, and of heroin taking in certain environments, were not eliminated by the blockade. For such individuals, the negative experience of experimenting with heroin and feeling little or no euphoria may contribute to the extinction of conditioned reflexes that underlie drug-seeking behavior (6). Needless to say, the staff does not encourage such dangerous experiments, but we recognize that for some individuals this type of self-experimentation might be a necessary step in reeducation and should not be regarded as a failure of treatment. Fortunately, experiments of this kind were the exception rather than the rule. The majority of patients have stopped heroin use completely after starting methadone treatment. This fact has been verified by repeated analyses of urine. For example, in a group of 174 patients, in which the analyses were done three times weekly for the first year of treatment, 55% did not show a single positive for self-administered narcotics. On the other hand, a minority of these patients, about 15%, continued to use heroin intermittently (e.g., on weekends) even though the euphoric effect was blocked. These tended to be isolated, schizoid individuals who were unable to find new friends or participate in ordinary activities.

The greatest surprise has been the high rate of social productivity, as defined by stable employment and responsibile behavior (Fig 3). This, of course, cannot be attributed to the medication, which merely blocks drug hunger and narcotic drug effects. The fact that the majority of patients have become productive citizens testifies to the devotion of the staff of the methadone program—physicians, nurses, older patients, counselors, and social workers. The success in making addicts into citi-

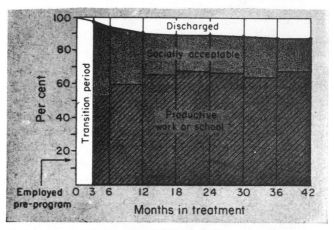

3. Status of 723 male addicts admitted to methadone
treatment. Rehabilitation was measured by productive
employment and crime-free status over four-year period.

zens also shows that an apparently hopeless criminal addict may have
ambition and intelligence that can work for rather than against society
when his pathological drug hunger is relieved by medical treatment.

REFERENCES

1. DOLE, V. P.; NYSWANDER, M. E.; and KREEK, M. J.: Narcotic Blockade, *Arch. Intern. Med.*
   118:304, 1966.
2. DOLE, V. P., and NYSWANDER, M.: A Medical Treatment for Diacetylmorphine (Heroin)
   Addiction: A Clinical Trial With Methadone Hydrochloride, *JAMA* 193:646-650
   (Aug. 23) 1965.
3. DOLE, V. P.; KIM, W. K.; and EGLITIS, I.: Detection of Narcotic Drugs, Tranquilizers,
   Amphetamines, and Barbiturates in Urine, *JAMA* 198:349-352 (Oct. 24) 1966.
4. BRILL, L., and JAFFE, J. H.: The Relevancy of Some Newer American Treatment Approaches for England, *Brit. J. Addict.* 62:375-386, 1967.
5. WIELAND, W.: Methadone Maintenance Treatment of Heroin Addiction: Beginning
   Treatment on an Outpatient Basis, read before the annual meeting of American
   Psychiatric Society, Boston, May 12, 1968.
6. WIKLER, A.: "Conditioning Factors in Opiate Addiction and Relapse," in Wilner, D. M.,
   and Kassebaum, G. G. (eds.): *Narcotics.* New York: McGraw-Hill Book Co., Inc.,
   1965, pp. 85-100.

26

ENDORPHINS AND ADDICTION

Avram Goldstein

I. THE ENDORPHINS—THEIR DISCOVERY AND SIGNIFICANCE

The exploration of endogenous opioids—one of the most extraordinary developments in the study of the mechanism and management of pain and anxiety—began in earnest barely eight years ago and has proceeded with an almost explosive rapidity to a point at which not only the structural detail shown in Figure 1 is known but many of the functional roles have also been established.

The starting point was a search for receptors in the human body utilized by exogenous drugs. At Stanford, the impetus for my coworkers and me was, more specifically, a consequence of our interest in the problem of addiction. Claude Bernard, in the middle of the nineteenth century, set out to study curare at the site of the body's response to the drug, and he did in fact localize that action. Now, more than a hundred years later, and with a twentieth century sophistication of technique, we were attempting to follow Bernard on a far more difficult trail.

The methodology and conceptual framework developed in the search for opiate receptors seem to me to be almost as important as the results. We based ourselves on the phenomenon of stereospecificity. We conceived of the receptors as locks and sought to determine whether such a lock could accommodate not only an opiate but its mirror-image isomer as well. If so, the situation would have been awkward because it would have precluded a binding assay. If the pharmacologically inactive isomer

Reprinted with permission from "Current Concepts in Postoperative Pain," *Hospital Practice*, January, 1978, Special Report.

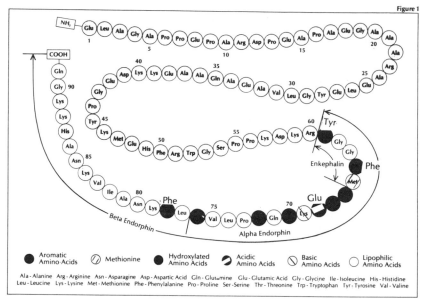

Figure 1

Amino acid sequence of the hormone beta-lipotropin is diagrammed above. The polypeptide segments that have been identified as endorphins and enkephalin are indicated. It is these segments that mimic the physiologic activities of naturally occurring opium alkaloids, strongly arguing for an identity in the molecular configuration of charges.

monopolized the receptor site, excluding all other binding, it would have been in effect an opiate antagonist.

What was learned concerning their species distribution was as fascinating as the physiologic siting of these receptors. Opiate receptor sites were found in all vertebrates and in no invertebrates. That told us something very important: Obviously, these opiate receptors were not a vestigial hangover but a refinement attendant upon a late stage of evolution. Now it seemed clear to the handful of investigators in the field at that time that such structures could not have evolved in order to react with a product of the opium poppy. It was evident to all of us that this intricate system was developed to interact with some endogenous ligands.

Our position was that of the child who opens a barn full of manure and, with a hope based on the overpowering evidence of his senses, states confidently: "There must be a pony in there some place."

The search for endogenous ligands went on simultaneously in a number of centers. Simon and Snyder were forging ahead in their laboratories on the basis of extensive mapping of receptor sites. Kosterlitz and Hughes in Aberdeen, and Terenius in Stockholm were equally active.

At Stanford we began our quest for an endogenous ligand that would resemble morphine pharmacologically. It is a pharmacologic axiom that

most exogenous drugs mimic endogenous substances. In this case, however, that seems to have been the wrong axiom to grind. In any case we
turned our attention away from that problematic objective to the peptides that play a well-recognized role as neurotransmitters. In 1975, we
found opioid activity in a rather large peptide in the pituitary (containing
31 amino acids) that proved to be a fragment of beta-lipotropin, the
pituitary hormone discovered by C. H. Li. Some months earlier, however, Hughes in Aberdeen had reported marked opioid characteristics
in a brain pentapeptide. His was far more readily purified than our
cumbersome compound.

It seemed unlikely that nature would have provided two distinct opioid
peptides, and it was therefore no surprise to discover that Hughes'
smaller peptide (enkephalin) turned out to match the sequence of a
segment of our larger one (endorphin).

Here then were the much sought endogenous ligands devised to bind
with the opiate receptors so strategically placed along the spinal cord,
in the pituitary, the brain, and the intestines. Both enkephalin and endorphin act on these sites precisely as does morphine.

In many ways, we were confronted with a most perplexing phenomenon, because we have here compounds with clearly disparate characteristics—on one hand, polypeptides, on the other, an alkaloid—
performing in identical fashion. The answer lies in the similarity of
"shape," the identical molecular configuration of charges, observable in
the peptides and in the alkaloid morphine. It is actually no more remarkable than the facility with which a plastic key and a metal key may
turn the same lock, though made of totally different materials.

That the configuration of a peptide within the brain or pituitary of
a vertebrate animal should precisely match that of a substance found in
an opium poppy must go down as one of nature's more bizarre coinci-
dences.

Research that began with a study of the causes and mechanisms of
morphine addiction has thus taken us deep into the central nervous and
endocrine systems of the human body, confronting us with hitherto
unknown possibilities and still greater mysteries.

We found, however—and this was vital to all subsequent progress
down that road—that the "wrong" isomer was in fact as ineffective as
a misshapen key. It proved totally inert, and the receptor site was thus
demonstrated to be truly stereospecific (see Figure 2). A binding assay
was thus possible.

Admittedly, that early demonstration had serious defects. The synthetic opiates we employed were not sufficiently potent to permit use at
low concentrations, and the nonspecific binding was far too great. Still,

Figure 2

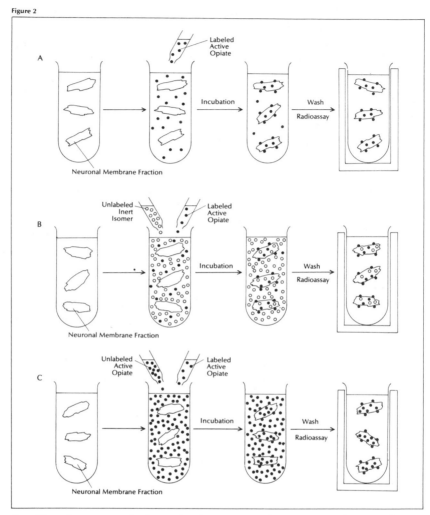

Competitive radioreceptor assay has been used to demonstrate the stereospecificity of opiates in relationship to surface receptors. In experiment depicted here, neuronal membrane fractions containing opiate receptors are incubated with isotope-labeled active opiates. After excess opiate is washed off, binding is measured by assaying the amount of bound radioactivity (A). If unlabeled inert isomer is added even in very large quantities (B), there is no reduction in radioactivity; clearly, even in excessive quantity, inert isomer cannot compete with active opiate for receptors. Finally (C), unlabeled active opiate is added in quantities 100-fold greater than needed to completely occupy receptor sites. Membrane-bound radioactivity drops substantially, since active unlabeled material overwhelms labeled in competing for specific receptors.

it established the directions for the search. Following these lines, Pert and Snyder at Johns Hopkins and Simon at New York University developed a vastly improved filtration assay that could wash out nonspecifically bound material.

This highly effective instrument of discovery made possible the pinpointing of receptors along the principal routes of pain stimuli: the medial pain pathways, at the first pain relay of the spinal cord, in the thalamus, the hypothalamus, and other parts of the brain. Moreover, opiate receptors were found as well in areas not associated with pain but with emotional responses and with hormone control. Concentrations of them were also noted in the amygdala and hippocampus, thought to be involved in reward systems and memory.

II. THE ENDORPHINS—THEIR PHYSIOLOGIC AND PATHOLOGIC POTENTIALS

The opioid characteristics of the endorphins have triggered intense curiosity about and investigation into the possible physiologic and pathophysiologic roles of these polypeptides. Some of the most active investigations have centered on the speculation that the endorphins may be involved in mental and emotional disorders. If such relationships were established, then an intriguing link between pain mechanisms and psychologic dysfunction would be forged. But one must stress the speculative nature of this research.

We can base some cautious optimism on the happy coincidence that endorphin has the happy faculty of acting on the same receptor, of turning the same lock as it were. One may assume, therefore, that it will have the same effects as morphine. And, indeed, there is now abundant evidence that endorphin does act precisely as morphine does.

Morphine combats the effect of stress, including that occasioned by physical pain. One may confidently expect that endorphin will do likewise. Morphine has the ability to release some pituitary hormones and to suppress the release of others. It has been found that endorphins perform similarly. Morphine is constipating, acting no doubt on opiate receptors that have been located in the intestinal tract. It may well be that endorphins have something to do with the control of intestinal motility.

When endorphin is injected into the brain, it produces analgesia just as morphine does, though it is more potent and its effect lasts longer. One investigator has shown that enkephalin injected at the spinal-cord level relieves pain just as morphine does.

Enkephalin, again like morphine, has been shown to stimulate the release of prolactin and growth hormone (see Figure 1).

Endorphin has also been shown to vary its effects according to species like its exogenous counterpart. In rats, it produces a catatonic episode in which the animal freezes in waxy rigidity in whatever position it is put until startled out of its trance state. Guillemin has produced the same catatonic trance-like state in rats by means of beta-endorphin.

In cats, on the other hand, endorphin (or morphine) produces hal-

Figure 1

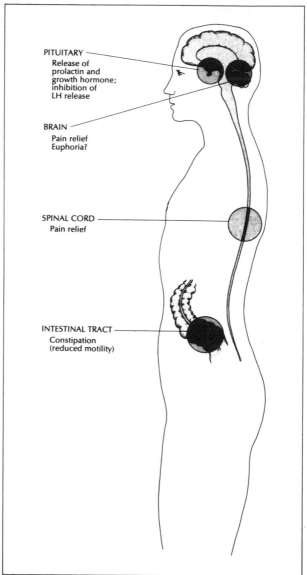

Body "map" shows organs in which endorphin receptors have been located, and lists some of the effects that have been shown for opiate analgesics and endorphins as they appear to relate to this distribution of specific receptors.

lucinatory mania—which can be startling, as a veterinarian discovered after he tried morphine on a tiger.

In 1973, even before the endogenous opiates were actually discovered (although their existence seemed almost certain), we suggested that a defect in a system that regulated mood, pain, and anxiety responses would almost inevitably result in behavioral disorders. We postulated such a defect could make one subject prone to addiction, to which another, whose endorphins were working normally, might prove invulnerable.

I do not mean to suggest that addiction is simply a matter of genetics, which may account for some inborn predisposition. Obviously addiction is a complex social phenomenon in which, I am sure, economics and lifestyles are more significant factors than the effectiveness of endorphins in any given population. However, the endorphin system may explain why it is that, given the same drug availability, some individuals will become addicted and others will not. It may elucidate the vulnerability factor in addiction.

Still another possibility is that addiction might be produced not by a constitutional defect in the endogenous system but by its suppression or severe impairment as a result of habitual use of exogenous opiates.

Guillemin has suggested that an excess of endorphins may be the significant underlying factor in catatonic schizophrenia. Although it is an intriguing hypothesis, it is one that must be approached very cautiously. One must, for example, ask why, if that hypothesis were true, naloxone should not be as effective a therapy for catatonic schizophrenia as it is for an overdose of heroin. And while the results of some studies do show a slight improvement among schizophrenics treated with naloxone, nobody would pretend that we have here a dramatic cure for that complex disorder. It cannot compare, for example, with the effectiveness of such neuroleptic drugs as phenothiazine. I think to suggest that schizophrenia is simply the result of an overproduction of endorphins might be an overly optimistic approach. Unfortunately the road to schizophrenia therapy is not going to be that simple.

The apparent improvements in schizophrenia when naloxone is administered—and they are minimal—may be attributed to the fact that chemical processes in the brain are so interrelated that any change in the workings of the system may provoke a change in schizophrenic behavior. It may be that schizophrenia is in fact not one disease but a complex of many disorders, one of which may be related to endorphin dysfunction. At this point, a role for endorphins is a possibility and nothing more.

Much more likely is that endorphins may play a role in determining pain threshold. One study has indeed shown interesting evidence linking insensitivity to pain with an overproduction of endorphins, but we shall have to wait for other studies to see whether this opens a new and promising road to the clinical uses of endorphins. This, too, may be a blind alley. One finds many such in this new terrain.

We ran down one such alley not long ago. We had before us the exciting, and now amply confirmed, data showing that the intractable pain of terminal cancer can be dramatically relieved by hypophysectomy. At Stanford, we had a middle-aged man suffering agonizing pain from a diffuse metastatic hypernephroma that had invaded the bone. A hypophysectomy was performed, and from the moment he regained consciousness after the operation, the patient was totally free of pain. Six months postsurgery, his cancer was far advanced but he remained perfectly pain-free. He consented to an experiment with naloxone. It was explained to him, of course, that if naloxone brought back his pain it would be short-lived and he would quickly regain his comfort. We injected a large dose of naloxone, but it had no effect whatsoever, indicating that the endorphin system was not involved.

I am certain we will go down many more such blind alleys before we arrive at a clear understanding of the role of endorphins in mental illness, in pain, and in homeostatic regulation. We can only assume that an entire system of potent, endogenous opioids acting on receptors must be relevant to the study and management of pain and anxiety.

III. THE ENDORPHINS AND PAIN—WHAT WE HAVE LEARNED

The hunters and trackers of endogenous opioids have borrowed a tool from the armamentarium of the addiction center—naloxone hydrochloride. This synthetic substance has the convenient characteristic of binding to an opiate receptor while manifesting no other unrelated effects. It simply monopolizes an opiate receptor site, denying it to the opiate. For many years it has been the standard and almost instantaneously efficient means of treatment for an overdose of heroin. It is that rare thing—a pure opiate antagonist.

Naloxone's competitive blockade is now used as a criterion for the presence of an opiate, in the sense that the conclusive test for opioid effect is evidence that it can be blocked and reversed by naloxone. If pain has been alleviated by an opiate—endogenous or exogenous— naloxone will quickly reverse that relief and reestablish the pain. If naloxone has no effect it must be assumed opiate receptors, and therefore opioids, are not involved.

The other indispensable technology for exploring endorphins is the radioimmunoassay, the technique for which Rosalyn Yalow, its codiscoverer (along with the late Solomon Berson), has just been awarded the Nobel Prize. Radioimmunoassay has superseded the clumsy and inconclusive bioassays to which we were confined in earlier pioneering days.

These two instrumentalities have made possible the charting of the body's own opiates, which has proceeded at an astounding pace in the last three years. It is now established that enkephalins follow the general pattern of neural transmitters and the almost identical pattern of opiate receptors.

At the subcellular level where the technique of immunofluorescence histology has located them (see Figure 1), opiate receptors are found in nerve terminals. That is precisely where one would expect to find neurotransmitters. It is there that we get a picture of the presynaptic inhibiting mechanisms of the enkephalins. For example, in the substantia gelatinosa there is a relay station in which a neurotransmitter emits a peptide known as substance P, which activates a pain signal. On that P neuron there are opiate receptors, and it is on those receptors that an enkephalin acts to inhibit the pain signal.

It appears that wherever there is a pain transmitter there is also an apparatus for inhibiting that transmitter.

The endorphins, those larger peptide configurations, were at first thought to be confined to the pituitary but are now known to be present in the brain as well, just as a number of hormones originally thought to be exclusively pituitary are also found in the brain (ACTH is one example.) One endorphin—beta-endorphin, a 31-amino-acid polypeptide—has been definitely located in the brain though, oddly enough, in cells that do not contain enkephalin.

At first it was thought that perhaps endorphin was produced in the pituitary and passed into the brain. However, we removed the pituitary of laboratory animals, waited a month, and found as much endorphin in brain as we had noted before. Clearly, it is made in the brain. This endorphin does contain enkephalin, making it a likely candidate for a role in competing with opiates.

There are then at least two opiate systems at work, though why this should be is still a mystery. And there are other questions in this still shadowy field in which we are taking our first steps. For example, we do not know why enkephalin is found in some places that are not at all associated with the transmission of pain signals. Nor do we know quite why these systems were evolved or precisely how they are activated. Pain that is constructive, that delivers a timely signal, that sets the animal to fight or flee is vital to survival. But pain that incapacitates, that produces

Figure 1

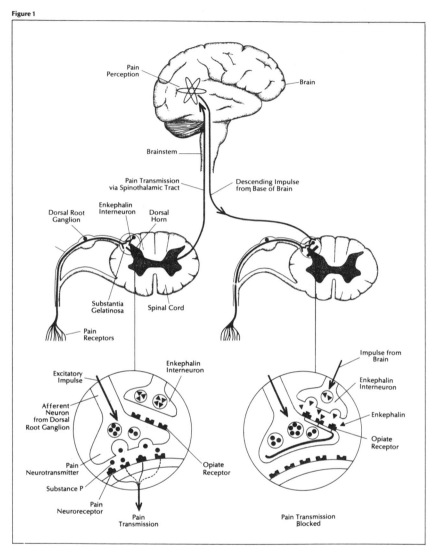

Immunofluorescence studies have located endorphin (enkephalin) receptors in close proximity and in blocking positions to pain receptors. The left side of the diagram shows the route of pain transmission from the dorsal root and dorsal horn to the brain. On the right, one sees the relationship of this pathway to localized enkephalin (and opiate) receptors.

anxiety, is obviously a handicap, and it may be that it is this sort of pain that triggers the endorphins. (I use the term in a generic sense to include enkephalins.)

A mouse in the clutches of a hawk must get the painful message that spurs him to action, but if he is to act he must have something that will temporarily shut off pain and anxiety and induce the euphoria—defined as a state of well-being—that enables him to act defensively.

We have tried to reproduce such situations in the laboratory with only indifferent success. Applying momentary heat to the feet of rats produced no sign of endorphin activity, judging by the failure of naloxone to alter the results. However, when we kept rats on a hot plate until they jumped off we did indeed find that an injection of naloxone resulted in a significantly quicker jump, suggesting greater pain and therefore the blocking of the moderating influence of enkephalins.

Severe electroshock in rats (up to 30 minutes of considerable stress) did produce evidence of endorphin activity. But whether it is the severity or the duration of the stimuli that triggers the analgesic effect we do not know.

We performed a number of painful tests on human volunteers, including an ice-water immersion test—which I underwent, myself, and can testify to its beastliness—with no evidence that the pain invoked an endorphin mechanism. The difficulty may be that though a laboratory experiment can produce pain it cannot evoke the anxiety of situations in the real world. This is probably because the subject knows that he can always terminate the experience if it becomes unbearable.

We are now interested in the more subtle, emotional aspects of endorphin action. There is evidence in animals that endorphins may play a direct role in reward mechanisms. An interesting sidelight on that point is the well-demonstrated ability of animals to self-administer morphine—a perversion of a natural endorphin system, it would appear.

We hope to test human subjects in other life situations. We have done an experiment in human sexual arousal and orgasm and found no endorphin activity.

An interesting by-product of endorphin research may be a scientific rationale for acupuncture. Pomeranz at the University of Toronto has shown in cats that applying needles to the points indicated on Chinese acupuncture charts does indeed prevent the firing of dorsal horn cells, which would normally take place in response to painful stimuli. That analgesic action was suppressed by naloxone, which indicates clearly that endorphins are involved.

The effect of acupuncture on the dorsal horn neurons is slow in onset (about five minutes after the needle puncture) and lasts up to three quarters of an hour. This would suggest that the mechanism involved is not in the nervous system where events take place in seconds or milliseconds. It seems more like a hormonal response.

Furthermore, when Pomeranz removed the pituitary in experimental mice he found that acupuncture lost all effect. It may be that acupuncture triggers a message that travels to the hypothalamus and down into the pituitary, where it releases a pituitary endorphin. Or perhaps the acupuncture triggers the release of endorphins elsewhere that require the interaction of a pituitary factor.

Acupuncture is only one of many analgesic phenomena that may ultimately be explained by this still tentatively explored system that manipulates mood, pain, and anxiety.

Section VI

RESEARCH ISSUES AND THE ADDICTIONS

There is a paucity of well-designed empirical research in the addictions. Nathan and Lansky (1978) have succinctly identified the major methodological problems responsible for this failing in addiction research. Although their work is heavily based on problems in the alco holism literature, the essence of their comments apply to work in the addictions as well. Further, Nathan and Lansky emphasize the importance of two areas often ignored in discussions on methodological problems in the social sciences: biased or selective literature reviews, and the important differences between statistical and clinical significance. Each of these areas deserves the reader's special attention.

If the experiment is considered the anvil of science on which is tested the viability of specific hypotheses, then theory is the vice that conceptually holds these ideas in place during such empirical examination. There has been a veritable legion of theoretical offerings in the addictions. These statements have often led to conceptual chaos, methodological artifact, and practical or applied confusion (in addition to Nathan & Lansky, 1978, see Gambino & Shaffer, 1979; Shaffer & Gambino, 1979; Peele, 1979, for discussions of these issues). Such conceptual/theoretical confusion often results in the poorly designed research that characterizes an immature science (as discussed earlier in the Introduction). In the brief and timely paper by Gendreau and Gendreau (1971), important design problems that had previously supported faulty conclusions about the "addiction prone" personality were identified and clarified. Gendreau and Gendreau also properly illustrate and expand upon Nathan and Lansky's warnings in the specific research area of heroin addiction. Gendreau and Gendreau demonstrate the importance of utilizing sound experimental design when attempting to examine a conceptual controversy.

Often, studies in the addictions are formulated and conducted as a result of pressure created by identified social "emergencies." Such pressure typically demands "quick" response and, therefore, "quick" results. Consequently, much of the data-base on which the current literature rests was produced by studies that utilized retrospective research designs. Typically, the patients who served as research subjects in these studies only crossed paths with the investigator because their heroin (or other drug) habit became unmanageable. As a result, they enrolled in a drug treatment program and only then became eligible to participate in "scientific" research. Variables antecedent to substance abuse (e.g., physiological, psychological, etc.) were *always* antecedent to treatment and most often to research efforts as well. The functional causal relationships between these variables remains unclear. Nathan and Lansky (1978) suggest the increased use of multivariate measures and analysis as a partial remedy for this problem. We strongly endorse this recommendation and suggest further that multivariate techniques be utilized within more and better *prospective* research designs. Vaillant's work (1966a, 1966b) is an example of this concept.

Vaillant's use of *longitudinal prospective* (rather than retrospective) design has yielded important and sometimes surprising results: for example, correcting the faulty notions that abstinence *requires* continued psychotherapy to be maintained or that "addicts *need* drugs for optimal adjustment" (1966b, p. 573). Careful attention should be paid to Vaillant's discussion about the journey from addiction to abstinence; particularly intriguing is his consideration of addiction as a disorder similar to adolescence.

Finally, we want to emphasize the importance of considering the differences between internal and external validity for the investigator contemplating empirical research. Specifically, it is not enough to have a study that is rigorously controlled, "clean" and, hence, internally valid. Such a design, however "tight," might yield equivocal results with respect to the actual phenomena of interest. For example, in a recent controversy about the relationship between psychiatric illness and drug abuse (McLellan, Woody, & O'Brien, 1979, 1980; Shaffer, Burglass, & Whitehead, 1980). Shaffer et al. suggest that McLellan et al. did not divide their subjects into mutually exclusive groups; i.e., users of psychostimulants, depressants, or narcotics, because all members of these groups had also used alcohol and marihuana. Consequently, Shaffer et al. argued that most of the subjects in this study were, in fact, polydrug users. McLellan et al. (1980) countered by stating that, "The concurrent (but not primary) use of alcohol and marihuana by most of our subjects are true, the fact that it applies to all the groups is the very reason why it is not relevant to the specific psychiatric effects found in the three groups" (p. 870). This controversy illustrates the fundamental difference between internal and external validity. Specifically, McLellan et al. (1980) supported the credibility of their work solely on the basis of internal validity, i.e., sound experimental design. Conversely, Shaffer et al.'s (1980) criticisms were based primarily on faulty external validity, i.e., the relevance of research findings for application to the larger population. To illustrate further, if the subjects observed in the McLellan study had used LSD instead of alcohol or marihuana, then the psychiatric effects noted would be more readily questioned and the causal role of psychiatric factors cast into considerable doubt. In terms of experimental design, the external validity of any study must be questioned when a major variable is confounded by the entrance of another *similar* variable into the design, even if the internal validity is not thereby affected.

If one could *replicate* the findings of McLellan et al. with a different patient population and fewer confounding factors, then the previous findings could be considered more robust and, therefore, externally valid. "There is no better procedure for assuring the internal and external validity of inferred relationships than to retest them using multiple research methodologies, using different controls depending on the variations of independent and dependent variables that are operating, and to probe the effects on different populations of research subjects" (Rosenthal & Rosnow, 1975, p. 95).

REFERENCES

GAMBINO, B., & SHAFFER, H. The concept of paradigm and the treatment of addiction. *Professional Psychology*, April 1979, *10*, 207-223.
GENDREAU, P., & GENDREAU, L. P. Research design and narcotic addiction proneness. *Canadian Psychiatric Association Journal*, 1971, *16*, 265-267.
McLELLAN, A. T., WOODY, G. E., & O'BRIEN, C. P. Development of psychiatric illness in drug abusers: Possible role of drug preferences. *New England Journal of Medicine*, 1979, *301*(24), 1310-1314.
McLELLAN, A. T., WOODY, G. E., & O'BRIEN, C. P. Psychiatric illness in drug abusers. *New England Journal of Medicine*, 1980, *302*(15), 870.
NATHAN, P. E., & LANSKY, D. Common methodological problems in research on the addictions. *Journal of Consulting and Clinical Psychology*, 1978, *46*, 713-726.
PEELE, S. Redefining addiction II. The meaning of addiction in our lives. *Journal of Psychedelic Drugs*, 1979, *11*, 289-297.
ROSENTHAL, R., & ROSNOW, R. L. *Primer of Methods for the Behavioral Sciences*. New York: Wiley & Sons, 1975.
SHAFFER, H., BURGLASS, M. E., & WHITEHEAD, J. Psychiatric illness in drug abusers. *New England Journal of Medicine*, 1980, *302*(15), 869.
SHAFFER, H., & GAMBINO, B. Addiction paradigms II: Theory, research and practice. *Journal of Psychedelic Drugs*, 1979, *11*(4), 299-303.
VAILLANT, G.E. A twelve-year follow-up of New York narcotic addicts: II. The natural history of chronic disease. *New England Journal of Medicine*, 1966, *275*, 1282-1288.(a)
VAILLANT, G. E. A twelve-year follow-up of New York narcotic addicts: IV. Some characteristics and determinants of abstinence. *American Journal of Psychiatry*, 1966, *123*(5), 573-584.(b)

27

COMMON METHODOLOGICAL PROBLEMS IN RESEARCH ON THE ADDICTIONS

Peter E. Nathan and David Lansky

Among the common methodological problems in research on the addictions reviewed in this article are (a) selective, incomplete, or biased reviews of the body of prior research from which a study has arisen; (b) reliance on inadequate or incomplete diagnostic criteria in choosing subjects for study; (c) choice of inappropriate comparison groups for treatment outcome research; (d) use of inadequate alcoholic analogues when alcoholic subjects are unavailable; (e) failure to adequately account for treatment dropouts in analysis of treatment outcome data; (f) unwarranted choice of single-subject over group designs in addictions research and vice versa; (g) failure to ensure that comparably trained, equivalently committed therapists provide both experimental and control treatments in treatment outcome studies; (h) failure to ensure that patients in both experimental and control treatments receive treatments as therapist- and time-intensive; (i) failure to follow patients for adequate lengths of time posttreatment; (j) failure to provide for adequate, multidimensional treatment outcome measures tapping a full range of patient behavior; (k) failure to exercise restraint, scientific modesty, and criticality in reporting results of one's own research; and

Reprinted with permission from the *Journal of Consulting and Clinical Psychology*, 1978, *46*, 713-726. Copyright 1978 by the American Psychological Association, Inc.

Preparation of this manuscript was facilitated by National Institute for Alcohol Abuse and Alcoholism Research Grant AA 00259 to the first author.

(l) failure to recognize important differences between statistical and clinical significance.

This article identifies common problems in research on the addictions. It also offers suggestions for remediating these methodological problems. The addictions considered in the article include alcoholism and the drug dependencies. Because the literature on alcoholism is much more extensive than that on drug addiction, most of the common errors reviewed are drawn from the alcoholism literature. Despite this focus, there is enough commonality between methods of research on alcoholism and drug dependence that criticism in one research area almost always has relevance to the other.

The first problems to be considered are those arising from inadequate, incomplete, or biased reviews of relevant literatures. Next, methodological shortcomings of subject selection, research procedure, and data analysis are detailed. Consideration of problems in the presentation of results and their interpretation and discussion concludes the article.

LITERATURE REVIEW AND STATEMENT OF THE PROBLEM

Although it might be considered gratuitous to begin this article by pointing out the impact that selective, incomplete, or biased reviews of research have on the impact of research findings, it is important, nonetheless, to recognize that the alcoholism researcher may be particularly liable to this temptation. Otherwise called "enlightened historical selectivity," this tendency comes easily to the addictions researcher who is forced to choose one position, from several, on such controversial matters as etiology (Sociocultural, genetic, metabolic/physiological, and behavioral views are foremost.) and treatment. (Dynamic, behavioral, medical and peer-group Alcoholics Anonymous treatments are available.) This breadth of available perspective has, in turn, been largely responsible for the proliferation and perpetuation of invalid "common truths" and unsubstantiated "old wives' tales" in this field.

Selective or biased reviews of the alcoholism literature have supported a variety of such "truths" through the years, including that alcoholism is a medical disorder (and that as a result, abstinence is the only appropriate treatment goal for alcoholics), that all alcoholics experience loss of control over their drinking, that "dry" alcoholics are the best therapists for other alcoholics, that alcoholics drink to reduce prevailing high levels of tension and anxiety, that alcoholics are oral-dependent individuals who have not come to terms with their needs for nurturance, and so on.

One area of alcoholism and drug addiction research—having to do with the etiology of alcohol and drug dependence—has been especially subject to the stultifying influence of selective biases on review and interpretation of research results. Since significant federal funding for alcoholism and drug research became available about a decade ago, unitary models of dependence have been largely disproven. Specifically, there do *not* appear to be characteristic personality patterns that differentiate drug abusers from nonabusers, there is clearly *not* a single route to alcohol or drug dependence, and alcoholics and nonalcoholics do *not* appear to metabolize ethanol in discernibly different ways at comparable levels of ingestion. Instead, the mechanism of dependence, the etiologic process, the personality structure of alcoholic and drug-dependent individuals, and their motivation for and response to treatment all depend on far more than intrapsychic or physiologic factors alone. To this end, the literature now supports a more sophisticated view, that of a complex individual system interacting with personal history and environmental factors to yield an addiction. Among the most clearly articulated of these new, more constructive points of view is the behavioral viewpoint on the addictions, well-stated by psychologists Miller and Eisler (1975):

> Within a social-learning framework alcohol and drug abuse are viewed as socially acquired, learned behavior patterns maintained by numerous antecedent cues and consequent reinforcers that may be of a psychological, sociological, or physiological nature. Such factors as reduction in anxiety, increased social recognition and peer approval, enhanced ability to exhibit more varied, spontaneous social behavior, or the avoidance of physiological withdrawal symptoms may maintain substance abuse. (p. 5)

From another perspective, that of tongue-in-cheek, Mark Keller (1972), alcoholism's long-time Dean of Letters, says the following about unidimensional theories of alcoholism:

> A splurge of reports, in the 1940's, of biochemical characteristics purporting to differentiate alcoholics from nonalcoholics stimulated me to review a voluminous related literature, implicating physical, social and psychological demarcators as well. The only conclusion I could derive, from the entirety of the reportage, took a form that became known, among colleagues, as Keller's Law: *The investigation of any trait in alcoholics will show that they have either more or less of it.* Accordingly, I then predicted that if sexadactyly should be investigated, alcoholics will yield either more or fewer six-toed and six-fingered people than a control population. (p. 1147)

SUBJECTS

Diagnostic criteria. The familiar problems that plague diagnostic decision makers called on to make diagnostic distinctions among psychiatric
patients (Chapman & Chapman, 1977; Goldberg, 1968; Nathan, 1967)
also confront the researcher who must select alcoholics from a general
population and, as important, assure that the subjects chosen are representative of an identifiable portion of the universe of alcoholics. It
might appear that choosing alcoholics must be easier than selecting schizophrenics or neurotics, because all alcoholics share a single stigma—they
drink too much. But the task is made more difficult than it might seem
by lack of consistency, in research reports, in detailing this hallmark of
the disorder. For example, descriptions of alcoholics recently studied by
psychologists range from "twenty subjects [who were] psychiatric patients
with a primary diagnosis of alcoholism" (Levine & Zigler, 1976, p. 141),
and "alcoholic Ss [subjects] [who] were volunteers from the patient population of the Alcoholism Treatment Program at the VA hospital"
(O'Leary, Radford, Chaney, & Schau, 1977, p. 580) to

> subjects [who] were three male veteran inpatient volunteers, ages
> 40, 50, and 55 years. They reported histories of chronic drinking
> of 15, 20, and 26 years, respectively. Each had experienced black-
> outs and delirium tremens as a result of drinking and had been
> hospitalized 9-20 times for alcohol-related problems. The sub-
> jects were each classified as binge drinkers consuming up to 140
> ounces of beer and 26-70 ounces of liquor per day when drink-
> ing. Drinking episodes ranged from 5-30 days followed by a 60-
> day (on the average) period of sobriety. (Doleys, Ciminero, Wal-
> lach, & Davidson, 1977, p. 207)

Leaving aside the question of which of these studies most carefully
ensured that its subjects were in fact alcoholics, it is clear that only the
latter article provides enough information to permit assessment of the
extent to which the subjects studied were comparable to alcoholics studied elsewhere.

The greatest possible detail about drinking pattern must be conveyed
in a research report. Above all, researchers—and their audience—must
become unwilling to consider men and women as alcoholics simply because they received that diagnosis from someone somewhere at some
time. Instead, hard signs of physical dependence, psychological dependence, and tolerance ought to be in evidence, along with indications
that alcohol has been a problem in living and that problems in family

relationships, vocational adjustment, and interpersonal relationships have followed from excessive alcohol consumption.

Although use of a broad range of assessment procedures is an essential aspect of alcohol and drug treatment research, the ultimate utility of these measures can only be gauged by reference to their respective reliability and validity estimates. It is, therefore, incumbent on the responsible researcher to assess and report the adequacy of these measures as applied to the subject population in question. Unfortunately, it is rare that the reliability and validity of assessment procedures are reported in alcohol and drug treatment studies.*

It is also important that age, sex, and socioeconomic status, at least, be summarized for all subject populations. As we have already observed, alcoholism does not wipe out the effect on behavior of subject variables such as demography, education, and social class.

Even more formidable assessment problems confront the drug researcher, since only very recently have attempts been made to measure quantity and frequency of drug ingestion (e.g., Mirin, Meyer, McNamee, & McDougle, 1976; Rawlins, Randall, Meyer, McNamee, & Mirin, 1976). As a consequence, diagnosis of drug dependence is from whatever signs of physical dependence are available, whereas differentiation among varieties of drug abusers must be confined to descriptive typologies (e.g., heroin addict, amphetamine addict, polydrug abuser, and so on). However, Carlin and Stauss (1977) recently explored the possibility of categorizing drug addicts along functional dimensions, including a streetwise/straight typology (e.g., legality of primary means of support, conventionality of dress and grooming, ability to buy drugs from street drug dealers, etc.) and a self-medication/recreational drug-use typology. The major point of their article is that use of these descriptors, in conjunction with the more common descriptive typology, provides more information about subjects than the descriptive typology alone.

Control and comparison groups. Another common subject selection problem is choice of comparison groups when one wishes to contrast alcohol or drug abusers with nonabusers. If subjects are inpatients, must the comparison group also be hospitalized? And if it is, should it be composed of hospitalized psychiatric patients, because, presumably, alcoholics and drug abusers are often victims of psychiatric disorder as well? By the same token, if subjects are outpatients, can comparison subjects be cho-

---

*For detailed information on unobtrusive approaches to the assessment of alcoholism and its concomitants, the reader can consult Briddell and Nathan (1976), Miller (1976) and Nathan and Briddell (1977).

sen from any non-drug-abusing group or must they be psychiatric out-patients? In the same vein, how necessary is it to match experimental and control groups by age, sex, socioeconomic status (SES), level of education, and treatment motivation (if the latter is relevant to the study)? Our view of this complex matter is that alcoholics or drug addicts whose addictions are accompanied by concurrent psychiatric disorder must be compared to age-, sex-, and SES-matched nonaddicted individuals whose psychiatric diagnoses approximate those of the alcoholics. We do not assume, of course, that all drug-dependent individuals—or even most of them—are psychiatrically disordered just because they abuse drugs or alcohol.

Though an obvious and well-accepted control procedure, it is probably worth noting here, in passing, that groups of patients to be compared on the basis of treatment outcome must have been chosen from the same patient population to begin with, then assigned to treatment groups in a way guaranteed to ensure comparability. Of equal importance, in this context, is selection of a proper comparison treatment for alcoholics or drug abusers undergoing a nonstandard treatment whose efficacy is being assessed. In this regard, it is probably worth noting that "no treatment" or waiting list controls may be unethical when one is dealing with severely disabled addict populations. As important, they may also be unfeasible, since alternative treatment sources are often freely available to the motivated alcoholic or drug abuser. Most important, one must ensure that the control treatment that matched patients do receive is as active, long lasting, and time intensive as the new treatment being evaluated. This important issue is discussed in greater detail later.

A related control issue, in this context, is the treatment motivation of experimental and control subjects of comparative treatment studies. Failure to assess subjects' treatment motivation in treatment outcome studies involving small numbers of subjects, a common failing, prevents one from knowing whether apparent differences in treatment efficacy, if found, reflect real differences in the power of one treatment to effect changes in behavior or whether that treatment group simply included individuals who were more highly treatment motivated. Researchers fail to undertake this necessary assessment because doing so inevitably reduces the size of the pool of potential subjects and because the assessment is really not so simple. Above all, subjects may not tell the truth about their treatment motivation, especially when financial, vocational, or judicial contingencies have brought them to treatment. But despite this problem, it is absolutely necessary to attempt to assess treatment motivation and to report results of that assessment in any study in which motivation for treatment could play a role in outcome.

Alcoholic analogues. Despite their omnipresence, alcoholics are not easy to locate for study. They are also not likely to be highly motivated to participate in psychological research (whose payoff to them may be unclear), are not always reliable in keeping appointments when they do agree to be subjects, and, when they are not drinking, they are apt to prefer working to participating in research. Because research designed to examine alcohol's effects on alcoholics can only include alcoholics in good physical and psychological health despite their chronic alcoholism, those who design such research find themselves with an even smaller pool of alcoholics ready, willing, and able to be research subjects.

For these reasons, researchers may choose to study *alcoholic analogue subjects,* who may be "problem drinkers" of one sort or another or, commonly, heavy-drinking college students. Though choice of such subjects is understandable, generalization from their behavior to that of alcoholics must be done with great care—if at all. For this reason, it is almost always preferable to study alcoholics than their analogues; it is practically impossible to control for all of the differences that separate alcoholics and nonalcoholics, some of which remain unknown. Among the most obvious of these differences are age, educational level, cognitive functioning, and rate of ethanol metabolism.

Above all, one must be chary about concluding that what is characteristic of the behavior of a group of problem or heavy drinkers is likely also to characterize the behavior of alcoholics—only more so! In all likelihood, such a conclusion is not justified.

The problem of treatment dropouts. Although the dropout problem for all kinds of psychological treatment is a serious one, it is especially so for alcoholics and drug addicts, both of whom are poorly motivated for treatment; variable in meeting vocational, familial, and personal obligations; and, often, in poor control of their behavior. A recent study of more than 14,000 chronic alcoholics treated at 44 federally funded alcoholism treatment centers throughout the country (Armor, Polich, & Stambul, 1976) revealed that fewer than 25% of these clients continued in treatment for as long as 3 consecutive months. Moreover, of the original sample of 14,000, 6-month follow-up data on only 2,371 clients were reported. Both figures suggest something of the scope of the attrition problem facing the addictions treatment outcome researcher.

Given, then, that substantial numbers of alcoholics and drug addicts drop from treatment in its midst and that as many more who complete treatment cannot be located for follow-up, how is one to compare two or more treatment methods on both the short and long term? To begin with, one must include in any statistical analysis of differences among treatment groups subjects who dropped from treatment; these subjects should be considered treatment failures regardless of the rationalizations some may have given for the decision to terminate. The unintentional deception that can result if this rule is not followed is illustrated by an article published a few years ago comparing groups of alcoholics receiving two "active" treatments, both involving the administration of electric shock, and two "inactive" placebo treatments. On comparing the four groups in terms of average length of abstinence immediately following treatment, the study's authors concluded that one of the active treatments was associated with significantly longer periods of abstinence than the other three treatments. Inspection of the data on which this conclusion was drawn, however, reveals that 13 active treatment subjects dropped from treatment in its midst, whereas only 1 placebo treatment subject did so; this fact was not taken into account in the significance testing of posttreatment abstinence rates, which only compared subjects who had completed treatment. Since many of the active treatment subjects dropped from treatment because they found electric shock aversive, to conclude from the abstinence rates of subjects who were motivated enough to endure shock and remain in treatment that the active treatment was more effective than the placebo is deceptive, however unintentional.

Although most readers doubtless agree that patients who drop from treatment must be considered treatment failures for comparative purposes, it is more difficult to find agreement on how to handle treated subjects who cannot be located for follow-up. Is one to conclude that all subjects who cannot be found at a follow-up interval have returned to drinking or drug taking, have remained "dry" or "clean," or are using alcohol and drugs in about the same proportions as subjects who could be located? Though all three stances are defensible, the most conservative approach to this problem is to consider all patients unlocated at follow-up to be treatment failures (a position recommended by the American Medical Association, 1956; Pattison, Sobell, & Sobell, 1977; Sobell, 1978).

Before having to accept this admittedly unsatisfactory solution to the problem, though, one ought to take every step necessary to ensure that as many patients as possible are available for follow-up assessment. Ways to achieve this desirable goal are summarized later in this article in the section entitled *Follow-up*.

Who to study? It is inevitable that most of the subjects in alcoholism and drug treatment research will be male skid-row or "blue collar" alcoholics and ghetto-dwelling drug addicts. The reasons are that these individuals are often unemployed and, hence, available for intensive, long-term study; even if employed, they are more likely to be clients of publically funded clinics whose clientele is more available to researchers than are the patients of private psychologists and psychiatrists. Another is that this population of alcoholics and drug abusers is more likely than any other to reach the attention of the judicial system, and subsequently to be remanded to treatment by the courts; such court referrals constitute an important source of subjects for treatment evaluation studies. This is especially important, since it is clear that data on treatment outcome for court-referred drug addicts—whatever their socioeconomic status—cannot readily be generalized to drug abusers referred for different reasons. Unfortunately, few alcohol or drug treatment reports include explicit descriptions of referral sources.

As a result of these and other similar factors, most of our data on drinking patterns, patterns of drug use, and response to treatment are from this group of subjects, even though it is not representative of the total universe of drug abusers and alcoholics. It has been estimated, for example, that fewer than 5% of all alcoholics are of the skid-row variety (Armor et al., 1976).

With these observations in mind, we offer two remedial suggestions: (a) Every effort should be made to study socially and economically advantaged alcoholics and drug abusers as well as more readily available groups. Sources of such persons include autonomous Alcoholics Anonymous groups; private clinicians who might agree to cooperate with researchers they know and trust; and private hospital administrators, whose interest in research collaboration might reflect their wish to gain professional credibility by associating with a university's research efforts. (b) If the usual groups of skid-row alcoholics and destitute heroin addicts are the only populations available for study, the researcher must make clear that generalizations from his/her data can only be to comparable groups of intellectually and vocationally limited individuals, that few alcoholics and drug-dependent individuals are as impoverished in so many ways as are these overstudied individuals.

PROCEDURE: COMPARATIVE TREATMENT STUDIES

Group versus single-subject designs. The same design dilemma faces the alcoholism or drug treatment researcher as confronts any other clinical researcher who must choose between group and single-subject designs. Group designs permit more comfortable generalization of findings from one population to another, because they enable statistical testing of differences in the efficacy of one treatment procedure and another among substantial groups of individuals. At the same time, group designs sacrifice the fine-grained analysis of the temporal dynamics of behavior change provided by single-subject designs. As important, they do not permit the "return to baseline" implicit in the single-subject ABA design that is necessary to establish that it was the treatment, rather than time, motivation, or expectancy, that brought about the observed changes in behavior.

Because so much of the research on alcoholism treatment by psychologists during the past 5 years has been behavioral, much of the literature reports single-subject designs. By contrast, the older literature reported results predominantly from group designs. It is possible, in fact, to retain the virtues of both designs by ensuring that group designs provide for thorough and reliable pretreatment and posttreatment assessment of behavior, carefully matched experimental and control treatment subjects, and suitably prolonged follow-ups.

Several recent studies comparing alcoholism treatment methods have achieved this desirable blending of the strengths of single-subject and group designs, among them comparisons of abstinence-oriented and controlled-drinking-oriented behavior modification programs (Sobell & Sobell, 1976), behavioral family counseling, electrical aversion, covert sensitization, and systematic desensitization (Hedberg & Campbell, 1974), and two broad-spectrum behavioral treatment packages (Vogler, Compton, & Weissbach, 1975). All three projects provided for comprehensive pretreatment and posttreatment assessment of drinking behavior and vocational, familial, and interpersonal effectiveness; follow-up periods extending to or beyond a year, accompanied by procedures to minimize subject attrition during the follow-up period; treatment groups matched for relevant demographic and treatment motivation variables; and careful attention to comparability of "active" and "placebo" treatments. Unfortunately, the blending of constructive design elements contained in these studies is not generally characteristic of the field.

Who are the therapists? It is important to ensure that the treatments contrasted in comparative treatment studies be provided by comparably trained, equally committed therapists. To compare treatment outcomes when one treatment is given by experienced therapists and the other by graduate students, or when one is administered by clinicians committed to the treatment they are providing while the other is offered by men and women convinced that what they are doing has value, represents poor research design. Yet many researchers have made precisely this design error when comparing one or another combination of innovative therapeutic approaches with what is euphemistically termed *standard hospital milieu therapy*. The latter, which may include alcohol or drug education, group therapy, occasional personal counseling, and the opportunity to participate in an Alcoholics Anonymous or Synanon group, is usually provided by undertrained, underpaid state hospital workers whose enthusiasm for their work, insight into its value, and level of clinical training are rarely equal to those administering the new treatment approach. When the new therapeutic package turns out to be more efficacious than the standard one in such comparative studies, one cannot be certain that it was actually more active or that it was provided by committed therapists whose enthusiasm for their work was infectious.

We recommend that no new therapeutic package be compared to "standard hospital treatment milieu," so often a euphemism for virtually no treatment at all. Instead, the separate components of novel treatment packages might more profitably be compared to each other, as well as to the package as a whole, in this way permitting assessment of each component's contribution to the overall package's effectiveness. For those researchers wishing to compare their efforts to some "standard" success rate for alcoholism treatment, two choices are among those possible: Armor et al.'s (1976) recent survey data, suggesting that 70% of the clients treated at typical alcoholism clinics across the country show short-term improvement in drinking rate, make for rigorous comparisons; Ditman's (1967) earlier conclusion that the success of Alcoholics Anonymous, often the alcoholic's initial treatment resource, is only between 30% and 35% makes for much more comfortable ones. Our own view of the matter is that abstinence beyond a year by 40% or more of patients treated by *any* technique surpasses current expectations.

Treatment variables. To justify meaningful comparisons among different treatments, it is axiomatic (a) that all patients in all treatment groups must have received about the same number of hours of individual and group treatment and (b) that the intervals between treatment sessions must have been comparable. It is necessary to ensure comparability of treatments in this way because there is a considerable clinical treatment literature that attests to the therapeutic impact of the relationship between therapist and patient, an impact independent of the therapeutic methods that the therapist chooses to use (Smith & Glass, 1977).

In practice, this straightforward control procedure can present problems. Comparing an experimental treatment to "standard hospital milieu" treatment, for example, might prove impossible if this control is taken seriously: Most experimental treatment programs provide individual or group treatment—or both—administered by highly trained and experienced clinical researchers and their students, whereas standard treatment, customarily administered by hospital workers whose training and motivation may be inferior, is also likely to involve much less 1:1 contact and small group treatment. In similar fashion, comparison of methadone maintenance to psychotherapy is frequently confounded, since methadone programs usually involve the drug addict in less treatment time and less intimate therapist contact than do most psychotherapeutic treatments.

A related matter has to do with the scope of treatment issues addressed—the range of problem behaviors confronted. Consider how different the scope of treatment was for experimental and control subjects in a recently reported, widely cited behavioral treatment package for alcoholics:

> *Experimental Subjects:* Procedures included subjects being videotaped while intoxicated under experimental conditions, providing subjects when sober with videotape self-confrontation of their own drunken behaviors, shaping of appropriate controlled drinking or nondrinking behaviors . . . the availability of alcoholic beverages throughout treatment, and behavior change training sessions. [The latter] is a summary phrase to describe sessions which concentrated upon determining setting events for each subject's drinking, training the subject to generate a series of possible alternative responses to those situations to evaluate each of the delineated alternatives for potential short- and long-term consequences, and then to exercise the response which could be expected to incur the fewest self-destructive long-term consequences. Behavior change training sessions consisted of discussion, role playing, assertiveness training, role reversal or other appropriate behavioral techniques.

> *Control Subjects:* Control subjects received conventional treatment procedures which could include group therapy, chemotherapy, Alcoholics Anonymous, physiotherapy and other traditional services. (Sobell & Sobell, 1973, p. 601)

Although the range and diversity of potential treatments available to control subjects in this study could have been as great as those provided to experimental subjects, one is left with the distinct impression that the scope of treatment offered to experimental subjects—the specific problem areas that the treatments were designed to confront—was both better targeted and more comprehensive than that available to control subjects. In other words, *the treatment package offered to experimental subjects was not only different from but better than that provided control subjects.*

One resolves this common design problem by confronting the fundamental difficulty of premature comparison of the efficacy of comprehensive treatment packages, by resigning oneself to the necessity to compare the components of a treatment package separately before attempting to assess the overall efficacy of the package itself. It was this strategy that guided Wilson, Leaf, and Hathan's (1975) assessment of the efficacy of electrical aversion, a common element of broad-spectrum behavioral treatment for alcoholism. Their subjects received lengthy conditioning trials of electrical aversion, followed directly by ad libitum access to beverage alcohol. When subjects showed absolutely no evidence of conditioned aversion to ethanol, by drinking during the posttreatment period with the same enthusiasm for alcohol that they have shown pretreatment, it was concluded that electrical aversion, either by itself or within a broad-spectrum treatment package, did not have the therapeutic power many had presumed it to have.

Follow-up. Although it is obvious that the longer the follow-up interval posttreatment, the more sure one can be of data on treatment efficacy, no one knows how *short* the follow-up period can be and still reflect ultimate treatment efficacy. Nonetheless, most alcohol and drug researchers question any follow-up interval that fails to extend to 1 year or more posttreatment. They believe that such an interval is inadequate to assess the long-term effects of treatment for alcoholism or drug dependence, given that many alcoholics and drug abusers spontaneously modify or cease drug or alcohol ingestion on their own for periods extending beyond a year. We believe that a 2-year follow-up of treatment for alcoholism or drug dependence is necessary to provide a suitably comprehensive view of the power of the treatment to effect lasting change.

A 2-year follow-up period, however, presents formidable subject attrition problems. Given the transient nature of the existence of many alcoholics and drug addicts, how does one keep contact over that time with men and women whose residences, jobs, and lives change so much and so often? Sobell (1978), a clinical researcher with great experience in maintaining contact with alcoholic clients over lengthy follow-up intervals, suggests the following set of coordinated steps to minimize attrition of subjects during a follow-up period: (a) Allow enough time and develop enough persistence to locate as many follow-up subjects as possible; do not settle for a majority of subjects or even for most of them. (b) Explain to subjects at the end of treatment why follow-up contacts are scheduled, when they can expect to be contacted for follow-up, the kinds of information to be requested, and how this information will be used. (c) Identify as many collateral sources of information about subjects as possible during treatment. (d) Maintain continuity of contact with patients during the follow-up interval by keeping in touch every few weeks, even if follow-up information is not required until 6-month or 1-year marks. (e) Be prepared to consult official records (e.g., jail, hospital, welfare, driver records, etc.) to locate lost subjects. Parenthetically, maintaining this kind of frequent contact for follow-up purposes also serves as an important source of low-cost "continuing care" that may help maintain therapeutic gains first achieved during treatment. In this instance, then, good research design and good patient care go hand in hand.

A frequently ignored follow-up issue of relevance to both alcohol and drug treatment studies is that a treatment program may be highly effective in attaining desired goals while patients are actively involved in the program, only to appear to fail when patients return to nonsupportive or destructive environments. Unfortunately, a follow-up assessment 3 or 6 months posttreatment will not reveal this Treatment × Environment interaction (Gotestam, Melin, & Öst, 1976). Under these circumstances, assessment of outcome immediately after treatment has ended and then again during a follow-up period much more clearly delineates dynamics of improvement and determinants of relapse.

Outcome measures. A variety of direct and self-report measures of drinking behavior have been developed. The Cahalan quantity-frequency index (Cahalan & Cisin, 1968), the Michigan Alcoholism Screening Test (MAST; see Selzer, Vinokur, & Wilson, 1977), and Marlatt's behaviorally oriented Drinking History questionnaire (Marlatt, 1975) are the most widely used self-report measures of drinking. Although use of such measures opens the investigator to criticism on grounds of the relative unreliability of self-report data, several studies have recently reported that alcoholics' and drug addicts' self-reports on drinking and drug ingestion may be far more accurate than previously believed (Cox & Longwell, 1974; Sobell, 1978; Homer & Ross, Note 1). Regardless of these data, however, we prefer direct measures of drinking behavior, including blood alcohol determinations taken at unannounced intervals (e.g., Miller, 1975), taste test or other drinking analogue methods (e.g., Marlatt, Demming, & Reid, 1973), or, simply, ad libitum drinking opportunities (Schaefer, Sobell, & Mills, 1971). The latter two methods, however, cannot be used to assess dry alcoholics, since they provide the opportunity for alcohol ingestion; this assessment problem is considered in greater detail by Nathan and Lansky (1978). Whatever outcome measures are ultimately selected for use, the point discussed earlier in regard to the issues of reliability and validity is relevant here as well: These measures are relatively uninterpretable unless reliability and validity estimates for the population under study are reported.

There are other measures of treatment outcome that relate less directly to drinking or drug ingestion. One of the most thorough tests of these pretreatment and posttreatment measures was provided by Armor et al.'s (1976) recent national study of 44 alcoholism treatment centers scattered around the country. A complex of vocational, marital, and social indicators of relevance to alcoholism were tapped; direct reports from employers, clinicians, relatives, and others in a position to comment on job stability and marital adjustment were elicited. In some instances, these indices of behavior change showed more dramatic improvement following treatment than did direct measures of change in alcohol consumption.

In similar fashion, treatment goals for drug abusers extend far beyond mere reduction of the frequency of drug abuse; goals are often set to include improved employment status, widened spheres of non-drug-related social contacts, and improved physical health (Anderson & Nutter, 1975; McCabe, Kurland, & Sullivan, 1975). As a result, pretreatment and posttreatment measures must tap information that directly reflects the status of these socially desirous variables, frequently a most difficult task.

Whichever combination of direct and indirect indicators of change-in-life functioning is chosen, it is important that follow-up intervals be circumscribed enough to permit reliable recall of the data requested. To ask an alcoholic or drug addict to recollect quantity and frequency of alcohol or drug ingestion or quality of marital or vocational adjustment over a 6-month or 1-year period with any reliability is obviously impossible; to request such recall for a 2-week period is both more reasonable and, likely, will prove more reliable.

PROCEDURE: OTHER STUDIES

Nature of the analogue in analogue studies. One of the most common thrusts of alcoholism research that is not treatment oriented involves the use of alcoholic analogues. Such research might describe "typical" drinking patterns of chronic alcoholics, college students, or middle-class women. It might investigate the effects of alcohol on psychological, social, or cognitive functioning. Or the research could inquire into the impact of one or another environmental variables, designed to induce stress or anger, for example, on consequent drinking. All of this research could be undertaken analogically. Typical drinking in the real world can be inferred from patterns of drinking in the laboratory; under certain circumstances, the effects of large amounts of alcohol on cognitive functioning can be predicted from the effects of small doses; in some cases, the impact of stress on drinking can be studied by first creating artificial stress in the laboratory—an environmental condition analogous to real-life drinking stress—and then measuring consequent drinking behavior.

Reasons for undertaking analogue research instead of research in the real world are many. Alcoholics and drug addicts are hard to find, even harder to study. Giving alcohol in large doses to anyone, especially to an alcoholic, is difficult; giving hard drugs to anyone, especially to a drug addict, is virtually impossible. For these and other reasons, analogue research on the addictions stands between no research and the researcher. But there are important caveats to observe in undertaking analogue research in this field. They include, above all, assuring oneself—and one's professional audience—that the analogue one has chosen to use is not stretched so far as to bear only vague resemblance to the phenomenon in the real world. For instance, the laboratory drinking behavior of college sophomores cannot be considered representative of the drinking of adults in neighborhood taverns or at home. Similarly, the absence of an impact on intelligence test performance of moderate blood alcohol levels during a single test session has little relevance to possible cognitive deficits suffered by long-term heavy drinkers. Finally, stress induced in a laboratory might not be at all comparable to stress in the real world, especially when the latter stress derives from *things that matter* and the former stress does not.

The obvious solution to these potential problems is to avoid analogue studies, when possible. But when it is not possible to do so, as is so often the case, what then? In that event, one must document, to the extent possible, the nature of the relationship between the analogue and the real world. The burden of proof of the relevance of an analogue to the natural environment is on the investigator, not his or her audience!

Experimenter bias. By now virtually every psychologist knows of the pitfalls of experimenter bias, known to many as the "Rosenthal effect" (Rosenthal, 1966). In essence, experimenter bias refers to the unintentional bias that experimenters bring to their interactions with experimental subjects that can, in some cases, affect data.

Although it is doubtful that experimenter bias plays a more serious role in research on alcoholism and drug dependence than it does elsewhere, it can—and does—play a role that must be anticipated. Examples include the following: (a) In studies of free ad libitum drinking, especially those taking place in controlled laboratory settings, it is entirely possible for staff unintentionally to bias subjects toward either more or less drinking. This possibility is so real that we actively seek to reduce interaction between drinking subjects and staff to an absolute minimum in our own laboratory drinking studies. (b) In studies in which the effects of stressors on drinking or of alcohol on response to stressors is the focus, the investigator must ensure that the effects of the stressor derive from its real impact, not from his/her unintentional conveyance of expectations about those effects. In such studies, postexperimental questionnaires must affirm that the subject did perceive the stress stimulus as a stressor. (c) In studies in which alcohol's effect on other behaviors is being examined (e.g., its impact on projective responses, interpersonal facility, or psychomotor behavior), it is just as important to ensure that hypothesized effects are not translated into observed effects, because the experimenters betray their expectations to drinking subjects. To this end, careful inquiry at the conclusion of the study as to subjects' perception of its intent is frequently most enlightening.

The demography of alcoholism and drug dependence. As emphasized above, it is crucially important to control for variables other than variety of alcoholism or drug dependence in comparative treatment studies. Similar controls—or, at the least, awareness of the importance of such variables as age, sex, race, and socioeconomic status when experimental controls are impossible—are also necessary in studies exploring the impact of alcoholism on behavior. To fail to account for these variables is to run the risk of attributing to alcoholism or drug abuse responsibility for a particular behavior, a Rorschach percept, a Minnesota Multiphasic Personality Inventory (MMPI) or Wechsler Adult Intelligence Scale response pattern—or a treatment outcome—when, in fact, these behaviors may derive instead from the complex of ethnic, educational, or socioeconomic factors associated with alcoholism or drug dependence.

RESULTS

On reporting results. It is tempting, when reporting the results of a study, to be optimistic about their significance, even a bit grandiose about their staying power. Human nature being what it is, it is hard to be overly critical of the natural human tendency to see in one's own efforts what one might not see in those of others.

On the other hand, although overestimation of the significance of a new nodule on the backside of a personality theory can be tolerated, misleading, immodest, or unrealistic reporting of the results of comparative treatment studies goes beyond bad form. When read by persons unequipped to separate an inflated claim from a barely significant probability value, such reporting could result in the misapplication of unproven methods.

The point we wish to make here is a simple one: It is incumbent on the serious researcher to report data parsimoniously, modestly, and completely, even when data in their entirety are more confusing and less unequivocally interpretable than data that have been selectively pruned. Although improper presentation of data is a snare for every researcher, it is particularly so in fields such as alcoholism and drug dependence.

In these fields, little is known; the stakes are high for persons who develop viable theories of etiology or useful therapeutic approaches; and rapid, independent confirmation or disconfirmation of new findings is difficult. As a consequence, a series of revolutionary findings have swept the field, including several genetic theories of etiology, a variety of new, "sure fire" diagnostic methods, novel behavioral treatment procedures that do not require abstinence, and innovative prevention programs guaranteed to reduce prevalence of these disorders. Unfortunately, like similar claims made of new discoveries about the schizophrenias in the late 1950s and early 1960s, the light of day—and independent replication—has either diminished or disproved most of these epochal findings.

Although Job was not necessarily speaking of psychological science when he concluded that there is nothing new under the sun, it might be wisest to heed his words until, or unless, independent confirmation supports your Nobel-prize-winning discovery, especially if you work in alcoholism or drug dependence!

Clinical versus statistical significance. It is as possible to overinterpret statistically significant as marginally or wholly insignificant differences among groups, because statistically significant differences may fail to achieve clinical significance. Although not conclusive, the following list includes three instances: (a) Psychological test patterns that differentiate groups at .05 or .01 levels rarely prove helpful in differentiating for diagnostic purposes. For example, alcoholics and drug abusers often differ from nonpsychiatric controls or unselected psychiatric patients by scoring higher on the Depression, Psychopathic Deviate, and Mania subscales of the MMPI; to draw similar diagnostic distinctions on the basis of symptoms of depression, mania, and psychopathic behavior alone, however, is rarely sufficient. (b) Statistically significant differences in the efficacy of one treatment approach over another, no matter what the level of difference in efficacy or how it was judged, are inadequate bases for selection of treatment unless or until cross-validation of the promising approach, with different therapists and different patient groups and in different settings, confirms the general utility of the technique. Electrical aversion, a promising behavioral technique that made excellent theoretical sense and showed exciting promise when first applied, has since proven itself to be of little value as a therapeutic technique on extensive cross-validation. Methadone maintenance may be in the midst of suffering the same ignominious fate. (c) Studies demonstrating the significant impact of a specific etiologic factor on a specific disorder do not, perforce, prove that every patient possessed of that factor will develop the resultant disorder or that every patient carrying that diagnostic label can point to that etiologic factor. In the case of alcoholism, for example, recent research by Goodwin and Guze (1974) strongly suggests the role of genetic factors in the etiology of alcoholism. Significantly more Danish children of alcoholic parents given up for adoption developed alcoholism than did children of nonalcoholic parents. But despite this significant difference in outcome, the contribution of the genetic factor was only partial: Some children of nonalcoholic natural parents became alcoholics as adults; most children of alcoholic parents successfully avoided alcoholism.

Do statistically significant differences among groups ever have significance clinically? In our experience, such differences have clinical significance only when all or most of one group shows one pattern and few or none of another does so; in such a rare event, however, it is doubtful that one would feel the need to point to statistical confirmation for such an obvious relationship. This issue, of course, is one of the touchstones of the applied behavior analysts, most of whom have chosen to dispense with statistics in favor of research designs permitting identification of the "active ingredients" of behavior change regimens capable of modifying a given target behavior every time it (or they) is applied.

DISCUSSION

Issues of generalization. Throughout this article, we have urged the reader to adopt a conservative, essentially modest, approach to his/her data and to claims or conclusions deriving therefrom. For the same reasons, we wish to suggest a spirit of modesty in the Discussion section of a research paper. Two essential features of this attitude are worth emphasizing. (a) Discussion of results might well begin with a section that details limits on generalization from the data reported. If only males over the age of 40 were studied and prior data suggest that the problem under investigation is not limited to that group, it is well to point out that conclusions from the research may refer only to older males, perhaps even older males from the geographic or sociocultural group studied (if those variables might also affect generalizability). (b) Even in the absence of specific methodological constraints on generalizability, it is wisest and most sound to limit the extent to which one lays claim for the widespread or universal relevance of one's findings. A host of variables specific to one's subject sample, procedure, or data analysis, unknown or undetected during the research, could later come back to haunt one. The classic example of such an embarrassment, of course, is the unfortunate team of biochemists who reported discovery of a "schizophrenic" blood portion, only to have to report some years later that their sample of schizophrenics had consumed so much coffee that the coffee's metabolic residuals had stamped their subjects' plasma as abnormal!

Bias in discussion. Beyond overblown claims of the merits of a new therapeutic approach or unwarranted generalizations beyond sample populations, the most common problem arising from discussion of alcoholism and drug dependence data comes when the author does not discuss data in terms of prior research *on both sides* of his/her position.

Although this approach to science sounds unthinkable, it is surprisingly easy to adopt a position, accept it fully, then view as well done and careful only work that supports that position. To this end, one of the most cherished, widely held views by alcoholism workers has long been that the only treatment goal for alcoholics can be abstinence. This position has continued to keep its supporters, of whom there are many, from more recent data suggesting that conventional, abstinence-oriented treatment for alcoholism is relatively ineffective (Pattison et al., 1977) and that some alcoholics do return to a controlled pattern of drinking either after treatment or in its absence (Pomerleau, Pertschuk, Adkins, & Brady, in press; Sobell & Sobell, 1976). Nonetheless, one reads startlingly ad hominum criticisms of researchers who have acknowledged the possibility that the new data on controlled drinking might justify a change in thinking. A similar lack of objectivity characterizes those who hold to the belief that alcoholism is a medical disease, wholly or largely, despite evidence to the effect that social-learning mechanisms, sociocultural influences, and psychological phenomena also play important etiologic roles in the disorder.

REFERENCE NOTE

1. HOMER, A. L., & ROSS, S. M. *The reliability and validity of interview data from drug and alcohol abusers.* Paper presented at the National Drug Abuse Conference, San Francisco, May 1977.

REFERENCES

AMERICAN MEDICAL ASSOCIATION, Committee on Alcoholism. Hospitalization of patients with alcoholism. *Journal of the American Medical Association,* 1956, *162,* 750.
ANDERSON, G. S., & NUTTER, R. W. Clients and outcomes of a methadone treatment program. *International Journal of the Addictions,* 1975, *10,* 937-948.
ARMOR, D. J., POLICH, J. M., & STAMBUL, H. B. *Alcolism and treatment.* Santa Monica, Calif.: The Rand Corporation, 1976.
BRIDDELL, D. W., & NATHAN, P. E. Behavior assessment and modification with alcoholics: Current status and future trends. In M. Hersen, R. M. Eisler, & P. M. Miller (Eds.), *Progress in behavior modification.* New York: Academic Press, 1976.
CAHALAN, D., & CISIN, I. H. American drinking practices: Summary of findings from a national probability sample: II. Measurement of massed versus spaced drinking. *Quarterly Journal of Studies on Alcohol,* 1968, *29,* 642-656.
CARLIN, A. S., & STAUSS, F. F. Descriptive and functional classifications of drug abusers. *Journal of Consulting and Clinical Psychology,* 1977, 45, 222-227.
CHAPMAN, L. J., & CHAPMAN, J. P. Selection of subjects in studies of schizophrenic cognition.

Journal of Abnormal Psychology, 1977, *86*, 10-15.

COX, T. J., & LONGWELL, B. Reliability of interview data concerning current heroin use from heroin addicts on methadone. *International Journal of the Addictions*, 1974, *9*, 161-165.

DITMAN, K. S. Review and evaluation of current drug therapies in alcoholism. *International Journal of Psychiatry*, 1967, *3*, 248-258.

DOLEYS, D. M., CIMINERO, A. R., WALLACH, E. S., & DAVIDSON, R. S. Responding by alcoholics during aversive conditioning. *Behavior Modification*, 1977, *1*, 205-220.

GOLDBERG, L. R. Simple models or simple processes? Some research on clinical judgments. *American Psychologist*, 1968, *23*, 483-496.

GOODWIN, D. W., & GUZE, S. B. Heredity and alcoholism. In B. Kissin & H. Begleiter (Eds.), *The biology of alcoholism* (Vol. 3). New York: Plenum Press, 1974.

GOTESTAM, K. G., MELIN, L., & ÖST, L-G. Behavioral techniques in the treatment of drug abuse: An evaluative review. *Addictive Behaviors*, 1976, *1*, 205-225.

HEDBERG, A. G., & CAMPBELL, L. A comparison of four behavioral treatments of alcoholism. *Journal of Behavior Therapy and Experimental Psychiatry*, 1974, *5*, 251-256.

KELLER, M. The oddities of alcoholics. *Quarterly Journal of Studies on Alcohol*, 1972, *33*, 1147-1148.

LEVINE, J., & ZIGLER, E. Humor responses of high and low premorbid competence alcoholic and nonalcoholic patients. *Addictive Behaviors*, 1976, *1*, 139-150.

MARLATT, G. A. The drinking profile: A questionnaire for the behavioral assessment of alcoholism. In E. J. Mash & L. G. Terdal (Eds.), *Behavior therapy assessment: Diagnosis and evaluation*. New York: Springer, 1975.

MARLATT, G. A., DEMMING, G., & REID, J. B. Loss of control drinking in alcoholics: An experimental analogue. *Journal of Abnormal Psychology*, 1973, *81*, 233-241.

MCCABE, O. L., KURLAND, A. A., & SULLIVAN, O. Paroled narcotic addicts in a verified abstinence program: Results of a five-year study. *International Journal of the Addictions*, 1975, *10*, 211-228.

MILLER, P. M. A behavioral intervention program for chronic drunkenness offenders. *Archives of General Psychiatry*, 1975, *32*, 915-918.

MILLER, P. M., *Behavorial treatment of alcoholism* New York: Pergamon Press, 1976.

MILLER, P. M. & EISLER, R. M. Alcohol and drug abuse. In W. E. Craighead, A. E. Kazdin, & M. J. Mahoney (Eds.), *Behavior modification principles, issues, and applications.* Boston: Houghton Mifflin, 1975.

MIRIN, S. M., MEYER, R. E., MCNAMEE, H. B., & MCDOUGLE, M. Psychopathology, craving, and mood during heroin acquisition: An experimental study. *International Journal of the Addictions*, 1976, *11*, 525-544.

NATHAN, P. E. *Cues, decisions, and diagnoses.* New York: Academic Press, 1967.

NATHAN, P. F., & BRIDDELL, D. W. Behavioral assessment and treatment of alcoholism. In B. Kissin & H. Begleiter (Eds.) *The biology of alcoholism* (Vol. 5). New York: Plenum Press, 1977.

NATHAN, P. E., & LANSKY, D. Management of the chronic alcoholic. In J. P. Brady & H. K. Brodie (Eds.), *Controversy in psychiatry.* Philadelphia, Penn.: Saunders, 1978.

O'LEARY, M. R., RADFORD, L. M., CHANEY, E. F., & SCHAU, E. J. Assessment of cognitive recovery in alcoholics by use of the Trail-Making Test. *Journal of Clinical Psychology*, 1977, *33*, 579-582.

PATTISON, E. M., SOBELL, M. B., & SOBELL, L. C. (Eds.). *Emerging concepts of alcohol dependence.* New York: Springer, 1977.

POMERLEAU, O. F., PERTSCHUK, M., ADKINS, D., & BRADY, J. P. A comparison of behavioral and traditional treatment for middle income problem drinkers. *Behavior Therapy*, in press.

RAWLINS, M., RANDALL, M., MEYER, R. E., MCNAMEE, H. B., & MIRIN, S. M. Aftercare on narcotic antagonists: Prospects and problems. *International Journal of the Addictions*, 1976, *11*, 501-512.

ROSENTHAL, R. *Experimenter effects in behavioral research.* New York: Appleton-Century-Crofts, 1966.

SCHAEFER, H. H., SOBELL, M. B., & MILLS, K. C. Baseline drinking behavior in alcoholics and social drinkers: Kinds of drinks and sip magnitude. *Behaviour Research and Therapy*, 1971, *9*, 23-27.

SELZER, M. L., VINOKUR, A., & WILSON, T. D. A psychosocial comparison of drunken drivers and alcoholics. *Journal of Studies on Alcohol*, 1977, *38*, 1294-1312.

SMITH, M. L., & GLASS, G. V. Meta-analysis of psychotherapy outcome studies. *American Psychologist*, 1977, *32*, 752-760.

SOBELL, L. C. A critique of alcoholism treatment evaluation. In G. A. Marlatt & P. E. Nathan (Eds.), *Behavioral assessment and treatment of alcoholism*. New Brunswick, N.J.: Rutgers University Center of Alcohol Studies, 1978.

SOBELL, M. B., & SOBELL, L. C. Alcoholics treated by individualized behavior therapy: One-year treatment outcome. *Behaviour Research and Therapy*, 1973, *11*, 599-618.

SOBELL, M. B., & SOBELL, L. C. Second-year treatment outcome of alcoholics treated by individualized behavior therapy. *Behaviour Research and Therapy*, 1976, *14*, 279-288.

VOGLER, R. E., COMPTON, J. V., & WEISSBACH, T. A. Integrated behavior change techniques for alcoholics. *Journal of Consulting and Clinical Psychology*, 1975, *43*, 233-243.

WILSON, G. T., LEAF, R., & NATHAN, P. E. The aversive control of excessive drinking by chronic alcoholics in the laboratory setting. *Journal of Applied Behavior Analysis*, 1975, *8*, 13-26.

28

RESEARCH DESIGN AND NARCOTIC ADDICTION PRONENESS

Paul Gendreau and L. P. Gendreau

According to previous arguments, supported in part by experimental data (1,2) narcotic addicts do not necessarily have unique personality traits which predispose them toward the specific effects of heroin. Basic to the argument is that earlier studies claiming to have found personality traits peculiar to narcotic addicts did not use control groups or in the cases where control groups were used the control procedures were inadequate. Where addicts and non-addicts were compared, the non-addict groups seemed to differ in that they, a) came from a different socioeconomic level, b) did not have a criminal record comparable to the addict group (in Canada, at least, 90 per cent of addicts are classed as criminal addicts, many of whom have lengthly criminal records) and, c) had different age and I.Q. distributions (2, 8)—two factors which should be controlled for when using criminal samples. There had also been no attempt to study non-addicts who had reasonable opportunity to obtain drugs but did not develop a heroin addiction. This latter control is useful, for these types of subjects must necessarily come from fairly similar socioeconomic levels and must have undergone living patterns somewhat akin to the addicts.

Reprinted with permission from the *Canadian Psychiatric Association Journal*, 1971, *16*, 265-267.

Modification of paper presented at the Canadian Psychiatric Association Meeting, Winnipeg, Man., June, 1970.

Paul Gendreau, Ph.D. is Asst. Prof., Trent University, Peterborough, Ont.

L. P. Gendreau, M.D. is Special Lecturer, School of Criminology, Univ. of Ottawa, Ottawa, Ont.

TABLE I
MEAN SCORES (NON-K CORRECTED) OF ADDICTS AND NON-ADDICTS ON THE MMPI

	MMPI Scales											
	L	F	K	Hs	D	Hy	Pd	Mf	Pa	Pt	Sc	Ma
Addicts	3.5	7.8	14.7	6.6	23.2	22.4	25.3	25.3	11.0	15.5	14.6	20.2
Non-addicts	3.9	8.0	14.2	6.6	22.6	21.2	24.9	24.1	11.0	15.6	15.3	20.0

When the above noted controls were adhered to in selecting a group of nonaddicts (2) personality differences between the addicts and non-addicts became negligible. Table I presents a comparison of fifty-one criminal addicts and eight-two criminal non-addicts on the Minnesota Multiphasic Personality Inventory (MMPI), a test previously used in reporting personality differences between the two groups. No significant differences were found when using two-tailed t-test comparisons. Even chance expectation would favour a significant effect being found on one of the twelve comparisons.

In one of three other papers not reviewed previously (2), relating to the addiction-prone theory (6), it was found that addicts answered some nineteen items differently than did non-addicts on the MMPI. It appears that these items were directly related to personality characteristics which are peculiar to addicts, but non-addicts were not compared as to I.Q., extent of criminal background and opportunity to obtain drugs. A second study implicated social anxiety as the factor predisposing a subject to take heroin (4). In this instance only three case histories were reported. Martin and Inglis (7) compared twenty-four female addicts and twenty-four female non-addicts. The composition of the non-addict group followed the criteria outlined by Gendreau and Gendreau (2, 3). The addicts studied by Martin and Inglis were not necessarily more anxious, introverted or neurotic than the non-addicted controls on the basis of test scores obtained on the Taylor Manifest Anxiety Scale, the Maudsley Personality Inventory and the Porteus Maze Q index.

The Martin and Inglis data and the results of the study reported (2) strictly mean that the tests employed failed to detect personality differences between addicts and non-addicts. However, if other psychometric instruments are to be used the control procedures outlined here should be observed. With the MMPI the differences purportedly found between addicts and non-addicts were not replicated when these control group criteria were applied.

There are other aspects concerning control procedures which had been overlooked to date. Given a hypothetical experiment in which the experimenter, employing an adequate control group, reported significant difference on personality scales between addicts and non-addicts, it would be impossible to determine whether such differences were causes of or due to the effects of heroin addiction. The hypothetical example, like existing studies supporting addiction-proneness, would be *ex post facto*. The confounding feature in such a design is the non-random assignment of subjects (9). The often unstated assumption of "addiction-prone" theorists is that presumed differences between addicts and non-addicts were not influenced by the drug. This assumption remains questionable, particularly since heroin has marked physiological effects and forces the addict to alter many aspects of his life. Matching also does not solve the issue (9, p. 78)—the only proper design (which for most practical purposes is too arduous) remains one in which subjects are randomly selected and then followed up and tested periodically over a lengthy time interval. Those subjects who eventually develop an addiction can be compared to those who do not. However, even in this hypothetical example it would be difficult to determine whether personality factors *per se* rather than pharmacological or sociological factors produced the heroin dependence.

While rejecting the idea of a causal connection between addiction and specific personality traits, it is recognized that psychological factors may be crucial in defining a given treatment for an addict. That is, clinical experience indicates that addicts display a wide variety of personality traits and in some cases severe psychopathology exists. This is important when choosing the optimal behaviour modification technique (1). Finally, an aspect of research concerning narcotic addicts which has so far been overlooked is that they may display individual differences in psychophysiological responsivity. Martin and Inglis (7) reported that pain thresholds for addicts were lower than those for non-addicts. Further work involving a signal detection analysis of the problem would shed light on whether addicts are more responsive or more sensitive to pain stimuli. An examination of the thresholds of addicts who are off heroin for varying time periods would also clarify to what extent the use of heroin itself is a determinant. This type of research is stressed because it may be linked closely with the sociological conditioning theory of addiction of Lindesmith (5). One intriguing possibility is that if addicts respond differentially to pain this fact may help to explain the very fast conditioning rates—the association between withdrawal stress and heroin intake seen in heroin addiction. The status of these assumptions should be examined by much needed empirical work.

REFERENCES

1. GENDREAU, P.: Addiction-proneness: Fact or myth? *New Scientist,* 1970, *45,* 616-617.
2. GENDREAU, P., and GENDREAU, L. P.: The 'addiction-prone' personality: A study of Canadian heroin addicts. *Canadian Journal of Behavioural Science,* 1970a, *2,* 18-25.
3. GENDREAU, P., and GENDREAU, L. P.: Narcotic addiction-proneness: A re-evaluation. Paper presented at the Canadian Psychiatric Association Meeting, Winnipeg, 1970b.
4. KRAFT, T.: Drug addiction and personality disorder. *British Journal of Addictions,* 1970, *64,* 403-408.
5. LINDESMITH, A.: *Addiction and Opiates.* Chicago: Aldine, 1968.
6. LOMBARDI, D., O'BRIEN, B., and ISELE, F.: Differential responses of addicts and non-addicts on the MMPI. *Journal of Projective Techniques and Personality Assessment,* 1968, *32,* 479-482.
7. MARTIN, J., and INGLIS, J.: Pain tolerance and narcotic addiction. *British Journal of Social and Clinical Psychology,* 1965, *4,* 224-229.
8. STANTON, J.: Group personality profile related to aspects of anti-social behaviour. *Journal of Criminal Law, Criminology and Police Science,* 1956, *47,* 340-347.
9. UNDERWOOD, B.: *Psychological Research.* Appleton-Century-Crofts, New York, 1957.

29

A TWELVE-YEAR FOLLOW-UP OF NEW YORK NARCOTIC ADDICTS: IV. SOME CHARACTERISTICS AND DETERMINANTS OF ABSTINENCE

George E. Vaillant

Thirty urban narcotic addicts who over a 12-year period achieved stable abstinences were compared with 30 chronic addicts. Abstinence was associated with certain changes in defensive style but did not result in emergence of new psychiatric symptomatology. It occurred most often in addicts with a prior history of regular employment and a stable early childhood. Compulsory community supervision, discovery of substitutes for narcotics, and gratifying nonfamily object relationships appeared to be important factors in producing abstinence.

One of the chief difficulties in the treatment of urban narcotic addiction is that so little is known about the determinants of abstinence.

Reprinted with permission from the *American Journal of Psychiatry*, 1966, 123, 573-585. Copyright 1966, the American Psychiatric Association.

Read at the 122nd annual meeting of the American Psychiatric Association, Atlantic City, N. J., May 9-13, 1966.

When this work was undertaken, Dr. Vaillant was Staff Psychiatrist, U. S. Public Health Service Hospital, Lexington, Ky.

This work was supported by Public Health Service grant H-65-1 from the Division of Hospitals.

The author wishes to thank John Merrifield, M.D., and Leston Havens, M.D., for their helpful criticisms and suggestions.

One reason for our ignorance is that the abstinent addict neither seeks medical nor attracts legal attention. In large part addiction has been conceptualized in terms of the chronically relapsing addict. As a result, it is difficult to know what really constitutes effective treatment for addicts, and it is impossible to appreciate the determinants or to predict the consequences of abstinence from narcotics.

To supplement our information on abstinent addicts, the writer, in a 12-year follow-up of 100 male heroin addicts from New York City, made a special effort to study those who did well. This paper is a description of the 30 addicts from that study who achieved and have maintained stable abstinences for at least three years. The findings shed light on the premorbid characteristics that distinguished these addicts from those who remained chronically addicted. The findings also suggest that abstinence depends more upon the addict's discovering gratifying alternatives than upon treatment per se.

Contrary to what might have been expected, abstinence did not elicit new psychopathology. The results lend no support to therapeutic nihilism or to the position that addicts *need* drugs for optimal adjustment.

The methods employed in the follow-up have been described in detail elsewhere (16). Briefly, 100 young, male, New York City (but otherwise unselected) addicts first admitted to Lexington between August 1, 1952, and January 31, 1953, were chosen for follow-up. In 1965 an attempt was made to interview all addicts who had done well and the relatives of all who had remained addicted. Second, all available institutional records on each addict were examined. These included city, state, and federal arrest records, and the records of the Federal Bureau of Narcotics. Excellent cooperation was obtained from the New York state and city departments of hygiene. Finally, extensive and prospectively gathered follow-up protocols were available on 95 percent of the patients for from three to six years after they left Lexington. These were generously made available to the writer by Leon Brill, who had directed the United States Public Health Service follow-up project responsible for their collection.

Extensive demographic data were available from the original Lexington charts and these data were coded and punched on cards before final outcome was known. When available evidence suggested the likelihood that the addict had achieved a stable abstinence, every effort was made to interview the ex-addict personally. If the addict was living out of New York City, the interview was conducted by telephone.

The interview usually lasted from 60 to 90 minutes. During this time an effort was made to determine the following: a) whom the addict lived with; b) the stability of his address; c) the important people in his life;

d) whether or not he had maintained cordial relations with his family of origin; e) his type of employment and approximate salary; f) his dependence on others; and g) medical and psychiatric problems, if any. Especial attention during the interview was paid to: reasons for abstinence; what, if anything, had filled the place that drugs once had occupied in the life of the addict; and the ways in which the addict now handled stress with special attention to psychological defenses.

For the purposes of discussion the 30 "best" outcomes were chosen from the total sample of 100 addicts. These will be referred to as *ex-addicts*. All shared the following characteristics: a) residence in the community for a minimum of three years without the use of narcotic drugs; b) the maintenance of such abstinence until the present time or until death; and c) no conviction for a narcotic or property offense for at least four years.

The group of 30 ex-addicts was compared to the 30 "worst" outcomes. These will be referred to as *chronic addicts* and all shared the following characteristics: a) they had spent less than 20 percent of the time since Lexington abstinent in the community; b) excluding time in prison, they had been actively addicted in the community for at least five years; and c) ten years after admission to Lexington they were still alive.

DEFINITION OF ABSTINENCE

Table 1 shows the kind of evidence that was obtained to support abstinence. Direct face-to-face interviews could be obtained with only 17 of the 30 ex-addicts. Four of the six cases interviewed by telephone were not living in New York City, the other two ex-addicts consented to discuss over the phone their previous addiction and their present adjustment, but they refused face-to-face interview. According to their relatives and to other evidence, both these men suffered from alcoholism. One ex-addict could be contacted only by mail.

In the seven instances where the addict was not contacted, two were dead, four refused interview, and one was out of the country. In six of these seven cases a relative was interviewed by this author. According to relatives, two of the ex-addicts who refused interview were engaged in, though not convicted of, illegal activities, one was a borderline paranoid psychotic who despite ten years of frequently confirmed abstinence had refused interview, and the mother of the last ex-addict would not reveal his address because his wife did not know of his prior addiction. During the period of alleged abstinence an average of three contacts by various agencies at different points in time confirmed abstinence for each ex-addict.

TABLE 1
Evidence of Abstinence for the 30 Ex-Addicts

METHOD OF DETERMINING ABSTINENCE	PERCENTAGE OF EX-ADDICTS FOR WHOM METHOD COULD BE USED
By some contact with ex-addict*	87
By personal interview with ex-addict	57
By interview of relative	70
By an agency confirming abstinence	93
By regular employment during alleged abstinence	70
By documented absence of convictions	70
By stable address for last two years	53
By at least four of the above	87

*Contact was obtained by telephone in six cases, by mail in one case, and by death certificate in two cases.

As can be seen from Table 1, in 87 percent of the cases corroboration of abstinence was obtained from at least four independent sources. The ex-addict for whom abstinence was least certain was a man known to be without arrest for six years and who, according to both his mother and his common-law wife, was not using narcotics. "An agency confirming abstinence" (Table I) refers to a report of abstinence by a social agency or a law enforcement officer who had had contact with the addict during the period of alleged abstinence. "Regular employment" indicates that according to social security records the ex-addict worked for at least 75 percent of the time abstinent. "Documented absence of convictions" indicated that an up-to-date New York State or FBI fingerprint record was obtained and supported the fact that the addict had not been arrested for the previous four years. For the two addicts who died, death certificates were obtained that supported their alleged abstinence.

RESULTS

Clearly, abstinence is a relative term. Severity of addiction prior to abstinence, length of abstinence, and circumstances of abstinence are important variables. Although prior to abstinence the average ex-addict in this study spent a total of 5.8 years addicted or in jail, five addicts had such "small" habits that they did not require narcotics during their period of withdrawal in 1952. One of these probably never had used opiates on even a daily basis.

All the addicts in our study were abstinent and in the community for at least three years. The average duration of abstinence was 7.7 years and of employment 6.0 years. Sixty percent were supporting wives and their children, if any. Only 20 percent were using their pharmacological substances to a degree that was clearly detrimental, and only four ex-addicts continued to engage in illegal activities. Worthy of emphasis is the fact that by 1964 only one of the 30 addicts remained under any external supervision or parole.

Out of the original 100 under study, besides the 30 ex-addicts there were 11 other addicts who achieved significant abstinence but who are not included because they did not exactly fit the particular criteria chosen. Four addicts achieved three years of abstinence in the community but then subsequently relapsed. Five other addicts probably fulfilled all the criteria to be classed as ex-addicts, but since their addiction status and address in the last two years was not definitely known, they were excluded. Finally, two others at time of death had been abstinent for less than two years.

Contrary to prevailing opinion, the ex-addicts in this study did not seem to "burn out" as they reached their mid-30s. Five addicts achieved permanent abstinence between 20 and 25, eleven between 26 and 30, nine between 31 and 35, five between 36 and 40. The average age of the 100 addicts on admission was 25. Thus, on the average two percent of the original sample became abstinent each year.

Table 2 shows the important differences in outcome between the 30 ex-addicts and the 30 chronic addicts. In general, after leaving Lexington the former were more likely to have achieved independence from home, to have created families, and to have held down jobs. It should be emphasized, however, that differences between the two groups became more apparent with the passage of time.

In terms of their criminal history after Lexington, as expected, the chronic addicts committed a greater number of crimes, but 77 percent of the ex-addicts had at least one conviction after Lexington. In both groups, for every six addicts convicted of drug-offenses, one addict was convicted of a crime against persons and four addicts were convicted for crimes against property. Thus, type of criminality did not distinguish the two groups.

Table 3 shows that on admission to Lexington the two groups were quite similar for many of the variables studied. At first glance there appears to be a preponderance of Negroes among the chronic addicts.

TABLE 2
Differences Between Ex-Addicts and Chronic Addicts After Lexington

FACTORS	30 EX-ADDICTS	30 CHRONIC ADDICTS
Abstinent for more than two years	100%	0%
Employed for half of adult life	63%	0%
Living with wife	57%	20%
Ever married	87%	60%
Living with female relatives after 30	40%	67%
Children	67%	37%
Received a year of compulsory supervision	47%	9%
Average number of drug hospitalizations	1.6	5.2
Average number of convictions	2.8	7.7
Time after Lexington in jail	1.3 years	2.7 years
Time after Lexington actually addicted	1.6 years	6.4 years
Time after Lexington known to be abstinent	7.7 years	0.8 years

TABLE 3
Similarities Between Ex-Addicts and Chronic Addicts

FACTORS	EX-ADDICTS n = 30	CHRONIC ADDICTS n = 30
	(IN PERCENT)	
Negro	47	57
White	53	43
Lexington admission voluntary	80	83
Heroin drug of choice	77	87
Home broken before 16	57	50
Reached 11th grade in school	50	50
Antisocial before drugs	53	53
Ever in mental hospital	7	13
Ever called schizoid or schizophrenic	27	17
Known family history of addiction	30	27
Known family history of criminality	30	33
Known family history of alcoholism	9	13

Prior to 1962, however, five white—but no Negro—addicts died as a direct result of addiction. These five were not included in the group of chronic addicts. In terms of broken homes, mental illness, and delinquency prior to addiction, the two groups were fairly similar. The two groups did not differ in the incidence of familial drug addiction, alcoholism, or crime. The nativity of the addicts did not differentiate the two groups. Virtually all the members from both groups first obtained narcotics through illegal channels.

As might be expected, a history of never having been physiologically addicted was prognostically favorable and having been physiologically addicted for over three years was unfavorable. However, in general there was little difference in the length of addiction before Lexington—2.0 years for the average ex-addict and 2.5 years for the average chronic addict. Of even more significance is the fact that severity of addiction, as measured by the amount of methadone required during the withdrawal period at Lexington, was the same for both groups. During the first day of withdrawal the average ex-addict received 16 mg. and the average chronic addict 17 mg. of methadone. Within limits, then, future chronicity of addiction was not significantly correlated with the quantity of narcotic injected in the past.

Although there were some suggestive differences in psychiatric diagnoses between the ex-addicts and chronic addicts, none of the differences observed approached statistical significance. Symptoms of overt anxiety or depression were recorded somewhat more frequently for the ex-addicts when first admitted to Lexington. In terms of diagnosis, slightly more of the ex-addicts were initially labeled passive dependent personalities, or neurotic, and more of the chronic addicts were called inadequate personalities, or sociopathic. Thus, ex-addicts appeared somewhat more "reactive." The fact that more significant differences in diagnosis did not emerge, despite profound difference in outcome, may be due to defects in our nomenclature for conceptualizing the character disorders.

Table 4 points out some of the relevant differences between the ex-addicts and chronic addicts that could be noted upon their admission to Lexington. The most important difference appeared to be the chronic addict's inability, prior to admission, to find or to keep gainful employment (civilian, academic, or military). Absence of stable work history, then, rather than presence of chronic addiction history, seemed best able to predict subsequent chronicity of addiction.

The prognosis for addicts who first became addicted after 25 seemed markedly better; but as a group the chronic addicts (average age 23.9) were only slightly younger on admission to Lexington than the ex-addicts

TABLE 4
Prognostically Significant Differences Between Ex-Addicts and Chronic Addicts and Their Relevance to Parole

FACTORS	EX-ADDICTS n = 30	CHRONIC ADDICTS n = 30	ADDICTS WITH PAROLE n = 26	ADDICTS WITHOUT PAROLE n = 74
		(IN PERCENT)		
Graduated from high school	33*	17	12	22
Some military service	70*	37	54	43
Four + years of employment prior to Lexington	53*	6	23	19
No opiates before 21	60*	37	46	38
Addicted less than three years before Lexington	77	53	73	57
No parental loss before six	77	60	77	70
No parent-child cultural disparity	40	23	42	36

*Indicates that the difference between the ex-addicts and the other 70 addicts in the study is significant at 0.05 level of confidence (chi-square).

(average age 26.2). Broken homes per se were not correlated with chronicity of addiction, but almost twice as many chronic addicts had homes broken before six. Chronic addicts were more apt to have parents from an alien culture. (By this is meant that New York-born addicts with at least one parent from a foreign country or, if Negro, with at least one Southern-born parent, were more apt to remain addicted.) The total number of addicts was too small to assess the relative importance of these factors to each other.

In Table 4 the items refer to relatively objective factors that can be determined when an addict is admitted for treatment. On admission in 1952, 73 percent of the chronic addicts had three or fewer of the seven factors in Table 4 present and 67 percent of the ex-addicts had four or more present. To validate these prognostic factors, it would be necessary to use a separate cohort of addicts and to follow them for at least ten years.

Table 5 indicates factors known to be associated with the sustained abstinences of the 30 ex-addicts and with 27 shorter abstinences—of at least a year—achieved by other addicts in the study. As reasons for abstinence, addicts themselves most often cited a substitute for narcotics, a new and meaningful relationship, or moving to areas with little drug use. Many addicts also explained their abstinence with statements like "something inside me just changed" or "I got tired of the life." However, such statements also occur with high frequency among most voluntary

TABLE 5
Factors Associated with Successful and Unsuccessful Abstinences

FACTORS	SUSTAINED ABSTINENCE OF EX-ADDICTS (n = 30)	SHORT ABSTINENCES OF OTHER ADDICTS (n = 27)
	(IN PERCENT)	
Nonparental compulsory supervision	47	63
Substitute for narcotics	60	19
New meaningful relationship	63	26
Left endemic drug-use area	30	37
Illness	3	8

admissions to Lexington, a majority of whom subsequently relapse, and therefore these statements have dubious validity.

Sutstitutes for narcotics were varied. In one ex-addict, the alleged drug substitute was his wife's cooking accompanied by a marked increase in weight. Also cited as substitutes for drugs were: marihuana in one case, chlordiazepoxide (100 mg. per day) in another case, and a fundamentalist religious sect in a third. Several abstinent addicts did become very conscious of food, and several joined evangelical or mystical religious sects. One worked hard for Alcoholics Anonymous. Others became very concerned with possessions.

In 14 cases the principal direct substitute was alcohol. In some ex-addicts alcohol was used to excess only during the first year of abstinence; four addicts engaged in sustained but not incapacitating heavy drinking; and in six cases use of alcohol led to impaired health or diminished occupational efficiency.

Employment and new meaningful nonparental relationships represented more constructive alternatives to addiction. Although long-term follow-up (17) suggests that addicts—even when not addicted—have extraordinarily poor work records, at last follow-up 70 percent of the ex-addicts were regularly employed and 37 percent were making more than $100 a week. Four were irregularly employed; three were unemployed or supporting themselves by activities like bookmaking and policy; and two were on welfare.

In general, when addicts cited another person as the reason for their abstinence, wives, girl friends, or children were most often named. Often such significant people were dependent on the addict rather than vice versa. Often, the new wife was an abstinent addict or an alcoholic herself. Other addicts cited an employer who trusted and respected them. However, addicts uniformly agreed that abstinence was usually achieved for themselves and never for parents. Ex-addicts often found friends who also became abstinent while the chronic addicts claimed that no addict they knew had ever been cured. Whatever the reality, addicts flatly denied that their parents had helped them in any way to achieve abstinence.

Our findings are similar to O'Donnell's findings among white Southern addicts (12) in that addicts did not attribute their abstinence to help from parents, social workers, or physicians. In contrast to O'Donnell's findings, no abstinent addict in this study gave up drugs because they were simply no longer available. Seventy percent continued to live in areas of high drug use and only a small fraction gave up drugs because of being too ill to "hustle" for them.

Compulsory supervision (usually probation or parole) seemed to be very important in producing abstinence. Addicts rarely gave such supervision as a reason for abstinence; but elsewhere the high correlation between compulsory supervision and abstinence has been documented (16). As shown in Table 2, although the 30 ex-addicts received an average of only 2.8 convictions, 47 percent received at least a year of compulsory supervision. On the other hand, the 30 chronic addicts received an average of 7.7 convictions; but only nine percent ever received a year of compulsory supervision. The fact that the ex-addicts received far more compulsory supervision than the chronic addicts appeared to be predominantly due to the fact that receiving parole caused the addict to become abstinent. The explanation was not that only addicts with good prognosis got parole. Table 4 shows that the addicts who received a year or more of parole did not appear to show significantly more favorable prognostic factors than the addicts who never received such parole.

It is worth noting that, on the one hand, compulsory supervision seemed more important among addicts who did not sustain their abstinence than among those who did. On the other hand, the "formation of a new and meaningful relationship" (see Table 5) was cited more frequently by addicts who did sustain their abstinence. In other words, addicts capable of finding on their own an alternative source of gratification to addiction (e.g., marriage or jobs) seemed less dependent upon external control for their abstinence. Admittedly, addicts with transient abstinences were less well studied.

With the exception of the fairly high incidence of alcoholism (mild to severe), the ex-addicts were in good health. Only two, one of whom was a severe alcoholic, had psychopathology to the degree that it interfered with employment or maintenance of interpersonal relationships. None of the 100 addicts in the study experienced psychotic or near-psychotic breaks in response to abstinence in the community. Only one ex-addict used tranquilizers regularly. Only one had required psychiatric care at any time while abstinent. None were psychiatrically more symptomatic off drugs than they had been while on drugs. Psychosomatic illness was uncommon: one patient had high blood pressure, one suffered from gastritis, and one from dermatitis. In other words, when the symptom of addiction was given up, it was not usually replaced by another symptom.

RESULTS OF INTERVIEWS

It is difficult to reduce the quality of impressions gained from psychiatric interviews to a statistical format. For this reason the following data are more impressionistic than the preceding results. It was an exciting experience to talk with the ex-addicts. As a group, despite great social deprivation and initial psychological vulnerability, the ex-addicts had achieved relative psychiatric and social health. Although often living in areas of New York with the highest prevalence of addiction, their apartments, their way of life, and their relatively stable families offered sharp contrast to the lurid and hopeless newspaper headlines about New York City's addicts.

Few of the ex-addicts interviewed appeared mentally ill in the conventional use of the term. Most were getting on well with themselves and with their associates, and were without somatic equivalents. Nevertheless, they were uniformly immature. Men of 40 retained an adolescent willingness to see all viewpoints and manifested a childlike delight at being important enough to be interviewed by a stranger even though such an interview meant reliving past memories. Few addicts terminated the interview willingly; many wished to see me again.

Few of the addicts seemed to know who they were or where they were going. Although they had achieved a certain mastery over their need to escape from life, they retained a lack of faith in their ability to master life itself. "I still feel something is missing inside:" "I never am sure that I will not go back:" "How does one stop drinking?" were representative complaints. Nevertheless, most ex-addicts related well and warmly. They gave as well as asked. Their manner was both charming and dependent. Although somewhat narcissistic, their ability to interact with others went deeper than the facile mechanical role-playing of the psychopath or the constricted, if more honest, interaction of the schizoid character.

During the course of therapy psychiatrists often note that a patient will give up acting out only to become depressed or to develop psychosomatic symptoms. Thus, a common but poorly documented hypothesis exists that as sociopaths mature, they develop depressions and a high incidence of psychosomatic illnesses. These ex-addicts were neither overtly depressed nor did they somatize their problems. This discrepancy seems worth emphasizing. Perhaps the differences between ex-addicts and the patient acting out in therapy can be understood by the fact that the adaptations seen in these addicts were long-term rather than short-term psychological adjustments. Thus, when a long-term change in defensive style is made, it may be less apt to produce substitute symptoms.

Over the previous decade few of the addicts admitted to having sought medical or psychiatric attention of any kind. None related to the interviewer as a doctor who would pay attention to their physical complaints. Only one, who had a bona fide illness predating his addiction, could be called hypochondriacal.

The defensive style of the ex-addicts during the interview resembled that of some Christian Scientists; often the ex-addicts appeared to have handled traumatic events by isolation, by hypomanic suppression and denial, and by a deliberate searching for the silver lining.

As in adolescence, the use of altruism as a defense was frequent. Although the frequent efforts of the ex-addicts to help others were sincere, they were rarely sustained and often demonstrated both the wish to be cared for and a continuing difficulty in accepting and channeling overt aggression. Several ex-addicts reported that they experienced sudden, poorly controlled outbursts of anger. Yet at the same time many ex-addicts showed themselves more able to tolerate and to use aggression constructively than in the past. Another addict observed that the impulse to relapse was associated with outbursts of anger toward his brother, so together they would go off to a sporting event and the temptation to return to drugs would pass.

Like the Canadian abstinent addicts described by Haslam (8), many of the ex-addicts employed reaction formation. One addict, who gave up drugs on his own initiative, attributed his abstinence to his profound disgust at being able to obtain narcotics legally in England.

Increased expressions of creativity were also evident. One ex-Harlem street gang member experimented with interior decorating; another slum-raised ex-addict found that his daily visits to the suburban site where his house was being erected galvanized his interest in the same way that drug seeking had in the past. As already noted, many ex-addicts achieved stable heterosexual relationships.

Several addicts were frankly puzzled why they had become abstinent. None really understood it. None were aware of the association of parole with abstinence. Few could conceptualize the fact that they had found different ways of solving emotional difficulties. The almost magical way they described their cure was reminiscent of the way adolescents look at achieving sudden athletic prowess or popularity with the opposite sex.

The results of every scientific investigation are distorted by the methods used to investigate them. Thus, despite efforts to remain a neutral observer, the interviewer may at times have appeared to the ex-addicts as a stranger, a USPHS officer, an "investigator," and quite probably an aggressor.

DISCUSSION

Although many follow-up studies of addicts exist, long-term follow-ups are uncommon. The most important finding of the present study was that 12 years after first Lexington admission, between 30-40 percent of urban addicts achieved the type of stable abstinence described. Table 6 summarizes the literature on long-term follow-up of addicts. All the studies but the one by Duvall and associates (3) describe addicts whose initial source of narcotics had been from doctors. In terms of eventual abstinance, Table 6 suggests that delinquent urban addicts do not differ dramatically from other more socially privileged groups. However, in a five-year follow-up of doctor addicts who also received strict compulsory supervision, Jones observed a 92 percent rate of abstinence (10). In the present study the urban addicts who received compulsory supervision also fared better than the average. Thus, there is hope that with improved methods of treatment the abstinence figures in Table 6 can be raised.

It is unlikely that the ex-addicts were different at 20 from the young delinquent addicts of today. It is well to remember that more than half the ex-addicts in this study began the use of illegal drugs in their teens. They were charter members of that group of delinquent urban addicts who in the early postwar period caused nationwide alarm over the growing wave of adolescent addiction.

Once the addict gave up drugs, he experienced relatively little difficulty in being accepted by his community. Jobs were found without undue difficulty and the abstinent addict was not molested by the police. The 100 addicts in this study received over 300 convictions; yet in retrospect only two of these were known to be "bum raps." Some addicts said that one of the first benefits of abstinence was that suddenly the

TABLE 6
Summary of Long-Term Follow-ups of Narcotic Addicts

INVESTIGATOR	n (STILL LIVING AT TIME OF FOLLOW-UP)	PERCENT ABSTINENT IN THE COMMUNITY	
		AN AVERAGE OF FIVE YEARS AFTER ADMISSION	AN AVERAGE OF TEN YEARS AFTER ADMISSION
Duvall and associates (3)	353*	25	
O'Donnell (11)	162	44 (14)**	
O'Donnell (11)	116		52 (24)**
Retterstöl and Sund (13)	30	23	
Schwarz (14)	89		40
Vaillant (16)	94	22	
Vaillant (16)	89		37

*Contact had been lost with 12 percent of 401 addicts still alive five years after hospitalization and these unknown outcomes were not included by Duvall and associates in their calculation of abstinence.

**Numbers in parenthesis refer to the percentage who not only were abstinent from narcotics but who also were not misusing barbiturates or alcohol.

police treated them with respect. This is important in view of the fact that some observers regard addicts as made and maintained by the community's need for scapegoats.

I suspect that our picture of the addict, like our picture of the alcoholic, is largely a creation of the addict himself. This is not to say that the early insults in the addict's life were of his own making, or that the community does not often condemn in the addict what it unconsciously loathes in itself, or that there are not contagious factors to addiction. Rather, I am suggesting that once addicted, the addict uses his addiction in a highly personal and often intrapunitive manner that has relatively little relationship to his need for opiates per se.

Unlike the abstinent alcoholic who, when abstinent, may show severe psychopathology (4), the ex-addicts as a group tolerated abstinence well. When questioned directly, ex-addicts did not believe legalization of drugs would have been helpful to them. They were glad to be abstinent. Several addicts said that the achievement of abstinence produced a real euphoria. One addict said that "being clean was like being reborn."

In general, ego strength, or the ability to live effectively, productively, and happily over a period of time, is powerfully correlated with the ability to have lived successfully over a past period of time. The natural history of mental illness appears largely unrelated to the severity of psychiatric symptoms at any fixed point.

Thus, it is not surprising that a good premorbid adjustment (late onset of delinquency, high school graduation, regular employment, and late onset of addiction) was a better predictor of abstinence than the fact that the addict had a "small" habit or obtained his drugs quasilegally. A reactive or an acute onset of addiction in response to a real stress or conscious depression also appeared to bode well, but such data were not systematically gathered. Davies and associates found that acute onset, good previous work history, and an affective diagnosis were related to remission in alcoholism (2). Retterstöl and Sund noted that acute and reactive onset, overt depressive affect, and good premorbid adjustment predicted remission from addiction to barbiturates as well as to morphine (13).

These same factors also predict remission in schizophrenia (15) and in psychotic depression (1) far more effectively than the severity of manifest clinical symptoms. The absence of such favorable factors should not discourage the energetic treatment of addicts who lack them; but the fact that addicts with a favorable prognosis recovered with little treatment may help to focus attention on elements important in the rehabilitation of addicts.

When the ex-addicts were compared to the Gluecks' reformed criminals (5, 6), there was again a good deal of similarity. For the Gluecks, poor prior work history was the most powerful predictor of chronic recidivism. They found that early onset of delinquency, failure to marry, and failure to complete high school were also correlated with poor outcome. Like the present study they found that homes broken before 16, type of criminality, social status, and birth rank were not important predictors. Nevertheless, in a more recent work comparing delinquents with normals, they document that disruption of the home before six is a worse prognostic factor than broken homes per se (7). However, the Gluecks found that the persistent delinquent tended to permanently separate from home too early (6). This is in sharp contrast to the chronic addicts in the present study who appeared to experience great difficulty in ever separating themselves from their parents (see Table 2).

Relapse to drugs seemed to result more from a poverty of familiar alternatives than because drugs powerfully answered the addict's needs. For instance, receiving a sentence sufficiently severe to result in a year or more of parole was certainly a favorable prognostic factor. Probably this is because abstinence can be best induced by giving the addict something that he did not have before, rather than by depriving him of what little he already has.

Hospitalization and prison often fail because they simply take away drugs, while parole or other compulsory community supervision may succeed because they give the addict the control and support that he needs to remain at work. The dependent wife or child or the trusting employer gives to the addict an admittedly symbiotic relationship but one in which he will not feel either guilty or used. In a long-term follow-up of habitual prisoners, West noted that here too the most common correlate of crime-free periods was stable, if "dependent or semi-parasitic," human relationships (18). The fact that the addict had worked in the past also offered him an alternative to drugs in the future. Finally, alcohol provided the ex-addict with a socially approved addiction.

The tendency of the ex-addicts but not the chronic addicts to use alcohol deserves special comment. The Gluecks noticed that as adult or adolescent criminal offenders matured past 30, an increasing number of them turned to alcohol (5,6). O'Donnell, in his long-term follow-up of Kentucky addicts, noted an increased misuse of alcohol (12). Many of the present ex-addicts admitted using alcohol compulsively at times of conscious stress, and at least a third used alcohol more than they wished. This is in contrast to the fact that many young active addicts will say that the use of alcohol makes them feel dangerously passive and vulnerable or that they find the use of alcohol actually dysphoric. A relevant and probably related fact is that opiates blunt both aggressive and sexual impulses while alcohol often facilitates impulsive behavior. Certainly, the interrelationships between use of alcohol, abstinence from narcotics, delinquency, and maturity are complex and deserve further study.

For heuristic purposes it is helpful to compare the abstinent addict to the maturing adolescent. In this way some of the complicated adjustments that lead to abstinence may be put into perspective. One task in maturation for both addict and adolescent is to achieve independence from the familial matrix to which each finds himself bound, and towards which each finds himself ambivalently angry and intolerant. In order to achieve independence each must find substitute objects to love and each must find appropriate channels for aggressive and sexual instincts that up to this point have been either focused toward family of origin, biologically latent or, in the case of the addict, narcotized. Finally, in achieving independence both addict and adolescent must be able to find and to sustain independent responsibility. For most this means steady employment. Thus, I am suggesting that addicts improve when they master their instincts, not when their instincts "burn out."

Like the addict, the early adolescent handles his conflicts by hostile withdrawal, by petty social rebellion, and by solitary instinctual self-gratification. Depressive affect is rarely permitted into consciousness and is often dealt with by manic or physical overactivity. In follow-up studies of normal adolescents, Hathaway and Monachesi have demonstrated that, compared to adults, adolescents score higher on the psychopathic deviancy scale of the MMPI (9).

Similar to the maturing adolescent, the ex-addicts seemed to give up their war against society at the same time that they permitted themselves extrafamilial intimacy with others. Although both often cloak it under altruism, the abstinent addict and the adolescent finally learn to accept their aggression. The maturing adolescent through identification and probably through internalized parental supervision achieves independent work patterns. The ex-addict, perhaps because he had lacked the proper parental objects to identify with or to incorporate, often learned work habits only under external supervision.

When the abstinent addict is looked at in this light, answers—albeit speculative ones—are provided to certain of the paradoxes in the paper. First, it is usual for severe chronic psychiatric illness to become worse with time, not better; and second, defensive styles in adults often remain relatively stable over time. However, if addiction is conceptualized as a form of immaturity, then it is not surprising to find that: a) the disorder, like adolescence, gets better with time; b) when symptoms are removed, they need not be replaced with others; and c) ex-addicts can manifest new defenses. If the addict's chief defect is related to immaturity, it is not surprising that stable early object relations and previous ability to achieve independence (e.g. employment) should be more important to prognosis than drug use per se.

Finally, the goals of treatment must be to assist the addict to pass into late adolescence, as it were. He must be helped to find the best possible dependency object, to sustain employment via external support, and to discover a more mature way to deal with his instinctual needs than solitary gratification. His childlike behavior must not be arbitrarily condemned, but neither should it be regarded as the best of which he is capable. Perhaps the best way for society to regard addiction is the same way that it regards the truancy that addiction rather resembles. The management of truancy is compulsory yet supportive supervision, not arbitrary punishment or "broadminded" toleration. In order to show that comparison between addicts and adolescents is more than facile analogy, however, it will be necessary, ten years from now, to show that the ex-addicts finally have become "adults."

SUMMARY

In a 12-year follow-up of 100 New York City addicts admitted to the Lexington USPHS Hospital, an attempt was made to study intensively the 30 best outcomes. These men had achieved and maintained until the present time stable abstinences of at least three years' duration.

Correlated with eventual abstinence were the prior ability to hold down a job, an intact home until age six, and a late onset of addiction. Unrelated to outcome were family pathology, amount of drug used, and previous criminal behavior. Compulsory supervision, a substitute addiction, and the establishment of a stable nonparental relationship appeared to facilitate abstinence. Understanding parents, unavailability of drugs, voluntary hospitalization, and psychiatric intervention seemed less important. No evidence was found that addicts, as a group, when they become abstinent develop other incapacitating mental illnesses. The importance of the predominant psychological defenses employed in abstinence was shown. The addict's journey from addiction to abstinence was compared to the vicissitudes of adolescence.

REFERENCES

1. ASTRUP, C., FOSSUM, A., and HOLMBOE, R.: A Follow-Up Study of 270 Patients with Acute Affective Psychoses. Oslo: Oslo University Press, 1959.
2. DAVIES, D. L., SHEPHERD, M., and MYERS, E.: The Two Years' Prognosis of 50 Alcohol Addicts After Treatment in Hospital, Quart. J. Stud. Alcohol 17:485-502, 1956.
3. DUVALL, H. J., LOCKE, B. Z., and BRILL, L.: Follow-Up Study of Narcotic Drug Addicts Five Years After Hospitalization, Public Health Rep. 78:185-193, 1963.
4. GERARD, D. L., SAENGER, C., and WILE, R.: The Abstinent Alcoholic, Arch. Gen. Psychiat. 6:83-95, 1962.
5. GLUECK, S., and GLUECK, E.: Juvenile Delinquents Grown Up. New York: Commonwealth Fund, 1940.
6. GLUECK, S., and GLUECK, E.: Criminal Careers in Retrospect. New York: Commonwealth Fund, 1943.
7. GLUECK, S., and GLUECK, E.: Unraveling Juvenile Delinquency. New York: Commonwealth Fund, 1950.
8. HASLAM, P.: The Maturation Process in Addiction, Canad. J. Correction 6:28-30, 1964.
9. HATHAWAY, S. R., and MONACHESI, E. D.: Adolescent Personality and Behavior. Minneapolis: University of Minnesota Press, 1963.
10. JONES, L. E.: How 92% Beat the Dope Habit, Bull. Los Angeles County Medical Association 88:19, 37-40, 1958.
11. O'DONNELL, J. A.: personal communication.
12. O'DONNELL, J. A.: A Follow-Up of Narcotic Addicts: Mortality, Relapse and Abstinence, Amer. J. Orthopsychiat. 34:948-954, 1964.
13. RETTERSTÖL, N., and SUND, A.: Drug Addiction and Habituation. Oslo: Universitetsforlaget, 1964.
14. SCHWARZ, H.: Weitere Untersuchungen zur Prognose des Morphinismus, Monatschr. f. Psychiat. u. Neurol. 84:257-280, 1932.
15. VAILLANT, G. E.: Prospective Prediction of Schizophrenic Remission, Arch. Gen. Psychiat. 11:509-518, 1964.
16. VAILLANT, G. E.: A 12-Year Follow-Up of New York Narcotic Addicts: I. The Relation of Treatment to Outcome, Amer. J. Psychiat. 122:727-737, 1966.
17. VAILLANT, G. E.: A 12-Year Follow-Up of New York Narcotic Addicts: II. The Natural History of a Chronic Disease, New Eng. J. Med.,275: 1282-1288, 1966.
18. WEST, D. J.: The Habitual Prisoner. London: Macmillan, 1963.

EPILOGUE: REFLECTIONS AND PERSPECTIVES ON THE HISTORY AND FUTURE OF THE ADDICTIONS

Howard Shaffer and Milton Earl Burglass

"Would you tell me, please, which way I ought to go from here?"
"That depends a good deal on where you want to get to," said the Cat.
"I don't much care where—", said Alice.
"Then it doesn't matter which way you go," said the Cat.

(Alice In Wonderland, by Lewis Carroll).

Reflecting on the history of a discipline is a difficult and ambitious task—a task limited by one's place in history and the operative paradigm(s) of the day. Nevertheless, much can be learned by surveying a field and assessing its roots. The addictions are rooted in a multitude of disciplines: history, sociology, psychology, medicine, physiology, pharmacology, philosophy, politics, witchcraft and religion, to name only a few. As a result of this complexity, the following discussion is *not* an attempt to examine comprehensively everything that has come before, but rather to highlight and distill central themes that we believe will have a major impact on future conceptualizations, considerations and treatments of addictive behavior.

THE JOURNEY

The history of addictive behavior is nested within a lexicon of confusing connotative meanings. References to "dope fiends," "junkies," "addicts," "speed freaks," etc. are commonplace. What is the full meaning and implication of these labels? Is getting "high" the equivalent of being "intoxicated"? Is being high the opposite of being "low"; non-intoxicated (pure) the opposite of intoxicated? These labels have important implicit meaning beyond simple semantics; these concepts reflect a society, cul-

481

ture, and/or historical time that made important distinctions between licit and illicit substances. Moreover, these labels euphemistically identify "enemies" of societies' mainstream: the dependent, morally corrupt, and socially impoverished. Since Zinberg (1974), Szasz (1974), and Apsler (1978) have examined these issues in detail, the following discussion will focus on the myriad of explanations offered to account for addictive behavior.

The perspectives offered to explain the addictions have evolved through a meandering and, perhaps, circuitous course. Early explanations viewed addicts as morally depraved. As it became clear that a great variety of people were represented among addicts, it became necessary to offer an explanation for their behavior that placed lesser responsibility on the deviant ethics and morals of the user and greater culpability on the individual's inherent weaknesses. This gave nourishment to the psychoanalytic perspectives that were concerned with the ego regressive and eventually ego adaptive mechanisms associated with pharmacologically altered states of consciousness. These views still exist and flourish today. Views that placed responsibility on the individual's environment were also founded during this period, e.g., sociologic theories. Only the more psychosocially interactive models still remain (e.g., Zinberg, Harding, & Winkeller, 1977; Becker, 1967). The popularity of behavioral psychology and the dissatisfaction with imprecise analytic formulations of addiction provided the context for the emergence of behavioral theories of drug abuse during the 1960s. These approaches practically eliminated "personal responsibility" from drug use; contemporary physiologic (e.g., Dole & Nyswander, 1967; Goldstein, 1976) and political oppression (Szasz, 1974) models may be perceived as the major impetus for the total elimination of personal responsibility for addictive behavior.

SUBSTANCES OF ABUSE

As perspectives evolved and reduced the importance of personal responsibility in addiction, the substances that one could abuse multiplied. Now, for example, one can become addicted to hard and soft drugs, caffeine, nicotine, social relationships, "junk food," and work (e.g., workaholic). Wherever one chooses to look addictive behavior can be identified—the "cures" are often nearby as well (e.g., smoke-enders, health spas, diet workshops, drug clinics, etc.). It almost seems that as society has attempted to control the behavior of its constituents it has become a controlled society. Perhaps, our society is in its "anal phase" of development with all the implicit struggles concerning self and other control. This hypothesis may not be so farfetched if one considers the emergence and more recent understanding of the social sanctions, mores, folkways, and rituals associated with the use of consciousness-altering substances. The interested reader should consult Becker (1967) and Zinberg et al. (1977) for excellent examinations of these issues.

PARADIGMS AND ADDICTION

Individuals working to explain addictive behavior and those attempting to treat these problems have not shared a unitary set of rules and standards. For example, theorists and practitioners still debate the necessity, efficacy, rationality, and even the morality of treating addictive behavior by substituting alternative drugs and/or promoting required abstinence instead of treating the "underlying" disorder. Similar controversy surrounds the issue of whether or not excessive drug use even requires treatment! These differences of perspective and variety of standard have resulted in an even more confusing state of treatment. To illustrate, the treatment for narcotic addiction may entail the use of methadone as an opiate substitute, naltrexone as an antagonist, or a treatment plan utilizing both drugs sequentially. Conversely drug-free therapies may include the therapeutic community or a variety of outpatient treatments.

Reflecting the variety of "schools" from which these are derived, the competing theoretical orientations offered to explain addictive behavior often suggest mechanisms that are inherent in the discipline and background of the theorists who authored them. Thus, physicians Dole and Nyswander (1967) offered a theory of opiate addiction based on metabolic deficiency; sociologists Lindesmith (1938) and Becker (1967) contributed major sociological perspectives concerned primarily with social/cultural environmental influences. Similar discipline identifications were present in the work of psychoanalysts (Federn, 1972; Khantzian, 1974, 1975, 1978; Rado, 1933; and Zinberg, 1974, 1975), and behaviorists (Gilbert, 1976; O'Brien, 1975).

These theoretical explanations (as well as those not specifically mentioned) have *not* been "accepted examples of actual practice . . . models from which spring particular coherent traditions of scientific research" (Kuhn, 1970, p. 10). These models have *not* precipitated a paradigm for the addictions, that is, an accepted and shared framework within which practitioners and researchers work. Consequently, without an operative paradigm, work in the addictions is *not* governed by the same scientific rules and standards. This state of disagreement leads to the inevitable conclusion that the addictions are in a pre-paradigm period. This pre-paradigm state of development "is regularly marked by frequent and

deep debates over legitimate methods, problems, and standards of solution, though these serve rather to define schools rather than to produce
agreement" (Kuhn, 1970, pp. 47-48). Although Kuhn's statement above
was not originally directed toward the addictions, he precisely describes
the present position of the field of drug treatment and theory.

Without a paradigm the important parameters of addiction are difficult to identify; even more difficult is the process of scientific agreement
and validation since the evidence intended to support the constructs of
abuse, addiction, and dependence is clouded in controversy and philosophical argument. Kuhn noted, "In the absence of a paradigm all of
the facts that could possibly pertain to the development of a given science
are likely to seem equally relevant" (1970, p. 15). The relevance of addiction theory for practice is similarly confusing since theories of addiction
are not primarily concerned (if at all) with the translation of theory to
practice; theories concerned with the etiology of addiction are not equivalent to theories of abstinence. An examination of "practice" theories
(Shaffer & Gambino, 1979) in the addictions further suggests that practitioners are being guided presently by "implicit," unarticulated paradigms. For example, some practitioners believe that rehabilitation cannot
proceed while one is chemically dependent. This implicit paradigm precludes methadone maintenance as a transitional treatment leading to
more constructive and developmentally viable coping mechanisms (e.g.,
internal, psychological skills). Other practitioners are more concerned
with responsible drug use and the decisions inherent in using or not
using drugs. Is using drugs "less" inherently better than using drugs
"responsibly?" Does the use of drugs automatically create problems for
the user or does *how* one uses drugs determine whether or not the drug
use will be or become problematic— Many models of addiction implicitly
consider drug use pathological. Other theories view drug use neutrally,
while still others view it as a welcome opportunity to explore alternate
states of consciousness (Weil, 1972).

Since the Kuhnian framework for paradigmatic analysis was originally
formulated for the natural sciences, it should only be utilized to examine
the addictions if we accept the assumption that addictive behavior is
subject to scientific or quasi-scientific principles. Street addicts do not
behave on the basis of the scientific method, however; nor do they concern themselves with the formal aspects of causal analyses. Addicts behaviorally provide practical definitions of addiction. Further, these
pragmatic definitions of addiction are not developed under the rigorous
scrutiny of scientific experimentation. The scientific perspective was invoked originally to explain addictive behavior when more simple alter-

natives failed to provide an effective method for producing abstinence. In an effort to provide "treatment" for an "unnatural" state, healers resorted to scientific orientations to facilitate their interventions and promote abstinence or culturally prescribed drug use. If addiction is conceptualized within an alternative framework, theology, for example, the notion of science and its paradigms might not be necessary or relevant to treatment efforts. The self-help movement nicely illustrates an effective (Quinones, Doyle, Sheffet, & Louria, 1979) and popular nonscience approach to drug treatment. Instead of requiring adherence to the scientific method, these self-help approaches created (and perhaps coerced) reference groups, social orders, surrogate families and different patterns of behavior from followers. We can conclude that if we adopt a paradigmatic framework (a scientific analysis), then theories of addiction are in a pre-paradigmatic level of development, or, alternatively, addictive behavior may not be subject to traditional scientific methods and, therefore, new alternative models of addiction are required to more fully explain this pattern of behavior. For the purposes of the present discussion, we shall accept the former assumption.

Shaffer and his associates (Gambino & Shaffer, 1979; Khantzian & Shaffer, in press; Shaffer, 1977; Shaffer & Gambino, 1979) have attempted to distill underlying themes from the assortment of available theoretical positions. They have suggested five key principles to consider while attempting to explain addictive behavior and/or evaluate theoretical positions: First, it is important to come to terms with the *individual differences* among drug users if explanations of addiction are to be relevant and practical. Second, drug users are self-determining agents; an adequate model of addiction should include an examination of *drug-use motivation.* Third, an analysis of the *settings and contexts* within which drugs are used is fundamental to a complete understanding of addiction. Particular interest should be paid to the dynamics of social and cultural rituals and ceremonies that implicitly and explicitly control drug use. Fourth, an adequate explanation of addiction must allow for *unconsciously motivated behavior.* Fifth, and finally, *drugs alter the perceived experience of the user;* thus, after drug use, a user's experience is altered. This change in experience (both the expected and unexpected) notes the importance of the cybernetic aspects of drug use. Taken together these guidelines provide a point of reference for the evaluation of past and future models of addiction.

In the next section, we will consider an illustrative model of addiction that integrates the points above and much of the inconsistent data that are associated with the pre-paradigm period of addiction theory.

ADDICTION AS A NATURAL PROCESS: PERSPECTIVES ON A SPECIAL CASE OF ADAPTATION

As we have discussed, addictive behavior has been viewed from a variety of perspectives. Addicts have been portrayed as weak-willed, morally corrupt, sociopathic, psychopathic, socially impoverished, developmental failures, developmentally regressed, organically impaired, subjects of conditioning, victims of political oppression, and psychosocially dependent. Further, addictive behavior has consistently demonstrated a remarkable capacity to resist treatment interventions; these difficulties have been observed during the treatment of heroin addiction, polydrug addiction, cigarette smoking, alcoholism, and overeating. If addiction is such a pathological unnatural state, what makes it so difficult to alter this pattern of existence? The plethora of available formulations concerning the addictions has failed to satisfactorily answer this question. This may be due to the pre-paradigmatic state of controversy concerning addiction theory or it may be due to one or many key assumptions that have been made about addictive behavior.

Explanations of addiction often reflect a disciplinary view inherently limited by the theoretical and methodological parameters of that field. For example, Dole and Nyswander (1966) warned that, "Heroin addiction is a medical problem—one that will be solved by medical research or not at all" (p. 2011). Such formulations are restricted further since most were developed as a result of social pressure rather than scientific motivation, that is, in an attempt to control the behavior of illicit drug users and/or to produce abstinence instead of understanding drug use. The pre-paradigmatic state of addiction theory and the failure of these models to generate effective treatments may be due, in part, to the consequences of applying methods primarily developed for application elsewhere.

Every culture has posed questions about states of consciousness and the substances used to alter these states; often the explanations offered have been divorced from experimentation and even careful comparative observation. However, "science is based on a willingness to challenge old dogma, on an openness to see the universe as it really is. Accordingly, science sometimes requires courage—at the very least the courage to question the conventional wisdom" (Sagan, 1979, p. 12). Consequently, as a result of careful clinical observation focused inductively on the *functional* aspects of addiction, the following discussion will challenge the traditional view of addiction as a pathological state and instead consider adaptation as a natural meta-cause for addictive behavior. In other words, rather than impose a preconceived ideology, we will consider the etiology of addiction to be based on natural developmental processes and examine the implications of this conceptualization for adaptive mechanisms. Before considering the relationship between adaptation and addiction, a brief digression will reveal how adaptation was selected as an example of a working alternative model.

If we assume that the traditional models offered to explain addiction are represented by the following set A (A_1, A_2, A_3, ... A_n), then we have identified the factors considered to be causally associated with addictive behavior. Some of the elements of this set can also be assumed to represent sets of interactive causes and account for more of the variance associated with addictive behavior than other elements of the same set.

At a higher level of analysis, we can assume the existence of a set B (B_1, B_2, B_3, ... B_n), that represents the causal processes responsible for the existence of the elements of set A; therefore, set B is assumed to represent the natural causes for addiction, or the "meta-causes." One meta-cause that is referred to by every element of set A, either directly (e.g., Becker, 1967; Khantzian, 1974, 1975, 1978; Wurmser, 1974; Zinberg, 1974, 1975; Zinberg et al. 1977) or indirectly (e.g., Dole & Nyswander, 1967; Gilbert, 1976; Wikler, 1965, 1973) is adaptation. That is to say, at the personal level of analysis individuals naturally attempt to fit in with their intra- and interpersonal environments in the pursuit of survival.

Adaptation and Addiction

Adaptation is not a conscious process as is willpower or diligent effort. It is almost entirely unconscious and it is characterized by concepts usually associated only with defense mechanisms: reaction-formation, denial, projection, sublimation, repression, etc. Typically, defense mechanisms have been examined in order to understand the dynamics of psychopathology. Be that as it may, our present interest resides in how individuals change their environment and themselves in order to adapt to life. Vaillant (1977) has examined the concept of adaptation in detail, using the concepts of adaptation and defense mechanisms interchangeably. Vaillant offers the analogy between defense mechanisms and "the means by which an oyster, confronted with a grain of sand, creates a pearl" (p. 7).

In order to consider addictive behavior as a natural and therefore adaptive process, this behavior must begin in the service of the organism. Early formulations of addiction focused on the *euphorigenic* experiences associated with drug use. The destructive consequences of addictive behavior have almost uniformly been related to the legal status of the drug

﹍sed and the purity of chemistry (also often a function of the social policies in vogue). More recently, euphoria also has come to be considered as the cessation of dysphoria. Khantzian (1974, 1975) has suggested that individuals self-medicate dysphoric states and select drugs to accomplish this purpose; even if one accepts this premise, initial drug use is almost always trial and error. In addition, set and setting (Zinberg, 1974) have a powerful effect in determining whether or not a substance will accomplish its purpose (e.g., reduction of dysphoria or production of another alternate state of consciousness).

Drug use may also serve to protect one's self-image. Jones and Berglas (1978) hypothesized a "self-handicapping" strategy to explain why some people turn to alcohol. They suggest that one reason for using alcohol (drugs can be substituted generally for alcohol, although Jones and Berglas only discussed alcohol) is:

> to avoid the implications of negative feedback for failure and to enhance the impact of positive feedback for success . . . by finding or creating impediments that make good performance less likely, the strategist nicely protects his sense of self-competence. If the person does poorly, the source of failure is externalized in the impediment . . . If the person does well, then he or she has done well in spite of less than optimum conditions (p. 201).

Thus, individuals may initially use drugs as a hoped for solution to current distress, to "act out" unresolved conflicts (e.g., the use of drugs to upset parents, identify with parents, or escape from a situation that has no physical exit), to protect their self-image, for recreation or enjoyment (i.e., no special reasons), or some combination of these. Depending upon the set, setting and substance (Zinberg, 1974), such drug use may (a) resolve or intensify pre-existing problems or (b) create totally new problems for users who are just trying to "fit in" with their reference group or self-handicap themselves.

If we accept the premise that patterns of human behavior emerge as a result of the interplay between an individual's characteristics and the environmental presses encountered during development, then patterns of addictive behavior should be considered to have similar roots. Compared to other adaptive behavior patterns, however, addictive behavior is characterized by inherent *paradox*. Once established, addictive behavior sustains its original adaptive purpose, but precipitates and contributes to the development and maintenance of new stressful situations (e.g., obtaining illicit drugs from criminals on a regular basis). Concurrently, secondary gain is associated with these newly created situations. Thus, for example, the compulsive narcotic addict may be considered disabled and therefore be supported by welfare without having to work for a living; this individual might similarly avoid other social or familial obligations because s/he is not considered to be able to control their behavior. Moreover, the intrapersonal (e.g., impulse management, dysphoric effect) or interpersonal (e.g., recreational drug use, peer pressure) situations that were adapted to vis-à-vis drug availability and use will probably elicit similar responses during future encounters, further increasing the likelihood of continued drug use. In short, addiction is characterized by behavior patterns that were adaptive originally, but because of the paradox and persistence of this behavior, adaptation in other contexts becomes inhibited; addictive behavior restricts alternative behaviors; distorts, reduces, or eliminates feedback about the addictive behavior; and therefore limits the individual's capacity to self-correct or readapt.

Within the present analysis, the concept of addiction is not limited to individual behavior and can be applied to social systems as well. For example, the industrial revolution created a new economic and social system; in a broader context, this natural adaptation to the needs of our world community has, years later, threatened its existence through some of the consequences of its maintenance: pollution, inflation, nuclear waste, etc. Are we addicted to industry? If we sustain our present industrial activities and concurrently believe that we are destroying the fabric of our society, then the answer is yes. If we readapt in a manner that permits us to fit in better with our immediate environment and the broader context of our sphere, then, perhaps, we have been rehabilitated.

The inability of individuals to adapt positively to their environment has been considered characteristic of sociopathic or psychopathic personalities. However, Vaillant (1975) noted that, if one examines these behavior patterns in the microcontext of an individual's immediate social environment, then sense can be made of behaviors that previously appeared incomprehensible. Similar understanding can be gleaned from a microanalysis of the adaptive purposes served by an individual's original drug use. The following formulation emerges from an adaptive perspective: Individuals adapt to life situations. This adaptation can be characterized by (a) unconscious intrapsychic adjustment (defense mechanism), (b) the development of psychological or somatic symptomatology, unconsciously motivated, that permits escape from a stressful situation, (c) artificial exogenous defenses (e.g., drug use), (d) a conscious decision to escape the situation (if possible), (e) a decision to reconceptualize personal (e.g., cognitive, affective, and behavioral) and social dimensions (e.g., a stressful situation), or (f) some combination of the above. Adaptations that facilitate intrapersonal and interpersonal life management will be maintained by the individual while others will atrophy.

Each adaptation considered above changes the individual's life context and, therefore, the individual. For example, consider adolescents who use opiates to control their newly emerging feelings of sexuality, aggression and depression (perhaps because their parents will not accept or permit such emotional expression). Their drug involvement creates a new social situation that brings them in contact with criminals, the need for large amounts of cash, and a physiological/emotional roller coaster (particularly if short-acting narcotics are used). These environmental presses often stimulate new affective responses with which coping is difficult. Since the individual's prior adaptation (using opiates) was experienced as successful, these new problems are often responded to similarly, with more opiates. Eventually, dependence arises and the cycle escalates without apparent escape. The following clinical vignette will illustrate these points.

The Case of Mr. E. Mr. E. is a 25-year-old caucasion male of Italian Catholic descent. He has been using opiates for the past 11 years. Originally, he was introduced to drugs by his older brother and his brother's friends—a group he enjoyed "hanging around with." Although Mr. E. reports feeling nauseous at first, he continued to use heroin in order to be accepted socially by this group. Mr. E. soon found that using heroin made him feel more "normal" and kept him from "jumping out of his skin." Heroin also kept him from feeling the overwhelming rage and uncontrollable aggression that he attributes to his belief that he was different from other young men his age. Mr. E. became addicted shortly after this comforting discovery and began to seek his own supply of heroin and other narcotics from a "street pusher." Mr. E.'s parents learned of his drug use and asked him to leave home; he agreed in order to "spare his parents any anguish." While on the street, Mr. E. committed a variety of crimes in order to support his habit and eventually was prosecuted and sentenced to jail. After release, Mr. E. became involved in methadone maintenance treatment as a consequence of a motorcycle accident and subsequent hospitalization. Eventually he got a full-time job as a machinist and moved home. Currently, he is in treatment with the expressed goal of seeking nonpharmacological means to alleviate his "anger and anxiety" so that he can "lead a normal life."

This vignette illustrates the escalating intrapsychic distress and interpersonal social pressures associated with drug use that often lead to ego regression (Zinberg, 1975). Further, these patterns were only interrupted by external factors. Finally, the case of Mr. E. reflects his ongoing need to "fit in" with the social environment and the "normality" of his reference group.

The Adaptive Illustration: How Does It Measure Up? Given the paradigmatic analysis offered previously (Gambino & Shaffer, 1979; Shaffer, 1977; Shaffer & Gambino, 1979), we can assess the utility of the adaptive model for future development and empirical analysis. First, this model emphasizes the importance of individual differences and the necessity to examine drug use motivation, both conscious and unconscious, since behavior that is adaptive for one individual may be irrelevant for another. This emphasis is consistent with three of the five principles offered by Gambino and Shaffer (1979): (1) individual differences, (2) self-determination and conscious drug use motivation, and (3) unconsciously motivated drug use.

In the adaptive model, the set and setting are considered to have a powerful effect in determining the user's perceived experience produced by drug use. That is to say, if drugs are used within culturally defined norms and prescribed settings, no paradox is manifest and, therefore, no substance abuse or addiction arises. The identification of a paradox will vary among cultures, historical moments, and drugs. The notion of adaptation as an alternative model of addiction thus satisfies the final paradigmatic principles of Gambino and Shaffer: (4) the role of settings and context in drug use, and (5) that drug use alters the user's perceived experience.

One might argue that the adaptation model of addictive behavior is all encompassing and not subject to disproval; that is, all behavior may be considered the results of adaptation. In order to assess the adaptive model, it is important to determine whether addictive behaviors are discarded when nonparadoxical alternative coping mechanisms are available, learned, and ready for use. Similarly, it is important to identify behavior patterns that may be considered addictive but exist in the absence of an apparent paradox. Such a finding would argue against addiction as a natural product of adaptation. Finally, the model of adaptation is advanced here primarily for its illustrative, heuristic and provocative value. Specifically, it is presented as an alternative perspective for the models that assume existing psychopathology as the sole cause for deviant behavior. Consequently, it is hoped that this discussion will stimulate new questions, raise old questions for reevaluation, and stimulate new and creative conceptual approaches to addictive behavior—if so, these ideas will have satisfied their purpose.

As we await the development of this or other new models of addictive ehavior, we can speculate about future addictive behavior and the corresponding substances of abuse. The final section of this chapter will consider these issues.

THE PHARMACOLOGY OF THE FUTURE: THINKING HIGH

During the past decade, scientists verified that individuals were capable of controlling many aspects of their autonomic nervous system. Biofeedback, meditation, and the relaxation response became common ways of reducing stress, changing blood pressure, and altering electrical activity in the brain. Years ago, the conscious control of these bodily functions would have been eschewed as simple fantasy. Today it is commonplace.

Predicting the future of the addictions is no simple task. The ability of scientists—social scientists in particular—to predict is poor. In the addictions, however, patterns do seem to be emerging—for example, the trend for theories of addictive behavior to evolve from macrolevel explanations to microlevel explanations. Presently there is growing interest in the increasing evidence supporting the existence and production of endogenous psychoactive substances (ENPAS) in the central nervous system. For example, endorphins (endogenous opiate-like substances) and the corresponding receptor sites in the central nervous system have already been identified. The role that ENPAS play in our day-to-day lives remains to be explored. It has been determined, however, that ENPAS play a major role in the experience of emotion and pain. As we learn more about the production of ENPAS and their function, it may be possible someday to regulate the production of these substances through conscious control. Should this fiction of today become a fact of tomorrow, it might be possible for people to govern their conscious experience by concentrating in such a manner that the delicate balance of ENPAS in the central nervous system is altered. Much as one would use modern technology (e.g., biofeedback equipment) to gain conscious control over the flow of blood in order to reduce migraine headaches, so too might one learn to use future technology or other purposeful means to increase or decrease the production of ENPAS in the central nervous system. If one could consciously change the balance of ENPAS in their system to reduce pain or depression, control unacceptable anger and aggression, or facilitate falling asleep, few would be critical of such an adaptive skill. However, let us now consider the consequences of inducing an alternate state of consciousness such as getting "high" through conscious mechanisms—"thinking high."

Thinking high implies the ability to alter levels of consciousness with relative immediacy by purposefully increasing the production of ENPAS. Consequently, thinking high implies that one need not get involved with illicit substances in order to achieve a "high" state. The explanation and control of alternate states of consciousness have concerned society since the beginning of recorded history. Thinking should be no exception.

Whether via illicit or licit means (e.g., heroin versus alcohol or marihuana versus tobacco), societies have been concerned with the states of consciousness of its members. Societies have also tended to legislate where, how and when individuals may use substances to alter consciousness. Szasz (1974) has suggested that in this way anti-establishment groups can be suppressed and pro-establishment groups organized and controlled. The culturally prescribed folkways and mores of consciousness altering have even pervaded the realm of sleep (a universally shared state of alternate consciousness). For example, in the United States there is great concern among its citizens that they sleep enough, fall asleep quick enough, and sustain a restful, peaceful sleep; all of these prescriptions are the result of cultural propaganda. These concerns are not accounted for by individual differences, familial history, learning, or even scientific evidence. If cultures generate mores concerning sleep, we should not be surprised at the concern expressed toward other states of alternate consciousness.

As a young child whirls away in dizzy delight, one usually hears an elder express concern about the child somehow "hurting" himself or herself. Years later similar concerns are echoed during legislative debate about the age at which one can legally alter consciousness with culturally prescribed drugs. Ultimately legislators concern themselves with how consciousness is altered (usually via drugs) during the waning moments of life and the onset of death. Somehow these different states of consciousness have come to imply "badness" or "madness." Zinberg (1977) has noted that shifts in consciousness are neither good nor bad, just *alternate* states—as opposed to altered states with the connotation of disruption, distortion, and destruction of a proper state.

If one can learn to think high without exogenous drugs, as we have described, then a high state should be considered natural by definition. In spite of its natural occurrence, we may anticipate that some factions of our society will seek to legislatively regulate high thinking. Perhaps, the future will bring thinking high "dens"; *licensed* teachers who will instruct the young on how to acquire high thinking skills; advanced workshops for aspiring high thinkers; controversies about when one is old enough to think high; technological means to measure high states vis-à-vis endorphin levels, perhaps to check on driving under the influence of improper thoughts! Since history does tend to repeat itself, we might also anticipate that those who do choose to think high will be accused of being morally depraved, weak-willed, and, in some circles, possessed.

Eventually "uncontrolled" thinking high will require treatment. Since the present discussion is science fiction, let us assume that the technology of the future has kept pace with the "thinking" of the future. First, treatment might include some form of confrontation or censure for thinking high; if this fails to produce an alternative mode of "thought," then, perhaps, exogenous opiates will be administered (by licensed programs) to inhibit or control an individual's ability to produce endogenous opiates—endorphins. Further, some treatment programs may even develop "maintenance" components for persistent high thinkers.

Any analysis of future addictions would be incomplete without considering future social science controversies. For example, does *some* high thinking lead to further or more high thinking? Is it possible to think high only on selected occasions, chipping? Are regular high thinkers of different personality types than those who choose not to think high? It is easy to fantasize about the future of high states, but let us not get too carried away. Really, *who* would be concerned about *how* others think anyway? Since Galileo, Darwin, Freud, and Einstein each received intense criticism for thinking differently about the universe or its parts, one can only imagine how "high thinking" will be viewed. Perhaps the more things change, the more they will stay the same.

Considering the history of consciousness altering and addictive behaviors, it appears safe to conclude that "better living through chemistry" has become a way of contemporary life. It is here to stay. Even strict prohibitionist efforts on the part of regulating agencies have been unable to eliminate the use of substances to alter consciousness. If the concept of thinking high becomes a reality of the future, then it is even more unlikely that consciousness altering will disappear. Therefore, our future scientific endeavors should be focused on an examination of the multitude of factors that contribute to an individual's decision to alter consciousness and the methods employed to achieve such alternate states.

SUMMARY

The present chapter briefly reviewed the history of addiction theory and concluded that the field lacked a suitable paradigm. Moreover, the pre-paradigm stage of theory development in the addictions was considered to be characterized by frequent and deep debates that served to identify "schools" of thought rather than resolve differences. In order to illustrate an alternative position, without imposing the inherent limitations of existing models, we considered addiction as a natural state and, therefore, a developmental consequence of adaptation. Finally, the chapter closed with a hypothetical discussion of the pharmacology of the future, thinking high, and its implications.

REFERENCES

APSLER, R. Untangling the conceptual jungle of drug abuse. *Contemporary Drug Problems,* 1978, *7,* 55-80.

BECKER, H. History, culture and subjective experience: An exploration of the social basis of drug induced experiences. *Journal of Health and Social Behavior,* 1967, *8,* 163-176.

DOLE, V.P. & NYSWANDER, M.E. Rehabilitation of heroin addicts after blockade with methadone. *New York State Journal of Medicine,* 1966, *66,* 2011-2017.

DOLE, V. P., & NYSWANDER, M. E. Rehabilitation of the street addict. *Archives of Environmental Health,* 1967, *14,* 447-480.

FEDERN, E. A psycho-social view of "drug abuse" in adolescence. *Child Psychiatry and Human Development,* 1972, *3,* 10-20.

GAMBINO, B., & SHAFFER, H. The concept of paradigm and the treatment of addiction. *Professional Psychology,* 1979, *10,* 207-223.

GILBERT, R. M. Drug abuse as excessive behavior. *Canadian Psychological Review,* 1976, *17,* 231-240.

GOLDSTEIN, A. Opioid peptides (endorphins) in pituitary and brain. *Science,* 1976, *193,* 1081-1086.

JONES, E. E., & BERGLAS, S. Control of attributions about the self through self-handicapping strategies: The appeal of alcohol and the role of underachievement. *Personality and Social Psychology Bulletin,* 1978, *4* (2), 200-206.

KHANTZIAN, E. J. Opiate addiction: A critique of theory and some implications for treatment. *American Journal of Psychotherapy,* 1974, *27,* 59-70.

KHANTZIAN, E. J. Self selection and progression in drug dependence. *Psychiatry Digest,* 1975, *36,* 19-22.

KHANTZIAN, E. J. The ego, the self and opiate addiction: Theoretical and treatment considerations. *The International Review of Psycho-Analysis,* 1978, *5* (2), 189-198.

KHANTZIAN, E. J., & SHAFFER, H. A contemporary psychoanalytic view of addiction theory and treatment. In J. Lowinson & P. Ruiz (Eds.), *Substance Abuse in the United States: Problems and Perspectives.* Baltimore: Williams & Wilkins, in press.

KUHN, T. S. *The Structure of Scientific Revolutions* (2nd ed.). Chicago: University of Chicago Press, 1970.

LINDESMITH, A.R. A sociological theory of drug addiction. *American Journal of Sociology,* 1938, *43,* 593-613.

O'BRIEN, C. P. Experimental analysis of conditioning factors in human narcotic addiction. *Pharmacological Review,* 1975, *27,* 535-543.

QUINONES, M. A., DOYLE, K. M., SHEFFET, A., & LOURIA, D. B. Evaluation of drug abuse rehabilitation efforts: A review. *American Journal of Public Health,* 1979, *69,* 1164-1169.

RADO, S. The psychoanalysis of pharmacothymia (drug addiction). *Psychoanalytic Quarterly* 1933, *2,* 1-23.

SAGAN, C. *Broca's Brain: Reflections on the Romance of Science.* New York: Random House, 1979.

SHAFFER, H. Theories of addiction: In search of a paradigm. In H. Shaffer (Ed.), *Myths and Realities: A Book about Drug Issues.* Boston: Zucker, 1977.

SHAFFER, H., & GAMBINO, B. Addiction paradigms II: Theory, research, and practice. *Journal of Psychedelic Drugs,* 1979, *11* (4), 299-304.

SZASZ, T. *Ceremonial Chemistry.* New York: Anchor Press, 1974.

AILLANT, G. Sociopathy as a human process. *Archives of General Psychiatry*, 1975, *32*, 178-183.

VAILLANT, G. *Adaptation to Life*. Boston: Little, Brown, 1977.

WEIL, A. *The Natural Mind*. New York: Houghton Mifflin, 1972.

WIKLER, A. Conditioning factors in opiate addiction and relapse. In D. N. Wilner & G.G. Kassebaum (Eds.), *Narcotics*. New York: McGraw-Hill, 1965.

WIKLER, A. Dynamics of drug dependence: Implications of a conditioning theory for research and treatment. *Archives of General Psychiatry*, 1973, *28*, 611-616.

WURMSER, L. Psychoanalytic considerations of the etiology of compulsive drug use. *Journal of the American Psychoanalytic Association*, 1974, *22*, 820-843.

ZINBERG, N. E. High states, A beginning study. *National Drug Abuse Council*, 1974, (Sept), 1-50.

ZINBERG, N. E. Addiction and ego function. *The Psychoanalytic Study of the Child*, 1975, *30*, 567-588.

ZINBERG, N. E. (Ed.). *Alternate States of Consciousness*. New York: Free Press, 1977.

ZINBERG, N. E., HARDING, W. M., & WINKELLER, M. A study of social regulatory mechanisms in controlled illicit drug users. *Journal of Drug Issues*, 1977, *7*, 117-133.

MORE CLASSICS: AN ANNOTATED
BIBLIOGRAPHY

The following references are presented here because space and/or consistency precluded a complete presentation in this text. Nonetheless, these works are "classic" and deserve to be consulted, cited, and discussed. It is also important to note that the editorial introductions which preceded each section also include "classic" references that we have not annotated here. The text of each section identifies the substance of those articles; therefore, we elected to keep these annotations to a minimum. Finally, this chapter will close with a short list of other important annotated bibliographies in the addictions which the interested reader can consult.

Bunce, R. Social and political sources of drug effects: The case of bad trips on Psychedelics. *Journal of Drug Issues*, 1979, *9*, 213-233.
   This study reviews empirical evidence that lends support to Becker's (1967) explanation of drug "psychosis." This is a well written and integrated paper; it should not be missed by anyone interested in the social/cultural effects on drug use and experience.

Burglass, M. E., & Duffy, M. G. *Thresholds. A Manual for the Correctional Counselor*. Cambridge, Mass: Correctional Solutions Foundation Press, 1974.
   A practical manual describing the cognitive methods and approach to therapy utilized in the national Thresholds Program in prisons and drug treatment facilities.

Clark, W. H. Chemical Ecstasy. *Psychedelic Drugs and Religion*. New York: Sheed and Ward, 1969
   Offers numerous case studies of drug-induced religious experiences, including the experiments done by Timothy Leary at Harvard Divinity School.

Cleckley, H. *The Mask of Sanity*. St. Louis: C. V. Mosby Co., 1976.
   A comprehensive, vivid description of the "psychopathic" personality; rich case material is used to illustrate conceptual detail. This is a timeless classic.

Densen-Gerber, J., Hochstedler, R., Rohrs, C., & Scott, T. Coercive management of addicts. *New England Journal of Medicine*, 1972, *286*, 609-610.
   Retort to Thomas Szasz regarding compulsory intervention with addicts. The position reflected in this paper is consistent with that of most Therapeutic Communities.

de Ropp, R. S. *Drugs and the Mind*. New York: St. Martin's Press, 1957.
   This work emphasizes repeatedly that in order to understand the course of history one must understand man's efforts to escape from one's own "sweating self" and to experience even temporary states of euphoria or relief of discomfort regardless

of the cost. This is a broad-based book that reflects the history of its time and the social transitions that were occurring then and how these influenced the author's thoughts about drugs.

Dole, V. P., & Nyswander, M. E. A medical treatment for diacetylmorphine (heroin) addiction. *Journal of the American Medical Association,* 1965, *193,* 646-650.
A progress report on the methadone maintenance of 22 patients, previously addicted to heroin, which demonstrated that methadone reduces the craving for narcotics and induces a sufficient tolerance to block the average illegal dose of heroin. This paper was partially responsible for the continuation of efforts that eventually led to methadone maintenance as a widespread treatment modality.

Dole, V. P. Narcotic addiction, physical dependence and relapse. *New England Journal of Medicine,* 1972, *286,* 988-992.
Examines the experimental animal literature in order to consider what can be generalized to human problems so that these can be treated or prevented. Neurochemical determinants of behavior are hypothesized and considered important for future research.

DuPont, R. L., & Green, M. H. The dynamics of a heroin addiction epidemic. *Science,* 1973, *181,* 716-722.
Excellent discussion of the rationale supporting the public health problem of heroin addiction for which methadone seemed the solution.

Freedman, A. M. Drugs and society: An ecological approach. *Comprehensive Psychiatry,* 1972, *13,* 411-420.
A brilliant exposition of the relationship that exists between drugs, drug use and the sociocultural context. One must look at the consequences involved when interventions occur in any aspect of the ecology—including the drug environment. Drug use can alter the psychoecology of our social environment.

Freud, S. *Cocaine Papers.* Edited by Robert Byck. New York: New American Library, 1974.
Contains Freud's early positive views of cocaine as a treatment for morphine dependence and depression; this also reflects Freud's later retractions of his earlier endorsements.

Fuller, J. G. *The Day of St. Anthony's Fire.* New York: Macmillan, 1968.
This is an incredible account of the events occurring in a small village in France during May, 1951 when an LSD-like substance contaminated the bread supply of the entire area. This account is particularly relevant to the sociological/cultural and expectancy models of drug effects since this is an actual account of unexpected drug effects.

Furst, P. T. (Ed.) *Flesh of the Gods. The Ritual Use of Hallucinogens.* New York: Praeger Publishers, 1972.
Provides an articulate cultural/historical framework for the psychedelic experience.

Goldstein, A. Opiate receptors. *Life Sciences,* 1974, *14,* 615-623.
Reviews the scientific efforts designed to identify the opiate receptors and the structure and function of the drug-receptor interaction.

Goldstein, A. Heroin addiction and the role of methadone in its treatment. *Archives of General Psychiatry,* 1972, *26,* 291-297.
An insightful analysis of the utility of methadone in treating heroin addiction. Particularly useful is Goldstein's suggestion of how time limited treatment might proceed when methadone is involved.

Goldstein, A., Hansteen, R. W., & Horns, W. H. Control of methadone dosage by patients. *Journal of the American Medical Association,* 1975, *234,* 734-737.
Explodes the enduring notion that addicts will always take the maximum amount of drug available to them. Tragically disregarded by most treatment programs!

Grinspoon, L. *Marihuana Reconsidered.* Cambridge: Harvard University Press, 1971.
A complete and classic description of marihuana, its history, pharmacology, effects, and place in our society. Prospective readers should note that with the exception of the chapter on chemistry and pharmacology, the author intended this book for the nonspecialist reader. As with Grinspoon's other work, the tone is scientific, scholarly and rational.

Grinspoon, L., & Bakalar, J.B. *Cocaine. A Drug and its Social Evolution.* New York: Basic Books, 1976.
A comprehensive examination of cocaine; included are discussions of its history, medicinal uses, abuse potential and cultural context.

Grinspoon, L., & Bakalar, J. *Psychedel. Drugs Reconsidered.* New York: Basic Books, 1979.
This is a comprehensive and au.horitative review of psychedelic substances. One of the rare attempts to logically and rationally understand drugs that alter consciousness.

Grinspoon, L., & Hedblom, P. *The Speed Culture. Amphetamine Use and Abuse in America.* Cambridge: Harvard University Press, 1975.
Another comprehensive, detailed, and rational work from Grinspoon. Once again, the authors have achieved their purpose, an understandable text for the nonspecialist reader.

Hess, A.G. *Chasing the Dragon.* Amsterdam: North-Holland Publishing Co., 1965.
An interesting and detailed account of the history and treatment of drug addiction in Hong Kong.

Himmelsbach, C.K. Clinical studies of drug addiction. Physical dependence, withdrawal and recovery. *Archives of Internal Medicine,* 1942, *69,* 766-772.
This study reports the results of a longitudinal examination of 21 persons addicted to morphine or its derivatives from the addicted state through withdrawal to the ninth month of total abstinence. The data are of interest to the physician who is learning about the effects of narcotics on tolerance and physical dependence.

Hughes, H. M. (Ed.). *The Fantastic Lodge.* Boston: Houghton Mifflin, 1961.
An articulate autobiographical statement of a female heroin addict.

Huxley, Aldous. *The Doors of Perception.* New York: Harper & Row, 1954.
A personal account of Huxley's experience with mescaline. This is a first rate literary exposition of a personal "psychedelic" experience.

Isbell, H., & Vogel, V. H. The addiction liability of methadone (amidone, dolophine, 10820) and its use in the treatment of the morphine abstinence syndrome. *American Journal of Psychiatry,* 1948, *105,* 909-914.
An empirical and conceptual demonstration that methadone is dependence inducing (i.e., methadone has a high "addiction" liability).

Isbell, H., & White, W. M. Clinical characteristics of addictions. *American Journal of Medicine,* 1953, *14,* 558-565.
Would have been on any list of classics in the 1950s.

Jaffe, J. H. Drug addiction and drug abuse. In L. S. Goodman and A. Gilman (Eds.), *The Pharmacological Basis of Therapeutics* (4th Ed.), New York: Macmillan, 1970, pp. 276-313.
Worth reading for the excellent and careful definitions of tolerance, dependence, and addiction and other basic terms used in the addictions.

Khantzian, E. J., Mack, J. E., & Schatzberg, A. F. Heroin use as an attempt to cope: Clinical observations. *American Journal of Psychiatry,* 1974, *131,* 160-164.
Authors suggest that addicts' use of opiates reflects a unique and characteristic way of dealing with their human problems. Five case studies are discussed and, these illuminate the presentation. This paper is an early step in Khantzian's self-selection model.

Larkowitz, D. The adolescent drug addict: An Adlerian view. *Journal of Individual Psychology,* 1961, *17,* 68-79.
One-of-a-kind analysis of the problem from the Adlerian perspective. Formulations concerning aspects of power in the development of addiction are interesting.

Larner, J. (Ed.), *The Addict in the Street.* New York: Grove Press, Inc., 1964.
Transcripts of interviews with street addicts make up the entire contents of this book. These interviews provide an interesting perspective on what addicts are thinking and talking about and how they got involved with drug abuse. This is particularly useful for the fledgling counselor who would like to become more familiar with "street" language.

Lewin, L. *Phantastica, Narcotic, and Stimulant Drugs.* London: Kegan, Paul, Trench and

Trubner, 1931.
  First book devoted to research and experimental chemotherapy. Is a foundation
  of modern psychopharmacology.
Lindesmith, A. R. *Opiate addiction.* Bloomington, Ind: Principia Press, 1947.
  A fascianting step forward for its time—still relevant today—this book emphasizes
  the importance of cognitive, labeling and self-concept factors in the addiction proc-
  ess. This work is a pioneer effort and remains vital today.
Louria, D. B. *The Drug Scene.* New York: McGraw-Hill, 1968.
  A semi-personal account of drug abuse and its scope. The aim of this book originally
  was to correct a misinformed public.
Martin, W. R. Opioid antagonists. *Pharmacological Reviews,* 1967, *19,* 463-521.
  An extremely detailed and technical review of the antagonist literature. Particularly
  relevant for physicians and physiologists. The paper includes discussions on: chemical structure of antagonists; biochemical considerations; agonistic actions; antagonistic actions; and clinical applications for other uses.
McDougall, W. A. A chemical theory of temperament applied to introversion and ex-
  troversion. *Journal of Abnormal and Social Psychology,* 1929, *24,* 293-309.
  A remarkable account of how "substances" may be secreted such that temperament
  is affected. Although this paper is empirically outdated, the concepts expressed are
  just beginning to be understood with respect to endorphins in particular and endogenous psychoactive substances in general.
Maris, R. W. Deviance as therapy: The paradox of the self-destructive female. *Journal of
  Health and Social Behavior,* 1971, *12,* 113-124.
  This paper is conceptually thought provoking as it considers abusive behavior to
  be part of an adaptive process. The methods and data analysis are particularly
  impressive; in fact, the path analysis techniques used here are becoming more
  common throughout the social sciences when difficult, complex data are being
  examined.
McGlothlin, W. H. (Ed.), Chemical comforts of man: The future. *The Journal of Social
  Issues,* 1971, *27*(3), 1-125.
  A comprehensive presentation of the issues that affected the field of substance
  abuse and, more importantly, that can be expected to shape its future. Many of the
  predictions have been demonstrated to be accurate since this journal was issued.
Musto, D. F. The Marijuana Act of 1937. *Archives of General Psychiatry,* 1972, *26,* 101-108.
  A brief but excellent analysis of the history of current marihuana laws, but readily
  applicable to other drug control laws and policies.
Musto, D. *The American Disease.* New Haven: Yale University Press, 1973.
  This is a remarkably well organized and detailed view of narcotics control. Musto
  views America's concern with narcotics as more than a medical or legal problem;
  instead, he considers narcotics control to be a political problem. This book is worthwhile for anyone seeking a sophisticated account of the dynamics associated with
  licit and illicit drugs.
Pattison, M., Bishop, L. A., & Linsky, A. S. Changes in public attitudes on narcotic addiction. *American Journal of Psychiatry,* 1968, *125,* 160-166.
  This paper illustrated that public attitudes reflect the ongoing human attitudes
  toward humanity and do not represent fadish isolated beliefs about addicts. This
  article also traces the issue of responsiblity as discussed in the present epilogue.
Platt, J.J., & Labate, C. *Heroin Addiction.* New York: John Wiley & Sons, 1976.
  One of the most comprehensive, best organized, and rational volumes on the subject
  of heroin addiction.
Smith, D. E., & Wesson, D. R. Phenobarbital technique for treatment of barbiturate dependence. *Archives of General Psychiatry,* 1971, *24,* 56-60.
  A technique for withdrawal of patients who are physically dependent upon barbiturates is described. This technique is based on the substitution of phenobarbital,
  a long-acting barbiturate. Comments and case illustrations serve to enlighten the
  reader. This article has become a standard of clinical practice.

United States Treasury Department. Bureau of Narcotics. *Digest of Court Decisions under the Harrison Narcotic Law and Other Related Statutes.* Washington, D.C.: United States Printing Office, 1931.
This is an anthology of decisions that have set precedent for current legal decisions. This volume should interest the legally inclined.
Vaillant, G. E. A twelve-year follow-up of New York narcotic addicts: I. The relation of treatment to outcome. *American Journal of Psychiatry,* 1966(a), *122,* 727-737.
This study provides evidence that, perhaps, addicts "mature out" of their addiction. Further, enforced abstinence was found useful for many addicts; nevertheless, addicts were characterized as a variable group in need of prescriptive treatment.
Vaillant, G. E. A twelve-year follow-up of New York narcotic Addicts: II. The natural history of a chronic disease. *New England Journal of Medicine,* 1966(b), *275,* 1282-1288.
This article views addiction as a chronic disease and follows its natural course in 50 urban addicts from adolescence until their 40th birthday. Mortality of addicts was found to be two to five times greater than expected and the inability to sustain employment was considered as antecedent to or even a cause of addiction.
Vaillant, G. E. A twelve-year follow-up of New York narcotic addicts: III. Some social and psychiatric characteristics. *Archives of General Psychiatry,* 1966(c), *15,* 599-609.
In this continuing sequence, the author reports that addicts are often deprived sociologically as well as by the loss of a parent. Delinquency often preceded drug use rather than followed it. Further, the author compares and contrasts addicts with chronically delinquent nonaddicts—two groups more similar than had previously been thought.
Vaillant, G. E. A twenty-year follow-up of New York narcotic addicts. *Archives of General Psychiatry,* 1973, *29,* 237-241.
This prospective follow-up supports the author's previous findings that suggest the need for strict community supervision. Addicts who were treated but not punished often died, while those who were "punished" by parole tended to survive and achieve stable community abstinence. In general, this study found that urban addicts who achieved more than three years of abstinence could usually maintain this abstinence indefinitely. Support for methadone maintenance and vocational programs can be found in this paper.
Vaillant, G. E. *Adaptation to Life.* Boston: Little, Brown, 1977.
Among a variety of other assets, this book illustrates how "successful" individuals use substances in order to adapt to their lives. This volume brings "to life" a multitude of textbook concepts; it should not be missed by any clinician.
Wesson, D.R., Gat, G.R., & Smith, D.E. Treatment techniques for narcotic withdrawal with special reference to mixed narcotic-sedative addictions. *Journal of Psychedelic Drugs,* 1971, *4*(2), 118-123.
Foundation article for the current medical management of the mixed addictions.
Wikler, A. Diagnosis and treatment of drug dependence of the barbiturate type. *American Journal of Psychiatry,* 1968, *125,* 758-765.
An early and complete discussion of the symptoms and treatment approaches for drug dependence of the barbiturate type.
Wikler, A. (Ed.), *The Addictive States.* Baltimore: Williams & Wilkins, 1969.
These articles are commonly referenced in the addiction literature; when published this volume provided a timely perspective on the field.
Wikler, A., & Rasor, W. Psychiatric aspects of drug addiction. *American Journal of Medicine,* 1953, *24,* 566-570.
This paper presents a review of the symptomatological, psychoanalytic, and pharmacodynamic formulations of drug addiction. Particular emphasis is placed on the latter model. The authors conclude that different classes of drugs alter patterns of behavior in different ways. This work is an early statement about the self-selection and adaptation models of drug use that have followed. This paper was part of a symposium on drug abuse; the other papers (also quite good) are presented in the

same issue of the *American Journal of Medicine*.

Wilner, D. M., & Kassebaum, G. G. (Eds.), *Narcotics*. New York: McGraw-Hill, 1965.
An excellent collection of articles dealing with a variety of drug related issues; these articles are cited often throughout the literature.

Wishnie, H. *The Impulsive Personality. Understanding People with Destructive Character Disorders*. New York: Plenum, 1977.
A practical manual that vividly describes Wishnie's unique approach to therapy with impulse-ridden patients.

Yablonsky, L. *The Tunnel Back: Synanon*. New York: Macmillan, 1965.
An entertaining discussion of Synanon and its "inner" workings. This is informative, nontechnical, and one of the only comprehensive discussions of the Synanon concept.

Zinberg, N. E., & Jacobson, R. C. The natural history of "chipping." *American Journal of Psychiatry*, 1976, *133*, 37-40.
Five case histories illustrate the concept of "chipping"—the controlled use of opiates. Social regulatory mechanisms were found to concurrently permit and limit illicit drug use. Controlled use may be more prevalent than previously thought.

Annotated Bibliographies in the Addictions

Ajami, A. M. Drugs: *An Annotated Bibliography and Guide to the Literature*. Boston: G. K. Hall & Co., 1973.

Langrod, J. A bibliography of the methadone maintenance treatment of heroin addiction. *International Journal of the Addictions*, 1970, *5*, 581-591.

Sells, H. F. *A Bibliography on Drug Dependence*. Fort Worth, Texas: The Texas Christian University Press, 1967.

United States Department of Health, Education, and Welfare. *Annotated Bibliography of Papers from the Addiction Research Center, 1935-1975*. Washington, D.C.: U.S. Government Printing Office, 1978.

Weise, C. E., & Price, S. F. *The Benzodiazepines—Patterns of Use. An Annotated Bibliography*. Ontario: Addiction Research Foundation, 1975.